Peter Gritzmann · Rainer Hettich
Reiner Horst · Ekkehard Sachs (Eds.)

Operations Research '91

Extended Abstracts of the 16th Symposium
on Operations Research
held at the University of Trier
at September 9-11, 1991

With 44 Figures

Physica-Verlag
A Springer-Verlag Company

Prof. Dr. Peter Gritzmann
Prof. Dr. Rainer Hettich
Prof. Dr. Reiner Horst
Prof. Dr. Ekkehard Sachs

Universität Trier
FB IV, Mathematik
Postfach 38 25
D-5500 Trier
Germany

ISBN-13: 978-3-7908-0608-3 e-ISBN: 978-3-642-48417-9
DOI: 10.1007/978-3-642-48417-9

Printing: Weihert-Druck, Darmstadt

7100/7130-543210 - Printed on acid-free paper

Preface

The purpose of this volume is to reflect the scientific activities during the **16th Symposium on Operations Research** which took place at the **University of Trier** from September 9 through September 11, 1991.

The Symposia on Operations Research are the annual conferences of the **Gesellschaft für Mathematik, Ökonomie und Operations Research (GMÖOR)**. This society which was founded in 1977 pursues the goal to support and facilitate research, development, application and education in an area where mathematics, economics, operations research, computer science and system theory come together.

The 16th Symposium on Operations Research stood under the auspices of the Ministerpräsident of the state of Rheinland-Pfalz, Rudolf Scharping. The opening addresses were given by the president of the Universität Trier, Professor Hasler, by the Minister für Wissenschaft und Weiterbildung, Professor Zöllner, and by Professor Hettich, on behalf of the organizers. These addresses are printed as part of the introductory material of this volume.

The conference was attended by 351 participants from 29 countries; more than 70% of the participants gave lectures on their current reseach interests, surveys on special topics or software demonstrations. They made the meeting truely a successful international forum for scientific exchange.

The conference was highlighted by the award of the society's scientific prize in memoriam Rudolf Henn to Professor R.E. Burkard, Technical University Graz, and his plenary GMÖOR-Award winner lecture on *Convexity and Discrete Optimization.*

According to the interdisciplinary character of the GMÖOR (and of the field of operations research) numerous subjects were covered. A classification of these areas was facilitated by the division of the talks into 13 different sections. These sections and the section chairmen are listed below.

Optimization: Theory and Modelling
D. Pallaschke
Optimization: Computational Methods
W. Oettli, J. Zowe
Combinatorial Optimization and Discrete Mathematics
A. Bachem
Combinatorial Problems in VLSI, Scientific Computing
G. Alefeld, T. Lengauer, R.H. Möhring
Systems and Control Theory
G. Feichtinger, H.W. Knobloch
Stochastic and Dynamic Optimization, Queueing, Scheduling
M. Schäl, R. Schaßberger
Stochastics, Econometrics
G. Bamberg, N. Schmitz
Mathematical Economics and Game Theory
W. Eichhorn, S. Tijs
Utility, Risk, Insurance
W.R. Heilmann, K. Mosler
Financial Engineering
K.H. Vollmer
Computer Science in Business and Economics
W. Stucky
Knowledge Engineering
W. Mellis, M. Richter
Production and Manufacturing
K.P. Kistner.

Fifty minutes plenary and invited lectures were given by

S. Axsäter, B. Betrò, A. Brandt, P. Brucker, J.E. Dennis, E. Dierker, H. Föllmer, P. Hansen, K. Helmes, C. Hipp, T.C. Hu, A. Ioffe, D. Klatte, V. Klee, H. König, J. Lehn, U. Leopold-Wildburger, M. Maschler, L. Montrucchio, B. Pasik-Duncan, F. Potra, H.J. Prömel, M. Richter, R. Richter, O. Schlecht, D. Schmeidler, A. Sølvberg, J. Wijngaard, J. Willems, W. Wolf, F. Wysotzki.

All other talks were 20–25 minute presentations.

The present volume is designated to serve as a documentation of the scientific activities at the conference. It consists of extended abstracts that were provided by the speakers. In view of the goal of this volume every speaker was invited to submit an extended abstract of his/her talk to be published in this book. The extended abstracts did not undergo any refereeing process whatsoever, hence the full responsibility of their content lies with the authors.

The extended abstracts are ordered as follows: the extended abstract of the GMÖOR-Award winner is followed by the abstracts of the plenary lectures (which are not officially attributed to any section), printed in alphabetical order. Then the remaining abstracts are printed sectionwise (and within a section in alphabetical order). Since the invited presentations are part of their section they are put in their alphabetical place.

We would like to close by expressing our deepest gratitude to all the numerous people – far too many to be listed here individually – who helped us in organizing the symposium and in putting together this volume.

Trier, September 1991

Peter Gritzmann
Rainer Hettich
Reiner Horst
Ekkehard Sachs

Minister Zöllner, Mr. President, Ladies and Gentlemen,

It is a good tradition that the local president or rector at the beginning of such a conference should make some official noises so that the latecomers will not miss anything of real importance. I am quite happy to fulfill this useful function, also to provide the Minister with a quiet auditorium because he will speak after myself. But let me add that it gives me real pleasure and satisfaction to see that the Gesellschaft für Mathematik, Ökonomie und Operations Research has chosen Trier as the venue of the 16th Symposium this year. I am particularly happy that this conference can be opened in the presence of our new Minister of Higher Education, Research and Further Education, my ex-colleague Minister Zöllner, because interdisciplinarity – both a difficult word and a difficult thing – is one of his main concerns when he looks at the state of universities at the present moment; and certainly nothing could be more interdisciplinary than the applied science of Operations Research. I would like to thank the local organizers for their efforts in preparing this conference in Trier, the composition of this local committee also reflects the interdisciplinary character of your endeavors. There is a gang of four from our Mathematics Department; four colleagues who are specialized in problems of optimization and closely collaborate with the other members of the committee who come from the fields of Computer Science, Applied Computer Science and Business Management. I have noted with great satisfaction that these very active colleagues are already making contributions to the regional usefulness and regional elements of this young university. They have collaborated in the fields of agriculture – the agriculture which is characteristic of the region –; they have already solved problems for the wine-growing industry in the Mosel-valley; they have been dealing with problems of the dairy industry; questions of an efficient milk collection. I recall that in the Swiss surroundings in which I grew up the farmers used to have a special breed of dog which in the evening with a little cart transported the day's milk to the next dairy and in addition to that the dogs were excellent guard dogs for the farm and the best companions of the family. I do not think that even the most advanced operations research can improve on this efficient use of resources. However, this predisposes a landscape dotted with little dairies and of course, there, the question of efficiency is another aspect and is seen in a different way.

Ladies and Gentlemen, the services of our Operations Research experts could have been used also for the organization of this day, since as I mentioned our Minister is our guest today. This is the first official visit to our university and he has to or he wishes to open two important congresses in addition to having conversations with the authorities of the university. This poses some problems and I would like to ask for your kind understanding if the Minister and I are forced to leave this opening ceremony before we really would have liked to, but we will all meet again at the reception tonight; and as you probably have seen in your congress information you will be lumped together with a bunch of philosophers then, philosophers who are decidedly unapplied. Therefore it may be quite a productive mixture in a social context tonight.

Ladies and Gentlemen, I am welcoming you on a campus which will have to accommodate in the next winter term between 10,000 and 11,000 students. A campus, which in its present form is designed for just under 6,000 students. This shows you that holding this conference in November would have been an absolute impracticability and impossibility; when the new intake comes in, the beginners or for our American colleagues, the freshmen, will fill this hall twice over. So I have to welcome them twice over. This is a situation which is characteristic of all German universities; it is not specific to Trier, but it illustrates the difficulties under which research is done in this country at this present moment, especially in fields which are so popular with the present student generation as anything concerned with business management. Perhaps you will also have a few minutes to note the not quite unattractive contrast between this new university – we are this year 21 years old – according to anglo–saxon traditions we have just reached maturity – this young dynamic and a bit 'poppy' university and the ancient city of Trier down in the valley. I hope you will be able to do that. Perhaps a parting piece of good advice: Should you have any contact with the locals of Trier, never cast any doubt on the historic fact that Trier is definitely the oldest city in Germany.

I wish you a very fruitful and pleasant congress in our university. Thank you very much. I have now the honour to ask Minister Zöllner to address you.

Trier, September 1991

Prof. Dr. J. Hasler
President of the University of Trier

Sehr geehrter Herr Hasler, meine Damen und Herren,

es ist mir eine besondere Freude, Sie heute im Namen der Landesregierung zu diesem Symposium begrüßen zu können. Ich freue mich insbesondere, die Grüße des Ministerpräsidenten, der die Schirmherrschaft über diese Veranstaltung übernommen hat, zu überbringen. Ich will diesen Kongreß nicht allzulange von der eigentlichen Arbeit abhalten, aber die Gelegenheit nutzen, einige grundsätzliche Bemerkungen zu machen.

Die neue Landesregierung in Rheinland-Pfalz legt großen Wert auf die Weiterentwicklung der Wissenschaften und Hochschulen, nicht nur wegen der Wissenschaft und wegen der Hochschulen selbst, sondern wegen der Bedeutung von Wissenschaft und Hochschulen für die Struktur und die Weiterentwicklung des Landes insgesamt. Das hat Konsequenzen. Erste Konsequenz ist natürlich die Schaffung der entsprechenden Rahmenbedingungen. Ein Thema, das Herr Hasler schon angedeutet hat, das uns in der Alltagsarbeit sehr beschäftigt und das nicht so ohne weiteres lösbar ist. Neben diesem materiellen Hintergrund ist die inhaltliche Weiterentwicklung der Hochschulen von ganz zentraler, wenn nicht entscheidenderer Bedeutung. Und hier sind es aus unserer Sicht im wesentlichen fünf Punkte, die wir im Auge behalten müssen, wenn wir die Wissenschaft und die Weiterentwicklung der Hochschulen vorantreiben wollen.

Zum einen ist es die Interdisziplinarität, die fächerübergreifende Zusammenarbeit nicht nur in der Forschung – und das betone ich ausdrücklich –, sondern auch in der Lehre. Etwas, das wir mit dem Schlagwort „Studium integrale“ verstärkt in das Bewußtsein auch der Hochschulen rücken wollen. Gemeint ist, schon im Studium die Voraussetzung für ein fächerübergreifenden Verständnis zu schaffen, das letzten Endes Teamarbeit und Kooperation im Berufsleben erst ermöglicht.

Die Hochschulen müssen, gerade weil sie den aktuellen Wissensstand vermitteln, Methoden und Angebote entwickeln, die ein echtes Weiterbildungsstudium und damit lebenslanges Lernen ermöglichen. Ein „Studium continuum“ ist die Aufgabe der Zukunft, und sie muß heute angepackt werden, selbst wenn wir als Hochschulen unter der Last der Überlast im wahrsten Sinne des Wortes leiden. Wenn wir heute die Weichen nicht stellen, so wird das morgen für uns in Zukunft verschlossen sein.

Zum dritten geht es um die stärkere Orientierung der Forschung und der Wissenschaft an der gesellschaftlichen Relevanz und zwar weit über den reinen technischen Anwendungsbezug hinaus.

Zum vierten müssen die Hochschulen sich vermehrt als hochspezialisierte Dienstleistungs- und Beratungsinstitutionen für die Gesellschaft zur Verfügung stellen.

Und als letzten Punkt möchte ich ein auch für die Region hier besonderes Anliegen formulieren: Es ist wichtig, daß die regionalpolitische Verankerung der Hochschulen gestärkt wird.

Vor diesem Hintergrund, so hoffe ich, wird deutlich, daß meine Freude zu Beginn kein Lippenbekenntnis und keine bloße Höflichkeit war. Ich freue mich besonders, diesen Kongreß heute hier eröffnen zu können, denn wie kaum ein anderes Fach, wie kaum eine andere Disziplin verkörpern sie in ihrer Arbeit wesentliche Punkte, die ich genannt habe und sie sind sicher ein Vorbild für andere Fächer, ein Vorbild für die interdisziplinäre Zusammenarbeit von Mathematikern, Informatikern und Wirtschaftswissenschaftlern, für die Zusammenarbeit und für die Möglichkeit des Nebeneinanders von Grundlagenforschung – hervorragender Grundlagenforschung – und von konkreten Praxisproblemen. Und – wie hier in Trier gezeigt – ist es auch möglich, daß dieser Wissenschaftszweig ganz konkrete und wichtige regionalpolitische Probleme behandelt. Insofern ist es besonders sinnvoll, daß der Kongreß in Trier stattfindet. Die Universität Trier, die möglicherweise in den Augen einiger als geisteswissenschaftliche Fakultät „abgestempelt“ wurde und bei der möglicherweise die Angst bestand, daß sie von der großen Welle des Technologietransfers in der Wissenschaftsförderung überrollt werden könnte, ist der überzeugende Beweis dafür, daß Hochschulen mehr als technisch orientierten Anwendungsbezug liefern können, daß es um Wissenstransfer geht. Daß gerade die Hochschule hier in Trier mit ihrer sicher spezifischen Fächerausrichtung diesen wichtigen Kongreß veranstaltet, freut mich besonders und ich bedanke mich bei den Organisatoren.

Ich hoffe, daß Sie gute Arbeit, daß Sie harte Arbeit vor sich haben, aber ich hoffe auch, daß Sie die Chance haben – wie Herr Hasler gesagt hat –, sich in dieser schönen Stadt Trier etwas zu erholen und die schöne Landschaft kennenzulernen. Ich wünsche Ihnen viel Erfolg.

Trier, September 1991

Prof. Dr. E. J. Zöllner
Minister für Wissenschaft und
Weiterbildung des Landes Rheinland-Pfalz

Sehr geehrter Herr Minister, Herr Präsident, dear Participants, Guests and Colleagues,

On behalf of the organization committee I have the pleasure to welcome you to this 16th Symposium on Operations Research.

Three years ago the Gesellschaft für Mathematik, Ökonomie und Operations Research entrusted us with the organization of its 1991 annual meeting. We appreciate very much the society's and its president's support during all that time, but also the extend of autonomy traditionally given to the local organizers with respect to the scientific and social program.

Operations Research comprises a large variety of mathematical, statistical and informational theories and methods to analyse complex situations and to contribute to responsible decisionmaking, planning and the efficient use of resources. In a world of increasing complexity and scarce natural resources we believe that there will be a growing need for such approaches in many fields of our society.

Traditionally this symposium is intented to be an international forum for scientific exchange at the frontiers of Operations Research in Mathematics, Statistics, Economics and Computer Science. We hope that the division into 13 sections (which certainly can be disputed), reflects on the one hand the variety of fields engaged without, on the other hand, separating too many subjects which belong together. We believe that the approximately 300 presentations including 32 plenary and invited lectures and a number of computer demonstrations reflect the state of the art in Operations Research as well as the actual challenges. Besides many contributions on recent advances in the classical fields we expect exciting presentations on new interactions with fields like Computer Science or Knowledge Engineering as well as an intense dialogue between theory and the numerous applications. We would not have succeeded in attracting so many distinguished speakers from all over the world without the engagement and the advice of the section chairmen. Many thanks to all of them.

Finally, let me express our gratitudes to the government of Rheinland–Pfalz, the city of Trier, the Deutsche Forschungsgemeinschaft, the University of Trier, the Freundeskreis of our university and all the sponsors who have supported us. We gratefully acknowledge the help and advice of many people inside and outside the university, the dedication and engagement of our colleagues, assistants and secretaries and many students. Without their help we could not have done all the organization.

Let me close with the hope that you will enjoy this conference and also your stay in Trier.

Trier, September 1991

Prof. Dr. R. Hettich
(on behalf of the organizers)

Contents

Section 1: Optimization: Theory and Modelling

Section 2: Optimization: Computational Methods

Section 4: Combinatorial Problems in VLSI, Scientific Computing

Section 5: Systems and Control Theory

Section 6: Stochastic and Dynamic Optimization, Queueing, Scheduling

Section 7: Stochastics, Econometrics

Section 8: Mathematical Economics and Game Theory

Section 9: Utility, Risk, Insurance

Section 10: Financial Engineering

Section 11: Computer Science in Business and Economics

Section 12: Knowledge Engineering

Section 13: Production and Manufacturing

THE ROLE OF CONVEXITY IN DISCRETE OPTIMIZATION

- Extended Abstract -

Rainer E. Burkard
Mathematisches Institut, Technische Universität Graz
Kopernikusgasse 24, A-8010 GRAZ (Austria)

Though the notions of convex sets and discrete programming seem in an first instance quite unrelated, convexity plays a remarkable role in discrete programming. Discrete optimization problems ask for maximizing or minimizing functions in real variables where some or all of the variables are supposed to take only integer values. We distinguish two main problems: mixed-integer programming problems where some variables are restricted to integral values and combinatorial optimization problems with zero-one variables.

A first application of convexity arises in methods for solving mixed-integer programs. In branch and bound methods for problems with a convex objective function and constraints of the form $f_i(\mathbf{x})\leq 0$ with convex functions f_i, $i=1,2,\ldots,m$ we can fix one variable in the branching step due to the convexity of the level sets of the objective function. Thus the size of the subproblems reduces. Further cutting plane methods can be designed for convex mixed-integer programming problems and Benders' decomposition uses as basic step that the solution set of a linear program can be written as convex hull of its vertices (provided it is bounded).

The feasibility of an integer linear program is equivalent with the existence of a solution of a linear diophantine inequality system. Thus these questions are strongly connected with questions of the geometry of numbers. Of particular interest is the question which computational effort is needed to decide whether an integer program has a feasible solution or not. It can be shown that for deciding whether the integer program max $\langle \mathbf{c},\mathbf{x}\rangle$ s.t. $\mathbf{Ax} \leq \mathbf{b}$, $\mathbf{x}\geq\mathbf{0}$ is infeasible, has a finite solution or is unbounded just the points $\mathbf{x}=(x_j)$ with $0 \leq x_j \leq [2 \max(m,n)^2 K]$ have to be investigated, where K is a bound on the coefficients of the inequality system $\mathbf{Ax} \leq \mathbf{b}$. Therefore integer programs lie in the complexity class NP and can be solved by enumeration. Bank et al. showed that this remains even true, if the constraint set is described by (quasi-)convex polynomials with integer-valued coefficients.

Of special interest in integer programming are integral polyhedra which contain an integral point in each of its nonempty faces. The importance of integral polyhedra lies in the fact that the integer linear program whose set of feasible points forms an integral polyhedron can be solved via linear programming. Thus it is an important question which systems of linear inequalities lead to integral polyhedra. An important result in this respect is due to Hoffman and Kruskal. An $(m\times d)$-matrix A is called *totally unimodular,* if any regular square submatrix of A has determinant +1 or -1.

Theorem (Hoffman and Kruskal, 1956)
Let A be an integral matrix. Then the following two statements are equivalent:
1. The polyhedron $P(A,b):=\{ \mathbf{Ax \le b, x \ge 0} \}$ *has for any integral vector* b *for which* $P(A,b)$ *is non-empty only integral vertices.*
2. The matrix A is totally unimodular.

This theorem raises the question to determine whether a given matrix is totally unimodular or not. Seymour [1980] has shown that this question can be settled in polynomial time. The theorem of Hoffman and Kruskal settles the question which systems of linear inequalities lead for *arbitrary* right hand side **b** to an integral polyhedron. More difficult is the analogue question when we specify the right hand side **b** or allow **b** to vary in a certain set. Typical results in this respect concern set packing, set partitioning and set covering problems. Let A be an (m×d)-matrix with only 0 and 1 entries. The set packing problem asks for integral solutions of $\mathbf{Ax \le 1, x \ge 0}$, where the m components of the vector **1** all equal 1. The set partitioning problems asks for integer solutions of $Ax=\mathbf{1}$, $\mathbf{x \ge 0}$ and the set covering problem asks for integral solutions of $\mathbf{Ax \ge 1}$, $\mathbf{x \ge 0}$. A (0,1)-matrix is called *balanced*, if it does not contain a square submatrix of odd order with row and column sums 2.
A result in the style of the Theorem of Hoffman and Kruskal is due to Berge. Berge considers slightly modified packing and covering polyhedra by allowing superfluous rows in the inequality systems.

Theorem (Berge, 1972)
Let A *be a matrix with* 0 *and* 1 *entries and no zero row or column. Then the following statements are equivalent:*
1. The polyhedron $\{ \mathbf{x}: \mathbf{Ax \le b}, \mathbf{x \ge 0} \}$ *is integral for all* **b** *with* $b_i \in \{1, \infty\}$.
2. The polyhedron $\{ \mathbf{x}: \mathbf{Ax \ge b}, \mathbf{x \ge 0} \}$ *is integral for all* **b** *with* $b_i \in \{0,1\}$.
3. The matrix A *is balanced.*

Unfortunately up to now no polynomial algorithm is known to test whether a given (0,1)-matrix is balanced or not.
Another important approach to combinatorial optimization problems is *polyhedral combinatorics*. Here we consider the convex hull of all feasible solutions of a combinatorial optimization problem and try to describe this convex polytope by linear inequality systems.
The polyhedral description of assignment problems, network flow problems, matching

problems and optimization problems in matroids or for the intersection of two matroids is completely known. But the polyhedral approach proved also extremely useful for NP-hard problems for which the corresponding polyhedral description is not fully known. A well-known example in this respect is the travelling salesman problem. Since the number of all known facets of the travelling salesman polytope is too large to be used in a linear programming formulation for this problem, the following *cutting plane approach* is applied with much success:

Some of the facet defining inequalities are used in a linear programming relaxation for the problem. If the corresponding linear program yields a fractional (or an infinite) solution, a *cutting plane* is constructed which separates this solution from the convex hull of all feasible solutions of the given problem. The cutting plane is added as an additional constraint to the linear program and this is resolved. Of particular practical importance is the solution of the so-called *separation problem*: given an infeasible point, generate automatically a cutting plane which separates this point from the convex hull of all feasible solutions. Problem specific techniques have been developed to tackle this problem.

This approach has successfully been applied to large travelling salesman problems, to the *linear ordering problem*, to *set packing* and *set partitioning*, the *stable set problem* or recently to the *three-index assignment problem*. It requires the availability of a code for solving large linear programs and needs detailed investigations on how the separation problem can be handled.

Finally, the data of a combinatorial optimization problem may arise from convex geometric configurations. In such instances an optimal solution can often be found faster than in the general case by using methods from computational geometry. This is a rather new, but promising area of research.

Combinatorial optimization problems which have been investigated in this way are *spanning tree problems*, *Steiner tree problems* and *Euclidean matching problems*. These problems have nowadays found increasing interest in connection with planar lay-out problems as a tool for VLSI design.

Using Voronoi diagrams and the relative neighborhood graph the following result can be shown for minimum spanning tree problems:

Theorem

Let n points be given in the plane. A minimum spanning tree for these points can be computed in O(n log n) time. If the points lie on the boundary of a convex polygon and are given in their cyclic order, then a minimum spanning tree for these points can be constructed in linear time.

A similar result has recently be shown by Monma, Paterson, Suri and Yao for computing

maximum spanning trees, i.e. trees whose total length is maximum.
Let us now turn to the *Steiner tree problem*. Provan (1988) showed the following result:

Theorem (Provan)
If the n terminals of a Euclidean Steiner tree problem lie on the boundary of a convex polygon in the plane, then there is a fully polynomial approximation scheme for this problem, i.e. there is an algorithm which for any $\varepsilon>0$ *constructs a Steiner tree T of length l(T) such that* $l(T) \leq (1+\varepsilon)\cdot Opt$, *where Opt is the optimal value of the problem. The running time of the algorithm is polynomial in n and* $1/\varepsilon$.

Finally we mention a result on Euclidean matching problems:

Theorem (Marcotte and Suri,1989)
Given a set V of 2n points on the boundary of a convex polygon whose edges are assigned weights equal to the Euclidean distance of their endpoints, then a minimum weight matching can be found in O(n log n) steps. A maximum weight matching can be determined in linear time O(n).

As a by-product of their method the authors get a fast algorithm for deciding whether a given matching is a minimum weight matching or not. This *verification problem* can be solved in $O(n\ \alpha(n))$ time where $\alpha(n)$ is the extremely slow growing inverse Ackermann function.
When we color the vertices red and blue and allow only edges between a red and a blue vertex, we get an *assignment problem*. Marcotte and Suri [1989b] showed that this assignment problem can be solved in O(n log n) steps provided the vertices lie again on the boundary of a convex polygon in the plane.

The full version of this paper appears in the *Handbook of Convex Geometry*, ed. by P.Gruber and J.Wills, Amsterdam: North Holland 1992.

DIRECT SEARCH METHODS ON PARALLEL MACHINES

J. E. DENNIS
VIRGINIA TORCZON
DEPARTMENT OF MATHEMATICAL SCIENCES
RICE UNIVERSITY
HOUSTON, TX 77251-1892, U.S.A.

Direct search methods are methods designed to solve unconstrained minimization problems of the form:

$$\min_{x \in \mathbb{R}^n} f(x),$$

where $f : \mathbb{R}^n \to \mathbb{R}$. These methods are distinguished by the fact that they neither use nor require explicit derivative information; the search for a local minimizer is driven solely by function information. Popular methods in this class include the factorial design algorithm of Box [1], the pattern search algorithm of Hooke and Jeeves [4], and the simplex method of Nelder and Mead [5].

Our interest in these methods is twofold. First, the very simplicity of the direct search methods suggested to us that they would be ideal candidates for parallelization. Second, their popularity suggested to us that any performance improvements that could be made due to parallelization would be of immediate use. As evidence of the popularity of direct search methods, we note that in the 1989 Science Citation Index [6], the original paper of Nelder and Mead has over 215 citations. By contrast, the paper of Fletcher and Powell [3] which introduced the variable metric secant update (now known as the DFP update) for quasi-Newton methods is apparently the most widely cited paper in the literature on quasi-Newton methods. It has 112 citations. The popularity of the direct search methods is further evidenced by the fact that variants of the Nelder-Mead simplex algorithm appear as options in most commercially available optimization software packages, including NAG, IMSL, and Matlab.

The simplicity and flexibility of direct search methods have allowed us to develop a family of parallel direct search algorithms that can be easily tailored to fit any computing environment. Our work has concentrated on distributed memory multiprocessors, such as the Intel iPSC/860 and the Intel Touchstone Delta, but the algorithms we propose are amenable to a variety of architectures: they are simple enough to be run sequentially on a personal computer and yet flexible enough to be run on a network of workstations or even a network of machines with varying architectural features. The key reason for the flexibility of the parallel methods lies in the fact that they are *scalable*—the number of processors that can be used is independent of the dimension of the problem to be solved. A special feature of this approach is the ease with which algorithms can be generated to take advantage of any number of processors and to adapt to any cost ratio of communication to function evaluation. The importance of scalability has become clear, if still not widely appreciated in the numerical optimization community, with the advent of machines that contain a large number of very fast processors, such as the Intel Touchstone Delta.

The parallel direct search schemes we propose [2] are based on the multidirectional search algorithm, a direct search method introduced by Dennis and Torczon [7]. We have chosen to use the multidirectional search algorithm as the core algorithm for our parallel direct search schemes because it is supported by a strong convergence theorem [8] that places minimal assumptions on the function; we require only that the function be continuously differentiable over a compact level set to guarantee convergence to the set of stationary points. Our numerical experiments suggest that the convergence theorem is borne out in practice: these methods have good global convergence properties and, in addition, are usually insensitive to noise in the function values. Furthermore, there is an interesting connection between the convergence theory for the basic multidirectional search algorithm and the parallel properties of the family of direct search methods we propose: we can interpret these methods as intelligent adaptive grid search algorithms.

Finally, we have experience which suggests that these methods can be extremely useful as experimental tools, particularly when little is known about the function to be minimized. One promising observation to be made is that the information generated by these methods could be used to drive visualization tools for solution diagnostics—an exciting possibility which we have yet to exploit. Of greatest significance, however, is the fact that these methods can successfully tackle problems which are not amenable to derivative based optimization algorithms.

REFERENCES

[1] G. E. P. Box, *Evolutionary operation: A method for increasing industrial productivity*, Applied Statistics, VI (1957), pp. 81–101.

[2] J. E. Dennis, Jr. and V. Torczon, *Direct search methods on parallel machines*, SIAM Journal on Optimization, 1 (1991).

[3] R. Fletcher and M. J. D. Powell, *A rapidly convergent descent method for minimization*, The Computer Journal, 6 (1963), pp. 163–168.

[4] R. Hooke and T. A. Jeeves, *"Direct search" solution of numerical and statistical problems*, Journal of the Association for Computing Machinery, 8 (1961), pp. 212–229.

[5] J. A. Nelder and R. Mead, *A simplex method for function minimization*, The Computer Journal, 7 (1965), pp. 308–313.

[6] SCI, *Science Citation Index Annual 1989*. Institute for Scientific Information, Inc., Philadelphia, Pennsylvania.

[7] V. Torczon, *Multi-Directional Search: A Direct Search Algorithm for Parallel Machines*, PhD thesis, Rice University, Houston, Texas, 1989. Available as Tech. Rep. 90–7, Department of Mathematical Sciences, Rice University, Houston, Texas 77251–1892.

[8] ——, *On the convergence of the multidirectional search algorithm*, SIAM Journal on Optimization, 1 (1991), pp. 123–145.

A Probabilistic Look at Options and at the Underlying Randomness

by Hans Föllmer

Consider an option based on a financial asset whose price fluctuation is modelled by a stochastic process (S_t) over some probability space $(\Omega, \mathcal{F}, P)$. Let H denote the resulting pay-off; for a call option with exercise price c and terminal time T we would have $H = (S_T - c)^+$. Instead of computing the fair price of such an option as the expected value $E[H]$ with respect to P, possibly modified by a risk premium, the Black-Scholes formula computes the price as the expected value $E^*[H]$ with respect to a new measure P^* which turns (S_t) into a martingale. We review the basic argument, both from a probabilistic and an economic point of view. It involves the Itô representation of H as a stochastic integral of the price process and the interpretation of the integrand as a dynamical hedging strategy. Such hedging strategies induce a technical demand for the financial asset. Thus the question arises: What is the impact of such strategies on the underlying price process?

Motivated by this question, we have a closer look at the structure of P. We review the arguments which led to the introduction of Brownian motion by L. Bachelier (1900) and of geometric Brownian motion by P.A. Samuelson as mathematical models for price fluctuation on a speculative market, and more recent attempts to justify the now canonical model of geometric Brownian motion as a *rational expectations equilibrium* of plans, prices and price expectations. We also recall the *efficient market hypothesis* that price fluctuation is induced by uncertainty about the fundamentals. However, recent experiments by Smith et al. (1988) have shown that uncertainty about the fundamentals is certainly not the only source of randomness, and that we need a more detailed micreconomic description of the randomness generated by interacting agents.

We then describe work in progress with Martin Schweizer (University of Bonn) on the microeconomic description of price fluctuation as a sequence of temporary equilibria induced by random excess demands of agents $i \in I$ and on the convergence of such discrete time models to a diffusion model. Under classical i.i.d. assumptions we are led to the canonical model of geometric Brownian motion. A richer structure appears if we distinguish different types af agents, e.g., *noise traders* and *information traders* in the sense of Black (1986). We consider an explicit model where the invariance principle leads us to a geometric Ornstein-Uhlenbeck process. Under stationary fundamentals, information traders produce an equilibrium described by a recurrent Ornstein-Uhlenbeck process, while noise traders produce an unstable situation where the Ornstein-Uhlenbeck process is transient. Following a suggestion by A. Kirman, we assume that the proportion between noise and information traders changes in a random fashion. We are then led to an Ornstein-Uhlenbeck process in a random environment. For this model, we discuss the existence of an equilibrium distribution, using mathematical techniques developped by Barnsley et al. (1988) in the analysis of random algorithms for the generation of images. Typically, the equilibrium distribution has a fractal structure: It is a mixture of log-normal distributions where the mixing measure is continuous but often singular. Coming back to the effect of hedging strategies, we now note that the demand induced by Black-Scholes hedging strategies has the structure of the demand of noise traders. We should thus expect that Black-Scholes trading increases the transient component of the process. Even if information traders remain so dominant that there does exists an equilibrium distribution, the instability induced by the transient component is reflected in the fact that the mixing measure has no longer bounded support.

References

M.F. Barnsley and J.H. Elton (1988), "A New Class of Markov Processes for Image Encoding ", Advances in Applied Probability 20, 14-32

F.Black and M. Scholes (1973), "The Pricing of Options and Corporate Liabilities", Journal of Political Economy 81, 637-659

F. Black (1986), "Noise ", Journal of Finance XLI/3, 529-543

D. Duffie (1988): "Security Markets. Stochastic Models", Academic Press

H. Föllmer, "Probabilistic Aspects of Options", Preprint University of Bonn (1991)

H Föllmer and M. Schweizer (1990): "Hedging by Sequential Regression: An Introduction to the Mathematics of Option Trading", The ASTIN Bulletin 18/2, 147-160

V.L. Smith, G.L. Suchanek and A.W. Williams (1988), "Bubbles, Crashes, and Endogeneous Expectiastions in Experimental Spot Asset Markets", Econometrica 56/5, 1119-1151

PSEUDORANDOM NUMBER GENERATORS

Jürgen Lehn
Technische Hochschule Darmstadt
D–6100 Darmstadt, Schlossgartenstr. 7

Sequences of pseudorandom numbers are needed for applications of stochastic simulation. Usually they are generated in the computer by a deterministic algorithm which produces a sequence of standard pseudorandom numbers, i.e. a sequence of numbers which "behave" as a realization of a sequence of independent identically distributed random variables having a uniform distribution on the unit interval. In a second step these standard pseudorandom numbers are often transformed in order to fit a given (non–uniform) distribution. For example, Devroy's book [4] is devoted to this problem. This paper deals only with algorithms producing sequences of standard pseudorandom numbers. Such algorithms are called pseudorandom number generators. Many users of simulation techniques do not think about the pseudorandom number generators implemented in their computers and use the standard software at hand. This habitude is dangerous since the "stochastic quality" of the pseudorandom number sequences is fundamental for the results of stochastic simulation and many pseudorandom number generators in use have serious defects (see e.g. [2], [6], p.10, and [26], p.18). The present paper gives a survey on methods for generating deterministic sequences of real numbers which can be used as standard pseudorandom number sequences. Special emphasis is given to generation methods which have been studied by the author's research group at Darmstadt Technical University.

Most frequently pseudorandom numbers are generated by the linear congruential method which goes back to Lehmer [16]. A linear congruential generator is defined by

$$x_i \equiv a \cdot x_{i-1} + b \pmod m$$

for a multiplier a, a shift b, a seed x_0, and a modulus m which is a large integer. The other parameters x_0, a and b are integers too, taken between 0 and $m-1$. If $b = 0$, then the generator is called multiplicative congruential. If the parameters are chosen carefully, then the sequence of numbers $u_i = x_i/m$, $i = 0, 1, 2, \ldots$, can be taken as a sequence of standard pseudorandom numbers. Because of the simple linear structure of the generation formula, the points $(x_0, x_1, \ldots, x_{k-1})$, $(x_1, x_2, \ldots, x_k)$, ... lie on a shifted lattice which is part of the full integer lattice $\mathbb{Z}^k$. A basis of the shifted lattice is given by $\vec{c}_1 = (1, a, a^2, \ldots, a^{k-1})$, $\vec{c}_2 = (0, m, 0, \ldots, 0)$, ... , $\vec{c}_k = (0, 0, 0, \ldots, m)$. It follows that the points $(x_0, x_1, \ldots, x_{k-1})$, $(x_1, x_2, \ldots, x_k)$, ... as well as the points $(u_0, u_1, \ldots, u_{k-1})$, $(u_1, u_2, \ldots, u_k)$, ... are carried by a finite number of hyperplanes (see Marsaglia [17]). Since the generated sequence $x_0, x_1, x_2, \ldots$ is periodic with period length $\leq m$, the parameters a and b of the recursion formula should be chosen in such a way that maximum period length m is achieved and that the sequence of points $(x_0, x_1, \ldots, x_{k-1}), (x_1, x_2, \ldots, x_k)$, ... does not concentrate on too few hyperplanes in $\mathbb{R}^k$ (for reasonable dimensions $k = 2, 3, \ldots$). The lattice structure of linear congruential pseudorandom number generators has been studied extensively (see for example the survey paper of Niederreiter [24] or Chapter 3 of [15]). The value of the modulus m is often chosen with respect to the word length of the computer. Since the number of hyperplanes carrying the shifted lattice is essentially determined by the multiplier a and the modulus m (the influence of the choice of b can be neglected) the problem is to find a "good" multiplier a for a given modulus m. Fishman and Moore carried out an exhaustive search for "good" multipliers a with respect to $m = 2^{32} - 1$ as well as $m = 2^{32}$ and partial search with respect to $m = 2^{48}$ (see [11] and [12]). The results show that, among others, the following generators can be recommended for stochastic simulations:

$$\begin{aligned} x_i &\equiv 742938285 \cdot x_{i-1} \pmod{2^{31}-1} \\ x_i &\equiv 1099087573 \cdot x_{i-1} + 1 \pmod{2^{32}} \\ x_i &\equiv 68909602460261 \cdot x_{i-1} + 1 \pmod{2^{48}} \end{aligned}$$

A criterion for selecting "good" multipliers a can be based on the maximum distance between the hyperplanes carrying the generated lattice (see Dieter [5] and [6]). Another way of analyzing the lattice structure is the calculation of a Minkowski reduced basis $\vec{e}_1, \vec{e}_2, \ldots, \vec{e}_k$ from the lattice basis $\vec{c}_1, \vec{c}_2, \ldots, \vec{c}_k$ mentioned above by an algorithm of Afflerbach and Grothe [3]. Since $\vec{e}_1, \vec{e}_2, \ldots, \vec{e}_k$ is in some sense a basis of shortest vectors with $|\vec{e}_1| \le |\vec{e}_2| \le \ldots \le |\vec{e}_k|$ describing the unit cell of the lattice, the Beyer ratios $q_k = |\vec{e}_1|/|\vec{e}_k|$, $k = 2, 3, \ldots$, can be used for selecting the multipliers a. One is interested in generators with q_k close to 1 (up to a certain dimension k, e.g. $k \le 20$). The search for a "good" multiplier a can also be based on the k–dimensional discrepancy which will be defined below. Upper and lower bounds for the discrepancy are due to Niederreiter [19]. Other criteria for selecting "good" multipliers can be found e.g. in [1] and [15].

As a generalization of the linear congruential method Knuth [15] introduced the multi-recursive generators

$$x_i \equiv a_1 \cdot x_{i-1} + \ldots + a_r \cdot x_{i-r} \pmod{p}$$

for recursion depth r and prime modulus p. The multipliers $a_1, \ldots, a_r$ and the starting values $x_0, \ldots, x_{r-1}$ are integers between 0 and $p-1$ and at least one of the integers $x_0, \ldots, x_{r-1}$ is different from zero. Maximum period length $p^r - 1$ is attained, if the polynomial $\lambda^r - a_1\lambda^{r-1} - \ldots - a_{r-1}\lambda - a_r$ is a primitive polynomial mod p. The matrix generator (see [13], [20], and [27]) generalizes this method. It is defined by

$$\vec{x}_i \equiv A \cdot \vec{x}_{i-1} \pmod{p}$$

where $\vec{x}_i$ is an r–vector with integer components, A an $r \times r$ matrix with integer entries, all integers between 0 and $p-1$, and a starting vector $\vec{x}_0 \neq \vec{0}$. Then a sequence of pseudorandom vectors (uniformly distributed in the hypercube $[0,1]^r$) is obtained by the normalization $\vec{u}_i = (1/p) \cdot \vec{x}_i$, $i = 0, 1, 2, \ldots$, and maximum period length $p^r - 1$ is attained by the sequence of r–vectors if the characteristic polynomial of the matrix A is a primitive polynomial mod p. Since the generated vectors lie on sublattices of $\mathbb{Z}^k$ $(k > r)$, the matrix generators can be analyzed in a similar way as the linear congruential generators. Grothe [14] carried out a search for "good" matrices up to $r = 6$ for different prime moduli p. For $r = 3$ and $p = 2^{31} - 1 = 2147483647$ he found that the matrix generator

$$\vec{x}_i \equiv A \cdot \vec{x}_{i-1} \pmod{2^{31}-1}$$

with

$$A = \begin{pmatrix} 387449180 & 221426589 & 1716832824 \\ 353640677 & 1110867971 & 1059928315 \\ 1382810819 & 1921776773 & 1528193766 \end{pmatrix}$$

is a good one in the sense that it has lattices in higher dimensions with reasonable values for the Beyer ratios. The period length $p^r - 1$ of this generator is approximatly 10^{28}.

In an attempt to get rid of the lattice structure of the linear congruential and matrix generators the inversive congruential method was introduced in [8]. The inversive congruential generator is defined by

$$x_i \equiv a \cdot \overline{x}_{i-1} + b \pmod p$$

where p is a prime modulus, the starting value x_0 as well as the coefficients a and b are integers between 0 and $p-1$, and $\overline{x}$ is defined in the following way: Observe that for any $x \in \{1,2,\ldots,p-1\}$ there is exactly one $\overline{x} \in \{1,2,\ldots,p-1\}$ with $x \cdot \overline{x} \equiv 1 \pmod p$. This $\overline{x}$ is the multiplicative inverse of x in the finite field $GF(p)$ of order p. Together with $\overline{0} = 0$ this defines $\overline{x}$. A method for calculating $\overline{x}$ (if $x \neq 0$) is based on the Euclidean algorithm: Set $\alpha_0 = p$, $\alpha_1 = x$, $\beta_0 = 0$, $\beta_1 = 1$, and $i = 1$. As long as $\alpha_i > 1$ set $\alpha_{i+1} \equiv \alpha_{i-1} \pmod{\alpha_i}$ with $0 < \alpha_{i+1} < \alpha_i$, $\beta_{i+1} = \beta_{i-1} - (\alpha_{i-1} - \alpha_{i+1}) \cdot \beta_i/\alpha_i$, and increase i by 1. Then $\overline{x} \equiv \beta_i \pmod p$. Asymptotically one needs $O(\log p)$ steps of iteration (cf. [15], Sec. 4.5). Therefore, the generation of inversive congruential pseudorandom numbers takes more time than is needed if the linear congruential method is applied. A sequence of inversive congruential pseudorandom numbers in $[0,1]$ is attained from $x_0, x_1, x_2, \ldots$ by the normalization $u_i = x_i/p$, $i = 0,1,2,\ldots$, and the sequence has maximum period length p, if the polynomial $\lambda^2 - b\lambda - a$ is a primitive polynomial mod p. In [10] generators with maximum period length are given for different prime moduli p. Two of them are

$$\begin{aligned} x_i &\equiv \overline{x}_{i-1} + 1 \pmod{2^{31} - 1} \\ x_i &\equiv \overline{x}_{i-1} + 5 \pmod{2^{47} - 297} \end{aligned}$$

Observe that $a = 1$ in both cases. This has advantages for doing the integer calculations on computers with short word length. The inversive congruential generators and several modifications have been studied extensively during the last years. The results show that inversive congruential generators have very different properties from those of linear congruential generators. They do not create lattice structures. They pass Marsaglia's lattice test (cf. [18]) in all dimensions $k \leq (p+1)/2$, i.e. the coarsest lattice containing all points $(x_0, x_1, \ldots, x_{k-1})$, $(x_1, x_2, \ldots, x_k)$, ... is the full integer lattice $\mathbb{Z}^k$ (see [7], [21]). Moreover, in a recent paper [9] Eichenauer–Herrmann proved the remarkable result that (for arbitrary k) there is no hyperplane in $\mathbb{R}^k$ containing more than k of these points. Another result showing that these generators produce sequences which "behave" very randomly is due to Niederreiter [22]. For inversive congruential generators with maximum period length p he studied the k–dimensional discrepancy of the (normalized) sequence $(u_0, u_1, \ldots, u_{k-1})$, $(u_1, u_2, \ldots, u_k)$, ... of points in the hypercube $[0,1]^k$ which is defined by

$$D_p^{(k)} = \sup_I |F(I) - V(I)|$$

where the supremum is taken over all subintervals I of $[0,1]^k$ with one vertex at the origin. $F(I)$ is the relative frequency of points falling into I and $V(I)$ denotes the k–dimensional volume of I. He derived the asymptotic formula

$$D_p^{(k)} = O\left(p^{-1/2} (\log p)^k\right)$$

for $2 \leq k < p$ and improved this result in [23] by showing that the discrepancy $D_p^{(k)}$ has on the average an order of magnitude between $p^{-1/2}$ and $p^{-1/2}(\log p)^k$. This is the range of magnitudes where the discrepancy of p independent identically distributed random vectors (uniformly distributed in $[0,1]^k$) can be found according to the law of iterated logarithm for discrepancies. Such a result cannot be proved for linear congruential generators. This shows again that there is a substantial difference between inversive and linear congruential generators (see [24] and [25] for a discussion of this result). The inversive congruential generators need more generation time than the linear congruential generators. But they seem to be important alternatives if one would like to run a Monte Carlo program many times using quite different sources of random numbers before taking the answers of the program seriously, a policy which has been suggested by Knuth (see [15], p.156).

References

[1] Afflerbach, L.: *On the assessment of linear congruential generators.* J. Comp. Appl. Math. 31 (1990) 3–10

[2] Afflerbach,L.: *The pseudo-random number generators in Commodore and Apple microcomputers.* Statist. Papers 26 (1985) 321–333

[3] Afflerbach L. and Grothe, H.: *Calculation of Minkowski reduced lattice bases.* Computing 35 (1985) 269–276

[4] Devroy, L.: *Non-Uniform Random Variate Generation.* New York: Springer Verlag 1986

[5] Dieter, U.: *How to calculate shortest vectors in a lattice.* Math. Comp. 29 (1975) 827–833

[6] Dieter, U.: *Probleme bei der Erzeugung gleichverteilter Zufallszahlen.* in: Afflerbach, L. and Lehn, J. (eds.): Zufallszahlen und Simulationen. Stuttgart, Teubner Verlag 1986, 7-20

[7] Eichenauer, J.; Grothe, H.; and Lehn, J.: *Marsaglia's lattice test and non-linear congruential pseudo random number generators.* Metrika 35 (1988) 241–250

[8] Eichenauer, J. and Lehn, J.: *A non-linear congruential pseudo random number generator.* Statist. Papers 27 (1986) 315–326

[9] Eichenauer–Herrmann, J.: *Inversive congruential pseudorandom numbers avoid the planes.* Math. Comp. 56 (1991) 297–301

[10] Eichenauer–Herrmann, J.: *Inversive congruential pseudorandom numbers: a tutorial.* Darmstadt, Fachbereich Mathematik: Preprint Nr. 1405 (to appear in Int. Stat. Rev.)

[11] Fishman, G.S.: *Multiplicative congruential random number generators with modulus 2^β: An exhaustive analysis for $\beta = 32$ and a partial analysis for $\beta = 48$.* Math. Comp. 54 (1990) 331-344

[12] Fishman, G.S. and Moore, L.R.: *An exhaustive analysis of multiplicative congruential random number generators with modulus* $2^{31}-1$. SIAM J. Sci. Statist. Comp. 7 (1986) 24–45; Erratum, ibid. 7, 1058

[13] Grothe, H.: *Matrix–Generatoren.* in: Afflerbach, L.; Lehn, J. (eds.): Zufallszahlen und Simulationen. Stuttgart: Teubner Verlag 1986, 29–34

[14] Grothe, H.: *Matrix–Generatoren zur Erzeugung gleichverteilter Pseudozufallsvektoren.* Thesis, Darmstadt (1988)

[15] Knuth, D.E.: *The Art of Computer Programming.* Reading (Mass.): Addison–Wesley 1969, Vol. 2, 1st ed.

[16] Lehmer, D.H.: *Mathematical methods in large–scale computing units.* Proc. 2nd Symposium on Large–Scale Digital Calculating Machinery. Cambridge, Mass.: Harvard Univ. Press 1951, 141–146

[17] Marsaglia, G.: *Random numbers fall mainly in the planes.* Proc. Nat. Acad. Sci. USA 61 (1968) 25–28

[18] Marsaglia, G.: *The lattice structure of linear congruential sequences.* in: Zaremba, S.K. (ed.): Applications of Number Theory to Numerical Analysis. New York: Academic Press 1972, 249–285

[19] Niederreiter, H.: *The serial test for pseudo–random numbers generated by the linear congruential method.* Numer. Math. 46 (1985) 51–68

[20] Niederreiter, H.: *A pseudorandom vector generator based on finite field arithmetic.* Math. Japonica 31 (1986) 759–774

[21] Niederreiter, H.: *Remarks on nonlinear congruential pseudorandom numbers.* Metrika 35 (1988) 321–328

[22] Niederreiter, H.: *The serial test for congruential pseudorandom numbers generated by inversions.* Math. Comp. 52 (1989) 135–144

[23] Niederreiter, H.: *Lower bounds for the discrepancy of inversive congruential pseudorandom numbers.* Math. Comp. 55 (1990) 277–287

[24] Niederreiter, H.: *Recent trends in random number and random vector generation.* Ann. Operations Research 31 (1991) 323–346

[25] Niederreiter, H.: *Nonlinear methods for pseudorandom number and vector generation.* Proc. Internat. Workshop on Computationally–Intensive Methods in Simulation and Stochastic Optimization, Laxenburg 1990 (to appear)

[26] Ripley, B.D.: *Stochastic Simulation.* New York: John Wiley & Sons 1987

[27] Tahmi, E.–H.: *Contribution aux générateurs des vecteurs pseudo–aléatoires.* Thesis, Algers (1982)

Learning, Inferences and Iterations

Extended Abstract

Michael M. Richter, Kaiserslautern

The concept of learning is studied in several disciplines such as Artificial Intelligence, Mathematics or Cognitive Sciences. All these approaches are somehow related to each other but they also show some fundamental differences. The lack of a uniform terminology makes a comparison difficult. We will give here some prototypical examples of different methods, discuss some of their relations and make some first steps towards an integrated view.

One mathematical discipline which deals with learning is logic. In this view learning is a type of inference which takes place in some logical calculus. In fact, all the three basic types of inferences, namely deduction, induction and analogical reasoning have their counterparts in machine learning. The first two types have in addition a long tradition in logic; e.g. induction was extensively studied by Francis Bacon and in this century by Rudolf Carnap. Induction reasoning generates a general concept from individual examples. In simple cases this can be carried out by antiunification algorithms, a more general form is given by various version space algorithms. They all lead to a universally quantified formula which has the examples as instance. The top-down-inductive-decision-tree (TDIDT) algorithms add a new feature. Each path in the tree still represents a concept but has in addition an information theoretic aspect which takes care of the desire for a fast classification. A numerical coding transforms the problem into the investigation of subsets of the $\mathbb{R}^n$ which leads to various geometric investigations. Instead of predicates one talks about half-planes, convex sets etc.. In the case of Boolean functions in principle the geometrical and the logical terminology are equivalent; e.g. the conjunction of predicates describing half-planes corresponds to a convex set. A detailed analysis can be, however, arbitrarily difficult. As an example we mention the notion of the entropy potential. For a finite set S and

$$B = \{0,1\},\ f{:}B^S \to B,\ U \subseteq S \quad \text{and } g, h \in B^u$$

we put

$$g \equiv_f h \Leftrightarrow [g', h' \in B^S,\ g' \upharpoonright U = g,\ h' \upharpoonright U = h \Rightarrow f(g)=f(h)]$$

The entropy potential is

<u>Def:</u> (i) $\mu_f(U) = \text{card}\ (B^S/{\equiv_f})$

(ii) $C(f) = \max (\mu_f (U) \mid \subseteq S)$

This is related to the Vapnik-Chervonenkis dimension by

$$V(\dim(f) = \max (m \,/\, \exists\, U, \mu_f(U) = 2^m)$$

Both, C(f) and VCdim(f) are indicators of decomposability and hence of definability of f.

Analogical reasoning is in its simplest form of the following type :
Given a problem a, select a known problem a' from a case base such that a and a' are "most similar" and use the solution for a' also as a solution for a.

Here the fundamental notion of analogical reasoning appears, namely that the of a similarity. Similarity can be defined as a function sim(x,y) with values in [0,1]. The dual to a similarity is that of a distance d(x,y). Note that such a distance in general will not be a metric because the triangle inequality is not required. There are many such functions and the question of what is a "good" function can only be decided a posteriori. That means, a similarity function should also be "learned". In principle, such a function is also a general law like a predicate, but it follows different rules. The relation between logical predicates and similarity has not yet been sufficiently clarified.

We take a closer look to analogical reasoning by investigating the PATDEX system (Pattern Directed Expert system), developed at Kaiserslautern. Here the above notions are refined in different ways.

Finally, we report on an experimental scenario in which different learning methods can be evaluated according to various criteria. The system is implemented in Smalltalk 80 and experiments were carried out for TDIDT algorithms, PATDEX and Baysian classification. The results show that the systems are difficult to compare ; one of the problems is to find the right level of abstraction for a comparison. We regard this as a major research problem for the near future.

References:

M. Stadler: Ein Vergleich von fallbasierten induktive und statistischen Lernverfahren für die Klassifikation. Diplomarbeit Kaiserslautern 1991.

M.M. Richter, S. Weß: Similarity, Uncertainty and Case-Based Reasoning in PATDEX. In: Frontiers of Computing, Ed. R.S. Boyer,

X. Li: On the entropy potential of binary functions. Preprint Kaiserslautern, 1991.

BAYESIAN METHODS IN GLOBAL OPTIMIZATION

Bruno Betrò
CNR - IAMI
via Ampère 56
I-20131 Milano

The basic problem in global optimization is the one of properly assessing a performance criterion for global optimum seeking algorithms, because of the lack of manageable analytical characterizations of the global optimum. In order to cope with this difficulty, the idea has been introduced of superimposing to the global optimization problem a probabilistic structure and to set up accuracy criteria consequently. Then Bayes theorem provides the basic tool for adapting the probabilistic structure to information gained about the problem itself after a certain number of function evaluations. Methods derived within this framework will be referred to as Bayesian methods. Following [1], an overview is presented of different probabilistic formulations of the global optimization problem and of related Bayesian methods as yet proposed.

THE RANDOM FUNCTION APPROACH

The approach is based on the idea of introducing a probabilistic model for the objective function f in the form of a random function $f(x,\omega)$, where ω belongs to some measurable space Ω over which a probability P is defined. The actual function to be optimized is seen as a realization $f(x)$ of $f(x,\omega)$.

Then, given a sequential n-step optimization strategy S_n, its effectiveness for the function f can be measured by the difference $L(S_n, f) = \max_x f(x) - f_n^*$, $f_n^* = \max_{1\leq i\leq n} f(x_i)$, where $x_1, \ldots, x_n$ is the sequence of points generated by S_n.

Over the class $\{f(x,\omega)\}$ a measure of the performance of S_n is given by

$$E(L(S_n, f)) = \int L(S_n, f)P(d\omega) = E(\max_x f(x)) - E(f_n^*),$$

so that an optimal strategy S_n^* can be defined as any strategy such that $E(f_n^{**}) = \sup_{S_n} E(f_n^*)$, where f_n^{**} is the largest function value attained by S_n^*.

The determination of S_n^* can take profit of a standard dynamic programming approach. However, it is well known that serious problems arise from a computational point of view in dealing with Bellman equations even for moderate n; it is therefore usual practice to derive suboptimal strategies. Effective suboptimal strategies have been actually proposed in the one-dimensional case, exploiting the fact that the Wiener process provides a manageable stochastic model of continuous univariate multimodal functions.

In the multi-dimensional case, the easiest way to model an unknown continuous function is to consider Gaussian random functions. Unfortunately, serious problems arise in deriving even suboptimal strategies, as the choice of the next point at which to evaluate the function typically reduces to a new global optimization problem. Several attempts have been made to circumvent such drawback. An attractive idea is that of reducing the multi-dimensional problem to an one-dimensional one by means of Peano maps.

A PROBABILISTIC MODEL FOR THE MULTISTART METHOD

It is an obvious observation that a global optimization problem would be solved once all local minima were discovered. It is therefore common practice to try to reach all local maxima starting a local search from n points randomly (uniformly) drawn in the search domain K. The procedure is usually referred to as *multistart* method. If the number of local maxima is finite, and apart from pathological situations, the procedure will achieve its goal with positive probability p; furthermore, p increases as the number of trials increases, so that n is usually taken large. It is conceivable that if it were possible to obtain information about p during the search procedure, then some stopping criterion could be set up avoiding to spend local searches superfluously.

It is useful to state the problem as follows. Assume that in K there is a finite number of local maxima, say $x_1^*, \ldots, x_k^*$. Let A be a search algorithm which, starting from a point x in K leads to some point $A(x)$ in K. Define $X_i^* \equiv \{x \in K : A(x) = x_i^*\}$, $i = 1, \ldots, k$ and assume that the set of starting points causing A not to converge to a local maximum has null Lebesgue measure. Let the quantity $\theta_i = m(X_i^*)/m(K)$ be the *share* of x_i^*.

If $X_1, \ldots, X_n$ are *i.i.d.* random variables uniformly distributed in K, then $P\{X_j \in X_i^*\} = \theta_i$, $j = 1, \ldots, n$, $i = 1, \ldots, k$. The application of A to the X_j's will lead to find N_i times the maximum x_i^*, with $N_i \geq 0$ and $\sum_{i=1}^k N_i = n$. Given the number of maxima k and the shares $\theta_1, \ldots, \theta_k$, then the vector $< N_1, \ldots, N_k >$ has a multinomial distribution. As k and $\theta_1, \ldots, \theta_k$ are unknown, it is sensible to infer about them on the basis of the available observations; this problem is a problem of inference about a multinomial distribution with an unknown number of classes.

Once a prior distribution on the parameter space $\Theta = \{< \theta_1, \ldots, \theta_k >, k = 1, 2, \ldots, \sum_{i=1}^k \theta_i = 1, \theta_i \geq 0\}$ is specified, the Bayes Theorem enables to obtain the posterior distribution of the unknown parameters k and $\theta_1, \ldots, \theta_k$, given the number of different maxima identified and their frequencies in the sample. Then a standard decision theoretic setting enables to decide in an optimal way whether all the local maxima have been reached or not.

Another possibility is to consider that the number of local searches is not fixed in advance, but these latter are started sequentially. Then after each of them is completed it is possible to decide whether to continue or not according to some criterion comparing the results obtained so far with the benefit expected from starting new searches.

A drawback of the approach is that the function values at the maxima are not taken into account. However, it has been recently observed that in the case that different maxima have different values, it is possible to incorporate ordering information about the maxima induced by their function values.

A BAYESIAN MODEL FOR OPTIMUM VALUES SAMPLED BY THE MULTISTART

The approach mentioned in the previous section is unable to deal explicitly with function values, neglecting this way important information about the structure of the problem. A way of circumventing this situation is based on the following ideas.

Let $t_i = f(x_i^*)$, $i = 1, \ldots, n$, be the optimum values sampled by the multistart methods after n steps. Assume that each local search has a fixed cost $c > 0$, expressed in the same units as f, and that the cost connected with stopping at step n is $L(t_1, \ldots, t_n; c) = -t_{(n)} + nc$ where $t_{(n)} = max_{i=1,\ldots,n} t_i$. This cost combines the cost of a new local search with the gain corresponding to a unit increase in the maximum observed value. The observations t_i are independent realizations of a random variable T whose distribution F is unknown (except for trivial cases).

Following the ideas of Bayesian nonparametric analysis, a class of random distribution functions in the family of ***neutral to the right*** can be introduced as a model for the unknown distribution function. A class in this family is described by the process $F(t) = 1 - \exp(-Y(t))$, where $Y(t)$ is a stochastic process a.s. nondecreasing and right continuous with $\lim_{t\to-\infty} Y(t) = 0$ and $\lim_{t\to\infty} Y(t) = \infty$.

In particular, considering a simple homogeneous model, it is possible to derive suboptimal stopping rules of the k−step look ahead (k*−sla*) type. A k*-sla* rule calls for stopping the sampling process as soon as the current cost is not greater than the cost expected if at most k further observations are taken. Under a stochastic model for F, the 1-*sla* is found to be the rule which prescribes stopping as soon as $\int_{t_{(n)}}^{\infty}(1 - \hat{F}_n(t))dt \leq c$, where $\hat{F}_n(t) = E(F(t) \mid t_1, \ldots, t_n)$ is easily obtainable within the simple homogeneous model.

The effectiveness of both 1-*sla* and 2-*sla* rules has been tested for randomly generated problems in up to six dimensions and with various degrees of complexity and for randomly generated distribution functions $F(t)$. The results show that the percentage of failures in finding the global maximum is low, with a moderate number of local searches performed before stopping.

REFERENCES

[1] Betrò B. (1991), Bayesian Methods in Global Optimization, *Journal of Global Optimization* **1**, 1-14.

OPTIMIZATION OF DISCRETE MANUFACTURING PROCESSES - BRANCH AND BOUND METHOD

Ewa Dudek-Dyduch
Institute of Automatics, Academy of Mining and Metallurgy
al. Mickiewicza 30, 30-059 Kraków, Poland

There are three kinds of papers connected with the branch and bound method (B&B). The very general ones (artifical intelligence level), the papers presenting algorithms for fixed problems and the papers considering the method applied to some class of problems (e.g. the discrete programming. The papers dealing with B&B applied to optimization of control of discrete manufacturing processes are usually of the second kind. This paper is aimed at generalization and formal discussion of given there algorithms, thus it belongs to the last group. It uses the mathematical model of the vast class of discrete manufacturing processes, proposed in the earlier author's papers. Basing on the introduced there formalism, a new classification of fundamental conception of algorithms is presented, different types of lower bounds are defined and domination rules for lower bounds are determinated. The paper refers to algorithms that do not use the discrete programming model.

DISCRETE MANUFACTURING PROCESS & MULTISTAGE DECISION PROCESS

Discrete manufacturing processes (DMP) consist in performing some tasks on a set of machines, subject to several constraints imposed on the tasks, machines, resources, time and their mutual relationships. A vast class of discrete manufacturing processes has been formally defined in the earlier author's paper [1] as follows.

Definition 1. The individual discrete process P is a process that is univocally determined by the quadruple $P = (s_0, f, S_N, S_F)$ where:

$f: U \times S \to S$ is a partial function called a transition function, (it has not to be defined for all elements of the set $U \times S$)

U is a set of control decisions or control signals,

$S = X \times T$ is a set named set of generalized states,

X is a set of proper states, $T \subset \mathbb{R}^{+} \cup \{0\}$ is a subset of non negative real numbers representing the time instants,

$s_o = (x_o, t_o)$, $S_N \subset S$, $S_F \subset S$ are respectively: an initial generalized state, a set of not admissible generalized states, and a set of final generalized states, i.e. states in which we want the process to take place at the end. (The word "generalized" will be often omitted).
The transition function is defined by means of two functions, $f = (f_x, f_t)$ where $f_x : U \times X \times T \to X$ determines the next state and $f_t : U \times X \times T \to T$ determines the next time instant; there is assumed that the difference $\Delta t = f_t(u,x,t) - t$ has a value which is both finite and positive.

Function f was defined as a partial function. Thanks to it, all limitations concerning the control decisions can be taken into account by means of the so-called sets of possible decisions in state s, denoted as $U_p(s)$ and defined as: $U_p(s) = \{ u \in U : (u,s) \in \text{Dom } f \}$.

At the same time an individual process P is represented by a set of its trajectories. A trajectory that ends in the set of final states is an admissible one and the control sequence determining the admissible trajectory is an admissible control sequence.

The task of optimization of DMP control lies in finding of such a sequence of admissible controls $\tilde{u}$ which minimizes a certain criterion Q . The optimization task is univocally determined by the pair (P,Q) where process P represents all the task limitations. A defined problem of control optimization DMP is such a set of optimization tasks which have a commonly determined set of data, common (parametric) definition of set of individual DMP and common (parametric) definition of criterion functions.

Definition 2. Multistage decision (constructing) process is a process P defined by the following six (U, Y, y_o, f, Y_N, Y_F) where the individual values are defined analogously as in definition 1, so U is a decision set, Y is set of states, y_o, Y_N, Y_F are distinguished initial state and sets of not admissible and final states, respectively, f is a partial function $f : U \times Y \to Y$ defined by means of the function $g : Y \to 2^U$ in the following way: $(u,y) \in \text{Dom } f \Leftrightarrow u \in g(y)$. Thus function $g(y)$ determines the decision subset $U_p(y)$, for wchich function f is determined in the state y.

Let us distinguish two basic ways of constructing the searched control sequence. The first one lies in recurrence generation of control sequence according to the discrete model of DMP; the second one - in the construction of the sequence by the determination of its elements in any order different than the order of occurance in the sequence $\tilde{u}$. The multistage process of control sequence generation (following the DMP model) will be called a natural process, whereas others will be called loose processes.

CLASSIFICATION OF ALGORITHMS AND LOWER BOUNDS

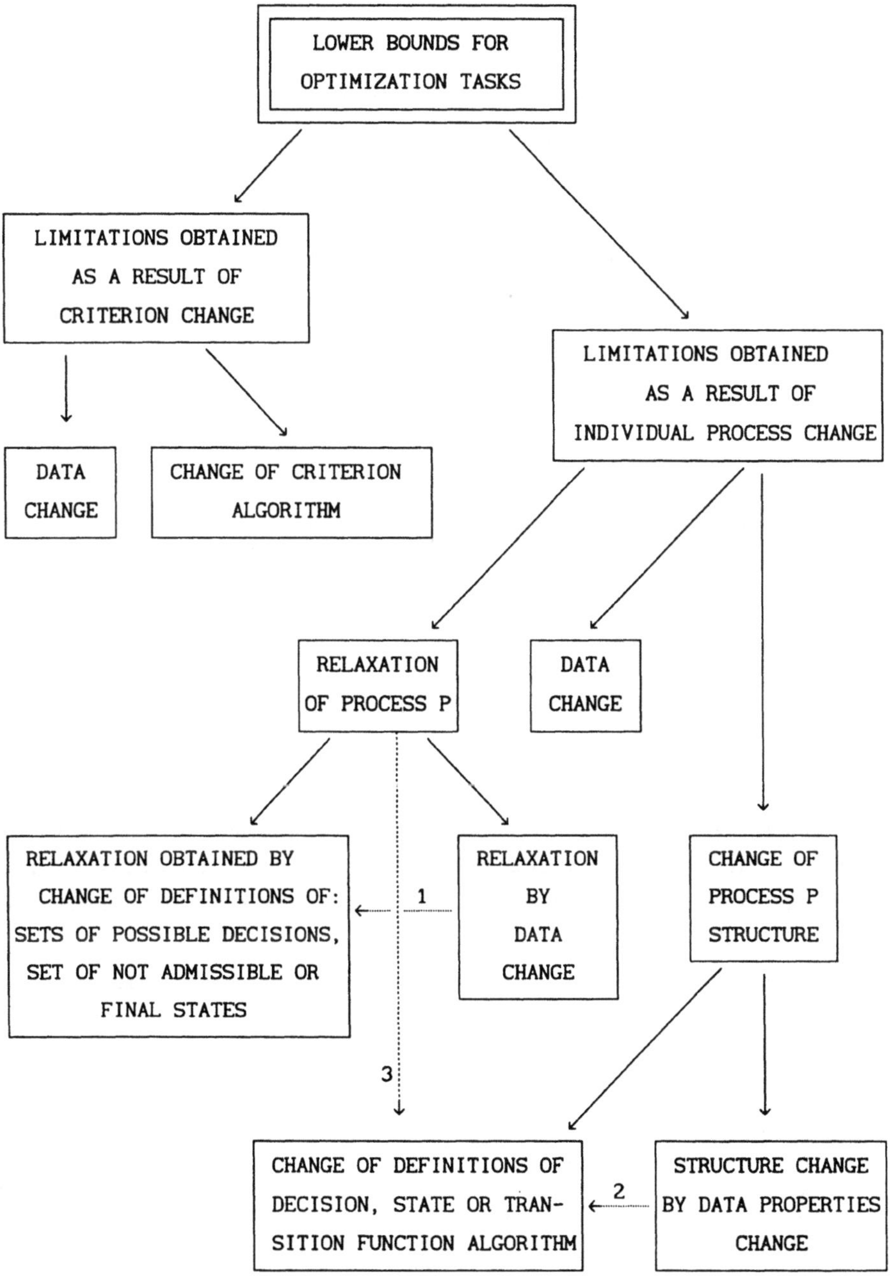

Fig.1 Types for lower bounds for a task, obtained as a result of its model change. The broken lines indicate additional consequences of some changes.

Using the introduced division of multistage processes we may distinguish the following types of algorithms.

B&B algorithms optimizing control of DMP:

- improving algorithms,
- constructing algorithms:
  - algorithms using decomposition,
  - algorithms using natural multistage processes,
  - algorithms using loose multistage processes.

EXAMPLES: algorithm for salesman problem presented in [4] belongs to constructing algorithms using a loose process; algorithms presented in [2], [3] belong to the improving ones.

Classification of lower bounds

The concept of determining the lower bounds significantly depends on the fact to which of the above mentioned types belonges the analysed algorithm. Taking into account the way of determining, the following groups of lower bounds can be distinguished:

1) bounds obtained as a partial value of the control or decision sequence of a suitable multistage process,
2) bounds obtained in the course of solution of another problem or task,
3) bounds obtained from the combination of two former types.

Considering the second group, one must pay attention that the lower bounds for a task differ from the lower bound for a problem. Fig. 1 presents the types of lower bounds only for a task. The lower bounds of problem can be defined analogously.

Let us stress the significance of the given DMP model in the discussion of the B&B algorithms optimizing DMP control. Firstly, it enables a uniform way of defining the searched object in the form of a control sequence. Secondly it is a refference for the discussion of other constructions of the searched object. Thirdly, it enables to formally define and compare different lower bounds and at the end to give their domination rules.

REFERENCES

1. Dudek-Dyduch E.: Scheduling some class of discrete processes, Proc.of 12th IMACS World Congress, Paryż 1988.
2. Grabowski J.: A new formulation and solution of the sequencing problem : mathematical model, Zastosowania Matematyki Nr 15, 1976, 325-343.
3. Grabowski J.: A new formulation and solution of the sequencing problem: algorithm, Zastosowania Matematyki Nr 15, 1977, 463-474.
4. Sysło M.M., Deo N., Kowalik J.S.: Discrete Optimization Algorithms, Prentice-Hall, Englewood Cliffs 1983.

Model estimation of air traffic control sectors capacity for solving the air traffic flow management problem

Gładyś Sylwester Malarski Marek
Jasiński Sławomir Skorupski Jacek

Warsaw University of Technology, Institute of Transport

Abstract

Civil aviation air traffic undergoes many random disturbances. Air traffic controllers watch the real traffic and ensure that it is free from collision hazards in the whole airspace - the ATC sector - under their control. The ATFM service takes care that the flow capacity in each sector, called capacity of the air traffic sector, is not exceeded. In the paper an original method of model estimation of the capacity of the designed ATC sectors is described. In this method an experimentally established statistical relationship between the random variables of control load and the air traffic density is used. The capacity of a sector was found from the joint probability distribution of such a two-dimensional random variable model determined as a quantile of adequate order. This method was verified in practice by determining the capacity of the designed new ATC sectors in FIR Warsaw.

Introduction

Civil air traffic in suitably organized airspaces (FIR) is in keeping with precise rules and subject to air traffic control (ATC). Air traffic in FIR is initially planned and coordinated, however its realization undergoes many random disturbances. The ATC services watch the real realization of this traffic and take measures to eliminate collision hazards. The air traffic controller is the principal person of the air traffic control system. He is personally responsible for security in the whole airspace - the ATC sector - under his control. If the density of the controllers operations begins to exceed the limits of the capacity of human memory, the security of flights reduced.

The air traffic flow management service (ATFM) minds that the flow capacity, called the sector capacity, not be exceeded in any of the ATC sectors. In practice, the capacity of the ATC sector is understood as a number of planes that are in the sector in a given period of time, for which it is possible to provide ATC service.

The published materials allow to determinate only the capacity of the existing sector. In the available literature there is no method of estimating the capacity of planned ATC sectors.

Definition of the ATC sector capacity

Traffic density is a quantity characterizing the air traffic in the ATC sector. It is defined as a number of planes residing in the ATC sector for one hour. The traffic density distribution depends on the realization of a flight schedule which is subject to many disturbances. Meteorological factors and other traffic limitations make the air traffic process a random process and the traffic density (X) characterizing it a random variable of step character.

The flight of plane through the sector initiating a series of entries submitted to the ATC sector controller. The total time of servicing all the entries taking placed in one hour is the quantity characterizing the control load. Control the ATC sector is thus a random process. The control load (T) in the ATC sector is a random variable depending on air traffic density.

Air traffic density and control load can be treated as interdependent random variables with an appropriate joint probability distribution (Fig.1a).

If the dependence of control load on traffic density is accounted for, it is possible to determine certain boundary values of density x_{p_X} and load t_{p_T}, for which the probability of realization of a two-dimensional random variable (X,T) beyond the area defined by (x_{p_X}, t_{p_T}) will be smaller than the set value:

$$p_{XT} = F_{XT}\,(x_{p_X}, t_{p_T})$$

where: F_{XT} is the distribution function of the two-dimensional random variable (X,T). There may be many pairs (x_{p_X}, t_{p_T}) which fulfill the above condition. So in practice it is possible to define x_{p_X} and t_{p_T} as a position parameters of suitable edge distribution of the random variable X and the random variable T in the distribution of the two-dimensional random variable (X,T). Let x_{p_X} be a quantile of the order p_X, and t_{p_T} a quantil of the order p_T (Fig.1b), then:

$$\{\, x_{p_X} : [P(X \le x_{p_X}) \ge p_X] \wedge [P(X \ge x_{p_X}) \ge 1-p_X] \}$$

$$\{\, t_{p_T} : F_T(t_{p_T}) = p_T \,\}$$

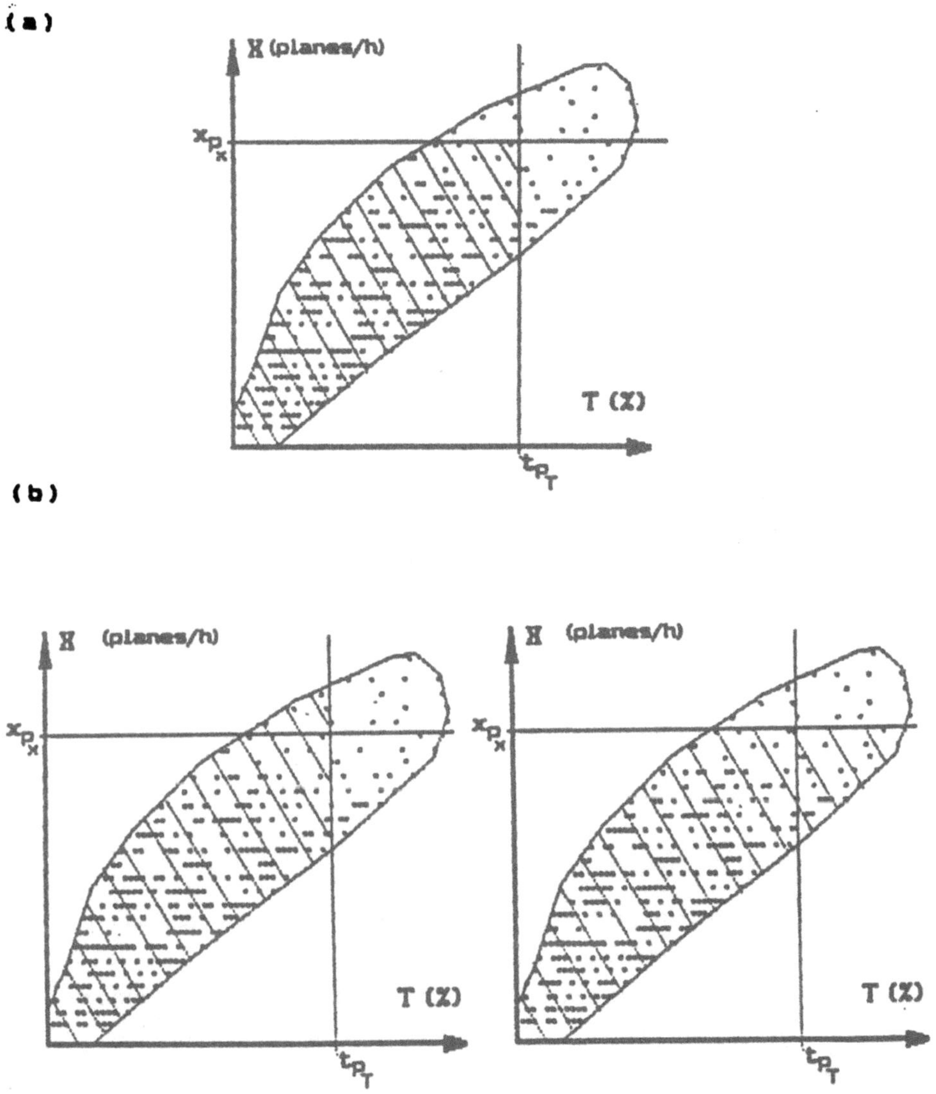

Fig. 1. A statistical sample collected from a general population with a joint probability destribution (X,T)

The determined value of the quantile x_{P_X} gives the capacity of the ATC sector. This capacity can thus be defined as follows:

The capacity of the ATC sector with a given organization is the quantil x_{P_X} of the order P_X of the distribution of the number of planes residing in the ATC sector for one hour (traffic density) which can be serviced by ATC at a given admissible control load measured by the quantil t_{P_T} of the order P_T on the load distribution.

Method of determining the ATC sector capacity

The method makes use of the stochastic relationship between the random variables X (traffic density) and T (control load). The method was implemented by building a simulation model of the air traffic system and its control (ATCS). This model allows to estimate the level of control load in given time intervals for various organizations of the ATCS system.

There exist standards defining the increments of the elementary work unit that correspond to the general rules of control. Thus, by using standard weight-coefficients S_i (recommended by ICAO documents), we can determined for the j-t plane and given time interval Δt_W the quantity

$$W_j = \sum_{i=1}^{N_j} S_i$$

where: W_j - coefficient of the increase of the elementary work unit connected with control of the j-t plane,

S_i - coefficient of the increase of the elementary work unit for the i-t change of flight conditions,

N_j - number of changes of flight conditions of the j-t plane.

Every elementary unit of work is executed within the mean time τ. This time depends only on the degree of control automation. The time of work t_{W_j} required by the controller for control corresponds to each plane residing in the ATC sector (in the time interval Δt_W):

$$t_{W_j} = W_j * \tau$$

That total time of controller's work in the examined interval is:

$$t_W = \sum_{j=1}^{m} t_{W_j}$$

where m is the number of planes in the sector submitted to control in time Δt_W. Comparison of the calculated value t_W with the length of the time interval allows us to determining the control load of air traffic in the sector in a given time interval:

$$T = \frac{t_W}{\Delta t_W} * 100\ \%$$

If we assume that the time interval $\Delta t_W = 1$, we obtained the control load which can be related to air traffic density occurring in the given hour.

The proposed method of determining the capacity of the sector of air traffic control has been split into two steps. In step 1 the suitable parameters of edge distributions of the variable (X,T) are determined for real traffic. As a result of experiments simulating the real air traffic process in the chosen ATC sector a statistical sample was obtained from a general population with a joint distribution (X,T). Beside, a fixed value of control load t_{P_T} in the ATC sector was assumed. From the distribution function of the edge distribution of control load we found the order of the quantile $P_T$of the assumed control load t_{P_T}. The order of the quantile p_X of the assumed value x_{P_X} was determined from the distribution function of the edge distribution of traffic density. The determined values:

- probability P_T that the control load in the ATC sector will not exceed the value t_{P_T}

$$P_T = P\{\ T < t_{P_T}\} = F_{XT}\ (\ \infty\ ,\ t_{P_T}\ )$$

- Probability P_X that the traffic density will not exceed the capacity of the sector x_{P_X}

$$\{ P_X: [P(X \le x_{p_X}) \ge p_X] \wedge [P(X \ge x_{p_X}) \ge 1-p_X] \}$$

are quantities that are established in step 2 of the method.

Estimation of the capacity of sectors in the designed ATCS systems (step 2) consists in carrying out simulation experiments of operation of the designed system. If we set the organization of airspace, the method of traffic control and the flow structure of planes, we should simulate traffic of a density selected so that the probability of control load in the ATC sector not exceeding approximately the value t_{P_T} is equal to P_T. Next density x_{P_X} should be determined in such a way that the probability of being exceeded is not greater than $1 - P_X$. The value x_{P_X} determined in such a way defines the capacity of the designed air traffic control sector. The general scheme of this algorithm is shown in Fig.2.

Application of the presented method makes it possible to compare the control loads in ATC sectors of the same traffic density and to measure the capacity of ATC sectors.

The simulation program algorithms have been written in Professional Fortran. The simulation experiments have been carried out on an IBM PC/AT compatible computer.

Verifying simulation experiments

The results obtained by the developed method for the eastern ATC sector in FIR Warsaw on the simulation model [$x_{P_X(\text{eastern})}$ = 13 planes / hour] were in agreement with those obtained experimentally in the Center of Air Traffic Control.

When checking the practical usefulness of the developed method of determining the capacity of the designed sector, a series of iterational experiments were carried in which the effec of changes of traffic density upon control load in the designed southern ATC sector was examined. The following results were obtained:

Intensity [planes/24 hours]	170	180	190	200
$t_{0.78(\text{nothern})}$[%]	67	75	77	81

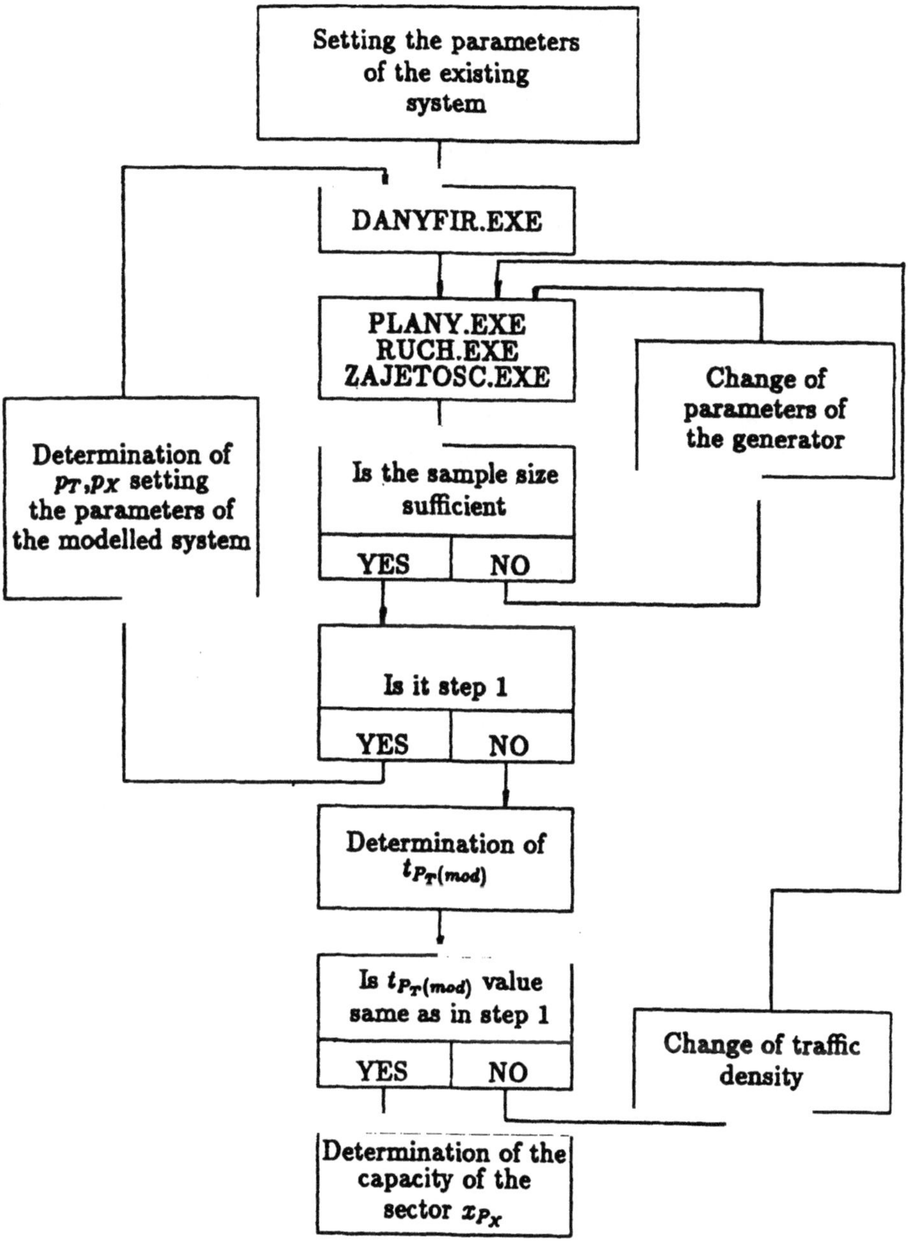

Fig. 2. General scheme of the algorithm for determining the capacity of the sector

At density up to 200 planes per 24 hours it was found that the control load in the designed sector is in accordance with the accepted previously comparative load $t_{P_T} = 80\% \pm 2\%$. The value of the quantile $x_{0.75}$ was determined from the distribution of variable (X,T) obtained for traffic of such density. The obtained result $x_{0.75}$ = 13 planes/hour is the capacity of the designed southern ATC sector.

Reference

1. *A Method of Estimating the Capacity of Air Traffic Sectors - An Interim Report.* CAA(UK) DORA Research Paper 7301, 7402.
2. *Air Traffic Management Table for the Eurregion 1981 - 1985.* Part 5 ATM, ICAO 26/4/85.
3. Arad B.A. *The Control Load and Sector Design* - Controller, 1972, 11, N 1-4, p.20-27.
4. Malarski M., Gładyś S., Urbanik A. *Model Analysis of Air Traffic Control System in FIR Warsaw Performed in View of its Modernization.* Transportation Forum, Toronto 1988.
5. *Re - assessment of the capacity of the control sectors of Maastricht UAC.* Eurocontrol, Ref. OPS/131/4, 1984.
6. *The Air Traffic Controller's Contribution to ATC System Capacity in Manual and Automated Environments.* Stanford Research Institute Report No. FAA-RD 72-63.

Models For Analysis of Air Traffic Control Systems in FIR Warsaw Performed in View of its Modernisation

Sylwester Gladys   Skorupski Jacek
Malarski Marek   Jasinski Slawomir

Warsaw University of Technology, Institute of Transport

I. Introduction

Airspace over the whole territory of Poland and partially over the Baltic Sea is organized into one Flight Information Region FIR Warsaw. The air traffic in FIR Warsaw is not too heavy. FIR Warsaw is divided presently into three control sectors. In all sectors air traffic control services are equipped in radars. Radar control is performed so that in case of a radar failure or servicing it is always possible to switch from radar control into procedural one. Such system of the air traffic control satisfies safety requirements at average traffic density. In peak hours, especially while procedural control is performed the system works at its capacity limits. Models for analysis of the ATC system in FIR Warsaw aim at the selection of methods and techniques of the air traffic control system modernisation.

II. Problem formulation

Air traffic control systems (ATC systems) belong to the class of complex systems with hierarchical structure of organization and control. It can be divided into several levels.

There are specific tasks assigned to each level. The time horizon of the decision making and time necessary to find the solution and accuracy of the decisions are features discriminating between the levels.

The activities provided on each level can be described in the following way:

L_1 level : information on air situation and constraints are processed into decisions determining separations between airplanes. Flight safety is used as the criterion. This is a regulation level which consists in trajectory tracking.

L_2 level : analysis leading to creation of the flight plans with regard to safety and flowability of the air traffic. The decisions taken on this level possess a character of local optimization with respect to given criteria.

L_3 level : analysis of the predicted traffic situation in whole FIR or in one of the control sectors determinating control decisions preventing excessive load which would exceed ATC sector capacity.

Because of the planned increase of the air traffic density it was necessary to undertake research on ATC system modernisation. ATC system modernisation should ensure:

- increase of flight safety,
- increase of system capacity,
- delay reduction,

Due to ATC system complexity as well as to the necessity of flight safety maintenance it is impossible to carry out experiments on actually working ATC system.

ATC system is so complex, that the elaboration of the analytical model of the whole system is impossible. That is why a set of detailed system simulation models was constructed. These simulation computer models were elaborated for different parts of ATC system: airways crossing, airway segment, terminal area and so on. Solely for the ATC control stand (service facility) a partial analytical model was successfully constructed.

III. Air traffic and ATC system simulation model

The structure of the modeled ATC system is defined by various information necessary for the creation of input variables, reception of functional relations determining mutual relationship between subsystems, as well as behavior of objects in the area of each subsystem.

Model input information include characteristics of the air space, airways network, structure of the aircraft flow, characteristics of control objects and ATC system, auxiliary data.

The simulated air space comprises the controlled area of FIR

Warsaw. It is characterized by the network :

$$S = \langle G, \{x_i\}, \{y_j\} \rangle$$

defined by:

- graph $G = \langle K, U, P \rangle$,
- set of functions $\{x_i\}$, $i = 1,2,\ldots,I$ defined on the set of graph nodes,
- set of functions $\{y_j\}$, $j = 1,2,\ldots,J$ defined on the set of graph branches.

Graph G is an ordinary graph consisting of the set of nodes $K = \{k_i\}$, $i = 1,2,\ldots,n$ constituting characteristic points of controlled space, and of a set of graph branches $U = \{u_j\}$, $j = 1,2,\ldots,m$ corresponding to segments of airways between selected control points. The relationship $P \subset K \times K$ defining incidence of points and segments is univocally characterized by a binary matrix of graph nodes contiguity. Functions $\{x_i\}: K \longrightarrow R$, $i = 1,2,\ldots,I$ assign parameters to the control points. These parameters are: code, name, identifier of affiliation to control sector, index of position report duty and so on.

Functions $\{y_j\}: U \longrightarrow R$, $j = 1,2,\ldots,J$ assign length, magnetic angle of the way, upper and lower flight level limitations to the airway segments.

The set of points was expanded by a set $L = \{l_1, l_2, \ldots, l_s\}$ which is a set of additional sources and outflows of the network symbolizing points from which an inflight into FIR area occurs.

In the graph G a set of routes G_r was distinguished. A route M_j is an ordered set of control points $k_i \in K$ and segments $u_j \in U$ connecting certain pairs of points. Because graph G is an ordinary graph then route M_j can be univocally presented quoting only the set of controlled points.

$$M_j = \{ k_1, k_2, \ldots, k_n \}_j$$

where $k_i \in K$, $i = 1,2,\ldots,n$, $(k_i , k_{i+1}) \subset P$.

A route extended by an additional source and an additional outflow is called a flight route.

$T_j = \{ l_a, k_1, k_2, \ldots, k_n, l_b \}_j$, l_a , $l_b \in L$

With each source l_a several routes M_a , which create a subgraph in the form of a tree, may be incident. The number of tree branches is given in the set $G_0 = \{ g_1, g_2, \ldots, g_n \}$, where g_i denotes the number of routes outgoing from the i-th control point, and n denotes a maximal number of the control point.

Parameters of aircrafts appearing in FIR Warsaw elaborated by Polish Civil Aviation Administration have been analyzed. Three groups of aircrafts were determined. Beneath stated parameters were taken into consideration:

- optimal and maximal flight levels,
- optimal velocity on optimal level,
- minimal velocity,
- optimal and maximal acceleration,
- optimal and maximal deceleration,
- mean value of climbing and descending velocity,
- in relation to the flight level :
    - optimal and maximal velocity distribution,
    - optimal and maximal climbing velocity,
    - optimal and maximal descending velocity,

ATC system characteristics depend on the kind of performed control : procedural, procedural aided by radar, and radar control. The kind of control is related to the degree of ATC system automatization. Regarding the kind of the performed control different kinds of applied separations between aircrafts were given. Agreements concerning the control transfer between FIR sectors were included in model.

Air traffic analysis with regard to determination of different classes of flights was performed. Taking into account the meaning, frequency of occurrence; a classification of the following types of flights was adopted:

- scheduled flights,
- civil nonscheduled flights,
- military flights.

Additional requirements for each kind of flights were determined.

The structure of aircrafts flow Φ in the modeled airways network S is described by the functions defined on the set of routes G_r. For each flight route the schedule is planned with regard to the type of the aircraft, kind of flight, cruising flight level, inflight level, outflight level.

Thus $\Phi = \{ G_r : f(G_r) \subset T \times P \times H \times R \}$,where :

f - function assigning :

T - distribution of the inflight time,

P - distribution of aircraft types,

H - distribution of flight levels used,

R - distribution of flight kinds.

Auxiliary data include: additional restrictions on the points, segments, parameters of the meteorological situation.

There are special programs to prepare input data in the above described way. It is called source form of the data. Different variants of the simulated space, airways network, flight routes and traffic density can be achieved by means of the change of the source form data .

IV. Inflight aircraft flow modeling

The basic structural unit at the examination of the air traffic processes and its control is constituted by a control sector. Decisions connected with organization of ATC in most of the cases comprise much larger areas, including several sectors. In relation to this there is a possibility of modeling the whole FIR area together with the possibility to divide it into separate sectors.

Taking into account the given structure of the traffic routes network **S** and flow parameters **Φ**, aircraft characteristics **A**, restrictions on flights, meteorological conditions and other interferences **E** flight schedules for the whole modeled space are formulated. Vector of the i-th aircraft flight plan:

$\{ N, M_j, p, r, t_{pow}, t_{we}, t_{wl}, H_{wl}, v_{wl}, H_{przel}, \Delta t_{wy}, H_{wy} \}$

consists of the following elements:

N - aircraft number,

M_j - flight route (number of the route),

p - aircraft type,

r - flight kind,

t_{pow} - time of inflight announcement,

t_{we} - time of entering the traffic situation,

t_{wl} - inflight time,

H_{wl} - inflight level,

v_{wl} - velocity in the moment of inflight,

H_{przel} - cruising flight level,

Δt_{wy} - period of time after which removal of the object from the traffic situation after leaving the outflight point occurs

H_{wy} - outflight level.

On the basis of the given aircraft flow structure Φ adequate cumulative distribution functions are created. They are used in order to construct program data generators.
The sequence of generating data is given below.
- the inflight point into the area is generated,
- for the indicated inflight point the inflight time t_{wl} is generated,
- for the indicated inflight point outflight point is generated, flight route number M_j is determined,
- for the determined route the aircraft type p is generated,
- for the determined flight route and aircraft type flight levels are generated : cruising flight level H_{przel}, inflight flight level H_{wl} and outflight flight level H_{wy},
- for the determined flight route time on leaving from the traffic situation Δt_{wy} is generated,
- for the determined inflight time the flight kind r is generated.

During the simulation experiments the influence of the following factors on traffic and control processes were examined:
Π_Q - variant of the space organization, division into ATC sectors,
Π_G - variant of the aircraft flow structure, flight density,
Π_K - degree of ATC processes automatizatiton (different control kinds),
Π_E - degree of restrictions and external interferences.

V. Simulation of the air traffic in the FIR area.

Process of simulation of the air traffic reduces itself to the servicing of the aircraft flow according to adequate ATC rules, and in such order as they appear naturally under control. An aircraft flight through the controlled area initiates a chain of events, which induce a reaction from the ATC system. An event in the model corresponds to the change in the state of the ATC system caused by the dislocation of an object in the area or by activities undertaken by the control services aiming at provision of flight safety.

With regard to the character of activity the set of events R may be divided into disjoint subsets R_i:

$$R = \bigcup_i R_i, \quad i = 1,2,3,4$$

Subset R_1 includes events directly connected with the process of movement, with the dislocation of aircrafts in the control area. Subset R_2 comprises events related to the execution of the basic work by the sector controller, ie. connected with receiving, transferring an aircraft control, guiding the aircraft within the control sector.

Events connected with prediction of collision situations (conflicts), taking decisions aiming at conflict solution belong to subset R_3.

The remaining events such as interference in communication, repeated inquiries, recession control are accounted to subset R_4. Occurrence of such events has not been taken into account in this model.

Time flow is realized in the model by means of the method of fixed time increments. Current time is increased by a fixed value (time increment).

VI. Result Analysis

The results of the simulation are contained in different sets. One of them contains full description of the traffic situation in the area with the accuracy determined by the updated time increment. Moreover for all the objects their current coordinates are quoted: flight velocity, flight level, distance to the next flight route control point and so on. Simulation results allow for the estimation of the object performance in short, few-minute time intervals. They also allow for the checkup of the realization against the adopted assumptions. Paralelly another set is created, where parameters connected with the process of traffic control are recorded. The set constitutes the base for the further processing of the simulation results.

As an example of the results mean aircraft flight time is presented:

CONTROL SECTOR NO 1

MEAN TIME OF AIRCRAFT STAY IN TRAFFIC BLOCK

ALL TYPES 22 min

1 AIRCRAFT TYPE 19 min

2 AIRCRAFT TYPE 26 min

3 AIRCRAFT TYPE 35 min

Mean numbers of aircrafts in each sector, the mean number of aircrafts in the ATC system, traffic density were also found out.

The obtained simulation results can be used to determine the capacity of the ATC sector in FIR Warsaw.

VII. Conclusions

Having created a set of air traffic and ATC simulation models an effective tool for the analysis of designed modernisation changes in the air traffic was achieved. "ATC sector capacity" or "FIR capacity" can be used as the criteria of the designed changes estimation. Data for the further analysis of the traffic control process itself can be gained as well as the data for the controller's work analysis.

VIII. Bibliography

[1] Reassessment of the Capacity of the Control Sectors of Maastricht UAC, Eurocotrol, Ref. OPS/131/4 1984.

[2] Air Traffic Management Table for the European 1981 - 1985 Air Navigation Plan , European Region, Part 5 ATM ICAO 1985.

[3] G.A.Krizanowskij : Woprosy ocenki effektiwnosti procesow UWD, Leningrad 1983, in Russian.

[4] Modelirowanije sistiem UWD i pilotazno-nawigacjonnych kompleksow, Kiev 1985, in Russian.

[5] Chosen Problems of Analysis, Design and Modernisation of Air Traffic Control Systems, CPBP 02.19.02.05, Warsaw 1987, in Polish.

[6] J.L.Goodwin, R.L.Ford Random : Air Traffic Generation for Computer Models, J. Navigation 1985, 38, No. 2.

[7] B.Korzan : Elements of the theory of graphs and Networks. Methods and Applications, Warsaw 1978, in Polish.

[8] A.Urbanik : Chosen Problems of Air Traffic Control Systems Modelling, IIIrd Inter. Symp. on Systems Analysis in Simulation Berlin 1988.

[9] Procedures for Air Navigation Services, Doc 4444-RAC/501/10, ICAO 1970.

SECOND ORDER ANALYSIS IN SEMI-INFINITE PROGRAMMING

Alexander Ioffe
Department of Mathematics
Technion - Israel Institut of Technology
Haifa 32000, Israel

1. Consider the problem of minimizing the function

$$f(x) = \max_{y \in Y(x)} f_o(x,y) \tag{1}$$

where f_o is a continuous function on $\mathcal{X}\times\mathcal{Y}$ (both $\mathcal{X}$ and $\mathcal{Y}$ being finite dimensional spaces), $Y(x)$ a compact-valued map from X into Y and either

(a) Y does not depend on x and f_o is continuous together with its first and second order derivatives with respect to x, or

(b) $Y(x) = \{y\colon f_i(x,y) \le 0,\ i = 1,\dots,k;\ f_i(x,y) = 0,\ i = k+1,\dots,m\}$ and all functions f_i, $i = 0,\dots,m$ are of class C^2.

We are interested in calculating or estimating the Hadamard type directional derivatives if $f(\cdot)$ of the first and the second order, namely the *lower contingent derivative* and the *lower second order epi-derivative*

$$f'_-(x;h) = \liminf_{t\to 0,\ h'\to h} t^{-1}(f(x+th') - f(x))$$

$$f''_-(x;v,h) = \liminf_{t\to 0,\ h'\to h} t^{-2}(f(x+th') - f(x) - v\cdot h').$$

Their special role in optimization is determined by the fact that both the strongest necessary and the weakest sufficient conditions for a minimum can be established only in terms of these derivatives or their equivalents.

2. For earlier results we refer to Girsanov [1], Pshenichniy [2] (the formula for the standard first order Dini directional derivative in case (1a)); Demyanov [3], [4] (formulae for the first and second order Dini derivatives for (1b) with concave internal maximization) ; Kawasaki [5] (a formula for the upper second order Dini derivative in (1a)); Wetterling [6], Hettich-Jongen [7], Jongen-Wetterling-Zwier [8] (analysis of (1b) under linear independence and strong second order sufficient conditions in the internal maximization problem). In [6]-[8] f_i does not depend on x for $i = 1,\dots,m$; this assumption seems to have been dropped in Still [9]. It is also absent in an earlier study by Shapiro [10] whose approach is close to that of

[6]-[8]. Common to them is the use of the implicit function theorem (thanks to LIC) with subsequent reduction to a standard problem with finitely many constraints. Darkovskii and Levitin [11] considered a more general situation with LIC replaced by the Mangasarian-Fromowitz constraint qualification.

3. In what follows we fix an x and set

$$Y_o = \{y:\ f_o(x,y) = f(x)\}.$$

For (1a) we set further

$$K = \{h:\ \nabla_x f_o(x,y) \le 0,\ \forall\ y\in Y_o\};$$
$$\Omega = \{\mu\in P(Y_o):\ \int\nabla_x f_o(y,x)d\mu = 0\}$$

($P(Y_o)$ is the set of probability measures on Y_o). We set further for $y\notin Y_o$

$$e(y,h) = \limsup_{\xi\to Y_o} \sup_{t>0} t^{-2}[f_o(x,y) + t\nabla_x f_o(x,y)\cdot h + t^2\nabla_x^2 f_o(x,y)(h,h) - f(x)].$$

THEOREM 1. *The following inequality always holds in* (1a) *for* $h\in K$:

$$f''_-(x;0,h) \le \max_{\mu\in\Omega} \int[e(y,h) + w(y,h)]d\mu.$$

and if the lim sup *in* (2) *is actually a limit for all* $y\in Y_o$, *then* (3) *holds as an equality. Consequently,*

$$\max_{\mu\in\Omega} \int[e(y,h) + w(y,h)]d\mu \ge 0,\quad \forall\ h\in K \tag{3}$$

is a necessary and, if the lim sup *in* (2) *is a limit for all* $y\in Y_o$, *then*

$$\max_{\mu\in\Omega} \int[e(y,h) + w(y,h)]d\mu > 0,\quad \forall\ h\in K\setminus\{0\} \tag{4}$$

is a sufficient condition for $f(\cdot)$ *to have a local minimum at* x.

The necessary condition (3) is a slight extension of that obtained in [12] by Kawasaki (Y is an arbitrary compact, not a unit interval) but the second part of the theorem is much stronger than the corresponding result of [5]. A proof of the theorem may be found in [13].

4. We consider (1b) next. For every $y\in Y_o$ we assume that the Mangasarian-Fromowitz constraint qualification is satisfied and set

$$J(y) = \{j:\ 1\le j\le k,\ \ f_j(x,y) = 0\}\cup\{0\};$$
$$\mathcal{M}(\mu,x,y) = f_o(x,y) + \sum\mu_j f_j(x,y) \quad (\text{here } \mu = (\mu_1,\dots,\mu_m));$$
$$\mathrm{M}(y) = \{\mu:\ \mu_j\ge 0,\ j=1,\dots,k;\ \mu_j=0 \text{ if } j\notin J(y);\ \nabla_y\mathcal{M}(\mu,x,y) = 0\};$$
$$C(y) = \{\xi\in Y:\ \nabla_y f_j(x,y) \le 0,\ j\in J(y);\ \ \nabla_y f_j(x,y) = 0,\ j=k+1,\dots,m\};$$
$$a_1(h) = \sup_{y\in Y_o} \sup_{\xi\in C(y)} \min_{\mu\in \mathrm{M}(y)} ((1/2)\nabla_y^2\mathcal{M}(\mu,x,y)(\xi,\xi) + \nabla_x\mathcal{M}(\mu,x,y)\cdot h);$$

$$a_o(h) = \max_{y\in Y_o} \min_{\mu\in M(y)} \nabla_x \mathcal{M}(\mu,x,y)\cdot h;$$

$$Y_{oh} = \{y\in Y_o\colon \min_{\mu\in M(y)} \nabla_x \mathcal{M}(\mu,x,y)\cdot h = a_o(h)\};$$

$$C_h(y) = \{\xi\colon\ p_o(y,h,\xi)\le a_o(h);\ p_j(y,h,\xi)\le 0,\ j\in J(y);\ p_j(y,h,\xi)=0,\ k+1\le j\le m\},$$

where $p_j(y,h,\xi) = \nabla_x f_j(x,y)\cdot h + \nabla_y f_j(x,y)\cdot\xi;$

$$M_h(y) = \{\mu\in M(y)\colon \nabla_y \mathcal{M}(\mu,x,y) = a_o(y)\};$$

$$b(h,w) = \sup_{y\in Y_{oh}} \sup_{\xi\in C_h(y)} \min_{\mu\in M_h(y)} (\nabla^2\mathcal{M}(\mu,x,y)((h,\xi),(h,\xi)) + 2\nabla_x\mathcal{M}(\mu,x,y)\cdot w).$$

THEOREM 2. *$f'_-(x;h) \ge a_1(h) \ge a_o(h)$. It follows that if $f(\cdot)$ have a minimum at x then $a_1(h) \ge 0$ $\forall$ h. The equality $f'(x;h) = a_1(h)$ holds if and only if for any $\varepsilon>0$ there are a $y\in Y_o$ and a bounded curve $\xi(t)$ such that*

$$y(t) = y+\sqrt{t}\xi(t) \in Y(x+th) \quad \text{and} \quad f_o(x+th,y(t)) \ge f(x+th) - t\varepsilon.$$

A proof of the first statement and the "if" part of the second may be found in [14], similar results were also mentioned by Gfrerer at the conference in Lambrecht. The corresponding necessary and sufficient condition for $f'(x;h) = a_o(h)$ was established by Lempio and Maurer [15]. Observe that the inequalities in the first part do not need the MF constrained qualification [16].

THEOREM 3. *Consider the lower parabolic derivative* (see [4], [14])

$$d^2_-f(x;h,w) = \liminf_{t\to 0} t^{-2}(f(x+th+t^2w) - f(x) - a_o(h)).$$

The inequality $d^2_-f(x;h,w) \ge b(h,w)$ is always valid. The equalities $f'(x;h) = a_o(h)$ and $d^2_-f(x;h,w) = b(h,w)$ hold together if and only if for any $\varepsilon>0$ there are $y\in Y_{oh}$ and a bounded curve $\xi(t)$ such that

$$y(t) = y+t\xi(t) \in Y(x+th+t^2w), \quad f_o(x(t),y(t)) \ge f(x+th+t^2w,y(t)) - t^2\varepsilon.$$

If, under the condition of the second part of the theorem, $f(\cdot)$ has a minimum at x, then we conclude that $b(h,w) \ge 0$ for all w and all h such that $a_o(h) = 0$. But sufficient conditions need lower second order epiderivatives. The connection between them and lower parabolic derivatives is not completely clear. In two cases, however , we can be sure that $f''_-(x;v,h) = \inf_w d^2_-f(x;h,w)$, namely, when ($\alpha$) f_j are concave functions of y for $j = 0,\dots,k$ and affine for $j = k+1,\dots,m$, and (β) Y_o is a finite set and at every point of Y_o the strong second order sufficient condition (as introduced by Shapiro [17]) is satisfied. The sufficient conditions obtained in [4], [8], [11] fall into these two categories.

REFERENCES

1. I.V. Girsanov, Differentiability of solutions of problems of mathematical programming, Abstracts of the conference on application of methods of functional analysis to nonlinear problems, Baku 1965.

2. B.N. Pshenichniy, *Necessary Conditions for an Extremum*, M. Dekker 1971.

3. V.F. Demyanov, Algorithms for solving minimax problems, Journal Computer System Sci. **2** (1968),342-380.

4. V.F. Demyanov, *Directional Differentiability*, Leningrad Univ. Press 1974.

5. H. Kawasaki, The upper and lower second order directional derivatives for a sup-type function, Math. Programming **41** (1988), 327-329.

6. W. Wetterling, Definitheitsbeddingungen für relative Extrema bei Optimierungs und Approximationsaufgaben, Numer. Math **15** (1970), 122-136.

7. R. Hettich and H.Th. Jongen, Semi-infinite programming: condions of optimality and applications, Lect. Notes Control Inf. Sci. v.7, Springer 1978.

8. H.Th. Jongen, W. Wetterling and G.G. Zwier, On sufficient conditions for local optimality in semi-infinite programming, Optimization **18** (1987),165-178

9. G. Still, Optimality conditions for generalized semi-infinite programming problem, 6th French-German Conference on Optimization, Lambrecht 1991

10. A. Shapiro, Second-order derivatives of extremal-value functions and optimality conditions for semi-infinite programs, Math Oper. Res **10** (1985), 280-299.

11. B.S. Darhovskii and E.S. Levitin, Quadratic optimality conditions for problems of semi-infinite programming, Trans. Mascow Math. Soc. **48** (1985), 163-210.

12. H. Kawasaki, Second order necessary optimality conditions for minimizing a sup-type function, Math. Programming **49** (1991), 213-229

13. A.D. Ioffe, Variational analysis of a composite function: a formula the lower second order epi-derivative, J. Math Anal Appl. to appear

14. F. Bonnans, A. Ioffe and A. Shapiro, Expansions of exact and approximate solutions in nonlinear programming, to appear.

15. F. Lempio and H. Maurer, Differential stability in infinite-dimensional nonlinear programming, Appl. Math. Optim. **6** (1980), 139-152.

16. A.D. Ioffe, On sensitivity analysis of nonlinear programs in Banach spaces. An approach via composite unconstrained optimization, submitted

17. A. Shapiro, Sensitivity analysis of nonlinear programs and diiferentiability properties of metric projection, SIAM J. Control Optimizattion **26** (1988), 628-645.

EXTREMAL SPHERES AND SEMI-INFINITE DUALITY THEORY

Friedrich Juhnke
Fakultät für Mathematik
Technische Universität "Otto von Guericke" Magdeburg
PSF 4120, D-O-3010 Magdeburg

Let $\mathbb{K}$ be the class of all nonempty compact convex sets of the n-dimensional Euclidean vector space $\mathbb{R}^n$. For $K \in \mathbb{K}$ we denote the inradius ϱ and the circumradius R by

$$\varrho = \varrho(K) := \sup \{ r \;/\; B(x,r) \subseteq K \}, \tag{1}$$
$$R = R(K) := \inf \{ r \;/\; B(x,r) \supseteq K \}, \tag{2}$$

where $B(x,r) := \{ t \in \mathbb{R}^n \,/\, \|t - x\| \leq r \}$.

Furthermore the width Δ and the diameter D of K are defined by

$$\Delta = \Delta(K) := \inf_{u \in \partial B} \left\{ \max_{t \in K} u^T t - \min_{t \in K} u^T t \right\}, \tag{3}$$

$$D = D(K) := \sup_{u \in \partial B} \left\{ \max_{t \in K} u^T t - \min_{t \in K} u^T t \right\} \tag{4}$$

$$= \sup_{t,y \in K} \|t - y\|$$

as the minimal (maximal) distance between two parallel supporting hyperplanes of K.

B(x,r) is an inscribed resp. circumscribed sphere of K iff the inequality

$$u^T x + r \leq k(u) \tag{5a}$$

respectively

$$u^T x + r \geq k(u) \tag{5b}$$

is fulfilled for every $u \in \partial B$.

k stands for the Minkowski support function of K,

$$k(u) := \sup \{ u^T t \,/\, t \in K \}, \tag{6}$$

such that K can be described by

$$K = \{ t \in \mathbb{R}^n \,/\, u^T t \leq k(u), \quad u \in \partial B \}. \tag{7}$$

∂B denotes the boundary of the unit ball $B := B(0,1)$;
$u^T x + r$ is the support function of $B(x,r)$.

Consequently, an insphere $B(x^0,\rho)$ resp. the circumsphere $B(x^1,R)$ of K is obtainable as solution of the following linear semi-infinite optimization problem (8a) resp. (8b):

$$\max \left\{ z_p(x,r) \;/\; \binom{x}{r} \in M_{Pi} \right\} \tag{8a}$$

$$\min \left\{ z_p(x,r) \;/\; \binom{x}{r} \in M_{Pc} \right\} \tag{8b}$$

with

$$z_p(x,r) := (0^T,1)\binom{x}{r} \;,$$

$$M_{Pi} := \left\{ \binom{x}{r} \in \mathbb{R}^{n+1} \;/\; \forall u \in \partial B:\; (u^T,1)\binom{x}{r} \leq k(u) \right\}, \tag{9a}$$

$$M_{Pc} := \left\{ \binom{x}{r} \in \mathbb{R}^{n+1} \;/\; \forall u \in \partial B:\; (u^T,1)\binom{x}{r} \geq k(u) \right\}. \tag{9b}$$

As the corresponding dual problem to (8a) we obtain

$$\min \left\{ z_D(\sigma,\lambda) \;/\; (\sigma,\lambda) \in M_D \right\} \quad ; \tag{10a}$$

the dual to (8b) reads as follows

$$\max \left\{ z_D(\sigma,\lambda) \;/\; (\sigma,\lambda) \in M_D \right\} \quad , \tag{10b}$$

where

$$\sigma := (u^1,\dots,u^q) \;,\quad \lambda := (\lambda_1,\dots,\lambda_q)$$

$$z_D(\sigma,\lambda) := \sum_{i=1}^{q} k(u^i)\,\lambda_i \tag{11}$$

$$M_D = \left\{ (\sigma,\lambda) \;\middle|\; \begin{array}{rcl} u^1,\dots,u^q & \in & \partial B \\ \lambda_1,\dots,\lambda_q & \geq & 0 \\ \sum_{i=1}^{q} u^i \lambda_i & = & 0 \\ \sum_{i=1}^{q} \lambda_i & = & 1 \end{array} \right\}. \tag{12}$$

The primal problems (8a), (8b) as well as the dual problems (10a), (10b) are superconsistent ones: The primal feasible regions M_{Pi}, M_{Pc} contain Slater-points, the gradient $\binom{0}{1}$ of the primal objective function is an inner point of the moment cone

$$\text{cone}\left\{ \binom{u}{1} \;/\; u \in \partial B \right\} \subseteq \mathbb{R}^{n+1}$$

generated by the normal vectors of the primal restriction hyperplanes. Therefore together with the continuity of $(k(u),\ u^T,\ 1)$ we obtain the solvability of both problems (8) and (10).

Let (σ,λ) be an optimal solution of the dual problem (10a) resp. (10b) with a minimal number q of positive components $u_1, \ldots, u_q$. Then (σ,λ) is automatically a basic solution of the feasible region M_D. We have $q \leq n+1$ and the complementarity

$$\lambda_i(k(u^i) - u^{i^T} x^o - \rho) = 0,\ i = 1,\ldots,q \tag{13}$$

results from duality properties.

1. In the case of the insphere we obtain

$$z_p(x^o,\rho) = \rho = \sum_{i=1}^{q} k(u^i)\,\lambda_i = z_D(\sigma,\lambda) \tag{14a}$$

for the optimal values of the objective functions. Choosing a nonempty proper subset J of $I := \{1, \ldots, q\}$ with m elements, $m < q$, we can see that the vector $d := \sum_{i \in J} \lambda_i u^i$ is always a nonzero one.

It can be verified that

$$\Delta(K) \leq \frac{1}{\|d\|}\left(\sum_{i \in J} \lambda_i\ k(u^i) + \sum_{i \in I \setminus J} \lambda_i\ k(u^i)\right) = \frac{\rho}{\|d\|},$$

(cf. (14a)) and - after a few combinatorial considerations -

$$\frac{\Delta(K)}{\rho(K)} \leq \min_{\substack{J \neq \emptyset \\ I \setminus J \neq \emptyset}} \frac{1}{\left\|\sum_{i \in J} \lambda_i\ u^i\right\|} \leq \min_{m=1,\ldots,q-1} \frac{q\sqrt{q-1}}{\sqrt{m(q-m)}}$$

$$\leq \begin{cases} 2\sqrt{q-1} & \text{for q even} \\[2ex] \dfrac{2q}{\sqrt{q+1}} & \text{for q odd} \end{cases}$$

This leads on account of $q \leq n + 1$ to the Steinhagen's inequality

$$\frac{\Delta(K)}{\varrho(K)} \leq \begin{cases} 2\sqrt{n} & \text{for n odd} \\ \frac{2n+2}{\sqrt{n+2}} & \text{for n even} \end{cases}$$

2. In the case of the circumsphere we have the corresponding duality property

$$R = \sum_{i=1}^{q} k(u^i)\lambda_i \qquad (14b)$$

with respect to the optimal values of the objective functions.
The points

$$y^i := x^1 + Ru^i, \quad i = 1,\dots,q$$

are boundary points of both the circumsphere $B(x^1,R)$ and the convex body K. Applying the restrictions of M_D we obtain

$$\sum_{i=1}^{q} \lambda_i y^i = x^1 + R \sum_{i=1}^{q} \lambda_i u^i = x^1$$

which implies

$$x^1 \in \operatorname{conv}\{y^1,\dots,y^q\} \subseteq \operatorname{conv}(\partial B \cap K).$$

Conversely, if $B(x,r)$ is any sphere containing K with the property $x \in \operatorname{conv}(\partial B(x,r) \cap K)$, then $B(x,r)$ can be shown to be the circumsphere of K (using duality properties only).
Further we have

$$\|y^i - y^j\|^2 = R^2\|u^i - u^j\|^2 = 2R^2 - 2R^2 u^{i^T} u^j .$$

Per definition of M_D follows

$$2R^2 = \sum_{i=1}^{q} \lambda_i \|y^i - y^j\|^2 = \sum_{\substack{i,j=1 \\ i = j}}^{q} \lambda_i \lambda_j \|y^i - y^j\|^2$$

$$2R^2 \leq D^2 \left(1 - \sum_{i=1}^{q} \lambda_i^{\,2}\right) \leq D^2\left(1 - \frac{1}{q}\right),$$

hence

$$R \leq D\sqrt{\frac{q-1}{2q}}$$

and on account of $q \leq n + 1$ we obtain the Jung inequality

$$R(K) \leq D(K)\sqrt{\frac{n}{2n+2}} \; .$$

References

[1] Alexander, R.: The width and diameter of a simplex. Geometriae Dedicata 6 (1977), 87-94

[2] Elzinga, D.J., D.W.Hearn: The minimum covering sphere problem, Management Science 19 (1972), 96-104

[3] Gericke, H.: Über die größte Kugel in einer konvexen Punktmenge, Math. Zeitschr. 40(1936), 317-320

[4] Glashoff, K., S.A. Gustafson: Linear Optimization and Approximation. Springer-Verlag New York 1983

[5] Hettich, R. (ed.): Semi-infinite programming. Proceedings of a workshop, Bad Honnef 1978. Lecture Notes in Control and Information Science 15, Springer Berlin 1979

[6] Juhnke, F.: Inradius und Dicke konvexer Körper aus optimierungstheoretischer Sicht, Beitr. z. Algebra u. Geometrie 27(1988), 13-20

[7] Juhnke, F.: Das Umkugelproblem und lineare semiinfinite Optimierung, Beitr. z. Algebra u. Geometrie 28(1989), 147-156

[8] Jung, H.E.W.: Über die kleinste Kugel, die eine räumliche Figur einschließt, Journ. Reine Ang. Math. 123 (1901), 241-257

[9] Steinhagen, P.: Über die größte Kugel in einer konvexen Punktmenge, Abh. Math. Sem. Univ. Hamburg 1 (1922), 15-26

FINDING LARGEST SIMPLICES (PRELIMINARY REPORT)

Victor Klee
Department of Mathematics
University of Washington
Seattle, Washington 98195, U.S.A.

Many of the basic problems of computational geometry are well understood only in low-dimensional cases. That is especially true of most geometric optimization problems except those that can be directly transformed into problems of linear or concave maximization. In the case of unrestricted dimension, nonconcave geometric maximization problems provide a fertile testing ground for methods of global optimization, for such problems typically present many local maxima that are not global maxima, and even the local maxima may be hard to find and recognize. That is often true even of problems involving the simplest sorts of convex polytopes (parallelotopes, cubes, simplices, etc.). As an indication of the current state of knowledge (or ignorance!) concerning high-dimensional geometric optimization problems, we here survey the fragmentary situation with respect to the following two problems concerning largest simplices (where k and d are integers with $1 \le k \le d$).

$\mathcal{P}(d,k)$: Given a convex d-polytope P, find the maximum of the k-measures of the k-simplices contained in P.

$\mathcal{C}(d,k)$: What is the maximum of the k-measures of k-simplices contained in the unit d-cube $[0,1]^d$?

In describing the computational difficulty of $\mathcal{P}(d,k)$, it must be specified whether the polytope P is presented as the convex hull of a finite set ($\mathcal{V}$*-presented*) or as an intersection of halfspaces ($\mathcal{H}$*-presented*). The maximum is always attained by some k-simplex that is *bound* to P (i.e., all of its vertices are among those of P). Since there are determinantal formulas for the k-measure of a k-simplex in $\mathbb{R}^d$ in terms of the coordinates of its vertices, it is easy to produce a finite algorithm for $\mathcal{P}(d,k)$. However, for most fixed k or d-k it is unclear how the intrinsic complexity of the problem is related to the containing dimension d.

The problem $\mathcal{P}(d,1)$ merely asks for the diameter of P. There is an obvious polynomial-time algorithm when P is $\mathscr{V}$-presented, and at least when d ∈ {2,3} there are algorithms significantly better than the obvious one (see [4] for references.) However, for $\mathscr{H}$-presented P the problem $\mathscr{P}(d,1)$ is $\mathbb{NP}$-complete in the case of variable d (Gritzmann and Klee [4]).

As was shown by Dobkin and Snyder [3], the problem $\mathscr{P}(2,2)$ (finding a largest triangle in a convex polygon P) admits a linear-time algorithm when P is presented as a sequence of vertices corresponding to a traversal of P's boundary.

When a k-simplex S is bound to a polytope P, a *move* for S is the process of replacing a single vertex v of S by a vertex of P that is adjacent (joined by an edge of P) to v. The move is called *fair* (*good*) if it produces a k-simplex at least as large as (larger than) S. In attacking $\mathscr{P}(d,k)$ for a particular P, the following properties (that P may have or lack) are of interest: $L_1(k)$ - starting from an arbitrary bound k-simplex that is not largest, there is a sequence of fair moves that leads to a largest k-simplex; $L_2(k)$ - whenever a bound k-simplex admits a fair move, it admits a sequence of fair moves that ends with a good move; $L_3(k)$ - each largest k-simplex in P is bound.

The following table lists all possible combinations of truth-values for the $L_i(d)$.

$L_1(d)$	t	t	t	t	f	f	f	f
$L_2(d)$	t	t	f	f	t	t	f	f
$L_3(d)$	t	f	t	f	t	f	t	f

Klee and Larman [7] have shown that the combinations in columns 2, 3, and 6 never arise, and that there are convex polygons exhibiting all the other combinations.

Some success has been attained [7] in deciding which of the properties $L_i(d)$ are possessed by the d-cube. The d-cube has $L_1(d)$ if and only if $d \leq 4$. It has $L_2(d)$ for d ∈ {3,4,5} but not for d ∈ {2,6,10}. It has $L_3(d)$ for d ∈ {4,5} and also whenever d + 1 is an H-number; and it lacks $L_3(d)$ when d ∈ {2,6,10}. (An H-*number* is a positive integer n such that there exists an Hadamard matrix of order n (see [5]). This implies that n is 1, 2, or a multiple of 4, and a long-standing conjecture asserts that every multiple of 4 is an H-number.)

The following problem is related to $\mathcal{E}(d,d)$ when $k = d$.

$\mathcal{E}(d,k)$: Is there at least one regular simplex among the k-simplices of maximum k-measure in a d-cube?

Result (3) below is closely related to an observation of Coxeter [2], and (1) and (2) two appear in [8].

(1) When $k \in \{2,3\}$, the answer to $\mathcal{E}(d,k)$ is affirmative if and only if d is a multiple of 3.

(2) The answer to $\mathcal{E}(d,4)$ is always negative.

(3) The answer to $\mathcal{E}(d,d)$ is affirmative if and only if $d + 1$ is an H-number.

We close by summarizing the situation for $\mathcal{E}(d,d)$. With the aid of the standard determinantal formula for the volume of a simplex, $\mathcal{E}(d,d)$ is seen to be equivalent to the problem of finding the maximum of the determinant of a $\{-1,1\}$-matrix of order $d + 1$. This is called the *Hadamard determinant problem.* It subsumes the *Hadamard matrix problem,* which "merely" asks whether every multiple of 4 is an H-number. It is not hard to see that whenever $d + 1$ is an H-number, the answer to $\mathcal{E}(d,d)$ is

$$\frac{(d + 1)^{(d+1)/2}}{d!2^d}.$$

Thus when $d + 1$ is a multiple of 4, the problem $\mathcal{E}(d,d)$ is roughly equivalent to the Hadamard matrix problem. However, the situation is much more complicated when $d + 1$ is not a multiple of 4.

There is not enough space to list even the main original references for the H-matrix problem or the H-determinant problem. Instead, we refer to the survey of Hedayat and Wallis [6] for the former, and for the latter to the surveys of Brenner and Cummings [1] and Smith [9] (and to [7]). And we mention (in alphabetical order) the following authors who have solved cases of the H-determinant problem for matrix orders that are not multiples of 4: K.N. Bhattacharya, T. Chadjipantelidis, J.H.E. Cohn, H. Ehlich, N.Farmakias, Z. Galil, J. Kiefer, S. Kouniuas, T.J. Mitchell, C. Moyssiades, D. Raghavarao, T.V. Trung, J. Williamson, C.H. Yang, K. Zeller. As a result of the efforts of all of these researchers, here is the situation for $\mathscr{C}(d,d)$ when $d + 1$ is not a multiple of 4.

When $d \equiv 0 \pmod 4$, the answer to $\mathscr{C}(d,d)$ is known only for $d \in \{4,8,12,20,24,40,60\}$;

when $d \equiv 1 \pmod 4$, the answer to $\mathscr{C}(d,d)$ is known only when $d \leq 102$ and $2d$ is the sum of two squares;

when $d \equiv 2 \pmod 4$, the answer to $\mathscr{C}(d,d)$ is known only for $d \in \{2,6,10\}$.

Thus the first open case of $\mathscr{C}(d,d)$ is for $d = 14$.

REFERENCES

[1] J. Brenner and L. Cummings, The Hadamard maximum determinant problem. *Amer. Math. Monthly*. **79** (1972) 626-630.

[2] H. S. M. Coxeter, Regular compound polytopes in more than four dimensions. *J. Math. Physics*, **12** (1933) 334-345.

[3] D.P. Dobkin and L. Snyder, On a general method for maximizing and minimizing among certain geometric problems. *Proc. 20th IEEE Sympos. Found. Comput. Sci. 1983*, 9-17.

[4] P. Gritzmann and V. Klee, Computational complexity of inner and outer j-radii of convex polytopes. *Math. Prog.*, to appear.

[5] J. Hadamard, Résolution d'une question relativ aux déterminants. *Bull. Sci. Math.*, **28** (1893) 240-246.

[6] A. Hedayat and W.D. Wallis, Hadamard matrices and their applications. *Ann. Statistics*, **6** (1978) 1184-1238.

[7] V. Klee and D.G. Larman, Simplices, cubes, and the Hadamard determinant problem, working title of a paper in preparation.

[8] V. Klee and D.G. Larman, Largest k-simplices in d-cubes: When can they be regular?, working title of a paper in preparation.

[9] W.D. Smith, Polytope triangulations in d-space, improving Hadamard's inequality, and maximal volumes of regular polytopes in hyperbolic d-space, unpublished report, Princeton, 1987.

OPTIMAL WELL PLACEMENT AND MANAGEMENT

ROBERT MICHAEL LEWIS
DEPARTMENT OF MATHEMATICAL SCIENCES
RICE UNIVERSITY
HOUSTON, TEXAS 77251-1892, U.S.A.

In the past decade nonlinear programming techniques have been applied to problems in the optimal management of groundwater resources and petroleum reservoirs ([4], [5], [3]). We will discuss two problems from these areas, the optimal design of groundwater pollution treatment strategies and the optimal design of enhanced oil recovery strategies.

In the treatment of groundwater pollution the objective is to minimize the cost of pollution remediation subject to constraints on water quality and pumping rates. In petroleum reservoir management the problem is that of designing enhanced oil recovery strategies in order to maximize the amount of oil recovered, subject to technological and economic constraints.

In the solution of these design problems, we need to decide the following:

1. the number of wells—well enumeration,
2. the location of wells—well placement, and
3. the operation of the wells—well management.

The operation of the wells is represented as a discretized function of time; the values are treated as continuously varying variables in the optimization. On the other hand, the number of wells and their locations are discrete variables (the location of the wells typically must fall on the grid points of some manner of discretization of a differential equation). This leads to mixed discrete-continuous optimization problems.

These design problems are complicated by limited and inaccurate knowledge of subterranean geology. We can attempt to improve this knowledge by using field observations to identify such unknown properties as rock permeability and porosity. This leads to another problem:

4. parameter identification—history matching.

History matching is a problem of great importance in the petroleum industry.

The solution of all the aforementioned problems requires techniques for large-scale nonlinear programming. These problems are computationally intensive due to the large number of variables and the expense of the evaluation of functions, gradients, and hessians. Moreover, the design problems contain a discrete optimization component.

The dominant cost is that of flow-in-porous-media simulations, which involves the solution of complex systems of partial differential equations (p.d.e.). We have concentrated our efforts to date on a nonlinear programming approach that exploits computational parallelism in the solution of the attendant differential equations.

Our idea is to make explicit in the nonlinear programming formulation the constraints that are implicit in domain decomposition methods for p.d.e. In a typical domain decomposition method, the region over which the p.d.e. is to be solved is divided into smaller regions, and the p.d.e. is then solved on each of the smaller regions in parallel. Some manner of correction is made and the subdomain solutions are continued until the solutions on the collection of subdomains represents the solution on the original domain. Conceptually, this corresponds to obtaining feasibility with respect to a constraint which expresses the consistency of the subdomain solutions.

In our approach, we make this implicit constraint explicit and add it as a constraint in the nonlinear programming problem. Our optimization algorithm produces iterates which are infeasible with respect to this constraint. This means that we never exactly solve the p.d.e. Instead, the progress of the optimization drives the accuracy with which we solve the p.d.e.: We only solve the p.d.e. accurately (which is equivalent to feasibility with respect to a constraint) only as we achieve optimality for the constrained problem.

We have begun an parallel implementation of this approach for a simple instance of the history matching problem. In our model problem we seek to identify the coefficient in an elliptic p.d.e. describing incompressible flow. As our domain decomposition method we use a non-overlapping decomposition method devised by Glowinski and Wheeler [2].

Our work is applicable to other environmental problems which involve the control of some sort of dispersive effect. Such problems include the problem of choosing the locations of industrial facilities along rivers or lakes in order to minimize ecological damage [6], and the problem of determining optimal strategies for river-borne disease vector control [1].

REFERENCES

[1] A. Chalifour and M. C. Delfour, *Optimal distribution of larvicide in running waters*, SIAM Journal on Optimization, (to appear).

[2] R. Glowinski and M. F. Wheeler, *Domain decomposition and mixed finite element methods for elliptic problems*, in Domain Decomposition Methods for Partial Differential Equations, R. Glowinski, G. Golub, G. Meurant, and J. Periaux, eds., Philadelphia, 1988, SIAM.

[3] S. M. Gorelick, *Large scale nonlinear deterministic and stochastic optimization: Formulations involving simulation of subsurface contamination*, Mathematical Programming, 48 (1990), pp. 19–39.

[4] S. M. Gorelick, C. I. Voss, P. E. Gill, W. Murray, M. A. Saunders, and M. H. Wright, *Aquifer reclamation design: The use of contaminant transport simulation combined with nonlinear programming*, Water Resources Research, 20 (1984), pp. 415–427.

[5] L. Lasdon, P. E. Coffman, R. MacDonald, and K. Sepehrnoori, *Optimal hydrocarbon reservoir production policies*, Operations Research, 34 (1986), pp. 40–54.

[6] G. I. Marchuk, *Mathematical Models in Environmental Problems*, North-Holland, Amsterdam, 1986.

THE OPTIMAL VALUE FUNCTION IN QUASIDIFFERENTIABLE PROGRAMMING

Bernd Luderer
Fachbereich Mathematik
Technische Universität Chemnitz
PF 964, DO - 9010 Chemnitz

This paper is dedicated to the study of the nonconvex nonsmooth mathematical programming problem

$$(P) \qquad \begin{cases} f(x,y) \longrightarrow \inf; \\ g(x,y) \le 0, \end{cases}$$

where the functions $f: R^n \times R^m \longrightarrow R^1$ and $g: R^n \times R^m \longrightarrow R^p$ are assumed to be continuous and quasidifferentiable in the sense of Dem'yanov and Rubinov [1]. In our approach, the vectors x and y are regarded as two groups of variables, and we decompose problem (P) by fixing the vector y. In doing so, at the lower level we get smaller and possibly easier subproblems to be solved. Let S(y) and P(y) be the sets of feasible and optimal, resp., solutions in the lower-level problem for fixed y. At the upper level we obtain the implicitly defined optimal value function

$$p(y) = \inf_x \{ f(x,y) \mid g(x,y) \le 0 \}$$

($p(y) = +\infty$ if $\nexists$ x: $g(x,y) \le 0$). Now one has to solve the problem

$$p(y) \longrightarrow \inf_y .$$

In order to find directions of descent of the function p or to decide whether a current iteration point is inf-stationary in the sense of [1], it is important to derive estimates for the Dini directional derivative p^+ of p. This is the main concern of the present paper. The results presented here for quasidifferentiable programs generalize results from Gauvin and Dubeau [2] and others.

Definition. A function $f: R^n \longrightarrow R^1$ is called quasidifferentiable at the point x, if it is directionally differentiable at this point and there exist two compact convex sets $\underline{\partial} f(x), \overline{\partial} f(x) \subset R^n$ such that the directional derivative can be expressed as

$$f'(x;r) = \max\{\langle a,r\rangle \mid a \in \underline{\partial} f(x)\} + \min\{\langle b,r\rangle \mid b \in \overline{\partial} f(x) .$$

The pair $Df(x)=[\underline{\partial}f(x), \overline{\partial}f(x)]$ is said to be the quasidifferential of the function f at the point x. Let $f_y(x)$ denote the function f(x,y) for fixed y and $Df_y(x)=[\underline{\partial}f_y(x), \overline{\partial}f_y(x)]$ be the corresponding quasidifferential (analogously f_x, g_{iy}, g_{ix}). Now, for fixed $r \in R^m$, $y \in R^m$, $x \in P(y)$, we define the sets

$$V(r,x,y)=\{v \in \overline{\partial}f_y(x) \mid \exists \hat{v}: (v,\hat{v}) \in \overline{\partial}f(x,y), \langle \hat{v},r\rangle = \min\{\langle z,r\rangle \mid z \in \overline{\partial}f_x(y)\}\},$$

$$W_i(r,x,y)=\{w_i \in \overline{\partial}g_{iy}(x) \mid \exists \hat{w}_i: (w_i,\hat{w}_i) \in \overline{\partial}g_i(x,y), \langle \hat{w}_i,r\rangle = \min\{\langle z,r\rangle \mid z \in \overline{\partial}g_{ix}(y)\}\},$$

$i=1,\dots,p$.

Theorem 1 [ ]. In (P), assume f and g to be quasidifferentiable. Let $r \in R^m$ be a fixed direction and $y \in R^m$ a point such that $S(y) \neq \emptyset$. Finally, let some constraint qualification be satisfied. Then

$$p^+(y;r) \leq \inf_{x \in P(y)} \inf_{\substack{v \in V(r,x,y) \\ w_i \in W_i(r,x,y)}} \max_{\lambda \in \Lambda(x,y,v,w)} L'_{x,\lambda}(y;r), \qquad (1)$$

where $w=(w_1,\dots,w_p)$. Here $\lambda=(\lambda_1,\dots,\lambda_p)$ are Lagrange multipliers associated with g_i, and Λ is the set of all such multipliers depending, of course, on fixed elements $v \in V$ and $w_i \in W_i$.

Corollary. If, under the assumptions of Theorem 1, the functions f and g_i are additive with respect to x and y, i.e. $f(x,y) = f_1(x)+f_2(y)$, $g_i(x,y)=g_{1i}(x)+g_{2i}(y)$, then $V(r,x,y) = \overline{\partial}f_1(x)$, $W_i(r,x,y) = \overline{\partial}g_{1i}(x)$.

Theorem 2. Let, under the assumptions of the Corollary, the expression on the ride-hand side in (1) be nonnegative for any $r \in R^m$. Then (x,y) is an inf-stationary point to (P) $\forall\, x \in P(y)$.

References

[1] Dem'yanov V.F., Rubinov A.M.: Quasidifferential Calculus, Optimization Software, Publ. Division, New York 1986.

[2] Gauvin J., Dubeau F.: Differential properties of the marginal function in mathematical programming, Mathematical Programming Study 19 (1982), 101-119.

[3] Luderer B.: Directional derivative estimates for the optimal value function of a quasidifferentiable programming problem, Mathematical Programming (to appear).

DYNAMIZATION OF THE PROMETHEE TYPE PROBLEMS

Cvjetan M. Redžić
Faculty of Economics, University of Banja Luka
Postbox 129, 78000 – Banja Luka

and

Tihomir M. Hunjak
Faculty of Information and Organization, University of Zagreb
Postbox 84, 42000 – Varaždin

Introduction

We define multistage process as the one which can be divided into more stages so that the results of the previous stage affects the course of the following stage. Since in each step of multistage processes decisions are made about further management of process, it is logic that we look for such order of decisions, or such management of process and thus we achieve the optimal effect in relation to some chosen optimal criterion.

We can consider the possibility of dynamization of the PROMETHEE /2/, /3/, type problem on N stages management horizon. We want to select the alternatives which, including all the deviations, will be optimal, i.e., we look for such management that evolution of the system is still on watched management horizon.

The state of system in each stage of process is determined by its configuration in that stage. Assuming that the initial stage x_N of our analyzed system is determined by matrix of decision A_N $(I \times J)$, whose elements are evaluations of alternatives a_j, $j = 1, ..., J$, $a_j \in K$ (K is set of alternatives), by the criteria z_i, $i = 1, ..., I$

$$z_{ij} = z_i(a_j). \tag{1.1}$$

Because of heterogeneity criteria space, we will use, in further consideration the normalized matrix A_N^*, whose elements can be determined in following way

$$z_{ij}^* = \frac{z_{ij}}{\left(\sum_{j=1}^{I} z_{ij}^2\right)^{0.5}}. \tag{1.2}$$

Considering this it follows

$$x_N = A_N^*. \tag{1.3}$$

Decision a_N, in N stage is also determined by normalized matrix of decision A_N^* which results in

$$a_N = x_N. \tag{1.4}$$

Transformation operator p_N transforms stage of system x_N in stage x_{N-1}, figure 1, we get

$$x_{N-1} = \left(A_N^*, \Delta_N^T\right)^T = p_N\left(x_N, a_N\right). \tag{1.5}$$

Matrix Δ_N $(J \times J)$ is a symmetric one whose elements d_{Njk}^*, $j,k = 1,...,J$, are distances among columns of normalized matrix A_N^*, determined by

$$d_{Njk}^* = \left(\sum_{i=1}^{I}\left(z_{Nij}^* - z_{Nik}^*\right)^2\right)^{0.5}, \quad d_{jj}^* = 0, \quad j,k = 1,...,J. \tag{1.6}$$

By means of (1.5) we have included, in stage x_{N-1}, all the deviations from the previous stage, and thus we have introduced prehistory in the process.

Proceeding in the same way through the whole horizon, the whole process can be shown as in the figure 1.

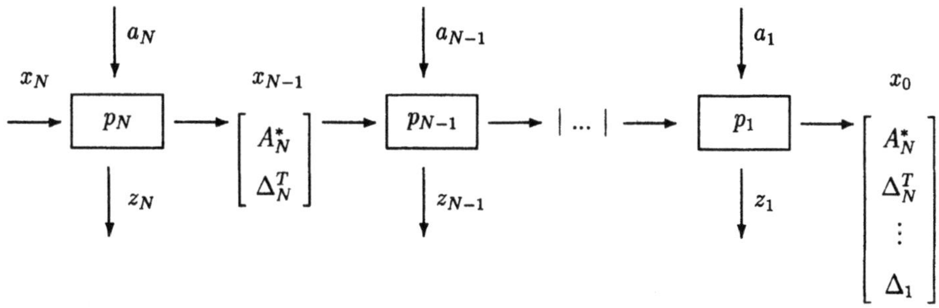

Figure 1.

Generally, the stage x_{n-1} is given as

$$x_{n-1} = \left(A_N^*, \Delta_N^T, ..., \Delta_n^T\right)^T = p_n\left(x_n, a_n\right), \tag{1.7}$$

where

$$x_n = \left(A_N^*, \Delta_N^T, ..., \Delta_{n+1}^T\right)^T. \tag{1.8}$$

Vector function of global criterion

Assuming minimization of the sum square deviations, in each stage described by (1.6), we can consider vector function as criterion function. Thus in n stage we have the following multicriteria 0–1 programming problem

$$\min h_n = h_n(h_{n1}, ..., h_{nJ}) \tag{2.1}$$

subject to:

$$d^*_{nkj} = t_{n+1}(d^*_{n+1kj}) \tag{2.2}$$

$$\sum_{j=1}^{J} \delta_j = 1 \tag{2.3}$$

$$\delta_j \in \{0,1\}. \tag{2.4}$$

The components of vector h_n are

$$\begin{aligned} h_{n1} &= d^{*2}_{n11}\,\delta_1 + d^{*2}_{n12}\,\delta_2 + \cdots + d^{*2}_{n1J}\,\delta_J \\ &\cdots\cdots\cdots\cdots\cdots\cdots \\ h_{nJ} &= d^{*2}_{nJ1}\,\delta_1 + d^{*2}_{nJ2}\,\delta_2 + \cdots + d^{*2}_{nJJ}\,\delta_J \end{aligned} \tag{2.5}$$

The condition (2.2) shows the dependence of deviations from n stage from deviations in $n+1$ stage.

The problem (2.1) – (2.4) can be solved by means of the compromise efficient solution of the multicriteria 0–1 programming problems, /7/.

Conclusion

The basic problem which should be solved in searching the possibility of application of dynamization to the problems of the PROMETHEE type is the identification of criterion function in dynamization case. In this paper we have treated the criterion function as vector function, and by means of 0–1 programming we have chosen the best alternatives in each stage.

The solution obtained in that way is degenerated. In order to avoid degeneration it is necessary to introduce, in each step, additional stage criteria, that is, to introduce constraint to d^*_{ij}.

References

Bellman R. and Kalaba R.: Dynamic Programming and Modern Control Theory, Academic Press, New York, 1966.

Brans J.P. and Vincke Ph.: Preference Ranking Organization Method for Enrichment Evaluations (The PROMETHEE Method for Multiple Criteria Decision–Making), Management Science, Vol. 31, No. 6, 1985.

Brans J.P., Vincke Ph. and Mareschal B.: How to select and how to rank projects: The PROMETHEE method, Operational Research, pp. 228–238, 1986.

Carraway L.R., Morin L.T. and Moskowitz H.: Generalized dynamic programming for multicriteria optimization, EJOR 44, pp. 95–104, 1990.

Ecker J.C. and Shomaker N.E.: Selecting Subsets from the Set of Nondominated Vectors in Multiple Objective Linear Programming, Control and Optimization, Vol. 19, No. 4, pp. 505–515, 1981.

Hunjak T.: Programming support for determined compromise efficient solution of multicriteria 0–1 problem programming SYM'OP'IS, 1988.

Mareschal B.: Etude theorique et practique des methodes de surclassment en analyse multicritere, Memoar presente en vue de l'obtention du grade de licencie en Sciences Mathematiques, Universite libre de Bruxelles, 1982/83.

Nemhauser I.G.: Introduction to Dynamic Programming, J. Wiley and Sons, New York - London - Sydney, 1966.

Opricović S.: Multicriterion optimization, Science book, Beograd, 1986.

Redžić C.: The PROMETHEE method dynamization, Ph.D. diss., Faculty of Economics, Univerzity Banja Luka, 1990.

Roy B. and Vincke Ph.: Multicriteria analysis: survey and new directions, EJOR 8, pp. 207–218, 1981.

Rupnik V. and Vrečko J.: Programming package ABSEVAL 1.0, Faculty of Economics, Ljubljana, 1988.

FIRST-ORDER CHARACTERIZATIONS OF GENERALIZED MONOTONE MAPS

Siegfried Schaible
Graduate School of Management
University of California
Riverside, CA 92521, USA

Stepan Karamardian
Graduate School of Management
University of California
Riverside, CA 92521, USA

Jean-Pierre Crouzeix
Mathématiques Appliquées
Université Blaise Pascal
F-63177 Aubière, France

Recently, various kinds of generalized monotonicity were introduced for maps [3]. In case of gradient maps, different types of generalized monotonicity of the gradient correspond to different types of generalized convexity of the underlying function. This gives rise to first-order characterizations of generalized convex functions involving gradients only, not known so far [2].

For generalized convex functions several second-order characterizations are known [2]. The earliest one, involving the gradient and the Hessian, was derived by Arrow and Enthoven [1]. From the point of view of the related gradient map, it can be interpreted as a first-order characterization in terms of the gradient map itself and its Jacobian.

In the present paper we derive first-order characterizations of generalized monotonicity for maps which are not necessarily gradient maps [4]. Among others, the concept of quasimonotonicity (QM) and pseudomonotonicity (PM) is introduced in [3]. A PM map is QM, but the reverse is not true.

Let S be a subset of the n-dimensional Euclidean space $\Re^n$ and F a map from S into $\Re^n$. We assume that S is open and convex and F is differentiable with Jacobian matrix $J_F(x)$ evaluated at x.

It turns out that the following property holds true for all QM (and hence PM) maps:

$$\text{(P)} \quad v^T F(x) = 0 \quad \Rightarrow \quad v^T J_F(x) v \geq 0 \quad \text{for all} \quad x \in S \quad \text{and} \quad v \in \Re^n.$$

However, this necessary condition is not sufficient for QM or PM maps. Sufficient conditions are derived for QM and for PM maps which involve in addition to (P) properties of the one-dimensional restriction $\Psi_{x,v}(t) = v^T F(x + tv)$ [4].

Additional results are derived for strictly pseudomonotone maps, also introduced in [3].

The results can be specialized to the affine case $F(x) = Mx + q$ where M is an $n \times n$-matrix and $q \in \Re^n$. It is well known that such a map is a gradientmap if and only if M is symmetric. Then the underlying function is the quadratic $f(x) = \frac{1}{2}x^T Mx + q^T x$. The reader is referred to [2], [5] where generalized convex quadratic functions are characterized by certain properties of the symmetric matrix M, thus providing conditions for generalized monotone maps of the above form when M is symmetric. Hence, the results in the case where M is not necessarily symmetric may be considered as generalizations of those in the above mentioned references.

It turns out that in the affine case the above property (P) is both necessary and sufficient for QM (and PM) maps on open convex sets [4].

References

[1] Arrow, K. J. and A. C. Enthoven, *Quasi-concave Programming*, Econometrica, 29, pp. 779–800 (1961).

[2] Avriel, M., W.E. Diewert, S. Schaible and I. Zang, *Generalized Concavity*, Plenum Publishing Corporation, New York, New York (1988).

[3] Karamardian, S. and S. Schaible, *Seven Kinds of Monotone Maps*, Journal of Optimization Theory and Applications, 66, pp. 37–46 (1990).

[4] Karamardian, S., Schaible, S. and J.P. Crouzeix, *Characterizations of Generalized Monotone Maps*, Working Paper 90-23, Graduate School of Management, University of California, Riverside (1991).

[5] Schaible, S. *Quasiconvex, Pseudoconvex and Strictly Pseudoconvex Quadratic Functions*, Journal of Optimization Theory and Applications 35, pp. 303–338 (1981).

EXTENDED DOMINATION SETS IN VECTOR OPTIMIZATION

Petra Weidner

Martin–Luther–Universität Halle–Wittenberg

Fachbereich Mathematik und Informatik

Postfach, D–O–4010 Halle (Saale), Germany

A vector optimization problem can be given in the following form:

Determine efficient elements of a feasible point set F in a linear topological space Y with respect to the domination set $D \subset Y$.

Here, $y^o \in F$ is said to be an efficient element of F with respect to D iff $F \cap (y^o - D) \subset \{y^o\}$ holds. From now on, $Eff(F, D)$ will denote the efficient point set of F with respect to D.
For $Y = \mathbf{R}^l$, $D = \mathbf{R}^l_+$ and $F = f(X)$ with $f = (f_1, \ldots, f_l)^T$, $f_i : X \to \mathbf{R}$ $\forall i = 1(1)l$, one obtains the classical optimality notion in multicriteria optimization:
$f(x^o) \in Eff(F, \mathbf{R}^l_+) \iff \bar{\exists} x \in X : \quad f_i(x) \leq f_i(x^o) \quad \forall i = 1(1)l$ and $f(x) \neq f(x^o)$.
We will call these special efficient points Pareto–optima of F.
There exist various methods for the computation of Pareto–minima. Most of them work with parameter–depending optimization problems which have scalar–valued objective functions. The solutions of many of these problems can be geometrically interpreted:

The parameters fix a point $a \in Y$, a vector $k \in Y$ and a set $C \subset Y$. The optimal point set of the scalar problem is the set $F \cap (a - cl\, C + tk)$ with the smallest real number t for which this set is non–empty.

Methods fitting into this scheme with $C = D$ are Gembicki's goal attainment method [8], scalar problems by Germeier [10], the minimization of the weighted Chebyshev–norm [3], STEM [1], the method of the displaced ideal with L_∞–norm [17], the SWT method [11], the ϵ–restriction method [5] and the method of satisfactory goals [2] among others. These methods turn out to be special cases of a scalarization introduced by Pascoletti and Serafini [12]. They have the disadvantage that Pareto–optimality of an optimal solution is only guaranteed if the optimal solution is a unique one [14], [13]. In order to avoid uniqueness requirements, we replace the domination set D in the scalarizing problem of Pascoletti and Serafini by some extension $C \subset Y$ and get the problem

$$
\begin{aligned}
(P_{a,k,C}): \quad & t \to \min \\
& y \in a - cl\, C + tk \\
& y \in F,\ t \in \mathbf{R}.
\end{aligned}
$$

The geometrical interpretation given above remains valid, and in $Y = \mathbf{R}^l$ the problem $(P_{a,k,C})$ is e.g. equivalent to problems of Wierzbicki [16], Choo and Atkins [4], Dubov [6] and Ester [7], where for each of these special cases C depends on parameters in a certain way. The importance of these methods is based on the following fact.

Proposition [14]:

(a) Assume that $C \subsetneqq \mathbf{R}^l$ is some convex cone with $\mathbf{R}^l_+ \setminus \{0\} \subset int\, C$ and that $y \in F$ is an optimal solution of some problem $(P_{a,k,C})$ with $a \in \mathbf{R}^l$ and $k \in int\, C$. Then y is an element of the properly efficient point set $G\text{-}Eff(F)$ of F in the sense of Geoffrion [9].

(b) For each $y \in G\text{-}Eff(F)$ there exists some convex cone $C \subsetneqq \mathbf{R}^l_+$ with $\mathbf{R}^l_+ \setminus \{0\} \subset int\, C$, $k \in int\, C$ and $a \in \mathbf{R}^l$ such that y is a unique optimal solution of $(P_{a,k,C})$.

$G\text{-}Eff(F)$ is dense in $Eff(F, \mathbf{R}^l_+)$, if F is closed and if there exist some $u \in \mathbf{R}^l$ and some convex cone H with $\mathbf{R}^l_+ \setminus \{0\} \subset int\, H$ and $(F - u) \cap -int\, H = \emptyset$ [14]. Consequently, the set of Pareto–optima can be approximated under these assumptions by the optimal solutions of the problems mentioned above.
The results are presented in detail in [14], some of them also in [13] and [15].

References

[1] R. Benayoun, O.I. Larichev, J. DeMontgolfier, and J. Tergny. Linear programming with multiple objective functions. The method of constraints. *Automat. Remote Control*, 32(8):1257–1264, 1971.

[2] R.G. Benson. *Interactive multiple criteria optimization using satisfactory goals.* PhD thesis, University of Iowa, 1975.

[3] V.J. Bowman. On the relationship of the Tchebycheff norm and the efficient frontier of multiple–criteria objectives. In H. Thiriez and S. Zionts, editors, *Multiple criteria decision making*, pages 76–86. Lect.Notes Econ.Math.Syst. 130, 1976.

[4] E.U. Choo and D.R. Atkins. Proper efficiency in nonconvex multicriteria programming. *Math. Ops. Res.*, 8(3):467–470, 1983.

[5] J.L. Cohon and D.H. Marks. A review and evaluation of multiobjective programming techniques. *Water Resources Research*, 11(7):208–220, 1975.

[6] J.A. Dubov. Ustojčivost' optimal'nych po Pareto vektor'nych ocenok i ϵ–ravnomernye rešenija. *Avtom. telem.*, (6):139–146, 1981.

[7] J. Ester and B. Schwartz. Ein erweitertes Effizienztheorem. *MOS, Ser. Optim.*, 14:331–342, 1983.

[8] F. Gembicki. *Performance and sensitivity optimization: a vector index approach.* PhD thesis, Case Western Research University, 1974.

[9] A.M. Geoffrion. Proper efficiency and the theory of vector maximization. *J. Math. Anal. Appl.*, 22:618–630, 1968.

[10] J.B. Germeier. *Einführung in die Theorie der Operationsforschung.* Akademie–Verlag, Berlin, 1974.

[11] Y.Y. Haimes and W.A. Hall. Multiobjectives in water resources systems analysis: the surrogate worth trade–off method. *Water Resources Research*, 10(4):615–624, 1974.

[12] A. Pascoletti and P. Serafini. Scalarizing vector optimization problems. *J. Optim. Theory Appl.*, 42:499–524, 1984.

[13] P. Weidner. An approach to different scalarizations in vector optimization. *Wiss. Z. TH Ilmenau*, 36(3):103–110, 1990.

[14] P. Weidner. Ein Trennungskonzept und seine Anwendung auf Vektoroptimierungsverfahren. Dissertation B, Martin–Luther–Univ. Halle–Wittenberg, 1990.

[15] P. Weidner. Verallgemeinerte Tschebyscheff–Normen in der Vektoroptimierung. *Wiss. Z. TH Ilmenau*, 37(3):101–114, 1991.

[16] A.P. Wierzbicki. The use of reference objectives in multiobjective optimization. In G. Fandel and T. Gal, editors, *Multiple criteria decision making – theory and application*, pages 468–486. Springer–Verlag, 1980.

[17] M. Zeleny. A concept of compromise solutions and the method of the displaced ideal. *Comput. and Oper. Res.*, 1(3–4):479–496, 1974.

ON SOME OPEN PROBLEMS IN CONVEX ANALYSIS

Constantin Zălinescu
Faculty of Mathematics, University of Iași, 6600-Iași, România

In this paper we answer some open problems raised by Rodrigues-Simons [6] and Simons [7]. The answers are given using the celebrated perturbation function method. The starting point for the problems raised in [6] and [7] is to find weaker conditions to have

(1) $(f+g\circ A)^*(x^*) = \min\{f^*(x^*-A^*y^*) + g^*(y^*) \mid y^*\in Y^*\}$,

where X, Y are locally convex spaces, $f:X \to \overline{\mathbb{R}}$, $g:Y \to \overline{\mathbb{R}}$ are proper convex functions and $A:X \to Y$ is a linear operator.

As it is well known, relations of type (1) are equivalent to duality results (with attainement of the dual) and can be used to state formulae for ε-subdifferentials.

In the finite dimensional case such a condition (see [3]) is

(2) $0 \in {}^{i}(A(\mathrm{dom}\, f) - \mathrm{dom}\, g)$,

where ${}^{i}D$ denotes the relative algebraic interior of $D \subset X$. In the sequel D^{i} and ${}^{ic}D$ will denote ${}^{i}D$ when span D = X and span D is a closed subspace, respectively.

An important effort was made to extend this finite dimensional result to the infinite dimensional case. The most common condition for A continuous, met in many books and papers, is that there exists $x \in \mathrm{dom}\, f \cap A^{-1}(\mathrm{dom}\, g)$ such that g is continuous at Ax. Weaker conditions are furnished by results of Rockafellar [4]: f and g are lower semicontinuous (l.s.c.), X, Y are Banach spaces and

(3) $0 \in (A(\mathrm{dom}\, f) - \mathrm{dom}\, g)^{i}$,

Rockafellar obtained this kind of result using the following theorem ([4, Th. 18(c)]).

Theorem A. Let X, Y be Banach spaces and $\Phi:X \times Y \to \overline{\mathbb{R}}$ be a proper l.s.c. convex function. Then (4) $\Rightarrow$ (5), where

(4) $0 \in (P_Y(\mathrm{dom}\, \Phi))^{i}$,

(5) $\inf_{x\in X}\Phi(x,0) = \max_{y^*\in Y^*} -\Phi^*(0,y^*)$.

Moreover, the mapping $y \to \inf_{x\in X}\Phi(x,y)$ is continuous at 0.

In [8] we got the algebraic version of Theorem A:

Theorem B. Let X, Y be linear spaces and $\Phi: X \times Y \to \overline{\mathbb{R}}$ be proper and convex. Then (5) holds with Y^* replaced by Y', the algebraic dual of Y, if

(6) $0 \in {}^{i}(P_Y(\text{dom } \Phi))$.

In fact, in [8, Th. 2.3] Th. B was stated in more general conditions. In [8, Th. 4.3] we obtained the topological version of Th. B. This says that Th. A is valid if X is a Frechet space and Y a barreled space (making use of Ursescu's Theorem). By using Th. B we got in [8] several formulae for conjugates and ε-subdifferentials in the algebraic case and pointed out how to obtain their topological versions; the details were furnished in [9]. We stated in [10, Th. 6]

Theorem C. Let X, Y be Frechet spaces and $\Phi: X \times Y \to \overline{\mathbb{R}}$ be a proper l.s.c. convex function. Then (5) holds if

(7) $0 \in {}^{ic}(P_Y(\text{dom } \Phi))$.

It is interesting to note that Jeyakumar [2, Prop. 3.1] obtained Th. C, too, without observing that this one is in [10] (cited in [2]). As an example of using Th. C, we pointed out ([10, Cor. 4]) that (1) holds if X = Y is a Frechet space, A = Id, f, g are proper l.s.c. convex functions and

(8) $0 \in {}^{ic}(\text{dom } f - \text{dom } g)$.

The same result was stated independently (using another method) by Attouch-Brezis [1] for X a Banach space. This result is also stated in [6, Cor. 7], [2, Lemma 3.1]. Of course, we could have restated all the results in [8] using Th. C. From such reformulations one obtains immediately the main results (Ths. 2.3 - 2.5, Cor. 3.1) from the paper [5] of Rodrigues and also [6, Th. 6].

Simons [7] looked for weakening the conditions on the functions and spaces envolved in (1). For such a purpose he stated in [7] a variant of the open mapping theorem. By using it he obtained (1), for example, in weaker conditions. Reformulating his open mapping theorem we get a generalization of Th. A, which permits us to obtain not only his results, but also to answer some problems raised in [6] and [7]. In the sequel X and Y are metrisable locally convex spaces. We also use the notions of cs-closed and cs-complete sets in the sense of [7] and the following hypotheses on the convex sets $D \subset X$ and $A \subset X \times Y$:

(H0) $0 \in {}^{i}D$ and span D is barreled,

(Hx) $\lambda_m \geq 0$, $(x_m, y_m) \in A$, $\Sigma_{m\geq 0}\lambda_m = 1$, $\Sigma_{m\geq 0}\lambda_m y_m = y$, $\Sigma_{m\geq 0}\lambda_m x_m$ is Cauchy then $\exists\, x = \Sigma_{m\geq 0}\lambda_m x_m$ and $(x,y) \in A$.

Note that (H0) is equivalent to $\cup_{i\geq 1} iD$ is a barreled subspace, used frequently in [7]; the letter x in (Hx) refers to the variable x. In the sequel we identify a multivalued mapping with its graph and we say that $f: X \to \mathbb{R}$ is cs-closed or cs-complete if epi f is so.

Theorem D. Let $\phi: X \times Y \to \overline{\mathbb{R}}$ be proper and convex. If $P_Y(\text{dom } \phi)$ satisfies (H0) and epi ϕ satisfies (Hx) then (5) holds.

Theorem 2 of [7] is obtained from Proposition 3, taking $\phi(x,u) = \chi(x)$ for $u \in Tx$, $= \infty$ otherwise, even for χ cs-closed instead of cs-convex and the conclusion with a linear functional instead of a sublinear one.

Proposition 1. Let $f: X \times Y \to \overline{\mathbb{R}}$ be a proper convex function and $A \subset X \times Y$. Suppose that $\cup\{A(x)-y \mid (x,y) \in \text{dom } f\}$ satisfies (H0), and (H1) or (H2) holds, where

(H1) f is cs-complete and A is cs-closed,

(H2) f is cs-closed and A is cs-complete.

Then there exists $u^* \in Y^*$ such that

(9) $\inf\{f(x,y) \mid y \in A(x)\} = \inf\{f(x,y) - \langle u,u^*\rangle \mid u+y \in A(x)\}$.

Taking A a linear operator and $f(x,y) = \chi(y)$ one obtains Theorem 3 of [4].

Proposition 2. Let $f: X \times Y \to \overline{\mathbb{R}}$ be a convex function with proper conjugate and $A: X \to Y$ a continuous linear operator. Suppose that $\{Ax - y \mid (x,y) \in \text{dom } f\}$ satisfies (H0), and (H1′) or (H2′) holds, where

(H1′) f is cs-complete,

(H2′) f is cs-closed and gr A is cs-complete.

Take $\varphi: X \to \overline{\mathbb{R}}$, $\varphi(x) = f(x,Ax)$. Then

(10) $\varphi^*(x^*) = \min\{f^*(x^*-A^*y^*,y^*) \mid y^* \in Y^*\}$.

Taking $f(x,y) = \varphi(x) + \psi(y)$ one obtains Th. 5 of [4] for non Frechet spaces.

By Prop. 2 we answer the Problem raised in [6], while by Prop. 1 we answer Problem 1 of [7]. In Prop. 2 we obtained a stronger form of [7, Th.5], but this one does not contain the result conjectured in Problem 3 of [7], where f, g are supposed to be l.s.c. proper convex functions and A linear with complete graph, but not continuous.

References

1. H. Attouch, H. Brézis, *Duality for the sum of convex functions in general Banach spaces*, in "Aspects of Mathematics and its applications", J. Barroso Ed. North Holland, (1986), 125-133.
2. V. Jeyakumar, *Duality and infinite dimensional optimization*, Nonlinear Anal., Theory Methods Appl. 15(1990), 1111-1122.
3. R.T. Rockafellar, *Convex Analysis*,Princeton University Press (1970).
4. R.T. Rockafellar, *Conjugate Duality and Optimization*, SIAM, Philadelphia (1974).
5. B. Rodrigues, *The Fenchel duality theorem in Fréchet spaces*, Optimization 21(1990), 13-22.
6. B. Rodrigues, S. Simons, *Conjugate functions and subdifferentials in non-normed situations for operators with complete graphs*, Nonlinear Anal. Theory Methods Appl. 12(1988), 1069-1078.
7. S. Simons, *The occasional distributivity of ∘ over $\overset{e}{+}$ and the change of variable formula for conjugate functions*, Nonlinear Anal., Theory Methods Appl. 14(1990), 1111-1120.
8. C. Zălinescu, *Duality for vectorial nonconvex optimization by convexification and applications*, An. Sti. Univ. "Al.I.Cuza" Iasi Sect. I a Mat. 29(3)(1983), 15-34.
9. C. Zălinescu, *Duality for vectorial convex optimization, conjugate operators and subdifferentials. The continuous case*, presented at the Conference "Mathematical Programming - Theory and Applications", Eisenach, 1984 (unpublished).
10. C. Zălinescu, *Solvability results for sublinear functions and operators*, Z. Oper. Res., Ser. A 31(1987), 79-101.

Fuzzy choice in design of complicated systems

Y. Below, S. Shafranskiyi.
(USSR)

The tasks of choice of the optimal in any sense project variant in some general set X of feasible technical projects are considered in this article.

Because in the real tasks of design purposes, restrictions, criterions of choice mostly are subjective, and in some cases not have clear definition, during constraction the theoretical models arise necessity of using the conseption of fuzzy objects Zadeh.

Thus, we considering the mechanism of the choise, which generate for arbitrary $X' \subseteq X$ numeric function $\mu_{X'}(x) : X' \to [0;1]$; for arbitrary $x \in X'$ value $\mu_{X'}(x)$ is the degree of optimum of the project x on subset X'. All information about optimality are contained in fuzzy set

$$\Psi(X) = \{ (x, \mu_X(x)), x \in X, \mu_X : X \to [0;1] \},$$

where Ψ - operator of fuzzy choice, which are defined on arbitrary subsets of the X.

Whith the purpose of development the general choice theory in article introduce characteristic condition for operators of fuzzy choice, investigate they correlation with known characterictic conditions for choice functions. Conseption of choice, which have variation on interval are introduced. This choice allow to combine formal procedures with application of empiric methods, what is especially important for design of qualitative new systems. The conditions, when the choice on the all general set of projects is equivalent with the choice on special subsets of X, are found out. This conditions are using in grounding of the decomposition approach for solve the task of choice are suggested in article. They based on agregation of structures of project definition (crossing on new formal level of definition of system).
Condition of agreement of the operators of the choice of adjacent levels and operator of agregation are introduced. Decomposition procedures, which is correspond to distinguished class of transformations for general and fuzzy choice are suggested. The concrete examples of application of this procedures are adduced.

A SUBGRADIENT PROJECTION METHOD IN LINEAR PROGRAMMING

Andrzej Cegielski
Institute of Mathematics, Higher College of Engineering,
ul. Podgórna 50, PL-65-246 Zielona Góra, Poland

Abstract.

In the paper a method is presented which evaluates a solution of a linear programming problem. From the parameters of primal and dual program a symmetric matrix game is constructed. The search for the solution of this game is reduced to a problem of the constrained convex minimization, where the minimized function is the maximum of finite number of affine functions and a standard simplex is the feasible region and the minimal value of the function is known. The subgradient method of Polyak is applied to solve this problem. The algorithm converges geometrically. On each iteration the projection onto a standard simplex is applied, for which a combinatorial algorithm is presented.

1. Reduction to a convex constrained optimization problem.

Consider the following linear programming problem:

$$\max \{ \langle c,x \rangle : Ax \le b,\ x \ge 0 \}$$

and its dual problem:

$$\min \{ \langle b,y \rangle : y^T A \ge c,\ y \ge 0 \},$$

where $c,x \in \mathbb{R}^m$, $b,y \in \mathbb{R}^n$ and A is an $(n \times m)$-matrix. Let P be the following $(p \times p)$-skew-symmetric matrix

$$P = \begin{bmatrix} \Phi & A^T & -c \\ -A & \Phi & b \\ c^T & -b^T & 0 \end{bmatrix}$$

where $p=m+n+1$. Consider a symmetric matrix game with the

pay-off matrix P. It can be easily shown that, if $z=(u,w,\lambda)\in\mathbb{R}^m\times\mathbb{R}^n\times\mathbb{R}$ is an optimal strategy in the matrix game P and $\lambda>0$ then $x=\frac{1}{\lambda}u$ and $y=\frac{1}{\lambda}w$ are optimal solutions of the primal and dual problems, respectively (see [3], [6]).

Now we give a method to evaluate a solution of the symmetric matrix game P. First we reduce the problem of the search for an optimal solution of the game P to a convex constrained optimization problem. From the von Neumann minimax theorem it follows that

$$\min_{s\in S}\max_{z\in S} s^T Pz = \max_{z\in S}\min_{s\in S} s^T Pz$$

where

$$S = \{ s\in\mathbb{R}^p : s^i \geq 0,\ \langle 1,s\rangle = 1 \}$$

is a $(p-1)$-dimensional standard simplex. Furthermore, observe that both sides of the above equality equal zero, since P is a symmetric game. It is easily to see that $\max_{z\in S} s^T Pz$ as well as $\min_{s\in S} s^T Pz$ are attained on extremal points e_k, $k\in K=\{1,2,\dots,p\}$ of S. Hence

$$\min_{s\in S}\max_{j\in K} s^T Pe_j = \max_{z\in S}\min_{i\in K} e_i^T Pz.$$

Then, of course, the search for optimal strategies in the game P is equivalent to the search for the minimum of the convex function

$$f(z) = \max_{j\in K} f_j(z) = \max_{j\in K} z^T Pe_j = \max_{j\in K} \langle z,p^{i\cdot}\rangle$$

on the standard simplex S. Futhermore, we know the minimal value $f^* = 0$ of f.

2. Application of the Polyak subgradient projection method.

The function f, as the maximum of finite number of affine functions, is Lipschitz continuous and satisfies the following property (so called sharp minimum property):

$$\exists l>0\quad \forall z\in S\quad f(z)-f(P_M(z)) \geq l\ \|z-P_M(z)\|,$$

where P_M is a metric projection onto the set $M = \operatorname{Argmin}_{z\in S} f(z)$. Therefore one can apply the Polyak subgradient projection method (see [5], [7]) for the search for a minimum of the function f, i.e. for the search for an optimal strategy of the game P (from which one obtains an optimal solution of the primal and dual linear programming problem).

Theorem. *Let the sequence* (z_k), $z_k=(u_k,w_k,\lambda_k)\in\mathbb{R}^m\times\mathbb{R}^n\times\mathbb{R}$ *be generated by the algorithm:*
$z_0 \in S$ *- arbitrary,*

$$z_{k+1} = P_S(z_k - \gamma\frac{\langle z_k,p^{\cdot r}\rangle}{\langle p^{\cdot r},p^{\cdot r}\rangle} Pe_r),$$

where $r\in I(z_k) = \{j\in K: f_j(z_k) = f(z_k)\}$, $\gamma\in(0,2)$. *Then* z_k *converges geometrically to an optimal solution* $z = (u,w,\lambda)$ *of the game P. If* $\lambda>0$ *then* $x=\frac{1}{\lambda}u$ *and* $y=\frac{1}{\lambda}w$ *are solutions of primal and dual linear programming problems, respectively.*

Similar methods was investigated by the author in [1]. In the mentioned paper, the search for an optimal solution of a matrix game is reduced to a convex constrained optimization problem for which the Polyak subgradient method is applied.

Now, we present a combinatorial algorithm of the metric projection P_S onto the standard simplex S.

Let $z_0\in\mathbb{R}^p$. If $z_0\in S$ then $z_0=P_S(z_0)$ and the algorithm terminates. Otherwise, let $I_0=(1,2,...,p)$. Suppose that, in the k-th step of the algorithm, one has obtained $z_k\in\mathbb{R}^p$ and $I_k\subset I_0$, $I_k\neq\emptyset$, $k=1,2,...$. In the $(k+1)$-st step one calculates

1° $z_{k+1} = (z^1_{k+1},...,z^p_{k+1})\in\mathbb{R}^p$, where

$$z^j_{k+1} = \begin{cases} |I_k|^{-1}(1-\sum_{i\in I_k} z^i_k)+z^j_k & \text{for } j\in I_k \\ 0 & \text{for } j\notin I_k \end{cases},$$

2° $I_{k+1} = \{i\in I_k: z^i_{k+1}\geq 0\}$

If $I_{k+1}=I_k$ then $z_{k+1}=P_S(z_0)$ and the algorithm terminates.
If $I_{k+1}\subsetneq I_k$ then one substitutes k by $k+1$ and one repeats 1° and 2°.

Theorem . *If* $I_{k+1}=I_k$ *for some* k, $k=1,2,...$, *then* $z_{k+1}=P_S(z_0)$. *It happens at most in the* p*-th iteration.*

Proof. see [2] or [4].

References.

1. Cegielski, A., ***A geometrically convergent subgradient projection method in matrix games***, submitted to Numerische Mathematik
2. Cegielski, A., ***An algorithm of the projection onto a standard simplex***, submitted to Journal of Optimization Theory and Applications.
3. Karlin, S., ***Mathematical methods and theory in games, programming and economics, Vol. I***, Reading, Massachusetts, Palo Alto, London, Addison-Wesley Publishing Company, Inc. 1962.
4. Michelot, C., ***A finite algorithm for finding the projection of a point onto the canonical simplex of*** $\mathbb{R}^n$, Journal of Optimization Theory and Applications, Vol. 50, No. 1, 195-200, (1986).
5. Polyak, B. T., ***Minimization of nonsmooth functionals***, USSR Computational Mathematics and Math. Physics, **9**, 14-39, (1969).
6. Szep, J., Forgo, F., ***Einfuehrung in die Spieltheorie***, Budapest, Akademiai Kiado 1983.
7. Shor, N. Z., ***Minimization methods for non-differentiable functions***, Berlin, Heidelberg, New York, Tokyo, Springer--Verlag 1985.

Copositivity and nonconvex optimization

GABRIELE DANNINGER, IMMANUEL M. BOMZE

Institut für Statistik und Informatik
Universität Wien
Universitätsstrasse 5, A-1010 Wien, Austria

Consider a quadratic minimization problem with a concave objective function, or equivalently, the problem

$$\begin{aligned} \tfrac{1}{2}x^TQx + c^Tx &\to \max \\ Ax &\leq b, \end{aligned} \tag{1}$$

where x^T denotes transpose of an $n \times 1$-vector $x \in \mathbb{R}^n$; Q is a symmetric, positive semidefinite $n \times n$-matrix; $c \in \mathbb{R}^n$; A is an $m \times n$-matrix; and $b \in \mathbb{R}^m$. The algorithm proposed in this paper is based on the characterization of global solutions $\overline{x}$ of (1) given by [HIRIART-URRUTY/LEMARECHAL 1990], see also [HIRIART-URRUTY 1989]. [HIRIART-URRUTY/LEMARECHAL 1990] start with the observation that a feasible point $\overline{x} \in M$ is a global solution to (1) if and only if (iff)

$$\partial_\varepsilon g(\overline{x}) \subseteq N_\varepsilon(M, \overline{x}) \quad \text{for all } \varepsilon > 0\,. \tag{2}$$

Here $g(x) = \frac{1}{2}x^TQx + c^Tx$ is the objective function,

$$\partial_\varepsilon g(\overline{x}) = \{y \in \mathbb{R}^n : g(x) - g(\overline{x}) \geq y^T(x - \overline{x}) - \varepsilon \quad \text{for all } x \in \mathbb{R}^n\}$$

is the ε-subdifferential of g at $\overline{x}$, while $M = \{x \in \mathbb{R}^n : Ax \leq b\}$ denotes the set of feasible points of (1) and

$$N_\varepsilon(M, \overline{x}) = \{y \in \mathbb{R}^n : y^T(x - \overline{x}) \leq \varepsilon \quad \text{for all } x \in M\}$$

is the set of ε-normal directions to M at $\overline{x}$. Since both $S(\varepsilon) = \partial_\varepsilon g(\overline{x})$ and $N(\varepsilon) = N_\varepsilon(M, \overline{x})$ are convex sets, the inclusion in (2) holds iff

$$\sigma_{S(\varepsilon)}(d) \leq \sigma_{N(\varepsilon)}(d) \quad \text{for all directions } d \in \mathbb{R}^n\,, \tag{3}$$

where for a set $Y \subseteq \mathbb{R}^n$, we denote by $\sigma_Y(d) = \sup\{d^T y : y \in Y\}$ the support functional of Y. With the help of the identities

$$\sigma_{S(\varepsilon)}(d) = d^T\overline{y} \quad \text{with} \quad \overline{y} = \begin{cases} Q\overline{x} + c + \sqrt{\frac{2\varepsilon}{d^TQd}}\,Qd, & \text{if } d^TQd > 0, \\ Q\overline{x} + c, & \text{otherwise,} \end{cases} \tag{4}$$

(observe that in any case $d^T\overline{y} = d^T(Q\overline{x} + c) + \sqrt{2\varepsilon\, d^TQd}$ holds) as well as

$$\sigma_{N(\varepsilon)}(d) = \varepsilon z(d) \quad \text{with} \quad z(d) = \begin{cases} \max\big[\{0\} \cup \{(Ad)_i/u_i : i \notin I\}\big], & \text{if } d \in \Gamma, \\ +\infty, & \text{otherwise,} \end{cases} \tag{5}$$

where we denote by $I = I(\overline{x}) := \{i \in \{1, \ldots, n\} : (A\overline{x})_i = b_i\}$ the set of binding constraints at $\overline{x}$; by $u_i := b_i - (A\overline{x})_i > 0$ the slack variables at $\overline{x}$, $i \notin I$; and the tangential cone of M at $\overline{x}$ by

$$\Gamma = \{d \in \mathbb{R}^n : (Ad)_i \leq 0 \quad \text{for all } i \in I\}\,;$$

condition (3) can be reformulated into

$$f_d(\delta) = \delta^2 z(d) - \delta\sqrt{2d^TQd} - d^T(Q\overline{x} + c) \geq 0 \quad \text{for all } d \in \mathbb{R}^n\,, \tag{6}$$

where $\delta = \sqrt{\varepsilon}$. Note that always $z(d) \geq 0$ and thus f_d is convex. So instead of (2) we shall check in the sequel the inequality $f_d(\delta) \geq 0$ for all $\delta \geq 0$, where $d \in \mathbb{R}^n$ is fixed, but arbitrary. According to (5), the relation $f_d(\delta) \geq 0$ is clearly satisfied for all $\delta \geq 0$ if $d \notin \Gamma$, so we only have to investigate directions d belonging to the tangential cone, as one would expect. In case of $z(d) > 0$, the function f_d attains its minimal value at $\delta^* = \frac{\sqrt{2d^TQd}}{2z(d)} > 0$, so that we have only to check $f_d(\delta^*) = -\frac{1}{2z(d)}d^TQd - d^T(Q\overline{x} + c) \geq 0$, which can be rephrased as

$$-d^TQd - 2d^T(Q\overline{x} + c)z(d) \geq 0\,, \tag{7}$$

which also has to hold if $z(d) = 0$, since then f_d is affine and thus has to have a non-negative slope in order to be non-negative for arbitrarily large δ. If we now denote by

$$\Gamma_i = \{d \in \Gamma : z(d) = \frac{(Ad)_i}{u_i}\}, \quad i \notin I, \tag{8}$$

and also

$$\Gamma_0 = \{d \in \mathbb{R}^n : Ad \leq o\} = \{d \in \Gamma : z(d) = 0\}, \tag{9}$$

condition (7) can further be reformulated into the conditions

$$d^T Q_i d \geq 0 \quad \text{for all } d \in \Gamma_i \text{ and all } i \in \{0, \ldots, n\} \setminus I, \tag{10}$$

where the symmetric $n \times n$-matrices Q_i are defined by

$$Q_i = \begin{cases} -Q, & \text{if } i = 0, \\ B_i - u_i Q, & \text{otherwise,} \end{cases} \tag{11}$$

and

$$B_i = -a_i(Q\overline{x} + c)^T - (Q\overline{x} + c)(a_i)^T, \tag{12}$$

where $(a_i)^T$ denotes the i-th row of A. Conditions (10) alone do not suffice to ensure validity of (2) and hence global optimality of $\overline{x}$. In addition we have to check whether

$$d^T(Q\overline{x} + c) \leq 0 \quad \text{for all } d \in \Gamma_0 \tag{13}$$

is satisfied. Conditions (10) and (13) together ensure (2) and hence global optimality, but the latter can be ignored if $\overline{x}$ is a KARUSH/KUHN/TUCKER point.

Therefore let us now consider the problem of determining whether or not

$$d^T Q d \geq 0 \quad \text{holds for all } d \in \Gamma, \tag{14}$$

where Q is a symmetric $n \times n$-matrix and $\Gamma \subseteq \mathbb{R}^n$ is defined by a set of (homogeneous) linear constraints, i.e. Γ is a polyhedral cone. If (14) pertains, the matrix Q is said to be "Γ-copositive". Of course (14) trivially holds if Q is positive semidefinite, or if Γ is trivial, i.e. $\Gamma = \{o\}$, but in general neither of these properties is shared by the matrices Q_i and the cones Γ_i occurring in the optimality criterion (10). In [BOMZE/DANNINGER 1991] an algorithm is described which both detects copositivity and returns a direction $d \in \Gamma$ with $d^T Q d < 0$ if (14) is invalid. This direction d will be used to "escape" from a local solution $\overline{x}$ of (1). In addition, the following procedure recognizes unsolvability of the problem (due to unboundedness of the objective function on the feasible region) and also generates an improving feasible direction d even if the starting point $\overline{x}$ does not satisfy the KARUSH/KUHN/TUCKER conditions (for sake of lucidity, we do not distinguish between vertices of M and those of the feasible set in standard form, i.e. including slack variables):

0. Generate a feasible vertex $\overline{x}$ of $M = \{x \in \mathbb{R}^n : Ax \leq b\}$ (if there is none, stop: the problem is infeasible). Check whether $Q_0 = -Q$ is Γ_0-copositive, where $\Gamma_0 = \{d \in \mathbb{R}^n : Ad \leq o\}$; if the answer is negative, stop: the problem is unbounded.

1. If the linear program

$$(Q\overline{x} + c)^T d \to \max$$
$$d \in \Gamma_0 \,,$$

is unbounded, stop: the problem is unbounded; else (13) is satisfied.

2. Determine $I = \{i : (A\overline{x})_i = b_i\}$, the tangential cone $\Gamma = \{d \in \mathbb{R}^n : (Ad)_i \leq 0 \text{ for all } i \in I\}$, and calculate the slack variables $u_i = (A\overline{x})_i - b_i$ for $i \notin I$. For all $i \in \{1, \ldots, n\} \setminus I$, check whether or not Q_i is Γ_i-copositive, where Γ_i is given by (8) and Q_i is calculated from (11) and (12).

3. If for all $i \in \{1, \ldots, n\} \setminus I$ the matrix Q_i is Γ_i-copositive, stop: $\overline{x}$ is a global solution of the problem (1). Else there is some $i \in \{1, \ldots, n\} \setminus I$ such that a direction $\overline{d} \in \Gamma_i$ is generated with $\overline{d}^T Q_i \overline{d} < 0$; then put

$$\overline{\delta} := \begin{cases} \max\{1, -\frac{\overline{d}^T(Q\overline{x}+c)}{\sqrt{\overline{d}^T Q \overline{d}}}\}, & \text{if } z(\overline{d}) = 0 \text{ (and hence } \overline{d}^T Q \overline{d} > 0), \\ \frac{1}{2}\sqrt{\frac{\overline{d}^T(Q\overline{x}+c)}{z(\overline{d})}}, & \text{if } z(\overline{d}) > 0, \text{ but } \overline{d}^T Q \overline{d} = 0, \\ \frac{\sqrt{2\overline{d}^T Q \overline{d}}}{2z(\overline{d})}, & \text{otherwise,} \end{cases}$$

calculate $\overline{\varepsilon} = \overline{\delta}^2$ and define $\overline{y} \in S(\overline{\varepsilon})$ as in (4). Solve the linear problem

$$\overline{y}^T x \to \max$$
$$x \in M \,,$$

by the simplex method starting at the vertex $\overline{x}$. Along the path of vertices v generated by this procedure, record their objective values $g(v)$ and pick that vertex, say $\overline{v}_i$, with the largest one. Replace $\overline{x}$ with $\overline{v}_i$ and go to step 1 (one may also repeat this step for all i such that Q_i is not Γ_i-copositive, then define $\overline{v}$ to be the vertex satisfying $g(\overline{v}) = \max_i g(\overline{v}_i)$, and replace $\overline{x}$ by $\overline{v}$).

References

BOMZE I.M./DANNINGER G. [1991]: A global optimization algorithm for concave quadratic problems. Technical Report **104**, Inst.f.Stat., Univ.Vienna (submitted).

HIRIART-URRUTY J.-B. [1989]: From Convex Optimization to Nonconvex Optimization, Part I: Necessary and sufficient conditions for Global Optimality, in: F.H. CLARKE et al. (eds.), Nonsmooth Optimization and Related Topics, 219–239, Plenum Press, New York.

HIRIART-URRUTY J.-B./LEMARECHAL C. [1990]: Testing necessary and sufficient conditions for global optimality in the problem of maximizing a convex quadratic function over a convex polyhedron, Preliminary report, Seminar of Numerical Analysis, Universitiy Paul Sabatier, Toulouse.

AN ALGORITHM FOR FINDING THE GLOBAL EXTREMUM OF A MULTIVARIATE LIPSCHITZ FUNCTION

Pham Canh Duong
Institut of Mathematics, Hanoi, Vietnam

1. Introduction

Let consider the following optimization problem

$$f(x) \to \min, \quad \text{s.t. } x \in \mathrm{D} \tag{1}$$

where $f(x)$ is a Lipschitz continuous function and D is a compact subset in $\mathbb{R}^n$. The method proposed in this paper is a generalization of an algorithm of S . A . Pijavskii [1] and B . Shubert [2].Unlike the algorithm proposed by R . H . Mladineo [3], our algorithm uses the approximating surface made up of simplicial based cones. The new method is simplier than that of Mladineo and much easier to implement.

2. Preliminaries

2.1. Extention of a Lipschitz function

Suppose that the constraint set D has the following properties

(i) int D $\neq \emptyset$;
(ii) $0 \in$ int D;
(iii) Every ray starting from 0 intersects with the boundary of D at a single point.

It is easy to show that every Lipschitz function $f(x)$ over such a set D may be extended to a Lipschitz function $F(x)$ over all of $\mathbb{R}^n$ with the same Lipschitz constant K by putting

$$F(x) = \begin{cases} f(x) & x \in \mathrm{D} \\ \mathrm{K}\|x - \tilde{x}\| + f(\tilde{x}) & x \notin \mathrm{D} \end{cases}$$

where $\tilde{x}$ is the intersection point of the line segment $[0, x]$ and the boundary of D. It is obvious that $f(x)$ and its extention $F(x)$ have the same set of global minima. This allows us to remove the constraint set D from consideration and replace the problem (1) by the following problem

$$F(x) \to \text{Global Min}, \quad x \in \mathbb{R}^n \tag{2}$$

2.2. Simplicial cones

Let

$$L = \{(x, y) | y \geq \mathrm{K}\|x\|\}$$

be the upward spherically based cone with slope K in $\mathbb{R}^{n+1}$. We denote by C the upward cone over the regular n–simplexe incribed in the cone L. The cone, similar to C, with the vertex at the point $x \in \mathbb{R}^{n+1}$ will be denoted by C(x). We also denote by $l_i(x), i = 0, \ldots, n$, the edges of C(x) and by $g_i(x)$ the hyperplane containing the facet opposite to $l_i(x)$.

3. Description of the algorithm

1. **Initialization.** Choose $z_0 = (0, x^0_{n+1}) \in \mathbb{R}^{n+1}$ so that the cone C(z_0) contains the graph of $F(x)$ in its interior. Denote by $G_0(x)$ the function which determine the upward cone surface $\partial C(z_0)$. We define

$$F_0(x) = G_0(x), \quad M_0 = x^0_{n+1}$$

2. **Step 1.** Choose $x_1 = 0 \in \mathbb{R}^n$ and define

$$F_1(x) = \max\{F_0(x), G_1(x)\}, \quad M_1 = \min_{x \in \mathbb{R}^n} F_1(x)$$

where by $G_1(x)$ we denote the function which determine the downward cone surface $-\partial C(z_1)$,with $z_1 = (0, F(0))$.

3. **Step k.** Choose x_k so that

$$F_{k-1}(x_k) = M_{k-1}$$

having chosen x_k, we define

$$F_k(x) = \max\{F_{k-1}(x), G_k(x)\}, \quad M_k = \min_{x \in \mathbb{R}^n} F_k(x)$$

where by $G_k(x)$ we denote the function that define the cone surface $-\partial C(z_k)$ with $z_k = (x_k, F(x_k))$.

Continuing in this way we obtain a sequence $\{x_k\}$ which converges to a global minimizer of $F(x)$. This fact will be established in the next section.

4. Convergence of the algorithm

The following theorem establishes the convergence of the above algorithm and gives a stoping rule for it.

Theorem 4.1. *Let ϕ be the global maximum of F, Φ, the set of global minimizers of F, x_n, M_n defined as in section 3, then*

$$\lim_{n \to \infty} F(x_n) = \phi,$$

$\{M_0, M_1, \ldots, M_n, \ldots\}$ *is non–decreasing and converges to ϕ, and*

$$\lim_{n \to \infty} \inf_{x \in \Phi} \|x - x_n\| = 0.$$

5. Computational implement

To implement the above algorithm we must find all the relative minima of the approximating surface $F_k(x)$ at step k. This may be done in a very simple way due to the following properties of the simplicial cone surfaces.

Denote by EM_k the set of local minima of F_{k-1} to be eliminated at step k, NM_k, the set of new local minima appearing at step k.

Proposition 5.1. $NM_k \subset -\partial C(z_k), z_k = (x_k, F(x_k))$

Proposition 5.2. *EM_k lies under the cone surface $-\partial C(z_k)$.*

Proposition 5.3. *For every relative minimum point $x \in NM_k$, if x belongs to the facet $g_i(z_k)$ of the cone $-\partial C(z_k)$ then there exists a point $y \in EM_k$ such that*

$$x = Pr_{g_i(z_k)} y$$

where $Pr_{g_i} y$ denotes the projection of y onto $g_i(z_k)$ and parallel to $l_i(.)$.

Proposition 5.4. *Let $y \in EM_k$. If the ray $l_i(y)$ does not intersect with any of the cones $C(y')$ for all $y' \in EM_k$, $y' \neq y$ then the point*

$$x = Pr_{g_i(z_k)} y$$

belongs to the set NM_k.

References

[1] S.A.Pijavskii, "An algorithm for finding the absolute extremum of a function", *USSR Computational Mathematics and Mathematical Physics* (1972) 57–67.

[2] B.Shubert, "A sequential method seeking the global maximum of a function", *SIAM Journal of Numerical Analysis* 9 (3) (1972) 379–388.

[3] R.H.Mladineo, "An algorithm for finding the global maximum of a multimodal, multivariate function", *Mathematical Programming* **34** (1986) 188–200.

QUASI-NEWTON DESCENT METHODS WITH INEXACT GRADIENTS

Ursula Felgenhauer
Department of Numerical Mathematics
Technical University Dresden
Mommsenstr.13, D-O-8027

Introduction

Consider the unconstrained minimization problem

$$f(x) \to \min \quad ; \quad x \in \mathbb{R}^n \quad , \tag{1}$$

where we assume

(A1) $f \in C^2$, $x_* = argmin\, f$ is regular and unique;

(A2) there are constants $m, M > 0$ such that

$$m\,\|z\|^2 \le z^T \nabla^2 f(x)\, z \le M\,\|z\|^2 \qquad \forall z \in \mathbb{R}^n, \forall x \quad . \tag{2}$$

Denote the gradient by $\nabla f = g$; the HESSE-matrix $\nabla^2 f = h$, and consider a quasi-Newton iteration in the form

$$x_{k+1} = x_k + \lambda_k s_k \tag{3}$$

with

$$\begin{aligned} H_k s_k &= -g_k && \text{search vector } s_k \text{ ;} \\ \lambda_k &= \Lambda(x_k, s_k\,;\, f, g) && \text{step length rule ;} \\ H_{k+1} &= \Psi(H_k, \Delta x_k, \Delta g_k) && \text{symm. secant update} \end{aligned}$$

where we require ($0 < m_k \le M_k$)

$$m_k\,\|z\|^2 \le z^T H_k z \le M_k\,\|z\|^2 \qquad \forall z \in \mathbb{R}^n \quad ; \tag{4}$$

H_0 - symmetric and positive definite ($H_0 \in S^+$).
For several classes of update formulas Ψ convergence results for the associated iterations are known with $\lambda_k = 1$ for ex. [local convergence] , see [2], or for so-called efficient ([7]) step lengths (together with some self-regularizing matrix correction as BFGS), [global/superlinear convergence] , cf. ([6], [1]). In practice stability properties of the iteration process are of additional interest; results in this direction exist, for example [3], [4], see also [5].

Gradient approximation influence

Besides of rounding effects (solution of the underlying linear systems etc.) an essential error source is connected with gradient approximation. Inexact gradients particularly

cause matrix perturbations, while the update formulas are commonly based on first order information only, so that this kind of errors has influence on the further iteration behavior (step length determination, approximation conditions) more than other ones.
In the papers cited above this question was treated mostly indirectly by general conditions for matrix deterioration or summarized matrix perturbation bounds. Our aim is to formulate restrictions about the gradient tolerances itself which yield appropriate asymptotic estimates for the algorithm. For general tolerance qualification denote

$$\tilde{g}_k = \tilde{g}(x_k, t_k) \qquad - \qquad \text{gradient approximation}\,;$$

$$\|\tilde{g}_k - g_k\| \leq t_k \leq \tau_k \|g_k\| \quad ,$$

we assume that $\tau_k \leq \bar{\tau} < 1 \quad \forall k$.
As a model iteration scheme we use Ψ – BFGS-formula; Λ – POWELL-WOLFE - criterium, so that for exact data the Theorem of POWELL ensures good convergence properties. The step size rule under consideration will be given by

$$0 < \alpha < 0.5 \quad , \quad \alpha < \beta < 1 \, ,$$

(P1') $\qquad f(x_k + \lambda s_k) - f(x_k) \leq \alpha \lambda \tilde{g}_k^T s_k + \lambda \epsilon \|s_k\|$

or (P1) $\qquad f(x_k + \lambda s_k) - f(x_k) \leq \alpha \lambda \tilde{g}_k^T s_k$

(P2) $\qquad \tilde{g}(x_k + \lambda s_k)^T s_k \geq \beta \tilde{g}(x_k)^T s_k$

General matrix updates with regularization

The first result concerns a regularized variant with GOLDSTEIN step length (P1) :

THEOREM 1 *Let (A1),(A2) hold and suppose, Ψ yields matrices with uniformly bounded condition numbers, i.e.*

$$m_k \geq m_H \quad ; \quad M_k \leq M_H \qquad \forall k .$$

(i) *If $t_k \leq \epsilon \, \forall k$, then for arbitrary x_0, H_0 there exist $\lambda_k > 0$ satisfying (P1'), and*

$$\| x_k - x_* \| \leq c_0 \left\{ \| x_0 - x_* \| \exp \left[-c_1 \sum_{i=0}^{k} \lambda_i \right] + c_2 \, \epsilon \right\}$$

(ii) *If for all k*

$$\tau_k \,/\, (1 - \tau_k) < (m_H / M_H)(1 - \alpha) \quad ,$$

then for arbitrary x_0, H_0 there exist $\lambda_k > 0$ with (P1). If further

$$\sum_{i=0}^{\infty} \lambda_i = +\infty \quad ,$$

then $\quad f_k \to f_* \quad$ *and* $\quad x_k \to x_*$.

Now consider the POWELL - WOLFE condition (P1) , (P2):

THEOREM 2 *Under the conditions of* Theor.1, (ii) *and the additional bound*

$$\tau_{k+1} \leq (m_H/M_H)(\beta - \alpha)\, m\,/\,(m + 4M)$$

there exist $\lambda_k > 0$ *satisfying (P1), (P2) , and* $\bar{\lambda}, \underline{\lambda} > 0$ *with*

$$\underline{\lambda} \leq \lambda_k \leq \bar{\lambda} \qquad \forall k \ .$$

The iteration $\{x_k\}$ *converges, and there are positive constants* κ, c *with*

$$\| x_k - x_* \| \leq c \exp(-\kappa k) \| x_0 - x_* \| \qquad .$$

The BFGS method with perturbed data

The next Theorems are valid for the BFGS formula without regularization. (The existence of step lengths will be explicitly required; for tolerance bounds that guarantee it cf. the preceeding Theorems.)

THEOREM 3 *Assume that (A1), (A2) hold and suppose, that for given* x_0, H_0 $\forall k$ *there exist* $\lambda_k > 0$ *with (P1), (P2). Let further the convexity condition hold in the form*

$$\exists \tilde{m} > 0 : \quad (\Delta\tilde{g}_k)^T (\Delta x_k) \geq \tilde{m} \| \Delta x_k \|^2 \qquad \forall k \ .$$

If

$$R_k(\tau) = \frac{(\tau_{k+1} + \tau_k) \|H_k\|}{(1 - \tau_k) \lambda_k} \leq r \qquad ,$$

where r *- sufficiently small, then*

$$\left\{ \prod_{j=1}^{k} \lambda_j \right\}^{1/k} \geq c_\lambda > 0 \qquad ,$$

and $\{x_k\}$ *converges to* x_* *at least r-linearly.*

THEOREM 4 *Let (A1), (A2) hold and assume that* $h = \nabla^2 f$ *is locally* LIPSCHITZ *- continous near* x_* *. Let* λ_k *be chosen with respect to (P1), (P2), where* $\lambda_k = 1$ *has to be accepted whenever possible. For given* $x_0 \in \mathrm{R}^n$, $H_0 \in S^+$ *there exists* $\tilde{\tau} > 0$ *so that for*

$$\tau_0 < \tilde{\tau} \qquad ; \qquad \tau_k \downarrow 0$$

and

$$\sum_{k=0}^{\infty} \| \Delta\tilde{g}_k - \Delta g_k \| \,/\, \|\Delta x_k\| < \infty$$

it follows that (Ψ *-* BFGS*) the sequences* $\{H_k\}, \{H_k^{-1}\}$ *are bounded and* $x_k \rightarrow x_*$ *at least q-superlinearly.*

Remark: The last condition in Theor.4 is connected with cancellation errors in the calculation of the update vectors; the given boundedness of their sum corresponds with conditions formulated by DENNIS and WALKER: $\sum \|M_k\| < \infty$, cf.[3]. The bounded deterioration property for the perturbed matrices ([4]) can be derived from the above condition as well.

References

[1] Byrd R.H., Nocedal J., Yuan Ya-Xiang *Global convergence of quasi-Newton methods on convex problems*, SIAM J.Numer.Anal., 24, 1987, 5, 1171-1190.

[2] Dennis jun. J.E., Moré J.J. *A characterization of superlinear convergence and its application to quasi-Newton methods*, Math.Comp.,28, 1974, 549-560.

[3] Dennis jun. J.E., Walker H.F. *Inaccuracy in quasi-Newton methods: local improvement theorems*, Math. Program. Study 22, 1984, 70-85.

[4] Dennis jun. J.E., Walker H.F. *Least change sparse secant update methods with inaccurate secant conditions* , SIAM J.Numer.Anal., 22, 1985, no.4, 760-778.

[5] Griewank A., Toint Ph. L. *Local convergence analysis for partitioned quasi-NEWTON updates* , Numer. Math. 39, 1982, 429-448.

[6] Powell M.J.D. *Some global convergence properties of variable metric algorithms without exact line search*, Nonlinear Programming, ed. Cottle R.W.,Lemke C.E., SIAM-AMS Proc., IX, AMS Providence, 1976.

[7] Warth W., Werner J. *Efficiente Schrittweitenfunktionen bei unrestringierten Optimierungsaufgaben*, Computing 19, 1977,59-72.

Iterative Methods for Quadratic Programming

Andreas Fischer and Klaus Schönefeld
Institut für Numertische Mathematik
Technische Universität Dresden
Mommsenstraße 13, O-8027 Dresden, BRD

In the present paper, we consider medium size quadratic programs

$$\begin{aligned} &\tfrac{1}{2}x^TCx + p^Tx = \min! \quad \text{s.t.} \quad x \in G \\ &G := \{x \in R^n \,|\, (A^Tx - b)^i \le 0,\, i \in I\} \ne \emptyset, \qquad I := \{1, ..., m\}, \end{aligned} \tag{1}$$

where C symmetric and positive definite. In contrast to finite methods for solving (1) (e.g. [3, 4, 7, 8, 9]), we consider infinite iteration processes, for instance penalty and NEWTON-type methods, and propose a general termination technique for these processes. In this way, it can be ensured under mild assumptions that after a finite number of steps the optimal solution is obtained, even if the normals of the active constraints are not linearly independent [2].
A vector $x^* \in R^n$ is the (unique) solution of the positive definite program (1) if and only if there is a vector $u^* \in R^m$ such that (x^*, u^*) fulfils the KUHN-TUCKER system

$$T(x,u) \quad := \quad \left[(Cx + p + Au)^T,\ \phi(g^1(x), u^1), \ldots, \phi(g^m(x), u^m)\right]^T = 0, \tag{2}$$

where the function ϕ is required to be locally Lipschitz-continuous and to satisfy the relation

$$\phi(a,b) = 0 \quad \text{if and only if} \quad a \le 0,\ b \ge 0,\ a\,b = 0.$$

Further, we define the sets

$$\begin{aligned} U^* \quad &:= \quad \{u^* \in R^m \,|\, (x^*, u^*) \text{ fulfils the KUHN-TUCKER conditions (2)}\}, \\ I(x) \quad &:= \quad \{i \in I \,|\, (A^Tx - b)^i = 0\}, \qquad I^* \ := \ I(x^*), \\ I^+(u^*) \quad &:= \quad \{i \in I^* \,|\, u^{*,i} > 0\}, \qquad I^0 \ := \ \{i \in I^* \,|\, u^{*,i} = 0 \text{ for all } u^* \in U^*\}. \end{aligned}$$

Let (x^*, u^*) be an arbitrary, but fixed KUHN-TUCKER point of (1), i.e. a solution of (2). Then (x^*, u^*) solves the linear system of equations and inequalities

$$Cx + p + Au \ = \ 0, \qquad (A^Tx - b)^i = 0 \quad (i \in I'), \qquad u^j = 0 \quad (j \notin I'), \tag{3}$$

$$(A^Tx - b)^j \ \le \ 0 \quad (j \notin I'), \tag{4}$$

$$u^i \ \ge \ 0 \quad (i \in I'). \tag{5}$$

where I' is an arbitrary index subset satisfying

$$I^+(u^*) \subseteq I' \subseteq I^*. \tag{6}$$

Conversely, for an arbitrary index subset $I' \subseteq I^*$ it holds

$$[(x,u) \text{ solves (3)-(5)}] \Longrightarrow [(x,u) \text{ satisfies (2)}].$$

BASIC ALGORITHM

S0 : Choose $(x_0, u_0) \in R^n \times R^m$ (e.g. $x_0 = -C^{-1}p$) and a constant $c > 0$. Set $k := -1$.

S1 : Set $k := k+1$. Compute a new approximation (x_{k+1}, u_{k+1}).

S2 : If $\|T(x_{k+1}, u_{k+1})\| \leq c$, then go to S3. Otherwise go to S1.

S3 : Set $c := c/2$ and $I_{k+1} := \{i \in I \mid u^i_{k+1} > |(A^T x_{k+1} - b)^i|\}$.
For $I' := I_{k+1}$ compute a solution of the system (3)-(5).
If such a solution exists, then stop. Otherwise go to S1.

REMARK 1 In order to treat the linear system (3)-(5) with $I' := I_{k+1}$ in step S3, we solve at first the equations (3). If this system of equations is solvable, then the definiteness of the matrix C implies that a solution consists of the unique vector x' and one (or possibly more than one) dual vector u'. If x' is feasible (4), then the question arises whether there exist related nonnegative dual variables in the system (3)-(5) or not. If the constraint normals $Ae^i (i \in I')$ are linearly independent, the answer is obvious. In the opposite case, this question can be formulated as a linear programming problem and standard procedures could be applied. In contrast to linear programming methods, the technique presented in this paper reduces the numerical effort under mild conditions in such a way that only a special QR-decomposition is necessary. It should be noted that this approach is independent of the optimization method taken in step S1. The method is only required to generate iterates whose distance to the set of KUHN-TUCKER points tends to zero.

ASSUMPTION A1

1) For each $x \in G$ the vectors a^i $(i \in I(x))$ are positive linearly independent.

2) card $I^+(u^*) \geq n^+ := \dim \operatorname{span}\{a^i \mid i \in I^* \setminus I^0\}$ for all $u^* \in U^*$.

3) The vectors a^i $(i \in I^0)$ are linearly independent.

ASSUMPTION A2

$$\lim_{k\to\infty} \|x_k - x^*\| = 0 \quad \text{and} \quad \lim_{k\to\infty} \min\{\|u_k - u^*\| \mid u^* \in U^*\} = 0.$$

THEOREM Let Assumption A1 be satisfied. Morover, the (infinite) sequence $\{(x_k, u_k)\}$ is required to fulfil Assumtion A2. Then, for k$\in$N sufficiently large, it holds:

a) There exists (at least) one index set J_k such that

$$A^{J_k} := [\ldots, a^i, \ldots]_{i \in J_k} \text{ has full column rank}, \quad \mathrm{card}(J_k \setminus I^0) = n^+, \tag{7}$$

$$I^0 \cap I_k \subseteq J_k \subseteq I_k, \tag{8}$$

$$u_k^i \geq \delta^* \quad (i \in J_k \setminus I^0) \quad \text{with some fixed } \delta^* > 0 \tag{9}$$

b) There is some $u_k^* \in U^*$ such that $I^+(u_k^*) \subseteq I_k \subseteq I^*$.

c) The system (3)-(5) taken with I_k instead of I' has (at least) one solution (x', u'). The primal part x' is uniquely determined by (3). In each solution of (3)-(5) the vector x' equals the minimizer x^* of problem (1).

d) A nonnegative solution $\hat{u}$ of the linear equation $Au + Cx^* + p = 0$ is given by

$$\begin{aligned} [\ldots, \hat{u}^j, \ldots]_{j \in J_k}^T &= -((A^{J_k})^T A^{J_k})^{-1} (A^{J_k})^T (Cx^* + p + \sum_{i \in I_k \setminus J_k} u_k^i a^i), \\ \hat{u}^j &= u_k^j \quad (j \in I_k \setminus J_k), \qquad \hat{u}^j = 0 \quad (j \in I \setminus I_k), \end{aligned}$$

i.e. $(x^*, \hat{u})$ is a KUHN-TUCKER *point of problem (1).*

REMARK 2 An index set J_k can be determined, for example, with the help of a modified and in general incomplete QR-factorization of the matrix $A_k := A^{I_k}$. Similarly to [6], by the use of HOUSEHOLDER-transformations it is possible to compute a (m_k, m_k)-permutation-matrix P_k, an orthogonal (n,n)-matrix Q_k, and a matrix $R_k = (r_k^{ij})$, integers $\check{j}_k$ and $\hat{j}_k \geq \check{j}_k$ such that $Q_k R_k = A_k P_k^T$,

$$\begin{aligned} r_k^{ij} &= 0 \quad \text{for} \quad i > j \text{ or } i > \hat{j}_k, \\ |r_k^{jj}| &\geq r \quad \text{for} \quad j = 1, \ldots, \hat{j}_k, \\ \bar{u}_k^T P_k^T e^j &\geq r \quad \text{for} \quad j = 1, \ldots, \check{j}_k, \end{aligned}$$

where $\bar{u}_k := [\ldots, u_k^i, \ldots]_{i \in I_k}^T \in R^{m_k}$ and $e^j \in R^{m_k}$ with $m_k := \mathrm{card} I_k$. The positive number $r \ll 1$ is used to decide numerically, whether a vector a^i, for an index $i \in I_k$, can be considered as linearly dependent from the set of vectors $\{A_k P_k^T e^j \mid j = 1, \ldots, i-1\}$ or not. Now, an index set J_k is given by those indices, which belong to the first $\check{j}_k$ columns of the matrix $A_k P_k^T$.

REMARK 3 Two iterative methods usuable in step S1 of the Basic Algorithm are sketched now (for more details see [1, 2]).
A first method is to minimize approximately the penalty function $S(\cdot, \mu_k)$ defined by

$$S(x, \mu) := \frac{1}{2} x^T C x + p^T x + \sum_{i \in I} \mu [\max\{0, (A^T x - b)^i\}]^3.$$

unless the new iterate x_{k+1} satisfies $\|\nabla_1 S(x_{k+1},\mu_k)\| \le (\frac{1}{2})^{k+1}$. The new dual iterate and the new penalty parameter are given by

$$u^i_{k+1} := 3\mu_k[\max\{0,(A^T x_{k+1}-b)^i\}]^2, \qquad \mu_{k+1} := 10\mu_k.$$

For this method the Assumption A2 can be guaranteed provided that the first statement of Assumption A1 is valid. The penalty function $S(.,\mu)$ is twice continuously differentiable and strictly convex, but not exact. In [5] problem (1) with box constraints is equivalently transformed into the minimization of an exact penalty function, which is twice continuously differentiable under strict complementarity.

An other way for an equivalent formulation of problem (1) without using penalties is given by the equation (2) with an appropriate functional ϕ, e.g. $\phi(a,b) := \sqrt{a^2+b^2}+a-b$. Thus, another iterative method for the step S1 consists in a damped and perturbed NEWTON-type method for solving $T(x,u) = 0$ (c.f. [1, 2]), where the merit function $\|T(.,.)\|_\infty$ is employed. Beside of global convergence properties, this method can be shown to possess a local quadratic rate of convergence under usual additional assumptions, however without requiring strict complementarity.

References

[1] K. Apel. Ein Newton-Typ-Algorithmus zur Lösung quadratischer Optimierungsaufgaben und eine Anwendung auf SQP-Methoden. Diplomarbeit, Technische Universität Dresden, Institut für Numerische Mathematik, 1991.

[2] A. Fischer and K. Schönefeld. Some iterative methods for quadratic programs. Technical report, 07-09-91, Technische Universität Dresden, 1991.

[3] R. Fletcher. A general quadratic programming algorithm. *Journal of the Institute of Mathematics and its Applications*, 7:76–91, 1971.

[4] D. Goldfarb and A. Idnani. A numerical stable dual method for solving strictly convex quadratic programs. *Mathematical Programming*, 27:1–33, 1983.

[5] L. Grippo and S. Lucidi. On the solution of a class of quadratic programs using a differentiable exact penalty function. In H.-J. Sebastian and K. Tammer, editors, *System modelling and optimization, Proceedings of the 14th IFIP-Conference Leipzig, GDR, July 3-7, 1989*, pages 764–773, Berlin, 1990. Springer-Verlag.

[6] A. Kielbasinski and H. Schwetlick. *Numerische lineare Algebra*. Deutscher Verlag der Wissenschaften, Berlin, 1988.

[7] M.J.D. Powell. ZQPCVX - A Fortran subroutine for convex quadratic programming. Technical report, DAMPT/1983/NA17, Department of Applied Mathematics and Theoretical Physics, University of Cambridge, 1983.

[8] B.N. Pšeničnyj and Ju.M. Danilin. *Numerische Methoden für Extremalaufgaben*. Deutscher Verlag der Wissenschaften, Berlin, 1982.

[9] K. Schittkowski and J. Stoer. A factorization method for the solution of constrained linear least squares problems allowing subsequent data changes. *Numerische Mathematik*, 31:431–463, 79.

ON THE NUMBER OF HOMOTOPY-INVARIANT SOLUTIONS FOR SYSTEMS OF POLYNOMIAL EQUATIONS

W. Forster
Department of Mathematics
University of Southampton
Southampton, England

There are many applications which lead to systems of polynomial equations (e.g. the application of the Kuhn-Tucker conditions to suitable nonlinear optimization problems). One way of solving systems of polynomial equations is by homotopy algorithms (deformation algorithms). One can set up homotopies in $\mathbb{R}^n$, but then one has to show

(i) that homotopy-paths do not cross, and

(ii) that the homotopy-paths converge to the right solutions.

One can impose stricter requirements and ask the following question: Is it possible to set up homotopies in a suitable space in such a way as to ensure that the number of solutions one starts with is a homotopy-invariant in this space. Homotopies in $\mathbb{R}^n$ in general do not satisfy this strict requirement (because $\mathbb{R}^n$ can be deformed into a point, or all homotopy-paths may converge to the same solution).

The material we will be using goes back to J. Nielsen [4]. He investigated the homotopy-invariance of fixed points on the torus.

We first consider one polynomial in one variable z . Using Nielsen's results we reinterpret the fundamental theorem of algebra in the following way. Given a polynomial

$$p(z) = a_n z^n + a_{n-1} z^{n-1} + \dots + a_0 ,$$

we want to find zeros, i.e. values of z such that $p(z) = 0$. We consider the polynomial p(z) as a map

$p(z) : \mathbb{C} \to \mathbb{C}$,

from the complex plane $\mathbb{C}$ to itself. For sufficiently large values of z we have $p(z) \neq 0$. In order to be able to use Nielsen's results we consider the map (for sufficiently large z)

$$\frac{p(z)}{|p(z)|} : \mathbf{S} \to \mathbf{S} ,$$

from the circle $\mathbf{S}$ to itself. For this map from $\mathbf{S}$ to a constant $\in \mathbf{S}$ we have a Nielsen number of n (= degree of polynomial). This number is invariant under homotopies, i.e. we can deform the circle $\mathbf{S}$ (as long as $p(z) \neq 0$) and we can get as close as we wish to the zeros of p(z). We can be sure that the homotopy-paths do not cross and that the homotopy-paths converge to n different solutions.

This approach can be generalized to a system of two equations in two variables. Consider the two polynomials (variables z_1 , z_2)

$$p_1(z_1 , z_2) : \hat{\mathbb{C}}_1 \times \hat{\mathbb{C}}_2 \to \hat{\mathbb{C}}_1 ,$$
$$p_2(z_1 , z_2) : \hat{\mathbb{C}}_1 \times \hat{\mathbb{C}}_2 \to \hat{\mathbb{C}}_2 ,$$

where $\hat{\mathbb{C}} = \mathbb{C} \cup \infty$ is the extended complex plane. If each polynomial has a dominant term, i.e. there is a term with the sum of the exponents strictly larger than the sum of the exponents in all other terms in that polynomial, then for sufficiently large values of z_1 and z_2 we have $p_1(z_1,z_2) \neq 0$ and $p_2(z_1,z_2) \neq 0$. For sufficiently large values of z_1 and z_2 we consider the maps

$$\frac{p_1(z_1,z_2)}{|p_1(z_1,z_2)|} : \mathbf{S}_1 \times \mathbf{S}_2 \to \mathbf{S}_1 ,$$

$$\frac{p_2(z_1,z_2)}{|p_2(z_1,z_2)|} : \mathbf{S}_1 \times \mathbf{S}_2 \to \mathbf{S}_2 ,$$

This can be considered as a map

$$P(p_1, p_2) : \mathbf{T}^2 \to \mathbf{T}^2 ,$$

i.e. as a map from the torus $\mathbf{T}^2 \equiv \mathbf{S}_1 \times \mathbf{S}_2$ to itself. The Nielsen number N of this map is the determinant of the exponents of the dominant terms.

$$N = \left|\det\begin{bmatrix} L_{11} & L_{12} \\ L_{21} & L_{22} \end{bmatrix}\right| ,$$

where L_{ji} is the exponent of the variable z_i in equation j (in the dominant term).

We can generalize this approach to systems of n equations in n variables. The Nielsen number for the n-dimensional torus is given in [1]. Therefore, for a system of n polynomials in n variables we have the following number of homotopy-invariant solution classes

$$N = \left|\det\begin{bmatrix} L_{11} & \cdots\cdots & L_{1n} \\ L_{n1} & \cdots\cdots & L_{nn} \end{bmatrix}\right| ,$$

where L_{ji} is the exponent of the variable z_i in equation j (in the dominant term of equation j).

If there is no dominant term in some of the equations, then we add an additional equation

$$z_0 = 0 ,$$

and add e.g. to all of the other equations (e.g. equation j) the following term

$$z_0^{d_j+1} \; z_j^{d_j} + \ldots ,$$

where d_j is the total degree of equation j (i.e. the maximum of the sums of the exponents in the terms of equation j). We have chosen the exponent $d_j + 1$ in order to make sure that this additional term goes to zero (even if $z_j^{d_j}$ tends to infinity).

The Nielsen number determines solution classes [3] and a solution from one solution class cannot be deformed into a solution from another solution class. It is therefore not necessary in simplicial homotopy algorithms [2] to show that homotopy-paths do not cross or that homotopy-paths converge to the right solutions.

REFERENCES:

1. Brooks, R.B.S, Brown, R.F., Pak, J., Taylor, D.H., Nielsen number of maps of tori, Proc. A.M.S., Vol. 52, pp. 398 - 400, 1975.

2. Forster, W., Computing 'all' solutions of systems of polynomial equations by simplicial fixed point algorithms, pp. 39 - 57 in: The computation and modelling of economic equilibria, Talman, A.J.J., van der Laan, G. (Eds.), North-Holland, Amsterdam, 1987.

3. Jiang, Boju, Lectures on Nielsen fixed point theory, American Mathematical Society, Providence, 1990.

4. Nielsen, J., Über die Minimalzahl der Fixpunkte bei den Abbildungstypen der Ringflächen, Mathematische Annalen, Vol. 82, pp. 83 - 93, 1921.

AN OUTER APPROXIMATION METHOD FOR SOLVING CANONICAL D.C. PROBLEMS*

János Fülöp
Laboratory of Operations Research and Decision Systems,
Computer and Automation Institute, Hungarian Academy of Sciences,
H-1518 P.O.Box 63, Budapest, Hungary.

1. INTRODUCTION

A real-valued function on $\mathbb{R}^n$ is called *d.c. function* if it can be represented as a difference of two convex functions on $\mathbb{R}^n$. Let f and g_i, $i=1,\dots,m$, be all d.c. functions. The global optimization problem

$$\text{minimize } f(x), \text{ subject to } g_i(x)\le 0, \; i=1,\dots,m, \tag{1.1}$$

is called *d.c. programming problem* [4]. A d.c. programming problem is *canonical* if it has the form

$$\text{minimize } c^T x, \text{ subject to } g(x)\le 0, \; h(x)\le 0, \tag{1.2}$$

where g is a convex and h is a concave function on $\mathbb{R}^n$, c is an n-vector and ^{T} is the sign of transposition. Any d.c. programming problem (1.1) can be transformed into an equivalent canonical form (1.2) at the possible expense of increasing the number of variables and constraints [4].

A polyhedral outer approximation method will be proposed for solving (1.2). This algorithm is a direct application of the polyhedral version of the outer approximation concept introduced by Horst, Thoai and Tuy [2-4]. The subproblems of the outer approximation method are linear programs with an additional reverse convex constraint. Finite algorithms are known for solving these subproblems [1,4].

2. THE POLYHEDRAL OUTER APPROXIMATION CONCEPT OF HORST, THOAI AND TUY

Although the outer approximation by polyhedral sets has been treated in the context of a more general outer approximation concept in [2-4], we deal only with the polyhedral case here.

Consider the mathematical programming problem

$$\text{(P):} \qquad \text{minimize } f(x), \text{ subject to } x\in D, \tag{2.1}$$

*Research partially supported by Hungarian Research Foundation, OTKA No.2568.

where $D=\{x\in\mathbb{R}^n|g(x)\le 0\}$, g is a convex and f is a lower semi-continuous real-valued function on $\mathbb{R}^n$. In [2-4] f is assumed to be continuous but it will be shown that the results are valid for lower semi-continuous f as well.

The polyhedral outer approximation method for solving (2.1) replaces it by a sequence of relaxed problems

$$(Q_k): \qquad \text{minimize } f(x), \text{ subject to } x\in D_k, \tag{2.2}$$

where D_k is a polyhedral set, $\mathbb{R}^n\supseteq D_1\supset D_2\supset\ldots\supseteq D$. It is assumed that each problem (Q_k) possesses an optimal solution x^k obtained by some available algorithm.

The polyhedral outer approximation method starts with $k\leftarrow 1$ and a polyhedral set $D_1\supseteq D$. In iteration k $(k=1,2,\ldots)$, solve (Q_k) obtaining an optimal solution $x^k\in\text{argmin } f(D_k)$. If $x^k\in D$, we can stop: x^k solves (P). Of course, if it turns out that $D_k=\emptyset$, we can also stop: (P) has no feasible solution. Otherwise, a linear function $\ell_k:\mathbb{R}^n\to\mathbb{R}$ is constructed such that

$$\ell_k(x)\le 0, \ \forall x\in D, \text{ and } \ell_k(x^k)>0. \tag{2.3}$$

Set $D_{k+1}=D_k\cap\{x\in\mathbb{R}^n|\ell_k(x)\le 0\}$, $k\leftarrow k+1$ and perform the next iteration.

In the polyhedral outer approximation method proposed by Horst, Thoai and Tuy [2-4], ℓ_k is defined by

$$\ell_k(x)=(p^k)^T(x-y^k)+\beta_k, \tag{2.4}$$

where $p^k\in\mathbb{R}^n$, $y^k\in D_1$ and $\beta_k\in\mathbb{R}$ are suitably chosen.

Let $D^o=\{x\in\mathbb{R}^n|g(x)<0\}$ and denote the subdifferential of g at x by $\partial g(x)$. Assume that $\partial g(x)\setminus\{0\}\neq\emptyset$, $\forall x\in\mathbb{R}^n\setminus D^o$. This assumption is fulfilled if $D^o\neq\emptyset$. For a set $A\subseteq\mathbb{R}^n$, denote the convex hull of A by conv A. The following proposition, proved in a more general context, is from [2-4].

Proposition 2.1: Let K be any compact subset of D^o. In (2.4) for each $k=1,2,\ldots$ choose

$$y^k\in\text{conv}(K\cup\{x^k\})\setminus D^o,\ p^k\in\partial g(y^k)\setminus\{0\},\ \beta_k=g(y^k), \tag{2.5}$$

where $x^k\in\text{argmin } f(D_k)$. Then every accumulation point of the sequence $\{x^k\}$ belongs to D and solves (P). □

In the proof of Proposition 2.1 in [2-4], the continuity of f is used only to show that from the obvious fact of $f(x^k)\le f(x)$, $\forall x\in D$, it follows $f(\bar{x})\le f(x)$, $\forall x\in D$, for any accumulation point $\bar{x}$ of the sequence $\{x^k\}$. However, this conclusion is valid for lower semi-continuous f as well since the set $\{y\in\mathbb{R}^n|f(y)\le\alpha\}$ is closed for every $\alpha\in\mathbb{R}$ [5].

The outer approximation methods based on Proposition 2.1 include several well-known cutting plane methods of convex and global optimization. The statement of Proposition 2.1 remains valid if (2.5) is changed to

$$y^k=\pi(x^k),\ p^k=x^k-y^k,\ \beta_k=0, \tag{2.6}$$

where $\pi(x)$ denotes the projection of $x\in\mathbb{R}^n$ on D [2-4].

3. POLYHEDRAL OUTER APPROXIMATION FOR SOLVING CANONICAL D.C. PROBLEMS

Consider the canonical d.c. problem (1.2). The feasible set of (1.2) is $D\cap H$, where $D=\{x\in\mathbb{R}^n|g(x)\le 0\}$ and $H=\{x\in\mathbb{R}^n|h(x)\le 0\}$. For the sake of simplicity, assume that D is bounded and $D^o\neq\emptyset$. Then (1.2) has a finite optimal solution if $D\cap H\neq\emptyset$.

We transcribe (1.2) into an equivalent form (2.1). Define the function f on $\mathbb{R}^n$ as follows:

$$f(x) = \begin{cases} c^T x/(1+|c^T x|) & \text{for } x\in H, \\ 1 & \text{for } x\notin H. \end{cases} \tag{3.1}$$

It is easy to see that $f(x)=\varphi(\bar{f}(x))$, where $\bar{f}$ is an extended-real-valued function on $\mathbb{R}^n$ defined by

$$\bar{f}(x) = \begin{cases} c^T x & \text{for } x\in H, \\ \infty & \text{for } x\notin H, \end{cases} \tag{3.2}$$

and φ is a real-valued function on the extended-real line $\bar{\mathbb{R}}$ defined by $\varphi(t)=t/(1+|t|)$, $t\in\mathbb{R}$, $\varphi(\infty)=1$, $\varphi(-\infty)=-1$. It is well-known that φ is a strictly monotone bijection of $\bar{\mathbb{R}}$ onto $[-1,1]$.

Proposition 3.1: f is lower semi-continuous on $\mathbb{R}^n$. □

Proposition 3.2: Problems (1.2) and (2.1), with f and D defined above, are equivalent in the following sense:

(*i*) $x\in D\cap H$ if and only if $x\in D$ and $f(x)<1$.

(*ii*) x^* is an optimal solutions of (1.2) if and only if x^* is an optimal solution of (2.1) such that $f(x^*)<1$. □

Consider a bounded polyhedron $D_k\supseteq D$ and the problem

$$(\bar{Q}_k):\qquad \text{minimize } c^T x, \text{ subject to } x\in D_k\cap H, \tag{3.3}$$

which is a relaxation of (1.2). The relation between (Q_k) and $(\bar{Q}_k)$ is obvious. In Proposition 3.2, replacing D, x^*, (1.2) and (2.1) by D_k, x^k, $(\bar{Q}_k)$ and (Q_k), respectively, we obtain

Proposition 3.3: Problems $(\bar{Q}_k)$ and (Q_k) are equivalent. □

Since all assumptions of the previous section are fulfilled, the polyhedral outer approximation method defined by Proposition 2.1 can be directly applied.

As D is bounded, we can start with a bounded polyhedron $D_1 \supseteq D$ and $k \leftarrow 1$. In iteration k, problem (Q_k) has to be solved. By Proposition 3.3, we can solve $(\bar{Q}_k)$ instead of (Q_k). Problem $(\bar{Q}_k)$ is a linear program with an additional reverse convex constraint and it can be solved by finite algorithms [1,4]. If it turns out that $D_k \cap H = \emptyset$, stop: (1.2) has no feasible solution. If for the optimal solution x^k of $(\bar{Q}_k)$, we have $g(x^k) \le 0$ and consequently $x^k \in D \cap H$, stop: x^k is an optimal solution of (1.2). Otherwise, construct $D_{k+1} = D_k \cap \{x \in \mathbb{R}^n \mid \ell_k(x) \le 0\}$ by (2.4)-(2.5), set $k \leftarrow k+1$ and perform the next iteration.

Proposition 3.4: If (1.2) has no feasible solution, then the algorithm presented above terminates in an iteration k detecting $D_k \cap H = \emptyset$. □

Proposition 3.5: If the algorithm presented above is infinite, then any accumulation point of the sequence $\{x^k\}$ solves (1.2). □

Since $D_k \supset D_{k+1}$ $(k=1,2,..)$, we have $c^T x^k \le c^T x^{k+1}$. Consequently, $c^T x^k$ is a lower bound on the optimum of $(\bar{Q}_{k+1})$. In some methods for solving problem $(\bar{Q}_{k+1})$, the addition of the inequality $c^T x \ge c^T x^k$ to the linear constraints determining D_{k+1} can be useful.

In [1], we presented a finite cutting plane method for solving linear programs with an additional reverse convex constraint. This method uses convexity and facial cuts. Of course, the cutting plane constraints generated during solving problem $(\bar{Q}_k)$ can be dropped after having found an optimal solution x^k. Strategies for dropping constraints generated by the outer approximation can be found in [2-4].

In contrast to other methods, the one presented in [1] does not assume that the problem is stable [4]. This is why the stability of the canonical d.c. problem (1.2) and that of the subproblems $(\bar{Q}_k)$ was not concerned here.

REFERENCES

[1] Fülöp, J.: A finite cutting plane method for solving linear programs with an additional reverse convex constraint. *European Journal of Operational Research* 44 (1990) 395-409.

[2] Horst, R., Thoai, N.V. and Tuy, H.: Outer approximation by polyhedral convex sets. *OR Spektrum* 9 (1987) 153-159.

[3] Horst, R., Thoai, N.V. and Tuy, H.: Outer approximation concept in global optimization. *Optimization* 20 (1989) 255-264.

[4] Horst, R. and Tuy, H.: *Global Optimization*. Springer, Berlin (1990).

[5] Rockafellar, R.T.: *Convex Analysis*. Princeton, New Jersey (1970).

USING EXACT ADDITIVE AND MULTIPLICATIVE PARTS IN QUASI-NEWTON METHODS

J. HUSCHENS
FB IV - MATHEMATIK; POSTFACH 3825
UNIVERSITÄT TRIER
5500 TRIER, FEDERAL REPUBLIC OF GERMANY

We consider approaches in algorithms for optimization, how certain problem inherent structure, that gives rise to a special form of the Hessian, can be exploited to construct suitable approximations to the Hessian. Taking the unconstrained nonlinear least squares problem:

$$\text{minimize} \quad f(x) = \frac{1}{2}R(x)^T R(x) = \frac{1}{2}\sum_{i=1}^{m} r_i(x)^2,$$

where $R : \mathbb{R}^n \to \mathbb{R}^m$ denotes the residual function, as an example for our considerations, it is apparent that the well-known algorithms for this problem like the Gauss-Newton method, the Levenberg-Marquardt method and Quasi-Newton methods [4, 7] work with different kinds of approximations to the Hessian:

$$\nabla^2 f(x) = J(x)^T J(x) + \sum_{i=1}^{m} r_i(x)\, \nabla^2 r_i(x),$$

where $J(x)$ denotes the Jacobian of R at x and $r_i(x)$ the i-th residual function. Defining $C(x) := J(x)^T J(x)$ and $S(x) := \sum_{i=1}^{m} r_i(x)\, \nabla^2 r_i(x)$ most of the well-known methods use the first order part $C(x)$ exactly and approximate only the second order term $S(x)$. Using the ideas from the framework of Quasi-Newton methods for the approximation of $S(x)$ Dennis,Gay,Welsch [2] proposed an algorithm based on the following approximation:

$$\nabla^2 f(x) \approx C(x) + A \quad ; \quad \nabla^2 f(x_+) \approx C(x_+) + A_+,$$

where A_+ is some kind of Quasi-Newton update for A. The theory for structured approximations based on this additive form $B = C(x) + A$ using an exact part $C(x)$ of the Hessian has been developed in [5], but gained further interest resulting in important contributions, mostly related to nonlinear least squares[3, 6] and also to constrained optimization [15].

In infinite-dimensional optimization these ideas have been used in the context of control problems [13, 14] and also, related to additive structure in the Jacobian, in algorithms for integral equations [12].

In our extension of this theory we concentrate on the problem, that Quasi-Newton approximations may fail to reflect the correct absolute size of the corresponding part of the Hessian, resulting for example in a loss of q-quadratic convergence in zero-residual nonlinear least squares problems. In order to address this point we consider approximations using exact additive and multiplicative structure in the form of:

$$B = C(x) + M(x)A,$$

where we assume in a neighborhood of the local solution x_* the following properties: $M(x) : \mathbb{R} \rightarrow \mathbb{R}$; $M(x) \geq M(x_*)$; $M(x) \geq \alpha\|x - x_*\|$, if $M(x_*) = 0$. This means that we introduce an exact multiplicative scalar valued part $M(x)$, which reflects the behaviour at the solution x_*. It is worth mentioning that $M(x) \equiv 1$ reduces this approach to the ideas discussed above. Approximations using the part $M(x)$ correspond in the context of nonlinear least squares to some kind of normalization:

$$\nabla^2 f(x) = C(x) + \|R(x)\| \sum_{i=1}^{m} \frac{r_i(x)}{\|R(x)\|} \nabla^2 r_i(x).$$

This means we now approximate the part $\sum_{i=1}^{m} \frac{r_i(x)}{\|R(x)\|} \nabla^2 r_i(x)$ by Quasi-Newton techniques and use $\|R(x)\|$ explicitly resulting in approximations of the form:

$$B = C(x) + \|R(x)\| A.$$

Using this kind of approximation and extending the approximation techniques to cover also the use of exact multiplicative parts results in an algorithm for the unconstrained nonlinear least squares problem, that obtains local q-quadratic convergence for zero-residual problems and q-superlinear convergence for nonzero-residual problems. These convergence results are due to a selfadapting property resulting from the exact use of multiplicative structure. For further details we refer to [10].

The application of this idea in constrained optimization is most striking in the case of constrained nonlinear least squares:

$$\begin{array}{ll} \min & f(x) = \frac{1}{2}R(x)^T R(x) \\ \text{s.t.} & g(x) = 0. \end{array}$$

The Hessian of the Augmented Lagrangian for this problem is given by:

$$\begin{aligned} \nabla_x^2 L(x, \lambda, C) &= J(x)^T J(x) + C\nabla g(x) \nabla g(x)^T \\ &\quad + \sum_{i=1}^{m} r_i(x) \cdot \nabla^2 r_i(x) + \sum_{i=1}^{k} \lambda_i \cdot \nabla^2 g_i(x) + C \sum_{i=1}^{k} g_i(x) \cdot \nabla^2 g_i(x). \end{aligned}$$

Using a totally structured approximation of the form:

$$B = J(x)^T J(x) + C\nabla g(x) \nabla g(x)^T + \sqrt{|L(x, \lambda, C)|}\ A$$

we can derive an algorithm using only exact first order information, that obtains a q-quadratic convergence rate for constrained zero-residual problems and a q-superlinear convergence rate for constrained nonzero-residual problems. The details of this application can be found in [9].

Finally the concept of totally structured approximations also carries over to Hilbert space applications. The formulation in a Hilbert space setting generalizes the results for finite-dimensional applications of totally structured approximations and also gives the generalization of approximations using exact additive parts to Hilbert space applications (see [11]). As an application in [11] infinite-dimensional nonlinear least squares problems in the form of parameter identification problems are discussed. Numerical comparisons to Gauss-Newton based approaches in this area (see e.g.[1, 8]) and the extension to constrained infinite-dimensional problems remain as future work.

REFERENCES

[1] H. Bock, *Randwertprobleme zur Parameteridentifizierung in Systemen nichtlinearer Differentialgleichungen*, Preprint Nr. 442, Universität Heidelberg, Institut für Angewandte Mathematik, SFB 123, D–6900 Heidelberg, West Germany, 1988.

[2] J. E. Dennis, D. M. Gay, and R. E.Welsch, *An adaptive nonlinear least-squares algorithm*, TOMS, 7 (1981), pp. 348–368.

[3] J. E. Dennis, H. J. Martinez, and R. A. Tapia, *Convergence theory for the structured BFGS secant method with an application to nonlinear least squares*, J. Optim. Theory Appl., 61 (1989), pp. 161–178.

[4] J. E. Dennis and R. B. Schnabel, *Numerical Methods for Unconstrained Optimization and Nonlinear Equations*, Prentice-Hall, Englewood Cliffs, N.J, 1983.

[5] J. E. Dennis and H. F. Walker, *Convergence theorems for least change secant update methods*, SIAM J. Numer. Anal., 18 (1981), pp. 949–987.

[6] J. Engels and H. Martinez, *Local and superlinear convergence for partially known quasi-Newton methods*, SIAM J. Optimization, 1 (1991), pp. 42–56.

[7] R. Fletcher, *Practical Methods of Optimization*, John Wiley and Sons, New York, 1987.

[8] M. Heinkenschloss, *Gauss-Newton Methods for Infinite Dimensional Least Squares Problems with Norm Constraints*, PhD thesis, Universität Trier, 1991.

[9] J.Huschens, *On a totally structured algorithm for constrained nonlinear least squares problems*, tech. rep., Universität Trier, 1991.

[10] ——, *On the use of product structure in secant methods for nonlinear least squares problems*, tech. rep., Universität Trier, 1991. (submitted for publication).

[11] ——, *Structured quasi-newton methods for optimization methods in Hilbert spaces*, tech. rep., Universität Trier, 1991.

[12] C. Kelley and J. Northrup, *A pointwise Quasi-Newton method for integral equations*, SIAM J. Numer. Anal., 25 (1988), pp. 1138–1155.

[13] C. T. Kelley and E. W. Sachs, *A pointwise Quasi-Newton method for unconstrained optimal control problems*, Numer. Math., 55 (1989), pp. 159–176.

[14] C. T. Kelley, E. W. Sachs, and B.Watson, *A pointwise Quasi-Newton method for unconstrained optimal control problems II.* JOTA, to appear.

[15] H. J. Martinez, *Local and Superlinear Convergence of Structured Secant Methods from the Convex Class*, PhD thesis, Rice University, 1988.

An Interval Method for Global Unconstrained Optimization

Christian Jansson
Informatik III, TU Hamburg-Harburg
Postfach 90 14 03, 2100 Hamburg 90

Introduction

A method for calculating the global minimum points of an unconstrained minimization problem $\min\{ f(x) \mid x \in X \}$ is presented. $f : X \to \mathbb{R}$ and

$$X := [\underline{X}, \overline{X}] := \left\{ x \in \mathbb{R}^n \mid \underline{X} \leq x \leq \overline{X} \right\} \subseteq \mathbb{R}^n$$

is an interval vector, i.e. a compact parallelepiped with sides parallel to the coordinate axes. This method is based on the tools of interval arithmetic and uses a special branch-and-bound technique in connection with a descent method. Besides the calculation of approximations of the global minimum value f^* and the set of all global minimum points X^* the algorithm provides a guaranteed lower and upper bound of f^*, i.e. the bounds calculated on a computer are always correct despite the presence of rounding errors and the nonlinearity of f. Derivatives of the function are not required.

Our experiments show that the method is extremeiy efficient and competitive with non-interval methods, the latter not providing guaranteed lower bounds.

The four basic operations for intervals $X, Y \subseteq \mathbb{R}$ are defined by

$$X * Y := \{ x * y \mid x \in X,\ y \in Y \}, \quad * \in \{+, -, \cdot, /\}. \tag{1}$$

These operations can easily be executed on a computer and require two real operations. For example, $[\underline{X}, \overline{X}] + [\underline{Y}, \overline{Y}] = [\underline{X} + \underline{Y}, \overline{X} + \overline{Y}]$. By definition, the interval operations (1) are *inclusion monotone*:

$$x \in X,\ y \in Y \quad \text{then} \quad x * y \in X * Y, \quad * \in \{+, -, \cdot, /\}. \tag{2}$$

From this fact it follows that lower and upper bounds for the range of functions can be computed by using the interval operations (1) instead of the real operations. A function F which is defined for all interval vectors $Y \subseteq X$ such that

$$F(Y) \supseteq \{ f(y) \mid y \in Y \} \tag{3}$$

is called an inclusion function.

For example, if $f(x) := x/(1-x)$ then we can replace each real variable by an interval variable yielding by (2) an inclusion function $F(X) := X/(1-X)$. F is defined for all intervals with $1 \notin X$. If $X := [2,3]$ then $F(X) = [2,3]/(1-[2,3]) = [-3,-1]$ where the true range of f over X is $[-2,-1.5]$. If $x \neq 0$ then $f(x) = 1/(1/x - 1)$ yields the inclusion function $G(X) := (1/(1/X-1))$ with $G([2,3]) = 1/(1/[2,3]-1) = [-2,-1.5]$.

In general, inclusion functions overestimate the range of the corresponding real function, but this overestimation tends to zero if the diameter of X tends to zero. Moreover, the overestimation depends on the arithmetic expression which is used for the inclusion function. A thorough treatment of the tools of interval arithmetic and the construction of inclusion functions can be found in [1], [2], [3]. For the application of interval arithmetic to optimization problems see also [4].

Method

In this section we explain roughly the main ideas how the method proceeds in the one-dimensional case. It is assumed that an inclusion function F of f is given.

During the minimization the initial box $Y := X$ is subdivided by repeated bisection. In each bisection step two pairs $\left(Y^{(1)}, F(Y^{(1)})\right)$, $\left(Y^{(2)}, F(Y^{(2)})\right)$ with $Y^{(1)} \cup Y^{(2)} = Y$ are calculated and are stored on a list S. Moreover, at some bisection steps a descent method is applied calculating an approximate local or global minimum $\tilde{x} \in X$. The value $f(\tilde{x})$ is used to update a smallest value μ of f currently known and to calculate a guaranteed upper bound of f^*. If $f(x) < \mu$ then we replace μ by $f(x)$. At the beginning we set $\mu := \infty$. Obviously, if during the bisection process the corresponding lower bound $\underline{F}(Y^{(j)}) > \mu$, $j \in 1,2$ then $Y^{(j)}$ cannot contain a global minimum point and therefore is discarded from the list S. Hence, the union of all boxes $Y^{(i)}$ of the list S contains always the set of all global minimum points X^*, the minimum $\underline{F}$ of all lower bounds $\underline{F}(Y^{(i)})$ of the list S is a guaranteed lower bound of the minimum value f^*. In addition $\underline{F} \leq f^* \leq \mu$ in each step of the process. In principle, $\mu - \underline{F}$ can be made arbitrarily small by repeated bisection.

The problem is how to incorporate the descent method in the bisection process. We do this by bisecting an interval Y from the list S three or four times and applying the descent method to the bisected interval with the smallest lower bound.

Numerical Results

Our method was applied to the six test functions considered in [5]. According to the authors these test functions well represent practical problems. In [5] six algorithms developed by Žilinskas, Strongin, Pijavskij, Shubert, Brent and Batishchev are compared according to these functions.

Our method calculates in each case all global minimum points and the global minimum value with relative accuracy 10^{-6}. The number of function evaluations, the global minimum value f^* and the guaranteed lower bounds $\underline{F}$ are given in table 1.

Function	NIF	NRF	f^*	$\underline{F}$	EFF
f1	20	9	−4.60131	−4.833	1.9
f2	20	17	−1.90596	−1.959	1.5
f3	110	37	−12.0312	−12.97	2.0
f4	18	14	−0.824239	−1.118	1.5
f5	24	21	−14.5927	−15.20	1.7
f6	44	31	−13.9223	−15.06	2.7

Table 1: Numerical Results

NIF resp. NRF denotes the number of interval resp. real function evaluations. The efficiency EFF is $2 \cdot \text{NIF} + \text{NRF}$ divided by the number of function evaluations of the best traditional method given in [5].

It follows that for all test functions the efficiency of our method is about two, whereas the efficiency of some methods tested in [5] varies drastically depending on the test functions. Moreover, our method provides guaranteed lower bounds $\underline{F}$ which describe in most cases the global minimum value very well. By continuing the bisection process the lower bounds can be improved. In the case of f4 we get $\underline{F} \doteq -0.8685$ using NIF = 40, NRF = 20.

There are several strategies adapting the method to the multi-dimensional case and handling also constrained global optimization methods. In this field our work is still in progress.

References

[1] Alefeld, G., Herzberger, J., Introduction to Interval Computations, Academic Press, New York, 1983

[2] Moore, R.E., Methods and Applications of Interval Analysis, SIAM, Philadelphia, 1971

[3] Ratschek, H., Rokne, J., Computer Methods for the Range of Functions, Ellis Horwood Limited, Chichester, 1984

[4] Ratschek, H., Rokne, J., New Computer Methods for Global Optimization, Ellis Horwood Limited, Chichester, 1988

[5] Törn, A., Zilinskas, A., Global Optimization, Springer-Verlag, Berlin, 1987

Fast Algorithms for Compact Fixed Point Problems

C. T. Kelley
Department of Mathematics
North Carolina State University
Raleigh, NC 27695-8205
USA

Compact fixed point problems arise in several applications such as semiconductor modeling [9], radiative transfer and neutron transport [5], and competitive systems [14]. In the general setting we consider nonlinear equations

$$\mathcal{F}(u) = u - \mathcal{K}(u) = 0 \tag{1}$$

where $\mathcal{K}$ is a completely continuous (compact) Lipschitz continuously differentiable map on a Banach space X. We make the standard assumptions that (1) has a solution u^* in X and that the Fréchet derivative $\mathcal{F}'(u^*)$ is nonsingular. We advocate solving (1) by Newton-like iterative methods. As is standard in the optimization literature [6] we will describe the methods in terms of the transition from current approximations (u_c, B_c) to $(u^*, \mathcal{F}'(u^*))$ to new approximations $(u_+, B+)$. The basic iteration is

$$u_+ = u_c - B_c\mathcal{F}(u_c)$$

after which $\mathcal{F}(u_+)$ is evaluated and a decision is made on whether or not to terminate the iteration. If it is decided to continue the iteration B_c is updated to B_+ and the iteration continues. The basic iteration itself has two parts, the solution of the linear equation for the step

$$B_c s = -\mathcal{F}(u_c),$$

and addition of the step to u_c to form u_+.

Newton's method uses $B_+ = \mathcal{F}'(u_+)$. In the finite dimensional case with dense unstructured Jacobian matrices and difference evaluation of derivatives the cost of evaluation of B_+ is N function evaluations, where N is the number of unknowns, and $O(N^3)$ floating point operations for factorization of the Jacobian matrix. Discretizations of infinite dimensional problems will incur similar costs. The local convergence rate for Newton's method is *q-quadratic*, that is

$$\|u_+ - u^*\| \le K\|u_c - u^*\|^2$$

for some $K > 0$ provided u_c is sufficiently near u^*.

One way to avoid the costs associated with Jacobian evaluation is to approximate $\mathcal{F}'(u^*)$ once and for all with a linear map B and never change it. If the map B is a sufficiently accurate approximation the iterates will converge but at a slower rate than is the case for Newton's method. If $\|B - \mathcal{F}'(u^*)\| \le \delta$ then

$$\|u_+ - u^*\| \le \bar{K}\delta\|u_c - u^*\|$$

for some $\bar{K} > 0$. In many cases, such as those considered here, the savings in derivative evaluation and matrix factorization are such that the increased number of iterates is more than offset by the lower cost per iterate.

The fast algorithms we consider are variations of the Atkinson-Brakhage [2], [4], algorithm for integral equations. We briefly describe that algorithm in a simple context and use that to illustrate the more complex examples to follow. Consider the equation

$$u(x) = \mathcal{K}(u)(x) = \int_0^1 k(x,y)u(y)\,dy + g(x) \tag{2}$$

where k and g are continuous and $u \in C[0,1]$ is to be found. We consider a sequence of quadrature rules, indexed with l, with nodal points $\{x_i^l\}_{i=1}^{N_l}$ and weights $\{w_i^l\}_{i=1}^{N_l}$. Such that

$$\lim_{l\to\infty} \sum_{i=1}^{N_l} f(x_i^l)w_i^l = \int_0^1 f(x)\,dx \tag{3}$$

for all $f \in C[0,1]$. We let K denote the linear integral operator in (2) and define the approximate operators

$$K_l u(x) = \sum_{j=1}^{N_l} k(x, x_j^l)u(x_j^l)w_j^l.$$

Equation (3) and the continuity of k implies that K_l is a collectively compact [1] sequence of operator that converges strongly to K. This in turn implies that if $I - K$ is an invertible operator so is $I - K_l$ for l sufficiently large and

$$(I - K_l)^{-1}g \to (I - K)^{-1}g$$

for all $g \in C[0,1]$.

However equations of the form $(I - K_l)u = g$ can be solved by factoring the $N_l \times N_l$ matrix with entries

$$\delta_{ij} - k(x_i^l, x_j^l)w_j^l,$$

solving the N_l dimensional system

$$U_i - \sum k(x_i^l, x_j^l)w_j^l U_j = g(x_i^l)$$

and using the equation to obtain

$$u(x) = g(x) + \sum_{j=1}^{N_l} k(x, x_j^l)U_j w_j^l.$$

Hence computing the action of $(I - K_l)^{-1}$ on several vectors requires a one time cost of $O(N_l^3)$ floating point operations for the matrix factorization and a cost of $O(N_l^2)$ floating point operations for each solve.

A second consequence of the strong convergence and collective compactness is the *norm* convergence of the sequence

$$A_l = I + (I - K_l)^{-1}K$$

to $(I - K)^{-1}$. In fact if we define

$$A_l^L = I + (I - K_l)^{-1}K_L$$

we have

$$\lim_{l\to\infty} \sup_{L\geq l} \|A_l^L - (I - K_L)^{-1}\| = 0.$$

This norm convergence is the basis for the Atkinson Brakhage iterative algorithm. To solve $(I - K_L)u = g$ for some large L would require $O(N_L^3)$ operations if done by a standard direct method. However the iterative method

$$u_+ = u_c - A_l^L(u_c - K_L u_c - g)$$

requires a startup cost of $O(N_l^3)$ operations for a coarse mesh matrix factorization and a cost of $O(N_L^2)$ operations for each iterate. The cost per iterate can be expressed in more detail as $N_L^2 + O(N_L)$ for the evaluation of $w = (u_c - K_L u_c - g)$ and again for the evaluation of $K_L w$ which must be done as part of $A_l^L w$. Following that is the cost of $O(N_l^2)$ for the application of $(I - K_l)^{-1}$. Hidden in all of this is the $O(N_L)$ cost for interpolation between grids.

The algorithm is made most efficient by refining the fine mesh as the iteration progresses. This was originally proposed in [10] and a cost analysis for the trapezoid rule was made in [3]. The iteration is of the form

$$u_+ = u_c - A_l^{L_c}\mathcal{F}_{L_c}(u_c)$$

where L_c is refined to L_+ after u_+ is computed. If l is sufficiently large only one iterate for each value of L is needed to maintain accuracy at the level of truncation. For the linear problem specified above

$$\mathcal{F}_{L_c}(u_c) = u_c - \mathcal{K}_{L_c}u_c = u_c - K_{L_c}u_c - g$$

but for general nonlinear compact fixed point problems the general scheme of the iteration is exactly the same. The role of K in the linear problem is played by the Fréchet derivative of $\mathcal{K}$ in the nonlinear case. The key point is the construction of norm convergent approximations to $(\mathcal{F}')^{-1}$ that can be efficiently evaluated. Details on construction of such approximations in more general settings may be found in [12] and [7] for example.

This talk will focus on implicit compact fixed point problems that come from elliptic systems of the form

$$\nabla^2 u = N(u, \nabla u)$$

where N is a bounded nonlinear operator such that $\nabla^{-2}N$ is completely continuous in an appropriate space. Treating multiplication by the inverse of ∇^2 as a preconditioner (which can be done by a fast Poisson solver, say) the equation becomes a compact fixed point problem of a more complicated type than an integral equation. Issues such a formation of A_l^L, proof of the collective compactness, and problems with nonsmooth nonlinearities will be mentioned with the integral equation being used as a model problem to solidify the ideas.

We have ignored the storage cost of $O(N_l^2)$ for storage of the matrix factorization but this may be a significant cost for the implicit compact fixed point problems discussed above. If l cannot be made large enough so that one iterate for each value of L is all that is needed either iterative methods for computation of A_l^L can be used as was done in [7] or Broyden's method can be used to accelerate convergence. Use of Broyden's method in this context has been analyzed in [11], [12], [13], and [8].

References

[1] P. M. ANSELONE, *Collectively Compact Operator Approximation Theory*, Prentice-Hall, Englewood Cliffs, NJ, 1971.

[2] K. E. ATKINSON, *Iterative variants of the Nyström method for the numerical solution of integral equations*, Numer. Math., 22 (1973), pp. 17–31.

[3] ——, *A survey of numerical methods for solving nonlinear integral equations*, Tech. Report 3, University of Iowa, Department of Mathematics, March 1990.

[4] H. BRAKHAGE, *Über die numerische Behandlung von Integralgleichungen nach der Quadraturformelmethode*, Numer. Math., 2 (1960), pp. 183–196.

[5] S. CHANDRASEKHAR, *Radiative Transfer*, Dover, New York, 1960.

[6] J. E. DENNIS AND R. B. SCHNABEL, *Numerical Methods for Nonlinear Equations and Unconstrained Optimization*, Prentice-Hall, Englewood Cliffs, N.J, 1983.

[7] M. HEINKENSCHLOSS, C. T. KELLEY, AND H. T. TRAN, *Fast algorithms for nonsmooth compact fixed point problems*. submitted for publication.

[8] D. M. HWANG AND C. T. KELLEY, *Convergence of Broyden's method in Banach spaces*. SIOPT, to appear.

[9] J. W. JEROME, *Newton's method for gradient equations based upon the fixed point map: convergence and complexity study*, Numer. Math., 55 (1989), pp. 619–632.

[10] C. T. KELLEY, *Operator prolongation methods for nonlinear equations*, in Computational Solution of Nonlinear Systems of Equations, E. L. Allgower and K. Georg, eds., vol. 26 of AMS Lectures in Applied Mathematics, American Mathematical Society, Providence, RI, 1990, pp. 359–388.

[11] C. T. KELLEY AND E. W. SACHS, *Approximate quasi-Newton methods*, Mathematical Programming, ser. B, 48 (1990), pp. 41–70.

[12] ——, *Fast algorithms for compact fixed point problems with inexact function evaluations*, SIAM J. on Sci. Stat. Comp., 12 (1991), pp. 725–742.

[13] ——, *A new proof of superlinear convergence for Broyden's method in Hilbert space*, SIAM J. on Optimization, 1 (1991), pp. 146–150.

[14] S. LENHART, V. PROTOPOPESCU, AND S. STOJANOVIC, *A mimimax problem for semilinear nonlocal competitive systems*. submitted for publication.

PARAMETRIC NONLINEAR OPTIMIZATION: STABILITY OF STATIONARY SOLUTIONS AND SOME APPLICATIONS

Diethard Klatte
Fachbereich Mathematik, Pädagogische Hochschule Halle-Köthen
Kröllwitzer Straße 44, 0-4050 Halle (Saale), Germany

For perturbed nonlinear programs (NLP) with twice continuously differentiable data, there is a well-developed theory of solution stability based on second-order conditions (SOC), cf., e.g., [2,3,9,11,12]. Motivations for this theory are manifold. For example, convergence analysis of optimization methods, the study of incorrect models, decomposition techniques, semi-infinite programming and input-output modelling lead to the question whether a stationary solution or a local/global minimizer of a NLP behaves stable in some sense. In the following, we give 2nd-order sufficient stability conditions for NLP, allowing some non-smoothness of initial data. The applications mentioned in the title particulary concern iterated local minimization and semi-infinite programming. For brevity of presentation, we refer in this connection only to the recent papers [5] and [6].

Consider a standard NLP depending on a parameter t varying in T,

$$P(t): \quad \min_x \left\{ f_o(x,t) \mid f_i(x,t)=0,\ i=1,\dots,p;\ f_j(x,t)\leq 0,\ j=p+1,\dots,m \right\},$$

where T is an open subset of R^s and f_i, $i=0,1,..,m$, are real-valued functions defined on $R^n \times T$. Denote by M(t) the constraint set of P(t). Let X be an open subset of R^n. Throughout the paper, let t^o be a fixed element of T, and let $x^o \in M(t^o) \cap X$. To have a uniform presentation here, we suppose that each f_i is of class $C^{1,1}$, i.e., f_i is continuously differentiable and has a locally Lipschitzian gradient mapping $Df_i(.,.)$ on X x T. Let $(x,u) \longmapsto l(x,u,t)$ be the usual Lagrange function to P(t), and put $l_{u,t} := l(.,u,t)$. $(x,u) \in K(t)$ means that the (m+n)-vector (x,u) satisfies the necessary Karush-Kuhn-Tucker conditions for x being a local minimizer to P(t). Further, let S(t) denote the set of stationary solutions to P(t), i.e., $S(t) := \{x \mid \exists\ u: (x,u) \in K(t)\}$, and let $LM(x,t) := \{u \mid (x,u) \in K(t)\}$ - the set of Lagrange multiplier vectors to x w.r.t. to P(t). By LICQ and MFCQ we abbreviate the well-known Linear Independence and Mangasarian-Fromovitz Constraint Qualifications, cf., e.g., [9,12]. We shall say that a multifunction F from T to R^N is <u>upper Hölder continuous</u> of order 1/2 at t^o if there are a neighborhood U of t^o and some $\beta > 0$ such that

$$\text{dist}\,(z,F(t^o)) \leq \beta\,||t - t^o||^{1/2} \qquad \forall t\in U \quad \forall z\in F(t).$$

When replacing the order 1/2 by 1, we use the notion "upper Lipschitz continuity". For $Y\subset R^N$ let $F\cap Y$ denote the multifunction $t \longmapsto F(t)\cap Y$.

A recent survey of second-order stability conditions for the class of programs studied here may be found in [6]. The following formulations are often specializations of the results in [6], but point out concisely the essence of the requirements for stability in weak or strong sense.

(1) Upper Hölder continuity of local solution sets. Let x^o be a local minimizer to $P(t^o)$ satisfying MFCQ and, with some $c>0$,

$$f_o(x,t^o) - f_o(x^o,t^o) \geq c\,||x - x^o||^2 \quad \text{for all } x\in M(t^o) \text{ near } x^o. \qquad (*)$$

Then there is some $r>0$ such that for all t near t^o,

a) $X(t) := \text{Argmin}_x\,(f_o(x,t)\mid x\in M(t)\wedge ||x-x^o|| \leq r)$ is nonempty,

b) $x\in X(t) \Longrightarrow x$ locally minimizes $f_o(.,t)$ on $M(t)$,

c) $X(.)$ is upper Hölder continuous at t^o of order 1/2 with $X(t^o) = \{x^o\}$.

([1, Thm. 4.6, Cor. 4.7], [6, Prop. 2.1])

(2) Upper Lipschitz continuity of LM(.,.). Let $x^o\in S(t^o)$, and suppose that MFCQ holds at x^o. Then $LM(.,.)$ is upper Lipschitz continuous at (x^o,t^o). ([5, Thm. 2.2], [6, Prop. 2.6])

Note that Proposition (2) is crucial to prove upper Lipschitz continuity of $K(.)$ under second-order assumptions. Similar to the case of NLP with twice differentiable (C^2) data, we need some kind of generalized second directional derivative. Given a $C^{1,1}$ function $g: R^N \longrightarrow R$, an appropriate concept is the following convex-set-valued mapping g''_{Cl} (cf. [4,5-7,10]):

$$g''_{Cl}(x;h,k) := \left\{ h^T H k \mid H\in\partial^2_{Cl}g(x)\right\},\ (x,h,k)\in R^N \times R^N \times R^N,$$

where $\partial^2_{Cl}g(x)$ is the generalized Hessian matrix (set) of g at x in Clarke's sense, for definition and calculus we refer to [4]. In particular, a second-order Taylor expansion holds in these terms ([4, Thm. 2.3]). For simplicity, we write $g''_{Cl}(x;h,k)>0$ instead of $v>0\ \forall v\in g''_{Cl}(x;h,k)$.

The following conditions naturally extend the standard and the strong SOC which are known to be essential for (sufficient and often also necessary) stability characterizations in the case of C^2 data, cf. [9,12].

We say that $(x,u)\in K(t)$ satisfies the standard second-order sufficient condition <u>SOSC</u> for $P(t)$ if $(l_{u,t})''_{Cl}(x;h,h)>0$ holds for all directions $h\in W(x,u,t)\setminus\{0\}$, where

$$I^+(u) := \{1,\dots,p\} \cup \{i \mid u_i > 0\}, \quad I(x,t) := \{j \mid j \geq p+1,\ f_j(x,t)=0\},$$
$$W^+(x,u,t) := \{h \mid h^T D_x f_i(x,t) = 0,\ i \in I^+(u)\},$$
$$W(x,u,t) := \{h \in W^+(x,u,t) \mid h^T D_x f_j(x,t) \leq 0,\ j \in I(x,t)\}.$$

We say that $(x,u) \in K(t)$ satisfies the strong second-order sufficient condition SSOSC for P(t) if $(1_{u,t})''_{Cl}(x;h,h) > 0$ holds for all $h \in W^+(x,u,t) \setminus \{0\}$.

(3) Strict local optimality. Let $x^o \in S(t^o)$. If for some $u^o \in LM(x^o,t^o)$, (x^o,u^o) satisfies SOSC for $P(t^o)$, then x^o is a local minimizer to $P(t^o)$ having property (*) (i.e., x^o is a strict local minimizer with order 2). ([8, Thm. 1], [6, Thm. 4.3]).

Obviously, (3) provides a sufficient condition for (1). The following proposition generalizes [12, Thm. 2.4] and [12, Cor. 4.3].

(4) Upper Lipschitz continuity of K(.). If $x^o \in S(t^o)$ satisfies MFCQ, and for each $u \in LM(x^o,t^o)$, SOSC holds at (x^o,u) for $P(t^o)$, then x^o is an isolated stationary solution (and also an isolated local minimizer) to $P(t^o)$. ([8, Thm. 2]).
Moreover, for some neighborhood V of x^o, the multifunction $K(.) \cap (V \times R^m)$ is upper Lipschitz continuous at t^o, where $K(t) \cap (V \times R^m) \neq \emptyset$ for t near t^o and $KT(t^o) \cap (V \times R^m) = \{x^o\} \times LM(x^o,t^o)$. ([6, Thm. 4.5]).

In view of the next two propositions we suppose that the (partial second directional derivative) multifunction $(x,u,t,h) \mapsto (1_{u,t})''_{Cl}(x;h,h)$ is closed and locally bounded on $\{x^o\} \times LM(x^o,t^o) \times \{t^o\} \times B$, where $B := \{h \mid \|h\|=1\}$. This ensures that SSOSC becomes the "uniform SOC" introduced in [7]. We note that the uniform SOC even allows more general formulations of (5) and (6) below, cf. [5-7].

(5) Strong stability of local minimizers. Let the assumptions of (4) be fulfilled but replace SOSC by SSOSC. Then for certain neighborhoods U of t^o and V of x^o, $S(.) \cap V$ is single-valued on U (say $S(t) \cap V = \{x(t)\}$) and upper Lipschitz continuous at t^o, where $x(t^o)=x^o$. Further, x(.) is Hölder continuous of order 1/2 on U, and for t in U, x(t) is a strict local minimizer with order 2 to P(t).
([7, Thm. 3.7], [5, Thm. 2.5], [6, Thm. 5.2, Cor. 5.3]).

(6) Strong stability of the Karush-Kuhn-Tucker map K(.). Let the assumptions of (5) be fulfilled but replace MFCQ by LICQ. Then for certain neighborhoods U of t^o and V of x^o, $K(.) \cap (V \times R^m)$ is single-valued (say equal to $\{(x(t),u(t)\}$) and Lipschitz continuous on U with $x(t^o)=x^o$. ([6, Cor. 5.5], [10, Thm.2]).

However, the hypotheses of (6) imply that such Karush-Kuhn-Tucker points are characterized, which are associated with a local minimizer x(t) to P(t). Note that Kummer [10] gives conditions for regularity of critical points of a system of locally Lipschitz equations being equivalent to the KKT system; these results allow to characterize strong stability of KT(.) in the sense of (6) also if x^{o} and x(t) are not local minimizers.

References

[1] Alt, W.: Lipschitzian perturbations of infinite optimization problems. In: A.V. Fiacco, ed., Mathematical Programming with Data Perturbations. M. Dekker, New York and Basel, 1983.

[2] Fiacco, A.V., ed.: Optimization with Data Perturbations. Annals of Operations Research 27 (1990).

[3] Fiacco, A.V. and G.P. McCormick: Nonlinear Programming: Sequential Unconstrained Minimization Techniques. Wiley, New York, 1968.

[4] Hiriart-Urruty, J.-B., J.J. Strodiot and V. Hien Nguyen: Generalized Hessian matrix and second-order optimality conditions for problems with C 1,1 - data. Appl. Math. Optim. 11 (1984), 43-56.

[5] Klatte, D.: Strong stability of stationary solutions and iterated local minimization. In: J. Guddat, H.Th. Jongen, B. Kummer, F. Nožička, eds., Parametric Optimization and Related Topics II. Akademie-Verlag, Berlin, 1991.

[6] Klatte, D.: Nonlinear optimization problems under data perturbations. In: W. Krabs and J. Zowe, eds., Proceedings der Sommerschule "Moderne Methoden der Optimierung" (Thurnau, 1990), Lecture Notes, Springer, Berlin-Heidelberg-New York, to appear. Manuscript, PH Halle, 1991.

[7] Klatte, D., B. Kummer and R. Walzebok: Conditions for optimality and strong stability in nonlinear programs without assuming twice differentiability of data. IIASA WP-89-089, Laxenburg/Austria, 1989.

[8] Klatte, D. and K. Tammer: On second-order sufficient optimality conditions for C 1,1 - optimization problems. optimization 19 (1988), 169-179.

[9] Kojima, M.: Strongly stable stationary solutions in nonlinear programs. In: S.M. Robinson, ed., Analysis and Computation of Fixed Points. Academic press, New York, 1980.

[10] Kummer, B.: An implicit function theorem for C 0,1 - equations and parametric C 1,1 - optimization. J. Math. Anal. Appl. (1991), to appear.

[11] Robinson, S.M.: Generalized equations and their solutions, Part I: Basic theory. Math. Programming Study 10 (1979), 128-141.

[12] Robinson, S.M.: Generalized equations and their solutions, Part II: Applications to nonlinear programming. Math. Programming Study 19 (1982), 200-221.

METHOD OF SOLVING ALTERNATIVE LINEAR SEMI - INFINITE PROGRAMMING PROBLEM

Vladimir G. Medvedev
Byelorussian State University, 220080, Minsk, USSR

Consider a alternative linear semi-infinite programming problem

$$c'x \longrightarrow max,$$
$$b_*(t) \le A(t)x \le b^*(t), \quad t \in T; \qquad \text{(ASIP)}$$
$$x \in X,$$

where

$$X = \bigcup_{s=1}^{k} X_s, \quad X_s = \left\{ x \in \mathbb{R}^n : f_*(s) \le G(s)x \le f^*(s), d_*(s) \le x \le d^*(s) \right\},$$

$G(s) \in \mathbb{R}^{q(s) \times n}$, $f^*(s), f_*(s) \in \mathbb{R}^{q(s)}$; $d_*(s), d^*(s) \in \mathbb{R}^n$, $s=1,2,\ldots,k$; $c, x \in \mathbb{R}^n$; $b^*(.), b_*(.) \in \mathbb{R}^m$; $A(.) \in \mathbb{R}^{m \times n}$; $T = \left\{ t \in \mathbb{R} : a \le t \le b \right\}$; $b_*(.), b^*(.), A(.) \in C^p(T)$, $p \ge 2$, $p \in \mathbb{Z}$.

We assume that there are vectors $v_s \in X_s$ such that

$$b_*(t) < A(t)v_s < b^*(t), \quad t \in T, \quad s=1,2,\ldots,k;$$

(Slater's condition).

The notions of a support feasible solution, a support, a support feasible solution structure, a finishing procedure are introduced for problem (ASIP). Based on these notions the criterion of optimality is proofed. A method of support problems is designed. The method based on principle of subsequent eliminating sets where constraints are violating consists of two procedures : 1) procedure of forming, solving and analysing the sequence of linear programming problems with small number of constraints, 2) finishing procedure. The method of support problems solves problem (ASIP) with a finite number of computations and allows to determine the optimal solution with any preassigned accuracy.

Numerical examples from the theory of optimal observation of dynamic systems with nonconvex a priory distribution of initial states are presented.

References

1. Rafail Gabasov, Faina M. Kirillova. New algorithms of solving extremal problems, in: A. Bensoussan, J.L. Lions, eds., Analysis and optimization of systems. Proceedings of the 9th International Conference (Antibes, June 12-15, 1990), Lecture Notes in Control and Information Sciences 144, pp. 570-579.

2. Vladimir G. Medvedev. Linear semi-infinite programming problems: theory, algorithms and numerical examples. Abstracts of International Soviet-Polish Seminar on Mathematical methods of Optimal Control and its applications (Minsk, May 16-19, 1989), pp. 190-191.

MULTICRITERIAL OPTIMAL CONTROL OF DYNAMIC MULTICONNECTED SYSTEM

B.V.Pelzwerger, Yu.B.Shtessel

Department of Applied Mathematics and Informatics,

Chelyabinsk State Technical University, Lenin ave.

76, Chelyabinsk, 454080, USSR.

Abstract

Linear dynamic system consisted of interconnected subsystems is considered. The quality of behavior of each subsystem is characterized by quadratic integral criterion. The problem of multicriterial optimal control synthesis in such systems is formulated and solved in the paper. The solution is obtained on the base of principle of proportional damages, which ensures the following properties

- the control law is obtained in linear form as in monocriterion optimization problem;

- the solution is invariant to the sort of metrics which characterized the distance between vector - criteria's current value and it's ideal one;

- optimal values of criteria of quality have relative losses to be inversely proportional to the coefficient of mutual importance comparative to their ideal values.

The numerical example was considered:

The keywords. Multicriterial control, dynamic system, optimality, Riccati equation, the principle of proportional damages.

A NEW METHOD FOR SOLVING GENERAL D.C. PROGRAMS AND APPLICATION TO SYSTEM OF QUADRATIC EQUATIONS

Thai Quynh Phong

LMC-IMAG, University J.Fourier (France)

We consider the following global optimization problem

$$(DCP) \qquad \min f_o(x) \text{ s.t. } x \in \Omega, g_j(x) \leq 0 \ (j = 1, \ldots, m)$$

where Ω is a closed convex set in R^n and all functions f_o, g_i are d.c. Here, d.c. stand for "difference of two convex functions". For detail discussion on d.c. functions and d.c. programming, we refer to the excellent monograph "Global Optimization" by R.Horst and H.Tuy.

The aim of this paper is to develop a new method for solving (DCP) which exploits the structure of the problem. The idea is borrowed from the Relief Indicator Method by Thach and Tuy for more general problem :

$$(P) \qquad \min f(x) \text{s.t. } x \in S$$

where f is a continous function and S is a compact set. Namely, using the concept of separator, one can construct a d.c. function $\phi(\alpha, x)$ depending on α such that (P) will be reduced to the parametric unconstrained d.c. minimization problem :

$$\text{find } \tilde{\alpha} \ \text{ such that } \min\{\phi(\tilde{\alpha}, x) : x \in R^n\} = 0$$

The function $\phi(\alpha, x)$ is called a relief indicator for f on S. We will see, in the sequel, that for (DCP) such a function can be constructed in more natural way, without using any separator.

By the properties of d.c. functions, we can rewrite (DCP) to the form

$$(Q) \qquad \min f(x) - g(x) \text{ s.t. } p(x) - q(x) \leq 0$$

where f, g, p, q are finite convex functions. For each $\alpha \in (-\infty, +\infty]$ we define

$$F(\alpha, x) = \max\{f(x) - g(x) - \alpha, p(x) - q(x)\}$$

which is a d.c. function of the form $h(\alpha, x) - k(x)$, where h, k are convex. Under the regularity condition

$$inf\{f(x) - g(x) : p(x) - q(x) < 0\} = inf\{f(x) - g(x) : p(x) - q(x) \leq 0\}$$

we can prove the fundamental theorem that states:

$$\alpha^* = \min(Q) \Leftrightarrow \min\{F(\alpha^*, x) : x \in R^n\} = 0$$

and any point x^* satisfying

$$0 = F(\alpha^*, x^*) = \min\{F(\alpha^*, x) : x \in R^n\}$$

is a global optimal solution of (Q). This allows us to reduce (Q) to the unconstrained d.c. minimization problem

$$\min\{h(\alpha^*, x) - k(x) : x \in R^n\}$$

By using an additional variable t, we can write it as an equivalent concave minimization problem $\min\{t - k(x) : h(\alpha^*, x) \leq t\}$ for which we can develop an outer approximation procedure. The difficulty is that the convex constraint

$$\tilde{D} = \{(x, t) : h(\alpha^*, x) \leq t\}$$

is not known explicitly. Therefore, at iteration k, the best value α_k so far obtained is used as an upper estimation of α^*. The algorithm will converge in the sense that $\alpha_k \to \alpha^*$ and any accumulation point of $\{\bar{x}_k\}$ such that $f(\bar{x}_k) - g(\bar{x}_k) = \alpha_k$ solves (Q).

As an application, we consider a system of quadratic equations

$$x^T A_j x = 0 \ (j = 1, \ldots, N), \ \|x\| = 1, x \in R^n$$

where A_j, $j = 1, \ldots, N$ are symmetric matrices of $n \times n$. It was shown that the well-known calibration problem in Computer Vision can be formulated as a solution of this system with $n = 4$. An approximate solution in terms of least squares will be provided by solving a global optimization problem

$$(R) \qquad \min\{\sum_{j=1}^{N}(x^T A_j x)^2 \ s.t. \ x \in R^n, \|x\| = 1\}$$

that is shown to be a problem of type (Q), but not regular. To apply the developed method, a regularization procedure is proposed which replaces (R) by a series of ϵ-perturbed problems, for which the regularity condition is verified.

PARALLEL DIRECT SEARCH METHODS APPLIED TO SEISMIC INVERSE PROBLEMS

VIRGINIA TORCZON
DEPARTMENT OF MATHEMATICAL SCIENCES
RICE UNIVERSITY
HOUSTON, TX 77251-1892, U.S.A.

The ultimate goal of this work is to improve the data processing techniques used to prospect for petroleum. The improvements will come from extracting detailed estimates of local parameter fluctuations in a model of the earth which may indicate lithological features associated with oil and gas deposits. Our hope is to further the evaluation of the widely-believed economic potential for finding and producing petroleum through more precise use of seismic data. A key component of this research lies in robust estimation of wave velocity models directly from waveform data. Interesting instances of this problem can be formulated via differential semblance optimization as a low (e.g., two- to four-) dimensional minimization problem [2], [3]. The catch is that while the number of control variables is small, the number of state variables is quite large. Thus an implementation of the objective function on a Stardent Titan, running at 20 Mflops, currently takes up to eight hours to return a function value. Noise in the data means that more than two digits in the value of the objective function is irrelevant. An analytic expression for the gradient is not yet available and a finite-difference approximation to the gradient appears fraught with numerical difficulties.

We have two reasons to believe that the parallel direct search schemes developed by Dennis and Torczon [1] provide a reasonable first approach towards solving these inverse problems in multidimensional wave propagation. First, the features of these problems, as outlined above, suggest that direct search methods may well be the optimization algorithms of choice for problems of this sort, as outlined below. Second, the magnitude of the computation involved suggests that any help that can be gained from parallel computation should be exploited. Perhaps the greatest advantage of the parallel direct search schemes is that they can immediately take full advantage of a large number of very fast processors—even for problems with a small number of control variables.

Direct search methods are methods designed to solve unconstrained minimization problems of the form:

$$\min_{\mathbf{x}\in\mathbb{R}^n} f(\mathbf{x}),$$

where $f : \mathbb{R}^n \rightarrow \mathbb{R}$. These methods are distinguished by the fact that they neither use nor require explicit derivative information; the search for a local minimizer is driven solely by function information.

The reasons for the popularity of direct search methods are several. First, in scientific settings it is often the case that there is no practical way to evaluate derivatives. Often function values are the result of either an experiment or a simulation so that there is no analytic expression for either the function or the gradient. For control problems, an alternative adjoint approach to derivative approximation might require weeks to derive. Furthermore, it is often the case that the function values are subject to a great deal of noise. Thus, finite-difference approximations to the gradient may cause gradient based methods to fail. As further consideration, if the function values only support a few significant digits in the solution, fast *local* convergence may be neither a reasonable nor useful requirement. Thus, any method with good *global* convergence properties might well be appropriate. The seismic inverse problems we are considering share most of these features, hence our belief that direct search methods may well be the best methods to bring to bear on these problems.

The multidirectional search algorithm, a direct search method developed by Dennis and Torczon [4], has two further advantages. First, it is supported by a strong global convergence theorem [5] that requires only that the function be continuously differentiable over a compact level set to guarantee convergence to the set of stationary points. Second, the basic algorithm can be used to form the core step in a family of *scalable* parallel direct search methods [1]. Our experience has shown that the algorithmic performance of these methods often improves dramatically as the number of processors increases [1]. Given the availability of the Intel Touchstone Delta machine, a distributed memory multiprocessor machine with a large number of very fast processors, our hope is that it may well be possible to find an approximate solution to the inverse problems in multidimensional wave propagation using the parallel direct search methods.

Both the algorithmic and computational details involved in solving these seismic inverse problems using the parallel direct search methods will be discussed in further detail.

REFERENCES

[1] J. E. Dennis, Jr. and V. Torczon, *Direct search methods on parallel machines*, SIAM Journal on Optimization, 1 (1991).

[2] W. W. Symes, *Velocity inversion: A case study in infinite-dimensional optimization*, Mathematical Programming, 48 (1990), pp. 71–102.

[3] W. W. Symes and J. J. Carazzone, *Velocity inversion by coherency optimization*, in Proceedings of the SIAM Workshop on Geophysical Inversion, J. B. Bednar, ed., 1991.

[4] V. Torczon, *Multi-Directional Search: A Direct Search Algorithm for Parallel Machines*, PhD thesis, Rice University, Houston, Texas, 1989. Available as Tech. Rep. 90–7, Department of Mathematical Sciences, Rice University, Houston, Texas 77251–1892.

[5] ——, *On the convergence of the multidirectional search algorithm*, SIAM Journal on Optimization, 1 (1991), pp. 123–145.

EXPLOITING MONOTONICITY IN CERTAIN GLOBAL OPTIMIZATION PROBLEMS

Hoang Tuy
Institute of Mathematics
P.O. Box 631, BoHo, Hanoi, Vietnam

1. A function $f:R^n \to R$ is said to be monotonic on a convex set $\Omega \subset R^n$ with respect to a cone $K \subset R^n$ if for any $u \in K$ (i.e. $u \geq 0$ in the ordering $\geq$ defined by K) we have $f(x+u) \geq f(x)$ $\forall x \in \Omega$. Functions with this monotonicity property occur in many global optimization problems arising from applications (in engineering design for instance). In a recent paper [4] we have developed a general approach for exploiting monotonicity in problems of the form

(P) minimize $f(x)$ subject to $x \in D$

where D is a polytope in R^n while $f(x)$ is a quasi-concave function, monotonic on a convex set $\Omega \supset D$, with respect to a polyhedral cone $K = \{u : Cu \geq 0\}$. It turns our that, due to monotonicity, the problem (P) can be decomposed into a connected sequence of much easier problems of dimension $k = \text{rank } C$, where usually $k << n$.

2. Of particular interest is the case when the matrix C has exactly two rows c^1, c^2, which are linearly independent, so that the monotonicity condition reads:

$$c^i u \geq 0 \ (i=1,2) \to f(x+u) \geq f(x) \quad \forall x \in \Omega \ . \qquad (1)$$

Examples of quasiconcave functions monotonic is this sense include: $f(x) = (c^1x+d_1)^{\alpha_1} (c^2x+d_2)^{\alpha_2}$ where $\alpha_1, \alpha_2 > 0$ and $c^ix+d_i > 0$ $(i=1,2)$ $\forall x \in \Omega$; $f(x) = f_1(c^1x+d_1) + f_2(c^2x+d_2)$ where $f_1(t)$, $f_2(t)$ are concave increasing functions of t ; etc... (see [4,5]).

When $f(x)$ is monotonic in the sense (1), problem (P) can be solved via the parametric linear program

$$(R_\alpha) \ \min \langle c^1+\alpha(c^2-c_1),x\rangle \quad \text{s.t. } x \in D \quad (0 \leq \alpha \leq 1).$$

More specifically, the following algorithm was proposed by Tuy and Tam [5].

<u>Algorithm 1</u>. Solve the parametric linear program (R_α) to obtain the breakpoints

$$\alpha_0 = 0 < \alpha_1 < \dots < \alpha_N = 1$$

along with the vectors x^j, $j=1,\dots,N$, such that x^j is a basic optimal solution of (R_α) for all $\alpha \in [\alpha_{j-1}, \alpha_j]$. Then an optimal solution of (P) is

$$x^{j^*} \text{ , with } j^* \in \arg\min \{f(x^j) : j=1,\dots,N\}$$

Computational experience has demonstrated the surprising efficiency of this algorithm which is similar to the parametric algorithm of Konno-Kuno [2] for the special case $f(x)=(c^1x+d_1)(c^2x+d_2)$ (however, in Konno-Kuno's algorithm the objective function of (R_α) is $\langle \alpha c^1 + \alpha^{-1}c^2, x\rangle$, $0<\alpha<+\infty$). Usually, solving (P) by this algorithm is only a bit more difficult than solving a linear program. As applied to the special concave mincost network flow problem with a single source, unbounded capacity and a single arc with nonlinear cost, this method yields an even <u>strongly polynomial</u> algorithm [3].

3. The condition on the quasiconcavity of f(x) can be replaced by the following weaker one:

(*) For any line segment $\Delta \subset D$ the minimum of f(x) over Δ can easily be determined

(this condition is fulfilled by any quadratic function). Under this weaker assumption, one can consider, instead of (R_α), the parametric linear program

$$(S_\alpha) \quad \min c^1x \quad \text{s.t. } x \in D \text{ , } c^2x = \alpha \text{ ,}$$

where $\alpha \in (-\infty, +\infty)$.

<u>Algorithm 2</u>. Solve the parametric linear program (S_α) to obtain the breakpoints

$$-\infty < \alpha_0 < \dots < \alpha < +\infty$$

along with the vectors u^j, v^j, $j=1,\dots,N$, such that $u^j+\alpha v^j$ is a basic optimal solution of (S_α) for all $\alpha \in [\alpha_{j-1}, \alpha_j]$. For each $j=1,\dots,N$ compute

$$x^j \in \operatorname{argmin} \{f(x) : x = u^j+\alpha v^j, \ \alpha_{j-1} \leq \alpha \leq \alpha_j\}$$

(see (*)). Then an optimal solution of (P) is

x^{j^*}, with $j^* \in \operatorname{argmin} \{f(x^j) : j=1,\ldots,N\}$.

When applied to the above mentioned special concave mincost network flow problem this algorithm provides an improvement of Guisewite-Pardalas' algorithm [1] (which has been shown to be polynomial). The improvement, which makes the algorithm strongly polynomial, consists in ordering the sinks simply by their increasing demands rather than by using a quantity U(t) the computation of which needs a time of O(log R), where R is the total demand of all sinks [1].

4. A more general and more difficult problem than (P) which is sometimes ecountered in the applications is the following

(Q) minimize $f(x) + g(x)$ s.t. $x \in D$,

where g(x) is a convex function, while f and D are as previously (note that f(x) is in general neither convex nor concave). Define

$$F(t) = \min \{f(x) : x \in D ,\ g(x) \leqslant t\}$$

and let $p_0 \leqslant g(x) \leqslant q_0 \ \forall x \in D$. Then (Q) is obviously equivalent to the univariate problem

$(\tilde{Q})$ minimize $t + F(t)$ s.t. $p_0 \leqslant t \leqslant q_0$.

For solving this problem a method which suggests itself is by branch and bound, where branching proceeds by bisection and bounding is based on the fact that for any segment $\Delta = [p,q]$ we have

$$\mu(\Delta) := p + F(q) \leqslant \min \{t + F(t) : t \in \Delta\}$$

(note that F(t) is nonincreasing). When g(x) is affine the value F(q) is computed by solving a problem of type (P) (by either of the previous algorithms). In the general case, the convex function g(x) can be approximated by an affine under-estimator : if $\bar{F}(q)$ is the resulting approximate value of F(q) then obviously $\bar{F}(q) \leqslant F(q)$, so that $\bar{\mu}(\Delta) := p + \bar{F}(q)$ can serve as a lower bound for $\min \{t + F(t) : t \in \Delta\}$. By suitably refining the affine underestimator of g(x) after each iteration, one can arrange for this branch and bound procedure to converge to a global optimal solution of $(\tilde{Q})$. For example, if $[p^k, q^k]$ is the interval to be subdivided at iteration k and x^k is the point such that $\bar{F}(q^k) = f(x^k)$ (solution of the bounding subproblem for this interval), it suffices to take $g(x^k) + \langle r^k, x-x^k \rangle$ as affine underestimator of $g(x)$ (r^k is a subgradient of $g(x)$ at point x^k).

REFERENCES

1. G.M. Guisewite and P.M. Pardalas, "A polynomial time solvable concave network flow problem", Preprint, Department of Computer Science, Pennsylvania State University, 1990.

2. H. Konno and T. Kuno, "Linear multiplicative programming", IHSS Report 89-13, Institute of Human and Social Sciences, Tokyo Institute of Technology (1989).

3. B. Klinz and H. Tuy, "A special concave network flow problem efficiently solvable by parametric method", preprint, Institute of Mathematics, Hanoi, 1991.

4. H. Tuy, "The complementary convex structure in global optimization", Proceedings, Conference on "Recent Advances in Global Optimization", Princeton, May 1991.

5. H. Tuy and B.T. Tam, "An efficient solution method for rank two quasiconcave minimization problems", Optimization, to appear (1991).

ESTIMATING THE COMPLEXITY OF PATH-FOLLOWING METHODS FOR LINEAR PROGRAMMING BY CURVATURE INTEGRALS

Gongyun Zhao
Institut für Angewandte Mathematik und Statistik
Universität Würzburg. Am Hubland
D-8700 Würzburg
Germany

In this work we study the complexity of certain *interior point methods*, which rapidly developed since Karmarkar published his work 1984, for solving a linear program and its dual

$$\begin{array}{llll} \min\limits_{x} c^T x & & \max\limits_{y,s} b^T y & \\ \quad Ax = b & (LP), & \quad A^T y + s = c & (LD) \\ \quad x \geq 0 & & \quad s \geq 0. & \end{array}$$

Here A is an $m \times n$-matrix, c is an n-vector and b is an m-vector. Let $z := (x, s, y)$.

An interior point algorithm starts from an interior feasible point $z_0 = (x_0, s_0, y_0)$, generating a series of points $\{z_k\}$ in the interior of the feasible region of (LP) and (LD) and parameters $r_0 > r_1 > \ldots$ in order to reduce the duality gap $r := x^T s/n$ from a given $r_0 := R_0 = x_0^T s_0/n$ to a smaller value R_1, that is, to $r_N \leq R_1$ for some N. The complexity considered here is measured by the number of steps (iterations) $r_k \to r_{k+1}$ needed by the algorithm to reduce the parameter r from R_0 to R_1, and the overhead at every iteration. In this work we focus our attention on the number of iterations N.

Upper bounds of the number of iterations N are usually estimated through the following steps:

i) For every iteration, one finds a lower bound of the relative step length $\epsilon_k \leq (r_k - r_{k+1})/r_k$, so that

$$\prod_{k=0}^{N-1} (1 - \epsilon_k) R_0 \geq r_N. \tag{1}$$

ii) In order to estimate N with $r_N \leq R_1$, one has to replace ϵ_k by their minimum $\hat{\epsilon} := \min_k \{\epsilon_k\}$. So from (1) follows

$$N \leq \ln \frac{R_1}{R_0} / \ln(1 - \hat{\epsilon}) \approx \frac{1}{\hat{\epsilon}} \ln \frac{R_0}{R_1}. \tag{2}$$

So far, the best estimate of $\hat{\epsilon}$ is $O(1/\sqrt{n})$, hence the best upper bound of N is $O(\sqrt{n} \ln(R_0/R_1))$.

In this work we only analyse a type of interior point algorithms, called *path-following algorithm*, but the results obtained here can certainly be used to other algorithms. We define a *ξ-trajectory* $z(r,\xi)$, especially the *central trajectory* with $\xi = e := (1,\ldots,1)^T$, for a fixed positive vector $\xi > 0$ with $e^T\xi = n$ and a real parameter $r \geq 0$, by relaxing the complementary slackness $x \circ s = 0$,

$$x \circ s = r\xi, \quad Ax = b, \quad A^Ty + s = c, \quad x \geq 0, s \geq 0. \qquad (LPD)_{r,\xi}$$

Here the operator "$\circ$" is defined by $x \circ s = (x_1s_1, \ldots, x_ns_n)^T$. It is known that for any fixed $\xi > 0$, the ξ-trajectory $z(r,\xi)$ tends to an optimal solution z^* of (LP) and (LD) as $t \to 0$. For any interior feasible point $z = (x,s,y)$, we can inversely define $r := x^Ts/n$ and $\xi := x \circ s/r$ with $e^T\xi = n$. A distance of z from the central trajectory is defined by $d(z) := \|\xi - e\|_2$.

Now we briefly describe our path-following algorithm which was proposed by G. Sonnevend [2]. Suppose z_k is the current point with $d(z_k) \leq T_0$, T_0 is a given constant. We go along the tangent $\bar{z}(r) := z_k + (r - r_k)\dot{z}(r_k)$, $r < r_k$ of the ξ_k-trajectory through the point z_k at r_k, till we reach a point $\bar{z}(r_{k+1})$ with $d(\bar{z}(r_{k+1})) = T_1(> T_0)$. Then follows a limited number of Newton iterations to find a new point z_{k+1}, such that $d(z_{k+1}) \leq T_0$ again, and keeping r_{k+1} unchanged.

It can be shown that the relative step length $\epsilon := (r_k - r_{k+1})/r_k$ of this algorithm is inversely proportional to a weighted curvature $\kappa(r_k,\xi_k)$ of the ξ_k-trajectory at r_k. Further we know that κ varies between 0 and $O(\sqrt{n})$, hence ϵ varies between 1 and $O(1/\sqrt{n})$. This implies that upper bounds for the number of iterations N may be much smaller than $O(\sqrt{n}\ln(R_0/R_1))$ (or $O(\sqrt{n}L)$ which is so far the best upper bound). But how can we achieve a smaller upper bound?

A promising way to improve the estimate is to connect the number of iterations N to the curvature integral $\int_{R_1}^{R_0} \kappa(r,e)dr$. Because: 1. the integral devided by $(R_0 - R_1)$ is the average bend of the central trajectory from R_0 to R_1, and it can be expected of a smaller value than $O(\sqrt{n})$; 2. the continuous integrand promises to use results of the Riemannian Geometry and other techniques dealing with continuous functions, cf. [1] and [2].

The following estimate, which is essentially due to G. Sonnevend,

$$N \approx \int_{R_1}^{R_0} \kappa(r,e)dr \qquad (3)$$

was stated without proof in [2]. Here we give a short description of a proof of the relation (3), (see [3] for details).

The proof consists of two parts: The first part shows the Lipschitz continuity of $\kappa(r,\xi)$ along a fixed ξ-trajectory, i.e.:

$$|\kappa(u,\xi) - \kappa(r,\xi)| \leq \kappa(r,\xi)\frac{r-u}{r-r'} \qquad \forall u \in [r',r]. \qquad (4)$$

Its difficulty lies in the particular Lipschitz constant $\kappa(r,\xi)/(r-r')$. From (4) follows immediately

$$\frac{T_1}{2} \leq \int_{r'}^{r} \kappa(u,\xi)du \leq \frac{3T_1}{2}, \qquad (4)$$

for any $0 < r' < r$ with

$$\kappa(r,\xi)(r - r') = T_1.$$

The second part estimates the difference of $\kappa(r,\xi)$ on different ξ-trajectories, i.e. $|\kappa(r,\xi)-\kappa(r,\xi')|$. This estimation is necessary since iterates generated by the algorithm lie on different ξ-trajectories and their contributions to the integral should be gathered up to the central trajectory, or any specified one.

References

[1] N. Karmarkar, Riemannian geometry underlying interior point methods, Mathematical Developments Arising from Linear Programming (J.C. Lagarias and M.J. Todd. Eds.), Contemporary Mathematics, Vol. 114, Amer. Math. Soc. 1990, pp. 51–76.

[2] G. Sonnevend, J. Stoer and G. Zhao, On the complexity of following the central path of linear programs by linear extrapolation II, presented at the International Symposium: Interior Point Methods for Linear Programming (the Netherlands, 1990), to appear in: Math. Progr. series B (eds. C. Roos and J.-P. Vial).

[3] G. Zhao and J. Stoer, Estimating the complexity of path-following methods for solving linear programs by curvature integrals, report No. 225, Schwerpunktprogram Anwendungsbezogene Optimierung und Steuerung. Inst. für Ang. Math. und Statistik, Universität Würzburg (1990), to appear in Appl. Math. & Optimization.

THE GROUP THEORETIC APPROACH AND DECOMPOSITION FOR INTEGER LINEAR PROGRAMMING

Igor L. Averbakh

By applying the group theoretic methods to integer linear programming (ILP) problems it is necessary to solve group minimization problems. The order of the finite abelian group arising is defined by the magnitude of the determinant of the LP–relaxation optimal basis and so may be enormously large. That is the major drawback of the group theoretic approach.

A possible way of overcoming this difficulty is using a decomposition, i.e. solving the group problem of large order by means of solving a number of subgroup subproblems of less order. Of course, it is unlikely to construct a decomposition algorithm efficient in general case. But quite often there are many zero coefficients in the group problem constraints and the coefficient matrix can be rearranged to a block–angular form (several efficient algorithms of such rearranging are known).

In our work methods for decomposing integer programs with a block structure and group constraints are developed. For block group minimization problems an algorithm of the iterative type is presented. Each iteration consists of: 1) solving several local group subproblems of small order; 2) obtaining for each subproblem several suboptimal irreducible solutions and prime cycles; 3) solving the master linking group problem which constructs the best possible solution from the suboptimal solutions and prime cycles of subproblems. Decomposition parameters (coefficients of local objective functions for subproblems) are chosen previously by two–level layering strategies technique. The method may be used for obtaining both optimal and ϵ–optimal solutions. Modifications of the algorithm for other types of block structures are presented. The efficiency of the method is confirmed by computational experiments.

A decomposition method for solving problems of a more general type–block integer programming problems with group coupling constraints is also presented. The type of block (local) constraints is inessential. Such problems may be used for obtaining bounds in implicit enumeration schemes, if the original ILP problem has a block-angular structure. A technique of construction an auxiliary problem of this type for strengthening the Langrangean relaxation bound for block-angular ILP problems is presented.

The cone of nondecreasing set functions

Martin Bellstedt and Heinz Dathe
Friedrich Schiller University Jena
Department of Applied Mathematics

January 22, 1992

1 Introduction

A real valued set function, defined on a finite set $E = \{1, ..., n\}$, is said to be nondecreasing if $r(I) \leq r(J)$, $\forall I \subseteq J \subseteq E$. Let 2^E be the set of all subsets of E and $n_0 = 2^{|E|}$. Every real valued function can be represented by a vector $x = (x_J)_{J \in 2^E}$, with $x_J = r(J)$. On the other hand, every $x \in R^{n_0}$ generates a real valued function $r : 2^E \rightarrow R$. Depending on the concrete situation we use the notation

$$F_m(E) = \{r : 2^E \rightarrow R \; ; \quad I \subseteq J \rightarrow r(I) \leq r(J) \; ; \quad \forall I \subseteq J \subseteq E\}$$

or

$$R_m^{n_0} = \{x \in R^{n_0} : x_I \leq x_J \; , \; \forall I \subseteq J \subseteq E\}$$

It is easy to see that $F_{m,0}(E) = \{r \in F_m(E) : r(\emptyset) = 0\}$ is a convex cone. In [2] we find a more general definition of a cone. If $c \in R$ then $F_{m,c}(E) = \{r \in F_m(E) : r(\emptyset) = c\}$ is a cone with the vertex $r(J) = c$, $\forall J \subseteq E$. Further we investigate the cone $F_{m,0}(E)$, because $F_{m,c}(E)$ differs from $F_{m,0}(E)$ only by a translation. We show that $F_{m,0}(E)$ is generated by all nondecreasing Boolean set functions.

2 Extreme rays of the cone of nondecreasing set functions

With

$$Q = \{[I, J] : I \subseteq J; I, J \in 2^E\}$$

we have

$$R_{m,0}^{n_0} = \{x \in R^{n_0} : x_I - x_J \leq 0, [I, J] \in Q, x_\emptyset = 0\} .$$

$R_{m,0}^{n_0}$ is the intersection of a finite number of halfspaces and from the theorem of Farkas-Minkowski-Weyl [3] it follows that the cone is finitely generated. Thus, we have to determine the functions and the number of functions for the given set E. We note that the subset $K \subset Q$ with $K = \{[I,J] \in Q : |I| = |J| - 1\}$ produces the nonredundant system of inequalities to describe the cone $R^{no}_{m,0}$. Hence we write the cone $R^{no}_{m,0}$ in the form:

$$R^{no}_{m,0} = \{x \in R^{no} : Ax \leq \theta\} \qquad \text{with} \quad A = \begin{pmatrix} a_{1\emptyset} & \cdots & a_{1E} \\ \vdots & \ddots & \vdots \\ a_{|K|\emptyset} & \cdots & a_{|K|E} \end{pmatrix},$$

$$a_{jI} = \begin{cases} 1 & \text{if } I = A; \\ -1 & \text{if } I = B; \\ 0 & \text{otherwise;} \end{cases}$$

and $[A, B]$ is the element of K which produces the j^{-th} row.

A matrix A is called unimodular if the value of all nonzero minors are $+1$ or -1.

Lemma 2.1.

The matrix A of the cone $R^n_{m,0} = \{x \in R^n : Ax \leq \Theta\}$ is unimodular.

Note that the matrix $\binom{A}{E}$ with the identity matrix E is also unimodular. The intersection of the cone $R^{no}_{m,0}$ and the unit cube of dimension n_0 is the polyhedron

$$P^{no}_{m,0} = \{x \in R^{no} : Ax \leq \theta; Ex \leq 1\} = \left\{x \in R^{no} : \begin{pmatrix} A \\ E \end{pmatrix} x \leq \begin{pmatrix} \theta \\ 1 \end{pmatrix}\right\}.$$

The next theorem on extremal points of polyhedrons can be found in [4].

Theorem 2.2.

Let A be a unimodular matrix and b an integer valued vector. Then the convex set $P = \{x \in R^n : Ax \leq b\}$ has only integer extremal points.

Since $P^{no}_{m,0}$ has a unimodular matrix A and a $(0,1)$ – vector b, we obtain that $P^{no}_{m,0}$ has only $(0,1)$ – extremal points. From this the next theorem follows.

Theorem 2.3.

The cone of nondecreasing set functions with $r(\emptyset) = 0$ can be generated by all nondecreasing Boolean set functions.

We have an interesting relationship between nondecreasing Boolean set functions and independence systems. A set system over E is a pair (E, F) with $F \subseteq 2^E$. The set system is called independent ([1]) if it satisfies:

$$(U1) \quad \emptyset \in F$$
$$(U2) \quad I \subseteq J \in F \quad \Rightarrow \quad I \in F$$

Each set $I \in F$ is said to be an independent set. For a given independence system $U = (E, F)$ we define a characteristic vector $x^F \in R^{n_0}$ in the following way:

$$x_J^F = \begin{cases} 1 & , J \in F \\ 0 & , \text{otherwise} \end{cases}$$

Let $\bar{x}^F \in R^{n_0}$ be a vector with $\bar{x}_J^F = 1 - x_J^F$, $J \in 2^E$. The following lemma is easy to prove.

Lemma 2.4.

A Boolean set function r is nondecreasing if and only if there exists an independence system $U = (E, F)$ with $r(J) = \bar{x}_J^F$, $\forall J \in 2^E$.

Remarks: An independence system is given by the set Γ of all maximal independent sets, $\Gamma = \{B \in F : \forall X \in F : B \not\subset X\}$. $B \in \Gamma$ is called a base of (E, F). All possible bases of independence systems over E are given by the set

$$S = \{I \subset 2^E : \forall K_1, K_2 \in I : K_1 \not\subset K_2\}.$$

$|S| - 1$ is the number of extremal rays wich generate the cone of nondecreasing set functions. For example:

$\|E\|$	1	2	3	4
$\|S\| - 1$	1	4	18	166

References

[1] Korte,B.: Kombinatorische Optimierung und algorithmische Prinzipien, Report No. 84355-OR, Bonn 1984

[2] Nocizka,F.: L.Grygarova, K.Lommatzsch, Geometrie konvexer Mengen und konvexe Algebra, Akademie-Verlag, Berlin 1988

[3] Schrijver,A.: Theory of linear and integer programming, John Wiley & Sons, New York 1986

[4] Vogel,W.: Lineares Optimieren, AVG Geest & Portig K.-G., Leipzig 1976

THEORETICAL AND EMPIRICAL RELATIONS BETWEEN THE DUALITY-GAP OF THE COMBINATORIAL P-MEDIAN PROBLEM AND THE SIMPLE PLANT LOCATION PROBLEM

Konrad Boenchendorf
Institut für Unternehmensforschung
Hochschule St. Gallen
Bodanstr. 6, CH-9000 St. Gallen

We consider the combinatorial version of the p-Median-Problem

$$(P1):\quad \min \sum_{ij} c_{ij}\, x_{ij}$$

$$\text{s. t.}\quad (1)\quad \sum_{i} x_{ij} = 1 \qquad \text{(for all j)}$$

$$(2)\quad 0 \leq x_{ij} \leq y_i \quad \in \{0,1\} \qquad \text{(for all ij)}$$

$$(3)\quad \sum_{i} y_i \leq p,$$

where the c_{ij} are the costs for supplying the total demand of customer j by supplier i, x_{ij} is the proportion of customer j's demand supplied by supplier i (w. l. o. g. $x_{ij} \in \{0,1\}$), y_i is 1 or 0 depending on whether the potential supplier i is used or not and where the total number of suppliers in use may not exceed a prespecified number p.

The nowadays most common approach to get lower bounds for this problem is to determine heuristically a feasible solution of the LP-Dual by a "dual ascent"-method.
In this paper we are mainly interested in the dual variable or Lagrangean multiplier M associated with (3). Therefore we consider the "intermediate" relaxation

$$(P2):\quad \max_{M}\ \min_{ij} \sum_{ij} x_{ij} = 1 + M\,(p - \sum_{i} y_i)$$

$$\text{s. t.}\quad (1)\quad (2),$$

which is a simple plant location problem with parametric fixed costs M. (Erlenkotter /2/ and earlier Bilde and Krarup /1/ have presented successful methods to determine the multipliers associated with (1) and (2).)

The optimal multiplier M for (P2) with respect to a given maximal number of suppliers p_0 is the slope resp. lies between the slopes of a function z(p) at p_0, where for any nonnegative **real** p

$$z(p) = \min \sum_{ij} c_{ij} x_{ij}$$

s. t. (3) holds and the x_{ij}, y_i are taken from the convex hull Q of the points satisfying (1) and (2).

In fact (P2) is equivalent to determining z(p) for integer p. Obviously z(p) is piecewise linear, convex and decreasing, moreover geometrical considerations show that z(p) can change its slope only at some integer values of p. It is the latter observation that makes z(p) more valuable than the corresponding function for the LP-Relaxation of (P1), because the statement about the slopes can be formulated as:

Proposition: Either

$$(4) \qquad \min_{R>p_0} \frac{v(p_0) - v(R)}{R - p_0} \leq M \leq \min_{r<p_0} \frac{v(r) - v(p_0)}{p_0 - r}$$

or

$$(5) \qquad M = \min_{r < p_0 < R} \frac{v(r) - v(R)}{R - r} ,$$

where v(p) is the optimal value of (P1).

If the slope of z(p) is changing at p_0, formula (4) is valid, otherwise formula (5). For practical purposes one can replace v(r) by the value of heuristical primal solutions; if the inequalities (4) are contradictious, (5) is used. As to our computational experience with data taken from the road-network of Switzerland this value of M is so good that in most cases it cannot be improved by local search, although it cannot be proved that M is also the best multiplier for the LP-Dual of (P1).

Moreover it is clear that the inequalities (4) are infeasible iff $z(p) < v(p)$, i.e. iff there is a duality-gap between (P1) and (P2).

This characterisation shows that a large duality-gap between (P1) and (P2) at p_0 can only occur if there are $r < p_0 < R$ so that it makes almost no difference whether r or p_0 suppliers are used but it makes a great difference whether p_0 or R suppliers are used. This observation supports the experience that a gap scarcely occurs for practical problems (we do have a few examples with small gaps).

As (P2) is a simple plant location problem we know from the experience of many researchers that in practice there is only a small duality-gap between (P2) and its LP-Dual, which is also the LP-Dual of (P1).

This together with our results concerning (P1) and (P2) shows that we can find lower bounds for the p-Median-Problem that are of the same quality as those for the simple plant location problem, a fact that was not so clear from former articles /3/.

REFERENCES

/1/ O. BILDE and J. KRARUP, "Sharp Lower Bounds and Efficient Algorithms for the Simple Plant Location Problem", Ann. Discrete Math. 1, 79-97 (1977).

/2/ D. ERLENKOTTER, "A Dual-Based Procedure for Uncapacitated Facility Location", Opns. Res. 26, 992-1009 (1978).

/3/ R.D. GALVAO, "A Dual-Bounded Algorithms for the p-Median Problem", Opns. Res. 28, 1112-1121 (1980).

"Monge"-property and efficient algorithms

Peter Brucker
Fachbereich Mathematik/Informatik
Universität Osnabrück
Postfach 44 69
D-4500 Osnabrück

In recent years there has been a growing interest in discrete optimization problems satisfying the "Monge"-property or related properties. In this survey some of the recent results on this topic will be presented.

1 Monge-property and related properties

Let $C = (c_{ij})$ be a real-valued mxn-matrix. Then C has

(i) **product property** if $c_{ij} - c_{ik} = f(i)h(k,j)$ for all i and all $k < j$ where $f(i)$ is a monicreasing function and $h(k,j) \geq 0$,

(ii) **generalized product property** if for all i,j we have $c_{ij} = a_i + b_j + c'_{ij}$ where $C' = (c'_{ij})$ has product property,

(iii) **Monge-property** if $c_{ik} - c_{jl} \leq c_{il} + c_{jk}$ for all $i < f, k < l$.

For each row $i = 1, \ldots, m$ of C let $j(i)$ be the leftmost column index containing the minimum value of row i.
Then C is

(iv) **monotone** if $j(i) \leq j(k)$ for all $i < k$,

(v) **totally monotone** if all its 2x2-minors are monotone.

The following theorem describes the relations between the five properties introduced.

Theorem 1: Between properties (i) to (v) the implications $(i) \Rightarrow (ii) \Rightarrow (iii) \Rightarrow (iv) \Rightarrow (v)$ hold. No two of these properties are equivalent.

For all properties defined so far we have (in an order-theoretic sense) corresponding dual properties. These dual properties are called convex while the properties defined in this section are called concave properties.

In the next section we will present examples of discrete optimizaton problems which satisfy one of the properties defined in this section. Due to these properties these problems can be solved very efficiently. The corresponding algorithms will be explained later.

2 Examples

2.1 All farthest neighbours (Aggarwal et al. [AKMSW87])

Consider a convex polygon P with n vertices. Then the matrix which contains all distances d_{ij} between the vertices of P as entries and which has additional negative entries as shown below for the case $n = 4$ is convex totally monotone.

$$\begin{pmatrix} 0 & d_{12} & d_{13} & d_{14} & -1 & -2 & -3 \\ -1 & 0 & d_{23} & d_{24} & d_{25} & -1 & -2 \\ -2 & -1 & 0 & d_{34} & d_{35} & d_{36} & -1 \\ -3 & -2 & -1 & 0 & d_{45} & d_{46} & d_{47} \end{pmatrix}$$

To find all farthest neigbours we have to calculate the row maxima of this matrix. This can be done in $0(n)$ steps as will be shown in the next section.

2.2 A text formatting problem (Hirschberg & Larmore [HL87])

In connection with text formatting we have the problem of breaking a paragraph optimally into lines. The text of a paragraph may be considered as a sequence $s : s_1, s_2, \ldots, s_n$ of syllables. Each line corresponds with a subsequence $s_i, s_{i+1}, \ldots, s_{j-1}$, and there is a penalty c_{ij} associated with this subsequence. The problem is to partition s into subsequences such that the total penalty of all subsequences is minimized. A typical penalty is $c_{ij} = (l_{ij} - w)^2$ where l_{ij} is the "natural length" of $s_i, s_{i+1}, \ldots, s_{j-1}$, and w is the width of the paragraph being formatted. The matrix $C = (c_{ij})$ defined by these penalties satisfies the Monge-property.

The text formatting problem is a special case of the following problem.

2.3 A path partitoning problem (Brucker [B91])

Given a path $1 \to 2 \to \cdots \to n-1 \to n$ and nonnegative weights c_{ij} associated with subpaths $i \to i+1 \to \cdots j-1$ $(1 \leq i < j \leq n)$. Find an integer $p(1 \leq p \leq n)$ and indices $1 = i_0 < i_1 < \cdots < i_p = n$ such that $\sum_{\nu=0}^{p-1} c_{i_\nu c_{i_{\nu+1}}}$ is minimized.

The following two examples also lead to special path partitioning problems.

2.4 A one machine batching problem (Alberts & Brucker [AB91])

Assume that n jobs $i = 1, \ldots, n$ with processing times p_i are to be processed on one machine in a given sequence (say $1, 2, \ldots, n$). Furthermore this job sequence must be split into batches. A batch is given by a subsequence $i, i+1, \ldots, j-1$. For each batch we have a set-up time s. The finish-time f_i of a job i in a batch is the finish-time of the last job in the batch. The problem we consider is to find a partitioning of the sequence $1, 2, \ldots, n$ into batches such that the weighted flow-time $\sum \alpha_i f_i$ is minimized.

The problem is a path partitioning problems with

$$c_{ij} + (\sum_{\nu=i}^{n} \alpha_\nu)(s + \sum_{\nu=1}^{j-1} p_\nu))$$

where c_{ij} is the "cost" induced by batch $i, i+1, \ldots, j-1$.

An easy calculation shows that for $i < j < k$ we have

$$c_{ik} - c_{ij} = f(i)h(j,k) \text{ with } f(i) = \sum_{\nu=i}^{n} \alpha_\nu \text{ and } h(j,k) = \sum_{\nu=j}^{k-1} p_\nu$$

Thus (c_{ij}) satisfies the product property.

2.5 The economic lot-size problem (Aggarwal & Park [AP91])

Let d_i be the demand for a product during period $i (i = 1, \ldots, n)$. This product may be produced in each period. $c_i(x)$ is the cost of producing x units of this product during period i. Furthermore let $h_i(y)$ the cost of storing y units of inverntory from period $i-1$ to period i. How many units of the product should be produced in each period such that

- the demand is satisfied in each period
- the sum of production and inventory cost is minimized?

Under the assumptions that for all i.

$$c_i(x) = \begin{cases} 0 & \text{if } x = 0 \\ c_i^0 + c_i^1 x & \text{if } x > 0 \end{cases}$$

$$h_i(y) = h_i y$$

$$c_i^1 \leq c_{i-1}^1 + h_i^1, \qquad d_i > 0 \tag{1}$$

the problem may be formulated as path partitioning problem with $c_{ij} = a_i + b_j + c'_{ij}$ where

$$\begin{aligned} a_i &= c_i^0 - c_i^1 d_{1i} + \sum_{\nu=1}^{i} h_\nu d_{1\nu}, \quad b_j = \sum_{\nu=1}^{j-1} h_\nu d_{\nu_j} \\ c'_{ij} &= (c_i^1 - \sum_{\nu=1}^{i} h_\nu) d_{1j}, \quad d_{ij} = d_i + \ldots + d_{j-1}. \end{aligned}$$

Due to property (1) the matrix $C' = (c'_{ij})$ has the product property. Thus $C = (c_{ij})$ has the generalized product property.

3 An efficient algorithm for finding all row (column) maxima (minima) of a matrix

All row maxima (minima) of a convex (concave) totally monotone mxn-matrix can be calculated in $0(m+n)$-time using a recursive algorithm due to Aggarwal et al. [AKMSW87].

In the literature this algoritm is known as SMAWK-algorithm. Using this algorithm all farthest neighbours of vertices in a convex polygon with n vertices can be calculated in $0(n)$-time.

Next we will show that the path partitioning problem may be reduced to an on-line version of finding all column minima of a quare matrix.

First notice that the path partitioning problem reduces to the problem of finding a shortest path from 1 to n in a netwoek $N = (V, E, c)$ with vertex set $V = \{1, \dots, n\}$ and $(i, j) \in E$ iff $i < j$. This problem can be solved by dynamic programming if we define $F(j)$ to be the length of a shortest path from 1 to j and solve the recursion

$$\begin{aligned} F(1) &:= 0 \\ F(j) &:= \min_{i<j}\{F(i) + c_{ij}\} \quad j = 2, \dots, n. \end{aligned}$$

Solving this recursion is equivalent to calculating the column minima of the matrix $F = (F_{ij})$ with

$$F_{ij} := \begin{cases} F(i) + c_{ij} & \text{if } i < j \\ \infty & \text{else.} \end{cases}$$

This is an on-line version of the column minima problem because the entries of column j depend on the column minima of columns $i = 1, \dots, j-1$. Let the transpose of F be totally monotone. Then it is not possible to solve this on-line problem by the SMAWK-algorithm. However two types of $0(n)$-algorithms have been developed to solve this problem:

- an on-line version of the SMAWK-algorithm (Larmore & Schieber [LS91])
- algorithms which use the SMAWK-algorithm as subroutine (Galil & Park [GP90], Klawe [K89]).

If (c_{ij}) is concave Monge then the transpose of F is concave totally monotone. Thus the path partitioning problem can be solved in $0(n)$-time.

All algorithms which solve the on-line column minima problem are sophisticated recursive procedures and not easy to implement. However, if the matrix $C = (c_{ij})$ has the generalized product property a very simple nonrecursive algorithm can be applied to solve the corresponding path partitioning problem (Brucker [B91]). Similar concepts have been used by Park [P91] to solve special n-city traveling salesman problems in $0(n)$-time.

4 Other results

Not all results in connection with Monge-arrays could be covered by this survey. Among the topics not covered are

- multidimensional Monge-arrays
  (Aggarwal & Park [AP88], Bein et al. [BBP90])
- recognition of Monge-arrays
  (Alon et al. [ACHS89], Cechlárová & Szabó [CS90])

- problems with botteneck objectives
  (Burkhard & van der Veen [BV90], Brucker [B91])

- Monge-arrays and parallel algorithms
  (Aggarwal & Park [AP89])

References

[AKMSW87] A.Aggarwal, M.M. Klawe, S. Moran, P. Shor, and R. Wilber. Geometric applications of a matrix-searching algorithm. Algorithmica 2, 195-208, 1987.

[AP88] A. Aggarwal and J.K. Park. Notes on searching in multidimensional monotone arrays. In Proceedings of the 29th Annual IEEE Symposium on Foundations of Computer Science, 497-512, 1988.

[AP89] A. Aggarwal and J.K. Park. Sequential searching in multidimensional monotone arrays. Research Report R.C.15128, IBM T.J. Watson Research Center, November 1989.

[AP91] A. Aggarwal and J.K. Park. Inproved algorithms for economic lot-size problems. Operations Research, 1991. To appear.

[AB91] S. Albers and P. Brucker. The complexity of one-machine batching problems. To appear in Discrete Applied Mathematics. 1991.

[ACHS89] N. Alon, S. Cosares, D.S. Hochbaum and R. Shamir. An algorithm for the detection and construction of Monge sequences. Linear Algebra and Its Applications, 114/115, 669-680, 1989.

[BBP90] W.W. Bein, P. Brucker, and P.K. Parthak. Monge properties in higher dimensions. Technical Report CS 90-11, University of New Mexico, October 1990.

[B91] P. Brucker. Efficient algorithms for some path partitioning problems. Osnabrücker Schriften zur Mathematik, Reihe P, Heft 142, 1991

[BV90] R.E. Burkard and J.A.A. van der Veen. Universal conditions for algebraic traveling salesman problems to be efficiently solvable. Report Nr. 163, Institut für Mathematik, Technische Universität Graz, 1990.

[CS90] K Cechlárová and P Szabó. On the Monge property of matrices. Discrete Mathematics, 81, 123-128, 1990.

[GP90] Z. Galil and K. Park. A linear-time algorithm for concave one-dimensional dynamic programming. Information Processing Letters, 33, 309-311, 1990.

[HL87] D.S. Hirschberg and L.L. Larmore. The least weight subsequence problem. SIAM Journal on Computing, 16, 628-638, 1987.

[K89] M.M. Klawe. A simple linear time algorithm for concave one-dimensional dynamic programming. Technical Report 89-16, University of British Columbia, 1989.

[LS91] L.L. Larmore and B. Schieber. On-line dynamic programming with applications to the prediction of RNA secondary structure. Journal of Algorithms, 1991. To appear.

[P91] J.K. Park. The Monge array: an abstraction and its applications. PhD Thesis, Department of Electrical Engineering and Computer Science, Massachusetts Institute of Technology, June 1991.

UNIVERSAL CONDITIONS FOR ALGEBRAIC TRAVELING SALESMAN PROBLEMS TO BE EFFICIENTLY SOLVABLE

R.E. Burkard
Mathematisches Institut
Technische Universität Graz
Kopernikusgasse 24
A-8010 Graz
Austria

J.A.A. van der Veen
Dept. Quantitative Methods
Nijenrode University
Straatweg 25
3621 BG Breukelen
The Netherlands

In recent years special cases of the Traveling Salesman Problem (TSP) solvable by polynomially bounded algorithms found considerable interest. Usually one considers TSPs with a sum as objective function, i.e. the cost of a tour is defined as a sum of all costs of single arcs of the tour. Another possibility is the Bottleneck TSP where the maximum cost of a single arc of the tour is minimized. A closer look shows that the special cases of TSPs fall into several classes. On one hand there are problems for which the sum problem but not the bottleneck problem is known to be efficiently solvable, e.g. if the nonsymmetric Demidenko conditions are fulfilled. On the other hand there are other special cases where the Bottleneck TSP can be solved efficiently, but not the corresponding sum case, e.g. if the cost matrix is a symmetric circulant or if it is graded. Finally, there are conditions which imply by their algebraic and combinatorial structure that both the sum and the bottleneck problem are solvable. In this paper it will be shown that these conditions are universal in the sense they guarantee to find efficiently an optimal solution in much more general cases, namely for the so-called algebraic TSP where the length of a tour is an algebraic composition of the cost coefficients that are elements of a commutative, totally ordered semigroup.

The Algebraic Traveling Salesman (ATSP) can be described more formally as follows. Let $(H,\ast,\leq)$ be a commutative, totally ordered semigroup. This is a set with an associative and commutative algebraic composition $\ast$ and an order relation $\leq$ such that the algebraic composition and the order relation are compatible (all a,b,c in H with $a \le b$ satisfy $a \blacklozenge c \le b \blacklozenge c$). The cost coefficient c[i,j] for traveling from i to j is an element of the semigroup $(H,\blacklozenge,\le)$. The cost of a tour $(1,i_2,i_3,\ldots,i_{n-1},i_n)$ is given by

$$c[1,i_2] \blacklozenge c[i_2,i_3] \blacklozenge \ldots \blacklozenge c[i_{n-1},i_n] \blacklozenge c[i_n,1].$$

The ATSP asks for a tour that minimizes this cost. This formulation generalizes the Sum TSP (H is the set of reals, and $\blacklozenge$ is the addition) and the Bottleneck TSP (H again the set of reals and $a \blacklozenge b := \mathrm{MAX}\{a,b\}$).

In the paper we will study conditions on distance matrices $C = (c_{ij})$ such that under these conditions there exists an optimal tour that is pyramidal. A Hamiltonian tour is pyramidal iff it is of the form

$$(1,i_1,i_2,\ldots,i_k,n,j_1,j_2,\ldots,j_{n-k-2})$$

with $i_1 < i_2 < \ldots < i_k$ and $j_1 > j_2 > \ldots > j_{n-k-2}$. First it is shown that a shortest pyramidal tour can be found in $O(n^2)$ time. The ATSP restricted to a class of distance matrices is called pyramidally solvable if with respect to every matrix in this class there is an optimal tour that is pyramidal. For instance it is shown that the ATSP restricted to symmetric Demidenko matrices (i.e. matrices such that $c_{ij} = c_{ji}$ for all i and j, and $c_{ij} \blacklozenge c_{kl} \le c_{ik} \blacklozenge c_{jl}$ for all $i < j < k < l$) is pyramidally solvable. Some other classes of matrices for which the ATSP is also pyramidally solvable are given.

Furthermore, we will treat algebraic TSPs fulfilling further axioms, like a divisor rule and weak cancellation rule. In this setting TSPs with Brownian ($c[i,j] = a[i]$ if $i < j$ and $c[i,j] = b[j]$ if $i > j$) are shown to be solvable in O(nlogn) time. Also, it is shown that TSPs with left-upper-triangular cost matrices ($c[i,j] = 0$ for all i,j such that $i + j \ge n+1$) can be solved efficiently.

ON THE MULTI-DEPOT VEHICLE ROUTING PROBLEM

J. Orestes CERDEIRA
Inst. Superior de Agronomia
Tapada da Ajuda, 1399 Lisboa – Codex, Portugal

1 – Introduction

The multi-depot vehicle routing problem deals with situations in which vehicles based at several depots are required to visit customers so as to fulfill known customers' requirements. Each vehicle leaves the depot where it is based, eventually returning to that same depot after visiting certain customers. It is asked to design a route for each vehicle so that each customer will be entirely supplied by a single vehicle, and the total cost of the distribution will be minimum.

We consider the multi-depot vehicle routing problem with vehicles of unbounded capacity, in short MDVRP. Using covers of the nodes by trees and matchings, we present a way of determining lower bounds on the cost of the optimal solutions. We also describe a class of algorithms for this problem, which includes polynomial time algorithms, and we show that if the triangle inequality holds, the costs of the resulting solutions are not greater than twice the optimal costs. Computational experience is reported.

2 – Formulation

Each instance of the MDVRP is described by an undirected weighted graph $G = (V, E, c)$, a subset K ($|K| = k$) of the node set V ($|V| = n$), and a function $nveic : K \to \mathbf{Z}^+$. Each node of G represents either a customer or a depot. K denotes the set of nodes representing depots. E is the edge set, and associated with each edge e we have the cost c_e of traveling directly between the two locations (customers or depots) represented by the extreme nodes of e. We assume there are no edges having both extreme nodes in K. If v is a node of K, $nveic_v$ is the number of vehicles based at the depot represented by v.

The MDVRP consists in determining $\sum_{v \in K} nveic_v$ cycles in graph G such that

i) each node v is included in exactly one cycle, if $v \in V - K$, and in exactly $nveic_v$ cycles, if $v \in K$,

ii) no two nodes from K appear in the same cycle, and

iii) the sum of the costs of all edges in these cycles is minimum.

Let T_k be the set of the $0-1$ incidence vectors of the covers of the nodes of G by k node-disjoint trees (i.e. the sets of $n-k$ edges which leave no node isolated, and free of cycles), such that no two nodes of K are included in the same tree. Let also M_k be the set of the $0-1$ incidence vectors of the sets of $\sum_{v \in K} nveic_v$ edges which cover all the nodes in K. Denoting by E_v the set of edges of G incident in node v, the MDVRP can be formulated as follows:

$$\min_{x \in T_k, y \in M_k} \sum_{e \in E} c_e (x_e + y_e) \tag{1}$$

subject to:

$$\sum_{e \in E_v} x_e = nveic_v \qquad \forall v \in K \tag{2}$$

$$\sum_{e \in E_v} y_e = nveic_v \qquad \forall v \in K \tag{3}$$

$$\sum_{e \in E_v} y_e \leq 1 \qquad \forall v \in V - K \tag{4}$$

$$\sum_{e \in E_v} (x_e + y_e) = 2 \qquad \forall v \in V - K \tag{5}$$

the set of edges defined by $x + y$ includes exactly $\sum_{v \in K} nveic_v$ cycles. (6)

3 – Lower Bounds

For each node $v \in V - K$, let $\lambda_v \in \mathbf{R}$ be the Lagrange multiplier associated with the corresponding constraint (5), and let $\lambda_v = 0$, $\forall v \in K$. If $e = [v_e, u_e]$ is an edge of G, let $\overline{c}_e = c_e - \lambda_{v_e} - \lambda_{u_e}$, and $\theta : \mathbf{R}^n \to \mathbf{R}$ be the function defined by

$$\theta(\lambda) = \min_{x \in T_k, y \in M_k} \sum_{e \in E} \overline{c}_e (x_e + y_e) + 2 \sum_{v \in V - K} \lambda_v \tag{7}$$

subject to: (2)–(4).

Given that (7), (2)–(4) is a relaxation of the MDVRP, for each feasible vector $\lambda \in \mathbf{R}^n$, $\theta(\lambda)$ is a lower bound on the value of (1) subject to (2)–(6). Moreover, determining $\theta(\lambda)$ can be achieved by solving the two following problems:

$$\min_{x \in T_k} \sum_{e \in E} \overline{c}_e x_e \tag{8}$$

subject to: (2), and

$$\min_{y \in M_k} \sum_{e \in E} \overline{c}_e y_e \tag{9}$$

subject to: (3), (4).

To solve problem (8), (2) there is an $O(n^2 + (\sum_{v \in K} nveic_v)^2 n)$ time algorithm [**1**,**2**]. Problem (9), (3), (4) can be solved as a matching problem in a bipartite graph in $O((\sum_{v \in K} nveic_v)^2 n)$ time.

Therefore we have an $O(n^2 + (\sum_{v \in K} nveic_v)^2 n)$ time algorithm to obtain the lower bound given by (7), (2)–(4) on the cost of the optimal solution of the MDVRP.

4 – Upper Bounds

Let x^* be the solution that

$$\min_{x \in T_k} \sum_{e \in E} c_e x_e \quad \text{subject to: (2)} ,$$

which, as we said before, can be obtained in $O(n^2 + (\sum_{v \in K} nveic_v)^2 n)$ time. From x^* we assign customers to vehicles. Let $E(x^*)$ be the set of edges defined by x^*, and $\widehat{E}(x^*)$ the set of all edges of $E(x^*)$ except those incident in the nodes of K. The customers represented by nodes v, u will be supplied by the same vehicle based at the depot represented by r iff v, u, r are all included in the same connected component of the graph $(V, E(x^*))$, and v, u appear in the same component of $(V, \widehat{E}(x^*))$. Let S_{v_i} be the set of nodes representing customers which will be supplied by the i-th vehicle based at depot represented by v. If we use an algorithm to solve the traveling salesman problem in the subgraph of G induced by $S_{v_i} \cup \{v\}$, for $i = 1, ..., nveic_v$ and for all $v \in K$, we obtain a feasible solution of the MDVRP. Suppose now the cost vector c satisfies the triangle inequality, i.e., $c_{[v,u]} + c_{[u,r]} \geq c_{[v,r]}$, $\forall\, v, u, r \in V$. There are several polynomial time algorithms for the traveling salesman problem which determine tours whose costs are not greater than twice the costs of the minimum spanning trees (see for example [6, 5]). With any choice of such an algorithm, the solutions of the MDVRP will be determined in polynomial time. Moreover, the costs of those solutions will be not greater than twice the optimal costs.

5 – Computational Results

In the computational tests we carried out, we use graphs with 50, 60, 70, 80, 90 and 100 nodes. In each of the six cases, ten different cost vectors satisfying the triangle inequality were considered. Each of these matrices results from applying Floyd's algorithm [3], for finding the shortest paths between all pairs of nodes, to a symmetric matrix with integer entries randomly selected in the range $[0, 100]$. For each graph we let the number of depots k be equal to $\lfloor \frac{n}{20} \rfloor$ and $\lfloor \frac{n}{15} \rfloor$. In each case we consider the three problems emerging by letting the number of vehicles, NV, be equal to $\lfloor \frac{n}{10} \rfloor$, $\lfloor \frac{n}{5} \rfloor$ and $\lfloor \frac{n}{3} \rfloor$. The assignment of vehicles to depots (i.e. the vector $(nveic_v)_{v \in K}$) was determined by generating a random partition of the number of vehicles with as many components as the number of depots k. The lower bounds LB were obtained according to the method described in section 3, at the end of n iterations of the subgradient method [4]. The upper bounds UB are the costs of the solutions determined by the algorithm of section 4, where the algorithm used to solve the traveling salesman problem works as follows. First a tour is obtained by the so-called minimum spanning tree algorithm [6, 5]. Next, the 3-optimal method appearing in [7, pg. 377–379] is used to improve that tour.

The main results are shown in figure 1. For the ten problems having the same node set, the same number of depots and the same number of vehicles, the average of the ratios $\frac{UB}{LB}$ is displayed in the 4-th and 9-th columns of the table. In the 5-th and 10-th columns we report the greatest value of these ratios among the ten problems.

n	k	NV	aver$\left(\frac{UB}{LB}\right)$	worst$\left(\frac{UB}{LB}\right)$	n	k	NV	aver$\left(\frac{UB}{LB}\right)$	worst$\left(\frac{UB}{LB}\right)$
50	2	5	1.102	1.170	80	4	8	1.123	1.188
		10	1.094	1.150			16	1.127	1.191
		16	1.078	1.127			26	1.078	1.132
	3	5	1.087	1.144		5	8	1.123	1.175
		10	1.099	1.125			16	1.107	1.160
		16	1.074	1.123			26	1.084	1.143
60	3	6	1.089	1.146	90	4	9	1.157	1.250
		12	1.087	1.146			18	1.147	1.240
		20	1.073	1.142			30	1.098	1.137
	4	6	1.094	1.164		6	9	1.164	1.252
		12	1.105	1.220			18	1.139	1.299
		20	1.079	1.141			30	1.119	1.207
70	3	7	1.098	1.174	100	5	10	1.151	1.284
		14	1.089	1.138			20	1.135	1.232
		23	1.057	1.087			33	1.081	1.147
	4	7	1.092	1.112		6	10	1.140	1.259
		14	1.091	1.135			20	1.120	1.226
		23	1.052	1.080			33	1.105	1.160

Fig.1

References

[1] S.M. BAAS and J.O. CERDEIRA, "Covering Nodes by k Node-Disjoint Trees with Additional Constraints", Memorandum nº 693, Faculteit der Toegepaste Wiskunde, Universiteit Twente, 1988.

[2] J.O. CERDEIRA, "Cobertura dos Vértices de um Grafo por k Árvores e Ciclos Disjuntos nos Vértices", Tese de Doutoramento, Faculdade de Ciências da Universidade de Lisboa, 1990.

[3] R.W. FLOYD, "Algorithm 97: Shortest Path", *Communications of the ACM*, 5, 1962, 345.

[4] M. HELD, P. WOLFE and H.P. CROWDER, "Validation of Subgradient Optimization, *Mathematical Programming*, 6, 1974, 62–88.

[5] D.S. JOHNSON and C.H. PAPADIMITRIOU, "Performance Guarantees for Heuristics", in *The Traveling Salesman Problem: A Guide Tour of Combinatorial Optimization*, Eds.: E.L. Lawler, J.K. Lenstra, A.H.G. Rinnooy Kan, D.B. Shmoys, John Wiley & Sons, New York, 1985, 145–180.

[6] C.H. PAPADIMITRIOU and K. STIEGLITZ, *Combinatorial Optimization: Algorithms and Complexity*, Prentice-Hall, New York, 1982.

[7] M.M. SYSLO, N. DEO and J.S. KOWALIK, *Discrete Optimization Algorithms with Pascal Programs*, Prentice-Hall, Englewood Cliffs, New York, 1983.

COMBINATORIAL MINIMIZATION WITH MULTIPLICATIVE OBJECTIVE FUNCTIONS

Do Duy Chinh, Nguyen Duc Nghia and Pham Canh Duong
Hanoi, Vietnam

1. INTRODUCTION.

This report concerns with the discrete minimization of the product of two convex positive functions with separable variables. The product of two convex separable functions might not be convex. Such a function may have multiple local minimizers. In [1] and, recently, in [2] the continuous case of this problems has been investigated. For its solution the authors proposed efficient algorithms, based on the use of linear parametric programming technique. Using the same approach in [3] a polynomial algorithm has been developed for the problem of finding a minimum product spanning tree on a two-weighted graph.

In this report we propose an efficient algorithm for finding the global minimum of the product of two convex positive separable functions over a general supermatroid.

2. MINIMIZING THE PRODUCT OF TWO SEPARABLE CONVEX FUNCTIONS OVER A GENERAL SUPERMATROID.

Let's consider the following discrete optimization problem :

$$\min \{ f(x).g(x) : x \in D \} \quad , \qquad (1)$$

where $f(x)$, $g(x)$ are positive and finite over an finite discrete set D.

To solve the problem (1), let's consider the next parametric problem P(t) :

$$\varphi(t) = \min \{ f(x) + t\, g(x) : x \in D \}, \qquad (2)$$

where t is a nonnegative real parameter.

It is known that the function $\varphi(t)$ is nondecreasing, continuous, concave and piecewise linear on $[0, +\infty)$ with finite number N of breaking points

$$0 < t_1 < t_2 < \dots < t_N < +\infty .$$

The following theorem shows the relationship between problem (1) and P(t).

Theorem 1. *Let x^i be an optimal solution of the problem (2) for every $t \in [t_{i-1}, t_i]$, $i = 1,\dots,N+1$ ($t_0 = 0$; $t_{N+1} = +\infty$). Then the optimal solution x^* of the problem (1) can be determined as :*

$$x^* = \arg\min \{ f(x^i).g(x^i) : i = 1,\dots,N+1 \}.$$

This theorem shows that the technique of the parametric combinatorial programming may be used to solve a combinatorial minimization problem with multiplicative objective functions. In further, we consider a special case of the problem (1) when D is a general supermatroid and f(x), g(x) are separable convex functions.

Now, we determine the set of feasible directions from a point x of D

$$fes(x,D) = \{ s : x + s \in D,\ s \in \{ e_i , - e_j , e_i - e_j \} \quad i, j = 1,\dots,n ,\ i \neq j \}.$$

Denote

$$\nabla^s f(x) = f(x+s) - f(x) ;$$

$$\nabla^s g(x) = g(x+s) - g(x) ;$$

$$F(x,t) = f(x) + tg(x);$$

$$fes_-(x,D) = \{ s : s \in fes(x,D) ,\ \nabla^s g(x) < 0 \} ;$$

$$fes_+(x,D) = \{ s : s \in fes(x,D) ,\ \nabla^s g(x) > 0 \} ;$$

$$t(s,x) = - \nabla^s f(x) / \nabla^s g(x);$$

Let D be a general supermatroid, f(x), g(x) be convex eparable functions. Then the point x^t will be an optimal solution to problem P(t) if and only if the following optimality criterion satisfies [5]

$$\nabla^s F(x,t) \geq 0 , \text{ for every } s \in fes (x^t,D)$$

For an optimal solution x^t of problem P(t), let denote

$$t_+(x^t) = t(s^+,x^t) = \min \{ t(s, x^t): t(s, x^t) \geq t,\ s \in fes_-(x^t,D) \};$$

$$t_-(x^t) = t(s^-,x^t) = \max \{ t(s,x^t): t(s,x^t) \leq t,\ s \in fes_+(x^t,D) \}.$$

We assume that $\max \{ \emptyset \} = 0$ and $\min \{ \emptyset \} = + \infty$.

Theorem 2 [4] *Let D be a general supermatroid, f(x) and g(x) be separable convex functions. Then*

a) x^t is an optimal solution of $P(t)$ for every $t \in [t_-(x^t), t_+(x^t)]$;

b) If $t_-(x^t) > 0$ then $x^t = x^t + s^-$ will be an optimal solution of $P(t_-(x^t))$;

c) If $t_+(x^t) < +\infty$ then $x^t = x^t + s^+$ will be an optimal solution of $P(t_+(x^t))$;

Corollary 1. *The points $t_+(x^t)$, $t_-(x^t)$ given by theorem 2 are breaking points of the function $\varphi(t)$.*

Combining theorem 1,2 we obtain the following algorithm for solving the considered problem.

ALGORITHM 1.

Initialization. Solve $P(0)$. Denote by x^1 the obtained optimal solution. Set $k = 1$, $t_0 = 0$, $x^* = x^1$.

k-iteration.

1. If $\nabla^s g(x^k) \geq 0$, $s \in fes(x^k, D)$, the solution x^* is an optimal solution of the problem (1), Stop; else calculate $t_+(x^k) = t(s^+, x^k) = \min\{ t(s, x^k): t(s,x^k) \geq t_{k-1}, s \in fes^-(x^k, D)\}$, and set $t_k = t_+(x^k)$, $x^{k+1} = x^k + s^+$.

2. If $t_k < +\infty$, and $t_k = t_{k-1}$ then set $x^* = \operatorname{argmin}\{ f(x^*). g(x^*), f(x^{k+1}). g(x^{k+1}) \}$, go to $(k+1)$-iteration.

From the theorem 1 it is not difficult to prove the following theorem.

Theorem 3. *The solution x^* given by the above described algorithm is an optimal solution of the problem (1).*

The computational results show that the average computational time for solving the parametric problem often is not greater than that one required for the problem $P(0)$. Moreover, the ratio between them is decreasing with the increase of the number of its variables. We note also that the number of breaking points of the problem under consideration approximately equals twice the number of its variables.

Now applying theorem 1 and 2 to a case when D is a general supermatroid and $f(x)$, $g(x)$ are linear functions implies

Corollary 2. *The problem of minimizing a product of two positive linear functions over a general supermatroid can be solved by solving less (n+1)(n+2)/2 the problems of minimizing a linear function over the same general supermatroid.*

Corollary 3 [3]. *The minimum product spanning tree problem can be solved by an algorithm of running time* $O(|E|^3 \log\log|V|)$.

REFERENCES

1. Gabasov R., Kirillova F.M. Methods of linear programming. Part III. Izd. BGU, Minsk, 1980. (in russ.).

2. Konno H., Kuno T. Linear multiplicative programming. IHHS Report 89-13, Institute of Human and Social Sciences, Tokyo Institute of Technology, September 1989.

3. Do Duy Chinh Some extremal problems on a polymatroid. Proc. of Conf. on Mathematical basic of Informatics. Hanoi, 1987, p. 18-23. (in vietnamese).

4. Do Duy Chinh The parametric methods for discrete convex optimization and its applications. ph. D. Thesis, Minsk, 1989. (in russ.).

5. Kovaliov M.M. Matroids in discrete optimization. Univer. Publisher. Minsk, 1987. (in russ.).

CONTRIBUTIONS TO TWO GRAPH-THEORETICAL CONJECTURES

Dieter GERNERT
Technische Universität München (Fak. WS)
Arcisstr. 21, D-8000 München 2

1. INTRODUCTION AND NOTATION

The following report outlines some partial results related to well-known graph-theoretical conjectures. These results were found with substantial use of the software system KBGRAPH, which is designed to support graph-theoretical proofs. Nevertheless this paper can be understood without any knowledge about that tool.

Very shortly, the knowledge-based system KBGRAPH is based upon a file of about 1400 theorems from graph theory. When attacking an undecided conjecture, known properties of a class of graphs - the class of possible counterexamples or a subclass thereof - are taken as the input, and the system will supply further properties of the considered class, particularly more severe inclusions for a lot of graph invariants. (For details see GERNERT (1989); for the original idea and two printed lists of relations between graph invariants see BRIGHAM and DUTTON (1991), with further references.)

Only undirected simple graphs (without loops and multiple edges) are considered. The following graph invariants will occur:

p = number of vertices
δ = minimal degree
Δ = maximal degree
χ = chromatic number
χ_1 = edge-chromatic number
σ = domination number
r = radius

d = diameter
g = girth
c = circumference
κ = vertex-connectivity number
γ = genus
c_3 = number of triangles.

2. THOMASSEN'S CONJECTURE

THOMASSEN (1986) made the following conjecture: Every 4-connected line-graph is hamiltonian.

This conjecture is important because it is equivalent to some other ones (see e.g. FLEISCHNER and JACKSON 1989). It is a practical strategy to consider not only the line-graphs addressed in the conjecture, but also the underlying root-graphs. As a consequence, let be G a graph such that its line-graph L(G) is a minimal counterexample: L(G) is 4-connected, but not hamiltonian.

These properties lead to the following conditions for G:

1. $p \geq c + \kappa + 1$
2. $2 \leq \kappa \leq 3$
3. $2 \leq \delta \leq 3$
4. $\kappa = \delta$
5. $3 \leq \Delta \leq p - 3$
6. $12 \leq c \leq p - 3$
7. $d \geq 4$
8. $\sigma \geq \delta + 2$
9. G has a claw (induced subgraph $K_{1,3}$).
10. G has no dominating cycle.
11. G is cyclically edge-4-connected (MARTIN 1976).
12. G has at least one edge not belonging to a triangle or a quadrilateral.

Next, conditions for L(G) can be derived:

1. $p(L(G)) \geqslant 24$
2. $4 \leqslant \kappa(L(G)) \leqslant 6$
3. $c(L(G)) \geqslant 19$
4. $c_3(L(G)) \geqslant 20$
5. $L(G)$ is not planar.
6. If $L(G)$ is regular, then $\delta = 3$ and $p(L(G)) \geqslant 30$.

Each of these statements can be reformulated in the sense of a partial proof: THOMASSEN's Conjecture is true e.g. for planar graphs, as well as for graph with less than 24 vertices etc., and for regular graphs with less than 30 vertices.

3. CYCLE DOUBLE COVER CONJECTURE

This conjecture, CDC for short, states: Every bridgeless graph has a cycle double cover, i.e. a cycle cover such that every edge belongs to exactly two cycles. For a survey see JAEGER (1985) where also connections to other conjectures are discussed and references concerning the origin are given.

A minimal counterexample to CDC must have the properties:

1. $\kappa = \delta = \Delta = 3$
2. G has no hamiltonian path.
3. $g \geqslant 8$ (GODDYN 1985, p. 25)
4. $\chi_1 = \Delta + 1 = 4$

Particularly the two latest conditions are very severe since it is even unknown whether snarks with $g \geqslant 7$ do exist at all (WATKINS and WILSON 1991).

An evaluation with KBGRAPH leads to new necessary conditions including:

1. $p \geqslant 32$
2. $\chi = 3$
3. $3 \leqslant \gamma \leqslant p/2$
4. $r \geqslant 4$

5. $c \geqslant 3g - 8$

6. G contains at least one odd cycle.

7. $\chi_1(L(G)) = \Delta(L(G)) + 1 = 5$

4. CONCLUDING REMARK

All readers are kindly invited to send open graph-theoretical problems together with partial results for a text with KBGRAPH, and also new relations between graph invariants which are likely to fit into the knowledge base.

REFERENCES

BRIGHAM, R.C., DUTTON, R.D., A compilation of relations between graph invariants - Supplement I. Networks 21 (1991) 421-455.

FLEISCHNER, H., JACKSON, B., A note concerning some conjectures on cyclically 4-edge connected 3-regular graphs. Annals Discr. Math. 41 (1989) 171-178.

GERNERT, D., A knowledge-based system for graph theory. Methods Oper. Res. 63 (1989) 457-464.

GODDYN, L., A girth requirement for the Double Cycle Cover Conjecture. Annals Discr. Math. 27 (1985) 13-26.

JAEGER, F., A survey of the Cycle Double Cover Conjecture. Annals Discr. Math. 27 (1985) 1-12.

MARTIN, P., Cycles hamiltoniens dans les graphes 4-réguliers. Aequationes Math. 14 (1976) 37-40.

THOMASSEN, C., Reflections on graph theory. J. Graph Theory 10 (1986) 309-324.

WATKINS, J.J., WILSON, R.J., A survey of snarks. In: Graph theory, combinatorics, and applications (Proc. Western Michigan Univ. 1988), ed. by Y. ALAVI et al., Wiley, New York 1991, vol. 2, p. 1129-1144.

Heuristics for several routing problems

Klaus Jansen
Department of Mathematics, University of Trier
Postbox 38 25, W-5500 Trier.

Abstract: This paper presents heuristics which are based on a tour splitting of a general routing tour for solving the general capacitated routing problem (GCRP). This problem is a generalization of the vehicle routing problem (VRP) and the capacitated arc routing problem (CARP).

1 Introduction

A difficult combinatorial optimization problem is to find an optimal route for a single vehicle on a given network. A network is given as a connected multi graph G consisting of a set V of nodes, a set E of edges and given positive weights (or costs, distances) $c : E \rightarrow \mathbb{R}^+$ on the edges. The general problem is to find a minimum tour containing specified nodes $V' \subset V$ and specified edges $E' \subset E$.

Most of the well known problems are defined on networks without allowing parallel edges. The problem of visiting all nodes in such a given network with minimum cost is the classical traveling salesman problem (TSP). The general TSP is usually defined as the problem of finding a tour of minimum total cost which visit each node exactly once. Here the TSP allows multiple visits and is a special case of the general TSP in which the costs satisfy the triangle inequality.

A modification of these problems is given by a capacity limit $q \in \mathbb{N}$ for the vehicles and by a demand $d(v), d(e) \in \mathbb{N}_0$ for each node v and edge e. Given a specified node $v_0 \in V$, the depot, the problem is to find a set of tours which passes through the depot where each node v with demand $d(v) > 0$ and each edge with demand $d(e) > 0$ is served at least once and where the total served-demand for each tour does not exceed the capacity q. In the general case it is not allowed to split the demand over different vehicles. Therefore we assume that $d(e), d(v) \leq q$. The objective is to minimize the total tour cost. We call this problem the general capacitated routing problem (GCRP).

The well-known capacitated problems can be classified as node routing and arc routing problems. The vehicle routing problem (VRP) corresponds to the TSP with given demands $d(v)$ for the nodes. An arc oriented problem is the capacitated arc routing problem (CARP) with demands $d(e) \geq 0$ for each edge.

2 Equal demand

In this section we look at the simpler case in which all demands $d(e), d(v)$ are zero or one. We define $V' = \{v \in V | d(v) > 0\}$ and $E' = \{e \in E | d(e) > 0\}$. The value of an optimum solution will be denoted with $R^*(V', E')$ and the value generated by a heuristic H with $R^H(V', E')$.

The first heuristic is called the first optimal tour partitioning (FOTP). It starts with the optimal GRP-tour through the nodes V' and edges E'. The path through the n customers is partitioned into $\lceil \frac{n}{q} \rceil$ disjoint segments (or paths) where each segment with exception of the last one contains q customers. After that splitting we get a set of tours by connecting the depot v_0 with the first and last customer of each segment.

A modification of this algorithm is known as the iterated optimal tour partitioning (IOTP). For that we choose as first segment $[x^{(1)}, \ldots, x^{(i)}]$ with $i \leq q$ and apply the FOTP heuristic to the rest tour. We do this for $1 \leq i \leq q$ and choose the best solution. For the general case, we get the following bound

2.1 Theorem:

$$\frac{R^{IOTP}(V', E')}{R^*(V', E')} \leq 2 - \frac{1}{q}.$$

□

For the case $E' = \emptyset$ the same bound was shown by Atinkemer and Gavish [1]. A clearly better approach is to search for a partition of the tour in segments with at most q elements. This can be done by the shortest path method. In papers of Beasley [3] or Mole, Johnson and Wells [9] partition algorithms base on this idea. This algorithm is called shortest optimal tour partitioning (SOTP).

From the definition it is clear, that $R^{SOTP} \leq R^{IOPT}$ and that $R^{IOPT} \leq (2 - \frac{1}{q})\, R^{SOPT}$ The bound $R^{IOTP} \leq (2 - \frac{1}{q}) R^*$ is approachable for each q; for examples see Jansen [7] and Li, Simchi-Levi [8]. Also the inequality $R^{SOTP} \leq (2 - \frac{1}{q}) R^*$ is satisfied. There is hope that there is a better bound for the SOTP heuristic, because the bound $R^{IOTP} \leq (2 - \frac{1}{q}) R^*$ is satisfied. Unfortunatly, there are examples [7] of CARP's with

$$R^{SOPT}(\emptyset, E_q) = (2 - \frac{1}{q})\; R^*(\emptyset, E_q).$$

We notice that the heuristics FOTP, IOTP and SOTP presuppose the availability of an optimal GRP tour. If the graph

$$G^* = (\{v | v \in e \in E' \text{ or } v \in V'\} \cup \{v_0\}, E')$$

is connected, the GRP tour can be generated in polynomial time. The general problem of finding such a tour is NP - hard. This means that these partitioning heuristics can only base on an approximation of this tour. We denote a tour partitioning heuristic which starts from an approximation of the optimal GRP tour with αTP where the length of each approximated tour is bounded by $\alpha T^*(V' \cup \{v_0\}, E')$. An upper bound of a solution produced by IαTP is given by Haimovich and Rinnooy Kan [5] for the VRP. We can generalize it for the general capacitated routing problem to:

$$R^{I\alpha TP}(V', E') \leq R^*(V', E') + \alpha(1 - \frac{1}{q}))R^*(V', E').$$

The GRP problem can be solved with an algorithm, which is a generalization of the known algorithm of Christofides [4], and with the approximation value $\alpha = \frac{3}{2}$. With this heuristic we get the upper bound $\frac{5}{2} - \frac{3}{2q}$.

3 Unequal demand

Let us now consider the case of unequal demands. We assume that it is not allowed to split the demand of a customer over several vehicles. There is a heuristic of Altinkemer and Gavish [2] for the vehicle routing problem. We can generalize this heuristic for the general capacitated routing problem GCRP and get the following bound for $R^{IOTP}(V', E')$ with $q_s = \lceil \frac{q}{2} \rceil$.

3.1 Theorem:

$$\frac{R^{IOTP}(V', E')}{R^*(V', E')} \leq (1 + \frac{q-1}{q_s}).$$

□

For even q we get as upper bound $3 - \frac{2}{q}$ and for odd q the bound $3 - \frac{4}{q+1}$. This result is also a generalization of the bound for the vehicle routing problem with even q of Haimovich and Rinnooy Kan [5]. For this algorithm there are examples with this bound, see also Jansen [7].

Now we want to consider an extension of the shortest path partitioning algorithm which was given for the VRP by Beasley [3] and Mole, Johnson and Wells [9]. Their algorthm is also a special case of our algorithm for the GCRP. We note that there are examples [7,8] with bounds close to three for the VRP and CARP.

For the IOTP and SOTP heuristics we need at first a GRP tour. But it is no polynomial algorithm known for the determination of the optimal GRP tour. Hence, in the general case we must approximate the GRP tour as for the equal-demand case. We can apply the same method as before and get

$$R^{I\alpha TP}(V',E') \leq \frac{q}{q_s}R^*(V',E') + \alpha(1-\frac{1}{q_s}))R^*(V',E').$$

With the approximation value $\alpha = \frac{3}{2}$ we get for even q the upper bound $\frac{7}{2} - \frac{3}{q}$ and for odd q the value $\frac{7}{2} - \frac{5}{q+1}$.

References

[1] K. Altinkemer and B. Gavish, Heuristics for equal weight delivery problems with constant error guarantees, Report Graduate School of Management, University of Rochester, 1985.

[2] K. Altinkemer and B. Gavish, Heuristics for unequal weight delivery problems with a fixed error guarantee, Operations Research Letters, 6 (1987) 149-158.

[3] J.E. Beasley, Route first- cluster second methods for vehicle routing, Omega 11 (1983) 403-408.

[4] N. Christofides, Worst case analysis of a new heuristic for the traveling salesman problem, Management science research report 388, Carnegie-Mellon University, Pittsburgh, PA, (1976).

[5] M. Haimovich and A.H.G. Rinnooy Kan, Bounds and heuristics for capacitated routing problems, Mathematics of Operations Research, 10 (1985) 527-542.

[6] M. Haimovich, A.H.G. Rinnooy Kan and L. Stougie, Analysis of heuristics for vehicle routing problems, in: B.L. Golden and A.A. Assad, ed., Vehicle Routing: Methods and Studies (North Holland, Amsterdam, 1988) 47-61.

[7] K. Jansen, Bounds for the general capacitated routing problem, to appear.

[8] C-L. Li and D. Simchi-Levi, Worst case analysis of heuristics for multidepot capacitated vehicle routing problems, ORSA J. on Computing 2 (1990) 64-73.

[9] R.H. Mole, D.G. Johnson and K. Wells, Combinatorial analysis for route first- cluster second vehicle routing, Omega 11 (1983) 507-512.

COMBINATORIAL OPTIMIZATION PROBLEMS IN PCB ASSEMBLY

Peter J.M. van Laarhoven
Centre for Quantitative Methods
Nederlandse Philips Bedrijven B.V.
P.O. Box 218, NL-5600 MD Eindhoven

We analyze combinatorial optimization problems arising in a component insertion line for printed circuit board mounting. Such a line consists of a number of fully automated placement machines, connected by an automated, carrierless conveyor system. Each machine has a placement device, consisting of an arm equipped with three placement heads. Each head may pick and place certain component types; there is some freedom in the choice of equipment for each head. Components are supplied to each machine by tape feeders (each containing components of only one type) which are placed at certain feeder positions along the machine.

Before actually operating such a line, a careful production preparation phase has to be completed, specifying for each printed circuit board type the exact way in which such a board should be mounted. Problems arising in this production preparation phase include: the choice of head equipments to be mounted on the arm of each machine, the choice of components to be placed at each machine (workload balancing), an assignment of feeders to feeder positions on each machine, clustering of components to be placed in one pick-and-place move of the arm, and the sequencing of component insertions at each machine; the problems should be solved in such a way that the total insertion time on the bottleneck machine (i.e. the slowest machine) is as small as possible.

Obviously, this series of problems is extremely complex; in order to reduce this complexity we have followed the usual approach of decomposing it into a hierarchy of related subproblems. Since most of these problems are generalizations of well-known NP-hard combinatorial optimization problems, and since the available time to develop the numerical control system was extremely short (three man months), most of our algorithms are based on simulated annealing, a general method to solve combinatorial optimization problems, which in recent years has been successfully applied to many large-scale practical optimization problems [Van Laarhoven and Aarts, 1987).

The numerical control system developed has been tested and implemented and has resulted in software, which is in use at several sites of Philips' Electronics. A more detailed description and numerical results can be found in [Van Laarhoven and Zijm, 1991].

References

Laarhoven, P.J.M. van, and Aarts, E.H.L., *Simulated Annealing: Theory and Applications*, Kluwer Academic Publishers, Dordrecht (1987).

Laarhoven, P.J.M. van, and Zijm, W.H.M., Production Preparation and Numerical Control in PCB Assembly, *International Journal of Flexible Manufacturing Systems*, in press (1991).

The Absolute Multi-Factor Evaluation Process

S. Mićković, V. Rupnik, A. Zajc,
MIPOS d.o.o., Reboljeva 16, YU-61000 Ljubljana

In the business world many decision problems involve a number of factors. When one possible alternative, which is expressed by several factors (attributes), is compared with other possible, ordinary rules of comparision are not usable. The aim of the presented evaluation process is to achieve simultaneous and mutually independent comparation of attributes and therefrom objective and unbiased decision making.

A general problem of comparation of a finite group of entities is a simple sorting task using the linear order relation when entities are described by only one attribute. In multi-dimensional problems entities are defined by several (N) attributes and can be therefore presented as N-dimensonal vectors. One of the ways to compare these vectors is to transform them into scalars and then to solve the one dimensional problem. But the scalarisation is a rather delicate process liable to a subjective choice of ponders or norming radikands and therefore mostly based on personal experience and estimations.

Evaluation method presented in this paper implements new kind of scalarisation which ensures higher degree of objectivity. Values of a k-th attribute of each of n entities are presented in a vector: $\xi_k = (r_{1k},...,r_{nk})^T$, $k=1,2,...,N$. Evaluation algorithm searches for a vector $x^\circ = (x_1^\circ,...,x_n^\circ)^T$ which is closest to all vectors ξ_k simultaneusly in the sense of any Holder metric. Components of this vector are a scalar measure for global quality of the first, second,..., n-th entity. Entities are then compared and sorted due to their global quality values.

Evaluation algorithm was tested on various cases of comparation problems and reached a reasonable degree of objectivity. Cross-correlation and regression tests of evaluation results showed that influence of attributes on the qlobal quality was connected also with the relations between attributes. Therefrom it may be concluded that objectivity of the evaluation process depends mostly on the proper selection of attributes and their quality.

References

Rupnik V. and Vrečko J. (1988) Programski paket Abseval 1.0. Ekonomska fakulteta Borisa Kidriča, Ljubljana

Mićković S. (1991) Izgradnja funkcionalnega, optimalnega, upravljalno orientiranega fluidnega modela, Ekonomska fakulteta Borisa Kidriča, Ljubljana

OPTIMAL SCHEDULING FOR LINEAR DYNAMIC PROCESSES

Wieslaw Wajs
Institute of Automatics, Academy of Mining and Metallurgy
al. Mickiewicza 30, 30-059 Krakow, Poland

Scheduling problems arise from situation that require the assignment of resources over a period of time to perform a set of activities. Typically, these problems may be viewed as the determination of an optimal sequence for activities on resources. When the activities are deterministic, these problems may be formulated as combinatorial optimization problems in the classical sense.

There is given a set of n models for the affect of heating and cooling a piece of metal. The models are denoted by index i for $i = 1, 2, ..., n$. Each model has the form of the Fourier equation (1).

$$\frac{\partial u_i}{\partial t} = \alpha_i \frac{\partial^2 u_i}{\partial x^2} + \beta_i \frac{\partial^2 u_i}{\partial y^2} + \gamma_i \frac{\partial^2 u_i}{\partial z^2} \tag{1}$$

Equation (1) describes the distribution of temperature u_i inside a piece of metal.

For each model for $i = 1, 2, ..., n$ two types of operations are realized. The first type of operations is realized for all models simultaneously. The beginning of operation of the first type is given as t_0. The second type of operations is realized only sequentially. None of the terms of beginning of operations of the second type is given. This term depends on the sequence of the performed operations.

There is a limitation that only one operation of the second type can be realized simultaneously.

The temperature on the edge of the area (X, Y, Z) for each model is given in the form of the boundary condition describing the course of temperature f_i.

The boundary conditions are given for the time interval between the beginning term t_0 to the term of termination of operation of the second type.

The time of termination $t_i + p_i$ of each operation of the second type depends on the sequence of realization of the operations.

There is a limitation that at the same time only one change of the function for the boundary condition can take place. This concerns the change of the boundary condition from the function $f_i(t)$ into function $g_i(t)$. Function $g_i(t)$ describes the boundary condition for the realization of the operations of the second type.

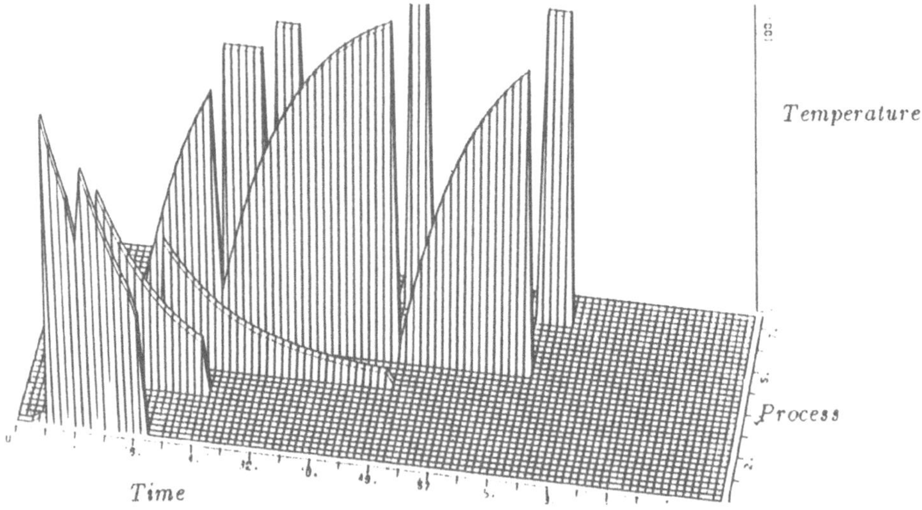

Fig. 1. A picture of realization of a sequence of operations for three models in a three-dimensional space.

The function for the boundary condition for operations of the first type, for all models, assumes the following form:

$$u_i(X,t) = f_i(t)$$
$$u_i(Y,t) = f_i(t) \qquad (2)$$
$$u_i(Z,t) = f_i(t)$$

Starting from term t_i the boundary condition for the model determined by the permutation changes.

$$u_i(X,t) = g_i(t)$$
$$u_i(Y,t) = g_i(t) \qquad (3)$$
$$u_i(Z,t) = g_i(t)$$

Time of duration of operation p_i and the connected term of termination of operation of the second type depends on fulfillment of the condition given by the difference of temperatures between the arbitrary point x, y, z and the point on the edge X, Y, Z for $-X < x < X$, $-Y < y < Y$, $-Z < z < Z$.

$$| u_i(X,t) - u_i(x,t) | = \varepsilon_x$$
$$| u_i(Y,t) - u_i(y,t) | = \varepsilon_y \qquad (4)$$
$$| u_i(Z,t) - u_i(z,t) | = \varepsilon_z$$

The initial value of the average temperature in the whole volume is given by:

$$u_i(x,y,z,0+) = u_0(x,y,z) \qquad (5)$$

Formulation of Optimization Task

There should be found such a permutation for the operation of the second type that the quality index

$$min(max(t_i)) \qquad (6)$$

reaches its minimum.

From the physical point of view this problem can be described in the following way. There was accumulated thermal energy in a volume of matter. The energy is scattered at the time of realization of operation of the first type, as the environment temperature is lower than inside the matter. Starting from the term t_i the temperature on the edge of the metal increases. When the operation of the second type is realized, the temperature in the whole mass increases. The change of control on the edge of the area takes place in n terms which depend on the form of permutation of the operations.

In such a situation two problems should be solved:

-finding the method of calculating the condition of the second-type operation from the equations:

$$| u_i(X,t) - u_i(x,t) | = \varepsilon_x$$
$$| u_i(Y,t) - u_i(y,t) | = \varepsilon_y \qquad (7)$$
$$| u_i(Z,t) - u_i(z,t) | = \varepsilon_z$$

which demand the solution of the Fourier equation for each realized sequence of operations, and

- finding an efficient (polynomial) algorithm of determining the optimum permutation for the given criterion.

Such a formulation of the problem has a reference to the packing problem. In the paper there has been considered the problem of packing objects which differs from the packing problem known from the literature by the fact that the packed objects change their size according to the relation

$$p_i = a_i * t + b_i \qquad (8)$$

when $a_i, t > 0; b_i \geq 0$.

Thus formulated problem may be referred to the problem of charging the furnace with metal pieces, and in which they are heated before rolling.

The metal awaiting the process gets cooler and cooler, losing the accumulated thermal energy.

Let us assume that at $t = t_0$ we pack the metal, for which the duration of the heating operation is given by the function

$$a_1 t + b_1. \tag{9}$$

The time of termination of heating will be described by relation

$$t_1 = t_0 + a_1 t_0 + b_1. \tag{10}$$

Term t_1 denotes end of heating when the first metal bit is packed, and the heating process starts at t_0 moment. When the second metal piece is paced first, then we get the following relation:

$$t_1 = t_0 + a_2 t_0 + b_2. \tag{11}$$

Each packing sequence of m pieces given a calculated value t_m for given t_0 and a_i, b_i for $i = 1, 2, ..., n$.

Optimization Method

The conducted simulations show to the possibility of registering the time of duration of the heating operation in the form of equation

$$\frac{dp_i(t)}{dt} = a_i \tag{12}$$

with the initial condition

$$p_i(t = t_0) = b_i \tag{13}$$

Such a simplification is admissible only in the case of a limited time interval, in which the relation between the cooling time and heating time approximately shows a linear dependence. Hence the time of operation is given by the formula

$$p_i(t) = a_i t + b_i. \tag{14}$$

No limitations are imposed on the order of the operations realization.

Problem

$$1 \mid n \mid p_i(t) = a_i t + b_i; a_i > 0; b_i > 0; t > 0 \mid min(max(t_i)) \tag{15}$$

performance index for the dynamic order task is given in the form

$$nim(max(t_i)) \tag{16}$$

Optimal scheduling for the task

$$1 \mid n \mid p_i(t) = a_i t + b_i; a_i > 0; b_i > 0; t > 0 \mid min(max(t_i))$$

when the relations for the dynamic processes are as in the below table

i	$p_i(t)$	t_i
0	0	t_0
1	$a_1 t_0 + b_1$	$(a_1 + 1)t_0 + b_1$
2	$a_2(a_1 t_0 + b_1) + b_2 = a_2 t_1 + b_2$	$(a_2 + 1)t_1 + b_2$
3	$a_3 t_2 + b_3$	$(a_3 + 1)t_2 + b_3$
...	....	....
n	$a_n t_{n-1} + b_n$	$(a_n + 1)t_{n-1} + b_n$

is given in the form of a sequence

$$\frac{a_1}{b_1} \geq \frac{a_2}{b_2} \geq \dots \frac{a_i}{b_i} \geq \dots \frac{a_{n-1}}{b_{n-1}} \geq \frac{a_n}{b_n}$$

Conclusions

The calculation complexity in the determination of the first element of optimal permutation can be determined as $O(nlogn)$.

References

1. Wajs W.(1990) *Optimal Control for Linear and Nonlinear Dynamic Processes* Proc. of the IXth World Congress IFAC Tallin
2. Rinnooy Kan A.H.G.(1976). *Machine scheduling problems.* Stenfet Krose, B. V., Leiden, Netherlands.
3. Lawler E.L. (1973) *Optimal sequencing to a single machine subject to precedence constraints* Management Sci. 19, 544-546.
4. Crank J., Nicolson P. (1947). *A Practical Method for Numerical the Heat-Construction Type* . Proc. Cambridge Philos. Soc 43, 50 - 67.
5. Carslaw H.,Jeager C.(1947) *Conduction of Heat in Solids* . Claredon Press, Oxford, 90 - 112.
6. Convay R.W., Maxwell W.L., Miller L.W.(1967) *Theory of Scheduling* Addison-Wesley, Reading, Mass.
7. Forsythe G.,Wasow W.R.(1960) *Finite-Difference Methods for Partial Differential Equations* John Willey and Sons, New York.

Packing Polyominoes

Joachim Wolffram

Lehrstuhl für Anwendungen des Operations Research, Universität Karlsruhe
Kaiserstr. 12, D–7500 Karlsruhe; Email:wolffram@andor.rz.uni–karlsruhe.de

Abstract

A *polyomino* is a connected figure consisting of unit squares joined at the edges. We consider the following *polyomino packing problem* (PPP): *Given a region R and a set S of n distinct polyominoes with associated values. How should copies of the polyominoes be placed into R so as to maximize their total value, whereby they are not allowed to overlap each other?* A lagrangean relaxation is presented which provides upper bounds for (PPP) using subgradient optimization. For the special case of packing copies of one polyomino into a rectangle, we present an exact tree search procedure which allows medium sized problems to be solved. We briefly describe tabu search heuristics for (PPP) which produce very good solutions.

1 Introduction

In the last decades there has been a lot of research in solving questions which arise in connection with polyominoes. Surprisingly, there is up to our knowledge only one article available (see [1]) which deals with (PPP). Only for the special case where all polyominoes of S are restricted to be of rectangular type a lot of algorithms have been proposed in the context of cutting stock problems [8].

In this extended abstract we give a short overview about our work and results on the polyomino packing problem we achieved so far. More detailed information, discussions and all proofs can be found in [10].

2 Definitions

Partition the plane into unit squares and declare one unit square as the origin $(0,0)$. Given the origin, every square can be identified by a unique *position* $(i,j) \in Z^2$. The positions are lexicographically ordered, e.g., $(i,j) \prec (k,l)$ if $i < k \vee (i = k \wedge j < l)$.

A *grid figure* in *normal position* is represented as $P \subset \{(i,j) \in Z^2 : i \geq 0,\ i = 0 \Rightarrow j \geq 0\}$ with $(0,0) \in P$. The point $(0,0) \in P$ is called the *origin* of P. To describe a translation of a grid figure P to a position p we use the notation $P^p = \{v + p : v \in P\}$.

A polyomino, as defined above, is a special kind of a grid figure. In the latter, P will always denote a polyomino unless specified else. Please note that all statements which will be made for polyominoes apply to grid figures as well.

The polyominoes have to be placed into a *grid pattern* which is given as $R = R_{r,c} \subset \{(i,j) \in Z^2 : (1,1) \leq (i,j) \leq (r,c)\}$. The empty pattern $R_{r,c} = \emptyset$ represents a $r \times c$ rectangular region.

A position p is called *fit position of P with respect to $R_{r,c}$* if the following holds: $P^p \cap R_{r,c} = \emptyset \wedge \forall q \in P^p : (1,1) \leq q \leq (r,c)$.

The lexicographically smallest fit position p of P with respect to R is called *first fit position.* The pattern R is called *full* if there exists no fit position for P.

The set $C(P) = \{c \in Z^2 : P \cap P^c \neq \emptyset\}$ is called the set of *collision vectors* of P.

The pattern R' is said to be *constructible* from $R^0 := R$ and P if there exists a sequence $e(R,R',P)=(p_j : j = 1,\ldots,k)$ such that $p_j \prec p_{j+1}, 1 \leq j < k$, p_{i+1} is a fit position for P in $R^i := R \cup \bigcup_{j=1}^{i} P^{p_j}$, $1 \leq i < k$, and $R^r = R'$.

We denote as $H^*(R,P)$ the set of full patterns which are constructible from R and P.

Given a sequence $e(R,R',P) = (p_j : j = 1,\ldots,k)$ and a fit position $p \succ p_k$ for P in R', then the pattern $R' \cup P^p$ is called an *expansion* of R'.

3 Optimal Packing of One Polyomino

The special case of (PPP) where one has to place a maximal number of copies of one polyomino into a region R will be denoted as (PPP_1). (PPP_1) is NP–complete because it contains instances of packing 3×3 rectangular polyominoes into a given region [5]. This implies the NP–completeness of (PPP). Based on powerful tabu search heuristics, which provide optimal or near optimal solutions for (PPP_1), it is possible to solve medium sized problems using a branch and bound algorithm. We will give a brief overview about this algorithm.

3.1 Enumeration of all full patterns

The basic idea for the enumeration scheme is to create recursively all sequences $e(R,\cdot,P)$ which lead to full patterns. At every recursion level a given pattern is expanded. If the pattern is not expandable and has no fit position, then the pattern is full. As we only need to compute full patterns, we can exploit the following observation:

Lemma 1 *Let p be the first fit position of P in R and let q be a fit position which satisfies $q \succ p + \max_{c \in C(P)} c$. Then*
$R \cup P^q$ can not be expanded to a full pattern.

Using Lemma 1 we obtain a recursive enumeration scheme for the elements of $H^*(R,P)$.

```
procedure e_pattern (R pattern, P polyomino, l position)
    if (there exists a fit position for P in R) then
        p := first fit position for P in R;
        A := {q : l ≺ q ⪯ p + max_{c∈C(P)} c, q fit position for P in R }
        if (A ≠ ∅) then
            ∀q ∈ A : e_pattern (R ∪ P^q, P, q);
        end;
    else
        H* := H* ∪ R;
    end;
```

To construct a correct and efficient branch and bound algorithm it is crucial not to miss any candidate solution and not to compute any candidate solution more than once. About *e_pattern* we can state the following:

Theorem 1 *Given a starting pattern R and a polyomino P. Executing* e_pattern $(R, P, (1,0))$ *will compute every element of $H^*(R,P)$ exactly once.*

3.2 Determination of an Upper Bound

Let $a_{pq} = 1$ if $q \in P^p$, e.g., P covers position q, if it is placed with its origin at position p, $a_{pq} = 0$ otherwise; $x_p = 1$ if polyomino P is placed with its origin at position p, $x_p = 0$ otherwise. Let $\bar{R}$ denote the set of all fit positions of P with respect to R. Using these definitions (PPP_1) can be formulated as an integer program:

$$
\begin{aligned}
Z_1 = \max \sum_{p \in \bar{R}} x_p & \\
\text{s.t.} \quad \sum_{p \in \bar{R}} a_{pq} x_p & \leq 1, \quad q \in R \\
x_p & \in \{0,1\} \quad p \in \bar{R}.
\end{aligned} \tag{1}
$$

To derive an upper bound for Z_1 we introduce lagrangean multipliers $\lambda_q \geq 0$, $q \in R$, and dualize the constraints (1). Then

$$
L_\lambda = \max \left\{ \sum_{p \in \bar{R}} (1 - \sum_{q \in R} \lambda_q a_{pq}) x_p + \sum_{q \in R} \lambda_q : x \in \{0,1\}^{|\bar{R}|}, |P| \sum_{p \in \bar{R}} x_p \leq |R| \right\} \tag{2}
$$

is an upper bound for $Z_1, \lambda \geq 0$. The inequality $|P| \sum_{p \in \bar{R}} x_p \leq |R|$ is called a *surrogate constraint.* Note that L_λ can easily be computed by just setting the $\lfloor |R|/|P| \rfloor$ variables with the biggest positive coefficients $1 - \sum_{q \in R} \lambda_q a_{\cdot q}$ to one. As we like to get the lowest upper bound for Z_1 obtainable from L_λ, we define the following lagrangean dual problem for (PPP_1):

$$
L_D = \min_{\lambda \geq 0} L_\lambda \tag{3}
$$

As we use the upper bound within the branch and bound algorithm, we are satisfied with a value *near* L_D. We use subgradient optimization [3] for computing this value.

Several other methods like dual ascent approaches [7] and n–opt like dual heuristics [4] produced good results for similar combinatorial problems. We tested several adaptations of these approaches for (PPP_1) without striking success. This seems to be caused by the *evenness* of the side constraints which rules out *domination* considerations.

By the *integrality property* of Geoffrion [3] we can state the following relationship between L_λ and the optimal value Z_{LP} of the LP–Relaxation of (PPP_1):

Theorem 2 $L_D = Z_{LP}$.

The LP–relaxation does not give tighter bounds on Z_1 than the lagrangean relaxation does. Moreover, we confirm the results of several authors [3] that solving the LP–relaxation is much more time consuming than computing bounds using subgradient optimization.

3.3 Branch and Bound

Including the computation of an upper bound for a given partial filled region R and the polyomino P as the first step of the procedure *e_pattern()* leads to a depth–first–search. Mostly the optimal solution can be found using the tabu search heuristics and we only have to verify the optimality of such a solution. Therefore depth–first–search is appropriate. However, there are quite a lot of refinements necessary to achieve an efficient branch and bound algorithm. See [10] for details.

Note that the enumeration scheme and the computation of the upper bound can be adapted for the general problem (PPP) in a straightforward way.

4 Tabu Search Techniques

The idea of tabu search was introduced by Glover. In the last years Glover and many other authors reported good results using this technique (see [6] for an overview).

We used tabu search in the following way for (PPP): Given a region R and polyominoes $P_1, \ldots, P_n$. Create a feasible solution by successively inserting the polyomino with the best value with respect to a valuation function. Find a subregion with minimal value. Declare the subregion as tabu. Delete the polyominoes from R which have fields in common with the subregion and declare some of them as tabu. Fill the subregion with polyominoes which were not declared tabu. Again, find a non–tabu subregion with minimal value. Iterate until a local stopping criterion is satisfied. Then, determine the *oldest* polyominoes in R, e.g., polyominoes at positions which were not removed for a long time, and declare them as tabu. Remove all polyominoes from R. Continue the whole process until a global stopping criterion is satisfied.

Note that this approach explicitly allows the objective value to get worse while cruising through the solution space. Hence there is a possibility to escape local optima. The tabu–states are used to prevent an immediately return to an escaped local optimum.

5 Computational Results

The tabu search heuristics produce very good results in a few minutes even for large problems on a 486 Unix system [10].

We solved all instances of packing pentominoes into squares up to a size of 15×15. The smaller problems up to 12×12 squares were solved in a few minutes, but some of the bigger problems took several hours.

The programs were written in the object oriented programming language *Eiffel* [9] which turned out to be excellent for our purposes.

References

[1] Beasley, J.E.: *An Exact Two–Dimensional Non–Guillotine Cutting Tree Search Procedure*; Operations Research 1985, 49–64

[2] Beasley, J.E.: *Bounds for Two–Dimensional Cutting*; J. Opl. Res. Soc.. Vol 36, No. 1, 1985, 71–74

[3] Fisher, M.L.: *The Lagrangian Relaxation Method for Solving Integer Programming Problems*; Management Science 27/1981, 1–18

[4] Fisher, M.L.; Kedia,P.: *Optimal Soution of Set Covering/Partitioning Problems Using Dual Heuristics*; Management Science Vol.36, No.6, June 1990, 674–688

[5] Fowler, R.J.; Paterson, M.S.; Tanimoto, L.: *Optimal Packing and Covering in the Plane are NP–Complete*; Information Processing Letters Vol.12, No.3, 1981, 133–137

[6] Glover,F.: *Tabu Search: A Tutorial*; Interfaces (1990), 20 (4), 74–94

[7] Guignard,M.; Rosenwein, M.B.: *An application-oriented guide for designing Lagrangean dual ascent algorithms*; EJOR 43(1989), 197–205

[8] Hinxman, A.I.: *The trim-loss and assortment problems: A Survey*; EJOR Research 5/1980, 8–18

[9] Meyer, B.: *Object–Oriented Software Construction*; Prentice Hall, 1988

[10] Wolffram, J.: *Packing Polyominoes*; Internal Report; Lehrstuhl für Anwendungen des Operations Research, Universität Karlsruhe, Germany

DISCRETE OPTIMIZATION PROBLEM WITH BRANCH STRUCTURE IN FOREST PLANNING

Lidija Zadnik Stirn
University of Ljubljana
Biotechnical Faculty, Forestry Department
Večna pot 83, 61000 Ljubljana, Yugoslavia.

The optimization problem presented in this paper arises from the problem of forest management. Forest is a very complicated renewable natural resource. It has to be managed with predescribed economic and environmental demands considering the given natural circumstances. The management of the forest involves sequences of relatively similar decisions which have a profound effect on current status of the forest as well as on the future forest conditions and they should be chosen with the aim to maximize the sum of returns. Methods of operations research and optimization models can be used as means to find a set of strategies which result in considerably improved decision making in forest management.

As presented at Ulm (1989) GMOER Conference on Operations Research (Zadnik, 1989) is the planning horizon divided into several equal periods i (i = 1,2,...,N) due to the exceptional length of the production period in forestry. The whole forest area is divided into E homogeneous forest elements, signed with e (e = 1,2,...,E), at the same time. The management of each element e is then presented as a discrete input-output process:

$$\underline{x}_{e,i+1} = f(\underline{x}_{e,i}, \underline{d}_{e,i}), \quad i=1,2,...,N; \; e=1,2,...,E; \qquad (1)$$

- $\underline{x}_{e,i}$ is the input vector which describes the state of the forest element e in period i. $\underline{x}_{e,i}$ consists of components $x_{e,i,1}, \ldots, x_{e,i,k}$ which present the type of the tree species on the element e, the total volume of timber, the average annual increment of the existing tree species, the quality of tree species, the developing stage - the age of the trees (there are four age groups distinguished), etc. All the components of vector $\underline{x}_{e,i} = x_{e,i,1},...,x_{e,i,k})$ are rendered discrete so that for each element e in each period i exists the same finite set X of possible vectors $\underline{x}_{e,i}$: $\underline{x}_{e,i} \in X$,
- $\underline{d}_{e,i}$ is the control vector and presents all possible silvicultural decisions as harvesting, clear cut, exchange of the existing tree species with a new one, thinning, improvement of the biological growth, etc. which can be undertaken on the forest element e with the state $\underline{x}_{e,i}$. There exists a finite set

D of silvicultural decisions $\underline{d}_{e,i} = (d_{e,i,1},\ldots,d_{e,i,m}) \in D$. These decisions are mutually exclusive at the same period and place, what means that at each period i and on each element e only one decision from the set D can be taken,
- $f(\underline{x}_{e,i},\underline{d}_{e,i})$ is the transition function which transforms the state $\underline{x}_{e,i}$ of the element e in period i to the state $\underline{x}_{e,i+1}$ in the period i+1. This function is defined empirically (Zadnik, 1990) for each possible state $\underline{x}_{e,i}$ and each possible decision $\underline{d}_{e,i}$ so that the function $f(\underline{x}_{e,i},\underline{d}_{e,i})$ (process (1)) is noted in the form of a table T_1.

On each element e with the state $\underline{x}_{e,i}$ each silvicultural decision from the set D brings about a certain effect $U(\underline{x}_{e,i},\underline{d}_{e,i})$ as net present value of the forest or wood removed, discounted profit, etc. These effects are for each possible state vector and decision determined empirically and gathered in the form of a table T_2. Under the assumption that the sum of effects $U(\underline{x}_{e,i},\underline{d}_{e,i})$ has to be maximized over all periods i the process (1) can be presented as the following optimization problem:

$$\max_{\underline{d}_{e,i}} \sum_{i=1}^{N} U(\underline{x}_{e,i},\underline{d}_{e,i}) \qquad i=1,2,\ldots,N \quad e=1,2,\ldots,E$$

$$\underline{x}_{e,i+1} = f(\underline{x}_{e,i},\underline{d}_{e,i}) \tag{2}$$

The optimal sequence of silvicultural decisions $d_{e,1,.}$, $d_{e,2,.}$, ..., $d_{e,N,.}$ which solves the problem (2) for each element e independently from other forest elements is determined on the base of tables T_1 and T_2 and by the use of Bellman's principle of optimality (Bellman, 1962). The results of problem (2) are presented in the form of tables T_e (e=1,2,...,E).

Table T_e: The optimal management of the forest element e

Period	State	Decision	Effect
1	$\underline{x}_{e,1}$	$d_{e,1,.}$	$U(\underline{x}_{e,1},d_{e,1,.})$
.			
.			
N	$\underline{x}_{e,N}$	$d_{e,N,.}$	$U(\underline{x}_{e,N},d_{e,N,.})$

The isolated optimal sequences of decisions gathered in tables T_e are then used to find a reciprocal co-ordination of all forest elements in order to manage the whole forest area in an optimal way. In solving the problem of optimal managing of the whole forest area which is the union of all E elements a predefined economic and environmental goals have to be achieved in each period i (i=1,2,...,N). This means in short that the sum of effects $U(\underline{x}_{e,i},\underline{d}_{e,i})$ over all forest elements e has to be maximized, the state of the entire forest area should ensure the permanence of approximately equal period yields and the quality of the existing tree species over all forest elements e has to be improved, what could be summarized as:

$$\max_{\underline{d}_{e,i}} \sum_{e=1}^{E} U(\underline{x}_{e,i},\underline{d}_{e,i})$$

$$\text{subject to:} \quad \sum_{e=1}^{E} x_{e,i+1,j}(\underline{x}_{e,i},\underline{d}_{e,i}) \geq \sum_{e=1}^{E} x_{e,i,j} \tag{3}$$

for all meaningful j=1,...,k.

THE METHOD

The problem (3) can be for i=1 and later analogue for i=2,...,N-1 written as:

$$\max z = U(\underline{x}_{1,1},d_{1,1,p})+U(\underline{x}_{2,1},d_{2,1,p})+ \dots +U(\underline{x}_{E,1},d_{E,1,p})$$

$$\text{subject to:} \quad x_{1,2,j}(d_{1,1,p}) + \dots + x_{E,2,p}(d_{E,1,p}) \geq C_j \tag{4}$$

$$j=1,\dots,k; \; p=1,\dots,m;$$

- $d_{e,1,p}$ are for e=1,...,E and p=1,...,m the unknown variables of the problem (4). They are nonnegative integers from the finite set (1,2,...,m) which presents the finite space of solutions of problem (4). $d_{e,1,p}=1$ if the first decision from the set D is undertaken on the element e, ... ,$d_{e,1,p}=m$ if the last decision from the set D is undertaken on the element e. The dimension of the problem (4) is somewhat reduced because at each element not all decisions are always possible (table T_1),
- $\underline{x}_{e,1}$ is the observed initial state vector of the element e,
- $U(\underline{x}_{e,1},d_{e,1,p})$ is calculated in dependence of each possible decision $d_{e,1,p} \in D$ by the use of table T_2,
- C_j is the constant calculated from the components of $\underline{x}_{e,1}$: $C_j = x_{1,1,j} + x_{2,1,j} + \dots + x_{E,1,j}$,
- $x_{e,2,j}(d_{e,1,p})$ is calculated in dependence of each possible $d_{e,1,p} \in D$ by the use of table T_1.

The problem (4) is a problem of branch structure as evident with variables $d_{e,1,p}$ (e=1,...,E). A complete decision tree in Fig. 1 helps to visualise the problem (4). Each level of the tree is identified with one forest element e, that means with one of the variables $d_{e,1,p}$. The number of nodes is exponential to the number of variables (there would be m^E nodes if for each element e all m decisions would be possible). Each path from the starting to the final node of the tree presents a solution but not all of them are feasible because not all of them satisfy the constraints of the problem (4). So it is reasonable

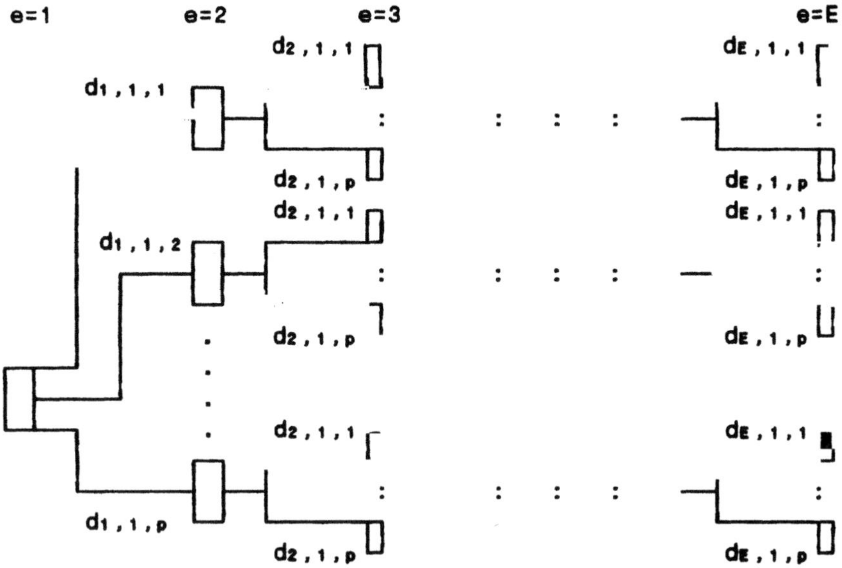

Figure 1: The complete decision tree of the problem (4)

to find the optimal solution of the problem (4) by using a procedure of branch and bound type (Beale, 1979) in which not the whole decision tree need to be presented and valued. Branching is developed as in Fig. 1, while the bound function is determined by functions z and C_j.

CONCLUSIONS

Dynamic programming procedure would be expected to use for solving the presented multistage decision problem. But the method based on the graph theory is more convenient because of great number of variables and constraints. It was possible to construct the tree of the problem only with computer due to great dimension of the problem. An example of 8 forest elements was calculated and the results confirm that the presented model could be practically used.

REFERENCES

- Beale,E.M.L., 1979. Branch and bound methods for math. prog. Annals of discrete math.5: 201-219.
- Bellman,R.E., 1962. Dynamic programming. Princeton Univ.
- Zadnik Stirn,L., 1989. An algorithm to find the optimal strategy in forest management. GMOER Conf. on Oper. Res. Ulm.
- Zadnik Stirn,L., 1990. Adaptive dynamic model for optimal forest management. For.Ecol.Manage.,31:167-188.

MAXIMUM FOLDING, A GENERALIZATION OF MAXIMUM MATCHING

T. C. Hu
Department of Computer Science and Engineering
University of California, San Diego
La Jolla, California, 92093-0114, USA

We shall introduce a unified graph model which represents various problems in VLSI, e.g., PLA folding, Gate-Matrix layout, and channel routing. Then we introduce an algorithm for folding a Weinberger's array [an array containing three kinds of entries, 0 (no connection), c (connection), t (transistors)]. It is shown that the folding of Weinberger's array is a generalization of the PLA folding, and equivalent to channel routing.

Given an undirected graph G = (V,E) where V is the set of vertices v_i ($i = 1, \cdots, n$) and E is the set of edges e_{ij} connecting v_i and v_j. The well-known maximum matching problem can be stated as follows:

Select maximum number of edges from the set E subject to the constraint that no two selected edges are incident to the same vertex.

Now let us formulate a similar problem called the maximum folding problem.

Given a graph G with its edges colored red, add maximum number of green edges between vertices not connected by red edges. In addition, the following two constraints must be satisfied.

(i) No two green edges are incident to the same vertex. In other words, in the green graph, no node has green degree more than one. This constraint will be referred to as the degree constraint.

(ii) After the green edges are added, there exists no cycle consisting of red and green edges alternatively (called the cycle constraint from now on). (See [2] [3] [4].)

Note that the cycle constraint makes the maximum folding problem different from the maximum matching problem. Constraint (i) is equivalent to the maximum matching. We can first draw all edges of a graph in red and its complement edges in green and then select a subset of green edges subject to constraint (i), which is the maximum matching problem. It is the addition of constraint (ii) which makes the problem NP-complete.

In the Programmable Logic Array (PLA), its personality matrix consists of 0's and 1's. Two columns of the PLA can be folded into a single physical column if the 1's in the two columns are in disjoint rows and we permute the rows of the (0,1) matrix such that all 1's in one column are in rows above 1's in the other column [1].

In the graph model, we represent columns by vertices of a graph and draw a red edge between the two vertices if the two corresponding columns have 1's in common rows. If we decide to fold two columns called T and B, we shall simply permute rows so that all 1's in the column T are in top rows and all 1's in the column B are in the bottom row. In the graph model, we would draw a directed green edge from the vertex B to the vertex T.

The maximum number of directed green edges means maximum number pairs of columns are folded.

The nonexistence of the alternating cycle means that a row permutation exists which permits the folding.

In the gate matrix layout, the problem can also be represented by a matrix of 0's and 1's just like PLA. The usual formulation is to permute columns in order to fold the rows. Here we shall state the problem as permuting rows to fold columns. However in gate matrix layout, more than two columns can be folded together. To accommodate this situation in the graph model, we allow green paths, each path consisting of several directed edges. The vertices in the same path represent columns folded into the same physical column.

Thus, we shall extend the original graph model. Given a graph G with undirected red edges, add maximum number of directed green edges subject to the following two constraints [2]:

(i) The indegree or outdegree of the green edges at a node is at most one. (This allows a directed green path.) (See [5].)

(ii) There exists no cycle formed by alternating single red edges and green paths. (Note that a green path is a generalization of a single directed green edge.)

A Transistor and Contact Array (TCA) comprises a grid of vertical and horizontal wires. A TCA can be represented by a matrix with three kinds of elements (0, ε, 1) where 0 indicates no connection, ε indicates a transistor and 1 indicates a contact. The problem is to permute rows so as to fold the maximum number of columns. For a given row, there is a sequence of ε's and 1's and the columns can be permuted as long as they do not disturb the relative orderings of ε's and 1's in the given row. The totality of all rows puts constraints on the permutations of all columns. In other words, the columns can be partitioned into subsets, each subset of columns can be treated as a PLA. Such a subset is called an interval set.

Once the row permutation is fixed, and the partitions of columns into interval sets is also determined, then we can use lexicographical ordering to fold the maximum number of columns within an interval set. After columns within every individual interval set are folded, there is still a problem of fitting all the columns between interval sets. Such a problem can be solved by dynamic programming techniques [5].

In the channel routing problem [6], pins are at the top and bottom parts of a channel and we have to connect all nets using one horizontal track per net. In the graph model, nodes are used to represent nets, and we draw a directed red edge between two nodes if there is a vertical constraint [7] between the two nets and we draw an undirected red edge between the two nodes if there is a horizontal constraint [7] between the two nets. In the red graph, we also fill in directed red edges implied by transitivity. If we decide to put three nets in one horizontal track, then we draw a green path connecting the three nodes. Here the degree constraint and cycle constraint have to be satisfied. The directed red edge plays the same role in restricting the top-to-bottom order of nets as in the left-to-right order of columns in TCA.

REFERENCES

1. Hachtel, G. D., A. R. Newton and A. L. Sangiovanni-Vincentelli, "An Algorithm for Optimal PLA Folding," *IEEE Transactions on Computer Aided Design of Integrated Circuits and Systems 1*, 2 (April 1982), pp. 63-77.
2. Hu, T. C. and Y. S. Kuo, "Optimum Reduction of Programmable Logic Array," *Proceedings of the 20th Design Automation Conference*, IEEE, 1983, pp. 553-558.
3. Hu, T. C. and Y. S. Kuo, "Graph Folding and VLSI Design," *Journal of Networks*, 17 (1987), pp. 19-37.
4. Luby, M, U. Vazirani and A. Sangiovanni-Vincentelli, "Some Theoretical Results on the Optimal PLA Folding Problem," *Proceedings of the 2nd International Conference on Circuits and Computers*, IEEE, September 1982, pp. 165-170.
5. Moerder, K. E., "Folding Algorithms for an Array of Transistors and Contacts," 1989 Ph.D. thesis (Advisor: T. C. Hu), University of California, San Diego, La Jolla, CA 92093.
6. Shing, M. T. and T. C. Hu, "Computational Complexity of Layout Problems," Chapter 8 in the book *Advances in CAD for VLSI*, Vol. 4, edited by T. Ohtsuki, published by North-Holland, 1986.
7. Yoshimura, T. and E. S. Kuh, "Efficient Algorithms for Channel Routing," *IEEE Trans. Vol. CAD-1*, Jan 1982, pp. 25-35. Also in the book *VLSI Circuit Layout: Theory and Design*, edited by T. C. Hu and E. S. Kuh, IEEE Press, 1985, pp. 180-190.

IMPLEMENTATION OF INTERIOR POINT METHODS ON PARALLEL AND VECTOR MACHINES

Florian A. Potra
Department of Mathematics
University of Iowa
Iowa City, Iowa 52242

The advent of interior point methods has revolutionized the field of mathematical programming. Although various interior point methods have been considered one way or another from the 50's, it was only after the publication of the seminal paper of Karmarkar (1984) that the scientific community engaged in an intensive theoretical and experimental study of interior point algorithms. On the theoretical side this research effort lead to improved computational complexity bounds for linear programming(LP), quadratic programming(QP), linear complementarity problems(LCP) and some convex programming problems. On the other hand the experimental work has resulted in a number of very efficient codes. These codes have performed consistently better than traditional methods, especially on very large problems. The vast amount of computation required for solving such problems often requires the use of supercomputers, wherefrom the need for studying different ways of implementing interior point methods on parallel and/or vector machines.

The first production code that successfully implemented interior point methods is contained in the integrated software-hardware KORBX system developed by AT&T. The software part consists in efficient variants of several different interior point algorithms, namely the primal affine, dual affine, primal-dual as well as power series versions. The KORBX processor is basically an Alliant FX/8 computer consisting of 8 vector processors with shared memory. The performance of the KORBX system, as benchmarked by the Military Airlift Command, is reported in Carolan, Hill, Kennington, Niemi and Wichmann(1990). The best known software package developed in an academic environment is OB1, an excellent code due to Lustig, Marsten and Shanno (1990a, 1990b, 1991a, 1991b). It consists of very efficient implementations of the primal-dual algorithm and of an improved version of the predictor-corrector method of Mehrota(1990). Most of the work required by any of the above mentioned algorithms is spent in solving linear systems of the form Mu=d, where M is a symmetric positive definite matrix of the form $M = ADA^T$. Here A is the rectangular matrix defining the linear constraints of the problem, and hence is constant at each iteration, and D is a diagonal scaling matrix that changes at each iteration. Of course the sparsity pattern of M is determined by the structure of the fix matrix A only. The most successfull method implemented so far in the solution of this linear systems is based on the Cholesky factorization of M. For increased performance on vector machines different column versions of the Cholesky factorization are used. For good practical performance it is crucial to improve the sparsity of the Cholesky factors. In OB1 this is accomplished by using permutations of the matrix M based on the multiple minimum degree heuristic of Liu, and the minimum local fill-in heuristic of Duff, Erisman and Reid. Performance is further increased by implementing the concepts of dense windows, supernodes, and loop unrolling. Efficient implementations must take into account the specifics of the architecture of the targeted machine. A very interesting discussion of this subject is given in a recent paper by Lustig, Marsten and Shanno (1991b), where very good performance of OB1 is reported on a number of machines, including the IBM RISC/6000 workstation and the CRAY Y-MP supercomputer.

A number of authors have tried to extend different interior point methods from linear programming to general convex programming. One such attempt is contained in Kortanek, Potra and Ye(1991) where the primal-dual potential reduction algorithm and the primal-dual path following algorithm are extended to linearly constrained convex programs. Both algorithms obtain a feasible primal-dual pair with duality gap less than ϵ in at most $O(\sqrt{n}|\log\epsilon|)$ iterations. At each iteration one has to approximately solve a nonlinear system. Explicit bounds for the norm of an acceptable residual are given. In Ye and Potra(1990) it is shown that for a class of entropy minimization problems one Newton step applied to the corresponding nonlinear system produces an acceptable residual. Thus only the solution of a linear system at each step is required for the implementation of the primal-dual potential reduction algorithm, the same as for LP. The resulting entropy optimization method was implemented by Han, Pardalos and Ye (1991) on an IBM 3090-600S and yielded very good results on some image reconstruction problems. The same problems were solved very recently on an Alliant FX/8 by an algorithm implemented by Potra and Shi(1991). They obtained better CPU timings than those reported by Han, Pardalos and Ye, which is quite remarkable taking into account the fact that the IBM 3090-600S is faster than the Alliant FX/8. This is explained by the fact that the primal-dual potential reduction algorithm has been modified so that it achieves a better reduction in practice of the primal-dual gap, and that as soon as the criterion described in Ye and Potra(1990) is satisfied one switches from the primal-dual algorithm to a pure Newton method that has quadratic convergence. Moreover, an efficient implementation of a conjugate gradient method is used for the solution of the corresponding linear systems. This method parallelizes very well, and by efficient use of hierarchical memories leads to superlinear speed-up in the number of processors.

References

[1] W. J. Carolan, J. E. Hill, J. L. Kennington, S. Niemi, and S. J. Wichmann. (1990). "An empirical evaluation of the KORBX algorithms for military airlift applications," *Operations Research* 38, No. 2, 240–248.

[2] C.-G. Han, P. M. Pardalos, and Y. Ye. (1991). "On interior point algorithms for entropy optimization problems," Preprint, Computer Science Department, Pennsylvania State University, University Park, PA.

[3] K. O. Kortanek, F. Potra and Y. Ye. (1991). "On some efficient interior point methods for nonlinear convex programming," *Linear Algebra and its Applications* 152, 169–189.

[4] I. J. Lustig, R. E. Marsten, and D. F. Shanno. (1990a). "On implementing Mehrotra's predictor-corrector interior point method for liner programming," Tech. Rep. SOR 90-03, Princeton University, Department of Civil Engineering and Operations Research, Princeton, NJ.

[5] I. J. Lustig, R. E. Marsten, and D. F. Shanno. (1990b). "The primal-dual interior point method on the Cray supercomputer." In T. Coleman and Y. Li, editors, Large-Scale Numerical Optimization, pp. 70–80, *SIAM*, Philadelphia.

[6] I. J. Lustig, R. E. Marsten, and D. F. Shanno. (1991). "Computational experience with a primal-dual interior point method for linear programming," *Journal of Linear Algebra and Its Applications* 152, 191–222.

[7] I. J. Lustig, R. E. Marsten, and D. F. Shanno. (1991b). "The interaction of algorithms and architectures for interior point methods." RUTCOR research report #36–91, Rutgers University, New Brunswick, New Jersey 08903-5062.

[8] S. Mehrotra. (1990). "On the implementation of a (primal-dual) interior point method," Tech. Rep. 90-03, Northwestern University, Department of Industrial Engineering and Management Sciences, Evanston, IL.

[9] F. A. Potra and Y. Shi. (1991). "An efficient interior point method for solving large scale entropy optimization problems," (in preparation).

[10] Y. Ye and F. Potra. (1990). "An interior-point algorithm for solving entropy optimization problems with globally linear and locally quadratic convergence rate." Technical report, Dept. of Management Sciences, The University of Iowa. Working Paper Series No. 90-22.

DEGREES OF CONTROLLABILITY

Peter Burgmeier
Institut für Mathematik
Technische Hochschule Köthen
Bernburger Str. 52-57 , O-4370 Köthen

Controllability is one of the central terms in control theory. Since the first researches about 30 years ago this field has developed into an independent domain with great practical importance and noteworthy versatility. But unfortunately very much several practical considerations have led to a lot of different conceptions, which in parts are contradictory and of which the linguistic multiplicity in the choice of denomination is characteristic. That's wy a new concept of definition of various controllability kinds in a uniform manner on one and the same foundation, applicable to lumped as well as to distributed parameter systems, was developed. It is completely described in detail in [1]. The common unitary base of these definitions are the so-called controllability sets (CS). But not only from this arises a great interest in qualitative and especially quantitative reflections about these ranges. Unfortunately, its exact computation is complicated and linked up to difficulties even for linear lumped parameter systems. Therefore approximations of these ranges are inevitable. One of it is the concept of degree of controllability as a simple measure of the size of the set of initial states that can be steered to the zero-state in a prescribed time which recently was developed and successfully used about 1980 to study qualitative properties of concrete control systems associated with large flexible spacecraft (see [2]). This concept will be explained in an essential comprehensive sense for linear lumped parameter systems and overmore, it will be transferred to a linear distributed parameter system.

LUMPED PARAMETER SYSTEMS

Consider

$$\dot{x}(t) = A(t)x(t) + f(t,u(t)) , \quad t \geq t_0, \tag{1}$$

where the state $x:[t_0,\infty[\to\mathbf{R}^n$, $A:[t_0,\infty[\to\mathbf{R}^{n,n}$ is piecewise continuous, $f:[t_0,\infty[*W\to\mathbf{R}^n$ is piecewise continuous in its first argument and continuous in its second, the control $u:[t_0,\infty[\to W$ is measurable with values in the control set $W\subset\mathbf{R}^r$ which is nonempty and compact. The set of all such admissible controls will be denoted by U, whereas

$$x(t) = x(t;t_0,x^0,u) , \quad t \geq t_0,$$

will denote the unique solution of (1) under a given initial condition $x(t_0) = x^0\in\mathbf{R}^n$ and an admissible control $u\in U$.

For a given nonempty set $X\subset\mathbf{R}^n$ of final states we define the X-controllability set (X-CS) of system (1) at time t_1 by

$$S(t_0,t_1,U,X) := \{x^0\in\mathbf{R}^n: \bigvee_{u\in U} x(t_1;t_0,x^0,u)\in X\}.$$

As simple measures of the size of the X-CS at time t_1 with respect to a given point $y\in\mathbf{R}^n$ we introduce two degrees.

Definition:

$$p_y(t_0,t_1,U,X) := \inf \{\|x-y\|: x\in\mathbf{R}^n\backslash S(t_0,t_1,U,X)\}$$

and

$$P_y(t_0,t_1,U,X) := \sup \{\|x-y\|: x\in S(t_0,t_1,U,X)\}$$

are called degree of X-controllability and degree of X-uncontrollability respectively with respect to y of system (1) at time t_1 by given t_0 and U, where $\|.\|$ denotes the Euclidian norm in $\mathbf{R}^n$.

For these degrees the following theorems are true:

Theorem 1: If X is closed and convex, then

$$p_y(t_0,t_1,U,X) = \max \{\hat{p}_y,0\} ,$$

where

$$\hat{p}_y := \min_{\|z^0\|=1} \left(z^{0T} y + \int_{t_0}^{t_1} \max_{w\in W} z^T(t)f(t,w)dt - \inf_{x^1\in X} z^T(t_1)x^1\right)$$

and z is the solution of the adjoint system

$$\dot{z}(t) = -A^T(t)z(t)\ ,\quad t\varepsilon[t_0,t_1],\qquad z(t_0) = z^0$$

($.^T$ denotes the transposition). ∎

Theorem 2:

$$\hat{p}_y < 0 \implies \{x\varepsilon\mathbf{R}^n:\ \|x-y\|<-\hat{p}_y\}\cap S(t_0,t_1,U,X) = \emptyset\ .$$ ∎

Theorem 3:

$$P_y(t_0,t_1,U,X) = \max_{\|z^0\|=1}\ (z^{0^T}y + \int_{t_0}^{t_1}\max_{w\varepsilon W} z^T(t)f(t,w)dt - \inf_{x^1\varepsilon X} z^T(t_1)x^1).$$ ∎

GOURSAT SYSTEMS

Consider the system of hyperbolic differential equations

$$\frac{\partial^2 Q(x)}{\partial x_1\partial x_2} + A_1(x)\frac{\partial Q(x)}{\partial x_1} + A_2(x)\frac{\partial Q(x)}{\partial x_2} + A(x)Q(x) = f(x,u(x)) \qquad (2)$$

for almost all $x=(x_1,x_2)\varepsilon]0,c_1[*]0,c_2[=:D\subset\mathbf{R}^2$,

$Q(x_1,0) = g_1(x_1),\ x_1\varepsilon]0,c_1[,\quad Q(0,x_2) = g_2(x_2),\ x_2\varepsilon]0,c_2[,$

with $A_1,\ \frac{\partial A_1}{\partial x_1},\ A_2,\ \frac{\partial A_2}{\partial x_2},\ A\varepsilon C(D,\mathbf{R}^{n,n}),\ u\varepsilon\mathbf{L}^p(D,W),\ p\varepsilon[1,\infty],\ W\neq\emptyset,$

$W\subset\mathbf{R}^r$, compact, $f:D*W\to\mathbf{R}^n$ is piecewise continuous in its first argument and continuous in its second, $g:=(g_1,g_2)\varepsilon\hat{\mathbf{W}}_0^{1,p}(D,\mathbf{R}^{n,2})$

$:= \{(g_1,g_2):\ g_i\varepsilon\mathbf{W}^{1,p}(]0,c_i[,\mathbf{R}^n),\ i=1,2,\ g_1(0)=g_2(0)\}.$

Under these assumptions (2) has a unique solution $Q\varepsilon\mathbf{W}_*^{2,p}(D,\mathbf{R}^n)$ which for each $X\varepsilon D$ can be given in the form

$$\begin{aligned}Q(X;g,u)=R(0,0;X)g_1(0) &+ \int_0^{X_1}R(x_1,0;X)[g_1'(x_1)+A_2(x_1,0)g_1(x_1)]dx_1+\\ &+\int_0^{X_2}R(0,x_2;X)[g_2'(x_2)+A_1(0,x_2)g_2(x_2)]dx_2 +\\ &+\int_0^{X_1}\int_0^{X_2}R(x_1,x_2;X)f(x_1,x_2,u(x_1,x_2))dx_2dx_1 =\end{aligned}$$

$$= q(X;g) + \int_0^X R(x;X)f(x,u(x))dx.$$

Here the RIEMANN function R is the unique solution of a corresponding adjoint problem and $\mathbf{W}_*^{2,p}$ denotes the BANACH space of functions f with two variables which together with their generalized derivatives f_{x_1}, f_{x_2}, $f_{x_1 x_2}$ belong to $\mathbf{L}^p$.

For a given nonempty set $Z \subseteq \mathbf{R}^n$ of "final states" we define the Z-controllability set (Z-CS) of system (2) at X by

$$S(X,U,Z) := \{g \varepsilon \hat{\mathbf{W}}_0^{1,p}: \bigvee_{u \varepsilon U} Q(X;g,u) \varepsilon Z\}$$

and its image $q(X;S) := \{q(X;g): g \varepsilon S = S(X,U,Z)\}$ with the linear continuous operator q(X). This subset of $\mathbf{R}^n$ can be approximated from the inside and the outside by corresponding degrees on analogous manner like in the above described lumped parameter case. And knowing the set q(X;S) or its approximation one can compute for given classes of initial functions the Z-CS of system (2) and its estimation respectively. Sometimes this is very easy.

[1] P. Burgmeier: Ein Beitrag zur Steuerbarkeit dynamischer Systeme, Diss. B, Halle, 1990.

[2] C. N. Viswanathan, R. M. Longman and P. W. Likins: A definition of the degree of controllability - A criterion for actuator placement, Proc. 2nd VPI&SU/AIAA Symp. of Dynamics and Control of Large Flexible Spacecraft, June 1979.

[3] P. Burgmeier: About controllability and controllability sets of higher order GOURSAT systems, optimization (to appear)

ON MODELING AND STABILIZATION OF FLEXIBLE BEAMS

Alexander V. Gnedin*
Institute of Control Sciences
Profsoyuznaya 65, 117342 Moscow, USSR

Suppression of vibrations in mechanical structures by the use of point dampers has received recently a considerable attention in the context of the Euler-Bernoulli beam equation [1,2,3,4,5]. In [1], a system of serially connected collinear beams with actuators and sensors co-located at joints was considered. It was proved that for a linear feedback scheme with control of shear and bending moment exponential stability can be achieved by a single stabilizer located at the free end point. In [2] it was proved that exponential stability holds for one cantilever beam with control solely of the bending moment at a free end.

In this report, we consider a system of serially connected non-collinear beams with controlled angles between them. One end of the structure is clamped under variable angle and another end is free. The free end and the joints between the links are loaded by concentrated masses. We derive a system of Euler-Bernoulli equations with specific boundary and in-span conditions to describe linear vibrations of the structure near a given nominal configuration and propose a linear feedback control scheme to damp the elastic energy of vibrations and to keep the beam close to the nominal configuration.

Consider the system of n flexible beams of unit length deflected from a given nominal, rigid-body, configuration. The nominal configuration is specified inambiguously by the nominal angles $\alpha_1,\dots,\alpha_n$ which can be different from the actual angles $\gamma_1,\dots,\gamma_n$ between the links. We regard the angular velocities $\dot\gamma_1,\dots,\dot\gamma_n$ as the control variables needed to stabilize the structure.

In the framework of the Euler-Bernoulli theory, the deflection of the i-th link is representable as a superposition of the transversal deflection from the corresponding segment of the nominal configuration, $w_i(x,t)$, and the longitudinal deflection, $z_i(t)$, $0 < x < 1$, $t \geq 0$. The transversal deflections satisfy the Euler-Bernoulli equations

$$m_i w_i''''(x,t) + EI\, \ddot{w}_i(x,t) = 0, \quad i= 1,\ldots n$$

(m_i is the mass density and EI is the flexural rigidity). This system is accomplished by the following boundary and in-span conditions derived by the Hamilton principle and a continuity argument (here M_i is the payload in the i-th joint):

$w_1(0,t) = 0$, $\dot{w}_1'(0,t) = \gamma_1(t)$ – clamped end,

$w_n''(1,t)=0$, $-EIw_n'''(1,t) + M_n \ddot{w}_n(1,t)=0$ – free end,

$w_i''(1,t)=w_{i+1}''(0,t)$ – in-span balance of moments,

$$EI(-w_i'''(1,t)+w_{i+1}'''(0,t)\cos\alpha_{i+1}) + M_i \ddot{w}_i(1,t) +$$

$$(m_{i+1}+M_{i+1})\ddot{z}_{i+1}(t)\sin\alpha_{i+1}+$$

$$\sum_{j=1}^{n-1} ((-EIw_{j+1}'''(0,t)\sin\alpha_{j+1}+(m_{j+1}+M_{j+1})\cos\alpha_{j+1}\ddot{z}_{j+1}(t))\sin\alpha_{i+1}\times$$

$$\sin\alpha_{i+1}\prod_{l=i+1}^{j-1}\cos\alpha_{l+1}=0$$ – in-span balance of shears,

$$\left.\begin{aligned} z_{i+1}(t) &= z_i(t)\cos\alpha_{i+1} + w_i(i,t)\sin\alpha_{i+1} \\ w_{i+1}(0,t) &= -z(t)\sin\alpha_{i+1}+ w(1,t)\cos\alpha_{i+1} \end{aligned}\right\}$$ continuity of deflections

$$\dot{w}_i'(0,t) - \dot{w}_{i-1}'(1,t) = \gamma_i(t)$$ – angle controls.

Note that by the first continuity equation we can derive recursively longitudinal deflections from the joints' transversal deflections.

We accept the sum $\mathcal{E} = \sum \mathcal{E}_i$ as a stability criterion, where

$$\mathcal{E}_i= \frac{1}{2} a_i|w_i'(1,t)-w_{i-1}'(0,t)|^2 + EI\int_0^1(w_i''(x,t)^2dx + (m_i+M_i)\dot{z}_i^2$$

$$(m_i+M_i)z_i^2 + \frac{1}{2} M_i\dot{w}_i^2(1,t) + m_i\int_0^1 \dot{w}_i^2(x,t)dx.$$

The first term here reflects a rigid-body deflection from the nominal configuration, whereas other terms constitute the elastic energy of the structure.

We introduce a linear feedback control in the form

$$\gamma_i(t) = -\sum_{j=1}^{n} k_{ij}(EIw''_j(0,t) - a_j(\gamma_j(t) - \alpha_j)),$$

where $K=(k_{ij})$ is an arbitrary positive n-matrix. With this feedback, the closed-loop system is dissipative in the sense that $\dot{\mathcal{E}} \leq 0$ for any initial state. We prove that the structure is stabilizable by any non-degenerate diagonal K; in the case all poles of the system lie in a domain $\mathrm{Re}\lambda < \beta$, with $\beta < 0$.

For the one-link structure we prove a stronger result: uniform exponential stabilizability holds for a point control at the clamped end. This result is complementary to the paper [2]. We provide also a frequency analysis of the closed-loop system.

*The work is supported by the A. von Humboldt Foundation during the author's visit to Ruhr University at Bochum

REFERENCES

[1] G. Chen, M.C. Delfour, A.M. Krall and G. Payne. Modeling stabilization and control of serially connected beams, SIAM J. Control Optim., 25(1987), pp.526-546.

[2] G. Chen, S.G. Krantz, D.W. Ma, C.E. Wayne and H.H. West. The Euler-Bernoulli beam equation with boundary energy dissipation, in: Operator Methods for Optimal Control Problems, Sung J. Lee, ed., Marcel Dekker, New York, 1988.

[3] G.Chen,S.G.Krantz, D.L.Russel, C.E.Wayne, H.H.West and M.P.Coleman. Analysis, designs and behavior of dissipative joints for coupled beams, SIAM J.Appl.Math., 49(1989), pp. 1665-1693.

[4] F.Conrad, Stabilization of beams by pointwise feedback control, SIAM J. Control Optim. 28(1990), pp. 423-437.

[5] S.G.Krantz and W.H. Paulsen. Asymptotic eigenfrequency distributions for the N-beam Euler-Bernoulli coupled beam with dissipative joints, preprint.

STABILIZATION OF A CLASS OF DISCRETE-TIME LINEAR UNCERTAIN SYSTEMS

Éva Gyurkovics
Department of Mathematics, Faculty of Mechanical Engineering,
University of Technology Budapest
Műegyetem rkp. 3, 1521 Budapest

Recently, much effort has been devoted to the problem of stabilizing discrete-time uncertain systems, see [1-6]. To obtain a stabilizing controller for such systems, the so-called matching condition is assumed to be valid. In [5] this notion was expanded introducing the "ℓth-step matching condition".

This work is concerned with the stabilization of discrete-time uncertain systems which are described by linear difference equations containing delayed controls. A weakened form of the matching condition is introduced and two types of control strategies are proposed. All of them renders the system to be asymptotically stable about a set containing the origin.

Consider an uncertain discrete-time system described by a difference equation of the form

$$\begin{aligned} x(k+1) &= [A + \Delta A(r(k))]\, x(k) + [B + \Delta B(r(k))]\, u(k) \\ &\quad [C + \Delta C(r(k))]\, u(k-1) + w(r(k)), \qquad k \in \mathbf{Z}, \end{aligned} \tag{1}$$

where $x(k) \in \mathbf{R}^n$ is the state, $u(k) \in \mathbf{R}^m$ is the control, $w(k) \in \mathbf{R}^n$ is the disturbance and $r(.) : \mathbf{Z} \to \mathcal{R} \in \mathbf{R}^p$ is the uncertainty. The coefficients are matrices of appropriate size and A is assumed to be invertible. The uncertainty bounding set $\mathcal{R}$ is compact and $\Delta A(.)$, $\Delta B(.)$, $\Delta C(.)$ and $w(.)$ depend continuously on the components of r. By introducing the new state variable $z(k) = (x(k)^T, u(k-1)^T)^T$, equation (1) takes the form

$$z(k+1) = [\mathcal{A} + \Delta\mathcal{A}(r(k))]\, z(k) + [\mathcal{B} + \Delta\mathcal{B}(r(k))]\, u(k) + \mathcal{H}\, w(r(k)), \tag{2}$$

where

$$\mathcal{A} = \begin{pmatrix} A & C \\ 0 & 0 \end{pmatrix}, \ \Delta\mathcal{A}(r) = \begin{pmatrix} \Delta A(r) & \Delta C(r) \\ 0 & 0 \end{pmatrix},$$

$$\mathcal{B} = \begin{pmatrix} B \\ I \end{pmatrix}, \ \Delta\mathcal{B}(r) = \begin{pmatrix} \Delta B(r) \\ 0 \end{pmatrix}, \ \mathcal{H} = \begin{pmatrix} I \\ 0 \end{pmatrix}.$$

For system (2), a feedback control $u(k) = p(z(k))$ should be determined, which yields the system

$$z(k+1) = \mathcal{A}z(k) + \mathcal{B}p(z(k)) + \mathcal{E}(z(k), p(z(k)), k) \tag{3}$$

where

$$\mathcal{E}(z, p(z), k) = \Delta\mathcal{A}(r(k))\, z + \Delta\mathcal{B}(r(k))\, p(z) + \mathcal{H}\, w(r(k)).$$

If system (2) satisfies appropriate matching condition, the methods proposed in [1-6] could be used to find the function p(.). However, for system (2), neither the usual, nor the ℓth-step matching condition is fulfilled.

In the sequel we utilise the following assumptions.

Assumption A1. The pair $(\mathcal{A}, \mathcal{B})$ is controllable.

Assumption A2. (Modified matching condition.) There are mappings D(.), E(.), F(.) and v(.) such that

$$\Delta A(r) = (B + A^{-1}C)D(r),\ \Delta B(r) = (B + A^{-1}C)E(r),$$

$$\Delta C(r) = (B + A^{-1}C)F(r),\ w(r) = (B + A^{-1}C)v(r).$$

Assumption A3. $B_1 := AB + C$ has full column rank.

Assumption A4. $|\lambda(A)| < 1$, i. e. the nominal free system is asymptotically stable.

Under the Assumption A4, for each $Q_1 = Q_1^T > 0$, the discrete-time Lyapunov equation

$$A^T P_1 A - P_1 = -Q_1$$

has a unique symmetric positive definite solution P_1. Let $S = B_1^T P_1 B_1$. Because of Assumption A2, S is positive definite.

Assumption A5.

$$0 \leq \rho_2 := \max_{r \in \mathcal{R}} \| E(r) \|_S < 1$$

Let $\rho_1 = \max_{r \in \mathcal{R}} \| (D(r)\ F(r)) \|$, $\rho_0 = \max_{r \in \mathcal{R}} \| v(r) \|$, $b_1 = \lambda_{max}^{1/2}(S)\rho_1/(1-\rho_2)$, $b_2 = \lambda_{max}^{1/2}(S)\rho_0/(1-\rho_2)$. Introduce the following functions:

$$\mu : \mathbf{R}^{n+m} \to \mathbf{R}^m,\ \mu(z) = B_1^T P_1(A^2\ AC)z, \quad \gamma : \mathbf{R}^{n+m} \to \mathbf{R},\ \gamma(z) = b_1 \| z \| + b_2.$$

Using these notations we can propose the following controllers.

Type I-1.

$$u(k) = p_1^I(z(k)) = \begin{cases} -\gamma(z(k))S^{-1}\mu(z(k))/ \| \mu(z(k)) \|_{S^{-1}} & \text{if } \mu(z(k)) \neq 0, \\ 0 & \text{if } \mu(z(k)) = 0. \end{cases}$$

Type I-2.

$$u(k) = p_2^I(z(k)) = \begin{cases} -\gamma(z(k))S^{-1}\mu(z(k))/ \| \mu(z(k)) \|_{S^{-1}} & \text{if } \| \mu(z(k)) \|_{S^{-1}} > \epsilon, \\ -\gamma(z(k))S^{-1}\mu(z(k))/\epsilon & \text{if } \| \mu(z(k)) \|_{S^{-1}} \leq \epsilon, \end{cases}$$

where $\epsilon > 0$ is arbitrary but fixed.

Remark. A controller, analogous to Type I-1 was proposed in [6] for the case of matched uncertainty independent of the input. This controller is however discontinuous. For practical considerations, it is desirable to modify it so that the "new" controller should be continuous and preserving the asymptotic stability of the closed-loop system about some set. This requirement is fulfilled by the control of Type I-2.

Lemma 1. Suppose that system (2) satisfies Assumptions A1-A5. Let

$$\mathcal{P}_1 = \begin{pmatrix} A^T P_1 A & A^T P_1 C \\ C^T P_1 A & C^T P_1 C + S \end{pmatrix}, \quad \mathcal{Q}_1 = \begin{pmatrix} A^T Q_1 A & A^T Q_1 C \\ C^T Q_1 A & C^T Q_1 C + S \end{pmatrix}$$

Then $V(z) = z^T \mathcal{P}_1 z$ is a Lyapunov function for the closed-loop system (3) and the Lyapunov forward difference satisfies the inequality

$$\Delta V(z(k), p_i^I(z(k)), k) \leq$$

$$\leq \begin{cases} -z^T(k)\mathcal{Q}_1 z(k) + \gamma^2(z(k)) & \text{if } \mu(z(k)) = 0 \text{ and } i = 1, \\ -z^T(k)\mathcal{Q}_1 z(k) + 2\gamma(z(k))\epsilon + 3\gamma^2(z(k)) & \text{if } \| \mu(z(k)) \|_{S^{-1}} \leq \epsilon, \\ & \gamma(z(k)) < \epsilon \text{ and } i = 2. \\ -z^T(k)\mathcal{Q}_1 z(k) + 5\gamma^2(z(k)) & \text{else.} \end{cases}$$

Theorem 1. Suppose that system (2) satisfies Assumptions A1-A4. If

$$b_1 < \sqrt{\lambda_{min}(\mathcal{P}_1)/5},$$

then system (3) is globally uniformly asymptotically stable about the set

$$\mathbf{B}(d_i) = \{z \in \mathbf{R}^{n+m} : z^T \mathcal{P}_1 z \leq d_i^2\},$$

where d_i $(i = 1, 2)$ is constant.

(The detailed expression of d_i is omitted here for brevity)

In the following we omit the Assumptions A3-A5.

In order to define a new controller let Q and R be symmetric positive definite matrices. Consider the algebraic Riccati equation

$$A^T P A - P - A^T P B_1 (R + B_1^T P B_1)^{-1} B_1^T P A = -Q. \tag{4}$$

It can be proven that under the Assumption A1, equation (4) has a unique positive definite solution P. We now propose the following controller.

Type II.

$$u(k) = p^{II}(z(k)) = -Kz(k), \quad \text{where } K = (R + B_1^T P B_1)^{-1} B_1^T P (A^2\ AC) z(k).$$

Remark. A controller, similar to Type II was proposed in [1] and investigated in [4].

Lemma 2. Suppose that system (2) satisfies Assumptions A1,A2, and let $P = P^T > 0$ be the solution of (4) with $R = R^T > 0$, and $Q = Q^T > 0$. Let

$$\mathcal{P} = \begin{pmatrix} A^T PA & A^T PC \\ C^T PA & C^T PC + R \end{pmatrix}, \quad \mathcal{Q} = \begin{pmatrix} A^T QA & A^T QC \\ C^T QA & C^T QC + R \end{pmatrix},$$

Then $V(z) = z^T \mathcal{P} z$ serves as a Lyapunov function for the closed-loop system (3), and the Lyapunov forward difference satisfies the inequality

$$\Delta V(z, p(z), k) \leq -\mu_1 \parallel z(k) \parallel^2 + \mu_2 \parallel z(k) \parallel + \mu_3,$$

where

$$\mu_1 = \lambda_{min}(\mathcal{Q}) - \lambda_{max}(B_1^T P B_1) a_1^2 - 2 \parallel RK \parallel a_1,$$

$$\mu_2 = 2(\parallel RK \parallel a_2 + \lambda_{max}(B_1^T P B_1) a_1 a_2), \quad \mu_3 = \lambda_{max}(B_1^T P B_1) a_2^2,$$

$$a_1 = \max_{r \in \mathcal{R}} (\parallel \begin{pmatrix} D(r) & F(r) \end{pmatrix} \parallel + \parallel K \parallel \parallel E(r) \parallel),$$

$$a_2 = \max_{r \in \mathcal{R}} \parallel v(r) \parallel,$$

Theorem 2. Suppose that system (2) satisfies Assumptions A1,A3. If $\mu_1 > 0$, then system (3) is globally uniformly asymptotically stable about the set

$$\mathbf{B}(d) = \{z \in \mathbf{R}^{n+m} : z^T \mathcal{P} z \leq d^2\},$$

where

$$d = \frac{\mu_2 \lambda_{max}(\mathcal{P}) + (\mu_2^2 \lambda_{max}^2(\mathcal{P}) + 4\mu_1 \mu_3 \lambda_{max}(\mathcal{P}) \lambda_{min}(\mathcal{P}))^{1/2}}{2\mu_1 \lambda_{min}^{1/2}(\mathcal{P})}.$$

References.

1. A. A. Bahnasawi, A. S. Al-Fuhaid, M. S. Mahmoud, IEE Proceedings, Vol. 136. Pt. D, No.1. 1989. pp. 47-52.

2. M. Corless, Proc. IFAC Workshop on Model Error Concepts and Compensation, Boston, 1985.

3. M. Corless, J. Manela, Proc. American Control Conference, Seattle, WA. 1986. pp. 515-520.

4. E. Gyurkovics, IEE Proceedings, Pt. D. to appear.

5. C. V. Hollot, M. Arabacioglu, Proc. American Control Conference, Minneapolis, MN. 1987. pp. 496-501.

6. M. E. Magaña, S. H. Żak, IEEE Trans. Aut. Control, vol 33. No. 9. 1988. pp. 887-891.

DYNAMICS OF POLLUTION, DEFINED BY FLUID MODELING

Marko Jurgele
Hydrometeorological Institute of Republic Slovenija
Vojkova 1b, YU-61000 Ljubljana

Nature changes and, unfortunately, it is also changed by thoughtless human interventions. And though we try to master the numerous consequences of pollution, ecologists are especially worried because of the consequences of **acid rain, greenhouse effect, of radioactive pollution and of the pollution of the sea and of drinking water sources.**

People are gradually becoming aware of their responsibility for nature and environment. They are increasingly interested in how long they can continue living in this vulnerable environment at the present rate of development. They would like to know whether an extended analysis of the present situation can result in forecasting the future development. The negative opinions that there is no correspondence between the models and the real life and that an extended analysis of weather conditions is of no use are not acceptable any more.

KINDS OF SYSTEMS AND MODELS

Environment can be treated as a global system with a nucleus and several shells. One of the shells is the ecological system with its own subshells. The systems can be divided into two groups. The first one are **deterministic** *systems based on causality, where on the basis of knowing the states of the system at a defined moment and the inner laws governing it, one can unambiguously determine the future state of the system. If on the basis of knowing the states of the system at the present moment and its inner laws it is only possible to establish a probability that the system will turn into one of a number of possible states, such a system is* **stochastic.** *The systems in nature are somewhere in the middle between these two extremes. They are neither deterministic nor chaotic. Their future states can be predicted with a greater or smaller degree of probability.*

Air pollution is governed by certain laws as well. They can be discovered to a moderate extent by the classical statistical analysis of time series or, more successfully, by the new modeling method, which belongs to experimental approaches and uses system theory and control theory. These operative models are based on a different philosophy altogether and supplement the present quantitative methodology of law determination.

Since the new experimental modeling approach pursues historical constituents, all relevant constituents of the model must have their corresponding history reviewed and filtered. This brings important dynamics into the model which we want to make as realistic as possible. Thus the model cannot be designed once and for all, it is fluid by continuously changing its structure, constraints, criteria and goals. The **fluid** *model itself adjusts to the system which has to be modeled because its structure depends upon the given data. Every system has a fluid model of its own, the same system has different models under different weather conditions.*

The approach is predictive since all processes are able to be predicted on the basis of the historical constituent. Our interest is focused on spaces rather than elements. A set of goals is to be based on a set of criteria. We are concerned with generalized criteria which bring an additional flexibility to the model. The extent to which this flexibility could be reached depends on how successful we are in assuring the dynamics of criteria to enter the model. An essential feature of fluid modeling is the seeking of relationships between criteria and goals. The assumption that a set of goals is based on a set of criteria excludes all such goals which are not harmonized with the criteria. Thereby the level of the reality (controllability) of the model is increased. The nucleus of the model depends on the input as well as on the output. A goal is not acceptable if there is not at least one criterion capable of expressing the given goal.

The fluid model must adjust to the changing of the system. This property relates to all constituents of the model, at least in principle. Hence the adaptivity of modeling is included into the definition of fluid modeling. The fluid modeling must be capable of forming a sequence of models.

To fluid modeling some special features are added. The functional model must be dynamized and turned into a control-oriented model. This operation enables us to return to non-control models as soon as we abandon the freedom of variation of some (control) variables. A common feature of the approach is the optimum of the goal function at every moment and the multi-criteria orientation. The control-oriented model complies with the special conditions for multiple criteria and multiple goals.

We do not have any advance data on the structure of the ecological system. Therefore the main question is the **structural identification.** *It is determined by the mathematical and statistical analysis of the time series of real measured data. The only adopted hypothesis is that the system can be described by an appropriate connection of systems containing linear algebraic and linear differential equations. First we must find those time series (*nucleus*), with the aid of which all other time series can be expressed by means of simple linear algebraic relations. In the next phase the determined nucleus is expressed by a linear differential model. The structure of the model is not uniform and depends on the criterion by which the vectors of the nucleus are chosen.*

*The picture of the dynamics of the phenomena is achieved by time series, which are a series of data of the same kind and are connected to successive time intervals or moments. Since the changes of a phenomenon are essentially time-dependent, the intervals between the single elements are necessarily equal. The time series is the numerical expression of time action of all factors influencing the phenomenon. These factors are numerous and their intensity and effect keep changing. The changes due to each factor cannot be brought out of the time series, yet the common effect of the factors can be gathered. The importance of the time series is based on the description of its structure (*__model__*), which is determined by observing only one variable (*__one-dimensional model__*) or several variables (*__multi-dimensional model__*). If only one-dimensional models are considered, the research cannot be expected to give reliable predictions for a longer period of time. The errors will be especially great in the case of variables affecting the observed time series in a different way from the one in the past.*

THE MODEL AND ITS NUCLEUS

The ecological system is dynamic by nature. In discrete dynamic systems the state of the system is expressed by the values of **n** *variables of the system at discrete time moments. The data base is represented by the set of* **n** *vectors in* **K***-dimensional vector space. The tone of the dynamic behavior of the ecological system is set by a group of characteristic variables, which are united in the nucleus by means of dynamic relations. In the nucleus all essential information on the dynamics of the ecological system is gathered. The variables outside the nucleus are derivations of the variables within the nucleus.*

How is the nucleus of the model to be established? If a vector is removed from a system of vectors, we get a new system of vectors and thereby any vector of the vector space can be linearly expressed. Since these vectors again represent a system of linearly dependent vectors, again at least one of them can be expressed as a linear combination of all the others. Thus we keep removing the vectors until we get a system of linearly independent vectors. The subset of these vectors is called the base.

We look for an appropriate criterion of seeking the base. The possible criteria are the smallest correlation and the smallest scalar product. By linear regression it is confirmed that the variables outside the base are sufficiently expressed as linear combinations of the variables of the base. The establishing of the variables of the base strongly depends on the choice of the first variable and on the length of the time series.

THE DETERMINATION OF THE NUCLEUS

The manner of determining the nucleus requires linear independence of input and output time series, thus the time series in the nucleus must be linearly independent. The chosen nucleus depends on the elected method, on the choice of the manner and criterion for determing the base and on the choice of the starting variables at seeking the base. Since the number of time series is comparatively greater than their length, the problem of non-uniformity of the nucleus is mathematically conditioned. Hence a great number of models can be obtained from the same base. And which model is the right one? As all established models are of equal value, it depends on the goal which form of the model and which time series in the nucleus is elected.

THE MODELING OF THE BASE

The basic task of pure experimental modeling is the determination of system inputs and outputs. On the basis of the course of the input and output variables, the contents of the system is established and we try to determine such a structure and such parameters of the model to give the most appropriate output in view of the given input. In these models we are not interested in the internal mechanism that has given rise to these relations but only in the input/output relations. These models with blurred functional connection within the system are simple, low-graded and also consider the surroundings of the system.

The system that contains several output variables, which are not mutually independent but connected by internal or external connections, is a multi-variable *system. In this case we also need information on the structure of the system, which cannot be established just on the basis of external behavior. The chosen model will react to the same input signals in the same way as the original model. This model is not the only one but just one of the set performing the same mapping with a completely different inner structure.*

It is characteristic of the model structure that it consists of a dynamic *part determined by the nucleus and of a* static *part. The behavior of the dynamic part is determined by a system of linear differential equations in the space of the states and by an appropriate mapping. The second part represents a static mapping between the variables of the nucleus and the variables outside the nucleus. Here the output time series that do not belong to the nucleus of the model are represented by a linear combination of the time series of the nucleus. The output variables of the nucleus are met by the time series established by computing the dynamic model of the nucleus. Numerical methods are used for establishing structural and parametric identifications of multi-variable systems. At the numerical method we are faced with the problem of solving the systems of linear equations and with the problem of unstability.*

DYNAMICS OF POLLUTION

The models for forecasting the concentrations of air pollution can be divided into two groups: the models based on physical laws and the models based on the bases of measured data. Successful predictions are obtained by using models based on linear regression and filtration technique (Kalman's or Box-Jenkis' algorithm). The best results are achieved at stationary time series when the regime does not change. However, models based on real data bases are more appropriate for the drawing up of a final hybrid model that should be an optimal, control-oriented fluid model and should encompass the ecological, economic and sociological aspects.

For determining the dynamics of pollution in Slovenija from October to April, two nuclei have to be determined, one for the city area of the capital Ljubljana and another for the broader area of Slovenija. One or more time series can remain in the nucleus.[1] *High correlation factors prove that the courses of the time series are very similar. In the nucleus of the city area only one of seven time series remained and the same was true of the broader area. Subsequently, the relation between the time series in the nucleus and the others was established by the linear regression model. To prepare a forecast, the representative(s) remaining in the nucleus was (were) modeled. Since by means of the representative(s) of the nucleus the whole system could be described, it was not necessary to model all time series of the system. This fact has proven to be exceptionally important and useful.*

At the process of seeking nuclei for the broader area of Slovenija and for the city area of Ljubljana, only one time series remained in the nucleus in either case. Could this finding be confirmed in another manner? In winter inversion takes place in Slovenija, which is not limited only to basins but reaches rather high. Only lowland measuring points took part in determining the nuclei and hence the inversion occurred at all measuring points at approximately the same time. The whole lowland area of Slovenija is a basin where all the processes take place. Due to the closeness of the area and the inversion, the course of all time series tallies. At a greater number of input time series more representatives could remain in the nucleus, yet they would not be very numerous in view of what has been said above. The basic finding of only one time series remaining in the nucleus of either area could be objected to. The objection could be based on the quick changes of the weather, which are not equal and simultaneous in all points of the observed area. However, the analysis was made upon ten-day average values of 24-hour measurements of single pollutants, thereby blurring any rapid changes, whereas the inversion in the winter months is quite stationary, which rather neutralizes the objections. The technique of fluid modeling can also be used for the time-series of the on-line automatic measuring net, which has a greater number of parameters and a half-hourly measuring interval. Since the value and the behavior of single parameters differ, a multidimensional model must be used. The establishing of the nuclei is of important practical value. As soon as the representatives of the system have been found, the number of the measuring points can be considerably reduced, which markedly decreases the cost of the measuring net. This is also true of any other measuring net that fulfills the basic conditions. In addition to the macro models, there are also useful the mezzo models for smaller areas or for the vicinity of emission sources. The mezzo model must cover all local peculiarities and the behavior of the parameters. They should conform to the local laws. For the mezzo models only the data of the automatic net can be used.

FUNCTIONAL, OPTIMAL, CONTROL-ORIENTED FLUID MODEL

Is it possible to make such a move in the present that the output of the ecological system will have a desired value in the future? The answer is yes. The final goal is a **functional, optimal, conttrol-oriented fluid model.** *This goal is reached by several steps.*

----

1. There has been used the PC-AT package Statistical Forecasting System (SFS) Ver. 1.0, developed in MIPOS, Ljubljana, Yugoslavia.

The dynamics of the system is affected by mutual connections of the states in different time periods, by accidental forces, by variables that cannot be influenced as well as by variables that can be influenced. When there are known the dynamic properties of the model for the variables that cannot be influenced, we control the variables that can be influenced in order to achieve the dynamic property of the model. The weather is a variable that cannot be influenced. Yet the weather conditions can be described by parameters. By the use of more recent global weather models, a greater amount of data and faster computers, the parametric description will become more accurate. At controlling, attention is paid to the stability of the system, to the reaction of the system to the variables that can be influenced, and to the capability of the system to repeat the elected output. In addition to the problem of the optimal control, there are also present the determination and evaluation of the parameters of the model and the seeking of the nucleus depending on the optimal output.

The final model is reached by two steps. The first step leads to the functional fluid model, where first the linear and then the general non-linear model are optimized. The output is optimized by the aid of the states of the system, the variables that can be influenced being disregarded. The second step leads to the control-oriented fluid model, where first the linear version and then the general model are optimized. The output is optimized by means of the variables that can be influenced.

REFERENCES

V. Rupnik: SOME EXPERIENCES WITH FLUID MODELING OF ECONOMIC SYSTEM; System Research (1985) Vol. 2. No. 3 page 211-219

S. A. Mićković: ON THE CLUSTERING METHOD BASED ON DISSIMILARITY MEASURE SPECIFIC FOR TIME SERIES; Research report, Jožef Stefan Institute (1989)

Đ. Juričić: A BLACK BOX APPROACH TO THE MODELING OF MACRO-ECONOMIC SYSTEM; Research report, Jožef Stefan Institute (1985)

S. A. Mićković, V. Rupnik: THE BUILDING OF A FUNCTIONAL, OPTIMAL, CONTROL-ORIENTED FLUID MODEL; Article

OPTIMAL ABATEMENT POLICIES WITHIN A STOCHASTIC DYNAMIC MODEL OF THE FIRM

Peter M. Kort
Economics Department
Tilburg University
P.O. Box 90153,
NL-5000 LE Tilburg

Nowadays, the improvement of environmental quality has become one of the most important objectives in the industrialized world. From an economic point of view one could argue that a non-polluted environment has become a scarce commodity. Consequently, environmental use is an allocation problem (Siebert (1987)) and should be taken into consideration by economic theory. This seems to be the reason that more and more books are devoted to environmental economics (e.g. Baumol and Oates (1988), Wicke (1982)).
An important question in this respect is what kind of policy instruments the government, in its role as social planner, should choose to reduce the level of pollution. One class of instruments includes direct controls by setting limits to the amount of effluent that the factories can discharge into a stream (Beavis and Dobbs (1986)). Another mechanism for the attainment of a given environmental target is the standard-price-approach (Baumol and Oates (1971)). The basic idea of this concept is to meet a given quantity of emissions by rationing the demand for emission permits by prices. The influence of an emissions tax on the economic behavior of government and firm is studied within a macroeconomic differential game framework by Gradus and Kort (1991). In Kort, Van Loon and Luptacik (1991) a deterministic dynamic model of the firm is developed to analyze the optimal reaction of the firm when the government imposes an emissions tax rate and offers a grant on investments in cleaner technologies and abatement activities.

In this paper we extend the work of Kort, Van Loon and Luptacik (1991) by introducing uncertainty into the analysis. To do so we extended a stochastic dynamic model of the firm developed by Bensoussan and Lesourne (1980) by incorporating activity analysis (cf. Van Loon (1983)). We considered two activities: the first one is productive but also causes pollution that is taxed by the government. The second one is non-productive but abates pollution so that tax payments are reduced.

It turned out that investments in the abatement activity can be optimal when the following conditions are satisfied:

- the reduction in emissions tax due to an additional abatement investment of one dollar has to be greater than the shareholders' time preference rate;
- the liquidity position of the firm has to be strong;
- the expected marginal earnings of productive investment must be lower than the reduction in emissions tax due to an additional abatement investment of one dollar.

References

Baumol, W.G., and Oates, W.E. (1971), "The use of standards and prices for protection of the environment", *Swedish Journal of Economics* 73, 42-54.

Baumol, W.G., and Oates, W.E. (1988), *The Theory of Environmental Policy*, second edition, Prentice Hall, Englewood Cliffs.

Beavis, B., and Dobbs, I.M. (1986), "The dynamics of optimal environmental regulation", *Journal of Economic Dynamics and Control* 10, 415-425.

Bensoussan, A., and Lesourne, J. (1980), "Optimal growth of a self-financing firm in an uncertain environment", in: A. Bensoussan et al. (eds.), *Applied Stochastic Control in Econometrics and Management Science*, North-Holland, Amsterdam, 235-269.

Gradus, R.H.J.M., and Kort, P.M. (1991), "Optimal taxation on profit and pollution within a macroeconomic framework", Research Memorandum FEW 484, Tilburg University, Tilburg, the Netherlands.

Kort, P.M., Loon, P.J.J.M. van, and Luptacik, M. (1991), "Optimal dynamic environmental policies of a profit maximizing firm", to appear in *Journal of Economics* 54, no. 3.

Loon, P.J.J.M. van (1983), *A Dynamic Theory of the Firm: Production, Finance and Investment*, Lecture Notes in Economics and Mathematical Systems 218, Springer, Berlin.

Siebert, H. (1987), *Economics of the Environment*, second edition, Springer, Berlin.

Wicke, L. (1982), *Umweltökonomie*, Verlag Franz Vahlen, München.

FLUID MODELLING: A STEP TOWARD MORE ADEQUATE MODELLING

S. Mićković, V. Rupnik,
MIPOS d.o.o., Reboljeva 16, YU-61000 Ljubljana

One of the main problems at modelling economic systems is changing of the structure of the system. It is especialy important for economic situation in Yugoslavia during last few years. It's characteristic is drastic changing of inner relationships as a consequence of the proposed economic reform and hyperinflation trends. This means that the structure of the existing economic system is changing (the structure between main macroeconimic sectors). When the a priori informations about model are unknown, an adaptive model is needed. Adaptability means that it is possible to: (1) change the values of parameters; (2) change the structure of the model so that it corresponds to the changes of the structure of the system under control; (3) modify goals and criterions according to the additional informations about surroundings; (4) change limitations control actions due to changes of available resources. The subject of researches in this work is the "structural adaptability" that is models with unknown input-output mapping operator.

Researches presented in this work are motivated by developing the new way of modelling which is more adequate compared with those already existing. Our concept of modelling/model:

- is adaptive mathematical representation of the observed system;

- don't pretend to force any of existing models;

- don't pretend to consider the model developed in moment t to be valid in moment $t' > t$;

- satisfy the concepts of controlability and observability.

In order to achieve this characteristics we start from the fluid modelling philosophy. Our tools are statistical clustering technique, dynamic programming and Kalman filtering. New concept of modelling/model can be considered as functional, optimal, control-oriented fluid (FOCOF) modelling/model. Till now in the literature are known only functional fluid models (Rupnik,V. (1985), Juričić, D.(1985) and Mićković, S.A. & Rupnik, V.(1989)).

We developed one of many possible "realizations" of fluid modelling: FOCOF model. The main feature of our model is that it can not be a priori designed. The model structure is derived from the data. A "fluid" model is one which adjusts itself to the system which has to be modeled. This can be achieved by introducing the ideas of a "kernel" of a model and "satellite submodels". Kernel (variables specifying "essential" dynamic behavior of the whole system which has to be modeled) and satellites (variables which don't belong to the kernel and which are conected to the kernel with regressions) can be, according to need, derived in any time moment. This means that the numbers of variables in kernel and satellites, number of satellites and relations between any two variables are not fixed over time. Parameter structure is assumed to be time function.

Introducing a kernel and an satellites the dimension of the system can be reduced without losing the great amount of informations. This is a consequence of eventually high correlations of variables. Decompozition on kernel and satellites enables to detect structural changes in model. Original approach to the derivation of kernel and satellites are given.

Controlability and observability are satisfied by solving the control problem. Adoptability of model is increased introducing a conection output - kernel. Thus, a fluid model quickly react on changes in system it describes.

Introduction of control variables can not be in automatic fashion. Use of a control variables should be based on a set of criteria and according to the nature of system under control. According to the above requirement, three different approaches about introducing the control variables are discussed. Objectivity of a fluid model is increased by solving a control problem in the case of non additive criterions. Thus, our fluid model is increased in functional, optimal, control oriented fluid (FOCOF) model.

FOCOF model is not developed only for economic systems. It can be applied to different fields as we already done in the case of air pollution system of the Kastela bay.

Results presented in this work are the beginning of the research concerning FOCOF modelling.

REFERENCES

1. V. Rupnik (1985), Some Experience with Fluid Modelling of Economic Systems, System Research Vol 2, No. 3, pp. 211–219.

2. S. A. Mićković (1989), On the Clustering Method Based on Dissimilarity Measure Specific for Time Series, IFCS–89, Virginia.

3. S. A. Mićković (1991), Izgradnja funkcionalnega, optimalnega. upravljalno orientiranega fluidnega modela, PHD, Ljubljana

4. H. Akaike (1980), On the Identification of State Space Models and their Use in Control: In. Directions in Time Series, Eds. D. R. Brillinger and G. C. Tiao, Institute of Mathematical Statistics, pp. 175–187.

5. B. D. O. Anderson and J. B. Moore (1979), Optimal Filtering Engelwood Cliffs, NJ: Prentice Hall.

6. Box – Jenkins (1970), Time Series Analysis Forecasting and Control, Holden–Day, San Francisco.

7. Sawaragi (1976), The Predictions of Air Pollution Levels by Nonphysical Models Based on Kalman Filtering Method; Jour. of Dynamic Systems. Measurement and Control 98, pp. 375–386.

Topics on Dynamics in Infinite Horizon Concave Problems

Luigi Montrucchio
University of Turin
Istituto di Matematica Finanziaria
Via Assarotti 3, 10121 Turin, Italy

Our concern in this paper is to present recent results on the dynamic behavior of the solutions to the general infinite-horizon, discrete-time, concave problem:

$$W_\delta(x_0) = \operatorname*{Sup}_{(x_t)} \sum_{t=0}^{\infty} V(x_t, x_{t+1})\delta^t \qquad \text{s.t.} \tag{P}$$

$$(x_t, x_{t+1}) \in D \quad \text{and } x_0 \text{ is given in } X \subseteq \mathbb{R}^n.$$

The main point discussed here will be the relationship between the dynamical complexity of optimal solutions to P and the discount factor δ running in *(0,1)*. Earlier results stated the fundamental role played by the discount factor. Such results can be summarized in two points which are however unsatisfactory:

i) any dynamic behavior is possible whenever the discount factor is small enough.

ii) very well-kown results (the so-called turpike theorems) assure that, under suitable conditions related to the curvature of the short-run utility V and for discount factors near *1* enough, all the optimal trajectories shrink and converge to an unique fixed point. So for low discounting the dynamic behavior is ***sim-***

ple.

It is worth noting the different nature of these two results to avoid misinterpretations. In fact, the first point says that, given a dynamical system $x_{t+1} = h(x_t)$, there is a discount factor $\delta^*(h)$, which depends on h, such that for any fixed $0 < \delta < \delta^*(h)$ there exists some well-behaved problem P having the optimal paths generated by the dynamical system $x_{t+1} = h(x_t)$. In other words, $h(x)$ is the optimal policy for some problem P. This was proved in Boldrin and Montrucchio (1986) where an estimate from below for $\delta^*(h)$ was also given. Below, we quote a new version of the theorem early given in Boldrin and Montrucchio (1986) which contains an improvement on the estimate of the discount factor.

Theorem 1 *Let $h: X \to X$ be any function of $C^{1,1}$ class which satisfies $(x,h(x)) \in D$ for all $x \in X$ where X is a convex and compact subset of $\mathbb{R}^n$. Then there exists a discount factor $\delta^*(h) > 0$ such that, for any fixed $\delta \in (0,\delta^*)$, one can find a concave utility function $V_\delta(x,y)$, defined on $X \times X$, so that h turns out to be the optimal policy for the problem (P) with short-run utility $V_\delta(x,y)$ and discount factor δ. Moreover, the following estimate holds:*

$$\delta^*(h) \geq \left(k_1 + \sqrt{k_0 k_2}\right)^{-2} > 0$$

where: $k_0 = \operatorname{Max}_{x,y\in X} |x - y|$, $k_1 = \operatorname{Max}_{x\in X} |Dh(x)|$ *and* k_2 *is the Lipschitz costant for* $Dh(x)$, *i.e.,* $|Dh(x_1) - Dh(x_2)| \leq k_2|x_1 - x_2|$ *for* x_1, x_2 *in* X.

Also, $V_\delta(x,y)$ can be chosen strongly concave, of class $C^{1,1}$, increasing in x and decreasing in y.

This theorem does not provide any information about which discount factors a dynamics $x_{t+1} = h(x_t)$ is not an optimal dynamics for any concave problem P. Actually, some chaotic behavior can coexist for discount factors whatever close to *1*. Note that this fact does not contrast with the turnpike results described at point *(ii)*. In fact, it affirms that, *given a problem P*, there exists a discount factor $\delta(V)$ such that the optimal dynamics is simple for any $\delta > \delta(V)$. As $\delta(V)$ depends on the curvature of V, the turnpike discount factor can be relegated whatever near 1.

In this paper we try to answer to a few questions raised in this preliminary discussion. In special way we provide estimates from above for the number $\delta^*(h)$. On this problem there are already two important papers (see Santos (1989) and Sorger (1990)).

All our results are based on a general theorem that proves the Holder (Lipschitz) continuous dependence of optima on initial conditions. Applying this theorem, we show that the mapping $x_0 \to \mathbf{h}_\delta(x) = (x_1, x_2, x_3, \ldots)$ sending the initial condition to the optimal sequence, seen as an element of Hilbert space $\ell_2(\delta)$, is Holder (Lipschitz) continuous in the strong topology. The precise formulation is:

Theorem 2 *Let problem P be given. Under the assumptions:*

i) x_0 *is interior to* X,

ii) $V(x,y)$ *is* (α,β)*-concave on* D *with* $\alpha,\beta \geq 0$ *and* $\alpha + \beta > 0$,

then the map $x \to \mathbf{h}_\delta(x)$ *is Holder continuous at* x_0 *whenever* $\mathbf{h}_\delta$ *maps* X *into* $\ell_2(\delta)$ *and* δ *is the discount factor. To be precise: there exist a constant* H *and a neighborhood* $\mathcal{V}(x_0)$ *of* x_0 *such that*

$$|\mathbf{h}_\delta(x') - \mathbf{h}_\delta(x'')| \leq H|x' - x''|^{1/2}$$

for all x' *and* x'' *in* $\mathcal{V}(x_0)$.

If in addition:

iii) the value function $W_\delta(x)$ *is concave-*γ *over* X *for some* γ,

then the map $x \to \mathbf{h}_\delta(x)$ *is Lipschitz continuous at* x_0. *More precisely:*

$$\sum_{t=1}^{\infty} |h_\delta^t(x) - h_\delta^t(x_0)|^2 \delta^t \leq K|x - x_0|^2$$

holds for all x *in* X. *Furthermore, one can take:*

$$K = \delta(\gamma - \alpha)(\alpha\delta + \beta)^{-1}.$$

Here $h_\delta^t(x)$ is the t-th iterate of the optimal policy $h_\delta(x)$. The (α,β)-concavity of $V(x,y)$ means that $V(x,y) + (1/2)\alpha|x|^2 + (1/2)\beta|y|^2$ is concave on D. It is a measure of strong concavity for the utility V. While concavity-γ means that $W_\delta(x) + (1/2)\gamma|x|^2$ is *convex* over X.

Theorem 2 has several implications which will be discussed in in this paper. They enable us to get several upper bounds for the maximal discount factor $\delta^*(h)$ in order that a given dynamics can be optimal for some strongly concave problem *P*.

Among other results, we find that a map with positive topological entropy does not generate an optimal dynamics for any strongly concave problem whenever the discount factor is large enough. Furthermore, a uniform estimate based on its topological entropy is provided. More precisely:

Theorem 3 *A necessary condition in order that h be a policy for some strongly concave problem is that the discount factor is not greater than* $\delta = exp(-\mathcal{H}/n)$, *where* $\mathcal{H}$ *is its topological entropy and* $n = dim\ X$, *i.e.,* $\delta^*(h) \leq exp(-\mathcal{H}/n)$.

We end the paper by showing as the Holder continuity formulated in Theorem 2 is also an useful tool for giving a few new turnpike results for the optimal paths of *P*.

References

Boldrin, M., L. Montrucchio, On the indeterminacy of capital accumulation paths, *Journal of Economic Theory*, 40, 26-39, 1986.

Santos, M.S., Smoothness of the Policy Function in Discrete Time Economic Models, University of Barcellona, 1989. Forthcoming Econometrica.

Sorger, G., *On Minimal Rate of Impatience for Complicated Optimal Growth Paths*, Institut fur Okonometrie und Operations Research, n.130, Vienna, 1990.

CONSTITUTIVE DISTRIBUTED PARAMETER MODELLING OF MOVING COORDINATE SYSTEMS (PART I)

Professor Dr. Eng. Wacław Niemiec
Mathematical Modelling and Control for
Distributed Parameter Systems
Silesian Technical University
Ul. Barska 33
PL - 33 -300 Nowy Sacz - Poland

The moving coordinate systems have underlying significance in classification of the system operations. In spite of this in the world literature these systems have not exactly been described from the point of view of the distributed parameter control of the physical aspects of the technological processes. In accordance with above the physical modelling of the technological processes for the phenomenally distributed parameter control is in convention of pertinent IFAC Meetings "a bridge between control science and technology". For the realization of this idea in my papers, for example [1–6] is given an original approach to the constitutive description of different kind active media in the constitutive way by the use of the definition of the following derivative $\frac{D}{Dt}$ [7] and the condition for partial differential equations of the continuity pertinent to balance $\frac{D}{Dt} = 0$ [7] as the constitutive invariance for continuous media with the space and time memories [8]. The choice of the state variables in this approach bases on the balance yield and quality control aspects of the activity of the moving coordinate systems [9]. For the considerations underlying significance has the reciprocity principle for the isotropic and anisotropic nonhomogeneous media with the source space and time memories [10].

The Determination of the Multicomponent and Multiactive Moving Coordinate Systems

The object of the considerations of this paper can be presented as follows:

<u>Definition 1.</u> Under multicomponent and multiactive media we understand these which

fulfil relations:

- for every state variable W and its every i component W_i for $i = 1, ..., I$ is fulfilled the balance relation

$$W = \sum_{i=1}^{I} W_i \tag{D1.1}$$

and

- for every source element pertinent to the balance of i component and j activity is:

$$\sum_{i=1}^{I} \sum_{j=1}^{J} S_{ij} L_j \tag{D1.2}$$

where: L_j — the mass factor of the source kg/molm^3.

Definition 2. The movement of the moving coordinate system is connected to the introduced a general field vector velocity $\underline{v}$ which is related to the i component field vector velocity $\underline{v}_i$ for $i = 1, ..., I$ according to formula (D1.1)

$$\underline{v} = \sum_{i=1}^{I} \underline{v}_i \tag{D2.1}$$

Consequently to the above formalization of the object of our considerations we introduce:

Definition 3. The activity j of the i component active media bases on both handside kinetics influences of the source:

$$i \xleftrightarrow[\text{kinetics}]{} j, \quad i = 1, ..., I; \; j = 1, ..., J \tag{D3.1}$$

pertinent to the physicochemical properties of the media.

For the considerations of this paper the following assumptions remain valid:

Assumption 1. All components I cooperate together with all J activities of the source elements independently to mass, energy and momentum balances.

And subsequently:

Assumption 2. The below listed physical phenomena of all I components of the multicomponent active media are decisive for the yield and quality aspects of the activity:

- diffusion concentration and enthalpy transport,
- heat transfer,
- field vector velocity.

Pressure has not influences on S_{ij} source elements for $i = 1, ..., I$ and $j = 1, ..., J$.

The Locally Distributed Parameters and Balance Formula

This chapter is devoted to the determination of the elements making the grounds of the mathematical approach presented in this paper. For the realization of this task we introduce:

Definition 4. The following geometrical relation is valid [1–6]

$$Z(x, y, z, t) \in \overline{\Omega}^{f}_{(a,b,c)\,t} \in \Omega_{Rt} \tag{D4.1}$$

where: $Z(x, y, z, t)$ — the point of equivalent multicomponent and multiactive medium source, $\overline{\Omega}^{f}_{(a,b,c)\,t}$ — the locally selected volume–time element of physicochemical conditions decisive for the source with dimensions a, b, c for the time t, Ω_{Rt} — working space volume–time.

Definition 5. For the chosen state variables of the multicomponent and multiactive media the following reciprocal relations are fulfilled; by $Q^R(\xi^R, \eta^R, \zeta^R, \tau) \in \Omega_{Rt}$ (D5.1)

is that

$$\begin{bmatrix} C(x, y, z, t) \\ T(x, y, z, t) \\ \underline{v}(x, y, z, t) \end{bmatrix} \longleftrightarrow \begin{bmatrix} C(\xi^R, \eta^R, \zeta^R, \tau) \\ T(\xi^R, \eta^R, \zeta^R, \tau) \\ \underline{v}(\xi^R, \eta^R, \zeta^R, \tau) \end{bmatrix}$$

$$Z(x, y, z, t) \longleftrightarrow Q^R(\xi^R, \eta^R, \zeta^R, \tau)$$

$$\overline{\Omega}^{f}_{(a,b,c)\,t} \qquad \Omega_{Rt} \tag{D5.2}$$

The formula (D5.2) for every component i is valid.

The element $\overline{\Omega}^{f}_{(a,b,c)\,t}$ is phenomenally closed and the influences of every phenomenon can be treated in the seperate way.

Definition 6. The balance formula of the phenomenal and source aspects of the multicomponent and multiactive media is written as:

$$\frac{\partial}{\partial t} \int_{\Omega^{f}_{(x,y,z)\,t}} \int\int \begin{pmatrix} \text{Whole} \\ \text{balance} \\ \text{form} \end{pmatrix} d\Omega^{f}_{(x,y,z)} =$$

$$\oint_{\underline{F}^{f}_{(x,y,z)\,t}} \oint \begin{bmatrix} \text{Sum of balance fluxes of} \\ \text{influences of physical} \\ \text{phenomena based on state} \\ \text{variables } W \text{ or } \sum_{i=1} W_i \end{bmatrix} d\underline{F}^{f}_{(x,y,z)} +$$

$$\int_{\Omega^{f}_{(x,y,z)\,t}} \int\int \left(\sum_{i=1}^{I} \sum_{j=1}^{J} S_{ij}\, L_j \right) d\Omega^{f}_{(x,y,z)} +$$

$$\int_{\Omega^{f}_{(x,y,z)\,t}} \int\int \begin{pmatrix} \text{Links between balances by} \\ \text{physical phenomena based} \\ \text{on state variables } \sum_{i=1} W_i \end{pmatrix} d\Omega^{f}_{(x,y,z)} \tag{D6.1}$$

The Partial Differential Constitutive State Equations of the Description of Multicomponent and Multiactive Continuous Media

As a consequence of the utilize of above considerations specially the formula (D6.1) one can deduce an original system of the partial differential constitutive state equations containing not only phenomenal but also source elements of the topic media:

$$\text{(I)} \quad \begin{aligned} \frac{DC}{Dt} &= D_c \nabla^2 C \mp C \operatorname{div} \underline{v} \pm \sum_{i=1}^{I} \sum_{j=1}^{J} A_{ij}(t)\, L_j && (1) \\ C \frac{DT}{Dt} &= \frac{\lambda_c}{c_p} \nabla^2 T \mp C\, T \operatorname{div} \underline{v} \pm \sum_{i=1}^{I} \sum_{j=1}^{J} \frac{B_{ij}(t)}{c_p} L_j + \sum_{i=1}^{I} \frac{H_{ci}}{c_p} D_{ci} \nabla^2 C_i && (2) \\ C \frac{D\underline{v}}{Dt} &= \eta_w \nabla^2 \underline{v} \mp C\, \underline{v} \operatorname{div} \underline{v} \pm \sum_{i=1}^{I} \sum_{j=1}^{J} M_{ij}(t)\, L_j + \frac{\eta_w}{3} \operatorname{grad} \operatorname{div} \underline{v} && (3) \end{aligned}$$

where: $\frac{D}{Dt} = \frac{\partial}{\partial t} \pm \underline{v}\, \mathrm{grad}$ — (sum of adequate gradient operations) [7], [1–6] and the partial differential equations of the continuity of the system (I) fulfil the condition $\frac{D}{Dt} = 0$ [7], [1–6].

Two cases of the systems of the partial differential equations of the continuity exist for the system (I):

<u>for the variable coefficients</u>; $D_c = D_c(x,y,z,t), D_{ci} = D_{ci}(x,y,z,t), \lambda_c = \lambda_c(x,y,z,t)$ and $\eta_w = \eta_w(x,y,z,t)$

$$\text{(II)} \quad \begin{aligned} \frac{\partial C}{\partial t} &= \operatorname{grad} D_c \operatorname{grad} C \mp \underline{v} \operatorname{grad} C && (1') \\ C\frac{\partial T}{\partial t} &= \frac{1}{c_p} \operatorname{grad} \lambda_c \operatorname{grad} T \mp \underline{v}\, C \operatorname{grad} T \left[+ \sum_{i=1}^{I} \frac{H_{ci}}{c_p} \operatorname{grad} D_{ci} \operatorname{grad} C_i \right]^* && (2') \\ \frac{\partial \underline{v}}{\partial t} &= \mp(\underline{v} \operatorname{grad})\, \underline{v} && (3') \end{aligned}$$

[ ]* — enclosed element only for thermic energy continuity form.

<u>for the constant coefficients</u>; $D_c \neq D_c(x,y,z,t), D_{ci} \neq D_{ci}(x,y,z,t), \lambda_c \neq \lambda_c(x,y,z,t)$ and $\eta_w \neq \eta_w(x,y,z,t)$

$$\text{(III)} \quad \begin{aligned} \frac{\partial C}{\partial t} &= \mp \underline{v} \operatorname{grad} C && (1'') \\ \frac{\partial T}{\partial t} &= \mp \underline{v} \operatorname{grad} T && (2'') \\ \frac{\partial \underline{v}}{\partial t} &= \mp(\underline{v} \operatorname{grad})\, \underline{v} && (3'') \end{aligned}$$

From the systems (II) and (III) we can easily have seen that system (I) is invariant to its physical coefficients [8]. In accordance with this idea it is possible to prove that the systems (II) and (III) represent groups of constitutive invariance for the system (I) [8].

The INPUT–OUTPUT Relation of the Constitutive Model

For presentation of the INPUT–OUTPUT relation for the multicomponent and multiactive media we need to introduce additionally the following idea:

<u>Definition 7.</u> The locally selected volume–time element $\overline{\Omega}^{f}_{(a,b,c)\,t}$ has outside oriented surface $\underline{F}^{f}_{(a,b,c)\,t}$ by the normal outside surface orientation vector $\underline{n}_f(z)$ which has underlying significance for the signs of the summations of the potential fields and the rotational field in adequate mass, energy and momentum balances as (-) or (+), but a,b,c for time t assure its cuboidal shape.

And nextly:

<u>Definition 8.</u> The working space volume–time Ω_{Rt} has outside oriented surface $\underline{F}_{Rt}$ by

the normal outside surface orientation vector $\underline{n}_R(z)$ which circulation depends to the distributed parameter control tasks by the use of the phenomenal boundary conditions. Continuing our considerations we need to stress here that all operations INPUT–OUTPUT have the following description:
INPUT (initial conditions) $\longrightarrow$ SOURCE (source functions) $\longrightarrow$ PROCESS (processing of the multicomponent and multiactive media) $\longrightarrow$ OUTPUT (resultant magnitudes of the PROCESS pertinent to its physical phenomena).
This interpretation involves decomposition of the system (I) for:

- the phenomenal partial differential equations of the potential fields; diffusion concentration and enthalpy transport, heat transfer, and
- the phenomenal partial differential equations in the forms of the following derivatives for the rotational field; field vector velocity.

From this point of view the variable coordinates point $Q^R(\xi^R, \eta^R, \zeta^R, \tau)$ can be presented as:

- for the potential fields $Q^R(\xi^R, \eta^R, \zeta^R, \tau) \equiv Q(\xi, \eta, \zeta, \tau)$, and
- for the rotational field $Q^R(\xi^R, \eta^R, \zeta^R, \tau) \equiv Q'(\xi', \eta', \zeta', \tau)$.

In accordance with above the following INPUT–OUTPUT transition is:

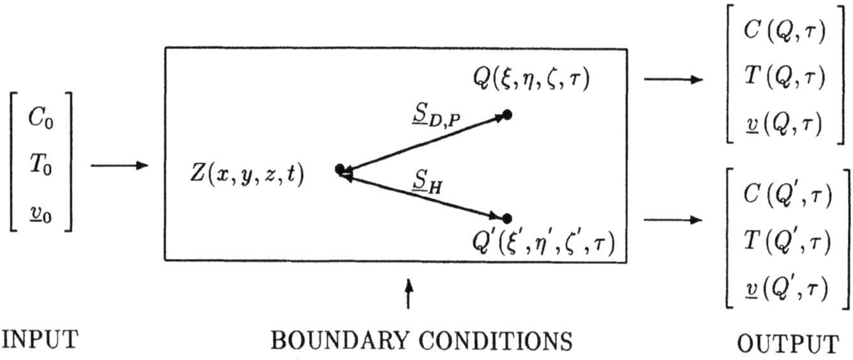

Fig. 1. The INPUT–OUTPUT phenomenal relation: $\underline{S}_{D,P}$ — the diffusion/heat transfer fluxes — potential fields, $\underline{S}_H$ — the turbulence stream — rotational field.

As we see from the above considerations the constitutive approach to the modelling of the moving coordinate systems possesses all significant features of the classic mathematical modelling in the sense of automatics [9]. The choice of the important state variables of the media makes possible on the real processing of these media by the use of their physical phenomena and their boundary conditions.

Conclusions

The following conclusions appear as a result of the considerations of this paper:

- very wide field of the applications of the presented constitutive distributed parameter modelling method,
- complete form of the constitutive description; phenomenal and kinetics yield and quality processing aspects,
- constitutive form of the system (I), its coefficients remain constant for analytical solution,
- bases on processing state variable which are accessible for measurement and control influences.

Notation

C — concentration kg/m^3, T — temperature K, $\underline{v}$ — velocity m/s,
whole coefficients: D_c — diffusion m^2/s, λ_c — heat transfer W/mK, c_p — specific warmth J/kgK, η_w — dynamic viscosity Ns/m^2,
i coefficients: D_{ci} — i component diffusion m^2/s, H_{ci} — i component own enthalpy J/kg,
source elements: $A_{ij}(t)$ — mass mol/s, $B_{ij}(t)$ — energy Jmol/kgs, $\underline{M}_{ij}(t)$ — momentum Nmol/kg, L_j — mass factor kg/molm^3.

References

[1] Niemiec, W.: On the constitutive theory of modelling and information for distributed parameter control of the continuous mass crystallization process: Part I: Partial differential constitutive state equations describing phenomena of the continuous mass crystallization process. Third Int'l Conference on Liquid Metal Engineering and Technology in Energy Production, Oxford, England, 9–13 April, 1984, Paper No. 191.

[2] Niemiec, W.: On modelling and information construction for control of distributed parameter chemical processes in fluid phase. 3^0 IFAC Symposium "Control of Distributed Parameter Systems", Toulouse, France, 29VI–2VII, 1982, Session 23.

[3] Niemiec, W.: The constitutive theory of modelling and information for phenomenal distributed parameter control of multicomponent chemical processes in gas, fluid and solid phase: Part I. 7th Miami Int'l Conference on Alternative Energy Sources, Miami Beach Florida, USA, 9–11 December, 1985, Session "Hydrocarbons/Energy transfer", pp. 579–588.

[4] Niemiec, W.: A mathematical model of the distributed parameters of the continuous mass crystallization process for the adaptive control: Part I "St. z Automatyki", 1989, pp. 81–118.

[5] Niemiec, W.: The mathematical analysis of the kinetics of the crystal growth reaction during the continuous mass crystallization process. 171st Meeting, The Electrochemical Society, Philadelphia, Pennsylvania, USA, 10–15 May, 1987, Paper No. 68.

[6] Niemiec, W.: On constitutive modelling and information for phenomenal distributed parameter control of multicomponent chemical processes in fluid– and solid-phase: Part I. Cavitation and Multiphase Flow Forum - 1985, San Diego, USA, Session FWA–2.

[7] Średniawa, B.: Hydrodynamika i teoria spężystości. Warszawa, PWN 1977.

For [8–10] see references to Part II.

CONSTITUTIVE DISTRIBUTED PARAMETER MODELLING OF MOVING COORDINATE SYSTEMS (PART II)

Professor Dr. Eng. Wacław Niemiec
Mathematical Modelling and Control for
Distributed Parameter Systems
Silesian Technical University
Ul. Barska 33
PL - 33 -300 Nowy Sacz - Poland

We concentrate our attention on the analytical solution of the deduced in Part I system of the partial differential constitutive state equations (I) from the point of view of the control theory [1]. For the realization of the constitutive distributed parameter control by the use of the physical phenomena of the multicomponent and multiactive media we need to obtain [1–7]:

- analytical solution of the system (I) by presence of the initial and boundary conditions,
- complete information for the phenomenally distributed parameter control,
- structure of the phenomenally distributed parameter control,
- optimization problems for the single physical phenomenon and whole system (I),
- an adaptive control concept.

Analytical Solution of the System (I) by Presence of the Initial and Boundary Conditions

The source elements for the system (I):

initial conditions (inside point $Z(x,y,z,t)$)

$$
(\mathrm{I}^s)\quad
\begin{aligned}
\frac{dC}{dt} &= \pm\sum_{i=1}^{I}\sum_{j=1}^{J} A_{ij}(t)\,L_j &(1)\\
C\frac{dT}{dt} &= \pm\sum_{i=1}^{I}\sum_{j=1}^{J} \frac{B_{ij}(t)}{c_p}\,L_j &(2)\\
C\frac{d\underline{v}}{dt} &= \pm\sum_{i=1}^{I}\sum_{j=1}^{J} \underline{M}_{ij}(t)\,L_j &(3)
\end{aligned}
$$

boundary conditions (boundary point $P(x,y,z,t)$)

$$
(\mathrm{I}^b)\quad
\begin{aligned}
\frac{dC}{dt} &= \mp\sum_{i=1}^{I}\sum_{j=1}^{J} A^b_{ij}(t)\,L_j\\
C\frac{dT}{dt} &= \mp\sum_{i=1}^{I}\sum_{j=1}^{J} \frac{B^b_{ij}(t)}{c_p}\,L_j\\
C\frac{d\underline{v}}{dt} &= \mp\sum_{i=1}^{I}\sum_{j=1}^{J} \underline{M}^b_{ij}(t)\,L_j
\end{aligned}
$$

Initial conditions

$C_0, T_0, \underline{v}_0 \quad C_{b0}, T_{b0}, \underline{v}_{b0}$

The analysis of the homogeneous part of the system (I):

Introducing definition of the rotational field: exists $\underline{B}$ vector potential of the fluid field so that $\underline{v} = \operatorname{rot}\underline{B}$ and $\operatorname{div}\operatorname{rot}\underline{B} \equiv 0$ [8–9] and from the idealization of the media [10] we have,

for the potential fields

$$
(\mathrm{I}^{hp})\quad
\begin{aligned}
\frac{\partial C}{\partial t} &= D_c\,\nabla^2 C &(1)\\
C\frac{\partial T}{\partial t} &= \frac{\lambda_c}{c_p}\,\nabla^2 T &(2)\\
C\frac{\partial T}{\partial t} &= \sum_{i=1}^{I} \frac{H_{ci}}{c_p}\,D_{ci}\,\nabla^2 C_i &(3)
\end{aligned}
$$

for the rotational field

$$
(\mathrm{I}^{hr})\quad
\begin{aligned}
\frac{DC}{Dt} &= \mp\operatorname{div}\underline{v}\\
C\frac{DT}{Dt} &= \mp C\,T\operatorname{div}\underline{v}\\
C\frac{D\underline{v}}{Dt} &= \eta_w\,\nabla^2\underline{v} \mp C\,\underline{v}\operatorname{div}\underline{v} + \frac{\eta_w}{3}\operatorname{grad}\operatorname{div}\underline{v}
\end{aligned}
$$

$$\frac{D}{Dt} = \frac{\partial}{\partial t} \pm \underline{v}\operatorname{grad}$$

In accordance with above the general formula governing the solutions of the phenomenal partial differential equations of the potential fields and the rotational field is:

$$
\begin{aligned}
W_{PH}(Z,t) = &\int_0^t \int\int_{\Omega_R}\int G_{Ph}(Z,t;Q^R,\tau)\,S^s(\tau)\,d\Omega_R(Q^R)\,d\tau +\\
&\left[\int_0^t \oint_{\underline{F}_{Rt}}\oint G^{xy}_{Ph}(P,t;Q^R,\tau)\,d\underline{F}^{xy}_R(Q^R) +\right.\\
&\int_0^t \oint_{\underline{F}_{Rt}}\oint G^{yz}_{Ph}(P,t;Q^R,\tau)\,d\underline{F}^{yz}_R(Q^R) +\\
&\left.\int_0^t \int_{\underline{F}_{Rt}}\int G^{zx}_{Ph}(P,t;Q^R,\tau)\,d\underline{F}^{zx}_R(Q^R)\right] S^b(\tau)\,d\tau \qquad (S.1)
\end{aligned}
$$

Complete solution of the system (I) by presence of the initial and boundary conditions fulfils the general formula:

$$\begin{bmatrix}\text{State}\\ \text{vector}\\ \text{of com-}\\ \text{plete}\\ \text{solution}\end{bmatrix} = \begin{bmatrix}\text{Source}\\ \text{state}\\ \text{vector}\\ \text{of point}\\ Z(x,y,z,t)\end{bmatrix} + \begin{bmatrix}\text{State vector}\\ \text{of phenomenal}\\ \text{solution of}\\ \text{potential fields}\\ Z \longleftarrow Q \longrightarrow P\end{bmatrix} + \begin{bmatrix}\text{State vector}\\ \text{of phenomenal}\\ \text{solutions of}\\ \text{rotational field}\\ Z \longleftarrow Q' \longrightarrow P\end{bmatrix} \quad \text{(S.2)}$$

Complete Information for the Phenomenally Distributed Parameter Control

Complete information approach for the phenomenally distributed parameter control comes straight from the classic control theory and contains:

- dynamical working space–time characteristics (formula (S.2)),
- statical working space characteristics (obtained from the formula (S.2) by the elimination of the time coordinates t and τ,
- dynamical phenomenal Green functions $G_{Ph}(Z,t;Q^R,\tau)$ as INPUT–OUTPUT dynamical transfer functions,
- statical phenomenal Green functions $G_{Ph}(Z;Q^R)$ as INPUT–OUTPUT statical transfer functions,

which can be used for the realization of the real control [11].

Structure of the Phenomenally Distributed Parameter Control

The procedure of the solution of the system (I) enables on formulation of the structure of the phenomenally distributed parameter control for every i component of multicomponent and multiactive media:

Phenomenal Green functions properties

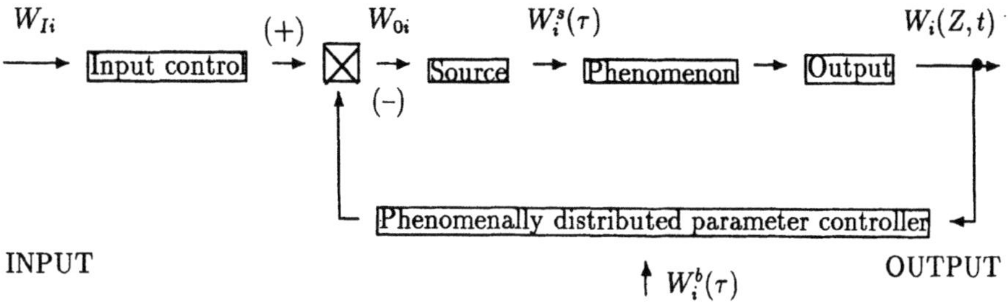

Fig. 1. A phenomenally distributed parameter control concept for the i component of the multicomponent and multiactive media

W_{Ii} — the i component INPUT state variable, W_{0i} — the i component INITIAL state variable, $W_i^s(\tau)$ — the i component SOURCE state variable, $W_i(Z,t)$ — the i component OUTPUT state variable, $W_i^b(\tau)$ — the i component BOUNDARY SOURCE state vector, all for $i = 1, ..., I$.

The structure from the Fig. 1 can subsequently be used to the higher forms of the yield and quality of the multicomponent and multiactive media processing aspects control by the use of pertinent physical phenomena.

Optimization Problems for the Single Phenomenon and Whole System (I)

For the optimization problems of the topic problems a very convenient assumption is that phenomenal index performance is equal to the state variable of result pertinent physical phenomenon — formula (S.1). In accordance with above opinion we are looking for minimum or maximum of the function:

$$\begin{matrix}\max\\ \text{or}\\ \min\end{matrix} \quad J^W_{Ph}(Z,t) = \begin{matrix}\max\\ \text{or}\\ \min\end{matrix} \quad W_{Ph}(Z,t) \tag{J.1}$$

The procedure of search of maximum or minimum of the formula (J.1) pertinent to the control tasks courses as follows:

- the first step is to intergate of the formula (S.1) to eliminate the variable coordinates
- the second step is maximum or minimum of the obtained function with respect to its constant coordinates (x, y, z, t) by the use of square forms [12].

For the whole form of the system (I) we introduce the state vector of index performances

$$\begin{bmatrix} J^C_{Ph}(Z,t) \\ J^T_{Ph}(Z,t) \\ J^{\underline{v}}_{Ph}(Z,t) \end{bmatrix} \tag{J.2}$$

With assumption that we consider only working space–time problems we have the resultant index performance in the form

$$[J_R(Z,t)] = \begin{bmatrix} J_{Ph}^{CD}(Z,t) \\ J_{Ph}^{TD}(Z,t) \\ 0 \end{bmatrix} + \begin{bmatrix} 0 \\ J_{Ph}^{TP}(Z,t) \\ 0 \end{bmatrix} + \begin{bmatrix} J_{Ph}^{CH}(Z,t) \\ J_{Ph}^{TH}(Z,t) \\ J_{Ph}^{\underline{v}H}(Z,t) \end{bmatrix} \tag{J.3}$$

Result Diffusion Heat transfer Turbulence

The analysis of the formula

$$\begin{matrix} \max \\ \text{or} \\ \min \end{matrix} \quad J_R(Z,t) \tag{J.4}$$

is going in the same way as for the formula (J.1).

The optimization considerations of this chapter for every i component with $i = 1, ..., I$ remain valid.

An Adaptive Control Concept

For the construction of the phenomenally distributed parameter Model Reference Adaptive Control System the following criterions of the construction of the error between Model and Plant can be considered:

- the error between dynamical working space–time charcteristics,
- the error between statical working space characteristics,
- the error between dynamical phenomenal Green functions,
- the error between statical phenomenal Green functions,
- the error between single phenomenal index performances,
- the error between whole index performances.

The choice of the error depends to the choice of the yield and quality control task by the processing of the multicomponent and multiactive media. On the above constructed errors pertinent to their choice from the asymptotic stability criterions necessary "adaptive laws" are deduced [11].

Conclusions

From above considerations can be seen that suggested in the paper an original constitutive approach to the control theory from the constitutive distributed parameter modelling of the moving coordinate systems fulfils all possible cases of the existing control theory. The considerations of this paper prove that the constitutive approach makes possible on more exact determination of the control realization pertinent to the process technology.

Notation

See notation to Part I and additionally boundary source elements: $A^b_{ij}(t)$ — mass mol/s, $B^b_{ij}(t)$ — energy Jmol/kgs, $\underline{M}^b_{ij}(t)$ — momentum Nmol/kg.

References (The end for Part I.)

[8] Morgan, A.: On the construction of constitutive equations for continuous media. Archiwum Mechaniki Stosowanej, vol. 17, 1965, No. 1, pp. 145–174.

[9] Wegrzyn, S.: Podstawy automatyki. Warszawa, PWN 1974.

[10] Nowacki, W.: Dynamiczne zagadnienia termospężystości. Warszawa, PWN 1966.

References

[1] Niemiec, W.: Part I of this paper.

[2] Niemiec, W.: On the constitutive theory of modelling and information for distributed parameter control of the continuous mass crystallization process: Part II. Third Int'l Conference on Liquid Metal Engineering and Technology in Energy Production, Oxford, England, 9–13 April, 1984, Paper No. 192.

[3] Niemiec, W.: On modelling and information construction for control of distributed parameter chemical processes in fluid phase. 3^0 IFAC Symposium "Control of Distributed Parameter Systems", Toulouse, France, 29VI–2VII, 1982, Session 23.

[4] Niemiec, W.: The constitutive theory of modelling and information for phenomenal distributed parameter control of multicomponent chemical processes in gas, fluid and solid phase: Part II. 7th Miami Int'l Conference on Alternative Energy Sources, Miami Beach Florida, USA, 9–11 December, 1985, Session "Hydrocarbons/Energy transfer", pp. 579–598.

[5] Niemiec, W.: A mathematical model of the distributed parameters of the continuous mass crystallization process for the adaptive control: Part II "Studia z Automatyki", 1989, pp. 119–162.

[6] Niemiec, W.: The mathematical analysis of the kinetics of the crystal growth reaction during the continuous mass crystallization process. 171st Meeting, The Electrochemical Society, Philadelphia, Pennsylvania, USA, 10–15 May, 1987, Paper No. 68.

[7] Niemiec, W.: On constitutive modelling and information for phenomenal distributed parameter control of multicomponent chemical processes in fluid– and solid-phase: Part II. Cavitation and Multiphase Flow Forum - 1985, San Diego, USA, Session FWA-2.

[8] Średniawa, B.: Hydrodynamika i teoria spężystości. Warszawa, PWN 1977.

[9] Trajdos, T.: Matematyka dla inżynierów. Warszawa, PWN 1974.

[10] Morgan, A.: On the construction of constitutive equations for continuous media. Archiwum Mechaniki Stosowanej, vol. 17, 1965, No. 1, pp. 145–174.

[11] Wegrzyn, S.: Podstawy automatyki. Warszawa, PWN 1974.

[12] Smirnow, W.: Matematyka wyższa. Warszawa, PWN 1966.

Controllability and Observability in a New Perspective

Jan C. Willems
Mathematics Institute
University of Groningen
P.O. Box 800
9700 AV Groningen
The Netherlands

1 Introduction

We start with some historical comments. The notion of controllability – related to the possibility of transferring the state of a system – has been introduced around 1960 and was soon to become one of the key concepts in control theory, related to the very possibility of exerting control. It enters as a crucial condition in (infinite time) LQG- and H_∞-control, in pole placement, in time optimal control, etc. Soon after the introduction of controllability, realization theory (which we prefer to call state representation theory) appeared on the scene. One of the important lessons which was learned from this development is that every transfer function and every convolution can be represented by a minimal state-space system and that minimality is equivalent to controllability and observability. This state of affairs has created the impression that controllability is not an intrinsic property of a dynamical system, but merely a property of a state realization, of a representation of a system.

We will now introduce a point of view which will make history out of these historical remarks and this folklore. Indeed, we will put forward a definition of controllability which is in principle applicable to any dynamical system. Thus, controllability will become a genuine property of a dynamical system.

2 Controllability

A *dynamical system* Σ is a triple $\Sigma = (\mathbb{T}, \mathbb{W}, \mathfrak{B})$ with $\mathbb{T} \subseteq \mathbb{R}$ the *time axis*, $\mathbb{W}$ the *signal space*, and $\mathfrak{B} \subseteq \mathbb{W}^{\mathbb{T}}$ the behavior.

Thus, a dynamical system is defined by $\mathbb{T}$, the time instants of interest; $\mathbb{W}$, the space in which the time signals which the system produces take on their values; and $\mathfrak{B}$, a family of $\mathbb{W}$-valued time trajectories. The sets $\mathbb{T}$ and $\mathbb{W}$ define the setting, the mathematization of the problem, while $\mathfrak{B}$ formalizes the laws which govern the system. According to the dynamical model Σ, time signals in $\mathfrak{B}$ can in principle occur, are compatible with the laws governing Σ, while those outside $\mathfrak{B}$ cannot occur, are prohibited.

A dynamical system $\Sigma = (\mathsf{T}, \mathsf{W}, \mathfrak{B})$ with $\mathsf{T} = \mathbb{Z}$ or $\mathbb{R}$ is said to be *time invariant* if $\sigma^t \mathfrak{B} = \mathfrak{B}$ for all $t \in \mathsf{T}$ (σ^t denotes the *backwards t-shift*: $(\sigma^t f)(t') := f(t'+t)$). If $\mathsf{T} = \mathbb{Z}$ then this condition is equivalent to $\sigma\mathfrak{B} = \mathfrak{B}$.

Let $\Sigma = (\mathsf{T}, \mathsf{W}, \mathfrak{B})$, $\mathsf{T} = \mathbb{Z}$ or $\mathbb{R}$, be a time-invariant dynamical system. Σ is said to be *controllable* if for all $w_1, w_2 \in \mathfrak{B}$ there exists a $t \in \mathsf{T}$, $t \geq 0$, and a $w : \mathsf{T} \cap [0,t] \to \mathsf{W}$ such that $w' \in \mathfrak{B}$, with $w' : \mathsf{T} \to \mathsf{W}$ defined by

$$w'(t') - \begin{cases} w_1(t') & \text{for } t' < 0 \\ w(t') & \text{for } 0 \leq t' \leq t \\ w_2(t'-t) & \text{for } t' > t. \end{cases}$$

In this definition, we should think of w_1 as a past trajectory, chosen by "nature", of w_2 as a desired future trajectory imposed by the "designer", and of w as a controlled trajectory judiciously selected by the "control engineer". Thus, a controllable system can eventually be steered to any desired trajectory, whatever be its past history.

3 Observability

In our view, observability will be a property of systems which produce two kinds of signals, one of which is observed, while the other should be deduced from the observed signal.

Let $\Sigma = (\mathsf{T}, \mathsf{W}_1 \times \mathsf{W}_2, \mathfrak{B})$ $\mathsf{T} = \mathbb{Z}$ or $\mathbb{R}$, be a time-invariant dynamical system. Then w_2 is said to be *observable* from w_1 in Σ if $\{(w_1', w_2'), (w_1'', w_2'') \in \mathfrak{B}$ and $w_1' = w_1''\} \Rightarrow \{w_2' = w_2''\}$. In other words, observability implies that there exists a map $F : \mathsf{W}_1^{\mathsf{T}} \to \mathsf{W}_2^{\mathsf{T}}$ such that $\{(w_1, w_2) \in \mathfrak{B}\} \Rightarrow \{w_2 = Fw_1\}$.

4 Sources

The point of view about dynamical systems, controllability, and observability put forward here has been developped in a series of papers. Particularly the last reference gives a broad view of this theory, including specific conditions for controllability and observability for a variety of classes of dynamical systems, in particular systems described by differential or difference equations.

References

[1] Willems, J.C., *System Theoretic Models for the Analysis of Physical Systems*, Ricerche di Automatica, Vol. 10, No. 2, pp. 71-106, 1979.

[2] Willems, J.C., *From Time Series to Dynamical Systems. Part I: Linear Time Invariant Systems; Part II: Exact Modelling; Part III: Approximate Modelling*, Automatica, Vol. 22, No. 5, pp. 561-580, 1986; Vol. 22, No. 6, pp. 675-694, 1986; Vol. 23, No. 1, pp. 87-115, 1987.

[3] Willems, J.C., *Models for Dynamics*, Dynamics Reported, Vol. 2, pp. 171-269, 1989.

[4] Willems, J.C., *Paradigms and Puzzles in the Theory of Dynamical Systems*, IEEE Transactions on Automatic Control. Vol. 36, pp. 259-294, 1991.

CONICAL APPROACH TO LINEAR DYNAMIC OPTIMIZATION

Paolo d'Alessandro
Department of Computer and Systems Science
University of Rome "LA SAPIENZA"
Via Eudòssiana 18, 00184 Roma, Italy

Elena De Santis
Department of Electrical Engineering
University of L'Aquila
67040 Poggio di Roio, Italy

A rather extensive literature has accumulated on input constrained dynamical systems (see e.g. [1], [2], [3]). The case of state constraints is analyzed in [4]. Here we use a dual conical condition [5] to investigate the linear dynamical optimization problem with state constraints, leaving the polyhedral structure of the problem intact. Our approach is based on the description of the evolution, backward in time, of the set of admissible states (that is initial states for which a feasible solution exists). First we give the expression of this set, which is of course a polyhedron, and then necessary and sufficient conditions of feasibility. In [6] we apply the approach to two possible relaxations of the concept of positive system. The ensuing conditions of positiveness involve a cone, which is the sum of the nonnegative orthant and a subspace, as well as its lineality space. The structure of this cone is described for arbitrary subspaces and the expression of the lineality space is given in the same general setting. Finally we extend our results to the case of optimality, following the usual approach of expressing the optimum problem as a parameterized feasibility problem.

Because of the numerical complexity of the dual conical optimality condition, our results have essentially a geometrical value, even though there are special cases, for which numerical computation can be easily performed. The computations for positive systems are instead straightforward.

The more numerical oriented approach given in [7] is based on a smoothing of the problem, that allows the application of standard techniques of dynamical optimization.

OPTIMIZATION PROBLEMS AND APPROACH

Consider a discrete time linear system S described by the recursive equations

$$x(t+1) = A\,x(t) + B\,u(t)$$
$$y(t+1) = C\,x(t+1)$$

with initial time $\bar{t} = 0$, initial state $x(0) = \bar{x}$, and with $x(t) \in R^n$, $u(t) \in R^p$, $y(t) \in R^q$.

The optimization problem addressed in this paper is defined by

$$\max \sum_{i=1}^{T} (f_i, x(i))$$

subject to $W(t)\,x(t) \le M_{xt} \qquad 0 < t \le T$

$V(t)\,u(t) \le M_{ut} \qquad 0 \le t < T$

where T is a given horizon of time

and subject to the dynamic equations of the system.

Obviously the inequalities are supposed to define nonvoid polyhedra. We have assumed a given initial state. This assumption might be expressed imposing a suitable constraint for the state at t=0. The extension of our theory to the case in which such constraint is a general one is trivial.

We are interested both in feasibility aspects of this problem and in the full optimization problem. Notice also that, being the dynamics time-invariant we make systematically reference to a zero initial time, but of course analogous results can be obtained for any other initial time.

The problem is feasible relative to an initial state $\bar{x}$ if there exists at least an input such that the corresponding evolution of the system S from the initial state $\bar{x}$ is consistent with respect to all the given constraints. As in [8] we shall call any state, relative to which the system is feasible, an admissible state. At this point we can define consistency of the system S as follows:

DEFINITION - A linear system S is consistent with respect to a set of constraints if the set of admissible initial states is nonvoid.

Of course, if the system is consistent and the initial state is fixed, there are feasible solutions if and only if the initial state belongs to the set of admissible states.

It was proved in [8] that with the above assumptions the set of admissible states is a polyhedron. Making reference for simplicity to the case of state only constraints, the general idea underlying our results is to consider a backward recursion, deriving at each step the set of admissible states at say t-1 with respect to the constraints at t, and then intersecting this polyhedron with the polyhedron defined by the constraints at t-1. The resulting polyhedron takes the place of the constraining set at t-1, starting from which another step can be performed. Starting from time T and arriving to time zero, the final polyhedron represents the set of admissible states. Of course, if at some step a void polyhedron is found, then the procedure is arrested and the system is not consistent. The usefulness of this procedure stems from the fact that, thanks to the machinery developed in [5], we are able to give an explicit expression of all those polyhedra.

To extend the results developed for the feasibility problem to the optimality problem, the simplest and most direct way is to incorporate the functional in the dynamics of the system (the resulting new linear system may or may not be, according to the cases, time invariant) and then express the optimality problem as a parameterized feasibility problem.

As a result, the polyhedron of admissible states at zero depends on a parameter h, and will be denoted by $P_0(h)$.

Thus the problem is to find an $\hat{h}$ such that

if $h \leq \hat{h}$ then $P_0(h)$ is nonvoid

whereas if $h > \hat{h}$ then $P_0(h)$ is void

Such an $\hat{h}$, if it exists, is the maximum of the problem, which therefore if feasible bounded. If, for any h, $P_0(h)$ is nonvoid then the problem is feasible unbounded and, finally, if $P_0(h)$ is void, for any h, then the problem is feasible unbounded. Applying the shortly outlined backward recursion, the maximum of the given problem is equal to the maximum of the following problem

maximize h subject to $Fh \leq K$

where both F and K are computed vectors and h is a scalar.

The interested reader is referred to [6] for the full version of this paper.

REFERENCES

[1] A. MARZOLLO, *Controllability and Optimization*, Lectures held at the Department of Automation and Information, University of Trieste, Courses and Lectures no. 17, International Center for Mechanical Sciences, Udine (Ialy) 1969.

[2] R. CONTI, *Processi di controllo lineari in R^n*, Quaderni dell'Unione Matematica Italiana, no. 30, Pitagora Ed., Bologna, 1985 (in Italian).

[3] P.d'ALESSANDRO, E. DE SANTIS, *Reachability in Input Constrained Discrete Time Linear Systems*, to appear on Automatica.

[4] E. DE SANTIS, *On reachability of constrained discrete time linear systems*, Report no. 38/90, Department of Electrical Engineering, University of L'Aquila.

[5] P.d'ALESSANDRO, M.DALLA MORA, E. DE SANTIS, *Techniques of Linear Programming Based on the Theory of Convex Cones*, Optimization, 20(1989) 6, 761-777.

[6] P.d'ALESSANDRO, E. DE SANTIS, *Conical theory of feasibility and optimality for dynamical linear systems*, Report no. 36/90, Department of Electrical Engineering, University of L'Aquila.

[7] PROPOI A., *Dynamic Linear Programming*, WP-79-38, International Institute for Applied System Analysis, Austria.

[8] P.d'ALESSANDRO, M.DALLA MORA, E. DE SANTIS, *On Consistency of Linear Linearly Constrained Discrete Time Systems*, International Journal of the Franklin Institute, vol. 319, no. 4, pp. 423-430, April 1985.

OPTIMAL CONTROL OF THE M/G/1 QUEUE WITH REPEATED VACATIONS

Eitan ALTMAN and Philippe NAIN
INRIA, Centre Sophia Antipolis
06565 Valbonne Cedex, France

Consider an M/G/1 queueing system where the server takes repeated vacations whenever the queue empties. At t_n, the end of the nth vacation, $n = 1, 2, ...$, the server has to decide whether or not to take another vacation. The decision may depend on all the history of the process (which includes the number of customers and the decisions made at the end of the previous vacations). The optimization problem typically arises when a switch-in cost is incurred each time the server is reactivated (turned on), and in the presence of an extra holding cost. One may wish to restrict to simple N-policies where the server is turned on at the end of each vacation if and only if the queue-length exceeds a fixed integer number N. A few recent papers address the problem of optimally choosing the integer N (see [2,3]). The contribution of this paper is to show that the policy which is average optimal among the subclass of N-policies is in fact overall optimal. We suggest a new approach which seems simpler than the approach recently proposed by Federgruen and So [1]. Key tools are the theory of Semi Markov Decision Processes (SMDP), the optimality principle and the value iteration algorithm. In particular, recent results by Sennotts [5] on average cost SMDPs are extended.

1 The Optimization Problem

Consider the M/G/1 queue of infinite capacity with arrival intensity $\lambda > 0$. Service times are i.i.d., distributed like a generic RV B with first and second moments b and $b^{(2)} < \infty$, resp. Assume $\rho := \lambda b < 1$. Whenever a busy period ends, the server takes a vacation whose duration is distributed like a generic RV D with Laplace-Stieltjes Transform (LST) $d^*(s)$, and with first and second moments $0 < d < \infty$ and $d^{(2)} < \infty$. At t_n, the server may take a new vacation (action v) or initiate a new service period if the system is nonempty (action s). Assume $t_1 = 0$. Arrivals, service times and vacation processes are mutually independent processes. The SMDP is characterized by (i) X_n := number of customers at t_n. (ii) A_n := action taken at t_n. (iii) *The cost:* Let $\gamma > 0$ be the cost incurred each time the server is restarted. In addition we consider holding cost per unit time and per customer. If action a is chosen in state x, then an immediate cost $z(x, a)$ is incurred, where

$$z(x,a) := \begin{cases} xd + \dfrac{\lambda d^{(2)}}{2}, & \text{if } a = v; \\ \dfrac{b}{2(1-\rho)}x^2 + \dfrac{\lambda b^{(2)} + b(1-\rho)}{2(1-\rho)^2}x + \dfrac{\lambda d^{(2)}}{2} + \gamma, & \text{if } a = s \text{ and } x \geq 1. \end{cases} \tag{1.1}$$

It can be shown that $z(x,a)$ represents the expectation of the total cost incurred between two consecutive decision epochs. (iv) *The transition times*: Let $\tau(x,a)$ be the conditional sojourn time in x given action a is chosen. If $a = v$ then $\tau(x,a)$ is distributed like D. If $a = s$ and $x \geq 1$ then $\tau(x,a)$ is distributed as the sum of x i.i.d. busy periods of an M/G/1 queue plus a vacation of length D. Let $\tau^*_{x,a}(\omega) := E[e^{-\omega\tau(x,a)}]$ be the LST of $\tau(x,a)$. Let $T^*(\omega)$ denote the LST of a busy period duration in an M/G/1 queue. Then

$$\tau^*_{x,a}(\omega) = \begin{cases} d^*(\omega), & \text{if } a = v \text{ and } x \in \mathbb{N}; \\ d^*(\omega)\,[T^*(\omega)]^x, & \text{if } a = s \text{ and } x \geq 1. \end{cases} \tag{1.2}$$

(v) *The transition law*. If the process is in x and action a is chosen then the next state will be y with the probability

$$P_{xy}(a) := \begin{cases} P_d(y), & \text{if } a = s \text{ and } x \geq 1; \\ P_d(y-x), & \text{if } a = v \text{ and } x \leq y; \\ 0, & \text{if } a = v \text{ and } x > y, \end{cases} \tag{1.3}$$

where $P_d(y)$ stands for the probability of y arrivals during a vacation period.

A policy $u \in \mathcal{U}$ is a sequence of measures on the action space $\{u_1, u_2 ...\}$ conditioned by the history of states and actions, where u_n is used at t_n.

Introduce the optimization problem **P**: given an initial state $x \in \mathbb{N}$, find $u \in \mathcal{U}$ that minimizes

$$\Phi(x,u) := \overline{\lim_{t\to\infty}} \frac{1}{t} E^u_x \left[\sum_{0 \leq t_n < t} z(X_n, A_n) \right].$$

2 The Discounted and Average Costs

To solve **P**, we first solve the discounted version of **P**.

Define

$$W_\alpha(x,u) := E^u_x \left[\sum_{n=1}^{\infty} z(X_n, A_n) \exp\left(-\alpha \sum_{j=1}^{n-1} \tau(X_j, A_j) \right) \right],$$

for $\alpha > 0$, $x \in \mathbb{N}$, $u \in \mathcal{U}$, and let $W_\alpha(x) := \inf_{u \in U} W_\alpha(x,u)$. A policy $u_\alpha \in \mathcal{U}$, $\alpha > 0$, is said to be α-discounted optimal if $W_\alpha(x) = W_\alpha(x, u_\alpha)$ for all $x \in \mathbb{N}$. Let $\mathcal{K}$ be the set of functions

$f : \mathbb{N} \to \mathbb{R}$ which grow at most polynomially in x. Define the Dynamic Programming (DP) operator $T_\alpha : \mathcal{K} \to \mathcal{K}$ by

$$T_\alpha f(x) := \min_a \left\{ z(x,a) + \tau^*_{x,a}(\alpha) \sum_{y=0}^{\infty} P_{xy}(a)\, f(y) \right\}, \quad f \in \mathcal{K},\ x \in \mathbb{N}. \tag{2.1}$$

The following results hold (see [4, Theorem 1]):

Proposition 2.1 *For any $\alpha > 0$, $W_\alpha(x)$ satisfies the optimality equation*

$$f(x) = T_\alpha f(x), \quad x \in \mathbb{N}, \tag{2.2}$$

and further

$$\lim_{n\to\infty} T^n_\alpha g(x) = W_\alpha(x), \quad x \in \mathbb{N},$$

for any function $g \in \mathcal{K}$. In addition, any stationary policy that minimizes the right-hand side of (2.2) is α-discounted optimal.

A set of functions $f_\alpha \in \mathcal{K}$, $\alpha > 0$, is said to satisfy condition **C1** if for any integers $x \in \mathbb{N}$, $k \in \mathbb{N}$, there exists a real number $\alpha_{x,k} > 0$ such that for any $r \in \mathbb{N}$ and for any α such that $0 < \alpha < \alpha_{x,k}$

$$f_\alpha(x+r+k) - [T^*(\alpha)]^k f_\alpha(x+r) \geq z(x+k,s) - z(x,s).$$

It is said to satisfy condition **C2** if for any $x \in \mathbb{N}$, $k \in \mathbb{N}$, and any $\alpha > 0$,

$$f_\alpha(x+k) - [T^*(\alpha)]^k f_\alpha(x) \geq k \min\left\{ d, \frac{\lambda b^{(2)}}{2(1-\rho)^2} \right\}.$$

Note that the function $f_\alpha(\cdot) := z(\cdot, s)$ satisfies **C1** and **C2** for all $\alpha > 0$. Also note from (1.1) that

$$z(x+k,s) - z(x,s) = z(k,s) + \frac{kbx}{1-\rho} - \frac{\lambda d^{(2)}}{2} - \gamma.$$

The optimality of a threshold policy is obtained following the following Lemmas.

Lemma 2.1 *W_α satisfies conditions* **C1** *and* **C2**.

Let u^*_α be a stationary policy that minimizes the right-hand side of the DP equation (2.2). Define N_0 to be the smallest integer larger or equal to $\gamma \{d/[1-\rho]\}^{-1}$.

Lemma 2.2 *There exists $\alpha^* > 0$ such that for all $\alpha \in (0, \alpha^*)$, $x \in \mathbb{N}$,*

$$u^*_\alpha(x) = v \quad \text{if} \quad 0 \leq x < L_\alpha; \tag{2.3}$$

$$u^*_\alpha(x) = s \quad \text{if} \quad L_\alpha \leq x < N_\alpha, \tag{2.4}$$

where $0 \leq L_\alpha \leq N_0 < \infty$, and $N_\alpha \to \infty$ when $\alpha \to 0$.

Proof. Using (1.2), (1.3) and (2.1), the DP equation (2.2) becomes

$$W_\alpha(x) = \min\left\{ z(x,v) + d^*(\alpha)\sum_{y=0}^{\infty} P_d(y)W_\alpha(x+y), z(x,s) + d^*(\alpha)\,[T^*(\alpha)]^x \sum_{y\geq 0} P_d(y)W_\alpha(y) \right\},$$

It can be shown that for any $x \geq N_0$, there exists $\alpha_x > 0$ such that for all $\alpha \in (0, \alpha_x)$, it is optimal to serve at state x, or equivalently

$$\Delta_\alpha(x) := z(x,v) - z(x,s) + d^*(\alpha)\sum_{y=0}^{\infty} P_d(y)\left(W_\alpha(x+y) - [T^*(\alpha)]^x\, W_\alpha(y)\right) > 0.$$

More precisely, we can show that for $x \geq N_0$, $\underline{\lim}_{\alpha\to 0}\Delta_\alpha(x) \geq xd[1-\rho]^{-1} - \gamma > 0$. The rest of the proof amounts to show that, for α small enough, the mapping $x \to \Delta_\alpha(x)$ is nondecreasing for $0 \leq x \leq N_0 - 1$.

From Lemma 2.2, we deduce that the limit as α converges to 0 of the α-discounted optimal policy u^*_α is a threshold policy with threshold $L \leq N_0$. Hence

Theorem 2.1 *An optimal threshold policy exists for* **P**.

Proof. If Assumptions 1-5 in Sennott [5, p. 250]) were to hold then the proof would follow from Theorem 2 in [5]. It can be shown that Assumptions 1, 3 and 4 hold but not 2 and 5. It can however be proved that weaker versions of Assumptions 2 and 5 are sufficient for Sennott's Theorem to hold, which establishes the proof.

References

[1] A. Federgruen and K. C. So, "Optimality of threshold policies in single-server queueing systems with server vacations", *Adv. Appl. Prob.* **23**, pp. 388-405 (1991).

[2] O. Kella, "The threshold policy in the M/G/1 queue with server vacations," *Nav. Res. Logist.*, vol. 36, 111-123, 1989.

[3] H. Lee and M. M. Srinivasan, "Control policies for the M^X/G/1 queueing system," *Management Sci.*, vol. 35, no. 6, 708-721, 1989.

[4] S. A. Lippman, "On dynamic programming wth unbounded rewards," *Management Sci.*, vol. 21, no. 11, 1225-1233, 1975.

[5] L. I. Sennott, "Average cost semi-Markov decision processes and the control of queueing systems," *Prob. in the Engineering and Informational Sci.*, vol. 3, 247-272, 1989.

ON DISCRETE TIME QUEUES INVOLVING BATCHES AND N-POLICY

Walter Böhm
Department of Statistics
University of Economics
Augasse 2-6, A-1090 Vienna

S.G. Mohanty
Department of Statistics
McMaster University
Hamilton, Canada L8S 4K1

There is increasing interest in discrete time queueing models and operating policies, especially in computer science. Two special models will be discussed. In both interarrival times and service times have a geometric distribution and the server will be turned on only if a prespecified number of customers is waiting. In the first model customers arrive in batches of a fixed size and there is single service. In the second model there are single arrivals and customers are served in batches of a fixed size. For both models the transient distribution of the queue length is derived by means of sample path combinatorics.

1 Batch arrivals

Consider the discrete time queueing process with the following arrival pattern and the service mechanism:

- arrival process: customers arrive in batches of a fixed size $R \geq 1$ according to a Bernoulli process with success probability α. Thus the interarrival times are i.i.d. geometric.

- service mechanism: a single server serves customers one at a time. The service times, which are independent of arrival times are i.i.d. random variables having a geometric distribution with parameter γ.

It may be realized that the batch arrival process as described is the discrete time analogue of $M/E_R/1$. In addition we assume that the system is operated according to N-policy strategy, which is explained as follows:

> whenever the server becomes empty the service is turned off and becomes active as soon as there are N ($N = cR, c$ being a positive integer) customers in the system.

Let Q_n denote the number of customers in the system at time n and Z_n the state of the system, which may be either idle or busy, to be represented by $\{Z_n = \omega\}$ and $\{Z_n = \sigma\}$, respectively. The bivariate process $\{(Q_n, Z_n), n \geq 0\}$ is a Markov chain.
The sample path segments of Q_n due to busy periods may be conveniently described in terms of a random walk process X_n, defined on the set of all integers, having the following one-step transition probabilities:

$$
\begin{aligned}
P(X_n = k + R | X_{n-1} = k) &= \alpha \\
P(X_n = k | X_{n-1} = k) &= \beta \\
P(X_n = k - 1 | X_{n-1} = k) &= \gamma,
\end{aligned}
$$

where $\beta = 1 - \alpha - \gamma$. For later reference let us denote

$$\begin{aligned} p_n(m,k) &= P(X_n = k | X_0 = m) \\ q_n(m) &= P(X_n = 0, X_i > 0, 0 \le i < n | X_0 = m) \\ s_n(m,k) &= P(X_n = k, X_i > 0, 0 \le i \le n | X_0 = m). \end{aligned} \tag{1}$$

We set $q_n(0) = \delta_{n0}$, where δ_{n0} denotes the Kronecker delta and $s_n(m,k) = 0$, whenever either k or $m \le 0$. It can be shown that

$$\begin{aligned} p_n(m,k) &= \binom{n;\alpha,\beta,\gamma}{n+k-m}_R \\ q_n(m) &= \frac{m}{n}\binom{n;\alpha,\beta,\gamma}{n-m}_R \\ s_n(m,k) &= \binom{n;\alpha,\beta,\gamma}{n+k-m}_R - \sum_{\nu\ge1}\frac{m}{\nu}\binom{\nu;\alpha,\beta,\gamma}{\nu-m}_R\binom{n-\nu;\alpha,\beta,\gamma}{n-\nu+k}_R \\ &= p_n(m,k) - q_n(m) * p_n(0,k), \end{aligned} \tag{2}$$

where $*$ denotes convolution and $\binom{n;\alpha,\beta,\gamma}{a}_R$ the coefficient of z^a in the expansion of $(\gamma + \beta z + \alpha z^R)^n$. During an idle period the process Q_n behaves like a Bernoulli process with success probability α, thus the duration of an idle period, which ends with an arrival, has a negative binomial distribution which we denote by

$$g_n(a) = \binom{n-1}{a-1}\alpha^a(1-\alpha)^{n-a}.$$

Theorem 1 *For $m, k > 0$, we have*

$$\begin{aligned} &P(Q_n = k, Z_n = \sigma | Q_0 = m, Z_0 = \sigma) = \\ &= s_n(m,k) + \sum_{i\ge1} g_n(ci) * [s_n(m+Ni,k) - s_n(m+N(i-1),k-N)]. \end{aligned} \tag{3}$$

Proof. The event $\{Q_n = k, Z_n = \sigma | Q_0 = m, Z_0 = \sigma\}$ may arise in two mutually exclusive ways: (a) the server has never been idle in the interval $(0,n)$, (b) there has been at least one completed idle period. In case (a) the probability of this event is $s_n(m,k)$.
To deal with case (b) assume that there have been $i \ge 1$ idle periods. Consider now the following mapping: In the path representing Q_n we cut out the i segments of idle periods. Next we form a new path by putting these segments of idle periods at the beginning and then concatenating the remaining segments of busy periods in their original order. The resulting path consists of two parts. The first part is a segment leading from height m to $m+Ni$ without going down. Clearly its probability is $g_n(ci)$. For evaluating the probability of the second part, we note that this path segment leads from height $m+Ni$ to a terminal point with height k, without touching or crossing the line $y = 0$. However, it has to touch or cross the line $y = N$, since the first point, where this happens, marks the beginning of the last busy period. This requirement will be automatically satisfied, if $k \le N$. If $k > N$, observe that the set of all paths leading from height $m + Ni$ to height k, which do not

touch or cross the line $y = 0$, is the disjoint union of the set of paths with same origin and terminus, which do not touch or cross $y = N$ and those paths, which do touch or cross this line. Hence the required probability is given by

$$s_n(m + Ni, k) - s_n(m + N(i-1), k - N).$$

In a similar way the distribution of Q_n can be derived if the server is idle at time n or at time 0.

2 Batch departures

Now we assume:

- arrival process: customers arrive one at a time according to a Bernoulli process with success probability α.
- service mechanism: a single server serves customers in batches of a fixed size $R \geq 1$. The service times, which are independent of arrival times are i.i.d. random variables having a geometric distribution with parameter γ.

It may be realized that the above process is the discrete time analogue of $E_R/M/1$. As earlier we assume N-policy strategy, which in the present case is as follows:

> whenever the queue length becomes less than R, the service is turned off and becomes active as soon as there are N $(N \geq R)$ customers in the system.

Again Q_n denotes the number of customers in the system at time n, including those which are in service at time n. Z_n denotes the state of the system, which may be either idle, i.e. $(Z_n = \omega)$ or busy, i.e. $(Z_n = \sigma)$. It follows from the above assumptions, that the vector process (Q_n, Z_n) is a Markov chain. We define, similar to the previous section, a discrete time random walk X_n^*, which has state space the set of all integers and one-step transition probabilities

$$\begin{aligned} P(X_n^* = k - R | X_{n-1}^* = k) &= \gamma \\ P(X_n^* = k | X_{n-1}^* = k) &= \beta \\ P(X_n^* = k + 1 | X_{n-1}^* = k) &= \alpha. \end{aligned}$$

The random walk X_n^* is dual to the process X_n defined in section 1, in the sense that $X_i^* = X_{n-i+1}, i = 0, 1, \ldots, n$. In that case,

$$\begin{aligned} p_n^*(m,k) &= P(X_n^* = k | X_0^* = m) \\ &= \bar{p}_n(k,m) \end{aligned} \tag{4}$$

and

$$\begin{aligned} s_n^*(m,k) &= P(X_n^* = k, X_i^* > 0, 0 \leq i \leq n | X_0^* = m) \\ &= \bar{s}_n(k,m) \\ &= \bar{p}_n(k,m) - \bar{q}_n(k) * \bar{p}_n(0,m), \end{aligned} \tag{5}$$

where $\bar{p}_n, \bar{q}_n$ and $\bar{s}_n$ are derived from p_n, q_n and s_n given in (1), by interchanging the probabilities α and γ.

Theorem 2 *For $k, m \geq R$, we have:*

$$P(Q_n = k, Z_n = \sigma | Q_n = m, Z_0 = \sigma) = \tag{6}$$

$$= \bar{s}_n(k - R + 1, m - R + 1) + \gamma \bar{s}_n(k - R + 1, N - R + 1) *$$

$$* \sum_{a>0} g_n(a) * \bar{s}_{n-1}(R, m + a - N)$$

Proof. As in Theorem 1 we consider two cases: (i) the server is never idle, (ii) the server is idle at least once. Let a denote the total number of arrivals during all completed idle periods. Clearly there will be no idle period, if and only if $a = 0$. Since a busy period terminates whenever the path of Q_n crosses the line $y = R$ downwards, the probability of (i) is $P(X_n^\star = k, X_i^\star > R - 1, 0 \leq i \leq n | X_0^\star = m)$, which equals $s_n^\star(m - R + 1, k - R + 1)$ and this gives the first term in (6).

Consider now the case $a > 0$, which implies that there is at least one completed idle period and construct the following bijective mapping: First, we cut out the segments due to idle periods and concatenate them to a path leading from height m to height $m + a$. At the terminal point of this path we append the concatenation of successive busy periods, yielding a path segment with the following properties: it starts at height $m + a$ and ends at height k. The point at which the path coming from height $m + a$ reaches the line $y = N$ for the first time, marks the beginning of the last busy period. It is clear that the path is not allowed to cross the line $y = R$. The problem of determining the probability of such a path is now a bit more complicated than in Theorem 1, since there are paths which cross $y = N$ from above in non lattice points. So paths, which cross the line $y = N$ for a first time in a non-lattice point are inadmissable and have to be excluded from further consideration. Consider now the segment of an admissable path from height $m + a$ to the point, where the last busy period begins. Its probability is conveniently derived by means of the basic process $X_n^\star$, in particular we find that this probability equals

$$P(X_n^\star = N, X_i^\star > N, 0 \leq i < n | X_0^\star = m + a),$$

which in turn equals $\gamma \bar{s}_{n-1}(R, m + a - N)$. The tail segment due to the last unfinished busy period has probability

$$\begin{aligned} P(X_n^\star = k, X_i^\star > R - 1, 0 \leq i \leq n | X_0^\star = N) &= s_n^\star(N - R + 1, k - R + 1) \\ &= \bar{s}_n(k - R + 1, N - R + 1). \end{aligned}$$

Taking into account that there have been $a > 0$ arrivals during idle periods, the result follows.

3 References

Böhm W., Mohanty, S.G. (1991) On discrete time Markovian N-policy queues involving batches. Submitted for publication.

Analysis of a communication network with bursty traffic streams

Andreas Brandt
Fachbereich Mathematik
Humboldt-Universität zu Berlin
P.O.Box 1297, O-1086 Berlin

The paper deals with the performance analysis of communication networks with channel allocation, where messages arrive from outside and have to be transmitted. The messages are divided into packets and are transmitted packetwise. The transmission is handled by an exchange processing unit (EPU) which has a buffer for packets. Two aspects are of importance:

1. performance characteristics of the network
2. performance characteristics of the EPU

Since, in reality, the dynamics of communication networks is very complicated, we have investigated both aspects separately.

In the first part of the paper the network aspect is analyzed by means of a queueing network model; the details are given in [3]: The network consists of n stations, where each station is equipped with k transmission channels and a waiting room for messages. Poisson arrival streams of messages enter the stations and require transmission to a destination station according to a given routing matrix. For a transmission one free channel is needed, both at the arrival and at the destination station. The transmission time is exponentially distributed. Messages get lost (possibly after a waiting time) if all channels are busy at the destination station. The queueing network model is of non-product form type. Hence, a heuristical approximation is given. The derived approximation leads to a system of nonlinear equations whose solution allow to compute the loss probabilities for messages. Explicit solutions can be derived for special cases. For the general case an efficient iterative numerical algorithm is given. Its convergence can be proved under weak assumptions.

Simulation studies show that the approximation is accurate enough for larger n.

In the second part of the paper we present an analytical model of the EPU and its analysis. The details can be found in [2]. The messages are divided into packets and transmitted packetwise, i.e. at the EPU a superposition of the arrival streams generated by many packet sources arrives. It is known that such packet streams are bursty traffics. Concepts for modelling bursty traffic streams as presented in [5] and [6] are shortly discussed. Our EPU is able to process only one packet and the processing time of each packet is constantly one time unit. Arriving packets finding the EPU busy are stored in a buffer. Thus the EPU is modelled as a single server for packets in discrete time. The packet arrival process is modelled as follows: Poisson distributed batches of messages arrive. Each message consists of a geometrically distributed number of packets, where the packets have a geometrically distributed (constant) spacing. A numerical algorithm for computing the stationary mean number of packets in the system is given in case of geometrically spacing and infinite buffer size. The numerical results show the burstiness of the packet stream arriving at the EPU. In case of finite buffer, an approximation for the packet loss probability, based on the analytical results, is proposed. Simulation results indicate that the packet loss probability depends dramatically on the burstiness of the arrival process. The proposed model of the EPU can be used to model transmission channels for voice sources in ISDN networks (ATM multiplexer). However, further investigations are necessary to get numerical algorithms, that are more tractable.

In the last part of the paper we show that the mathematical ideas given in [3] can be extended to analyze the following system (cf. Fig. 1); the details of the analysis are outlined in [1]:

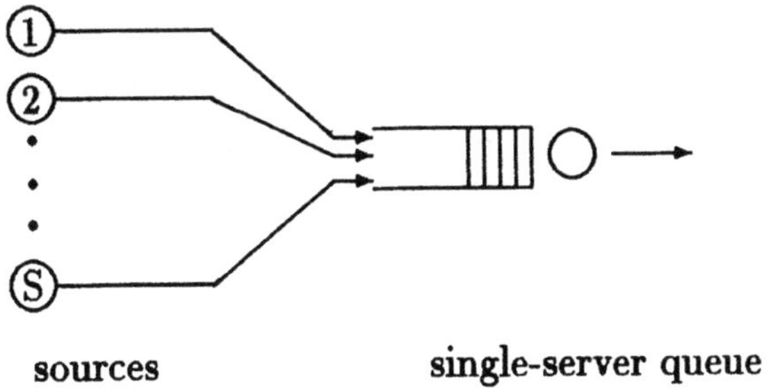

Fig. 1 The $\Sigma MMPP/D/1/\infty$ system

S independent sources generate packets which are served by a single server queue in discrete time and with infinite buffer. The packets require a time unit as service time. Each source (cf. Fig. 2) alternates between active and passive periods such that $Y_n^s = \mathbb{1}\{\text{source } s \text{ is active in frame } n\}$ is a discrete-time Markov chain (MC) with transition probabilities p_{ij}, $i, j \in \{0, 1\}$.

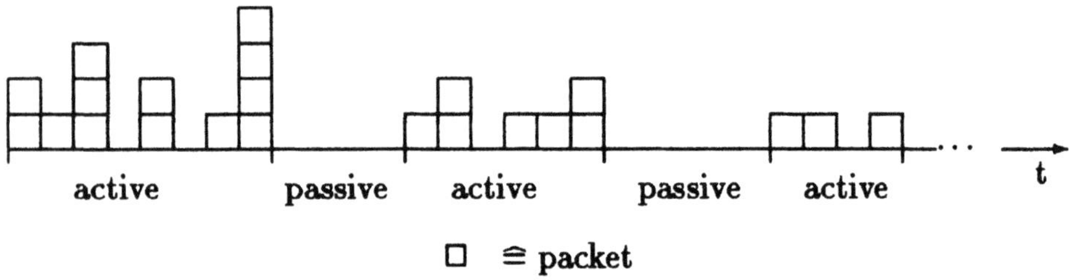

Fig. 2 Single packet source

If source $s \in \{1, \ldots, S\}$ is active, then a Poisson distributed number U_n^s of packets is generated in the n-th frame, otherwise no packets are generated. The model is a discrete time version of an $\Sigma MMPP/D/1/\infty$ system with $\lambda_0 = 0$, $\lambda_1 = \lambda$, cf. [4] and the references therein. The sequence $\{[X_n, R_n]\}$ of the number of packets in the system at the n-th frame and the number of active sources is a MC and has a stationary distribution $p(x, r)$, provided that $\varrho = \lambda S p_{o1}/(p_{o1} + p_{1o}) < 1$. The PGF $\Pi(u, v) = \sum_{x,r} p(x, r) u^x v^r$ satisfies the functional equation

$$\Pi(u, v) = \frac{A(v)}{u}(\Pi(u, h(u, v)) - (1 - u) g(v)) \tag{1}$$

where

$$A(v) = (p_{oo} + p_{o1} v)^S, \; h(u, v) = e^{-\lambda(1-u)} q(v), \; q(v) = \frac{p_{1o} + p_{11} v}{p_{oo} + p_{o1} v}$$

and $g(v) = \Pi(0, e^{-\lambda} q(v)) = \sum_{l=0}^{\infty} a_l v^l$ is the unknown boundary function. The stationary mean number of packets in the system can be computed via this boundary function without solving the functional equation. If $p_{o1} < p_{1o} < \frac{1}{2}$, which is often satisfied in applications, then one can construct the following transformations. Let

$$f(u, v) = \prod_{n=0}^{\infty} \frac{A(v(u))}{A(h^n(u, v))}, \quad w(u, v) = \prod_{n=0}^{\infty} \frac{q'(v(u))}{q'(h^n(u, v))},$$

where $v(u)$ is the unique solution of the equation $v = h(u,v)$ and $h^n(u,v) := h(u, h^{n-1}(u,v))$, $n \geq 1$ and $h^o(u,v) := v$. Define recursively:

$$\chi_o(u,v) \;:=\; f(u,v)\Pi(u,v),\ \chi_n(u,v) := w(u,v)\frac{\partial}{\partial v}\chi_{n-1}(u,v),\ n \geq 1,$$
$$c_o(u,v) \;:=\; A(v)f(u,v)g(v),\ c_n(u,v) := w(u,v)\frac{\partial}{\partial v}c_{n-1}(u,v),\ n \geq 1. \quad (2)$$

Then it can be shown that (1) yields for $v = v(u)$:

$$\chi_n(u, v(u))\alpha_n(u) = -(1-u)c_n(u, v(u)), \quad (3)$$

where $\alpha_n(u) = u - A(v(u))e^{-n\lambda(1-u)}(q'(v(u)))^n$. The functions $\alpha_n(u)$ have exactly one zero u_n in the unit disk D^1 and $u_n \in (0,1)$. For $u = u_n$ eq. (3) yields

$$c_n(u_n, v_n) = 0, \quad n \geq 1, \quad (4)$$

where $v_n = v(u_n)$. From (2) and (3) one can derive, for the unknown coefficients a_l, a linear system of equations whose coefficients can be computed recursively.

References

[1] Brandt, A.: A discrete time single server model with multiple two state discrete *MMPP* sources. Preprint Nr. 91-10 (1991), Humboldt-Universität zu Berlin

[2] Brandt, A., M. Brandt and H. Sulanke: A single server model for packetwise transmission of messages. Queueing Systems 6 (1990), 287-310; Part II: Analytical solution for the Poisson case- Preprint Nr. 229, Humboldt-Universität zu Berlin (1989)

[3] Brandt, A. and H. Sulanke: A queueing network model for a communication system with channel allocation. To appear in Probability in the Engineering and Informational Sciences 1991

[4] Fischer, W. and K. Meier-Hellstern: The *MMPP* cookbook. (submitted for publication)

[5] Heffes, H. and D.M. Lucantoni: A Markov modulated characterization of packetized voice and data traffic and related statistical multiplexer performance. IEEE J. Select. Areas Commun. vol. SAC-4 (1986), 856-868

[6] Nagarajan, R., J. Kurose and D. Towsley: Approximation techniques for computing packet loss in finite-buffered voice multiplexers. Infocom' 90 San Francisco, Juni 1990

MINIMIZING TOTAL TARDINESS WITH UNEQUAL RELEASE DATES

Chengbin Chu
Projet SAGEP, INRIA-Lorraine, CESCOM, Technopôle Metz 2000
4, rue Marconi, 57070 Metz, France

We consider the scheduling problem to minimize the total tardiness of a set of n jobs to be processed on a single machine which can perform only one job at a time. No preemption of jobs is allowed. Each job i has a release date r_i, a processing time p_i and a due date d_i. The objective is to find a schedule S which minimizes $T(S)=\sum_{i=1}^{n} T_i(S)=\sum_{i=1}^{n} \max(C_i(S)-d_i,0)$, where T(S) is the total tardiness of schedule S, $C_i(S)$ and $T_i(S)$ are respectively the completion time and the tardiness of job i in schedule S.

The problem considered has been proved to be NP-hard (Rinnooy Kan 1976). Although the single machine scheduling problem has been extensively studied (Gupta and Kyparisis 1987, Lawler *et al.* 1989), to the best of our knowledge, there is no published work on minimizing total tardiness with unequal release dates.

However, much attention has been paid to the problem with equal release dates which is also NP-hard (Du and Leung 1990). The theorems proved by Emmons (1969) to reduce problem size were widely used by several authors to construct exact algorithms. Most of them use the dynamic programming approach (Lawler 1977, Potts and Van Wassenhove 1982, Srinivasan 1971), among which the algorithm using decomposition approach proposed by Potts and Van Wassenhove (1982) was tested on problems with up to 100 jobs. This approach employs the method of Baker and Schrage (1978) for the problem with precedence constraints between jobs. Using Lagrangean relaxation, Fisher (1976) obtained a tight lower bound which was integrated in a branch and bound algorithm.

Our previous paper (Chu and Portmann 1991) addressed the problem of minimizing total tardiness with unequal release dates. We proved a sufficient condition for local optimality which can also be considered as a dynamic priority rule, defined a dominant subset (a dominant subset is one containing at least one optimal solution) called T-active subset, and proposed a number of heuristic algorithms.

In this paper, we present other dominance properties and a simple lower bound, and propose a branch and bound algorithm using these results.

DOMINANCE PROPERTIES AND LOWER BOUND

We do not present the dominance of T-active schedules (refer to Chu and Portmann 1991). We present here new dominance properties and the lower bound without proof. Their proofs can be found in Chu 1992. In the remainder, let J denote the set of the jobs to be scheduled.

Theorem 1. *If there is a job i such that* $i \in J$*, and* $\forall j \in J$, $p_i \leq p_j$, $d_i \leq d_j$*, there is an optimal schedule in which job i precedes any job k such that* $r_i \leq r_k$.

Theorem 2. *If* $\max_{i \in J}(r_i) \leq \min_{i \in J}(r_i + p_i)$ *and j and k are two jobs belonging to J such that* $r_j \leq r_k$, $r_j + p_j \leq r_k + p_k$ *and* $d_j \leq d_k$*, then job j dominates job k in the first position.*

Theorem 3. *Let* $j \in J$ *be a job such that* $r_j = \max_{i \in J}(r_i)$*, there is an optimal schedule in which job j is preceded by any job k such that* $p_j \geq p_k$ *and* $d_j \geq d_k$.

Theorem 4. *Given two jobs i,* $j \in J$*, if* $p_i \geq p_j$ *and* $r_i + p_i \leq r_j + p_j$ *and* $d_i \leq d_j$*, then job i dominates job j in the first position.*

The following theorem shows how to calculate a lower bound.

Theorem 5. *Given a problem* Π*, we construct a schedule* Σ *in which the jobs are scheduled according to SRPT (Shortest Remaining Processing Time),by relaxing the non preemption assumption . If* $(d'_1, d'_2, \ldots, d'_n)$ *is the series obtained by ordering the series* $(d_1, d_2, \ldots, d_n)$ *in non decreasing order, the following relation holds* $\sum_{i=1}^{n} \max(C_{[i]}(\Sigma) - d'_i, 0) \leq T^*(\Pi)$*, where* $C_{[i]}(\Sigma)$ *is the completion time of the job completed at the i-th position in* Σ. $T^*(\Pi)$ *is the optimal total tardiness of problem* Π.

BRANCH AND BOUND ALGORITHM

The branch and bound algorithm mixes a technique of "forward sequencing branching rule" and a technique of "backward sequencing branching rule". Each node is defined by a partial sequence P of jobs scheduled from the beginning of the schedule and a partial sequence Q of jobs scheduled at the end of the schedule. Initially, P and Q are empty sets. Q must be empty if there is at least one unscheduled job whose release date is strictly greater than the completion time of the sequence P.

When Q has to be empty, each descendant node is obtained by adding, *behind* the partial sequence P, a new job i, chosen among the unscheduled jobs. The choice of a job i is such that: (i) it is not necessarily be preceded by another unscheduled job according to Theorems 1 and 3, (ii) it is not dominated by another unscheduled job according to Theorems 2 and 4, and (iii) job i and the last job of P verify the conditions of a T-active schedule.

If the release dates of *all* the unscheduled jobs are smaller than the completion time of P, each descendant node is obtained by adding, a new job i, chosen among the unscheduled jobs *before* the partial sequence Q. The choice of job i is such that there is no unscheduled job j, according to Theorems of Emmons (1969). The job i and the first job of Q should also verify the conditions for a schedule to be T-active.

The lower bound is computed using Theorem 5. An upper bound is computed for each descendant node by completing the partial sequences with the heuristic NDPRTT (see Chu and Portmann 1991). For branching, we always select the node with the smallest lower bound.

The computational results reported in Chu 1992 show that the proposed algorithm can solve hard problems with up to 30 jobs and relatively "easy" problems with up to 230 jobs.

CONCLUSION

This work is the first attempt to tackle the scheduling problem for minimizing total tardiness with unequal release dates. We have presented some dominance properties, and provided a lower bound. Combined with our previous results, this allowed us to construct a branch and bound algorithm which is able to exactly solve difficult problems with up to 30 jobs and relatively easy problems with up to 230 jobs.

REFERENCES

Baker K.R., Schrage L.E. (1978), "Finding an Optimal Sequence by Dynamic Programming: An Extension to Precedence-Related Tasks", *Opns. Res.* **26**, 111-126

Chu C. (1992), "A Branch and Bound Algorithm to Minimize Total Tardiness with Different Release Dates", *Naval Research Logistics* **39**, to be published

Chu C., Portmann M.C. (1991), "Some New Efficient Methods to Solve the $n/1/r_i/\Sigma T_i$ Scheduling Problem", *Europ. J. Opnl. Res* **56**, to be published

Du J., Leung J.Y.-T. (1990), "Minimizing Total Tardiness on One Machine is NP-hard", *Math. Oper. Res.* **15**, 483-495

Emmons H. (1969), "One-Machine Sequencing to Minimize Certain Functions of Job Tardiness", *Opns. Res.* **17**, 701-715

Fisher M.L. (1976), "A Dual Algorithm for the One-Machine Scheduling Problem", *Math. Prog.* **11**, 229-251

Gupta S.K., Kyparisis J. (1987), "Single Machine Scheduling Research", *OMEGA Int. J. Mgmt. Sci.* **15**, 207-227

Lawler E.L. (1977), "A "Pseudopolynomial" Algorithm for Sequencing Jobs to Minimize Total Tardiness", *Ann. Disc. Math.* **1**, 331-342

Lawler E.L., Lenstra J.K., Rinnooy Kan A.H.G., Shmoy S.D.B. (1989), "Sequencing and Scheduling: Algorithms and Complexity", *Report* **BS-R8909**, Center for Mathematics and Computer Science, Amsterdam

Potts C.N., Van Wassenhove L.N. (1982), "A Decomposition Algorithm for the Single Machine Total Tardiness Problem", *Opns. Res. Lett.* **1**, 177-181

Rinnooy Kan A.H.G. (1976), *Machine Sequencing Problems: Classification, Complexity and Computation*, Nijhoff, The Hague

Srinivasan V. (1971), "A Hybrid Algorithm for the One-Machine Sequencing Problem to Minimize Total Tardiness", *Nav. Res. Logist. Quart.* **18**, 317-327

SIMULATED ANNEALING AND SCHEDULING IN MANUFACTURING SYSTEMS

Gérard FLEURY
Université Blaise PASCAL - CLERMONT FERRAND II
F63177 AUBIERE Cedex. FRANCE

Problem: For scheduling in manufacturing systems, the make-span, or total flow time, is the difference between the output date of the last job on the last machine, and the input date of the first job on the first machine. The problem is to find a schedule which minimises the make-span.

SIMULATED ANNEALING

*Notation: Let Ω be a finite set and $H:\Omega \to \mathbb{R}$ a cost function (Hamiltonian, or energy function), we look for a minimum for H, that is $y \in \Omega_{Min}=\{x/H(x)=MinH(\Omega)\}$.

The idea of simulated annealing comes from statistical physics, mainly the Ising model [See 5, 11 or 13]. It is known that if a Markov chain X, with finite set of states, is aperiodic, irreductible and homogeneous, then it has a unique stationary probability π_i and we have: $\forall i, \sum \pi_j P_{ji}=\pi_i$ [3].Then $\lim P\{X(n)=i/X(0)=x\}=\pi_i \ \forall x \ \forall i$. If, $\forall i, \forall j$, $P_{ij}.\pi_i=P_{ji}.\pi_j$ (detailed balance equation), then π is stationary for P.

Let be:

1) a stochastic symetric array P^*. P^*_{ij} is the probability to go from state i to state j, usually defined by a neighbourhood V(i) of i (having the same number of elements), such that: if $y \notin V(x)$, $P^*_{xy}=0$, and if $y \in V(x)$, $P^*_{xy}=\frac{1}{card(V(x))}$ and: $y \in V(x)$ if and only if $x \in V(y)$.

2) a probability π on Ω such that, if H(i)=H(j), then $\pi_i=\pi_j$. For instance, for a T>0:

$$P\{X=x\}=\frac{e^{-\frac{H(x)}{T}}}{Z(T)} \text{ with } Z(T)=\sum_x e^{-\frac{H(x)}{T}}$$

3) an array A verifiing, $\forall i, \forall j$, H(j)>H(i) implies $A_{ij}.\pi_i=\pi_j$.

Let us then construct the homogeneous Markov chain X with transition array P defined by: if X(n)=i, then X(n+1)=j with probability P_{ij} such that:

if $H(j) \le H(i)$ and $j \ne i$, then $P_{ij}=P^*_{ij}$, if H(j)>H(i) then $P_{ij}=P^*_{ij}.A_{ij}$

and $P_{ii}=1-\sum_{j \ne i} P_{ij}$

Under these conditions, the detailed balance equation is satisfied, therefore π is stationary (Metropolis dynamic) [8].

INHOMOGENEOUS ALGORITHM

The Markov chain X is defined by: $P\{X(n+1)=y/X(n)=x\}=P^*_{xy}.e^{-\frac{H(y)-H(x)}{T}}$ if H(y)>H(x), with $T=T_n=\frac{C}{\ln(n+1)}$.

Definition: We call local minimum, an element x of Ω which minimises H in V(x), their set is Ω_{Loc}. One says that x communicates with y at the height h when either x=y and $H(x) \le h$, or there exists a finite chain of neighbour elements and of energy at most h, going from x to y: it exists a finite sequence x_k $(0 \le k \le n)$ with, $x_0=x$ and $x_n=y$ and, $\forall k \in \{1;2;...;n\}$ $x_k \in V(x_{k-1})$ and $\forall k$, $H(x_k) \le h$. If x is a local minimum, its deapness is the minimal positive real d such that $\exists y \in \Omega$ verifiing $H(y)<H(x)$ and: x communicates with y at the height H(x)+d.

Theorem: (Hajek [10]) For x in Ω, let d_x its deapness, and let be $D=Max\{d_x / x \in \Omega_{Min} \backslash \Omega_{Loc}\}$:

If $\forall x, \forall y \in \Omega$, $\forall p>1$, $\exists L_0, L_1, ..., L_p$ in Ω with $L_0=x$ and $L_p=y$ and $\forall k$ in $\{0;1;...p-1\}$, $P^*_{L_k L_{k+1}}>0$

and, for $\forall x$ $\forall y$ inΩ,

x communicates with y at the height h if and only if y communicates with x at the height h

then:

$$\forall y \in \Omega, \lim P\{X(n) \in \Omega_{Min} / X(0)=y\}=1$$

if and only if

$$\forall n \in \mathbb{N}^*, T=\frac{C}{\ln(n+1)} \text{ with } C \ge D$$

THE FLOW-SHOP PROBLEM

In the usual applications of simulated annealing, (statistical physics, picture restoration), the neigbourhoods are geometrically defined. For scheduling, it seems natural to consider as neighbour of the schedule x, the schedule y obtained

1) by transposition of 2 jobs (contiguous or not): T
2) by transposition of 2 contiguous jobs: CT
3) by insertion of a job in another room: I

Remark: The property: $\forall x, \forall y \in \Omega$, $\forall p>1$, $\exists L_0, L_1, ..., L_p$ in Ω with $L_0=x$ and $L_p=y$ and $\forall k$ in $\{0;1;...p-1\}$, $P^*_{L_k L_{k+1}}>0$, which means that we can go from any state x to any other y by a finite number of neighbour states x , is valid in all these cases.

What is the bias of these choices of neighbourhood on the make-span? In the following, "at random" means the use of a uniform pseudo-random generator. One have considered 80 jobs in a flow-shop of 5 machines, service times on each machine are random natural integers, from 1 to 19 (included). All the following was done with the 26 same data. For each of them, we generated 900 couples (x;y) of schedules "at random": R. We did the same with a random choice of a schedule x, associated to 30 neighbour random schedules y chosen as above. We have below the means of the correlation coefficients obtained for each of the 26 data:

	correlation coefficient
R	0.000
T	0.951
CT	0.998
I	0.973

The correlation coefficient is high, in the three last cases, and justifies the name of neighborhood.

We have compared the results furnished by simulated annealing (Metropolis) corresponding to these three choices of neighbourhoods by a Student's test on the deviations between 26 couples of results: (T,I) and also (TC,I), and with different values of temperature. It appears that the difference between TC and I is higthly significative, and the difference between I and T is significative. It seems that we must avoid the neighbourhood associated to contiguous transpositions, and that insertion is the best method.

HEURISTICS

One will find a good catalog of Flow-shop heuristics in Han & Dejax [22], or Widmer [24]. We compared simulated annealing to the following heuristics (which seems to be the best ones (Widmer [24]):

CDS (Campbell, Dudek et Smith) [18]

RAES (Rapid Acces with Extensive Search,Dannenbring [21])

NEH (Nawaz, Enscore et Ham) [23]

To compare to simulated annealing, we can use the internal clock, and limit the duration of annealing by the duration of the best heuristic. But annealing is (with a good choice of parameter) an exact, but asymptotic method. We retained, for criterium, instead of the CPU time (depending on the machine, on the program, on intermediate mesures...), thenumber of calls of the energy function.

Some of the heuristics never use the energy function, but they are not the best ones. Our purpose was, perhaps, to use annealing with a simulation software, and therefore, this kind of time-mesuring seems more appropriate, for the time for the calculus of make-span for a more complicated workshop can strongly overlap the CPU-time used by the algorithm. We have chosen to compare annealing to the best method (which seems to be NEH, as shown by Widmer [24]), in the same time (with the above sense).

We have tested these methods with different flow-shops: 5, 15 or 25 machines and, 20, 40 or 80 jobs. Each time,wehave created 26 different data. With 20 jobs, the number of calls to function has been limitated (following NEH), to 200, with 40 jobs, to 800, and in the case of 80 jobs, to 3000. The service-times are integers at random from 1 to 19 included.

We have used the inhomogeneous algorithm, but, for short uses (less than 1000 calls), an homogoneous algorithm (with low T), seems to have been sufficient. We also tested the annealing withT=0 (stochastic descent), and, with a small number of calls (less than 300), it seems better than others.

To separate differences between all theses results,we consider the n=26 couples. We calculate the n differences between annealing and another method, and, if these numbers are normally distributed, with their mean M and their variance V, then

$$t = \frac{|M|}{\sqrt{\frac{V}{n-1}}}$$

follows a Student law with n-1 degrees of freedom. We have verified the hypothesis of normality of the differences by the Shapiro-Wilk test [see 1 or 2] (between annealing and NEH). The response always was positive.

Some of the results are below.

In our study, annealing is at least as good as any of the heuristics, but usually less rapid. Nevertheless annealing is better when the conditions are away from the 2-machines flow-shop problem. This can be explained by the fact that most of the heuristics use the idea of Johnson theorem to construct their schedule.

Annealing also is better when the number of jobs is high, for heuristics as NEH use a too great number of calls (which is $O(n^2)$ for NEH), to the energy function.

We have used other data, with several identical jobs. Annealing seems much better, for the heuristics often use sorting, and, therefore, group identical jobs together, which is not necessarily the best method.

5 MACHINES 80 JOBS
MINIMUM VALUE

THEORETICAL MINIMUM	CDS	RAES	NEH	ANNEALING 7/ln(n+1)	0 (3000 CALLS)	4/ln(n+1)
Means						
867.8	898	880.7	881.2	874.5	873.2	872.6
Standard deviations						
36.12	37.28	36.75	34.54	36.25	35.85	35.14

DEVIATIONS WITH ANNEALING (T=4/ln(n+1), 3000 CALLS)

	CDS	RAES	NEH	ANNEALING 7/ln(n+1)	0	
Means:	25.38	34	8.653	1.961	0.615	
Variance:	181.0	328.8	88.14	18.03	9.698	
Number:	26					
Degrees of freedom:		25				
Calculated T:	19.43	5.39	4.61	2.31	0.988	
Bounds for T:	(5% 2.060)		(1% 2.787)		(0,1%	3.725)
Conclusion:	≠	≠	≠	?	=	

Legend:
≠ the difference is hightly significative
? the difference is significative
= the difference is not significative.

CONCLUSION

Drawback

1) the relative slowness of annealing in front of heuristics, except for the best of them. It seems that annealing is to use for problems which necessitate a good optimum, or when one disregards CPU-time.

2) the difficulty of choice for the temperature. Slight difficulty, because it seems that it can be chosen low (and even null, if a relative minimum is sufficient, or if CPU-time is strongly limited).

Advantages:

1) Easy algorithm for programming,

2) The longer the algorithm runs, the better the results are, and different tries may lead to different results. Results are much better than those of heuristics, when the dimensions (number of jobs, or number of machines), of the problem are high.

4) One can use this algorithm for other manufacturing problems (one machine problem for instance), or more complicated:

delays for transportation between machines,

limitations in the internal ressources,

periodical indisponibility of machines,

possibility for a job, to use any of different machines for the same task, with different service-times.

In fact, one can use simulated annealing for scheduling in any workshop, as soon as it has a deterministic model and a well defined internal rule for conflicts.

BIBLIOGRAPHY

[1] BRATLEY, FOX, & SCHRAGE: A Guide to Simulation. Springer-Verlag.
[2] CEA: Statistique appliquée à l'exploitation des mesures. Masson. Paris.
[3] FELLER: an introduction to probability theory and applications. Wiley & Sons. New-York.
[4] HAMMERSLEY & HANDSCOMB: Les méthodes de Monte-Carlo. Dunod. Paris.

Simulated annealing

[5] AARTS & KORST: Simulated Annealing & Boltzman Machines. Wiley & Sons. New-York.
[6] CARNEVALI, COLETTI & PATARNELLO. Image processing by simulated annealing. IBM J. Res. Develop. vol 29 n° 6, nov 1985.
[7] GEMAN & GEMAN: Stochastic relaxation, Gibbs distribution & the Bayesian restoration of images. IEEE Trans. Pattern Analysis, Machine intel, vol PAMI-6, pp 721-741 nov 1984.
[8] GEMAN: Random fields & inverse problems in imaging. Lecture notes n° 1427. Ecole d'été de probabilités, St Flour XVII-1988. Springer-Verlag. pp.117-193.
[9] HAJEK. Cooling schedules for optimal annealing. Maths for Oper Res. 13 (2) 311-329, 1988.
[10] HAJEK. Optimization by simulated annealing, a necessary & sufficient condition for convergence.Lectures notes, Monograph series, vol 8, Institute of mathematical statistics, Haywar, California, pp.417-427.
[11] KIRKPATRICK & TOULOUSE: Configuration space analysis of travelling salesman problems. J Physique 46 (1985) 1277-1292.
[12] van LAARHOVEN & AARTS: Simulated Annealing: theory & applications. Reidel. Dordrecht.
[13] OTTEN & van GINNEKEN: The annealing algorithm. Kluwer academic publishers. London.
[14] PRUM: Processus sur un réseau et mesures de Gibbs. Masson.Paris.
[15] SIAARHUS & DREYFUS: La méthode du recuit simulé: théorie & applications.
[16] WONG, LEONG & LIU: Simulated annealing for VLSI design. Kluwer academic publishers. London.
[17] ZERUBIA & CHELLAPPA, Mean field annealing using compound Gauss-Markov random fields for edge detection & image restoration. INRIA, rapport de recherche n°1295, programme 6, octobre 1990.

Scheduling

[18] CAMPBELL, DUDEK & SMITH. A heuristic algorithm for the n jobs, m machines sequencing problem. Management science, 1970, 16, n°10, pp 630-637.
[19] CARLIER & CHRETIENNE: Problèmes d'ordonnancement: Masson. Paris.
[20] COFFMAN: Computer & job-shop scheduling theory. Wiley & Sons. New-York.
[21] DANNENBRING & DAVID: an evaluation of flow-shop sequencing heuristics. management science, 1977, 23, n°11, pp 1174-1182.
[22] HAN & DEJAX: Une heuristique pour le problème d'ordonnancement de type n/m//F/C avec la présence de machines goulots. Revue de Recherche Opérationnelle . 24, n°4, 1990, p.315-330.
[23] NAWAZ, ENSCORE & HAM. A heuristic algorithm for the n jobs, m machines sequencing problem. Omega, 1983, 22, n°1, pp 127-141.
[24] WIDMER Modèles mathématiques pour une gestion efficace des problèmes d'ateliers flexibles. Thèse. Ecole polytechnique de Lausanne.

On the Variance of Measurable Extremal Functions

Karl Frauendorfer
Institute for Operations Research
Moussonstr. 15
University of Zurich
Switzerland

We consider problems of the form

$$P(\eta,\xi) \qquad \rho(\eta,\xi) := \inf_x \; f(\eta,\xi,x) \tag{1}$$

with (η,ξ) representing a random vector of $\mathbf{R}^{K+L}$ with respect to the Borel algebra $\mathcal{B}^{K+L}$ and a given probability measure P with compact support Ω; f is supposed to be a *proper convex normal integrand* ensuring measurability of the extremal function $\rho(\eta,\xi)$ with respect to $\mathcal{B}^{K+L}$ (see Rockafellar 1976 [7]); further, $f\colon \mathbf{R}^{K+L} \times \mathbf{R}^n \to \mathbf{R}$ is assumed to be a *proper closed* saddle function (concave in η and convex in (ξ,x)) in the sense of Rockafellar 1970 [6].

We are focusing on the variance of the extremal function (itself a saddle function being concave in η and convex in ξ) given through

$$\mathrm{Var}\,[\rho(\eta,\xi)] = \int \rho^2(\eta,\xi)dP - [\int \rho(\eta,\xi)dP\,]^2 \tag{2}$$

Due to the fact that extremal functions are not available explicitly and the effort for solving problem (1) even for one specific outcome (η,ξ) might be cumbersome we start our investigations with concentrating on the derivation of an upper bound for $\mathrm{Var}\,[\rho(\eta,\xi)]$.

The intention to get some information on the variance of extremal functions stems e.g. from stochastic optimization, where problems $P(\eta,\xi)$ play an essential role in those models that allow stochasticity within the prices as well as within capacities. For solving stochastic optimization problems approximately one has to rely mostly on sample or empirical distributions as approximates for P (formulas for the terms in (2) are only available for highly structured models with properties like separability, sublinearity and distinguished probability measures). With substituting P by sample/empirical distributions it is well known that for achieving a certain accuracy of the approximate solution with respect to a pregiven confidence level one has to choose the proper sample size based on the underlying variance, or at least based on a corresponding upper bound. (Readers interested in stochastic optimization problems and methods are referred to e.g. Kall 1976 [5], Ermoliev and Wets 1988 [2], Wets 1989 [8].)

Let us now specify the frame in detail : to allow possible stochastic independences among components of (η,ξ) we write $(\eta,\xi)=\times_i(\eta^i,\xi^i)$ with (η^i,ξ^i), $i=1,\dots,I$, denoting random (sub)vectors being stochastically independent; the associated probability distributions are denoted P^i, $i=1,\dots,I$. The compact support of η^i,ξ^i - with respect to the marginal probability measures P^i - are assumed to be contained in a simplex given through Θ^i , Ξ^i being subsets of $\mathbf{R}^{K_i}$, $\mathbf{R}^{L_i}$. We therefore obtain with $\Theta := \times_i \Theta^i$, $\Xi := \times_i \Xi^i$ polytopes that are characterized through taking the crossproduct of a finite number of simplices, subsequently being called a **$\times$-simplex (crossimplex)**; obviously $\Theta\times\Xi$ and $\Theta^i\times\Xi^i$ are again $\times$-simplices that contain the support of the entire random vector (η,ξ) and of (η^i,ξ^i) in particular. The vertices of the simplices Θ^i, Ξ^i are denoted a_{ν_i} , b_{μ_i} with $\nu_i=0,\dots,K_i$, $\mu_i=0,\dots,L_i$ and $i=1,\dots,I$. In the case that all components of (η,ξ) are stochastically dependent this reduces to $I=1$ and Θ, Ξ being simplices. Last but not least, we assume $\rho(\eta,\xi)$ to be subdifferentiable on $\Theta\times\Xi$. This ensures the existence of multilinear approximates that support the extremal function on distinguished points of $\Theta\times\Xi$ depending only on P^i and $\Theta^i\times\Xi^i$ $(i=1,\dots,I)$.

Remark 1: $\times$-simplices might be seen as generalizations of hyperrectangles that obviously are crossproducts of intervals (one-dimensional simplices); moreover, $\times$-simplices have the nice property that one may easily evaluate the number of vertices, the number of edges (one-dimensional faces, or pairs of adjacent vertices) and the set of edges itself, due to the property that any two vertices of a simplex are adjacent. Further $\times$-simplices belong to the class of *simple polytopes* (see e.g. Brondsted 1983 [1]) that are characterized through the property that for any vertex the number of its adjacent vertices is equal to the dimension of the polytope.

Remark 2 : Due to the Fenchel-Rockafellar duality theory of convex analysis, subdifferentiability of extremal functions might be enforced through stability criterions for parametric optimization problems. This is under investigation by the author for problems of type (1) and will be summarized in a future work.

Remark 3 : Bounding the variance of extremal functions has been studied in Frauendorfer and Kall 1988 [4] for the special case of (1) being a linear (in x) program with stochasticity in the convex argument ξ (in the right hand side of the underlying linear stochastic program, respectively). Herein, we are concerned with the convex case (in x) and with stochasticity in the concave argument η as well as in the convex one ξ. For this case we apply a barycentric approximation scheme, having been worked out for solving stochastic two-stage optimization problems in Frauendorfer 1991 [3].

In [3] we disaggregate the probability measure P^i for all $i=1,\dots,I$ into K_i+1 mass distributions on the (facial) simplices $\{a_{\nu_i}\}\times\Xi^i$ for $\nu_i=0,\dots,K_i$. This induces (K_i+1) generalized barycenters - denoted (a_{ν_i},ξ_{ν_i}) - of these simplices. Assigning to the (generalized) barycenter (a_{ν_i},ξ_{ν_i}) a probability equal to the mass distributed on $\{a_{\nu_i}\}\times\Xi^i$ for any $\nu_i=0,\dots,K_i$

we obtain a discrete probability measure $P^{i,l}$ having the barycenters $\{(a_{\nu_i},\xi_{\nu_i}), \nu_i=0,...,K_i\}$ as support and having the property that $P^{i,l}$ solves a certain moment problem. Dually, we may construct a multilinear function $L(\times_i(\eta^i,\xi^i))$ - more precisely linear in η^i (i=1,..,I); ξ separately - with the property that $L(\times_i(\eta^i,\xi^i))$ supports the extremal function $\rho(\eta,\xi)$ from below on the generalized barycenters $\times_i(a_{\nu_i},\xi_{\nu_i})$ of the $\times$-simplices $\times_i [\{a_{\nu_i}\}\times\Xi^i]$. These lower approximates exist due to subdifferentiability of $\rho(\eta,\xi)$, solve the corresponding semiinfinite program and may be characterized to be that extremal approximate that maximize its expectation subject to all multilinear minorants of $\rho(\eta,\xi)$.
Due to symmetricity we may derive extremal upper approximates in a similar way : disagreggating the probability measure P^i for all i=1,...,I into L_i+1 mass distributions on the (facial) simplices $\Theta^i \times\{b_{\mu_i}\}$ for $\mu_i=0,...,L_i$, this induces (L_i+1) generalized barycenters - denoted (η_{μ_i},b_{μ_i}) - on these simplices. Assigning to barycenter (η_{μ_i},b_{μ_i}) a probability equal to the mass distributed on $\Theta^i \times\{b_{\mu_i}\}$ for any $\mu_i=0,...,L_i$ we obtain a discrete probability measure $P^{i,u}$ having the barycenters $\{(\eta_{\mu_i},b_{\mu_i}), \mu_i=0,...,L_i\}$ as support and having the property that $P^{i,u}$ solves a certain moment problem. Dually, we construct a multilinear function $U(\times_i (\eta^i,\xi^i))$ - more precisely linear in η, ξ^i (i=1,...,I) separately - with the property that $U(\times_i(\eta^i,\xi^i))$ supports the extremal function $\rho(\eta,\xi)$ from above on the generalized barycenters $\times_i(\eta_{\mu_i},b_{\mu_i})$ of the $\times$-simplices $\times_i [\Theta^i \times\{b_{\mu_i}\}]$. These upper approximates again exist due to subdifferentiability of $\rho(\eta,\xi)$, solve the corresponding semiinfinite program and may be characterized to be that extremal approximate that minimize its expectation subject to all multilinear majorants of $\rho(\eta,\xi)$.

Concerning the computational effort we have to stress that the above mentioned generalized barycenters are determined completely through the vertices of the $\times$-simplices $\Theta^i\times\Xi^i$, i=1,...,I and through the crossmoments of first order of η^i, ξ^i (i=1,...,I), and therefore are independent of problem (1) and $f(\eta,\xi,x)$ in particular. On the other hand, the lower approximate L supports ρ on $\times_i(a_{\nu_i},\xi_{\nu_i})$, and the upper approximate U supports ρ on $\times_i(\eta_{\mu_i},b_{\mu_i})$. For both, L and U, we have to know the dual solutions of (1) with respect to the generalized barycenters.

We therefore obtain on $\Theta\times\Xi$

$$L(\eta,\xi) \leq \rho(\eta,\xi) \leq U(\eta,\xi) \qquad (3)$$

and claim $L(\eta,\xi)$, $U(\eta,\xi)$ to be (computationally) easily integrable with respect to P as due to multilinearity of the approximates and stochastic independence, it suffices to use again the crossmoments of first order for determining the expectation of L and U.

For bounding the variance of $\rho(\eta,\xi)$ we write

$$\mathrm{Var}\,[\rho(\eta,\xi)] \leq |\,\mathrm{Var}[\rho(\eta,\xi)] - \mathrm{Var}[L(\eta,\xi)]\,| + \mathrm{Var}[L(\eta,\xi)] \qquad (4)$$

and use the following

Lemma 1 : Let $\Theta := \times_i \Theta^i$, $\Xi := \times_i \Xi^i$ be $\times$-simplices and $\phi(\eta,\xi)$ be linear in η^i, ξ^i (i=1,..,I) separately. Then, maximum and minimum of $\phi(\eta,\xi)$ with respect to the $\times$-simplex $\Theta\times\Xi$ are attained at some vertex of $\Theta\times\Xi$. Moreover, $\phi^2(\eta,\xi)$ is convex in η^i, ξ^i (i=1,...,I) separately, and the maximum with respect to $\Theta\times\Xi$ is attained at some vertex of $\Theta\times\Xi$.

Proof : The first assertion follows immediately from the fact that a linear function attains its extremum (with respect to a compact polytope) at a vertex; similarly, the second assertion is due to the fact that a convex function attains its maximum at a vertex. //

The term $|\mathrm{Var}[\rho(\eta,\xi)]-\mathrm{Var}[L(\eta,\xi)]|$ might be bounded from above through the expectations of L and U with respect to P, and $\max\{U(\eta,\xi)-L(\eta,\xi) \mid \forall\ (\eta,\xi)\in\Theta\times\Xi\}$; the latter is attained at a vertex due to Lemma 1 and setting $\phi(\eta,\xi) := U(\eta,\xi)-L(\eta,\xi)$. The second term in (4) is defined through

$$\mathrm{Var}[L(\eta,\xi)] = \int_{\Theta\times\Xi} L^2(\eta,\xi)dP - \Big[\int_{\Theta\times\Xi} L(\eta,\xi)dP \Big]^2 \qquad (5)$$

The expectation of L is known. To bound the expectation of L^2 we have to note that L^2 is convex in η^i, ξ (i=1,...,I) separately; due to the above, the maximum is attained at some vertex of $\Theta\times\Xi$; we so obtain upper bounds for both terms in (4) and hence for $\mathrm{Var}[\rho(\eta,\xi)]$.

Summarizing, we may state that - once the crossmoments of η^i, ξ^i (i=1,..,I) and the generalized barycenters are known - it requires to solve $\Sigma_i(\Pi_i(K_i+1)+\Pi_i(L_i+1))$ problems of type (1); the corresponding dual solutions define lower and upper approximates L and U that support $\rho(\eta,\xi)$ at the barycenters; finally, both approximates have to be evaluated at the vertices of $\Theta\times\Xi$, whose number is given through $\Pi_i[(K_i+1)*(L_i+1)]$. Therefore the entire effort behaves polynomially in the dimensions of the stochastically independent subvectors with order I.

References :

[1] *A. Brondsted* : An Introduction to Convex Polytopes; Graduate Text in Mathematics 90; Springer-Verlag New York (1983)

[2] *Y. Ermoliev, R.J.-B. Wets* : Numerical Techniques for Stochastic Optimization: Springer-Verlag Berlin, (1988)

[3] *K. Frauendorfer* : Stochastic Two-Stage Optimization, Manuscript, University of Zurich (1991)

[4] *K. Frauendorfer , P. Kall* : A Solution Method for SLP Recourse Problems with Arbitrary Distributions - The Independent Case; in: Problems of Control and Information Theory 17 (1988); p. 177-205.

[5] *P. Kall* : Stochastic Linear Programming; Springer-Verlag Berlin (1976)

[6] *R.T. Rockafellar* : Convex Analysis, Princeton University Press (1970)

[7] *R.T. Rockafellar* : Integral Functionals, Normal Integrands and Measurable Selections; in: Nonlinear Operators and the Calculus of Variations; Springer-Verlag, Lecture Notes in Mathematics 543, Berlin (1976) 157-207

[8] *R.J.-B. Wets* : Stochastic Programming; in: Handbook on Operations Research and Management Science, Vol. 1: Optimization (G.L.Nemhauser, A.H.G. Rinnoy Kan, M.J. Todd eds.) North-Holland 1989, 573-629

PERTURBATION ANALYSIS: BASICS FOR DERIVING HIGHER ORDER PROPAGATION RULES*

Wolfgang Geiselhart, Peter Kischka† and Ulrich Tüshaus
Institut für Unternehmensforschung (Operations Research)
Hochschule St. Gallen
Bodanstr. 6, CH-9000 St. Gallen

1 Introduction

Perturbation analysis of discrete event dynamic systems (DEDS) is a time domain based approach for the analysis and optimization (especially, the sensitivity analysis) of DEDS. It views a queueing network as a stochastic dynamical system evolving in time, and observes the sample realization of its trajectory. To this extent this is a similar viewpoint (and hence enjoys the same advantages) as the simulation approach to queueing systems. However, by observing a sample realization of the network trajectory, one uses analytic formulas, i.e., the so-called perturbation generation and propagation rules to derive answers to the question "*What* will happen *if* we repeat the sample trajectory exactly except for a (parameter) perturbation at some time t". The efficiency of this approach lies in the fact that one can answer a multitude of such *what-if questions* simultaneously while the sample trajectory is being observed. Thus compared with the brute force simulation study, perturbation analysis of DEDS has a computational advantage near by $M : 1$ where M is the number of *what-if questions* asked.

Perturbation analysis is based, as mentioned before, on the analysis of a sample trajectory, referred to as the nominal trajectory. Now, if we want to have answered (for simplification) one *what-if question*, we have to consider a new trajectory, say the perturbed trajectory, which, in general, differs from the nominal. In this context we can say the simulation approach is one method to produce (and observe) trajectories. To answer a *what-if question* we have at least two simulation runs to produce the nominal and perturbed trajectory. The main idea of perturbation analysis is to compute the perturbed trajectory by means of specific rules (especially, the propagation rules) in parallel to producing the nominal.

In this paper we mainly treat the propagation rules and their orders. In the next section we briefly discuss important components of perturbation analysis. Then we introduce the order of perturbation analysis, describe the distinctions between infinitesimal and finite perturbation analysis, and give "balance-equations" as a general framework for the perturbation propagation. Finally, we derive some higher order propagation rules and discuss their use.

2 Basics of perturbation analysis

A "tableau" (Fig. 1) is a completely general representation of a network's trajectory (for details, see [4]). The main components of a tableau are event sequences E_j - for each server of the queueing

*This paper was supported in part by Schweizerischer Nationalfonds zur Förderung der wissenschaftlichen Forschung (Grant 20-30302.90) and IBM Switzerland.

†Forschungsstelle für empirische Wirtschaftsforschung, Varnbüelstr. 14, CH-9000 St. Gallen.

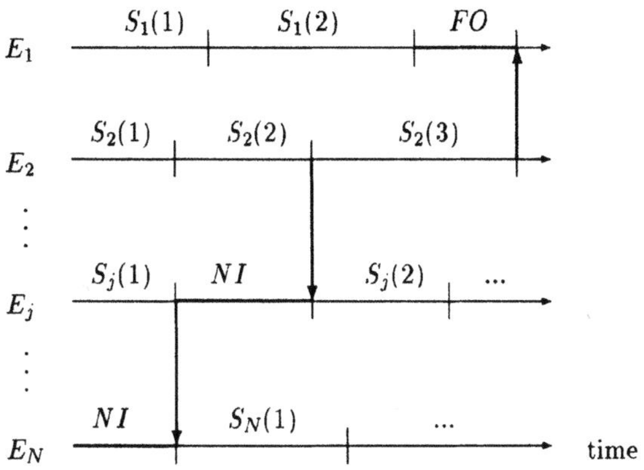

Figure 1: *Tableau*

network - and arrows: E_j is a series of consecutive sample service time durations, $S_j(\cdot)$, denoting a customer's service time at the jth server interspersed with NI (no input or idling) and FO (full output or blocking) periods. The arrows directed to the end of NI resp. FO periods are referred to as NI resp. FO terminators (for details, see [3], [4]). Let T and T' denote the tableaus representing the nominal and perturbed trajectory (for simplification we neglect the argument ω for the sample and write T instead of $T(\omega)$). This is also true for t_j resp. t'_j, a time instant when service termination occurs at server j in T resp. T'. (For details of this notation, see [3].) With this notation the next service termination instant at server j is defined as follows: $t_{j+1} = t_j + [FO]_j + [NI]_j + S_j(next)$; where $[FO]_j$ and $[NI]_j$ are the lengths of a possible NI or FO period which may occur direct after t_j, and $S_j(next)$ denotes the next customer's service time.

If we perturb a parameter, e.g., the mean of service time distribution of server j, then in T and T' the same event will take place at different time instants: t_j and $t'_j \overset{def}{=} t_j + \Delta_j$. Now perturbation analysis considers two points: a) perturbation generation, that is to compute locally generated Δ_j's in case a parameter of queueing system j is perturbed and b) perturbation propagation, that is to compute the propagation from Δ_j (Δ_j is a result from superposition of generation and propagation) to other servers. The common hierarchical classification scheme for the propagation rules moves along with the order of perturbation analysis. With a higher order the application area of perturbation analysis - as well as the implementation effort - increases.

3 The order of (finite) perturbation analysis

In T consider for this purpose three arbitrary service termination time instants t_i, t_j, and t_k belonging to the servers i, j, and k. Assume that we have the following relation in time: $t_i < t_j < t_k$. If this relation holds also in T', that is $t'_i < t'_j < t'_k$, then we say *deterministic-similarity* holds for these time instants. If, however, for example $t'_j < t'_i < t'_k$ holds in T' then we say a change of adjacent events (t_i and t_j) or of first order takes place. If $t'_k < t'_j < t'_i$ holds in T' then we say a change of second order (t_i and t_k) takes place. Finite perturbation analysis only considers changes in order of events up to a predefined limit. For example, "first order" finite perturbation analysis (FPA1) only considers the possibility that adjacent events might change order, and ignores any effects of changes in order beyond adjacent events. FPA0 is also referred to as infinitesimal perturbation analysis (IPA).

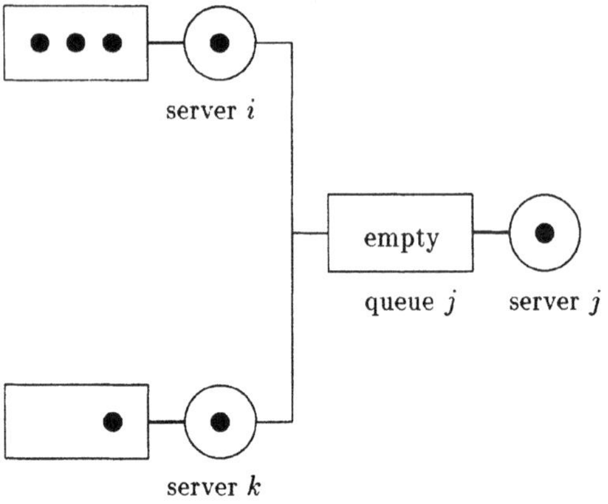

Figure 2: *Queueing network with one customer present at queueing system j.*

4 A general framework for perturbation propagation

Dealing with IPA, we make the *deterministic-similarity assumption* for all time instants. That means any effects of order changes are ignored. The propagation rules for IPA are as follows: $\Delta_{jnew} = \Delta_i$ in case server i is terminating a NI or FO period at server j.[1] We have to point out that perturbation propagation only occurs when NI or FO periods are terminated [3].

An important consequence of the *deterministic-similarity assumption* is that there is no NI or FO period eliminated or created if we compare T and T', and that we have the same terminators in T and T'. If, however, one relaxes this assumption - this is done step by step if higher order propagation rules are used - we have to analyze the following situations: A) NI or FO periods are eliminated in T'; B) NI or FO periods are created in T'; and C) in T' are other terminators than in T. The recognition whether or not such a situation arises depends on the order used: Assuming that we have in $t_i < t_k < t_j$ and $t'_j < t'_k < t'_i$ for the queueing network described by Fig. 2 then situation B arises and this is recognized only if an order greater than one is used. In general, the situation A, B, and C are not mutually exclusive.

Let $[NI]_j$ and $[NI]'_j$ be the length of a specific NI period in T and T' and define $[FO]_j$ and $[FO]'_j$ in the same manner. For the finite perturbation analysis we have the following general framework for perturbation propagation: (1) $\Delta_{jnew} = \Delta_j + [NI]'_j - [NI]_j$ for NI termination and (2) $\Delta_{jnew} = \Delta_j + [FO]'_j - [FO]_j$ for FO termination. We denote (1) and (2) as "balance-equations". The proof that the "balance equations" hold for nth order is outlined as follows:

Proposition: The "balance equations" hold for zero order (IPA).

Proof: Consider the NI case: Assume server i terminates a NI period at server j (the last customer leaves j at t_j and the next customer enters j at t_i). We have $t_j < t_i$ and $[NI]_j = (t_i - t_j)$. With *deterministic-similarity* we have further a) $t_j + \Delta_j < t_i + \Delta_i$ and b) $[NI]'_j = (t_i + \Delta_i) - (t_j + \Delta_j)$. Using (1) we get $\Delta_{jnew} = \Delta_i$. Theproof of the FO case proceeds in the same manner. *Q.E.D.*

To prove the "balance equations" for first order, the validity for all cases enumerated in [3] has to be checked. This is done in [2]. With the proof for zero and first order and the fact that the distinction between FPA1 and FPAn is to take more events into account to analyze the situations A, B, and C (see above), we have the "balance equations" as a general framework for perturbation

[1] Server i terminates a NI period of server j in case a customer passes from i to the idling j. A FO period at j is terminated by i if the queue belonging to i receives the blocked customer from j.

propagation.

5 Higher order propagation rules

In the section above we pointed out that to recognize whether or not situation A, B, or C arises, depends explicitly on the order of the propagation rules. In this section we propose a procedure for computing nth order propagations. In general, the procedure works as follows: for each situation A, B, or C we define an initial-state. Starting from this initial-state we have to observe a defined number of service termination time instants, e.g., $t_i < t_j < t_k$ (in the following abbreviated by $R = (t_i, t_j, t_k)$). Then we compute R' by ordering the perturbed service time instants belonging to the time instants from R in a non decreasing manner. Finally, we decide whether or not the situation A, B, or C takes place and compute the propagation with (1) resp. (2). For convenience let us treat the NI case first.

Let $p_R(t_j)$ be the position of t_j in R (e.g., $p_R(t_j) = 2$ in R above) and $p_{R'}(t'_j)$ the position of t'_j in R'. Further let $\mid R \mid$ denote the number of time instants in R. In the following we want to observe the evolution of perturbation at server j, with the servers i, k, and l delivering customers to j.

Situation A: Initial-state: NI at j (the last customer leaves j at t_j). We have to wait n events after t_j. Thus, we have $R = (t_j, t_i, ..., t_l, ..., t_k)^2$ with $\mid R \mid = n + 1$. Let t_i be this event for which $p_R(t_i) = 2$ holds. If $p_{R'}(t'_j) > 1$ then A occurs. With (1) we get $\Delta_{jnew} = \Delta_j - (t_i - t_j)$ as the rule for the perturbation propagation. (Note situation A means $[NI]'_j = 0$.)

Situation B: Initial-state: n customers present at queueing system j (this state is also referred to as potential no input with n customers present ($PNIn$) [3]). We have to wait $2n + 1$ events. Hence, we have $R = (t_l, ..., t_j, ..., t_{j+1}, ...)$ with $\mid R \mid = 2n + 1$. If $p_R(t_{j+n-1}) \leq 2n$ then we can get $R' = (t'_j, t'_{j+1}, ..., t'_{j+n-1}, t'_i, ...)$. That means B occurs. With (1) we get $\Delta_{jnew} = \Delta_j + ((t_i + \Delta_i) - (t_{j+n-1} + \Delta_j)) = \Delta_i + (t_i - t_{j+n-1})$ as the rule for the perturbation propagation.

Situation C: Initial-state: NI at j (the last customer leaves j at t_j). We have to wait $n + 1$ events after t_j. Thus we have $R = (t_j, t_i, ..., t_k, ...)$ and $\mid R \mid = n + 2$. C occurs if $p_{R'}(t'_j) = 1$ and $p_{R'}(t'_k) = 2$ with $k \neq i$. Using (1) we get $\Delta_{jnew} = \Delta_j + ((t_k + \Delta_k) - (t_j + \Delta_j)) - (t_i - t_j) = \Delta_k + (t_k - t_i)$ as the rule for the perturbation propagation.

To analyze the FO case is more difficult. In [5] we define a queueing system j as a composition of a real and a virtual queue and one server. In the virtual queue we have the customers who can not enter the real one because it is full. That means servers who send their customers to the virtual queue are blocked by j. The service termination time instants of customers in the real queue, supposing it has enough buffers, determine the FO termination points from the servers whose customers are in the virtual. Difficulties will arise for real queues with few buffers. The FO case based on this idea is discussed in [5].

6 Concluding remarks

Higher order propagation rules open new application areas for FPA. Even for single-class queueing networks with finite buffer sizes IPA estimates are biased [1]. To reduce this bias FPA1 is needed (see [1] and the references there). In [3] experiments show that first order rules give an exact prediction in a wider region than zero order rules do. An example for the need of higher order propagation rules is in [6]. In [6] higher order propagation rules for tandem queueing networks with infinite buffers (no FO periods occur) are formulated (a special case of the propagation rules above) the estimates did not converge to the true value till 11th order. The 0th-10th orders resulted in the same biased estimate.

---

[2] It is not necessary that the time instants in R belong to different servers.

References

[1] Cao, X.R.: First-Order Perturbation Analysis of a Simple Multi-Class Finite Source Queue. Performance Evaluation, vol. 7, pp. 31-41, 1987.

[2] Geiselhart, W., Kischka, P. und Lucca, H.: Grundzüge der Finiten Perturbations Analyse. Submitted for publication.

[3] Ho, Y.C., Cao, X., and Cassandras, C.: Infinitesimal and Finite Perturbation Analysis for Queueing Networks. Automatica, vol. 19, no. 4, pp. 439-445, 1983.

[4] Ho, Y.C. and Cao, X.: Perturbation Analysis and Optimization of Queueing Networks. Journal of Optimization Theory and Applications, vol. 40, no. 4, pp. 559-582, 1983.

[5] Institut für Unternehmensforschung an der HSG: Perturbations-Fortpflanzungsregeln mit höheren Ordnungen. Abschlußbericht zum Nationalfondsprojekt 21-25569.88, Beilage B.

[6] Jackman, J. and Johnson, M.E.: Sensitivity Analysis of Serial Transfer Lines Using Finite Perturbation Analysis. International Journal of Systems Science, vol. 20, no. 1, pp. 129-137, 1989.

[7] Suri, R.: Perturbation Analysis: The State of the Art and Research Issues Explained via the GI/G/1 Queue. Proceedings of the IEEE, vol. 77, no.1, pp. 114-137, 1989.

RECENT DEVELOPMENTS IN PARTIALLY OBSERVED CONTROL

Kurt Helmes
Department of Mathematics
University of Kentucky, Lexington, Ky, 40506
e–mail: kurt@ ms.uky.edu

Abstract. Recent robustness and reduction results for partially observed stochastic control problems by V. Beneš, and by R. Rishel & K. Helmes will be reviewed and applications will be discussed. Specifically, it will be shown that for certain linear quadratic problems with non–Gaussian disturbances a separation principle holds and the optimal control will be derived. It turns out that for such problems only the solution of a Ricatti equation and a particular and natural martingale on the observations need to be computed.

A LQ–Problem with General Disturbances

Motivated by applications (see Remark below) and the long–standing question to what extent the form of the control recipe known from Linear–**Q**uadratic–**G**aussian–theory (**LQG**),

(1) "gain coefficients" *times* "state",

is robust against modifications of the model assumptions (see [8], [15]), variants of the LQG–model have recently been analyzed by Helmes & Rishel ([11], [12]) and Beneš [2]. Consider the state equation

$$dx_t = (Ax_t + Bu_t)dt + dz_t, \quad x(0) = x_0, \tag{2}$$

and noise process (z_t) described by

$$dz_t = F(\eta_t)dt + dW_t. \tag{3}$$

Assume that (η_t) is a Markov process, F is a non–linear transformation, (W_t) is a vector Brownian motion and A, B are piecewise continuous matrix functions of appropriate dimensions. The objective is to minimize the performance index (final value criterion)

$$E\left[x_T'Qx_t + \int_0^T u_s'Nu_s ds\right] \tag{4}$$

among all $\mathcal{F}_t^x = \sigma(x_s,\ s \leq t)$–adapted control process (u_t) for which (1) has a unique strong solution; N is assumed to be positive definite and Q non–negative definite. For the special cases that (η_t) is either a jump Markov process with finitely many states or a diffusion process the optimal control has been derived in [11] and [12]. It turns out that the optimal control is of the form (1) provided the "state" is properly chosen. Except for technical difficulties the main steps of the analysis of the two cases are the same. So we shall explain these steps for the finite state jump Markov case. Let η_t take on values $a_1, \ldots, a_k$, and let it have initial distribution p_0 and generator matrix $\mathcal{G}$.

Step 1: *Introduce augmented co-ordinates,* $(t, x_t) \to (t, x_t, \pi_t)$.
To the coordinates t and x_t "add" the vector of conditional probabilities of η_t given $\mathcal{F}_t^z$,

$$\pi_t(i) = P\left[\eta_t = a_i | \mathcal{F}_t^z\right], \quad 1 \le i \le k. \tag{5}$$

Step 2: *Change co-ordinates,* $(t, x_t, \pi_t) \to (t, r_t, \pi_t)$.
Introduce the *"predicted miss"* r_t (sometimes called *"zero-effort miss"*) for every control process $(u_s)_{0 \le s \le T}$ by putting

$$\tilde{u}_s = \begin{cases} u_s, & s \le t \\ 0 & s > t, \end{cases} \tag{6}$$

and defining

$$r_t = E\left[x_T^{\tilde{u}} | \mathcal{F}_t^z\right]. \tag{7}$$

Step 3: *Evolution equations for* (r_t, π_t).
Show that (r_t, π_t) satisfy the system of stochastic differential equations:

$$dr_t = (Ar_t + Bu_t)dt + \sigma(t, \pi)d\nu_t, \tag{8}$$

$$d\pi_t = \mathcal{G}'\pi_t dt + \gamma(t, \pi)d\nu_t, \tag{9}$$

where

$$\begin{aligned}
\pi(0) &= p_0, \\
\gamma(\pi_t)(i) &= \left[F(a_i) - \hat{F}_t\right] \pi_t(i), \quad 1 \le i \le k, \\
\hat{F}_t := \pi_t(F) &= \sum_{i=1}^{k} F(a_i)\pi_t(i), \\
r(0) &= x_0 + \int_0^T \pi_0 \left(E_\bullet[F(\eta_s)]\right) ds \\
d\nu_t &= (F(\eta_t) - \hat{F}_t)dt + dW_t, \\
\sigma(t, \pi_t) &= 1 + \sum_{i=1}^{k} F(a_i) \left[\int_t^T d\tau e^{\mathcal{G}'(\tau - t)} \gamma(\pi_t)\right](i).
\end{aligned}$$

Step 4: *Verification Theorem.*

By making the "Ansatz"

$$V(t,r,\pi) = r'K(t)r + q(t,\pi), \tag{10}$$

where $K(t)$ satisfies the matrix Ricatti equation

$$\dot{K} + KA + A'K - KBN^{-1}B'K \equiv 0, \quad K(T) = Q, \tag{11}$$

and $q(t,\pi)$ satisfies the partial differential equation

$$q_t + q_\pi \mathcal{G}'\pi + \frac{1}{2}\operatorname{tr}[\gamma(t,\pi)\gamma'(t,\pi)q_{\pi\pi}] + \sigma\sigma' K(t) \equiv 0, \quad q(T,\pi) = 0, \tag{12}$$

verify that

$$u^*(t,r) = -N^{-1}B'K(t)r \tag{13}$$

is the optimal control of the stochastic control problem:

$$\min E\left[r_T'Qr_T + \int_0^T u_s'Nu_s ds\right] \tag{14}$$

subject to (8), (9) and (u_t) adapted to the past of (r_t, π_t). Moreover, show that (10) is the "value function" of this problem (see [8] for the terminology).

Step 5: *Admissibility.*
Finally, show that formula (13) defines an admissible control, i.e. show that (u_t^*) is $\mathcal{F}_t^x$-adapted and that Eq. 2 has a unique strong solution.

For the details of the arguments and the generalization to the case of a diffusion process we refer to [11] and [12]. In [2] Beneš has extended the previous results to the case where (z_t) is a general semi–martingale. Using convex and stochastic analysis he again shows that formula (13) gives the optimal control in terms of "predicted miss". For the case that A is time–independent, the martingale referred to in the abstract can be easily expressed in terms of the quantities introduced as $e^{-A'(T-t)}K(t)r_t$. But for the case of a general semi–martingale there is usually no expression equivalent to Eq. 8 which allows the predicted miss to be computed in a recursive way.

Remark. Important applications of the model described in the section arise in the context of pursuit–evasion problems when (η_t) describes the control actions of the evader and u^* suggests an "optimal" design for the pursuer. Other applications are modifications of the LQG–problems described, for instance, in [1], [10] and [14]. To see that already minor modifications of the LQG–assumptions can make it extremly difficult to determine – even theoretically – the optimal control, read [4], [9] and [13] when the distribution of the initial position is no longer Gaussian; cf., f.i., [3] and [6] for models with "hard constraints", [7] for a variation of the observation structure and [5] for a counter–example of the existence of a strict–sense optimal control.

REFERENCES

[1] Athans, M. (eds.): Special issue on the linear-quadratic-Gaussian estimation and control problem. *IEEE Transactions on Automatic Control*, **AC–16**, 527-547 (1971).

[2] Beneš, V.E.: Quadratic approximation by linear systems controlled from partial observations. Proc. Internat. Symp. in honor of M. Zakai, 1991.

[3] Beneš, V.E: and Karatzas, I.: Examples of optimal control for partially observable systems: Comparison, classical and martingale methods, *Stochastics*, **5**, 43–64 (1981).

[4] Beneš, V.E. and Karatzas, I.: Estimation and control for linear partially observable systems with non-Gaussian initial distribution. *Stochastic Processes and their Applications*, **14**, 233–248 (1983).

[5] Beneš, V.E. and Karatzas, I. and Rishel R.: The separation principle for a Bayesian adaptive control problem with no strict-sense optimal law. Proc. Workshop on Appl. Stoch. Analysis, Imperial College, London, 1989.

[6] Christopeit, N. and Helmes, K.: The separation principle for partially observed linear control systems: A general framework. Proc. E.N.S.T.-C.N.E.T. Colloquium, 1983, Korezilioglu, H., Mazziotti, G. and Szpirglas, J. (eds.). *Springer Lecture Notes in Control and Information Sciences*, **61**, 36–60 (1984).

[7] Christopeit, N. and Helmes, K.: On stochastic 'bang-bang' control for linear diffusions with point process observations. Proc. Workshop on Appl. Stoch. Analysis, Imperial College, London, 173–203 (1989).

[8] Fleming, W. and Rishel, R.: Deterministic and stochastic optimal control. Applications of Mathematics **1**, Springer–Verlag, 1975.

[9] Haussmann, U. G.: Examples of optimal controls for linear stochastic control systems with partial observations. *Stochastics*, **22**, 289–323 (1987).

[10] Heyman, D.P. and Sobel, M.: Handbook in Operations Research and Management Science, vol. 2. Amsterdam: North–Holland Publ. Co., 1990.

[11] Helmes, K. and Rishel, R.: The solution of a partially observed stochastic optimal control problem in terms of predicted miss. To appear in *IEEE Transactions on Automatic Control*, 1992.

[12] Helmes, K. and Rishel, R.: An optimal control depending on the conditional density of the unobserved state, to appear in Proc. 2nd US–French workshop on Appl. Stoch. Analysis, 1991, Karatzas,I. and Ocone, D. (eds).

[13] Makowski, A.: Filtering formulae for partially observed linear systems with non-Gaussian initial conditions, *Stochastics* **16**, 1–24 (1986).

[14] Pindyck, R.S.: Optimal planning for economic stabilization. Amsterdam: North–Holland Publ. Co., 1973.

[15] Wonham, W.M.: On the separation theorem of stochastic control. *SIAM J. Control*, **6**, 312–326 (1968).

Acknowledgment. This work was supported in part by Sonderforschungsbereich 303 while the author was visiting the Institute of Operations Research and Econometrics at the University of Bonn. The hospitality and stimulating atmosphere at the Econometrics Unit of the Institute is greatly appreciated.

AVERAGE OPTIMALITY OF MARKOV DECISION PROCESSES WITH UNBOUNDED COSTS

Onésimo Hernández–Lerma
Departamento de Matemáticas
CINVESTAV–IPN, A. Postal 14–740
07000 México, D.F., México

1 Introduccion

This paper considers Markov decision processes (MDPs) with *Borel* state space, *not* necessarily compact control constraint sets, and *unbounded* cost functions. The objective is to present some recent results on the existence of stationary optimal policies for MDPs with an *average cost* (AC) criterion. These results include extensions of recent works [7, 8, 9] based on the "vanishing discount factor" approach, as well as existence results for MDPs with *strictly unbounded* costs.

2 The decision model

Let (X, A, Q, c) be the usual (discrete–time, time–homogeneous) Markov decision model with state space X, action set A, transition law Q, and cost per stage c. Both X and A are assumed to be Borel spaces. All sets and functions introduced below are supposed to be Borel–measurable. For each $x \in X$, $A(x) \subset A$ is a nonempty set whose elements are the feasible actions when x is the state of the system. Let $K := \{(x, a) \mid x \in X, a \in A(x)\}$. The transition law $Q(dy \mid x, a)$ is a stochastic kernel on X given K, and the cost $c(x, a)$ is a real–valued function on K. Consider:

H1. $c(x, a)$ is nonnegative and lower semicontinuous.

H2. The multifunction $x \to A(x)$ is compact–valued.

H2'. The set $\{a \in A(x) \mid c(x, a) \leq r\}$ is compact for every $x \in X$ and $r \in R$.

H3. Q is strongly continuous [3, 7, 8].

H3'. Q is weakly continuous [3, 7, 8].

H4. There exist increasing sequences of compact sets $X_n \uparrow X$ and $A_n \uparrow A$ such that $K_n := X_n \times A_n$ is a subset of K and $\inf\{c(x, a) \mid (x, a) \notin K_n\} \to \infty$ as $n \to \infty$.

Performance criteria. As usual, a control *policy* is a sequence $\delta = \{\delta_t\}$, where $\delta_t(\cdot \mid h_t)$

is a conditional probability on A, given the history $h_t := (x_0, a_0, \ldots, x_{t-1}, a_{t-1}, x_t)$, and which satisfies the constraint $\delta_t(A(x_t) \mid h_t)=1$. Here x_t and a_t denote the state and action at time $t = 0, \ldots$, respectively.

Definition. Let F be the set of all measurable functions f from X to A such that $f(x) \in A(x)$ for all $x \in X$, and let Φ be the set of all the stochastic kernels $\varphi(da \mid x)$ on A given X satisfying that $\varphi(A(x) \mid x)=1$ for all $x \in X$. Then a policy $\delta = \{\delta_t\}$ is said to be a:

1. ***relaxed*** (or ***randomized stationary***) policy if there exists $\varphi \in \Phi$ such that $\delta_t(. \mid h_t) = \varphi(. \mid x_t)$ for all $h_t \in H_t$ and $t = 0, 1, \ldots$;
2. ***(pure*** or ***non–randomized) stationary*** policy if there exists $f \in F$ such that $\delta_t(. \mid h_t)$ is concentrated at $f(x_t)$ for all $h_t \in H_t$ and $t = 0, 1, \ldots$

Following a standard convention, we will identify F (resp.Φ) with the set of all stationary (resp. relaxed) policies.

Given a policy δ and the (initial) distribution ν of x_0, let $V_\alpha(\delta, \nu) := E_\nu^\delta \sum_{t=0}^{\infty} \alpha^t c(x_t, a_t)$ be the ***α–discounted cost,*** with discount factor $\alpha \in (0,1)$. The long–run expected ***average cost*** per unit time is defined as $J(\delta, \nu) := \limsup_{n\to\infty} n^{-1} E_\nu^\delta \sum_{t=0}^{n-1} c(x_t, a_t)$. If ν is concentrated at $x_0 = x$, then we write these cost functions as $V_\alpha(\delta, x)$ and $J(\delta, x)$, respectively. Let $j^* := \inf_\nu \inf_\delta J(\delta, \nu)$. If $J(\delta, \nu) = j^*$, then (δ, ν) is called a ***minimum pair*** [5]; it is called an ***almost surely*** (a.s.)–***minimum pair*** if $J(\delta, x) = j^*$ for ν–almost all x.

A policy δ^* is said to be (i) ***α–discount optimal,*** or (ii) ***average cost*** (AC–) ***optimal*** if $V_\alpha(\delta^*, .) = V_\alpha(.)$ or $J(\delta^*, .) = J(.)$, respectively, where $V_\alpha(x) := \inf_\delta V_\alpha(\delta, x)$, and $J(x) := \inf_\delta J(\delta, x)$, $x \in X$. Finally, δ^* is called ***strictly AC–optimal,*** if $J(\delta^*, x) = j^*$ for all x.

3 Optimality Results

To avoid a trivial situation, we ***assume throughout the following*** the existence of a policy δ and an initial distribution ν for which $J(\delta, \nu)$ is finite.

For each $x \in X$ and $\alpha \in (0,1)$, let $m_\alpha := \inf_x V_\alpha(x)$, $g_\alpha(x) := V_\alpha(x) - m_\alpha$.

Theorem 1. Suppose that for some $\beta \in (0,1)$, $\sup_{\beta<\alpha<1} g_\alpha(x) < \infty$ for every $x \in X$. Suppose further that either (a) H1, H2, H3, or (a$'$) H1, H2$'$, H3 hold. Then there exists a constant j, a nonnegative measurable function h on X, and a stationary policy $f^* \in F$ such that

$$j + h(x) \geq c(x, f^*(x)) + \int h(y)Q(dy \mid x, f^*(x)) \;\forall x. \tag{1}$$

Hence f^* is strictly AC–optimal, and $j = j^* = \lim_{\alpha\uparrow 1}(1-\alpha)m_\alpha$.

Proof. See Schal [8] when using (a), or Hernández–Lerma [4] when using (a'). □

Now define $h_\alpha(x) := V_\alpha(x) - V_\alpha(x^*)$ for $x \in X$ and $\alpha \in (0,1)$, where $x^* \in X$ is an arbitrary (but fixed) state.

Theorem 2. Suppose that there exists a constant $N \geq 0$, a nonnegative measurable function b on X, and a stationary policy f such that, for every $x \in X$ and $\alpha \in (0,1), V_\alpha(x) < \infty$, $-N \leq h_\alpha(x) \leq b(x)$, and $\int b(y)Q(dy \mid x, a) < \infty$. Suppose further that one of the following two conditions holds: (a) H1, H2, H3 and, in addition, the multifunction in H2 is upper semicontinuous; $(a')H1$, $H2'$, $H3$. Then the conclusion of Theorem 1 holds, with $j = j^*$.

Proof. Under (a), see [7]; under (a'), the proof (with some obvious changes) is as in [4, 7].□

Both Theorems 1 and 2 are examples of the so–called "vanishing discount factor" approach. A different, direct approach may be followed for MDPs with ***strictly unbounded*** costs, as in H4. Before stating the results, let us recall [5] that a relaxed policy $\varphi \in \Phi$ is said to be ***stable*** if there exists a probability measure $P = P_\varphi$ such that $P(.) = \int Q(. \mid x, \varphi)P(dx)$, and $J(\varphi, P) = \int c(x,\varphi)P(dx) =: J(\varphi) < \infty$, where $Q(. \mid x, \varphi) := \int Q(. \mid x, a)\varphi(da \mid x)$, and $c(x,\varphi) := \int c(x,a)\varphi(da \mid x)$.

Theorem 3. [5] Suppose that H1, H2$'$, H3$'$ and $H4$ hold. Then there exists a stable relaxed policy φ such that (φ, P_φ) is a minimum pair, or equivalently, it is an a.s.–minimum pair. (The equivalence is due to the fact that, if $\varphi \in \Phi$ is stable, then $J(\varphi) = \int J(\varphi, x)P_\varphi(dx)$). □

One may also obtain an inequality similar to (1), as follows.

Theorem 4. [5] Suppose the same hypotheses of Theorem 3, and let φ be a stable ***relaxed*** policy. Then (φ, P_φ) is a minimum pair if and only if there exists a nonnegative function h on X such that

$$j^* + h(x) \geq c(x,\varphi) + \int h(y)Q(dy \mid x, \varphi) \; P_\varphi - a.e. x \in X. \tag{2}$$

Moreover, if $\varphi \in F$ is a stable (non–randomized) ***stationary*** policy, then φ is strictly AC–optimal if and only there exists a function $h \geq 0$ such that (2) holds for *all* $x \in X$. □

Clearly, (2) implies

$$j^* + h(x) \geq \inf_{a\in A(x)} [c(x,a) + \int h(y)Q(dy \mid x, a)] P_\varphi\text{–a.e.}x. \tag{3}$$

On the other hand, one may obtain the existence of a measurable minimizer $f \in F$ of the right-hand side of (3). More precisely, we have:

Corollary 5. [5] In the hypotheses of Theorem 3, replace $H3'$ by $H3$. Then there exists a probability measure P on X, a measurable function $h \geq 0$, and a stationary policy $f^* \in F$ such that (1) holds, with $j = j^*$, for P–a.e.x. Hence f is strictly AC–optimal P–a.s. (i.e., (f, P) is an a.s.–minimum pair).

Remark. Additional results on the strictly unbounded case are given in [5]. For results related to Theorems 1 and 2, see [1, 2, 3, 6, 8].

References

[1] A. Arapostathis, V. Borkar, E. Fernández–Gaucherand, M. K. Ghosh, and S. I. Marcus. Controlled Markov processes with an average cost criterion: a survey. *SIAM J. Control Optim.* **29** (1991). In press.

[2] E. Fernández–Gaucherand, *Controlled Markov Processes on the Infinite Planning Horizon: Optimal and Adaptive Control.* Ph. D. Thesis, Univ. of Texas at Austin, 1991.

[3] O. Hernández–Lerma, *Lecture Notes on Discrete–Time Markov Control Processes.* IV CLAPEM, Mexico City, 1990.

[4] ———, Average optimality in dynamic programming on Borel spaces–unbounded costs and controls. *Syst. Control Lett.* **16** (1991).

[5] ———, Average optimality of controlled Markov chains with strictly unbounded costs. Preprint, 1991.

[6] ———, R. Montes–de–Oca and R. Cavazos–Cadena, Recurrence conditions for Markov decision processes with Borel state space:a survey. *Ann. O.R.* **29** (1991).

[7] ——— and J.B. Lasserre, Average cost optimal policies for Markov control processes with Borel state space and unbounded costs. Syst. Control Lett. **15** (1990), 349–356.

[8] M. Schal, Average optimality in dynamic programming with general state space. Preprint, 1990.

[9] L.I. Sennott, average cost optimal stationary policies in infinite state Markov decision processes with unbounded costs. *Oper. Res.* **37** (1989), 626–633.

OPTIMAL DETECTION OF A CHANGE IN THE FAILURE RATE OF A REPAIRABLE SYSTEM

Uwe Jensen
Institute of Applied Mathematics and Statistics
University Stuttgart-Hohenheim
Postfach 700 562/110, D-7000 Stuttgart 70

A technical system is considered which can work in one of N unobservable states. The states are labeled from 1 to N, where 1 stands for 'new' or 'in good condition' and N describes the state 'defect' or 'in bad condition'. The system fails from time to time and the failure rate depends on the unobservable state of the system.

The changes of the states are driven by a homogeneous Markov process (X_t), $t \in \mathbb{R}_+$ with values in $S = \{1,2, \dots ,N\}$ and infinitesimal parameters q_i, $q_{ij} < \infty$:

$$q_i = \lim_{h \to 0+} \frac{1}{h} P(X_h \neq i | X_0 = i),\ q_{ij} = \lim_{h \to 0+} \frac{1}{h} P(X_h = j | X_0 = i),\ i,j \in S,\ i \neq j.$$

The failure time points form a point process. After each failure a minimal repair is carried out immediately which leaves the state of the system unchanged.

The observed failure point process is linked with the unobservable state of the system by the intensity of this point process which may depend on the actual state of the system. So in different states the system works with different failure rates μ_j, $j \in S$.

The following two problems are investigated. The first one is to estimate the unobservable state at any time t given the failure point process observations up to this time t.

The second problem is to find an optimal time to stop processing the system with respect to the following reward structure: There is a gain of c_j per unit time in state j, and the costs for stopping in state j are k_j, $j \in S$. Stopping at time t the net gain Z_t is then

$$Z_t = \sum_{j=1}^{N} \int_0^t c_j U_s(j) ds - \sum_{j=1}^{N} k_j U_t(j),$$

where $U_t(j) = I_{\{X_t = j\}}$ denotes the indicator function.

RESULTS

Using a semimartingale representation of the indicator process $U_t(j)$ the estimation problem can be solved by methods of filtering theory. These methods yield an explicit expression for the conditional probability $\hat{U}_t(j)$ to be in state j at time t conditional on the failure point process observations up to time t. This is the starting point for a solution of the optimization problem.

Assume the following additional assumptions:

- $q_{ij} = 0$ for $i > j$;
- $r_j := c_j - \sum_{\nu=j+1}^{N} (k_\nu - k_j) q_{j\nu}$

  $r_1 \geq r_2 \geq \cdots \geq r_N = c_N,\ c_N < 0$ (non-increasing net gain rates)
- $0 < \mu_1 \leq \mu_2 \leq \cdots \leq \mu_N$ (non-decreasing failure rates).

If furthermore $q_{iN} \geq \mu_N - \mu_i$, i=1,..,N-1, then

$$\tau^* = \inf \{t \in \mathbb{R}_+ | \sum_{j=1}^{N} r_j \hat{U}_t(j) \leq 0\}$$

is an optimal stopping time in the sense of maximizing the expected net gain $E(Z_\tau)$, where τ ranges in the set of stopping times with respect to the failure point process.

A proof of this result and a more rigorous treatment of this problem can be found in [1] including further references. The so-called disruption or disorder or detection problem is a special case (N=2) of the model represented above and was treated among others by A. N. Shiryayev [2] in discrete time and by M. Yoshida [3] in continuous time .

REFERENCES

[1] Jensen, U.: Optimal stopping by means of point process observations with applications in reliability.
Manuscript, Stuttgart-Hohenheim 1991.

[2] Shiryayev, A. N.: Optimal stopping rules.
Springer, New York 1978.

[3] Yoshida, M.: On disorder problem with point processes.
Osaka J. Math. 23 (1986), 415 – 423.

SCHEDULING UNIT-LENGTH MULTIPROCESSOR TASKS ON DEDICATED PROCESSORS

Marek KUBALE
Institute of Informatics
Technical University of Gdańsk
PL-80-952 Gdańsk, Poland

EXTENDED ABSTRACT

Tasks that require for processing more than one facility at a time create a realistic model for scheduling in microprocessor environment. There are, for example, self-testing multi-microprocessor systems in which one processor is used to test others, or diagnostic systems in which tested elements are simultaneously stimulated and their outputs analyzed.

The problem under consideration is as follows. We are given a task set $T = \{T^1, T^2, \ldots, T^k\}$ with $|T^i| = n_i$ $(i = 1, \ldots, k)$ and $n_1+n_2+\ldots+n_k = n$. Each task belonging to T^i requires a set of i dedicated processors simultaneously. Each of tasks is independent of each other and requires a unit-length processing time. A processor set is $P = \{P_1, P_2, \ldots, P_m\}$. Each of processors can be assigned only one task at a time. The objective is to find a feasible schedule with the minimum makespan.

One can see that this problem is equivalent to that of coloring the edges of a hipergraph $H = (P,T)$ whose vertices correspond to processors and edges correspond to multiprocessor tasks. In particular, the strong chromatic index of H is equal to the optimal makespan. If $k = 2$ then the scheduling problem reduces to the classical edge-coloring problem and, hence, remains NP-hard in 2-processor tasks case. In that case the minimum makespan is either $\Delta(G)$ or $\Delta(G)+1$, where $\Delta(G)$ is the maximum vertex degree of a simple graph G. However, deciding which of these two possibilities holds is a well-known

NP-complete the chromatic index problem [5]. If k can take on any value from 2 to m then the minimum schedule length is at most 2^{m-1}. We improve this bound in some special cases, e.g. where $k = m/2$.

For the other special cases of multiprocessor task scheduling see a collection of papers by Błażewicz et al. [1,2,3,4].

References

[1] J. Błażewicz, M. Drabowski, J. Węglarz, Scheduling multiprocessor tasks to minimize schedule length, IEEE Trans. Comp. C-35 (1986), 389-393.

[2] J. Błażewicz, K. Ecker, Scheduling multiprocessor tasks under unit resource constraints, Proc. Int. Conf. on Optimization Techniques and Applications, Singapore (1987), 161-169.

[3] J. Błażewicz, M. Drozdowski, D. de Werra, J. Węglarz, Scheduling multiprocessor tasks to minimize maximum lateness, Technical University of Poznań (1991).

[4] J.Błażewicz, M. Drozdowski, G. Schmidt, D. de Werra, Scheduling independent multiprocessor tasks on a uniform k-processor system, Technical University of Poznań (1991).

[5] I. Holyer, The NP-completeness of edge-coloring, SIAM J. Comput. 10 (1981), 718-720.

[6] M. Kubale, The complexity of scheduling independent two-processor tasks on dedicated processors, Inf. Process. Lett. 24 (1987), 141-147.

TIME SERIES FORECASTING BY IMITATION OF PRECEDING PATTERNS

Barbara Motnikar, Drago Čepar, Peter Žunko,*
Marijan Ribarič, Boštjan Vovk
"Jožef Stefan" Institute, Jamova 39
***Faculty of Electrical and Computer Engineering, Tržaška 25**
61111 Ljubljana, Slovenia

Introduction

We propose a new approach to time series forecasting based on the imitation of the preceding local shapes of a given time series z_t, $t = 1, \dots, n$. We define a pattern $\vec{r} \equiv (z_{b(r)}, z_{b(r)+1}, \dots, z_{b(r)+s-1})$ as a sequence of s observations starting at index $b(r)$, where s is the pattern size and we compare various patterns by some similarity measure chosen in advance. In the belief that the similarity between two patterns can be extended to their subsequent observations, we try to find the pattern $\vec{r}_1$ among all possible patterns, that is most similar to the very last pattern $\vec{p}$ of the time series. Time series observations that follow the pattern $\vec{r}_1$ are transformed into forecasts of future observations (following $\vec{p}$). If there are k patterns sufficiently similar to $\vec{p}$, we rank them according to the similarity measure and denote them by $\vec{r}_1, \dots, \vec{r}_k$. Each of these patterns generates one potential forecast; and we calculate the actual forecast as their linear combination.

There are some points in the proposed method which require particular care, e.g. the normalization of the patterns to enable proper comparison, the definition of a similarity measure, the determination of the pattern size s, the number k of chosen similar patterns and their weights in the linear combination of forecasts.

Normalization

The aim of pattern comparison is to recognize the similarity of their shapes. As time series may be nonstationary, patterns with similar shapes may have different mean values and standard deviations. We therefore transform patterns so as to have zero means and unit standard deviations. Pattern $\vec{r}$ is normalized to its *shape* $\vec{R} \equiv (\vec{r} - \bar{r})/\sigma_r$, where $\bar{r}$ and σ_r denote the mean and standard deviation of the pattern $\vec{r}$; if the pattern standard deviation is zero, we put $\sigma_r = 1$. Other transformations (for instance inclination) may be also of some help in extracting the pattern's shape but are not considered here.

If $k = 1$ we define the forecast $\hat{z}_{n,1}(i)$ of z_{n+i}, that is the forecast from origin n for i time steps ahead, as: $\hat{z}_{n,1}(i) = \bar{p} + \sigma_p(z_{b(r_1)+s-1+i} - \bar{r}_1)/\sigma_{r_1}$, using the i-th observation $z_{b(r_1)+s-1+i}$ following the most similar pattern $\vec{r}_1$. If $k > 1$ we define the forecast $\hat{z}_{n,k}(i)$ as a combination of k forecasts generated from k similar patterns, weighted by w_j:

$$\hat{z}_{n,k}(i) = \bar{p} + \sigma_p \sum_{j=1}^{k} w_j (z_{b(r_j)+s-1+i} - \bar{r}_j)/\sigma_{r_j} \ . \qquad (1)$$

Similarity measure and the pattern size

We may choose various similarity measures for pattern comparison, depending on the purpose of the time series forecasting. Some of the possible distances are discused in [3]; the simplest of them is $D_1(\vec{p},\vec{r}) \equiv 1-\rho^2$, where ρ is the Pearson correlation coefficient between patterns $\vec{p}$ and $\vec{r}$. Another possibility is to define the distance between two patterns $\vec{p}$ and $\vec{r}$ as the weighted *sum of squared differences*:

$$D_2(\vec{p},\vec{r}) \equiv \sum_{i=1}^{s} \lambda_i [P(i) - R(i)]^2 , \tag{2}$$

where $P(i)$ and $R(i)$ are i-th components of the normalized patterns $\vec{P}$ and $\vec{R}$, respectively. The weights λ_i are the values of the time series partial autocorrelation function *pacf*: $\lambda_i \equiv |pacf(s-i+1)|$. Owing to this definition, similar patterns agree more in those components that have more impact on the patterns' first subsequent observations. Very often, the *pacf* turn out to be damped exponentials or damped sine waves.

Since values of the $pacf(j)$ converge to zero as j goes to $-\infty$, the pattern size s should be sufficiently large that $\lambda_1 = pacf(s)$ is very close to zero (its absolute value is lower than a very small value chosen in advance). When using distance D_2, therefore, the problem of the pattern size selection is not very sensitive if size s is large enough.

The number of similar patterns

It can be shown that the forecast errors greatly depend on the number k of similar patterns. To obtain the optimal k at which the forecast errors are as small as possible we use the following cross–validation technique:

For each possible k we successively predict all observations of the time series (but the first s of them). To forecast the observation z_t we consider the very last pattern p before this observation z_t; similar patterns $\vec{r}_1,\ldots,\vec{r}_k$ are chosen before and after the pattern p. Using a different number k of similar patterns we obtain different forecasts $\hat{z}_{t-1,k}(1)$ and corresponding errors $|z_t - \hat{z}_{t-1,k}(1)|$. The number k that leads to the minimal error $|z_t - \hat{z}_{t-1,k}(1)|$ is optimal in forecasting the observation z_t. For forecasting different observations z_t the optimal number of similar patterns is different but for many time series variations of these optimal k are small. To forecast future observations we select the number k of similar patterns that minimizes the mean absolute error

$$MAE(k) \equiv \sum_{t=s+1}^{n} |z_t - \hat{z}_{t-1,k}(1)|/(n-s) . \tag{3}$$

Weights

To calculate forecasts using (1) we need to choose weights w_j. Since the more similar patterns should have more impact on the forecasts, we define the weights for $j=1,\ldots,k$ as follows:

$$w_j = \frac{Const}{D_2(\vec{p}, \vec{r}_j) + \epsilon}, \tag{4}$$

where *Const* is determined by the requirement that the sum of weights is 1, and ϵ is an arbitrary small positive value used to prevent division by zero.

An example

Let us demonstrate the proposed method on the real time series E considered in [1], where the one hundred observations are Wolfer sunspot numbers. We will forecast the last 8 observations, which we omit from the input data. After calculating the time series pacf, we choose a pattern size $s = 20$. We use the algorithm described above for determination of the number k of similar patterns. In Table 1 the $MAE(k)$ at different k are calculated using (3).

k	1	2	3	4	5	6	7	8	9	10	11
MAE	16.30	12.42	11.59	12.42	11.65	12.03	12.09	12.55	12.61	12.78	12.94

Table 1: MAE(k) at different values of k.

The minimum of MAE(k) is reached at $k = 3$; it equals 11.59. So for the forecasting of the future observations we take $s = 20$ and $k = 3$. To test the reliability of our one-step-ahead forecasts, we reanalyzed the data by the Box–Jenkins method, see [1]; the corresponding mean absolute error is higher (11.95). This comparison shows that in this example the proposed method is better than the Box–Jenkins method for *one–step–ahead* forecasting. To compare the forecasts of more than one time–step–ahead, both methods were used to calculate the last 8 observations. The mean absolute forecast error obtained by the proposed approach is 11.62, while the Box–Jenkins approach leads to a higher error (14.81). The last 20 observations (pattern $\vec{p}$) and forecasts obtained by both methods are shown in Figure 1.

Conclusions

For applicability of most time series forecasting methods, some assumptions about the data or model should be satisfied (e.g. Gaussian time series, linearity of time series model). By the proposed approach, *imitation of the preceding patterns*, forecasts are calculated without assuming any particular model. Time series to be forecast can have any type of nonstationarity. The only assumption used is that time series local shape is occasionally approximately repeated.

The choices of similarity measure, weights, pattern size and the number of similar patterns are complicated interrelated tasks. In this paper, we have considered only the simplest case. The problem of determining the optimal number k of similar patterns is solved empirically, testing the prediction strength for various values of k.

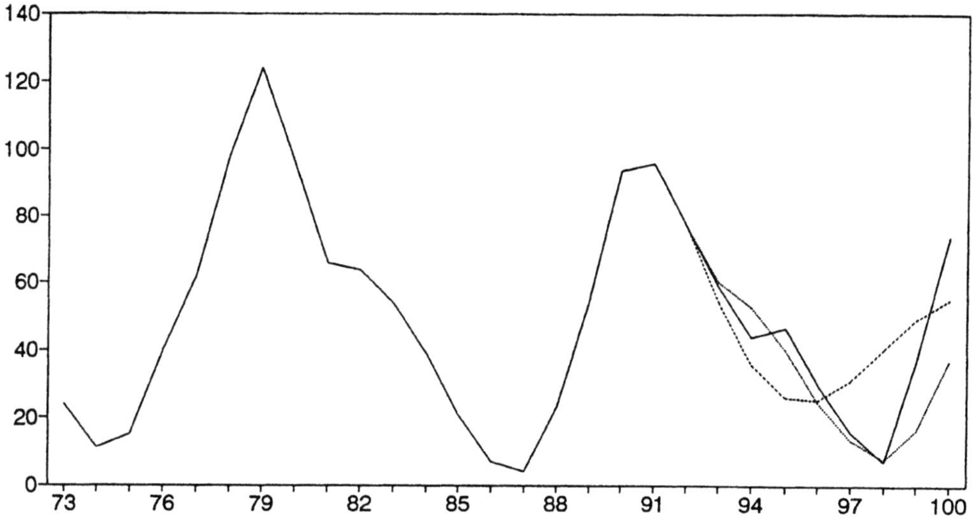

Figure 1: Comparison of forecasts of the last 8 observations of time series "Wolfer Sunspot numbers"; original observations (solid), forecasts by the proposed method (dotted) and Box–Jenkins' forecasts (dashed).

The problem of determining the optimal number k of similar patterns is solved empirically, testing the prediction strength for various values of k.

In future work, we intend to generalize the proposed approach to multi–input multi–output time series. The main idea is to use a computer to choose automatically the influential input time series and their contribution to the forecasting of future observations of output time series.

References

[1] G. E. P. Box, G. M. Jenkins (1970), Time Series Analysis: Forecasting and Control, Holden–Day, San Francisco.

[2] M. Ribarič et al.(1984), Computational methods for parsimonious data fitting, Compstat Lectures: 2. Lectures in Computational Statistics, Physica-Verlag, Vienna.

[3] Z. Bohte, D. Čepar, K. Košmelj (1980), Clustering of time series, Compstat, p. 587 - 593, Physica-Verlag, Vienna.

LIMIT THEOREMS OF PROBABILITY THEORY AND OPTIMALITY IN LINEAR STOCHASTIC EVOLUTION SYSTEMS

Bozenna Pasik-Duncan
Department of Mathematics
University of Kansas
Lawrence, Kansas, U.S.A.

A survey of some methods and results for the adaptive control of infinite dimensional stochastic systems is given. Adaptive control includes the identification of unknown parameters and the construction of an adaptive control law that is optimal for an ergodic cost criterion. Some approaches to identification are given that yield a family of strongly consistent estimates. The ergodic cost criterion is a quadratic functional of the state and the control. The behavior of such a quadratic functional is investigated using various measures of convergence to the optimal cost.

In the control or adaptive control of linear stochastic evolution systems with complete observations of the state it is important to know the asymptotic distribution of the quadratic cost or the asymptotic bounds for the fluctuation of the average cost around the optimal average cost. In this paper stochastic evolution systems are considered. These systems arise from a semigroup description of various infinite dimensional systems such as linear partial differential equations. These systems are often controlled and the quadratic costs provides a measure of the controlled performance. The optimal average cost as the limit of the average cost where the time goes to infinity can be regarded as optimality of the control with respect to the Law of Large Numbers. It is shown that the optimal control is optimal with respect to all principal Limit Theorems of Probability Theory: the Central Limit Theorem, the Arcsine Law and the Law of the Iterated Logarithm.

References:

[1] T. Duncan, B. Goldys, B. Pasik-Duncan: Adaptive Control of Linear Stochastic Evolution Systems, to appear in Stochastics.

[2] T. Duncan, B. Maslowski, B. Pasik-Duncan: Adaptive Boundary Control of Linear Distributed Parameter Systems, preprint.

[3] P. Mandl: Asymptotic ordering of probability distributions for linear controlled systems with quadratic cost. In Stochastic Differential Systems (N. Christopeit, K. Helmes, M. Kohlmann, editors), Lecture Notes in Control and Inf. Sc., Springer-Verlag, Berlin-Heidelberg 1986, 277-283.

[4] P. Mandl: Limit Theorems of Probability Theory and Optimality in Linear Controlled Systems with Quadratic Cost, Proceedings of 5th IFIP Conference on Stochastic Differential Systems.

[5] B. Pasik-Duncan: The Asymptotic Distribution of Some Quadratic Functionals of Linear Stochastic Evolution Systems, to appear in JOTA.

THE FULL-INFORMATION BEST CHOICE PROBLEM WITH TWO CHOICES

Zdzislaw Porosinski
Institute of Mathematics
Technical University of Wroclaw
Wyb. Wyspianskiego 27, PL-50-370 Wroclaw

INTRODUCTION

The following full-information best choice problem was studied by Gilbert and Mosteller (1966). A known number, say N, of *iid* *rv's* $Y_1, Y_2, \ldots, Y_N$ from a known continuous *df* F is observed sequentially. The objective is to maximize the probability of choosing the largest. After Y_n is observed it must be chosen (and the observation is terminated) or rejected (and the observation is continued). Neither recall nor uncertainty of selection is allowed and one choice must be made.

For a finite number of observations the so-called *monotone case* was obtained. The optimal strategy is to accept (if possible) the first Y_n which is largest one so far and exceeds a_n, where the sequence of optimal decision levels (a_n) is non-increasing.

The full-information best choice problem when the number of observation N is random was considered by Porosinski (1987, 1990). In this model the observer incurs an additional risk. Since N is unknown, if he rejects any observation, in case it was the last one he receives nothing. A class of *df's* of N for which the *monotone case* occurs was characterized and the solution for this case was given.

Tamaki (1980) studied, applying dynamic programming approach, the full-information problem of choosing the largest by accepting in twice when N is fixed. The optimal stopping rule turned out to be of *monotone* type as well.

In this paper the observer also is allowed to accept two observations but the number of observations is random. For some class of *df's* (being a subclass of IFR) the optimal strategy of *monotone* form is found.

PROBLEM FORMULATION AND METHODS

Let $Y_1, Y_2, Y_3, \ldots$ be an observed sequence of *iid* *rv's* with a continuous *df* F, defined on the probability space $(\Omega, \mathcal{F}, P)$. The number of observations K is a bounded *rv* independent of $(Y_n)_{n=1}^{\infty}$ with a known *df* $P(K=n)=p_n$, $(\pi_n=\sum_{m=n}^{N} p_m,\ \pi_N>0,\ \pi_{N+1}=0)$.

Let T be a set of all compound stopping variables (*csv's*), (Haggstrom, 1967) (σ,τ) with respect to family of σ-fields of information $(\mathcal{F}_n)_{n=1}^{N}$, where $\mathcal{F}_n=\sigma(Y_1,\ldots,Y_n,I_{\{K=0\}},\ldots I_{\{K=n-1\}})$ (I_A denotes the indicator function of A).

Let $M_n = \max(Y_1,\ldots,Y_n)$. Consider the following problem:

Find a *csv* $(\sigma,\tau)\in T$ such that

$$P(\sigma\le K, Y_\sigma=M_K \text{ or } \tau\le K, Y_\tau=M_K) = \sup_{(s,t)\in T} P(s\le K, Y_s=M_K \text{ or } t\le K, Y_t=M_K).$$

Let Z_{mn} be the gain after stopping at m*th* and n*th* observations, m<n. A *csv* (σ,τ) is said to be *optimal* in $T_m=\{(\sigma,\tau)\in T:\ \sigma\ge m\}$ (or in $T_{mn}=\{(\sigma,\tau)\in T:\ \sigma=m,\tau\ge n\}$) if $EZ_{\sigma\tau}=v_m$ (or $=v_{mn}$), where $v_m = \sup EZ_{st}$, $(s,t)\in T_m$, $v_{mn} = \sup EZ_{st}$, $(s,t)\in T_{mn}$.

If we tentatively assume that we stop for the first time after taking exactly m observations then the problem of finding an optimal *csv* $(m,\tau)\in T_{m,m+1}$ is equivalent to finding an optimal τ for $(Z_{mn},\mathcal{F}_{mn},n>m)$ (here $\mathcal{F}_{mn}=\mathcal{F}_n$). Thus $X_{mn}=\operatorname{ess\,sup} E_{mn}Z_{\sigma\tau}$, $(\sigma,\tau)\in T_{mn}$, should be calculated, where E_{mn} denotes the conditional expectation operator relative to $\mathcal{F}_{mn}$. X_{mn} fulfills the relation $X_{mn}=\max(Z_{mn},E_{mn}X_{m,n+1})$ a.s. Moreover, if (m,τ_{mn}) is defined by setting $\tau_{mn}=\inf\{k\ge n:\ X_{mk}=Z_{mk}\}$ (or ∞ if no such k exists), then (m,τ_{mn}) is optimal in T_{mn} (if $\tau_{mn}<\infty$ a.s.).

Now consider the application of optimal stopping theory to the sequence $(X_m,\mathcal{F}_m,m\ge1)$, where $X_m=E_mX_{m,m+1}$ (E_m denotes the conditional expectation with respect to $\mathcal{F}_m$). If $V_m=\operatorname{ess\,sup} E_mX_\sigma$, $\sigma\in S_m$, where S_m denotes the class of Markov moments relative to $(\mathcal{F}_n,n\ge1)$ such that $\sigma\ge m$, then $V_m = \max(X_m,E_mV_{m+1})$ a.s. Moreover, $\sigma_m=\inf\{k\ge m:\ X_k=V_k\}$ is optimal in S_m.

THEOREM (General solution). *Let* $\sigma=\inf\{m\ge1:\ X_m=V_m\}$. *On* $\{\sigma=m\}$, *let* $\tau=\inf\{n>m:\ Z_{mn}=X_{mn}\}$. *If* (σ,τ) *is finite-valued a.s., then* (σ,τ) *is an optimal csv.*

SOLUTION

Since F is known and continuous, without loss of generality it may be additionally assumed that Y has the uniform *df* on [0,1]. Because the *rv* K is bounded in our problem, X_{mn} and V_m can be determined by backward induction using the relations:

$$X_{mN}=Z_{mN} \quad \text{for } 1\le m<N, \qquad X_{mn}=\max(Z_{mn},E_nX_{m,n+1}) \quad \text{for } m<n<N,$$

$$V_{N-1}=X_{N-1}, \quad V_m=\max(X_m,E_mV_{m+1}) \quad \text{for } 1\le m<N-1.$$

If we define $Z_{mn} = P(K\ge m, Y_m=M_K \text{ or } K\ge n, Y_n=M_K \mid \mathcal{F}_n)$, $1\le m<n\le N$, then $E(Z_{\sigma\tau}) = P(\sigma\le K, Y_\sigma=M_K \text{ or } \tau\le K, Y_\tau=M_K)$. We obtain that $Z_{mn} = P(K\ge m, Y_m=M_K \mid \mathcal{F}_n) + P(K\ge n, Y_n=M_K \mid \mathcal{F}_n) = Q_{mn} + R_n$, where $Q_{mn}=Q_{mn}(Y_m)=\sum_{k=n}^{N}(p_k/\pi_n)Y_m^{k-n}$ if $Y_m=M_n$, $R_n=R_n(Y_n)=\sum_{k=n}^{N}(p_k/\pi_n)Y_n^{k-n}$ if $Y_n=M_n$ and $Q_{mn}=0$, $R_n=0$ otherwise. Further, we can show that $X_{mn}=Q_{mn}+\max(R_n,\alpha_n)$, where $\alpha_N=0$ and $\alpha_n=E_{n-1}\max(R_n,\alpha_n)$. A solution of this system is of the form $\alpha_n = \alpha_n(Y_1,\dots,Y_n) = F_{N-n}(M_n)$, where $F_0(x) = 0$ and

$$F_{k+1}(x) = \frac{\pi_{N-k}}{\pi_{N-k-1}}\left[xF_k(x)+\int_x^1 \max(R_k(y),F_k(y))dy\right].$$

Let $f_n(x)=\pi_{N-n}F_n(x)$, $r_n(x)=\pi_{N-n}R_n(x)$. Since $Z_{mn}=X_{mn} \leftrightarrow r_n=\max(r_n,\alpha_n)$ on $\{\sigma=m\}$, we should choose Y_n if $r_n(Y_n)\ge f_n(Y_n)$. This is te fundamental inequality for one choice problem with random number of observations and it has been considered in details by Porosinski (1987, 1990). The result is as follows.

LEMMA 1. *If the sequence* $(p_{n+1}/p_n)_{n=0}^{\infty}$ *is non-increasing, then an optimal stopping rule exists and is of the form*

$$\tau = \inf\{n: Y_n=M_n \ \textit{and} \ Y_n\ge b_n\}$$

where the decision number b_n *is the least root of the equation* $r_n(x)=f_n(x)$ *in* [0,1]. *The sequence* $(b_n)_{n=1}^{\infty}$ *is non-increasing.*

Now we can write $X_m = E_mX_{m,m+1} = E(Q_{m,m+1}|\mathcal{F}_m)+\alpha_m = R_m(Y_m)+\alpha_m$, and hence $V_m=\max(R_m+\alpha_m,\beta_m)$ for $m<N$, where $\beta_{N-1}=\alpha_{N-1}$ and $\beta_{m-1} = E_{m-1}\max(R_m+\alpha_m,\beta_m)$. A solution of this system is of the form $\beta_m= \beta_m(Y_1,\dots,Y_m) = G_{N-m}(M_m)$ for $m\le N-1$, where $G_1(x)=F_1(x)$ and

$$G_{k+1}(x) = \frac{\pi_{N-k}}{\pi_{N-k-1}}\left[x \max(F_k(x), G_k(x))+\int_x^1 \max(R_k(y)+F_k(y),G_k(y))dy\right].$$

If we set $g_m(x)=\pi_{N-m}G_m(x)$, then $g_k(x)\geq f_k(x)$ and

$$g_{k+1}(x) = x\, g_k(x) + \int_x^1 \max(r_k(y)+f_k(y), g_k(y))dy.$$

and the sequence of decision levels for the first choice is given by the following lemma.

LEMMA 2. *If the sequence* $(b_n)_{n=1}^N$ *is non-increasing, then there exist* $a_k\in[0,1]$ *such that* $g_k(x)\leq r_k(x)+f_k(x)$ *for* $x\geq a_k$ and $g_k(x)> r_k(x)+f_k(x)$ *for* $x<a_k$. *The sequence* $(a_k)_{k=1}^{N-1}$ *is non-increasing and* $a_k\leq b_k$.

In this way we have obtained an optimal solution for the problem determined by a pair of sequences $(a_m)_{m=1}^{N-1}$ and $(b_n)_{n=1}^N$:

THEOREM. *If the sequence* $(p_{n+1}/p_n)_{n=0}^N$ *is non-increasing, then a solution exists and an optimal csv* (σ,τ) *has the form*

$$\sigma = \inf\{m\leq N-1:\ Y_m=M_m \text{ and } Y_m\geq a_m\},$$

$$\tau = \inf\{n>m:\ Y_n=M_n \text{ and } Y_n\geq b_n\} \quad \text{on the set } \{\sigma=m\}.$$

The decision level b_n *is the least root of the equation* $r_n(x)=f_n(x)$ *in* $[0,1]$ *and* a_m *is the least in* $[0,b_m]$ *root of the equation* $g_m(x)=r_m(x)+f_m(x)$ *(*$a_m=0$ *if there is no such a root). The sequences* $(a_m)_{m=1}^{N-1}$ *and* $(b_n)_{n=1}^N$ *are non-increasing.*

Df's $(p_n)_{n=1}^\infty$, for which the sequence $(p_{n+1}/p_n)_{n=0}^\infty$ does not increase turns out to be (Porosinski, 1990) a subclass of the so-called IFR (*increasing failure rate*) *df's* (Barlow and Proschan, 1965).

References

Barlow R.E., Proschan F., Mathematical Theory of Reliability, Wiley, 1965, New York.

Gilbert J.P., Mosteller F. (1966) Recognizing the maximum of a sequence. J.Amer.Stat.Assoc. 61, 35-73.

Porosinski Z. (1987) The full-information best choice problem with a random number of observations. Stoch. Proc.Appl. 24, 293-307.

Porosinski Z., On the full information best choice problem, Proc. Conf. on Operations Research, Vienna, 1990, to appear.

Shiryaev A.N., Statistical sequential analysis, Nauka, 1969, Moskow (in Russian).

Tamaki M. (1980) Optimal selection with two choices - full information case. Math. Japonica 25, 359-368.

SOME NEW CONCEPTS IN THE CONTROL OF QUEUEING SYSTEMS

M. F. Ramalhoto
"Instituto Superior Técnico" (Technological University of Lisbon) and "Universidade Aberta"(Portuguese Open University)
Phone: 351/1/7143311 or 673351 Fax: 351/1/673229

So far, most of queueing research papers take the conditions of a queueing system as given, and merely attempts to compute such values as average waiting time, probability of the service being idle longer than x, etc., without allowing changes in the number of servers, in the service rates or in any other of the initial given conditions, as the system goes along. However, under a managerial point of view there is a need to actually control the queue, for instance, under the following rules: (1) If the queue exceeds b, introduce another server (or "k" servers, $k \geq 1$), if it falls below a, withdraw one server (or "k" servers, $k \geq 1$), where $b > a$. (2) If the queue exceeds b, shorten the service time (by deferring some tasks to be worked out later, or by reducing the quality of service). (3) Identify classes of service needed by customers (each class requiring a different service time and being of different "value") and treat the customers in separate queues, when the total queue length exceeds b. These considerations of control may require as well the construction of cost models, where costs are imputed to the use of alternative servicing facilities. The basic concept allows a wide variety of possible procedures to be designed and examined, thereby opening a new area of research.

In this contribution to the mentioned conference, the equilibrium probabilities of the number of customers in the system of the $M|M|c|\infty|FCFS$ queue under the rule (1), for one and two thresholds, is presented. A cost structure is introduced to assign a cost r_1 to each server, a cost r_2 to an idle server and a cost r_3 to a waiting customer. The average (global) cost is a linear function of r_1, r_2, r_3 and can be expressed in terms of the threshold in a quite revealing way concerning quality improvement in the service industry.

1. THE M|M|c|∞|FCFS QUEUEING SYSTEM UNDER THE RULE (1)

Let the M|M|c|∞|FCFS queue (a queueing system with **c** exponential identical servers with mean rates μ, unlimited queue size, first-come-first-served discipline, and Poisson arrivals with mean rate τ) be under the rule (1). If the service of one customer is completed when there are **a+1** customers in the system, and there are **c+k** servers operating, then **k** servers are removed and the customers who were in service are served by the remaining servers. For our purposes it is not necessary to specify which servers become idle.

For **b-a=1**, the number of customers in the system is clearly a birth-death process, where the mean arrival (birth) rate τ_j equals τ, for j= 0, 1, 2,..., and the mean service rate μ_j, when there are j customers in the system, for **c+k≤a** is

$$\mu j=\begin{cases} j\mu & , \quad \text{for } 1\le j<c \\ c\mu & , \quad \text{for } c\le j\le a \\ c+k)\mu & , \quad \text{for } \quad j>a \end{cases}$$

For **b-a>1**, the mean arrival rate remains constant and equal to τ but the mean service rate μ_j is more complicated. In this case the number of customers in the system is not a birth-death process as usually defined. In fact, for μ_j, with j between **a** and **b**, it is necessary to define two phases: (1) **phase upwards**, where there are **c** servers operating, because although **a** has been reached already, **b** has not, or because having revisited **a** (after **b** has been reached), **b** has not yet been revisited. (2) **phase downwards**, where there are **c+k** servers operating, because **b** has been reached and **a** has not yet been revisited after that. Therefore μ_j for **c+k≤a** is

$$\mu_j=\begin{cases} j\mu & , \quad \text{for } 1\le j<c \\ c\mu & , \quad \text{for } c\le j\le a \\ \mu_j^* & , \quad \text{for } a<j<b \\ (c+k)\mu & , \quad \text{for } \quad j\ge b \end{cases}$$

where $\mu j^* = c\mu$, if phase upwards and $\mu j^* = (c+k)\mu$, if phase downwards. If in both cases, **b-a=1** and **b-a>1, c+k>a** than the mean service rate $\mu_j = (c+k)\,\mu$ should be replaced by $\mu_j = \min((c+k), j)\mu$. For the purpose of the existence of the equilibrium probability distribution of the number of customers in the system, it is assumed that $\tau < (c+k)\mu$.

The equilibrium probability that there are j customers in the system, P_j, is for **b-a=1**

$$P_j = \begin{cases} 1/j!\ (\tau/\mu)^j\ P_o & \text{, for } 0 \le j \le c-1 \\ 1/c!\ (\tau/\mu)^c\ (\tau/c\mu)^{j-c}\ P_o & \text{, for } c \le j < a \\ 1/c!\ (\tau/\mu)^c\ (\tau/c\mu)^{a-c}\ (\tau/(c+k)\mu)^{j-a}\ P_o & \text{, for } j \ge a \end{cases}$$

By assumption $\tau < (c+k)\mu$, therefore $\tau = c\mu$ is allowed, and for P_o this case has to be considered separately.

$$P_o = [\sum_{j=0}^{c-1} (\tau/\mu)^j/j! + 1/c!\ (\tau/\mu)^c\ (1-(\tau/c\mu)^{a-c})/(1-(\tau/c\mu)) + 1/c!\ (\tau/\mu)^c\ (\tau/c\mu)^{a-c}\ (1/(1-(\tau/(c+k)\mu))]^{-1}, \text{ for } \tau \ne c\mu$$

$$P_o = [\sum_{j=0}^{c-1} c^j/j! + c^c/c!\ [(a-c) + (c+k)/k]]^{-1}, \text{ for } \tau = c\mu$$

In the case **b-a>1**, the number of customers in the system is no longer a birth-death process in the usual way, due to the states **a+1** to **b-1**, as already mentioned (see Ramalhoto (1991) for a brief discussion of this case).

COST STRUCTURE

In equilibrium the average cost is

$$E\,[\text{cost}] = \sum_{i=0}^{c-1} [c\ r_1 + (c-i)\ r_2]\ P_i + \sum_{i=c}^{a} [c r_1 + (i-c)\ r_3]\ P_i + \sum_{i=a+1}^{\infty} [\ (c+k)\ r_1 + (i-c-k) r_3]\ P_i$$

The average cost is a linear function of r_1, r_2, r_3. It can be expressed in terms of the integer parameter a as follows, for $b-a=1$, $\tau \neq c\mu$

$$E\ [cost] = (f_1+(f_2+f_3 a)(\tau/c\mu)^a)\ /\ (f_5+f_6(\tau/c\mu)^a)$$

Where f_1 depends on all the parameters c, k, r_1, r_2, r_3, $\tau/_\mu$; f_2 doesn't depend on r_2; f_3 doesn't depend on r_2 and r_1; and f_5 and f_6 don't depend on the costs. For $\tau=c\mu$

$$E\ [cost] = ((r_3/2)\ a^2+[cr_1+(\tfrac{1}{2}+c(1-k)/k)r_3]\ a+g_1)\ /\ (a+g_2)$$

Where g_1 is a function of c, k, r_1, r_2, r_3 and g_2 is a function just of c and k. In both cases, the importance of the cost r_3 in connection with the minimisation of E [cost] in a, is quite revealing concerning the quality improvement of the "service" provided. Furthermore, the cost r_2 appears in the average cost just through the functions f_1, g_1, respectively. It is not difficult to set up a computer program to minimize E [cost] in a. An inter-active computer program written in C and Fortran, using the E04ABF-NAG's routine, has been developed by Silva and it is currently under improvement.

The same Markovian queue under the rule (3) is also being studied. In the conference's presentation some graphs about this situation are shown. The main results will be published elsewhere.

Acknowledgements: The author would like to thank the Portuguese Open University (Universidade Aberta) and the Portuguese National Council for Scientifical Research and Technology (JNICT) for financial support.

REFERENCES

Ramalhoto, M. F., "Some Inventory Control Concepts in the Control of Queues", to be published in the Proceedings of the 22nd Annual Pittsburgh Conference on Modeling and Simulation, University of Pittsburgh, USA, May, 1991.

Some remarks on forecasting of stock dynamics

Rolf Reiner
II. Institut für theoretische Physik
Universität Stuttgart
Pfaffenwaldring 57/III
D-7000 Stuttgart 80

Matthias Ginter, Hermann Schnabl
Institut für Sozialforschung, Abt. Mikroökonomik
Universität Stuttgart
Breitscheidstraße 2c
D-7000 Stuttgart 1

The evolution of stock market still remains a highly interesting point in scientific discussion. Each new tool in computer science and regression analysis for handling time series will be used for investigations in the predicticability of stock returns. In particular, our paper gives some comments to results obtained from methods of nonlinear dynamics (for details see [1]) and predictions using neural networks (compare [2]). Schöneburg analyzed the possibility of predicting stock prices on a day-to-day basis [2], Scheinkman and LeBaron applied algorithms of nonlinear analysis to stock returns and found evidence that indicates the presence of nonlinear dependence on weekly returns [1]; on daily returns their conclusions are somewhat weaker.

In any case, to allow for prediction or to allow for theoretical conclusions a nontrivial structure has to be in the data. The purpose of our investigations was to check examples of stock returns, whether there exists a day-to-day structure in it or not. In order to discuss the principal possibilities of forecasting the relative daily variations of single stocks, we analyzed time series of BASF, RWE, SIEMENS stocks, and the index of the Frankfurter Allgemeine Zeitung (FAZ). The data source was delivered from DATASTREAM and includes daily values of these stocks starting in 1974. Until 1989 series of approximately 4000 points were available for our investigations.

To be sure to avoid any misinterpretation of our results we analyzed *relative changes*

$$k_i(t) = \frac{K_i(t) - K_i(t-1)}{K_i(t-1)} \tag{1}$$

instead of the original data $K_i(t)$. The index i characterizes the specific stock. Eq. (1) ensures that no kind of mid or long term trend remains in the records.

Fig. 1 gives a first impression of the data structure. The dependence of succesive values of $k_i(t)$ seems to be purely random.

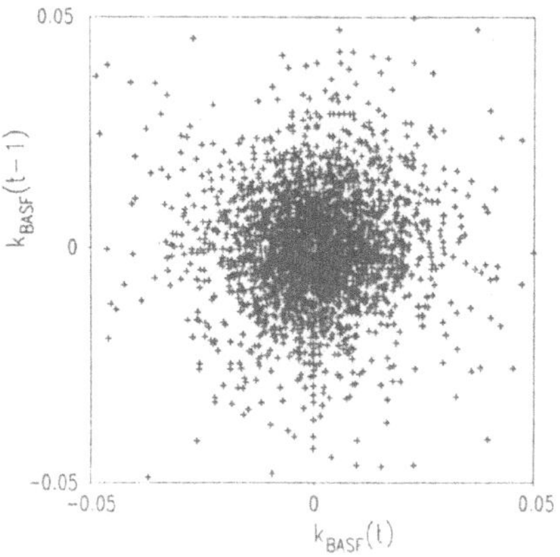

Fig. 1: Plot of $k_{BASF}(t\text{-}1)$ against $k_{BASF}(t)$.

Fourier analysis

In all cases we find a constant Fourier spectrum (compare Fig. 2), which gives rise to the conclusion that there is no kind of periodicity in the record. Even more, these results give evidence for a autocorrelation of type $\delta_{tt'}$, or in other words: there is no first or higher order autocorrelation in the time series. The constant power spectrum is an indication to purely white noise in the series.

Durbin-Watson test

Another test for detecting white noise was proposed from Anderson [3], calculating the ratio $R = c_1/c_0$ with

$$\sigma^2 c_0 = \sum_{t=1}^{T} \left[k_i(t) - \bar{k}_i\right] \left[k_i(t) - \bar{k}_i\right] \tag{2}$$

and

$$\sigma^2 c_1 = \sum_{t=1}^{T} \left[k_i(t) - \bar{k}_i\right] \left[k_i(t+1) - \bar{k}_i\right] \tag{3}$$

with $k_i(T+1) \equiv k_i(1)$. If the sample comes from a white noise then for large T R tends to have values near 0; if not, R tends to have values away from 0.

This test was further developed to the well known Durbin-Watson test (compare [4]), which allows to test the hypothesis of no first order serial correlation against the alternative there exists a serial correlation. The results of both statistics are depicted in table 1. The results of both tests are in complete agreement with the results of the power spectra: all series show the properties of white noise!

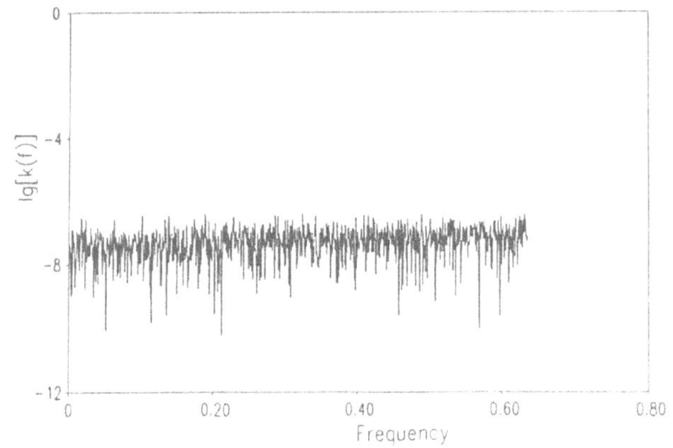

Fig. 2: Fourier spectrum of k_{BASF}.

Table 1: Statistics for testing serial correlation.

	BASF	RWE	SIEMENS	FAZ
R	-0.061	0.002	0.073	0.035
DW	2.12	2.00	1.85	1.93

Correlation dimension

Nevertheless, the above presented results do not exclude the possibility of a deterministic or quasideterministic behaviour of the series. The data might be the outcome of a system with deterministic chaotic behaviour. If so, Grassberger and Procaccia proposed a method to calculate the dimension of the underlying strange attractor, which gives the lower bound of the dimensionality (degrees of freedom) for the system [5].

In our examples we obtain similar results for all records. With growing embedding dimension D_E the dimension D_C of the "attractor" comes not to a saturation level (see Fig. 3). Thus, there exists no argument for the existence of such an attractor.

Even if such a finite dimension could be detected in further investigations, the complexity of a system consisting of at least 24 independent variables (which have to be identified!) contradicts the handling of these series for the prediction on a day-to-day basis.

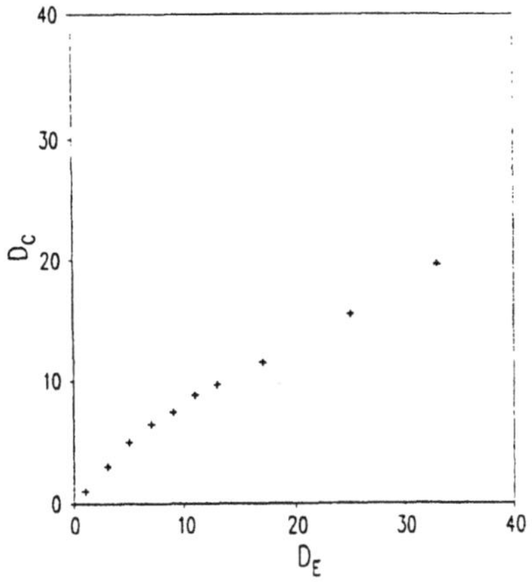

Fig. 3: Correlation dimension D_C versus embedding dimension D_E for k_{BASF}.

Conclusions

The above listed results give evidence for pure random behaviour in the day-to-day evolution of stock returns. The presence of white noise indicates, that there is no kind of "memory" in the records under investigation. Thus, we cannot confirm the conclusions presented in [1] and [2]. Indeed, Schöneburg as well as Scheinkman and LeBaron could not distinguish between day-to-day and mid or long term effects in the data. In particular, Schöneburg's results agree with our statistical examination, if they are not interpreted as a "day-to-day" prediction but as a "one-day prediction of trend".

Finally, it should be remarked, that a proper statistical examination of the empirical record should be the basis for any further investigation.

References

[1] J.A. Scheinkman, B. LeBaron, Nonlinear dynamics and stock returns, *Journal of Business* **62**/3 (1989) 311-337.

[2] E. Schöneburg, Stock price prediction using neural networks: A project report, *Neurocomputing* **2** (1990) 17-27.

[3] R.L. Anderson, Distribution of the serial correlation coefficient, *Ann.Math.Stat.* **13** (1942) 1-13.

[4] N.R. Draper, H. Smith, *Applied Regression Analysis,* 2nd ed. (Wiley, New York, 1982).

[5] P. Grassberger, I. Procaccia, Measuring the strangeness of strange attractors, *Phys.Rev.* D **9** (1983) 189.

SIMULATED ANNEALING — ABSORPTION & RECURRENT BEHAVIOUR IN TIME-INHOMOGENEOUS MARKOV CHAINS

Manh Tien TRAN
Institut für Mathematik, Universität Hildesheim
Samelsonplatz, D-3200 Hildesheim

Abstract: Simulated Annealing is a randomized algorithm which has been proposed for finding global optima in large NP-complete problems with cost functions which may have several local minima. A theoretical analysis of simulated annealing is based on the theory of time-inhomogeneous Markov chains. We analyze the asymptotic behaviour of time–inhomogeneous Markov chains with general state space. We consider an arbitrary partition $\{A, A^C\}$ of the state space Ω where A could be the set of optimal solutions. We give a necessary and sufficient condition for the "reachability" of A and a simple sufficient condition for the asymptotic absorption in A.

1 Introduction

Heuristic methods for combinatorial optimization problems are often based on local neighbourhood searches. At each iteration the current solution is replaced by one of its improving neighbours if the latter exists. The quality of the final solution depends heavely on the initial solution and the process tends to get trapped in local optima. To avoid these problems simulated annealing algorithms allow occasional changes that make the current solution worse. The transitions are governed by a generation mechanism and an acceptance function. Most simulated annealing algorithms can be modelled by using the theory of time-inhomogeneous Markov chains. Let A be the set of global optima or a set of desirable states. The most important properties to analyze are

1. Weak ergodicity: ("loss of memory") the asymptotic behaviour does not depend on the choice of the initial state.
2. Strong ergodicity: Does the process's distribution converge ?
3. Reachability of A: Is A reached from every starting point with probability 1 ?
4. Asymptotic absorption: Will the process finally be absorbed into A with probability 1 ?

Anily/Federgruen [1], Hajek [2] and Gelfand/Mitter [3] treated the two latter properties in the context of simulated annealing.

In this paper we consider a time-inhomogeneous Markov chain with

1. a measurable state space $(\Omega, \mathcal{A})$
2. a sequence of transition kernels $P_n(x, dy), n \in \mathbb{N}_0$ on $(\Omega, \mathcal{A})$.

Let $A \in \mathcal{A}$ (A could be the set of optimal solutions). We are interested in the following *global* behaviours

1. *Asymptotic recurrence*: Does the process reach A with probability 1 independently of starting time and place ?
2. *Asymptotic absorption*: Does the process converge to A with probability 1 independently of starting time and place ?

In section 2 we give a definition of as well as a necessary and sufficient condition for the asymptotic recurrence. Section 3 contains the definition and a simple sufficient condition for the asymptotic absorption.

2 Asymptotic Recurrence

2.1 Definition

A is said to be *asymptotically recurrent*

$$:\Longleftrightarrow \forall m \in \mathbb{N}_0 \quad \lim_{n\to\infty} \sup_{\omega\in\Omega} \mathbf{P}(X_\nu \in A^C \text{ for } \nu = m+1,\ldots,n | X_m = \omega) = 0$$

$$\Longleftrightarrow \forall m \in \mathbb{N}_0 \quad \lim_{n\to\infty} \sup_{\omega\in A^C} \mathbf{P}(X_\nu \in A^C \text{ for } \nu = m+1,\ldots,n | X_m = \omega) = 0$$

where A^C denotes the complement of A.

2.2 Remark

A is asymptotically recurrent

$\Rightarrow \forall m \geq 0 \quad \forall \omega \in \Omega \quad \mathbf{P}(X_n \text{ in } A \text{ i.o. } | X_m = \omega) = 1$

The converse is generally not true.

For example:

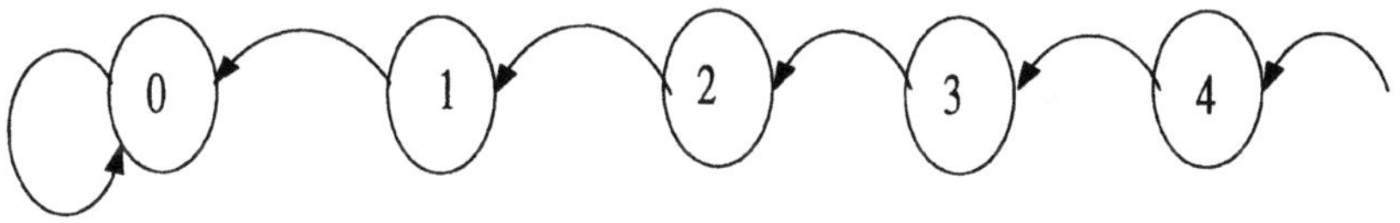

It is

$$\mathbf{P}(X_n = 0 \text{ i.o. } | X_m = j) = 1$$

but

$$\sup_{j\neq 0} \mathbf{P}(X_\nu \neq 0 \text{ for } \nu = m+1,\ldots,n | X_m = j) = 1$$

Let $(Q_n)_{n\geq 0}$ be substochastic kernels which arise by restricting $(P_n)_{n\geq 0}$ to $(A^C, A^C \cap \mathcal{A})$ and

$$Q_n(\omega, B) := P_n(\omega, B \cap A^C)$$
$$Q[m, n+1) := Q_m Q_{m+1} \cdots Q_n$$
$$\|Q_k\| := \sup_{\omega \in A^C} Q_k(\omega, A^C)$$

then

$$\|Q[m, n+1)\| = \sup_{\omega \in A^C} \mathbf{P}(X_\nu \in A^C \text{ for } \nu = m+1, \ldots, n | X_m = \omega)$$

2.3 Theorem

A asymptotically recurrent
$\iff \forall m \geq 0 \quad \lim_{n\to\infty} \|Q[m, n+1)\| = 0$
$\iff$ There exists a strictly increasing sequence (n_j) so that

$$\sum_{n=0}^{\infty} (1 - \|Q[n_j, n_{j+1})\|) = \infty$$

2.4 Proposition

A is **not** asymptotically recurrent, if for

$$\gamma_n := \inf_{\omega \in A^C} Q_n(\omega, A^C), \qquad n \in \mathbb{N}_0$$

we have

$$\sum_{j=0}^{\infty} (1 - \gamma_n) < \infty.$$

3 Asymptotic Absorption

3.1 Definition

A is said to be *asymptotically absorbing*

$$:\iff \forall m \geq 0 \lim_{n\to\infty} \sup_{\omega \in \Omega} \mathbf{P}(X_n \in A^C | X_m = \omega) = 0$$

3.2 Theorem

A asymptotically absorbing, if

1. A asymptotically recurrent
2. $\exists m \in \mathbb{N}_0 \quad \lim_{n\to\infty} \sum_{\nu=m}^{n} \sup_{\omega \in A} \mathbf{P}(X_\mu \in A^C, \mu = \nu+1, \ldots, n | X_\nu = \omega) = 0$

3.3 Theorem

Let

$$\alpha_n := \sup_{\omega \in A} \mathbf{P}(X_{n+1} \in A^C | X_n = \omega)$$
$$\beta_n := \inf_{\tilde{\omega} \in A^C} \mathbf{P}(X_{n+1} \in A | X_n = \tilde{\omega}).$$

i) $\sum_{n=0}^{\infty} \beta_n = \infty$,
ii) $\lim_{n\to\infty} \frac{\alpha_n}{\beta_n} = 0$,
iii) $\sum_{n=0}^{\infty} \alpha_n < \infty$,

Then we have

1. i) $\Rightarrow$ A asymptotically recurrent
2. i) + ii) $\Rightarrow$ A asymptotically absorbing
3. i) + ii) + iii) $\Rightarrow$ $\inf_{\omega \in \Omega} \mathbf{P}(\lim_{n\to\infty} \mathbf{1}_A(X_n) = 1 | X_m = \omega) = 1$

3.4 Remark

In case $|\Omega| < \infty$, we get the same implications if α_n, β_n in Theorem 3.3 are replaced by

$$\alpha_n := \sup_{\omega \in A, \omega' \in A^C} \mathbf{P}(X_{n+1} = \omega' | X_n = \omega),$$
$$\beta_n := \inf_{\omega \in A, \omega' \in A^C} \mathbf{P}(X_{n+1} = \omega | X_n = \omega').$$

References

1. Anily, S./ A. Federgruen: Simulated annealing methods with general acceptance probabilities, *Journ. of Applied Probability* **24**, 657–667, 1987.
2. Hajek, B: Cooling schedules for optimal annealing, *Mathematics of Operations Research* **13**, 311–329, 1988.
3. Gelfand, S.B./ S.K. Mitter: Analysis of simulated annealing for optimazation, *Proc. 24th IEEE Conf. on Decision and Control,* Ft. Lauderale, 779–786, 1985.

AN ALLOCATION PROBLEM IN STATISTICAL PROCESS CONTROL

Bernhard F. Arnold
Fachbereich Informatik/Mathematik
Fachhochschule München
Lothstraße 34, W-8000 München 2

In this paper the question is investigated how to allocate the sampling points at a production line. Obviously the sampling costs are minimized when there is only one sampling point at the end of the line; the disadvantage of this proceeding is that defects in the production system are detected possibly too long after they have occurred. This disadvantage can be circumvented by performing sampling actions after each part of the production line but of course, proceeding like this may be too costly. To come to a compromise an economic objective function is introduced and optimized.

This objective function which can more or less be interpreted as the average longterm profit per item produced is formulated within the framework of a shock-model approach (shock-models of statistical process control are also described e.g. in Uhlmann (1982) and in Montgomery (1985)) with the advantage that the concept of the renewal cycles can be applied. It may be considered as a generalization of von Collani's (1989) objective function and of the one investigated by Arnold (1990). In optimizing the here presented objective function the method of dynamic programming can be applied.

In order to obtain an optimal control policy it is assumed that the process under consideration is known from a technical and an economic point of view. Especially it is assumed that each of the mutually independent quality characteristics can be assigned to a special component of the production line and that the effects of the possible shocks are known from the technical as well as from the economic viewpoint. Furthermore, it is assumed that only one shock occurs per renewal cycle.

Numerical examples are given in the special case, where the in-control lifetime is exponentially distributed, the quality characteristics are normally distributed, the shocks effect only the means of the quality characteristics and the control policies consist of $\bar{x}$-charts used in parallel.

References

Arnold,B.F. (1990): An Economic $\bar{X}$-Chart Approach to the Joint Control of the Means of Independent Quality Characteristics. ZOR 34, 59-74.

Collani,E.v. (1989): The Economic Design of Control Charts. Teubner-Verlag, Stuttgart.

Montgomery,D.C. (1985): Introduction to Statistical Quality Control. Wiley, New York.

Uhlmann,W. (1982): Statistische Qualitätskontrolle. Teubner-Verlag, Stuttgart.

Length tests for goodnesss-of-fit

IMMANUEL M. BOMZE, ERHARD RESCHENHOFER

Institut für Statistik und Informatik
Universität Wien
Universitätsstrasse 5, A-1010 Wien, Austria

Consider an i.i.d. sample $X_1, \dots, X_n$ with distribution function F, which throughout is assumed to be twice continuously differentiable with support $[0,1]$ and strictly positive derivative on $[0,1]$. Denote by

$$0 = X_{0:n} \le X_{1:n} \le \cdots \le X_{n:n} \le X_{n+1:n} = 1$$

the order statistics, and the spacings by

$$e_{kn} = X_{k+1:n} - X_{k:n}\,, \quad 0 \le k \le n\,.$$

Then the length of the linearly interpolated empirical distribution function based upon this sample is given by

$$\ell_n(F) = \sum_{k=0}^{n-1} \sqrt{\tfrac{1}{n^2} + e_{kn}^2} + e_{nn} = \tfrac{1}{n} \sum_{k=0}^{n-1} h(ne_{kn}) + e_{nn}\,,$$

where $h(y) = \sqrt{1+y^2}$. Equally well, one could also consider $e_{0n} + \frac{1}{n}\sum_{k=1}^{n} h(ne_{kn})$ instead of $\ell_n(F)$.

In the context of time series analysis, the analogous test for GAUSSian white noise suggests the use of

$$L_n(F) = \frac{1}{n+1} \sum_{k=0}^{n} h((n+1)e_{kn})\,,$$

where F is here the spectral distribution function, frequencies being measured as a fraction of π. Since $L_n(F)$ and $\ell_n(F)$ have the same asymptotic properties, we shall investigate $L_n(F)$ instead of $\ell_n(F)$, the main reason being the symmetry of the former quantity.

The length test as proposed in [RESCHENHOFER/BOMZE 1991] rejects the null hypothesis that $F = F_0$, the equidistribution function on $[0,1]$, if L_n is too large. The smoothed length test is obtained by replacement of the e_{kn} in L_n by the smoothed spacings

$$q_{kn} = \frac{1}{m}\sum_{i=k-r}^{k+r} e_{in} = \frac{1}{m} t_{k-r:n}\,,$$

where $m = 2r+1 \sim \sqrt{n}$ and where $t_{j:n} = X_{j+m+1:n} - X_{j:n}$, $0 \le j \le n-m+1$, are the m-spacings of the sample $X_1, \ldots, X_n$. Hence the smoothed length test rejects the null hypothesis if M_n is too large, where

$$M_n(F) = \frac{1}{n+1}\sum_{k=r}^{n-r} h\big((n+1)q_{kn}\big)\,.$$

Critical values for both versions of the length test are given in Table 1 of [RESCHENHOFER/BOMZE 1991]. In the sequel we concentrate on the smoothed version, because both empirical evidence and theoretical investigations [BOMZE/RESCHENHOFER 1990] suggest that the latter is superior.

Let us denote by $G = F^{-1} : [0,1] \to [0,1]$ the inverse of F and by $g(x) = G'(x)$ its derivative. With the help of HALL's [1986] theory of higher order spacings, we obtain the limiting distribution of $M_n(F)$. For details see [RESCHENHOFER/BOMZE 1991].

Theorem 1:

(a) Under the null hypothesis $F = F_0$,

$$n^{3/4}[M_n(F_0) - \mu_{\mathrm{M},0}] \to \mathcal{N}(0, \sigma^2_{\mathrm{M},0}) \quad \text{in distribution as } n \to \infty\,,$$

where

$$\mu_{\mathrm{M},0} = \sqrt{2} - \frac{7}{4\sqrt{2n}} \quad \text{and} \quad \sigma^2_{\mathrm{M},0} = \tfrac{3}{8}\,.$$

(b) Under the alternative hypothesis $F \neq F_0$,

$$\sqrt{n}[M_n(F) - \mu_{\mathrm{M}}(F)] \to \mathcal{N}\big(0, \sigma^2_{\mathrm{M}}(F)\big) \quad \text{in distribution as } n \to \infty\,,$$

where

$$\mu_{\mathrm{M}}(F) = \ell(F) - \frac{\tau(F)}{\sqrt{n}}$$

and

$$\tau(F) = h\big(g(0)\big) - \frac{1}{2}\int_0^1 g^2(t) h''\big(g(t)\big)\,dt\,,$$

while $\sigma^2_{\mathrm{M}}(F) = \mathrm{Var}\,(Y)$ with $Y = 1/h\big(g(U)\big)$, U being a uniform-$[0,1]$ variate.

From Theorem 1 we see that $M_n(F) \to \ell(F)$ in probability as $n \to \infty$, where

$$\ell(F) = \int_0^1 h\big(g(t)\big)\,dt$$

denotes the length of the graph of G (and of F) on $[0,1]$. Moreover, observe that due to $h''(y) \le 1$ for all $y \ge 0$, we have

$$\tau(F) \ge h\big(g(0)\big) - \tfrac{1}{2} \ge \tfrac{1}{2}$$

so that $\mu_M(F) < \ell(F)$ holds, the difference vanishing with rate $n^{-1/2}$ as $n \to \infty$. This difference compensates for boundary effects in the smoothing procedure. Finally note that neither $\mu_M(F_0) = \mu_{M,0}$ nor $\sigma^2_M(F_0) = \sigma^2_{M,0}$ holds; indeed, we have $\sigma^2_M(F_0) = 0$ because then $Y = 1/\sqrt{2}$.

Now we compare the smoothed length test with the KOLMOGOROV/SMIRNOV test on basis of several asymptotic efficiency (ARE) criteria (see, e.g. [SERFLING 1980, p.315]). The asymptotic type-II error $\beta_M(F)$ at a (fixed) level α of the test based on M_n can be obtained in a straightforward manner: if $\Phi^{-1}(\gamma)$ denotes the γ-quantile of the standard normal distribution function Φ, then $\beta_M(F) = \Phi(b_M - a_M\sqrt{n})$ with

$$a_M = \frac{\ell(F) - \sqrt{2}}{\sigma_M(F)}, \quad b_M = \frac{7\sqrt{2}/8 + \tau(F)}{\sigma_M(F)} + \frac{\sigma^2_{M,0}}{\sigma_M(F)}\Phi^{-1}(1-\alpha)n^{-1/4}.$$

Theorem 2:

Let $F \neq F_0$ and assume that there is a unique $x \in (0,1)$ such that

$$\Delta(F) = \sup_{t\in[0,1]} |F(t) - t| = |F(x) - x|.$$

Denote by $\sigma^2_{KS}(F) = F(x)[1 - F(x)]$ the asymptotic variance of the normalized and centralized KOLMOGOROV/SMIRNOV test statistic under the alternative [SERFLING 1980, p.112]. Then the smoothed length test based on M_n is superior to the KOLMOGOROV/SMIRNOV test w.r.t. ARE in the sense of HODGES and LEHMANN, i.e.

$$\frac{\beta_M(F)}{\beta_{KS}(F)} \to 0 \quad \text{as } n \to \infty,$$

if and only if either (a) $\Delta(F)/\sigma_{KS}(F) < a_M$ or (b) $\Delta(F)/\sigma_{KS}(F) = a_M$ and

$$[\tfrac{7}{8}\sqrt{2} + \tau(F)]/\sigma_M(F) < \Psi^{-1}(1-\alpha)/\sigma_{KS}(F),$$

where Ψ denotes the limiting distribution of the KOLMOGOROV/SMIRNOV test statistic under the null hypothesis.

Proof: see [RESCHENHOFER/BOMZE 1991]. □

Of course, one can reverse the usual procedure by determining the significance levels $\alpha_i(F)$ through the (now fixed) type-II error β. Comparing then the rates of convergence of $\alpha_M(F)$ and $\alpha_{KS}(F)$ just means to compare convergence rates:

Theorem 3:

Let $F \neq F_0$. Then the smoothed length test based on M_n is superior to the KOLMOGOROV/SMIRNOV test w.r.t. ARE in the sense of BAHADUR:

$$\frac{\alpha_M(F)}{\alpha_{KS}(F)} \to 0 \quad \text{as } n \to \infty.$$

Proof: From the higher rate of convergence for $M_n(F_0) - \mu_{\mathrm{M},0}$ and from the form of Ψ [SERFLING 1980, p.62] it easily follows that the ratio $\alpha_{\mathrm{M}}(F)/\alpha_{\mathrm{KS}}(F)$ is of order $n^{-1/4}\exp(-cn^{3/2})$ for some $c > 0$. □

Let us finally discuss a criterion for comparisons of tests which is closely related to the ARE in PITMAN's sense. For the length test based on M_n, we consider smooth alternatives

$$F_n = F_0 + n^{-3/8}T$$

converging to the uniform distribution function at a rate of $n^{3/8}$. In this case, the asymptotic power amounts to

$$1 - \Phi[\Phi^{-1}(1-\alpha) - \frac{\|T'\|_2^2}{2\sqrt{3}}] \qquad (1)$$

and hence exceeds the level of significance [RESCHENHOFER/BOMZE 1991]. Note that the KOLMOGOROV/SMIRNOV test even is able to detect local alternatives only $n^{-1/2}$ apart from the null hypothesis [CHIBISOV 1961]. This rate cannot be obtained even if we choose a larger window for smoothing, i.e. if m grows faster than $\sqrt{n}$, provided $\frac{m}{n} \to 0$ [HALL 1986]. Hence the KOLMOGOROV/SMIRNOV test is superior to the (smoothed) length test w.r.t. the ARE in PITMAN's sense. However, the asymptotic power of the former does not only depend on the L^2-norm of T' as in (1), but also on the direction of T' [MILBRODT/STRASSER 1990]. In this sense, one may view the smoothed length test as "more uniform" than the KOLMOGOROV/SMIRNOV test (a similar statement holds also true for the test based on L_n, see [BOMZE/RESCHENHOFER 1990]).

References

BOMZE I.M./RESCHENHOFER E. [1990]: Smoothing improves the length test. Technical Report **85**, Inst. Statist., Univ. Vienna.

CHIBISOV D.M. [1961]: On the test of fit based on sample spacings. Theory Prob. Applic. **6**, 325–329.

HALL P. [1986]: On powerful distributional tests based on sample spacings. J. Multivar. Analysis **19** 201–224.

MILBRODT H./STRASSER H. [1990]: On the asymptotic power of the two-sided Kolmogorov/Smirnov test. J. Statistical Planning and Inference **26**, 1–23.

RESCHENHOFER E./BOMZE I.M. [1991]: Length tests for goodness of fit. Biometrika **78**, 207–216.

SERFLING R.F. [1980]: Approximation theorems of mathematical statistics. Wiley, New York.

Methods for Semiparametric Regression Analysis of Multivariate Correlated Event-History Data

Leo Brecht
Faculty of Economics and Statistics
University of Konstanz
P.O. Box 5560, FRG-7750 Konstanz

1. Introduction

For the analysis of univariate sojourn- or survival-times hazard-rate models are generally used. These models are also applicable for the *regression analysis* of multivariate sojourn-times. In this case it is possible to formulate the dependent process as a regression model, in which the independent process is modelled as a time dependent covariate. If one is interested, however, in the *correlation structure* of multivariate sojourn-times, it is necessary to develop new statistical models. This contribution presents methods to generate multivariate survivor functions and develops a semiparametric estimation procedure for the analysis of multivariate correlated sojourn-times. Further generalizations to handle other multivariate event-history data are sketched and it is shown how the concept applies to time discrete multivariate event data.

2. Generating Multivariate Survivor Functions

One approach to generate multivariate survivor functions is to generalize the principle of unobserved heterogeneity of univariate event-history analysis. This approach leads to multivariate frailty models.

Definition 2.1 *Let $\mathbf{X} \in \mathbb{R}^K$ be a non negative random vector with distribution function $G_X(\mathbf{x})$. A model with conditional survivor function given the variable $\mathbf{X} = \mathbf{x}$ of the form*

$$S(\mathbf{T} \geq \mathbf{t} \mid \mathbf{X} = \mathbf{x}) = exp\left(-\sum_{k=1}^{K} x_k \Lambda_k(t_k)\right) \tag{1}$$

with $\Lambda_k(t_k)$ the cumulative hazard function of component k, is called a multiplicative multivariate frailty-mixture model of dimension K.

With this definition it is possible to generate one class of multivariate survivor function by integrating out the random vector $\mathbf{X}$, stated in the following theorem:

Theorem 2.1 Let $\Lambda_1(t_1), \ldots, \Lambda_K(t_K)$ *be the cumulative hazard functions and $G_X(\mathbf{x})$ the K-variate mixture distribution with $\bar{G}_X(0) = 1$, $\bar{G}_X(\mathbf{x}) = 1 - G_X(\mathbf{x})$, and with univariate marginal distribution functions given by $G_k(x_k)$. Denote the Laplace transform of X_k and $\mathbf{X}$ as $\varphi_k(s_k)$ and $\varphi_X(\mathbf{s})$. If $F_k(t) = exp(-\Lambda_k(t_k))$, then*

$$S(\mathbf{t}) = \int \ldots \int F_1^{x_1}(t_1) \cdots F_K^{x_K}(t_K) dG_X(\mathbf{x})) \tag{2}$$

is a K-variate survivor function with marginal survivor functions

$$S_k(t_k) = \varphi_k(\Lambda_k(t_k)).$$

Proof: The proof is analogous to *Marshall/Olkin (1988).*

The principle can be extended to general mixture models with the following form:

$$S(\mathbf{t}) = \int \dots \int K(F_1^{x_1}(t_1), \dots, F_K^{x_K}(t_K))dG_X(\mathbf{x}) \tag{3}$$

where $F_k(t) = exp(-\varphi_k^{-1}(S_k(t)))$ and $K(\cdot)$ is a K-variate distribution function with univariate marginals uniform on $[0,1]$. Parametrizing the mixture distribution with a parameter α, called *association parameter*, we can measure the association with the estimated value of α. It is important to note that the marginal survivor function of model (3) is independent of the mixture distribution $G_X(\cdot)$, so that the association parameter is not identifiable from the marginal survivor function. Several special cases are generated from these model formulations, e.g. if one considers only univariate mixture distributions, or if one sets $K(\mathbf{t}) = \prod_{k=1}^{K} t_k$, with $0 \leq t_k \leq 1$. The main advantage of these models is that they can be formulated as a function of the Laplace transform of the mixture distribution, thus encompassing a rather wide class of multivariate survivor functions.

3. Semiparametric Estimation in Classes of Multivariate Survivor Functions

One approach of solving the inference problem of multivariate correlated sojourn-times was developed by *Clayton/Cuzick (1985)*, but only for a bivariate model, which is rather restrictive. Based on their method we develop a semiparametric estimation procedure for the class of frailty- and frailty-mixture models. With this procedure you can estimate the association parameter α as well as the vector β_k of regression parameters in a proportional hazards model given by $\lambda_k(t_k) = \lambda_{k0}(t_k)e^{\beta_k^t \mathbf{Z}_k}$, without knowledge of the hazard functions $\lambda_{k0}(t_k)$, where $\mathbf{Z}_k$ are the observed covariates of component k. The starting-point is a likelihood based on the ranks of the sojourn-times, which has to be generalized in the multivariate censored case. We restrict ourselves to model (2) with univariate mixture distribution $G_X(x,\alpha)$. Since $\Lambda_{k0}(\cdot)$ is strictly monotonically increasing, we get the following expression for the rank likelihood using the invariance principle of rank likelihoods and substitution of the variables

$$\int_{\mathbf{t}_1 \in \mathbf{R}_1} \cdots \int_{\mathbf{t}_K \in \mathbf{R}_K} \prod_{i=1}^{n} \int_{x_i=0}^{\infty} x_i^K \left(\prod_{k=1}^{K} e^{-x_i e^{\beta_k^t \mathbf{Z}_{ki}} t_{ki}} e^{\beta_k^t \mathbf{Z}_{ki}} \right) dG_X(x_i,\alpha) d\mathbf{t}_K \cdots d\mathbf{t}_1$$

$$= \int_{\mathbf{t}_1 \in \mathbf{R}_1} \cdots \int_{\mathbf{t}_K \in \mathbf{R}_K} \prod_{i=1}^{n} \left(\prod_{k=1}^{K} e^{\beta_k^t \mathbf{Z}_{ki}} \right) (-1)^K \varphi_{X_i}^{(K)} \left(\sum_{k=1}^{K} t_{ki} e^{\beta_k^t \mathbf{Z}_{ki}}, \alpha\right) d\mathbf{t}_K \cdots d\mathbf{t}_1.$$

with $\mathbf{R}_k$ the rank vector of the sojourn-times $\mathbf{t}_k$. Since the sojourn-times may be censored, some modifications are necessary. Therefore we generalize the vectors of the ranks $\mathbf{R}_1, ..., \mathbf{R}_K$ to $\mathbf{R}_1^G, ..., \mathbf{R}_K^G$ given by

$$R_{ki}^G = \begin{cases} (j,0), & t_{ki} \text{ uncensored, with rank } j \text{ under uncensored } t_{ki},\ \forall i, \\ (j,1), & t_{ki} \text{ censored, between } t_{k(j)} \text{ and } t_{k(j+1)} \text{ uncensored}, \\ (0,1), & t_{ki} \text{ censored and not greater than all uncensored times.} \end{cases}$$

Condition 3.1 Let $\varphi_X(s,\alpha) = E(e^{-sX})$ *be the Laplace transform of the frailty-variable* X, $\alpha \in \mathcal{A} \subset \bar{\mathbb{R}}^r$, $r \geq 1$. *Then the derivatives of* $\varphi_X(s,\alpha)$ *up to order* $K+1$ *exist and are continuous functions in* s, $K > 1$.

In the censored case under condition 3.1 we get using the censoring indicator $\delta_{ki} \in \{0,1\}$

$$\int_{\mathbf{t}_1 \in \mathbf{R}_1^G} \cdots \int_{t_K \in \mathbf{R}_K^G} \prod_{i=1}^{n} \left(\prod_{\substack{k=1 \\ \delta_{ki}=1}}^{K} e^{\beta_k^t \mathbf{Z}_{ki}} \right) (-1)^{\sum_{k=1}^K \delta_{ki}} \varphi_X^{(\sum_{k=1}^K \delta_{ki})}(\bar{\Lambda}_{0i},\alpha) dt_K \cdots dt_1,$$

with $\bar{\Lambda}_{0i} = \sum_{k=1}^{K} t_{ki} e^{\beta_k^t \mathbf{Z}_{ki}}$. To avoid integrating out the rank likelihood, the transformed sojourn-times are substituted by suitable rank-scores as in *Clayton/Cuzick (1985)* but the whole method can be derived for a general class of multivariate survivor functions. From there we get an efficient estimation procedure, with the following estimating equations

$$\sum_{i=1}^{n} l_j^{(i)}(\bar{t}_{1i},\cdots,\bar{t}_{Ki},\alpha,\beta_1,\cdots,\beta_K) = 0, \quad j = 1,2,$$

with the notation:

$$\begin{aligned} l_1^{(i)}(\cdot) &= \frac{\partial}{\partial \alpha} log\phi_i(\cdot), \quad l_{2,k}^{(i)}(\cdot) = \frac{\partial}{\partial \beta_k} log\phi_i(\cdot), \\ \phi_i(\bar{\Lambda}_{0i}) &= \left(\prod_{\substack{k=1 \\ \delta_{ki}=1}}^{K} e^{\beta_k^t \mathbf{Z}_{ki}} \right) (-1)^{\sum_{k=1}^K \delta_{ki}} \varphi_X^{(\sum_{k=1}^K \delta_{ki})}(\bar{\Lambda}_{0i},\alpha), \\ \bar{\Lambda}_{0i} &= \sum_{k=1}^{K} e^{\beta_k^t \mathbf{Z}_{ki}} \bar{t}_{ki}, \quad \bar{t}_{ki} = E(T_{ki} \mid \mathbf{R}_1^G,\cdots,\mathbf{R}_K^G). \end{aligned} \tag{4}$$

With the condition 3.1 we state the following theorem, where we represent the failure times $\mathbf{t}_i$ and the censoring indicators δ_i by $\mathbf{N}_i(\mathbf{t}) = (\mathbf{N}_{1i}(t_1),\ldots,\mathbf{N}_{Ki}(t_K))$ and $\mathbf{Y}_i(\mathbf{t}) = (\mathbf{Y}_{1i}(t_1),\ldots,\mathbf{Y}_{Ki}(t_K))$, with $N_{ki}(t_k) = I\{T_{ki} \leq t_k\}$ and $Y_{ki}(t_k) = \{T_{ki} > t_k\}$.

Theorem 3.1 *Let us consider a multiplicative multivariate frailty-model of dimension* K ($K \geq 1$). *The sojourn-times may be censored and conditionally independent given the frailty-variable* $X = x$. $g_X(x,\alpha)$ *is the density of the frailty-variable* X, $\varphi_X(s,\alpha)$ *their Laplace transform, satisfying the condition 3.1. If the number of uncensored variables in the* K*-tupel* $(t_{1i},\ldots,t_{Ki})$ *is* $\sum_{k=1}^{K} \delta_{ki} = \mu_i$, $\mu_i \in \{0,\ldots,K\}$ *then we get* $E(X_i|\mathbf{N}_i,\mathbf{Y}_i) = -\frac{\varphi_X^{(\mu_i+1)}(\bar{\Lambda}_i,\alpha)}{\varphi_X^{(\mu_i)}(\bar{\Lambda}_i,\alpha)}$ *with* $\varphi_X^{(\nu)}(\bar{\Lambda}_{0i},\alpha) = (\frac{\partial}{\partial s})^\nu \varphi_X(s,\alpha)|_{s=\bar{\Lambda}_i}$, $\nu \in \{0,\ldots,K+1\}$ *and* $\bar{\Lambda}_i = \sum_{k=1}^{K} \Lambda_k(t_{ki})$.

Proof: see *Brecht (1991a)*.

Using the following lemma it is possible to approximate the score vector $\bar{\mathbf{t}}_i$

Lemma 3.1 *We define*

$$\psi_{ki}(\mathbf{t}_i,\delta_i,\alpha,\beta) = log\phi_i(\mathbf{t}_i,\delta_i,\alpha,\beta) - log\phi_{i0}(\mathbf{t}_i,\delta_i,\beta) \tag{5}$$

and $\psi_{ki}^{(1)}(\mathbf{t}_i,\delta_i,\alpha,\beta)$ *as the partial derivative of* $\psi_{ki}(\cdot)$ *with respect to* t_{ki}, *where* $\phi_{i0}(\mathbf{t}_i,\delta_i)$ *is defined to*

$$\phi_{i0}(\mathbf{t}_i,\delta_i) = \left(\prod_{\substack{k=1\\ \delta_{ki}=1}}^{K} e^{\beta_k^t \mathbf{Z}_{ki}}\right) e^{-\sum_{k=1}^{K} t_{ki} e^{\beta_k^t \mathbf{Z}_{ki}}},$$

then we get

$$\psi_{ki}^{(1)}(\mathbf{t}_i,\delta_i,\alpha,\beta) = -(E(X_i \mid \mathbf{N}_i,\mathbf{Y}_i) - 1)e^{\beta_k^t \mathbf{Z}_{ki}}, \tag{6}$$

where $E(X_i \mid \mathbf{N}_i,\mathbf{Y}_i)$ *is given in theorem 3.1 by* $E(X_i|\mathbf{N}_i,\mathbf{Y}_i) = -\frac{\varphi_X^{(\mu_i+1)}(\bar\Lambda_{0i},\alpha)}{\varphi_X^{(\mu_i)}(\bar\Lambda_{0i},\alpha)}$ *with* $\bar\Lambda_{0i} = \sum_{k=1}^{K} e^{\beta_k^t \mathbf{Z}_{ki}} t_{ki}$.

Proof: see *Brecht (1991a)*.

Using this expression we can approximate the score-vector $\bar t_{ki} = E(T_{ki} \mid \mathbf{R}_1^G,\cdots,\mathbf{R}_K^G)$. The scores are given by

$$\bar t_{ki} = E(T_{ki} \mid \mathbf{R}_1^G,\cdots,\mathbf{R}_K^G) = \frac{\int_{\mathbf{R}_1^G}\cdots\int_{\mathbf{R}_K^G} t_{ki}\prod_{j=1}^{n}\phi_j(\mathbf{t}_j,\delta_j,\alpha,\beta)\,d\mathbf{t}_K\cdots d\mathbf{t}_1}{\int_{\mathbf{R}_1^G}\cdots\int_{\mathbf{R}_K^G}\prod_{j=1}^{n}\phi_j(\mathbf{t}_j,\delta_j,\alpha,\beta)\,d\mathbf{t}_K\cdots d\mathbf{t}_1}.$$

If we use the identity

$$e^{\psi_j(\mathbf{t}_j,\delta_j,\alpha,\beta)}\phi_{j0}(\mathbf{t}_j,\delta_j,\beta) = \phi_j(\mathbf{t}_j,\delta_j,\alpha,\beta)$$

we get

$$\bar t_{ki} = \frac{\int_{\mathbf{R}_1^G}\cdots\int_{\mathbf{R}_K^G} t_{ki}\exp\left(\sum_{j=1}^{n}\psi_j(\mathbf{t}_j,\delta_j,\alpha,\beta)\right)\prod_{j=1}^{n}\phi_{j0}(\mathbf{t}_j,\delta_j,\beta)\,d\mathbf{t}_K\cdots d\mathbf{t}_1}{\int_{\mathbf{R}_1^G}\cdots\int_{\mathbf{R}_K^G}\exp\left(\sum_{j=1}^{n}\psi_j(\mathbf{t}_j,\delta_j,\alpha,\beta)\right)\prod_{j=1}^{n}\phi_{j0}(\mathbf{t}_j,\delta_j,\beta)\,d\mathbf{t}_K\cdots d\mathbf{t}_1}.$$

After a Taylor series expansion of $\psi_j(\mathbf{t}_j,\delta_j,\alpha,\beta)$ around $\bar{\mathbf{t}}_j$ to first order, it follows

$$\bar t_{ki} \approx \frac{\int_{\mathbf{R}_k^G} t_{ki}\prod_{j=1}^{n} e^{-t_{kj}(e^{\beta_k^t \mathbf{Z}_{kj}} - \psi_{kj}^{(1)}(\bar{\mathbf{t}}_j,\delta_j,\alpha,\beta))}\,d\mathbf{t}_k}{\int_{\mathbf{R}_k^G}\prod_{j=1}^{n} e^{-t_{kj}(e^{\beta_k^t \mathbf{Z}_{kj}} - \psi_{kj}^{(1)}(\bar{\mathbf{t}}_j,\delta_j,\alpha,\beta))}\,d\mathbf{t}_k}.$$

All these integrals exist because $e^{\beta_k^t \mathbf{Z}_{kj}} - \psi_{kj}^{(1)}(\bar{\mathbf{t}}_j,\delta_j,\alpha,\beta) \geq 0$, and if we use lemma 3.1 we get the following approximation

$$\bar t_{ki} \approx \sum_{j:t_{kj}\leq t_{ki}} \delta_{kj}\left(\sum_{l\in\mathcal{R}_{kj}^G} e^{\beta_k^t \mathbf{Z}_{kl}} E(X_l|\mathbf{N}_l,\mathbf{Y}_l)\right)^{-1} \tag{7}$$

with $E(X_i|\mathbf{N}_i,\mathbf{Y}_i) = -\frac{\varphi_X^{(\mu_i+1)}(\bar\Lambda_{0i},\alpha)}{\varphi_X^{(\mu_i)}(\bar\Lambda_{0i},\alpha)}$, $\bar\Lambda_{0i} = \sum_{k=1}^{K} e^{\beta_k^t \mathbf{Z}_{ki}} t_{ki}$, and a risk-set $\mathcal{R}_{kj}^G$ given by

$$\mathcal{R}_{kj}^G = \begin{cases} \{l : t_{kl} \geq t_{kj}\}, & \delta_{kj} = 1, \\ \{l : t_{kl} \geq t_{kj^*},\ t_{kj^*} = \max\{t_{ki} : t_{ki} \leq t_{kj}, \delta_{ki} = 1, \forall i\}\}, & \delta_{kj} = 0. \end{cases}$$

For the iterative procedure a starting value is necessary. Here we apply an independence model and estimate the vector of regression parameters of each component using a partial likelihood approach and get $(\hat{\beta}_1, \ldots, \hat{\beta}_K)$. After this the iteration can start if we approximate the scores in the first step by

$$\tilde{t}_{ki}^{ind} \approx \sum_{j:t_{kj} \leq t_{ki}} \delta_{kj} \left(\sum_{l \in \mathcal{R}_{kj}^{G}} e^{\beta_k^t \mathbf{Z}_{kl}} \right)^{-1} . \tag{8}$$

The method of *Clayton/Cuzick* can be generalized to wide classes of multivariate survivor functions, especially to frailty-models, if we know the Laplace transform of the frailty variable and if we assume some differentiability conditions.

4. Generalizations to other multivariate data situations

One special case of the proposed model and method is to consider a multivariate survivor function without modelling the influence of covariates. The same procedure is applicable and we only have to estimate the association parameter. A case where no semiparametric estimation procedure has to be developed is the situation of multivariate time discrete sojourn-times. The generation of survivor functions is possible in the same way as for time continuous measurements. Other multivariate event-history data appear in models with multiple episodes. Dependent multi-episode-models are analyzed in *Brecht (1991b)* and are similiar to the proposed method. In dependent competing-risk models however, an identifiabilty requirement has to be fulfilled. It is possible to identify the model under some conditions and to estimate dependent competing-risks semiparamatrically in a similiar way.

References

BRECHT, L. (1991a): Ansätze zur semiparametrischen Regressionsanalyse multivariater korrelierter Verweildauermodelle. Diskussionspapier Nr. 129/s, Universität Konstanz.

BRECHT, L. (1991b): Neuere Regressionsansätze zur Analyse von Mehr-Episoden-Modelle. Diskussionspapier Nr. 132/s Universität Konstanz.

CLAYTON, D., CUZICK, J. (1985): Multivariate generalizations of the proportional hazards model. Journal of the Royal Statistical Society, Series A 148, 82-117.

MARSHALL, A.W., OLKIN, I. (1988): Families of multivariate distributions. Journal of the American Statistical Association 83, 834-841.

NATURAL GROWTH POPULATION PROJECTIONS

Drago Čepar, Lojze Gosar*, Erika Uršič
"Jožef Stefan" Institute, *Urban Planing Institute, Ljubljana

1 Introduction

With population projections future population size changes using present and past parameters and trends are estimated. The basic assumption of the underlying mathematical model is that some crucial demographic variables such as age-specific fertility and survival ratios remain unchanged. Therefore population projections serve as warning about future demographic processes if the existing parameters remain unchanged. We will concetrate on natural growth population projections. They forecast changes in the population structure based on fertility, mortality and population age distribution, without considering migrations. First we describe an annual model of population projections by natural increase which is considered in more detail in [1]. Then we describe, how to use this model, if data on one-year age groups are not available.

2 Annual model of population projections by natural increase

The basic variables of the model are the following. $N^t_{s,i}$ is the number of people by sex (s=1 for male and s=2 for female) belonging to i^{th} age group (it is [i,i+1) for i=0,1,...,84, whereas $N^t_{s,85}$ includes all people older than 84 years) in year t. One-year specific fertility ratio R_i represents the proportion between the number of babies who, during year t, were born by mothers belonging to i^{th} age group and number $N^t_{2,i}$. One-year specific survival ratio $P_{s,i}$ means a probability that a person, who is now i years old, will survive i+1 years. The survival ratio for infant children P'_s tells us how many children, who are not one year old yet, will survive until the end of the calendar year. R_i, $P_{s,i}$ and P'_s generally depend on time. But as we assume in our model that they remain unchanged, they are not fitted out with index t.

The inputs for the model are: initial year t_0; $N^{t_0}_{s,i}$ for s=1,2 and i=0,1,...,85; R_i for i=15,16,..,49; $P_{s,i}$ for s=1,2 and i=0,1,..,85; P'_s for s=1,2; final year T.

Our model is described by the following equations:

$$N^{t+1}_{s,i+1} = N^t_{s,i} \cdot P_{s,i}, \ i = 0,1,2,..,83, \ s = 1,2,$$

$$N^{t+1}_{s,85} = N^t_{s,84} \cdot P_{s,84} + N^t_{s,85} \cdot P_{s,85} \ , \quad B = 1/2 \cdot \sum_{j=15}^{49} (N^t_{2,j} + N^{t+1}_{2,j+1}) \cdot R_j \ , \qquad (1)$$

$$N^{t+1}_{1,0} = 0.517 \cdot B \cdot P'_1 \ , \quad N^{t+1}_{2,0} = 0.483 \cdot B \cdot P'_2 \ .$$

Constants 0.517 and 0.483 represent the ratio between live-born boys and girls. These parameters are considered global constants. They tell us that in global average among 1000 live-born children there are 483 girls and 517 boys.

Performing calculations (1) for $t = t_0, t_0+1, ..., T$ we obtain forecasts of the number of births and population sex and age distribution $N^t_{s,i}$ for years t_0 , t_0+1 , ..., T.

3 Transformation methodology

Population data for one-year age groups for different countries in the world are not always available. They are ussually collected for five-year age groups. In many demographic yearbooks, population data is given for the following age groups: 0 year, 1-4 years, 5-9 years, 10-14 years, ..., 80-84 years and the last age group 85+ years (people who are 85 years old or more). To allow for using model (1) we looked for a way of approximating the one-year age distribution, fertility and survival data by five-year data. Errors of estimations caused by those approximations were observed on specific cases. We will denote age group from i to j by index 'i-j'.

3.1 Age distribution

Five-year age group data can be expressed by one-year data as follows:

$$N^t_{s,0} = N^t_{s,0} \ , \quad N^t_{s,1-4} = \sum_{i=1}^{4} N^t_{s,i} \ , \quad N^t_{s,i-(i+4)} = \sum_{j=i}^{i+4} N^t_{s,j} \ , \quad i = 5, 10, .., 80 \ , \quad N^t_{s,85+} = N^t_{s,85} \ .$$

To get an approximation of one-year data from five-year data the most simple way is the following:

$$N^t_{s,0} = N^t_{s,0}, \quad N^t_{s,1} = N^t_{s,2} = N^t_{s,3} = N^t_{s,4} = \frac{1}{4} \cdot N^t_{s,1-4}, \quad N^t_{s,85} = N^t_{s,85+} \ ,$$

$$N^t_{s,i} = N^t_{s,i+1} = N^t_{s,i+2} = N^t_{s,i+3} = N^t_{s,i+4} = \frac{1}{5} \cdot N^t_{s,i-(i+4)}, \quad i = 5, 10, .., 80 \ . \tag{2}$$

The resulting population pyramid is staircased. We can reduce the errors caused by this method by reducing the height of the steps of step function (2) simultaneously taking into account the conditions $N^t_{s,1-4} = \sum_{i=1}^{4} {'N^t_{s,i}}$ and $N^t_{s,i-(i+4)} = \sum_{j=i}^{i+4} {'N^t_{s,j}}$ for i=5,10,..,80, where ${'N^t_{s,i}}$ are corrected values. The underlying equations are:

$${'N^t_{s,0}} = N^t_{s,0}, \quad {'N_{s,85}} = N_{s,85+}$$

$$a_s = N^t_{s,1}, \quad h_s = (N^t_{s,0} - a_s)/4, \quad {'N^t_{s,1}} = a_s + h_s, \quad {'N^t_{s,2}} = a_s + \frac{h_s}{2}, \quad {'N^t_{s,3}} = a_s - \frac{h_s}{2}, \quad {'N^t_{s,4}} = a_s - h_s$$

and for $i = 5, 10, ..., 80$:
$$H_{s,i} = (N^t_{s,i-3} - N^t_{s,i+2})/5, \quad {'N^t_{s,i}} = N^t_{s,i+2} + 2H_{s,i},$$

$${'N^t_{s,i+1}} = N^t_{s,i+2} + H_{s,i}, \quad {'N^t_{s,i+2}} = N^t_{s,i+2},$$

$${'N^t_{s,i+3}} = N^t_{s,i+2} - H_{s,i}, \quad {'N^t_{s,i+4}} = N^t_{s,i+2} - 2H_{s,i} \ .$$

3.2 Survival ratios

We denote five-year survival ratios by $P^5_{s,0}$, $P^5_{s,1-4}$, $P^5_{s,i-(i+4)}$, i=5,10,..,80, $P^5_{s,85+}$. Five-year survival ratio is the probability that a person, who belongs to the corresponding age group, will survive the next five years. Five-year survival ratios can be expresed as follows:

$$P^5_{s,0} = \frac{N^{t+5}_{s,5}}{N^t_{s,0}}, \quad P^5_{s,1-4} = \frac{N^{t+5}_{s,6} + N^{t+5}_{s,7} + N^{t+5}_{s,8} + N^{t+5}_{s,9}}{N^t_{s,1} + N^t_{s,2} + N^t_{s,3} + N^t_{s,4}}, \quad P^5_{s,85+} = \frac{\sum_{i=85}^{100} N^{t+5}_{s,i+5}}{\sum_{i=85}^{100} N^t_{s,i}},$$

$$P^5_{s,i-(i+4)} = \frac{N^{t+5}_{s,i+5} + N^{t+5}_{s,i+6} + N^{t+5}_{s,i+7} + N^{t+5}_{s,i+8} + N^{t+5}_{s,i+9}}{N^t_{s,i} + N^t_{s,i+1} + N^t_{s,i+2} + N^t_{s,i+3} + N^t_{s,i+4} + N^t_{s,i+5}}, \quad i = 5, 10, .., 80 .$$

The number of people, who are i years old in calendar year t and will survive the next five years is $N^{t+5}_{s,i+5} = N^t_{s,i} \cdot P_{s,i} \cdot P_{s,i+1} \cdot P_{s,i+2} \cdot P_{s,i+3} \cdot P_{s,i+4}$. For this computation all one-year survival ratios are needed at least to the age of 100 years; they are usually available in complete life tables.

To get one-year survival ratios from five year ratios we propose the following equations:

$$P_{s,0} = \sqrt[5]{P^5_{s,0}}, \quad P_{s,5} = \sqrt[5]{P^5_{s,1-4}}, \quad P_{s,i+4} = \sqrt[5]{P^5_{s,i-(i+4)}}, \quad i = 5, 10, .., 80 \; ; \quad P_{s,85} = \sqrt[5]{P^5_{s,85+}} \, .$$

We get the remaining ratios by linear interpolation given by equations:

$$d_s = \frac{1}{4}(P_{s,9} - P_{s,5}), \quad P_{s,i} = P_{s,5} - (5-i) \cdot d_s \, , \quad i = 1,2,3,4; \quad P_{s,i} = P_{s,5} + (i-5) \cdot d_s \, , \quad i = 6,7,8;$$

$$P_{s,i+k} = P_{s,i-1} + \frac{(k+1)}{5} \cdot (P_{s,i+4} - P_{s,i-1}) \quad for \quad k = 0,1,2,3, \quad i = 10, 15, .., 80 .$$

It is shown for the case of Slovenia, errors caused by this approximation are greater for $i \geq 74$ then for $i \leq 73$. We can reduce these errors using survival ratios of a specific country; we ourselves used Slovenia ones. $P_{s,i}$ is transformed into $'P_{s,i} = P^{SL}_{s,i} \cdot k_i \; , \; i = 74, ..., 85$, where $P^{SL}_{s,i}$ are Slovenian one-year survival ratios and $k_i = \sum_{j=i-10}^{i-1} P_{s,i} / \sum_{j=i-10}^{i-1} P^{SL}_{s,i}$.

3.3 Fertility ratios

Five-year ratio $R_{i-(i+4)}$ represents the proportion between the number of babies born by mothers belonging to the age group i-(i+4) in one year t and number $N^t_{2,i-(i+4)}$.

If we know the *total fertility rate* $T_f = \sum_{i=15}^{49} R_i$ and the five-year fertility ratios, R_i can be approximated as follows:

$$R_i = {}'R_i \cdot (T_f / \textstyle\sum_{i=15}^{49} {}'R_i) \, ,$$

where $'R_i = R^{SL}_i \cdot (R_{j-(j+4)} / R^{SL}_{j-(j+4)})$ *for* $j = 15, 20, ..., 45, \; i = j, j+1, j+2, j+3, j+4$. T_f is the average number of children one women gives birth to during her whole life. R^{SL}_i and $R^{SL}_{j-(j+4)}$ are one-year and five-year fertility ratios for Slovenian women.

3 Some empiric results

Results of population projections for some European countries are presented in Table 1. The last year for which a population pyramid is available is taken as the initial year t_0. Ratios R_i and $P_{s,i}$ are one-year ratios calculated from the latest available five-year ratios.

$country_{t_0}$	fertility	survival	1990	2000	2100	2200
$Austria_{88}$	'87	'87	7.61	7.56 (0.99)	2.47 (0.32)	0.59 (0.08)
$Belgium_{84}$	'83	'84	9.93	9.89 (0.99)	4.14 (0.42)	4.40 (0.14)
$Czechoslovakia_{86}$	'86	'86	15.75	16.37 (1.04)	15.54 (0.99)	13.30 (0.84)
$Denmark_{87}$	'87	'87	5.13	5.09 (0.99)	1.90 (0.37)	0.57 (0.11)
$Finland_{86}$	'86	'86	4.98	5.01 (1.01)	2.32 (0.47)	0.90 (0.18)
$France_{88}$	'87	'87	56.21	58.12 (1.04)	40.70 (0.72)	24.27 (0.43)
GDR_{88}	'85	'85	16.72	16.74 (1.00)	9.36 (0.56)	4.56 (0.27)
GFR_{86}	'86	'86	60.95	59.74 (0.98)	16.13 (0.26)	3.41 (0.06)
$Hungary_{87}$	'87	'87	10.60	10.57 (0.99)	6.39 (0.60)	3.51 (0.33)
$Iceland_{84}$	'84	'84	0.26	0.28 (1.10)	0.33 (1.31)	0.33 (1.30)
$Ireland_{86}$	'85	'85	3.67	4.06 (1.11)	7.49 (2.04)	12.04 (3.28)
$Italy_{87}$	'82	'84	57.75	58.63 (1.02)	25.29 (0.44)	8.65 (0.15)
$Norway_{87}$	'87	'87	4.22	4.30 (1.02)	2.65 (0.63)	1.37 (0.33)
$Poland_{87}$	'87	'87	38.42	40.55 (1.06)	47.84 (1.25)	51.50 (1.34)
$Portugal_{87}$	'87	'87	10.36	10.63 (1.03)	4.88 (0.47)	1.62 (0.16)
$Sweden_{87}$	'87	'87	8.46	8.50 (1.01)	5.68 (0.67)	3.54 (0.42)
$Switzerland_{87}$	'87	'87	6.60	6.64 (1.01)	2.61 (0.40)	0.83 (0.13)
United $Kingdom_{87}$	'87	'87	57.46	58.52 (1.02)	39.49 (0.69)	23.27 (0.40)
$Yugoslavia_{87}$	'87	'87	23.92	25.30 (1.06)	22.70 (0.95)	18.11 (0.76)

Table 1: Population forecasts for some European countries in millions. The ratios with respect to the year 1990 are written in parenthesis. The years for which fertility and survival ratios are used are written in the second and the third columns. Input data is taken from [2].

5 Conclusion

This methodology represents an efficient instrument for forecasting population trends. The population projections for European countries are not based on the latest data. In spite of that, results give indications about future trends, which are important for economy and society planning. If the fertility is unchanged and there are no migrations, the total number of people in the countries from Table 1 will decrease from about 399 million in 1990 to 177 million in 2200. In Poland, Island and Ireland the total population will increase by 50%. Population will decrease the most in Austria, Germany, Denmark, Switzerland, Belgium, Italy, Portugal and Finland. The error of forecast of a country's total population in 2200 due to approximation of one-year data by five-year data, observed on some specific cases, is up to 5%. The above described model can be improved to be able to cope with the assumption that fertility and mortality are variable in time.

References

[1] L.Gosar: Demografske projekcije v prostorskem planiranju, Ljubljana, januar 1980.
[2] United Nations: Demographic Yearbook, 1990.

PC–TSA 2.0 TIME SERIES ANALYSIS ON PC

D. Čepar, B. Motnikar, P. Pehani, Z. Radalj, B. Vovk
"Jožef Stefan" Institute, Jamova 39
YU - 61111 Ljubljana, Slovenia

1. Introduction

The *PC–TSA* is a menu driven user friendly software package for time series analysis running on an IBM PC or compatible. It enables time series modelling by an extended Box–Jenkins' approach. It can be used in many different fields of experimental data processing (financial, business, natural, technical and other types of time series). Some parts of the analysis are fully automatic to make handling the package very simple. So to work on a *PC–TSA* only basic statistical education is necessary.

Its first version based on Box–Jenkins approach (Box, Jenkins, 1970) generalised by Čepar, Dekleva (Čepar, Dekleva, 1986) was described by Čepar and Mićković (Čepar, Mićković, 1988). Later we have extended it by including the possibilities of analysing time series with missing data (Bole, Čepar, Radalj, 1990 and Čepar, Radalj, 1990) and computing forecast reliability for user defined confidence region (Bohte, Čepar, Motnikar, 1990 and Čepar, Motnikar, 1990).

We emphesize the following elements of the *PC–TSA* software package:

- data manipulation (enter, import, export, edit, save, generation of time series for a given model);
- data transformations for inducing stationarity (log, power, (seasonal) difference, move);
- calculation of statistics (descriptive, autocorrelation and partial autocorrelation function, mean–range plot);
- model identification and forecasting (automatic model identification, estimation of model parameters, missing observations, sensitivity of observations, forecasts, reliability of forecasts);
- high resolution graphic representation (time series plot, comparison of two time series);
- programability and controlability (batch procedure, default settings).

2. Data manipulation

The commands of this section enable the user to enter time series (in different ways: from floppy disk, hard disk or keyboard), to complete it (correct wrong observations, edit new observations, etc.), to save it, or to generate time series for a given model (described by given parameters). In short: in this section, the time series is prepared for further analysis.

3. Data transformations

The commands of this section transform a nonstationary time series to a stationary one. The nonstationarity can be eliminated by proper transformations. The user selects them on the basis of a mean–range plot (see Section 4) from four types: logarithming, powering, differencing and seasonal differencing. The first three transformations deal with trend and the nonconstant variance of time series, while the last transformation deals with seasonality (oscillating irregularities, consequences of calendar properties).

4. Calculation of statistics

The commands of this section calculate the following statistics: descriptive statistics (mean, variance, standard deviation, range, standard error of mean), autocorrelation and partial autocorrelation function. They also show the mean–range plot with the possible interpretations which help the user to select the proper transformation.

5. Model identification and forecasting

This section performs the following tasks:

- *identification of the optimal ARMA model and estimation of its parameters.* In the ARMA (p, q) model, p and q represent the maximal lags of previous observations and random impulses. By Box–Jenkins' approach orders p and q are determined by inspection of autocorrelation and partial autocorrelation functions. Model parameters are estimated by Marquardt algorithm. In our software package we choose the key–word "estimate" to estimate parameters of the chosen ARMA model. The software package offers the possibility of automatical determination of the orders p and q by stepwise application of one of several available goodness of fit and parsimony criteria (e.g. σ_a^2, AIC, BIC). We can choose forward stepwise algorithm by key–word "forward": the algorithm starts by chosen ARMA model (ARMA$(0,0)$ recommended) and proceeds by including parameters which improve criterial function. On each step decision whether to increase p or q is considered. Algorithm chooses the possibility which gives better criterial function. Algorithm stops when neither possibility causes a significant improvement of the criterial function. Backward algorithm effected by key- word "backward" starts by a chosen model (we recommend the model selected by forward algorithm) with supposedly too many parameters and proceeds by stepwise elimination of the least significant parameters. We suggest the consecutive use of forward and backward algorithms. Seasonal models can also be considered. This identification procedure is graficaly supported and illustrated by a tree structure representation (ARMATREE). The results of identification and estimation procedure are: orders of the optimal model, estimated parameters of the model, correlation matrix of parameters, roots of operator's polynoms, residual statistics, e.g. values of criterial functions, autocorrelation function.

- *estimation of the missing observations.* An iterative algorithm is used for the analysis of time series with missing observations and for estimation of missing observations. The importance of the missing observations is estimated to establish a preference order for eventually collecting the missing observations.
- *forecasting future observations.* A user has to enter the forecast origin, forecast lead time and confidence level. The results are forecasts of future observations with confidence intervals.
- *calculation of reliability of forecasts.* Procedure calculates probability that no future observation is outside region whose limits are determined by the user. The forecasts and their reliability have proved to be a powerful aid in planning and decision-making.

6. Graphic representation

All elements are supported by high resolution graphic. The time series plot can be displayed in extended or narrowed form, as line or dot plot, with or without confidence levels, with or without forecasts. Display and analysis of only a part of the time series is also possible as well as comparison of two time series. Low resolution graphics can be used on computers without a graphic card.

7. Programability and controlability

Batch procedure enables noninteractive execution of the program and so can save a lot of the user's time. Automatic processing of the *PC–TSA* can be controlled by prearranged list of commands on a file. Processing is controlled by more than twenty changeable parameters. Most of them keep their default values in most cases, which makes controll very simple.

8. System requirements

The software package *PC–TSA* requires the following hardware and software:

- PC compatible personal computer with:
  - two 360 K or one 1.2 M floppy disk or hard disk;
  - 640 K RAM,
  - graphic card HERCULES, CGA, EGA or VGA (for high resolution graphics);
- operating system MS DOS 3.0 or higher;
- mathematical co-processor is recommended.

9. Conclusions

The main advantages of the package are:

- Automatical and graphics supported model identification and parameter estimation.
- Analysis of time series with missing data.
- The possibility of computing reliability of forecasts for a user defined region.
- High resolution grafic support.

A software package *PC-TSA* has successfully proved its value in the following establishments in Ljubljana: "Ljubljanska banka", "Narodna banka" - banking, "Zavarovalna skupnost Triglav" - insurance, "Elektroinštitut Milan Vidmar" - planning of electricity supply. It is suitable also for demonstration and teaching purposes at universities. The possible ways of sharing our research and software results with other researchers are: purchase of the software package, analysis of data sent by mail (If we receive data - i.e. one time series - till the end of the year 1991, results of analysis will be returned free to the sender), seminars or visits and TEMPUS projects.

Acknowledgement
We thank Nataša Krajnc, Slaven Mićković, Erika Uršič and Aleš Zajc for their work on the described project.

References

Bohte Z., D. Čepar and B. Motnikar: "Confidence Level for the Region of Single Time Series Forecasts with Different Lead Times", Methods of Operations Research, Vol. 62, Proceedings of 14th Symposium on Operations Research, Ulm 1989, Anton Hain Verlag, p. 503–509, 1990

Bole V., D. Čepar and Z. Radalj: "Estimating missing values in time series", Methods of Operations Research, Vol. 58, Proceedings of 12th Symposium on Operations Research, Ulm 1989, Anton Hain Verlag, p. 510–516, 1990

Box G. E. P. and G. M. Jenkins, Time Series Analysis: Forecasting and Control, Holden–Day, San Francisco, 1970

Čepar D. and J. Dekleva: "On the generalized univariate ARIMA models and their identification", Methods of Operations Research 54, Konigstein, 1986

Čepar D. and S. Mićković: "PC–TSA – A Program for Time Series Analysis for the IBM PC", 8th International Symposium on Forecasting, Amsterdam, June 1988

Čepar D. and B. Motnikar: "Reliability of time series forecasts", Proceedings of 5th ECMI, Lahti, Kluwer Academic Press, 1990

Čepar D. and Z. Radalj: "Estimating Time Series with Missing Data", Proceedings of 5th ECMI, Lahti, Kluwer Academic Press, 1990

DETERMINATION OF ADMISSIBLE VALUES OF PARAMETERS FROM THE ESTIMATED ACCURACY OF DATA

Drago Čepar, Zoran Radalj, Marijan Ribarič, Boštjan Vovk
Department of Applied Mathematics, "Jožef Stefan" Institute
Yu 61111 Ljubljana, Slovenia

Abstract. In the traditional parameter estimation approach, confidence intervals for parameters are computed using statistical assumptions, such as the randomness of the sample and a normal distribution of errors. If these statistical assumptions are omitted, we can still estimate values of the model parameters, but the question is whether we can say anything about their confidence limits. We provide an affirmative answer by showing how for a given analytic expression we can determine admissible values of parameters that are compatible with the accuracy of experimental data. An estimate of relative importance of a particular datum for parameter estimation is obtained as a byproduct; it is defined by the number of occasions when this datum determines the extreme admissible values of parameters that are consistent with its accuracy. Use of the method is illustrated by a case study.

1. Introduction. Suppose that we know the function representing the natural law

$$f(x, \alpha_1, \ldots, \alpha_k) ,$$

where $\alpha_1, \ldots, \alpha_k$ are unknown free parameters. Given the measurements of a natural law y_i and estimates of their accuracy ϵ_i, for $i = 1, \ldots, N$, for certain values of independent variable x_i, we will consider the aproximation of experimental data by $f(x, \alpha_1, \ldots, \alpha_k)$. Our objective is to determine the domain of admissible values of parameters $\alpha_1, \ldots, \alpha_k$ consistent with the accuracy of experimental data.

The traditional approach in fitting experimental data is based on the assumption that y_i and $\epsilon_i = f_i - y_i$ are realizations of random variables distributed normally with the same variance σ^2. Using the least squares (LS) method, the parameters α_j and their standard errors $SE(\alpha_j)$ for $j = 1, \ldots, k$, are estimated by minimizing the expression $\epsilon_1^2 + \epsilon_2^2 + \ldots + \epsilon_N^2$.

Our method for determining admissible values of parameters α_j does not require any statistical assumptions about y_i or ϵ_i. The method is described in Section 2. In Section 3, we estimate the relative importance of a particular datum for parameter estimation. In Section 4, we illustrate the method by a case study.

2. The method proposed for parameter estimation. We define the domain $\mathcal{D}_\alpha$ of the admissible values of parameters $\alpha_1, \ldots, \alpha_k$ as consisting of those values that satisfy N inequalities

$$y_i - \epsilon_i \leq f(x_i, \alpha_1, \ldots, \alpha_k) \leq y_i + \epsilon_i , \qquad i = 1, \ldots, N . \tag{1}$$

The domain $\mathcal{D}_\alpha$ of admissible parameters can be constructed in two steps as shown in the following two–parameters case with α_1 and α_2:

(i) Computation of the initial values of parameters. We calculate initial values $\alpha_{1,0}$ and $\alpha_{2,0}$ by the LS method.

(ii) Determination of the domain $\mathcal{D}_\alpha$. We determine $\mathcal{D}_\alpha$ by testing which of the pairs $\alpha_1 = \alpha_{1,0}(1+\delta_1 \cdot l)$ and $\alpha_2 = \alpha_{2,0}(1+\delta_2 \cdot m)$, $l, m = -L, \ldots, L$, of discrete values of parameters satisfy inequalities (1) for some chosen values of L, δ_1 and δ_2. If a certain pair (α_1, α_2) satisfies inequalities (1) for all observations y_i, then it belongs to the domain of admissible parameters. Using the domain $\mathcal{D}_\alpha$, obtained on the discrete plane $\alpha_1 \otimes \alpha_2$ defined as

$$\alpha_1 \otimes \alpha_2 = \{(\alpha_1, \alpha_2) \ : \ \alpha_j = \alpha_{j,0}(1+\delta_j \cdot l) \quad for\ j = 1,2 \ \ and\ l = -L, \ldots, L\} \ ,$$

we proceed as follows:

1. If $\mathcal{D}_\alpha$ is an empty set, we vary the values of δ_j and/or L. If $\mathcal{D}_\alpha$ is still empty after varying δ_j and/or L we have to check observations y_i and/or estimates of accuracy ϵ_i.
2. If $\alpha_{j,0}(1+\delta_j \cdot L) \in \mathcal{D}_\alpha$ for $j = 1$ or 2, we increase the value of δ_j or L.
3. We proceed until we determine the maximal, closed domain $\mathcal{D}_\alpha$ of admissible values belonging to a certain discrete square plane $\alpha_1 \otimes \alpha_2$.

3. Relative importance of a particular datum. In the preceding section we determined a closed domain $\mathcal{D}_\alpha$ on the discrete plane $\alpha_1 \otimes \alpha_2$. Now we consider the boundary of the complementary set $\mathcal{D}_\alpha^{\mathcal{C}} \equiv \alpha_1 \otimes \alpha_2 - \mathcal{D}_\alpha$ of the domain $\mathcal{D}_\alpha$.

For each pair (α_1, α_2) on the boundary $\mathcal{B}(\mathcal{D}_\alpha^{\mathcal{C}})$ of $\mathcal{D}_\alpha^{\mathcal{C}}$ there exists at least one observation y_i for which the inequality from (1) does not hold. For each such observation y_i we count the number of pairs (α_1, α_2) on the boundary $\mathcal{B}(\mathcal{D}_\alpha^{\mathcal{C}})$ which do not satisfy the ith inequality in (1). We divide the obtained sum by the total number of pairs (α_1, α_2) on the boundary $\mathcal{B}(\mathcal{D}_\alpha^{\mathcal{C}})$. This ratio determines the relative importance of the particular observation y_i for parameter estimation. If we have an opportunity to repeat only one measurement, the observation y_i with the largest value of this ratio seems the most important, and should be chosen.

4. Case study. Since estimating directly the number of ants that populate a colony is very difficult, biologists use an indirect and easier approach to this problem as elaborated in [1]: If y is the colony size and x the number of foraging ants, we assume the relationship between y and x to be $y = \alpha_2 x^{\alpha_1}$; so, by counting the number of ants leaving a colony to forage on a regular basis, we can estimate the total colony size. Using the LS method, we approximate 15 observations given in Table 1 by the expression $\log \hat{y} = 0.86 \log x + 1.13$; the standard errors of estimates are $SE(\alpha_1) = \pm 0.17$, $SE(\log \alpha_2) = \pm 0.49$ and $\sigma_{\log \hat{y}} = 1.22$. To consider the same problem by the method proposed, we need the estimates of measurement accuracy ϵ_i. The authors of the study

i	x_i	y_i	i	x_i	y_i	i	x_i	y_i
1	45	280	6	823	2 769	11	611	8 834
2	74	222	7	647	2 828	12	4 119	12 584
3	118	288	8	446	3 229	13	850	12 605
4	70	601	9	765	3 762	14	11 600	34 661
5	220	1 205	10	338	7 551	15	64 512	139 043

Table 1: Actual colony sizes (y) and foraging sizes (x) for 15 colonies of red wood ants given in [1].

[2] estimated that the colony sizes given in Table 1 may deviate from the real value by a factor up to $\times$ 2. The domain $\mathcal{D}_\alpha$ of admissible values of the parameters obtained by our method with estimated relative accuracy of experimental data $\epsilon_i = 0.25y_i$ is shown in Fig. 1. The 10th and 3rd observations turned out to be the most important for the

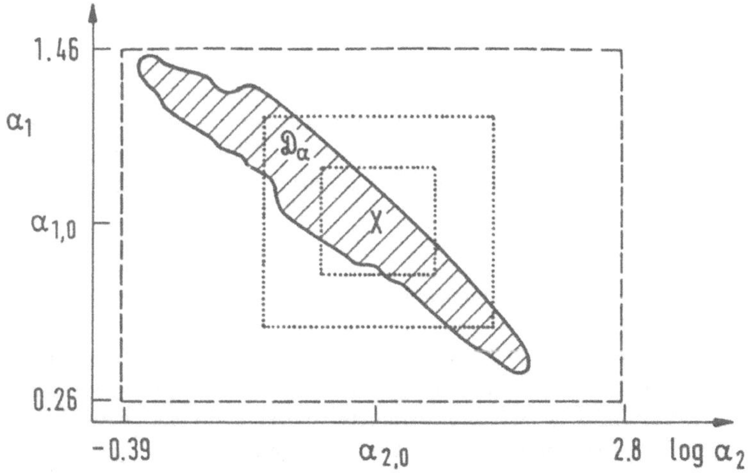

Figure 1: Shaded region is the domain $\mathcal{D}_\alpha$ of admissible values of parameters α_1 and α_2 determined by $\epsilon_i = 0.25y_i$, $L = 10$, $\delta_1 = 0.7$ and $\delta_2 = 1.5$ for analytic expression $\log y = \alpha_1 \cdot \log x + \log \alpha_2$. The discrete plane $\alpha_1 \otimes \alpha_2$ is bounded by a dashed line. The LS estimate $(\alpha_{1,0}, \alpha_{2,0})$ is denoted by $\times$ and the standard errors of estimates $SE(\alpha_1)$, $SE(\alpha_2)$ and $2SE(\alpha_1)$, $2SE(\alpha_2)$ are denoted by dots.

estimation of parameters α_1 and α_2; whereas the LS approach suggested the 10th and 13th observations are crucial, since they had the largest estimation errors.

For different numbers of ants counted on a foraging trail, we now compare the results of the LS approximation with the results obtained by the proposed method. The estimates of colony sizes obtained by the LS method and by the proposed one are given in Fig. 2. In our method, we inferred the extreme values of colony sizes from the domain of the admissible values of parameters $\mathcal{D}_\alpha$ given in Fig. 1.

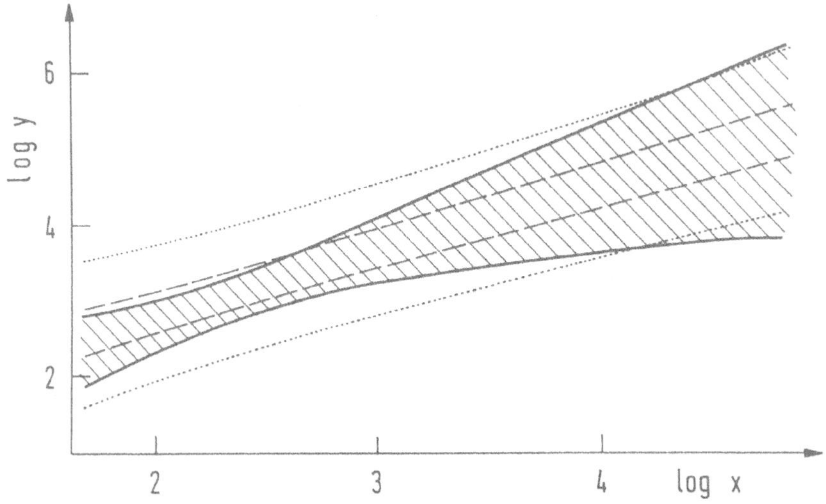

Figure 2: Shaded region is the range of admissible values of colony sizes obtained by our method. The dotted line represents the limits of the 99% confidence region and the dashed line represents the limits of the 60% confidence region for estimates of colony sizes obtained by the LS method.

5. Conclusion. Our method gives additional information about the interpolation of experimental data that is independent of statistical assumptions. Without any statistical assumptions, it enables us to infer the maximal uncertainty of the parameter estimates implied by the uncertainty of experimental data. The case study shows that the domain of the admissible values of parameters obtained by our method are not in contradiction with LS estimates. Fig. 2 shows that the region of estimates of colony sizes obtained by our method is larger than the 60% confidence region for LS estimates and smaller than the 99% confidence region for LS estimates.

References

[1] R. J. Larsen, M. L. Marx, *Statistics.* p. 57 - 58, Prentice – Hall International Editions (1990).

[2] Kruk–De Bruin, M., et al. *Estimates of the Number of Foraging Ants with the Lincoln–Index Method in Relation to the Colony Size of Formica Polyctena.* Journal of Animal Ecology, **46**, p. 463 - 468, (1977).

LFC-RESULTS FOR TESTS IN k-VARIATE LOCATION MODELS

Helmut Finner and Markus Roters

Universität Trier
Fachbereich IV - Mathematik/Statistik
Postfach 3825, 5500 Trier, Germany

INTRODUCTION

Let $X = (X_1, \ldots, X_k)$ be a k-variate random variable with values in IR^k. We assume that the distribution P_μ of X has a Lebesgue-density $f_\mu(x) = f(x - \mu)$ depending on a location parameter $\mu \in \Theta = IR^k$. If one is interested in testing hypotheses concerning the parameter μ, often the problem of determining least favourable parameter configurations (LFC's) occurs. A typical hypothesis is the homogeneity hypothesis $H: \mu_1 = \cdots = \mu_k$, or, if testing for material significance (cf. Hodges & Lehmann, 1954) is of interest, e.g. the hypotheses $H: \max_{1 \le i \le j \le k} |\mu_1 - \mu_j| \le \delta$, $H: \sum_{i=1}^k (\mu_i - \overline{\mu}_.)^2 \le \delta$, or $H: \sum_{i=1}^k |\mu_i - \overline{\mu}_.| \le \delta$, respectively, are appropriate. If $\le \delta$ is replaced by $\ge \delta$, we are in the situation of testing for equivalence.

Now let $A \subseteq IR^k$ denote the acceptance region for testing H versus $K = \Theta \setminus K$ and let $K' \subset K$. Then we are concerned with the following optimization problems: (a) find $\mu^* \in H$ such that $P_{\mu^*}(A) = \inf_{\mu \in H} P_\mu(A)$, and (b) find $\mu^{**} \in K'$ such that $P_{\mu^{**}}(A) = \sup_{\mu \in K'} P_\mu(A)$. A solution μ^* of (a) or μ^{**} of (b) is called an LFC. Problems of this kind occur in the following situations: (i) determination of level-α-tests, (ii) comparison of different tests, and (iii) determination of tests with guaranteed power (sample size calculation problem).

Several results were obtained in the recent literature for various distributional settings and hypotheses (cf. Chen et al. (1990), Finner & Roters (1991), Giani & Finner (1991), Hayter & Liu (1990a,b), Kunert (1990), Nelson (1985)). It has been shown in Finner & Roters (1991) that most of the hypotheses considered up to now are special cases of certain Φ_t-functions. Let $z = (z_1, \ldots, z_m) \in IR^m$, $z_i \ge 0$, $1 \le i \le m$, and define $\Phi_t(z) = (\frac{1}{m}\sum_{i=1}^m z_i^t)^{1/t}$ for $t \in IR \setminus \{0\}$, $\Phi_0(z) = (\prod_{i=1}^m z_i)^{1/m}$, $\Phi_{-\infty}(z) = \min_{1 \le i \le m} z_i$, and $\Phi_{+\infty}(z) = \max_{1 \le i \le m} z_i$. Let $D_1(\mu) = (|\mu_i - \overline{\mu}_.|, 1 \le i \le k)$ and $D_2(\mu) = (|\mu_i - \mu_j|, 1 \le i < j \le k)$. Then we use the functions $\Psi_i(t, \mu) = \Phi_t(D_i(\mu))$, $i = 1, 2$, as measures of dispersion to describe hypotheses or subsets of the alternative, e.g. $\max_{1 \le i < j \le k} |\mu_i - \mu_j| \le \delta$ is equivalent to $\Psi_2(+\infty, \mu) \le \delta$, and $\sum_{i=1}^k (\mu_i - \overline{\mu}_.)^2 \le \delta$ is equivalent to $\Psi_1(2, \mu) \le (\delta/k)^{1/2}$.

In terms of Ψ_i, $i = 1, 2$, we consider the optimization problems

$$OP_i(\inf, t): \quad P_\mu(B) \to \inf \quad \text{s.t. } \Psi_i(t,\mu) \leq \delta,\ 0 < t \leq +\infty,$$

$$OP_i(\sup, t): \quad P_\mu(B) \to \sup \quad \text{s.t. } \Psi_i(t,\mu) \geq \delta',\ -\infty \leq t \leq +\infty,$$

where B denotes an acceptance (or rejection) region. Here we assume that $B \in \mathcal{A} = \{A \in IB^k : A \text{ shift and permutation invariant and convex}\}$ while $P \in \mathcal{P}_0 = \{P : P$ has a permutation invariant, unimodal Lebesgue-density$\}$. Some results require different and/or additional assumptions, e.g. log-concavity and/or symmetry of f and convexity, shift invariance of B.

RESULTS

Theorem. Let $P \in \mathcal{P}_0$, $B \in \mathcal{A}$, $m = k/2$ for k even and $m = (k-1)/2$ for k odd. Then we have:

(a) $OP_1(\inf, t)$ has solutions of the type

(α) $(-\tau, \ldots, -\tau, 0, \tau, \ldots, \tau)$ with m $(-\tau)$'s, m τ's, k odd if $t = +\infty$,

(β) $(-\tau, \ldots, -\tau, \tau, \ldots, \tau)$ with m $(-\tau)$'s, m τ's, k even if $t = +\infty$,

(γ) $(-\tau, 0, \ldots, 0, \tau)$ with $(k-2)$ 0's if $0 < t \leq 1$.

(b) Let $\tau(r) = (0, \ldots, 0, \tau, \ldots, \tau)$ with r $0's$ and $(k-r)$ $\tau's$. Then a solution of $OP_1(\sup, t)$ is given by $\tau(r)$ for one

(α) $r \in \{1, k-1\}$ if $t = +\infty$,

(β) $r \in \{1, \ldots, k-1\}$ if $-\infty < t \leq 1$,

(γ) $r \in \{m, k-m\}$ if $t = -\infty$,

where τ is determined by $\Psi_1(t, \tau(r)) = \delta$.

(c) A solution of $OP_2(\sup, t)$ is of the type

(α) $(\tau, 2\tau, \ldots, k\tau)$ if $t = -\infty$,

(β) $(-\tau, \xi, \ldots, \xi, \tau)$ with $-\tau \leq \xi \leq \tau$ if $t = +\infty$.

(d) $OP_2(\inf, t)$ has a solution of the type

$\tau(r, \xi) = (-\tau, \ldots, -\tau, \xi, \tau, \ldots, \tau)$ with r $(-\tau)$'s, $(k-r-1)$ τ's, $-\tau < \xi \leq \tau$ for $r \in \{1, \ldots, k-2\}$ and $\xi = \tau$ for $r = k-1$ if $t = +\infty$.

The proof which may be found in Finner & Roters (1991) is based on the theory of majorization (cf. Marshall & Olkin (1979)) and makes essential use of Mudholkar's theorem (cf. Mudholkar (1966)) and some related results. Hayter & Liu (1990) proved that $\xi = 0$ holds in (c)(β) if $P \in \mathcal{P}_0$ is symmetric, whereas by virtue of Prekopa's theorem (cf. Prekopa (1973)) log-concavity of f, shift invariance and convexity of B imply $\xi = \tau$ in (d) (cf. Chen et al. (1990)). For $B = B_R = \{x \in IR^k : \max_{1 \leq i < j \leq k} |x_i - x_j| \leq c\}$ and f symmetric, $f(x) = \prod_{i=1}^k g(x_i)$ the solution in (d) is of the type $\tau(m, \tau)$ (cf. Giani & Finner

(1991)). Unfortunately, up to now no results are available for $1 < t < \infty$, except for the case $k = 3$ (cf. Kunert (1990) for $B = B_R$ and an ANOVA-model, cf. Finner & Roters (1991) for $t \neq 2$).

REFERENCES

Chen, H. J., Lam, K., Xiong, M. (1990). Inference on the dispersion of several location parameters. University of Georgia, Department of Statistics. Technical report Nr. 157.

David, H. A., Lachenbruch, P. A. and Brandis, H. P. (1972). The power function of range and studentized range tests in normal samples. Biometrika 59, 161-168.

Finner, H., Roters, M. (1991). Power considerations and LFC-results with respect to Φ_t-restrictions in k-variate location models. Submitted for publication to Statist. Decisions.

Giani, G., Finner, H. (1991). Some general results on least favourable parameter configurations with special reference to equivalence testing and the range statistic. J. Statist. Plann. Inference 28, 33-47.

Hayter, A. J., Liu, W. (1990a). The power function of the studentized range test. Ann. Statist. 18, 465-468.

Hayter, A. J., Liu, W. (1990b). Some minimax test procedures for comparing several normal means. Preprint 1990, University of Bath, United Kingdom.

Hodges, J. L., Jr., Lehmann, E. L. (1954). Testing the approximate validity of statistical hypotheses. J. Roy. Statist. Soc. (B) 16, 261-268.

Kunert, J. (1990). On the power of tests for multiple comparisons of three normal means. J. Amer. Statist. Assoc. 85, 808-812.

Marshall, A. W., Olkin, I. (1979). Inequalities: Theory of Majorization and its Applications. Academic Press, New York.

Mudholkar, G. S. (1966). The integral of an invariant unimodal function over an invariant convex set - an inequality and application. Proc. Amer. Math. Soc. 17, 1327-1333.

Nelson, P. R. (1985). Power curves for the analysis of means. Technometrics 27, 65-73.

Prekopa, A. (1973). On logarithmic concave measures and functions. Acta Scient. Mat. 34, 335-343.

MAKING USE OF THE WEIDLICH-HAAG-MODEL IN THE CASE OF REDUCED DATA SETS

P.Frankhauser
University of Stuttgart, Institute for Theoretical Physics,
Pfaffenwaldring 57, D-7000 Stuttgart 80, Germany
E-Mail: FRANK@DS0SYN51.BITNET

H.-P.Schwefel
University of Dortmund, Department of Computer Science
PO Box 500500 D-4600 Dortmund 50, Germany
E-Mail: UIN005@DDOHRZ11.BITNET

During the last years W.Weidlich and G.Haag have introduced a new method for the description of the dynamics of socio-economic processes, like migrations, settlement formation, or economic developments [1], [2].

The goal of the present paper is to focus on the estimation of the model parameters, when the method is applied to real world situtations and the data base is reduced. In particular it will be shown how the influence of model assumptions on the parameter estimation procedure may be tested. As an example, the case of interurban migration shall be discussed, where tests have been made on the base of French data.

The basic idea of the model is a stochastic description of the decision behaviour of social agents. It is assumed that there exists a mean behaviour of these agents with respect to the type of decision considered, e.g. to migrate from one city to an other. This decision behaviour is parameterized by introducing utility functions $u_i(t)$, which represent a measure for the attractivity of city i, mobility factors $f_{ij} = f_{ji}$ describing time independent distance effects between the two cities i, j and a global time dependent mobility $\nu(t)$, which measures the general disposition to migrate (for details cf. [2]).

For the formal description a *socio-configuration* $\mathbf{n} = (n_1, n_2, \ldots, n_i, \ldots, n_j, \ldots, n_L)$ is defined, where the n_k $(k = 1, 2, \ldots, L)$ are the inhabitant numbers of the L cities of the system considered. Changements in a given configuration occur by migration and birth-death processes. These processes are described by a probabilistic concept, where the time evolution of the probabilities to find a certain configuration is given by the *master equation*, well-known in statistical physics. Then the migration decisions define the transition rates between the different configurations. These *total migration rates* are related to the previously introduced parameters in the following way:

$$w(\mathbf{n}^{i+,j-}|\mathbf{n}) = n_j(t) \cdot \varpi(\mathbf{n}^{i+,j-}|\mathbf{n}) = n_j(t) \cdot \nu(t) \cdot f_{ij} \cdot e^{u_i(t)-u_j(t)} \tag{1}$$

where $\varpi(\mathbf{n}^{i+,j-}|\mathbf{n})$ is the *individual transition rate* for one agent to migrate from city j to i, which is multiplied by the number n_j of potential migrants in j. Since only differences of utility functions come into play, they are normalized to $\sum_{i=1}^{L} u_i = 0$. In the same way *individual birth/death rates* ρ_i are introduced for each city i, representing the difference between individual birth and death rate and related to the corresponding *total birth/death-rates*:

$$w(\mathbf{n}^{i\pm}|\mathbf{n}) = n_i(t) \cdot \rho_i^{\pm} \tag{2}$$

For practical applications, it is assumed that there exists a unimodal, highly peaked probability distribution, and thus the corresponding mean value equation can be derived:

$$\dot{n}_i = \sum_{i\neq j;j=1}^{L} \left\{ n_j \varpi(\mathbf{n}^{i+,j-}|\mathbf{n}) - n_i \varpi(\mathbf{n}^{i-,j+}|\mathbf{n}) \right\} + \rho_i n_i \tag{3}$$

$$\equiv \mathcal{W}_i + \rho_i n_i \tag{4}$$

where all inhabitant numbers and configurations are now mean values.

This formula assumes implicitly that the system of the L cities is *closed* with respect to migratory effects. Indeed, the changement of inhabitant numbers $\dot{n}_i$ consists only of the migratory balance $\mathcal{W}_i$ for city i and the amount of birth/death processes. In reality, however, immigrations/emigrations related to other communities, belonging to rural areas and foreign countries contribute to the total changements, too. Thus we should rewrite the equation (4) in a more correct way:

$$\dot{n}_i = \mathcal{W}_{i,\mathcal{U}} + \mathcal{W}_{i,\mathcal{D}} + \rho_i n_i \equiv \mathcal{W}_{i,\mathcal{U}} + \tilde{\rho}_i \tag{5}$$

where $\mathcal{W}_{i,\mathcal{U}}$ is the contribution of migrations within the system, $\mathcal{W}_{i,\mathcal{D}}$ the migratory contributions from and to outside, and $\tilde{\rho}_i = \mathcal{W}_{i,\mathcal{D}} + \rho_i n_i$ the total contribution, not resulting from migrations in the system itself. Thus a relation of the form (4) assumes that immigrations/emigrations may be be tackled like birth-death-processes, i.e. $\tilde{\rho}_i \stackrel{!}{=} \rho_i' \cdot n_i$

In order to analyze the dynamics of a real system, the model parameters $u_i(t)$, $\nu(t)$, and f_{ij} mut be estimated out of empirical data. Usually they are used to determine socio-economic key factors for the migration process. If empirical migration matrices are available, the relation (1) can serve to estimate the parameters in a quite convenient way. This method has been used for a comparitive study of interregional migration in 6 countries [2]. However, the *empirical transition matrix* will usually *not* be available, in particular if other types of problems are analyzed, like changements in the consumer behaviour. Even for the interurban migrations, in France, only for a subset of the 78 biggest cities such data were available; in general only inhabitant numbers are known.

The only possibility to determine the parameters is then to recur to the whole equation of motion (3). Let T denote the number of periods, then $L \cdot \left(T + \frac{1}{2}(L-1)\right)$ parameters would have to be estimated, whereas only $L \cdot T$ data are available [3].

Thus, for each time step the parameters were determined by combining three consecutive data sets: the set of each considered year t_m, those of the previous census date t_l and the next one, t_r. In particular, the time derivatives were approximated by finite differences, according to (cf. [3]):

$$\frac{\Delta x_i(t_m)}{\Delta t_m} \equiv \frac{n_i^{(e)}(t_r) - n_i^{(e)}(t_l)}{N^{(e)}(t_m)\cdot(t_r - t_l)} \qquad \text{(e): empirical values} \tag{6}$$

where the normalized numbers $x_i(t) \equiv \frac{n_i(t)^{(e)}}{N(t)^{(e)}}$ with $N(t)^{(e)} = \sum_{i=1}^{L} n_i(t)^{(e)}$ have been used. This yields the following function to be minimized:

$$\mathcal{Z}(\nu,\{u_i\}) \equiv \sum_{\kappa=l,m,r} \sum_{i=1}^{L} \left\{ \frac{\Delta x_i(t_\kappa)}{\Delta t_\kappa} - \rho_i'(t_\kappa)\, x_i(t_\kappa) - \right.$$
$$\left. - \left[\nu(t_m) \left(\sum_{j=1}^{L} x_j(t_\kappa)\, f_{ij}\, e^{u_i(t_m)-u_j(t_m)} - \sum_{j=1}^{L} x_i(t_\kappa)\, f_{ij}\, e^{u_j(t_m)-u_i(t_m)} \right) \right] \right\}^2 \tag{7}$$

An additional problem occurs, since city systems consist usually of a great number of units ($L = 1178$ in the French case). Thus a method for *reducing the number of units* was introduced, where the parameters were only determined for a small but varying number K of cities, whereas the other cities were tackled as a global hinterland $\mathcal{R}$ with its own parameters like its utility $u_{\mathcal{R}}$. It was shown, that this assumption is at least plausible [3]. Then in (7), the sum runs over $K+1$ units, instead of L.

Finally the time independent values f_{ij} were determined by using the usual method in the subset of 78 cities, where migration data were available. Then only $T \cdot L$ parameters have to be estimated by use of $3 \cdot T \cdot L$ empirical data. In the general case where such parameters are not available, we may use alternatively the ansatz: $f_{ij} = e^{-\beta \cdot d_{ij}}$ where d_{ij} are the geographical distances and solely one additional parameter β has to be estimated.

It can be expected that the parameter estimation may be influenced in the present case by some model assumptions, beeing not relevant when migration matrices are available. Indeed, the function $\mathcal{Z}(\nu, \{u_i\})$ depends on the the term $\rho_i'(t_\kappa)$, which consists not only of birth/death rates, but also of emigration/immigration rates, usually not known. It is evident, that these rates become the more important, the smaller we choose the number of cities in the system. In order to analyze these effects, different tests have been made for one census year (1975). In a first series *S1* a system $\mathcal{U}_{tot}$ has been used, containing all communities of France. Then it can be assumed, that the remaining parts of immigration/emigration are not so important. In order to test the influence of the term, we inserted into (7) for ρ_i' just the empirically known birth/death rates (model *S1.1*). Furtheron we investigated whether the alternative use of mean birth-death rates ρ_i' of the 78 biggest cities affects the results (model *S1.2*). These models neglect rigorously the emigration/immigration. Thus in a third series *S1.3* the mean rate of the *total* changement of the population numbers

$$\rho' = \rho_{\mathcal{U}_{tot}}' = \frac{\sum_{i \in \mathcal{U}_{tot}} \Delta n_i^{(e)}}{\sum_{i \in \mathcal{U}_{tot}} n_i^{(e)} \cdot \Delta t} \tag{8}$$

was used. Finally the reduced system of the 78 biggest cities served to compute the corresponding rate (model *S1.4*).

A second series *S2* was based the system of the 78 biggest cities, for which migration data and thus the migratory balance $\mathcal{W}_{i,\mathcal{U}}$, resulting from migrations within the system were known. Thus the utilities could be estimated directly out of migratory data (*S2.1*). A particularly interesting comparison arises, if alternatively again the mean rate (8) is used (*S2.2*). This may serve to analyze, how the results are influenced by the manner, in which system is closed. Additionally, the usual procedure based on the rate ansatz (1) was tested (*S2.3*). Finally the variation of the number K of cities could influence the results. Thus some models have been tested for varying $K = 5, 10, 20, 30, 50$.

The highly nonlinear form of the function $\mathcal{Z}(\nu, \{u_i\})$ requires a careful parameter estimation procedure, since many local minima must be expected, leading to unwanted results. Thus the program OASIS, developed at Jülich [4], has been used, which provides the possibility to combine different kinds of estimation methods and to change the method used during one run. In the present case, different combinations of the methods of Rosenbrock, of Powell, of Hooke and Jeeves as well as evolution strategies (cf. [5]) turned out to be very successful. For each series several runs with different combinations of methods have been performed.

The obtained results may be summerized as follows:

- A *unique solution* was found for every model, but it was *not* possible to determine the mobility in a non-ambiguous way. In any case at the end of the estimation procedure, an arbitrary further reduction of the value ν led to a spread of the utility functions. This effect may be explained by the fact that this parameter is directly influenced by the total amount of migration processess. Since the procedure was based on the mean value equations, only *balance data* were used. When the utilities were normalized with respect to their variance, stable results were obtained.

- Nevertheless stable solutions were observed for the *utility ranking* for all models.
- The utility ranking obtained depended however on the type of model. The influence of the different assumptions for the birth-death processes could be easily interpreted by comparing the empirical rates with the subsequently used mean values.
- The way in which the system was closed, led to important changes in the utility ranking. Indeed, it is evident that the estimated utilities refer to the importance of the city within the considered system. This becomes obvious, comparing the size of the hinterland for the differently defined systems *S1.4* and *S2.2*. Moreover, the comparison of the models *S2.1* and *S2.2* show that using migratory data, the utilities refer to the migratory fluxes whereas in the other cases the total changements in the population number are evaluated. This is confirmed by the results for *S2.4*. Here additionally the fact is important, that in the present case only changements of population numbers come into play, and not the *total amount* of migratory fluxes.
- The estimation procedure turned out to be robust in view of the variation of K since the utility rank within the set of previously considered cities was in general not affected by adding new ones.

In general the tests has proved that even if the mobility looses its importance, unique solutions are obtained for the utility ranks. These results could not only be related to model assumptions, but could describe rather well the socio-economic situation of the analyzed cities. For further applications the system should be chosen in such a way, that emigrations/immigrations are not important. The model *S1.1* must be considered as the most useful one. Thus empirical birth-death rates should be known in order to obtain realistic results.

The previous discussion has shown that even for a reduced data base, a parameter estimation procedure can be developed. Variations of the model turned out to be a powerful instrument to test the influence of model assumptions on the estimation results.

References

[1] W. Weidlich and G. Haag. *Concepts and Models of a Quantitative Sociology.* Springer Berlin, Heidelberg, New York (1983).

[2] W. Weidlich and G. Haag (Eds.). *Interregional Migration — Dynamic Theory and Comparative Analysis.* Springer Berlin, Heidelberg, New York (1988).

[3] P. Frankhauser. *Beschreibung der Evolution urbaner Systeme mit der Mastergleichung.* (1991). *Dr.rer.nat thesis at the University of Stuttgart.*

[4] F. Drepper, R. Heckler and H.-P. Schwefel. Combining Estimation, Simulation and Optimazation in Computed-aided Energy Planning. *Angewandte Systemanalyse* **2** (1981).

[5] H.-P. Schwefel. *Numerical Optimazation of Computer Models.* John Wiley (1981).

Economic Defects Inspection

Rainer Göb
Institut für Angewandte Mathematik und Statistik
Universität Würzburg
Sanderring 2, D-8700 Würzburg

Defectives inspection has always been treated as the essential field of interest for investigations on acceptance sampling, whereas defects inspection has received rather few attention only. Throughout, authors who consider defects inspection start from the rather unrealistic type B case (process inspection model): decision on acceptance/rejection of a production process by means of a single sample taken from the production process, where the operating characteristic (OC) function is conceived as a function of sample size n, acceptance number c, and process average number of defects per item λ. For calculation of a process OC function, the defects numbers of the items are assumed to be independent identically distributed random variables, all distributed according to a Poisson distribution with mean λ, hence the process OC is given by $\mathcal{F}_{n,c}(\lambda) = \sum_{k=0}^{c} \frac{(n\lambda)^k}{k!} e^{-n\lambda}$ (see *Burr*, *Hald*).

However, the essentially realistic model for shop applications is type A (lot inspection model): decision on acceptance/rejection of a finite lot by means of a single sample taken without replacement from the lot, where the operating characteristic (OC) function is conceived as a function of lot size N, sample size n, acceptance number c, number of defects in the lot K. In order to cover the lot inspection case in the approach sketched above it is assumed that the process OC is in any case a sufficiently good approximation of the lot OC (see *Burr*, p. 256, for instance) - an assumption necessarily unproved since the actual lot OC remains unknown. Clearly, on this basis defects plans can be treated as straightforward by-products of defectives plans: the Poisson OC replaces the hypergeometric OC or the binomial OC in a pattern derived from defectives plans; because of the simplicity of the Poisson OC, calculations become even easier; often, even the same calculations can be used since the Poisson OC is widely used as an approximation of the binomial OC or the hypergeometric OC. In such a way, defects plans were included into customary statistical sampling schemes like Dodge-Romig sampling tables or MIL-STD-105D. In economic acceptance sampling, a similar marginal treatment of defects plans is given in *Hald*. Beyond that, no explicit investigations on economic defects plans seem to exist. Neither the extensive bibliography in *Wetherill/Chiu* nor its updating in *von Collani*[2] lists any article explicitly dedicated to the problem of economic defects plans.

For modern quality control, both the steadily increasing complexity of products and the need for differentiated cost calculation involve a clear demand for economic defects sampling plans in the framework of the realistic lot inspection model. Calculation of the corresponding lot OC function requires an assumption on the probability distribution of the $\binom{N+K-1}{K}$ arrangements of the total number of defects K over the N elements of the lot. There is no generally applicable model which covers all situations occurring in practice, but essentially two models seem reasonable.

Equidistribution Model: Equidistribution of the $\binom{N+K-1}{K}$ arrangements of K defects over the N elements of the lot. The resulting OC function is given by $\mathcal{H}_{N,n,c}(K) = \sum_{k=0}^{c} \frac{\binom{n+k-1}{k}\binom{N-n+K-k-1}{K-k}}{\binom{N+K-1}{K}}$.

Poisson Model: The underlying production process satisfies the usual Poisson assumptions as used for derivation of the process OC, i.e. the defects numbers of the N items are assumed to be independent identically distributed random variables, all distributed according to a Poisson distribution with mean λ. The resulting lot OC function is given by $\mathcal{M}_{N,n,c}(K) = \sum_{k=0}^{c} \binom{K}{k} \left(\frac{n}{N}\right)^k \left(1-\frac{n}{N}\right)^{K-k}$.

An economic *cost model* recording all relevant cost factors (acceptance/rejection, sampling) can be constructed by adapting the classical linear cost model of defectives inspection (see *Hald, Uhlmann*) to the special purposes of defects inspection. The loss incurred by acceptance/rejection of a lot of size N is assumed to be a linear function $C_A^{(N)}/C_R^{(N)}$ of the number of defects in the lot K, where $C_A^{(N)}(K) < C_R^{(N)}(K)$ if $\frac{K}{N} < \lambda_0$, $C_A^{(N)}(K) > C_R^{(N)}(K)$ if $\frac{K}{N} > \lambda_0$, for *break even quality* λ_0. Sampling inspection has to be designed in a way so as to minimize the loss caused by economically wrong decisions, the so-called *avoidable loss*. The expected value of the avoidable loss incurred by application of a sampling plan (n,c) to a lot of size N containing K defects, the so-called *average avoidable loss* $R_{N,n,c}(K)$ is given by

$$R_{N,n,c}(K) = \begin{cases} \left(C_R^{(N)}(K) - C_A^{(N)}(K)\right) \cdot \left(1 - \mathcal{O}_{N,n,c}(K)\right), & \text{if } \frac{K}{N} \leq \lambda_0, \\ \left(C_A^{(N)}(K) - C_R^{(N)}(K)\right) \cdot \mathcal{O}_{N,n,c}(K), & \text{if } \frac{K}{N} > \lambda_0, \end{cases}$$

where $\mathcal{O}_{N,n,c}(K)$ is one of the OC functions introduced above. Sampling costs are assumed to be a linear function $d_1 n + d_2$ $(d_1 > 0,\ d_2 \geq 0)$ of the sample size n.

Models for acceptance inspection are essentially characterized by their attitudes towards prior information on lot quality. As an alternative to either of the antagonistic concepts which have influenced the history of economic acceptance sampling (minimax approach, Bayes approach) an intermediate approach has been suggested by *Krumbholz*: incomplete knowledge on lot quality represented by an admissible subset Γ of the set of distribution functions of lot quality. A typical representative is the *α-optimal sampling* *scheme* introduced for defectives sampling by E. von Collani, see *von Collani*[1],[2]. Transposed into the terminology of defects inspection the basic principle is as follows: Γ is the set of all distribution functions F of the lot average number of defects per item $\frac{\kappa}{N}$ satisfying $F(\lambda_0) = \alpha$, i.e. the probability $P\left(\frac{\kappa}{N} \leq \lambda_0\right) = \alpha$ is known to the inspection department. Sampling plans are to be designed in a way to give protection against the worst case possible under this restriction. Hence the appropriate economic objective function is given by

$$Z_{N,\alpha}(n,c) = \sup_{F\in\Gamma} E_F\left[R_{N,n,c}(\kappa)\right] + d_1 n + d_2 =$$

$$\alpha \cdot \max_{0\leq\frac{K}{N}\leq\lambda_0} R_{N,n,c}(K) + (1-\alpha)\cdot \sup_{\lambda_0\leq\frac{K}{N}} R_{N,n,c}(K) + d_1 n + d_2 .$$

References.

Burr, I.W. Statistical Quality Control Methods. Marcel Dekker, New York/Basel, 1976.

von Collani, E.

[1] The α-optimal Sampling Scheme. Journal of Quality Technology 18 (1986), 63-66.

[2] Wirtschaftliche Qualitätskontrolle - eine Übersicht über einige neue Ergebnisse. OR Spektrum 12 (1990): 1-23.

Dodge, H.F./*Romig*, H.G. Sampling Inspection Tables. 2nd ed. John Wiley, New York, 1959.

Hald, A. Statistical Theory of Sampling Inspection by Attributes. Academic Press, London/New York/Toronto/Sydney/San Francisco, 1981.

Krumbholz, W. Die Bestimmung einfacher Attributprüfpläne unter Berücksichtigung von unvollständiger Vorinformation. Allgemeines Statistisches Archiv 66 (1982), 240-253.

Uhlmann, W. Statistische Qualitätskontrolle. 2nd ed. Teubner Verlag, Stuttgart, 1982.

U.S. Department of Defense Military Standard, Sampling Procedures and Tables for Inspection by Attributes (MIL-STD-105D). U.S. Government Printing Office, Washington, D.C., 1963.

Wetherill, G.B./*Chiu*, W.K. A Review of Acceptance Sampling Schemes with Emphasis on the Economic Aspect. International Statistical Review 43 (1975): 191-209.

Generalized EWMA-Charts

Joseph J. Hoegel
Abt. Klinische Dokumentation
Universität Ulm
D-7900 Ulm

Hans W. Wolff
Abt. Stochastik
Universität Ulm
D-7900 Ulm

Introduction. The control problem of a production process with output $Y(t) = M(t) + \varepsilon(t)$ ($\varepsilon(t)$ being a white noise function with $E(\varepsilon(t)) = \sigma^2$ for all time points and $M(t) := E(Y(t))$) can be considered as the problem of monitoring the unknown expectation function $M(t)$. Because in practice we get observations only at dicrete time points t_n, $n \geq 1$, we have to control the sequence of expectations $M_n := M(t_n) = E(Y(t_n))$, $Y_n := Y(t_n) = M_n + \varepsilon_n$. Let us (as usual) define the process to be **in control** with respect to a given target M_0 iff $M_n \equiv M_0$. If there exists a time point ν such that $M_n = M_0$ $\forall n < \nu$ and $M_n \neq M_0$ $\forall n \geq \nu$ then the process is said to be in control up to time point $(\nu - 1)$ and **out of control** from time point ν and ν is called **change point**.

Basically our general approach of getting control schemes is to use a tracking procedure $\{X_n\}$ for a sequence $\{M_n\}$ of expectations given a sequence $\{Z_n\}$ of independent random variables with $E(Z_n) = M_n$. Such a procedure was proposed by Theodorescu and Wolff (1981) and further studied by e.g. Pakes (1982), Kormann, Theodorescu and Wolff (1987), Schnerring (1988) and Hoegel (1990). In the context of process control the random variables Z_n can be understood as sample means $Z_n := m^{-1} \Sigma Y_{n,j}$ where $Y_{n,j}$, $j = 1,\dots,m$, are observations of the r.v. $Y(t_n)$. The proposed updating algorithm is given by

(1) $X_{n+1} := (1-a_n) X_n + (a_n+A_n) Z_n, \quad n \geq 1,$

$X_1 = x_1$ being an arbitrary number, $\{a_n\}$ and $\{A_n\}$ are sequences of nonnegative real numbers satisfying either one of the following conditions:

(2) $\lim a_n = 0, \quad \Sigma a_n = \infty, \quad A_n^2 = o(a_n)$ or

(3) $\lim a_n = a, \quad 0 < a < 1, \quad \lim A_n = 0$.

Clearly for $A_n \equiv 0$ procedure (1) includes two important special cases both being well-known and widely studied:

(i) Shewhart chart (sample mean): choose $a_n \equiv 1$, $n \geq 1$, $x_1 = 0$.

(ii) Exponentially weighted moving average (**EWMA**) chart:
choose $a_n \equiv a$, $0 < a < 1$.

Moreover from (1) we can derive e.g. **CUSUM** and **MOSUM** charts (see Hoegel (1990), Hoegel and Wolff (1991)). Therefore the family of tracking procedures (1) implies a fruitful tool for constructing new control charts.

Generalized EWMA charts. Using the monitoring sequence $\{X_n\}$ given by (1) we propose as a generalization of the usual **EWMA** chart the following control procedure defined by the stopping time

$$(4) \quad N = N(L_1,L_2) = \begin{cases} \inf\{n \geq 1: X_{n+1} < L_1 \cup X_{n+1} > L_2 \\ \infty, \text{ if such n doesn't exist} \end{cases}$$

where at least one of the decision boundaries L_1 and L_2 is assumed to be finite. A general result about the behavior of the stopping time N is given by the following Theorem.

Theorem: Let $U_n := c_n(L_1 - (1-a_n) L_2)$ and $O_n := c_n(L_2 - (1-a_n) L_1)$ with $c_n := (a_n+A_n)^{-1} < \infty \ \forall n > n_0$. Suppose there exist a constant q, $0 < q < 1$, such that $P(U_n \leq Z_n \leq O_n) \leq q \ \forall \ n \geq n_0$, then it holds (i) $P(N = \infty) = 0$, (ii) $E(N^k) < \infty$, $k \in \mathbb{N}$.

However the main purpose of introducing the general **EWMA** is to indicate that variable weights (instead of a constant weight as in the usual **EWMA**) offer a lot of possibilities for a tailored design of control charts. Therefore we have studied the performance of these new procedures in terms of the average run length (**ARL**) and average time to signal (**ATS**) both for the in-control-state and for the out-of-control-state (also for **shifts and drifts**, see Hoegel (1990)).

The numerical calculation of the **ARL** and **ATS** were carried out by approximating the inhomogeneous Markov process (1) by a suitable inhomogeneous Markov chain. This technique is a generalization of the well-known procedure for the homogeneous case (e.g. for the standard **CUSUM** or **EWMA**) introduced by Brook and Evans (1972).

In our examples we have restricted ourselves to normally distributed errors and in addition to shifts or linear drifts. But our formulas fot the **ARL** and **ATS** can be used also for other distributions for the output variables and also for other kinds of drifts.

References

Brook, D.; Evans, D.A. (1972). An approach to the distribution of CUSUM run length. Biometrika 59, 539-550.

Hoegel, J. (1990). Trendverfolgungsverfahren und deren Anwendung in der statistischen Qualitätskontrolle. Dissertation, Universität Ulm.

Hoegel,J.; Wolff, H. (1991). Generalized CUSUM-charts. Paper presented at the 1991 Joint Statistical Meeting, Atlanta, Georgia. (to appear in the Proceedings of the Quality and Productivity Section).

Kormann, U.; Theodorescu, R.; Wolff, H. (1987). A dynamic method of moments. Statistics 18 (1), 131-140.

Pakes, A.G. (1982). Some remarks on the paper by Theodorescu and Wolff "Sequential estimation in the presence of trend". Australian Journal of Statistics 24 (1), 89-97.

Schnerring, J.. Lineare Lernregeln zur Schätzung zeitlich variabler Parameter in einem Hilbertraum. Dissertation, Universität Stuttgart, 1988.

Theodorescu, R.; Wolff, H. (1981). Sequential estimation in the presence of trend. Australian Journal of Statistics 23 (2), 196-203.

Gamma–minimax estimators with respect to unimodal priors

Katja Ickstadt
Fachbereich Mathematik
Technische Hochschule Darmstadt
Schloßgartenstr.7, D–6100 Darmstadt

For the description of statistical decision problems the so–called statistical game, a two person zero sum game between nature and the statistician, is often an appropriate model. Depending on the prior information the statistician has, one of the following optimality principles may be chosen. If the statistician has no prior information, he has to take into account all strategies of nature, i.e. all priors $\pi \in \Pi$ on the parameter space. In this situation he may apply the minimax principle. If he knows the strategy of nature, the Bayes principle could be applied. If he has vague prior information, the gamma–minimax principle as an intermediate approach between the first two principles enables him to make use of his information.

In the following it is assumed that available vague prior information leads to the class of unimodal priors with fixed mode θ_M over the bounded interval $[-m, m]$ defined by

$$\Gamma_U(\theta_M) \;=\; \{\nu\epsilon_{\theta_M} + (1-\nu)\tilde{\pi} \mid \nu \in [0,1],\ \tilde{\pi} \text{ having a unimodal density with mode } \theta_M\},$$

where ϵ_{θ_M} denotes the one point measure at the mode θ_M. If $\theta_M = 0$, the subset Γ_{SU} of $\Gamma_U(0)$ consisting of all symmetrical and unimodal priors, is of particular interest. This class Γ_{SU} is defined by

$$\Gamma_{SU} \;=\; \{\nu\epsilon_0 + (1-\nu)\tilde{\pi} \mid \nu \in [0,1],\ \tilde{\pi} \text{ having a unimodal and symmetrical density}\}.$$

Let Δ denote the set of strategies of the second player (the statistician) and let $R(\cdot,\delta)$, $\delta \in \Delta$, be any family of risk functions $R(\cdot,\delta) : [-m,m] \to [0,\infty)$. Then the pay–off function is given by the Bayes risk of $\delta \in \Delta$ with respect to $\pi \in \Pi$, which is defined by

$$r(\pi,\delta) = \int_{[-m,m]} R(\theta,\delta)\,\pi\,(d\theta)\,.$$

Let π_L and π_R denote the uniform distributions on $[-m, \theta_M]$ and on $[\theta_M, m]$, respectively, i.e. on the left and on the right of the mode. For $\lambda \in (0,1)$ put $\pi_\lambda = \lambda\pi_L + (1-\lambda)\pi_R$

and let π_u be the uniform distribution on $[-m, m]$. Furthermore let δ_λ and δ_u denote the Bayes strategies with respect to π_λ and π_u. Then the following theorem gives necessary and sufficient conditions for the pair $(\pi_\lambda, \delta_\lambda)$ being a saddle point in the statistical game $(\Gamma_U(\theta_M), \Delta, r)$ (cf. Eichenauer–Herrmann et al. (1991)).

Theorem 1 *Let δ_λ be a Bayes estimator with respect to the prior π_λ for some $\lambda \in (0,1)$. Suppose that its risk function $R(\cdot, \delta_\lambda)$ is quasiconvex on both intervals $[-m, \theta_M]$ and $[\theta_M, m]$. Then $(\pi_\lambda, \delta_\lambda)$ is a saddle point in the statistical game $(\Gamma_U(\theta_M), \Delta, r)$ if and only if*

$$R(\theta_M, \delta_\lambda) \le r(\pi_\lambda, \delta_\lambda) \quad \text{and} \quad r(\pi_L, \delta_\lambda) = r(\pi_R, \delta_\lambda).$$

In most applications the stronger assumptions of the following corollary are fulfilled.

Corollary 1 *Let δ_u be a Bayes estimator with respect to the prior π_u. Suppose that its risk function $R(\cdot, \delta_u)$ is symmetrical and quasiconvex on $[0, m]$. Then (π_u, δ_u) is a saddle point in the statistical game $(\Gamma_U(0), \Delta, r)$ if and only if*

$$R(0, \delta_u) \le r(\pi_u, \delta_u).$$

Because of $\pi_u \in \Gamma_{SU} \subset \Gamma_U(0)$, Corollary 1 remains valid if "$\Gamma_U(0)$" is replaced by "Γ_{SU}". This result will now be applied to two different examples.

Example 1: Estimation of a bounded normal mean

Consider the following problem: The mean $\theta \in [-m, m]$ of a normal distribution with variance 1 is to be estimated if the statistician has vague prior information of type Γ_{SU}. In this case the set Δ consists of all (non-randomized) estimators δ, i.e. of all functions $\delta : \mathbb{R} \to [-m, m]$. If squared error loss is assumed the risk function has the form

$$R(\theta, \delta) = \int_{\mathbb{R}} (\theta - \delta(x))^2 \varphi(x - \theta)\, dx,$$

where φ denotes the density of the standard normal distribution.

For this estimation problem the following result is known (cf. Olman and Shmundak (1985), Eichenauer–Herrmann (1990)). If δ_u denotes the Bayes estimator with respect to π_u, which is given explicitly in Berger (1985), then the pair (π_u, δ_u) is a saddle point in the statistical game (Γ_{SU}, Δ, r) for small parameter intervals, at least for $m \le 0.288$. But (π_u, δ_u) may still be a saddle point in this statistical game if $m > 0.288$. In order to determine the maximal length of the parameter interval such that (π_u, δ_u) is a saddle point in (Γ_{SU}, Δ, r), a numerical calculation has been performed. Because the risk function $R(\cdot,\delta_u)$ is symmetrical it has only to be checked numerically, whether $R(\cdot,\delta_u)$ is quasiconvex on $[0,m]$ and satisfies

$$R(0,\delta_u) \leq r(\pi_u,\delta_u)\,.$$

It turns out that the risk function has these properties for $m \leq 2.532$ (cf. Eichenauer–Herrmann et al. (1991)).

Example 2: Optimal pulse amplitude modulation (PAM) including timing jitter

For this transmission theoretic problem the following model of a transmission system gives a description.

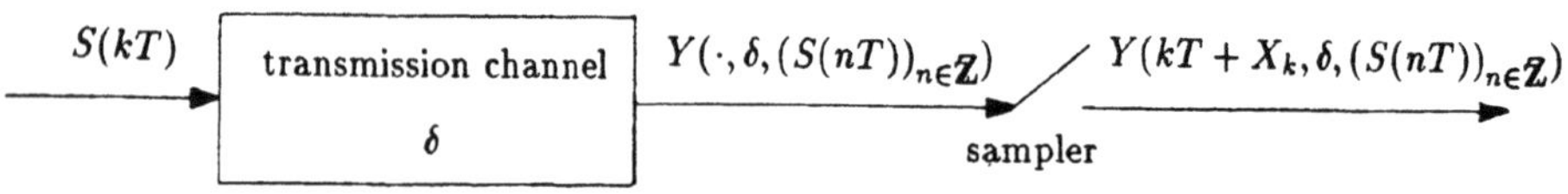

Figure 1: Transmission system

The PAM–signal values $S(kT)$, $k \in \mathbb{Z}$, are assumed to be identically distributed, pairwise uncorrelated random variables with mean 0 and variance 1. These $S(kT)$ pass the transmission channel described by the transmission function δ. At the receiver side a signal, i.e. a time depending function $Y(\cdot,\delta,(S(nT))_{n\in\mathbb{Z}}) : \mathbb{R} \to \mathbb{R}$ is received, which is sampled at times kT, $k \in \mathbb{Z}$, for decoding the PAM–signal values. Because of synchronization errors this sampler produces $Y(kT + X_k,\delta,(S(nT))_{n\in\mathbb{Z}})$ instead of $Y(kT,\delta,(S(nT))_{n\in\mathbb{Z}})$, where the independent identically distributed random variables X_k, $k \in \mathbb{Z}$, take their values in $[-m,m]$ with $m \in (0,T/2]$. They are called timing jitter.

In order to find a good transmission function the following two person zero sum game of the system designer against "nature" may be applied. Let us assume that the unknown distribution of the X_k (the jitter distribution π) is not known precisely, but that it is unimodal with mode 0. Then $\Gamma_U(0)$ is the set of all jitter distributions. The set Δ of all strategies for the system designer consists of all functions δ defined on the frequency range $[-B,B]$, where B denotes the so–called Nyquist bandwidth. The following integral has the same value for every time kT, $k \in \mathbb{Z}$. It may be defined as the pay–off function

$$r(\pi,\delta) = \int_{[-m,m]} E([S(kT) - Y(kT+\theta,\delta,(S(nT))_{n\in\mathbb{Z}})]^2)\,\pi(d\theta)$$

with $\pi \in \Pi$ and $\delta \in \Delta$. The values of the risk function are given by

$$R(\theta, \delta) = E([S(kT) - Y(kT + \theta, \delta, (S(nT))_{n\in\mathbb{Z}})]^2).$$

For the situation that no prior information is taken into account, the following result is known (cf. Krabs (1986)). For Nyquist bandwidth B and $m \in (0, T/2]$ the pair (π^*, δ^*) consisting of the two point distribution $\pi^* = 0.5\epsilon_{-m} + 0.5\epsilon_m$ and the strategy δ^* defined by

$$\delta^*(\omega) = \begin{cases} \cos(\omega m) & \omega \in [-B, B] \\ 0 & \text{otherwise} \end{cases}$$

form a saddle point in the statistical game (Π, Δ, r), with Π denoting the set of all jitter distributions. If prior information allows a restriction of Π to $\Gamma_U(0)$ (or, if symmetry is provided, to Γ_{SU}) Corollary 1 is applicable, since its assumptions are fulfilled. This corollary yields that for Nyquist bandwidth B and $m \in (0, T/2]$ the uniform distribution π_u and the Bayes strategy δ_u,

$$\delta_u(\omega) = \begin{cases} \frac{\sin(\omega m)}{\omega m} & \omega \in [-B, B]\backslash\{0\} \\ 1 & \omega = 0 \\ 0 & \text{otherwise} \end{cases}$$

with respect to π_u form a saddle point in $(\Gamma_U(0), \Delta, r)$ and in (Γ_{SU}, Δ, r), too. A comparison of the saddle points (π^*, δ^*) and (π_u, δ_u) shows that the Gamma-minimax approach yields the uniform distribution π_u as least favourable timing jitter, which is a more "natural" prior than the "artificial" two point distribution π^*.

References

Berger, J.O. (1985) Statistical decision theory and Bayesian analysis, 2nd ed., Springer, Berlin–Heidelberg–New York

Eichenauer–Herrmann, J. (1990) A gamma–minimax result for the class of symmetric and unimodal priors, Statist. Papers 31, 301–304

Eichenauer–Herrmann, J., Ickstadt, K. and Weiß, E. (1991) Gamma–minimax results for the class of unimodal priors, Preprint 1388, Fachbereich Mathematik, Technische Hochschule Darmstadt

Krabs, W. (1986) On the Determination of the Worst Sampling Error in a Communication System for Pulse–Amplitude–Modulated Signals by Solving an Approximation Problem, Math. Meth. in the Appl. Sci. 8, 256–268

Olman, V. and Shmundak, A. (1985) Minimax Bayes estimation of mean of normal law for the class of unimodal a priori distributions (in Russian), Proc. Acad. Sci. Estonian Physics Math. 34, 148–153

A BAYESIAN APPROACH FOR ESTIMATING INFANT MORTALITY IN DEVELOPING COUNTRIES

Maged G.Ishak
Institut fur Statistik und Mathematische Wirtschaftstheorie
Universität Karlsruhe
Kaiserstrasse 12. D-7500 Karlsruhe 1. Germany.

Mortality behaviour in a country is simply to be presented where reliable vital statistics data are available. This is not the case in most of developing countries. However, different direct and indirect methods of estimation are usually suggested to assess mortality experience either by adjusting the distorted official data or by employing data obtained from untraditional sources. An improved technique for estimating infant mortality level and pattern is introduced in this study. A Bayesian model for estimating infant mortality is suggested as a conveniet method for including all the prior information about the problem, and hence, to assure the best occupation of the available data.

INFANT MORTALITY MODEL

Studying the shape of infant mortality in various countries of the world, with a special consideration for the effect of under-registration problem, it has been found that the pattern in both developed and developing countries can be efficiently represented by using the following model;

$$\mathbf{Y_i} = \left\{ \begin{array}{lll} Ae^{-\alpha x_i} {x_i}^{\gamma} & * \; e^{u_i} & i = 1, \ldots, 4 \\ Be^{-\beta x_i} {x_i}^{\delta} & * \; e^{u_i} & i = 5, \ldots, 15 \end{array} \right\} \quad (1)$$

where: Y_i is the rate of mortality in the age interval i.

x_i is the age at death at the midpoint of the age interval i.

u_i is the disturbance variable.

The application of this model on infant mortality data from fourteen selected countries, including both developed and developing ones, has shown great efficiency, in which the χ^2 test of goodness of fit has reflected unsegnificant differencies in all cases. For example, while the schedual value at 9 degree of freedom and 95% segnificant level is 16.9, the calculated value for Egypt(1974-75) was 0.21 and in Federal Republic of Germany(1983) was 0.13.

THE BAYESIAN ESTIMATION

In almost all developing countries prior information about infant mortality levels and patterns can be usually provided from sample surveys, censuses or from infant mortality experience of other countries or areas that have identical socio-economic conditions and possess more reliable data. To assure the best occupation of these data when estimating the model's parameters, the Bayesian method is considered.The prior information is combined with the corrected data, i.e. after eliminating the effect of under-registration, via an informative natural conjugate prior function. Expressing the model in (1) in the linear form, the prior function would be in the form of normal-gamma joint function. Hence, the posterior distribution can be derived in the form;

$$P(B,\sigma/Z) \propto \sigma^{-n-k-m-1} exp[\frac{-1}{2\sigma^2}(ms^2 + (B-b)'D(B-b) + (Z-xB)'(Z-xB)] \qquad (2)$$

where: B is the unknown parameter's vector.
b is the mean vector of the prior distribution.
Z is the vector of the natural logarithm of the corrected data.
m,D,s^2 are the prior parameters depend on our prior information.

The published infant mortality data of Egypt in the average of the years 1974-75 have been used as an example of applying this model. Prior information about the likely values of the level and pattern parameters was deduced mainly from the considerably accurate data of Cairo governorate. In this sense, We have utilized the published data of Cairo in a series of ten years (1971-1981). The probability distribution of each of the pattern parameters $(\alpha, \gamma, \beta, \delta)$ has conveniently approached the normal shape. The mean values of these distributions were used as the prior mean values. These were calculated to be as follows;

$$E(\alpha) = 2.05 \qquad E(\gamma) = 0.42$$
$$E(\beta) = 0.26 \qquad E(\delta) = 1.1$$

On the other hand, the values of the level parameters (A,B) have showed a considerably strong linear relation to the corresponding infant mortality rates (IMR), in which the correlation coefficient (r) was relatively high in both equations. These were given as;

$$lnA = 2.75 + 0.0075\mathbf{IMR} \qquad r = 0.92$$
$$lnB = 1.26 + 0.0048\mathbf{IMR} \qquad r = 0.96$$

These equations are used respectively to derive the prior mean value of the level parameters. The prior variance for the first and the second component parameters can be derived by respectively employing the following two probability functions;

$$pr[E(\alpha) - 0.1E(\alpha) < \alpha < E(\alpha) + 0.1E(\alpha)] = 0.9$$
$$pr[E(\beta) - 0.1E(\beta) < \beta < E(\beta) + 0.1E(\beta)] = 0.7$$

Where α and β were taken as examples for the other first and second component parameters respectively.
The first equation implies our relatively big confidence on the prior information during the first month period, where the published data are known to be seriously defective. On the other hand, the bigger variance assumed in the second equation expreses the more trust provided to the published data of the next eleven months of life. Assuming a prior independence between the parameters, the above obtained quantities are sufficient to determine the prior mean vector b and the variance matrix D, and to specify the prior distribution.

Inferences about the unknown parameter vector B can be then deduced from either the multivariate normal conditional posterior distribution $P_1(B/\sigma, Z)$ or from the multivariate t marginal posterior distribution $P_2(B/Z)$.

As a Bayesian point estimation of B, we have adopted the posterior mean vector $\hat{B}$ as the optimal Bayesian estimator,if we consider either the quadratic loss function or the linear loss function.

The final results when applying this model to the data of Egypt are presented in table(1).

Table 1: Prior, Corrected, and Posterior Estimates of the Model's Parameters. Egypt(1974-75).

Parameter	Prior	Corrected	Bayesian
ln A	3.69	4.26	3.81
α	2.05	2.22	1.82
γ	-0.42	-0.136	-0.386
lnB	1.86	2.25	2.175
β	0.265	0.212	0.249
δ	1.1	0.69	0.88

Finally, the Bayesian estimation of the infant mortality model in Egypt for the average of the years (1974-75) can be given as;

$$Y_i = \left\{ \begin{array}{ll} 45.2e^{-1.82x_i}x_i^{-0.386} & i = 1, \ldots, 4 \\ 8.81e^{-0.249x_i}x_i^{0.88} & i = 5, \ldots, 15 \end{array} \right\}$$

RELIABILITY OF THE MODEL

To examine the compatibility and the admissibility of the results, the model is further applied to the five main subregions of Egypt namely, the metropolitan cities of Cairo and

Alexandria, urban-lower, rural-lower, urban-upper, and rural-upper. However, the admissibility of the results were examined in which the following criteria were considered;

a) The consistency in the estimated rates of mortality.

b) The consistency in the estimated values of the model's parameters.

c) The admissibility regarding the posterior variance of the parameters.

In all cases, the Bayesian estimates were considerably consistent and could reflect more acceptable and plausible differentials between the various subregions of Egypt. Moreover the Bayesian model could correct the wrong pattern reflected by the published data, specially during the neonatal period. This can be observed from Figure (1).

FIGURE 1 : NEONATAL MORTALITY RATES .RURAL UPPER.

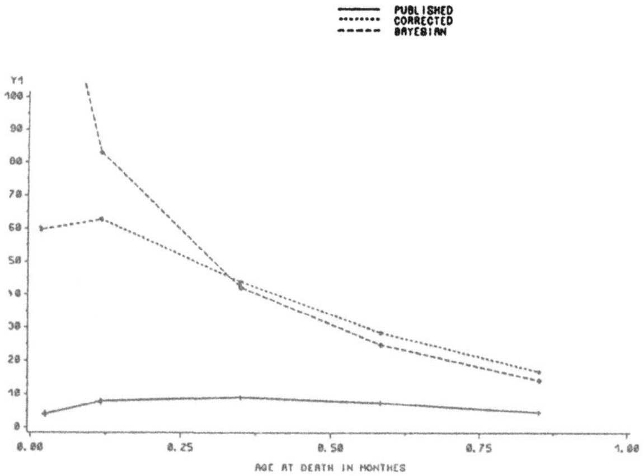

REFERENCES

Box,G.E.P., and G.C.Tiao (1973). Bayesian Infrences in Statistical Analysis. Reading, Mass.:Addison.Wesley.

Central Agency for Public Mobilization and Statistics. Births and Deaths Statistics (Annual Publication), for the years 1971-1981.Cairo.

Fienberg,S.E., and A.Zellner (1975). Studies in Bayesian Econometrics and Statistics. Amesterdam: North-Holland Publishing Company.

Judge,G.G., et al. (1982). Introduction to the Theory and Practice of Econometrics. New York: John Wiley & Sons.

National Academy Press (1982). "The Estimation of Recent Trend in Fertility and Mortality in Egypt". Report No.9, Washington.

Sayed,H.A., and M.Ishak (1987). "Some Demographic Implications of a General Model to Study Infant Mortality". Research Monograph Series No.16, Cairo: Cairo Demographic center.

United Nations (1983). Indirect Techniques for Demographic Estimation. Manual X. Department of International Economic and Social Affairs,Population Studies No.81.New York.

——. Demographic Year Book. (1980-1987). Department of International and Social Affairs, Statistical office. New York.

Vallin,J., and J.H. Pollard, and L.Heligman.(1984).Methodologies for Collection and Analysis of Mortality Data. Belgium: International Union for the Scientific Study of Population.

World Healh Organisation (1977). Manual of Mortality Analysis. Division of Health Statistics Dissemination of Statistical Information, Geneva.

Zellner,A. (1984). Basic Issues in Econometrics. Chicago: The Unversity of Chicago Press.

RECURRENCE RELATIONS FOR MOMENTS OF ORDER STATISTICS AND RECORD VALUES

Udo Kamps
Institute of Statistics
Aachen University of Technology
Wüllnerstr. 3, D–5100 Aachen

Recurrence relations and identities are often helpful to determine moments of order statistics. In comparison with direct computations via explicit expressions the application may lead to a reduced numerical effort and to a raised accuracy. Thus in the literature we find a lot of results for specific distributions, which are reviewed and developed in Balakrishnan et al. (1988); we also refer to Khan et al. (1983) in case of truncated distributions. Lin (1988) observes that there are similar recurrence relations for exponential, uniform, Pareto and logistic distributions, namely identities for the difference of moments of successive order statistics, and finds them to be characteristic properties. In Kamps (1991) a recurrence relation of this type and a characterization result are given for a class of probability distributions, so that some isolated identities are subsumed, and new ones are found. Such an approach yields recurrence relations valid for distributions with at least two parameters, and moments of non–integral orders; furthermore it provides structural properties and relationships of several probability distributions. In this paper the class of distributions is generalized, including power function, Pareto, Weibull, Burr XII and logistic distributions, and an analogous result for k–th record values is stated.

Let $X_1,\dots,X_n$ be iid random variables with distribution function F, and corresponding order statistics $X_{1,n} \le X_{2,n} \le \dots \le X_{n,n}$.

Theorem Let $\alpha \in \mathbb{R}$, $\beta \ge 0$ with $\alpha+\beta \ne 0$, and a function h_1 on (0,1) with

$$\frac{d}{dt} h_1(t) = \frac{1}{d}\, t^p\, (1-t)^{q-p-1} \quad \text{a.e. on } (0,1),$$

and constants $d > 0$, $p,q \in \mathbb{Z}$ be given, such that the expression $(\beta\, h_1(t))^{1/\beta}$ is defined if $\beta > 0$. Furthermore let F be given by

$$F^{-1}(t) = \begin{cases} \exp\{h_1(t)\}, & \beta = 0 \\ (\beta\, h_1(t))^{1/\beta}, & \beta > 0 \end{cases}, \quad t \in (0,1),$$

and let the moments $EX_{r,n}^{\alpha+\beta}$, $EX_{r-1,n}^{\alpha+\beta}$, $EX_{r+p,n+q}^{\alpha}$ of order statistics exist for some integers r,n with $2 \leq r \leq n$ and $1 \leq r+p \leq n+q$.

Then the recurrence relation

$$EX_{r,n}^{\alpha+\beta} - EX_{r-1,n}^{\alpha+\beta} = (\alpha+\beta)\, c_1\, EX_{r+p,n+q}^{\alpha} \quad \text{with} \quad c_1 = \frac{1}{d} \frac{\binom{n}{r-1}}{(r+p)\binom{n+q}{r+p}}$$

holds true.

In Azlarov, Volodin (1986), Lin (1988), and Kamps (1991) characterizations of distributions are given based on the validity of the above identity for a certain sequence with respect to r and n. Results of this type may be derived the same way here, and in connection with record values.

Let $X_1, X_2, \ldots$ be a sequence of iid random variables with continuous distribution function F. The k–th record times, $k \in \mathbb{N}$, are defined by $L^{(k)}(1) = 1$, and $L^{(k)}(r+1) = \min\{j;\, j > L^{(k)}(r),\, X_{j,j+k-1} > X_{L^{(k)}(r),L^{(k)}(r)+k-1}\}$, $r \in \mathbb{N}$.

Then the random variables $X_r^{(k)} := X_{L^{(k)}(r),L^{(k)}(r)+k-1}$ are named k–th record values.

In contrast to order statistics recurrence relations and identities for moments of record values have been considered in the literature only marginally.

Theorem Let $\alpha \in \mathbb{R}$, $\beta \geq 0$ with $\alpha+\beta \neq 0$, $k \in \mathbb{N}$, and a function h_2 on (0,1) with

$$\frac{d}{dt} h_2(t) = \frac{1}{d}(1-t)^{s-1}\left(\log \frac{1}{1-t}\right)^p \quad \text{a.e. on } (0,1),$$

and constants $d > 0$, $p,s \in \mathbb{Z}$, $k + s \geq 1$ be given, such that the expression $(\beta\, h_2(t))^{1/\beta}$ is defined if $\beta > 0$. Furthermore let F be given by

$$F^{-1}(t) = \begin{cases} \exp\{h_2(t)\}, & \beta = 0 \\ (\beta\, h_2(t))^{1/\beta}, & \beta > 0 \end{cases}, \quad t \in (0,1),$$

and let the moments $E(X_r^{(k)})^{\alpha+\beta}$, $E(X_{r-1}^{(k)})^{\alpha+\beta}$, $E(X_{r+p}^{(k+s)})^{\alpha}$ of record values exist for some integer $r \geq 2$ with $r+p \geq 1$.

Then the recurrence relation

$$E(X_r^{(k)})^{\alpha+\beta} - E(X_{r-1}^{(k)})^{\alpha+\beta} = (\alpha+\beta)\, c_2\, E(X_{r+p}^{(k+s)})^{\alpha} \quad \text{with} \quad c_2 = \frac{1}{d} \frac{k^{r-1}}{(k+s)^{r+p}} \frac{(r+p-1)!}{(r-1)!}$$

holds true.

References

Azlarov, T.A., Volodin, N.A. (1986), Characterization Problems Associated with the Exponential Distribution, Springer, New York.

Balakrishnan, N., Malik, H.J., Ahmed, S.E. (1988), Recurrence relations and identities for moments of order statistics, II: Specific continuous distributions, Commun. Statist.–Theory Meth. 17, 2657–2694.

Kamps, U. (1991), A general recurrence relation for moments of order statistics in a class of probability distributions and characterizations, Metrika 38, 215–225.

Khan, A.H., Yaqub, M., Parvez, S. (1983), Recurrence relations between moments of order statistics, Nav. Res. Log. Quart. 30, 419–441.

Lin, G.D. (1988), Characterizations of distributions via relationships between two moments of order statistics, J. Stat. Plan. Inf. 19, 73–80.

Statistical Quality Control of Data

H.-J. Lenz

Freie Universität Berlin
Inst. f. Statistik und Ökonometrie
Garystr. 21, W-1000 Berlin 33

E. Rödel
Humboldt-Universität zu Berlin
Fachbereich Informatik
Unter den Linden 6, PF 1297
O-1086 Berlin

1. Introduction

It's a matter of fact that there exist logical, arithmetic probabilistic or more general structural relations between variables in large data-sets, cf [1], [2].
If there are errors in the data then the underlying structural relations are violated. Thus the main objective of statistical quality control of data is to detect contradictions between the data and the structural relations given a-priori.

To illustrate the idea we give a simple example of a structural relationship which is equivalent to an aggregation.

> A bus company owns p busses which are operating in the public transport. The total consumption rate of fuel of all the busses can be computed by two different approaches. The consumption rate can either be measured by the reduction size of the company's stock of fuel or by summing over the consumption rates of the p busses. As there will be usually differences between their figures it is necessary to check the deviations and to analyse the sources of the errors.

We are considering in the following the structural relationships which can be described by a linear model. Using this approach we are able to detect the contradictions between the data and the structure by estimation and test procedures.

2. The model

Let $\xi = (\xi_1, \ldots, \xi_p)$ be a p-vector of the true values and H a (q x p) matrix, $q \leq p$ and Rank (H) = q.
We assume that ξ and $\zeta = H\,\xi$ are observable only with additive errors, i.e.

$$x = \xi + v \qquad (1)$$

$$z = H\,\xi + w\,, \quad \text{cf [3].} \qquad (2)$$

The vectors x and z represented a real record of data. The equation $\zeta = H\,\xi$ describes the q structural relationships of the components of ξ.

We make the following assumptions:

$$E(v) = 0, \quad E(w) = 0 \qquad (3)$$

$$E(vv') = P, \quad E(ww') = R \qquad (4)$$

v,w are stochastically independent, i.e. the covariance matrix Q of v and w is

$$Q = \begin{pmatrix} P & 0 \\ 0 & R \end{pmatrix}, \qquad (5)$$

where Rank (P) = p and Rank (R) = q.

Using the notation

$$y = \begin{pmatrix} x \\ z \end{pmatrix}, \quad J = \begin{pmatrix} I \\ H \end{pmatrix}, \quad n = \begin{pmatrix} v \\ w \end{pmatrix},$$

we get
$$y = J\,\xi + u\,. \tag{6}$$

Evidently, it follows
$$E\,y = J\,\xi\,,\quad E\,(uu') = Q, \tag{7}$$

where Q is given by an estimation from past data. It is often enough reasonable to assume that the submatrices P, R are of a diagonal form.

3. The Estimation of the Parameters ξ, ζ

Given the data x,z and the model parameters H,P,R we get the GLS-estimators $\hat{\xi}$, $\hat{\zeta}$ of ξ and ζ, respectively:

$$\hat{\xi} = x + K\,(\,z - Hx\,) \tag{8}$$

where

$$K = P\,H'\,(\,HPH' + R\,)^{-1}$$

and

$$\hat{\zeta} = H\,\hat{\xi}\,. \tag{9}$$

It holds true that
$$E\,(\hat{\xi}) = \xi\,,\quad \Sigma_{\hat{\xi}} = P - KHP \tag{10}$$

and
$$E\,(\hat{\zeta}) = \zeta\,,\quad \Sigma_{\hat{\zeta}} = H\,\Sigma_{\hat{\zeta}}\,H'\,. \tag{11}$$

4. The Tests

Evidently, the errors in the data-set cause large differences between the vectors $\hat{\xi}$ and x.
A usual measure of distance between two random vectors is the Mahalanobis distance which is in this case equal to

$$d(\hat{\xi},x) = (\hat{\xi}-x)' \, \Sigma^{+}_{\hat{\xi}-x} \, (\hat{\xi}-x) \qquad (12)$$

where $\Sigma^{+}_{\hat{\xi}-x}$ is the Moore inverse of

$\Sigma_{\hat{\xi}-x} = KHP$, see [4, p.443] .

If $u \sim N(0,Q)$ then $d(\hat{\xi},x) \sim \chi^2_q$, cf [4] . (13)

Under the assumption of normality one decides for errors in the data-set if

$$d(\hat{\xi},x) > \chi^2_{q;1-\alpha} \qquad (14)$$

for an appropriate $\alpha \in (0,1)$.

Such a decision can be interpreted in a way that the observed data-set (x,z) is inconsistent with the given structure. It could be that a deviation between $\hat{\xi}$ and x is not detected but there exists a large deviation between $\hat{z} = H\hat{\xi}$ and z, e.g. the z-values are wrongly recorded.

Under the same assumption as above we have

$$d(\hat{z},z) = (\hat{z}-z)' \, \Sigma^{-1}_{\hat{z}-z} \, (\hat{z}-z) \sim \chi^2_q \qquad (15)$$

where

$$\Sigma_{\hat{z}-z} = H \, (\Sigma_{\hat{\xi}} + P) \, H' \, . \qquad (16)$$

The test on "outliers" $\|\hat{z}-z\|$ is done in an analogous manner as in (14).

The tests presented so far check the consistency of the data and the structure. However, it is useful to test hypotheses about the domain of the data.

The simple hypotheses

$$H_{01}: \xi = \zeta_o$$

and

$$H_{02}: \zeta = \zeta_o$$

are rejected if

$$d(\hat{\xi},\xi_o) > \chi^2_{p;1-\alpha} \qquad (17)$$

and

$$d(\hat{\zeta},\zeta_o) > \chi^2_{q;1-\alpha} , \qquad (18)$$

respectively.

Using the appropriate covariance matrices in (10) and (11) d can be specified as follows:

$$d(\hat{\xi},\xi_o) = (\hat{\xi}-\xi_o)' \, \Sigma^{-1}_{\hat{\xi}} \, (\hat{\xi}-\xi_o) \qquad (19)$$

and

$$d(\hat{\zeta},\zeta_o) = (\hat{\zeta}-\zeta_o)' \, \Sigma^{-1}_{\hat{\zeta}} \, (\hat{\zeta}-\zeta_o) \; . \qquad (20)$$

The hypothesis

$$H_o: \xi \in I\,[a,b] \qquad (21)$$

is also of interest where

$$I[a,b] \subset \mathbb{R}^p$$

is a closed interval.

A natural test is provided by the statistic

$$d(\hat{\xi};\, a,b) = (\hat{\xi}-\hat{\xi}_o)' \, \Sigma^{-1}_{\hat{\xi}} \, (\hat{\xi}-\hat{\xi}_o) \qquad (22)$$

where $\hat{\xi}_o$ is uniquely defined by

$$\inf_{\xi \in I[a,b]} (\hat{\xi}-\xi)' \Sigma_{\hat{\xi}}^{-1} (\hat{\xi}-\xi) \tag{23}$$

$$= (\hat{\xi}-\hat{\xi}_o)' \Sigma_{\hat{\xi}}^{-1} (\hat{\xi}-\hat{\xi}_o) \ . \tag{24}$$

It holds true

$$d(\hat{\xi};a,b) \leq d(\hat{\xi},\xi) \quad \text{for all} \quad \xi \in I[a,b].$$

Therefore, we have under H_o

$$P\ (d(\hat{\xi};a,b) > \chi^2_{p;1-\alpha}) \ \leq \ P\ (d(\hat{\xi},\xi) > \chi^2_{p;1-\alpha}) \ = \ \alpha \ . \tag{25}$$

Analogously, we can test the hypothesis

$$H_o\colon \zeta \ \in \ I[c,d] \ .$$

References

[1] Wetherill, G.B., Gerson, M. (1986): Quality Assurance for Data Entry. An Integrated Approach, in: Preprints of the III rd Int.Workshop on Statistical Quality Control, Lynby

[2] Lenz, H.-J. (1989) : Knowledge-based Data Validation, Research Workshop on Expert Systems and Statistics, University of Edinburgh

[3] Schneeweiß, H. (1988): Personal Communication

[4] Rao, C.R. (1965): Linear Statistical Inference and its Applications, Wiley, New York etc.

THE URBAN MACRO-ECONOMIC MODEL SYSTEM

Shuxia Li
College of Management
Ocean University of Qingdao
Qingdao(266003), Sandong
PR. OF CHINA

In the Summer of 1989, the Government of Qingdao entrusted us to charge with a task, to make a Economic Model for designing the Eighth and Ninth Five-Year Plans of this city. So a research group was organized. In June of 1990 the Macro-Economic Model System of Qingdao (MEMSQ) was developed and a number of major economic indices forecasting, policy simulation, annual plan evaluations, economic structure analysis of this city were run. The modelling system was handed over to the Plan Committee of the City Government, and had been used in the process of designing the plans.

The Model System is a larger system. It is made up of five kinds of models, the Macro-Econometric Model (MEM), the Macro-Planning Evaluation Model (MPEM), the Macro-Planning Optimization Model (MPOM), the Macro-Optimization Control Model (MOCM) for Policy evaluation, and the Agricultural Macro-Econometric Model (AMEM).

1. The Macro-Econometric Model

This model constitutes the basis of the model system. There are 7 exogenous variables and 77 endogenous variables. These variables include most of the major economic indices. There are 77 equations, including 47 random equations, and 30 definition equations. This Econometric Model consists of 7 blocks, which are production, investment & fixed assets, labor demand & population, consumption & accumulation, financial income & expenditure, bank loan, and foreign trade & seaport transportation blocks. It is an economic equilibrium model. It has been used to forecast major economic indices for the City of Qingdao in the Eighth and Ninth Five-year Periods.

2. The Macro-Planning Evaluation Model

This model is derived from the Macro-Econometric Model by adding, deleting some equations, and changing industrial output value , agricultural output value and financial income into exogenous variables, and converting all others into endogenous variables. This model has been used for the evaluation of Qingdao's 1990 Annual Economic Plan. Through comparing the planned values and the predicted values of major economic indices, modifications for the Annual Plan were recommended.

3. The Macro-Planning Optimization Model

This model was set up by means of the MEM, Qingdao's 111-Industry Input-Output Table (1987) and applying optimization theory. Because of incomplete data, only the production block of the MEM has been optimized. Gross output values of the five major material production industries, which are industry, agriculture, transport and post, building industry, and commercial, were treated as decision variables, and national income as objective function. In accordance with the Three-Year Adjustment Policy of the Central Government of China, an Adjustment Optimization Model for 1990-1992 and an Optimization Model for 1993-1995 were constructed. The Production block of the MEM connected the MEM with the MPOM. The MPOM was inserted the MEM and run, which simulated the optimized state of the economic system of the city. So we had given economic structure analysis of the city. Using these models the optimization values of major economic indices for the Eighth Five--Year Plan had been forecasted. Therefore this model has higher applications value than the Macro-Econometric Model.

4. The Macro-Optimization Control Model for Policy Evaluation

The Macro-Planning Evaluation Model is a policy simulation model. It can be used to demonstrate the effects of different policies, but cannot be used to select the best policy.

The Macro-Optimization Control Model for Policy Evaluation was constructed by introducing the optimization control principles to the Macro-Econometric Model, taking the Macro-Econometric model as constraint, and some planning targets as objective function. Using this model the optimization values of policy variables could be obtained, thereby selecting the best policy. This model was also used to evaluate Qingdao's Annual Economic Plan (1990). Optimized values of major economic indices as given by this model were compared to their planned counterparts, which showed that the planned values of national income was lower than its optimized counterpart, and for other indices there was no significant difference between the two sets.

5. The Agricultural Macro-Econometric Model

This model is a sub-model of the Macro-Econometric Model. There are 4 exogenous variables which were taken from the Macro-Econometric Model, and 23 endogenous variables. It has 21 random equations and 2 definition equations. This model includes material output block, production values block, and an aggregate index block. It was used to predict the values of major agricultural economic indices for Qingdao's Eighth Five-year Period.

The Macro-Economic Model System of Qingdao had been used in the process of designing the Eighth and Ninth Five-Year Plans of the city. The services of the MEMSQ to the City Government have been immense.

References

Alt, W. (1984), "On the Approximation of infinite Optimization Problems with an Application to Optimal Control Problems,"Appl. Math. Opt., 12, 15-27.
Benjamin Reif (1973), Models in Urban and Regional Planning (Leonard Hill Books).
Chow, G.C. (1975), Analysis and Control of Dynamic Economic System (John Wiley & Sons, New York).
De Groot, M. (1970), Optimal Statistical Decisions. New York: McGraw-Hill Book Company.
Drud, A. (1976), "Method for Control of Complex Dynamic System," IMSOR on. 27, Univ. Lyngby (Denmark).
Eiselt, H. A. , Pederzoli, G. and Sandblom, C. L. (1984), Continuous Optimization Models (Walter de Gruyter & Co., Berlin-New York).
Fair, R. C. (1974), " An Evaluation of a Short Run Forecasting Model." International Economic Review, 15: 285-303.
Girlich,H. J. (1985), " Optimal Decision Rules. In: Sequential Methods in Statistics," Banach Center Publications,Vol. 16,115-122.
Gui Xianyun (1983), " Modelling and Optimization in System Planning in China," Lecture Notes in Control and Information Sciences System Modelling and Optimization Proceedings of the 11th 1-12.
Hu Yukui (1981), Systemical Dynamics (Forecast & Exploitation Company Science & Technology Consultative Service Center of China).
Intriligator, M. D. (1971), " Econometrics and Economic Forecasting," in J. M. English, Ed., The Economics of Engineering and Social Systems. New York: John Wiley & Sons,Inc.
John P. Wan de Geer (1980), Introduction to Multivariate Analysis for the Social Sciences (W. H. Freeman and Company San Francisco).
J. W. Forrester (1969), Urban Dynamics (M.I.T. Press).
Klein, L. R. (1971), "Forecasting and Policy Evaluation Using Large Scale Econometric Models: The State of the Art," in M.D. Intriligator, Ed., Frontiers of Quantitative Economics Amsterdam: North-Holland Publishing Co.
Klein, L. R. (1965), " What Kind of Macroeconomic Model for Developing Economies?" Indian Economic Journal, 13: 313-324.
Lasdon, L. S. (1973), Optimization Theory for Large Scale System (Macmillan,London).
Lasdon, L. and J. Mantell (1977), "Optimal Control of Large Econometric Models." Communication at NBER Conference on Control and Economics, New Haven (USA).
Minder, J., and V. Zarnowitz (1969), " The Evaluation of Economic Forecasts," in Mincer, Ed.
Mitchell, B. (1971), " Estimation of Large Econometric Models by Principal Component and Instrumental Variable Methods." Review of Economics and Statistics, 53: 140-146.
Murtagh, B. A. & M. A. Saunders (1978)," Large Scale Linearly Constrained Optimization," Math. Programming 14, 41-72.
Naylor, T.H. (1971), "Policy Simulation Experiments with Macroeconometric Models: The State of the Art," in M. D. Intriligator, Ed., Frontiers of Quantitative Economics. Amsterdam: North-Holland Publishing Co.
Naylor, T. H. (1971),Computer Simulation Experiments with models of Economic Systems. New York: John Wiley & Sons,Inc.
Polak, E. (1971), Computational Methods in Optimization (Academic Press, New York).
Rao, P., and R. L. Miller (1971), Applied Econometrics. Belmont, Calif.: Wadsworth Publishing Co., Inc.
Samuelson, P. A. (1975), " The Art and Science of Macro-Models," in Fromm and Klein, Eds.
Savas, E. S. (1981), " Urban Systems Analysis and Urban Policy" Lecture Notes in Control and Information Sciences System Modelling and Optimization Proceedings of the 10th IFIP Conference, 121-148.
Theil, Henri (1958), Economic Forecast and Policy (Amsterdam: North-Holland).
Theil, Henri (1964), Optimal Decision Rules for Government and Industry (Amsterdam: North-Holland).
The Statistics Bureau of Qingdao (1980-1989), Statistics Year Book of Qingdao (Qingdao Press).
The Statistics Bureau of Qingdao (1989), Brilliant 40-Year of Qingdao (Qingdao Press).

IMPROVEMENT OF STABILITY IN CLUSTER ANALYSIS AND PRINCIPAL COMPONENTS ANALYSIS BY SPECIAL WEIGHTING THE VARIABLES

Hans-Joachim Mucha
Karl-Weierstrass-Institute of Mathematics
Mohrenstrasse 39, D-O-1086 Berlin

Often the Euclidean metric applied to raw or standardized data leads to a bad result in cluster analysis (as well as in principal components analysis). A better one can be obtained in almost every case by using specific or adaptive weights. For instance the weights $q_{jj} = 1/\overline{x}_j^2$ can be used for nonnegative values x_{ij} (instead of $q_{jj} = 1/s_j^2$) in the squared weighted Euclidean distance

$$d_Q^2(\boldsymbol{x}_i, \boldsymbol{x}_{i'}) = (\boldsymbol{x}_i - \boldsymbol{x}_{i'})'\boldsymbol{Q}(\boldsymbol{x}_i - \boldsymbol{x}_{i'}) = \|\boldsymbol{x}_i - \boldsymbol{x}_{i'}\|_Q^2$$

between two observations $\boldsymbol{x}_i$ and $\boldsymbol{x}_{i'}$. Here $\boldsymbol{Q}$ is diagonal, $\overline{x}_j$ and s_j^2 are the mean value and the variance of variable j, respectively. In consequence these specific metrics should be used in principal components analysis too. In that way the principal components plot gives a good support in the interpretation of the results of cluster analysis.

A general applicable approach for measuring the stability (i.e. the quality) of results of cluster analysis will be presented. For instance this general approach allows us to assess the improvement of the stability in cluster analysis by using special weights of variables too.

INTRODUCTION

The structure of both row and column points of a (I*J)-data table $\mathbf{X}=(x_{ij})$, i=1,2,...,I, j=1,2,...,J, can be investigated. The data table $\boldsymbol{X}$ may contain various types of values; for example 0-1-values, measurements, frequencies, percentages, and a mixture of them. Without loss of generality we consider the cluster analysis of row points (observations) here only. Analysing $\mathbf{X}'=(x_{ji})$ instead of $\mathbf{X}$ the cluster analysis of variables is practicable in often the same way as clustering the observations (without any further considerations in the case of a contingency table $\mathbf{X}$, or a 0-1-matrix $\mathbf{X}$).

On the basis of statistical software we can get results in an easy way. For example, the cluster analysis presents a set of clusters in almost every case, independent on the existence or nonexistence of a cluster structure. In cluster analysis the problem of detecting the underlying number of classes is closely related to the problem of assessing the stability of the obtained cluster solutions. For example, an unusual high stability of a partition P(I,K) of I points into K clusters (K$\ll$I) indicates an inherent structure within the data under investigation. A partition P(I,K) allocates a positive integer, the so-called class membership, to every observation i, i=1,2,...,I. Hierarchical cluster analysis computes a sequence of partitions. Therefore in most applications it is sufficient to look at partitions as a general output of clustering. By analogy with the assumed relations between a cluster structure and stability, the determination of the number of factors in principal components analysis or correspondence analysis is also closely related to the stability of the computed axes. The use of both cluster analysis and principal components analysis is recommended in statistical applications (Jambu, 1983; Lebart, 1984).

SPECIFIC METRICS

For increasing the stability in cluster analysis specific (or adaptive) metrics should be applied instead of the "usual" standardization of data (Mucha, 1990a). For example, the K-means clustering (MacQueen, 1967) of the well-known Iris-data of Fisher (1936) is failed in the case of using the standard weights suggested by SAS or SPSS. The Iris-data consists of 3 given classes with 50 observations each. For this example the weights $q_{jj} = 1/\bar{x}_j^2$ can be used (instead of $q_{jj} = 1/s_j^2$) in the squared weighted Euclidean distance (see formula above). Generally we must require x_{ij} nonnegative and $\bar{x}_j$ positive.

We will give another important metric from the statistical point of view. An adaptive partitioning classification method is successfully demonstrated by Mucha (1991) for clustering the Iris-data. Starting with the standard weights $q_{jj} = 1/s_j^2$ (or other ones like for example the trivial weights $q_{jj} = 1$) the K-means method computes a partition P(I,K). In a repeated K-means clustering with P(I,K) as initial partition the weights

$$q_{jj} = 1/\bar{s}_j^2$$

are used. Here $\bar{s}_j$ is the pooled standard deviation of variable j over K clusters of the partition P(I,K):

$$\bar{s}_j^2 = 1/I \sum_{k=1}^{K} \sum_{i=1}^{I} \delta_{ik}(x_{ij} - \bar{x}_{kj})^2.$$

The indicator function δ_{ik} is 1 if the observation i comes from cluster k, or 0 otherwise, and $\bar{x}_{kj}$ is the mean value of variable j in the cluster k. The new obtained partition is used in a next K-means clustering, and so on. In this example a stable solution is reached after 5 cycles. Six misclassifications are counted. In consequence these specific metrics should be used in principal components analysis too. In that way the principal components plots give a good support in the interpretation of results of cluster analysis (Mucha,1991).

THE STABILITY OF RESULTS

It is difficult to validate a cluster structure. Multivariate graphics using factorial methods give appropriate tools for a better understanding of the data and for interpreting the cluster structure, respectively. These graphics are very useful tools for a validation of cluster structures too.

A "significant" stability of a partition P(I,K) indicates an inherent structure within the data table **X**, while on the other hand a low value of stability of P(I,K) results from data without a K-cluster structure (for example all observations come from the same uniform or normal distribution). Specific significance tests in cluster analysis are given for example by Bock (1985). A general applicable approach to measuring the stability in cluster analysis of observations or variables was presented in a detailed way by Mucha (1990a,b).

Generally, the performance of clustering methods were investigated (and compared one with another) in various simulation studies like by Bayne et al. (1980) and Milligan (1980), (1981). These studies give the user recommendations for selecting an appropriate cluster method. The investigators use computer-generated mixtures of probability distributions with known parameters as input data. Here the true partition is known beforehand.

In cluster analysis a new sample can't be drawn for assessing the degree of stability of a partition (for instance by the estimation of the error rate), because the true cluster membership of the observations is unknown in advance. Therefore no direct criteria for checking the cluster results exist. We distinguish between two fundamental ways of investigating the stability. Firstly, the internal stability measures the degree of independence of the cluster solution on random selection (or on random weighting) of observations. Secondly, the influence of adding randomly generated errors to the data on the cluster solution will be quantified (external stability).

The partition from clustering the whole original data points under investigation is crossed by the partition obtained in the cluster analysis of selected or disturbed data. Crossing the partitions results in a contingency table. Here in the contingency table the advantage arises that additionally the stability of each single cluster can be investigated (Mucha, 1990a, 1991). Several measures of comparing two partitions were presented for example by Rand (1971), and Hubert and Arabie (1985). A solution is stable if it is repeatable with a high degree of correspondence (high dependence in the contingency table). This procedure of sampling by random selection or disturbing and subsequent comparing should be repeated several times. For example the median (or mean respectively) of the values of Rand's measure per number k of classes (k=2,3,4,...) constitutes one point of a so-called reference curve (Mucha, 1991a). A confidence region around the curves facilitates the interpretation.

We can assume, that the data set with a true cluster structure (K clusters) has a "significantly" higher value of stability for K clusters than an unstructered one. That means, the cluster solutions of a sample drawn randomly from structured data are only slightly different from results obtained from other samples (internal stability), or the solutions are stable against small changes in the data (external stability). On the other hand clustering of randomly generated data without a cluster structure is characterised by low values of stability.

THE SOFTWARE **ClusCorr**

The software ClusCorr, which has been developed at IMath (Institute of Mathematics) is designed to include the most important known and lately developed procedures of data classification, and more generally, of univariate and multivariate data analysis including graphical representations. Both the internal and external stability can be investigated. Once more, statements like "the specific weights **Q** of variables are better for clustering than the specific weights **Q*** of variables" can be made. The software ClusCorr has many options for increasing the stability, for example outlier handling (see also Balakrishnan and Tiku (1988)), rank analysis, collapsing (Mucha, 1990b), or the concept of active and supplementary row points and/or columns points of a data table (Jambu and Lebeaux (1983), Greenacre (1984)). As a consequence of these options clusters with one or a few elements only will be avoided. That's important for the determination of the number of cluster as well as the investigation of stability.

ClusCorr is written in FORTRAN like its former issues, which were developed throughout the last dozen years (see for example: Mucha (1985)). The formulation of the desired cluster analysis and data analysis will be done by using the ClusCorr command language. In this way the software can be used interactively. On the other hand the batch mode is recommended for extensive analyses like for example simulation studies. We offer "ready for use" or customizable batch programs for various typical tasks of statistical analyses or simulation studies. More generally, both batch and interactive mode can be used alternately. In any case the commands are stored on a so-called Log-file during the work for further use.

However, the heart of ClusCorr is a system file with a so-called memory, which allows definite states whenever the work is interrupted. Another important benefit of ClusCorr is a 400 pages electronic book containing a comprehensive description of theory, methods, algorithms, software, and last not least a lot of examples of applications (Mucha, 1991).

References

Balakrishnan, N., Tiku, M.L. (1988): Robust classification procedures based on dichotomous and continuous variables. *Journal of Classification 5*, 53–80

Bayne, C.K., Beauchamp, J.J., Begovich, C.L., Kane, V.E. (1980): Monte Carlo comparisons of selected clustering procedures. *Pattern Recognition 12*, 51–62

Bock, H.H. (1985): On some significance tests in cluster analysis. *J. Classif. 2*, 77–108

Fisher, R.A. (1936): The use of multiple measurements in taxonomic problems. *Ann. Eugenics 7*, 179–188

Greenacre, M.J. (1984): Theory and application of correspondence analysis. *Academic Press*, London

Hubert, L.J., Arabie, P. (1985): Comparing partitions. *Journal of Classification 2*, 193–218

Jambu, M., Lebeaux, M.O. (1983): Cluster analysis and data analysis. *North-Holland*, Amsterdam

Lebart, L., Morineau, A., Warwick, K.M. (1984): Multivariate descriptive statistical analysis. Correspondence analysis and related techniques for large matrices. *Wiley*, New York

Mac Queen, J.B. (1967): Some methods for classification and analysis of multivariate observations. *Proc. 5th. Berkeley Symp. on Math. Stat. and Prob., University of California Press*, Berkeley

Milligan, G.W. (1980): An examination of the effect of six types of error perturbation on fifteen clustering algorithms. *Psychometrika 45*, 325–342

Milligan, G.W. (1981): A Monte Carlo study of thirty internal criterion measures for cluster analysis. *Psychometrika 46*, 187–199

Mucha, H.-J. (1985): CLUSTER - Program package for cluster analysis of observations and variables. *Statistical Software Newsletter 11 (2)*, 76–77

Mucha, H.-J. (1990a): Valuation of stabitity in cluster analysis. *Proceedings DIANA III*, Bechnye/Prague, 197–206

Mucha, H.-J. (1990b): Untersuchungen zur Stabilität in der Cluster- und faktoriellen Analyse mit der Software ClusCorr. In: Gladitz, J., Troitsch, K.G. (Eds.): Computer Aided Sociological Research. *Akademie-Verlag*, Berlin, 163–176

Mucha, H.-J. (1991): Clusteranalyse mit Mikrocomputern. (In preparation) *Akademie-Verlag*, Berlin

Rand, W.M. (1971): Objective criteria for the evaluation of clustering methods. *Journal American Statistic Ass. 66*, 846–850

BAYES OPTIMAL DESIGN OF MONITORING NETWORKS

Jürgen Pilz
Fachbereich Geowissenschaften
Bergakademie Freiberg
G.-Zeuner-Str. 12, D-9200 Freiberg (Sachs)

We are concerned with a particular problem of optimal design for random fields, namely the optimal placement of monitoring stations for monitoring regionalized environmental variables. The sparse literature on this problem is solely based on the variance of the well-known kriging predictor for spatial random fields, see e.g. Fedorov (1989) and Cressie et al. (1990). Here we consider a Bayesian version of the kriging predictor which allows the incorporation of prior knowledge about the trend behaviour of the regionalized variable under consideration. We derive a robust Bayes linear predictor which only requires approximate knowledge of the first and second order prior moments. Hereafter we consider the design problem for the (robust) Bayes linear predictor on the basis of the maximum and the integrated Bayes risk over the region of interest. Finally, we present some results for the case where there is only a finite number of potential sites from which the optimal choice is to be made. This particularly pertains to the problem of adding a few additional stations to an existing network.

BAYES LINEAR PREDICTION OF RANDOM FIELDS

Consider a random field $\{Z(x): x \in D\}$ defined over some subset D of R^d (d=2 or 3) with

$$E\,Z(x) = \theta_1 f_1(x) + \ldots + \theta_k f_k(x) = \theta' f(x) \tag{1}$$

where $f(x)=(f_1(x),\ldots,f_k(x))'$ is a vector of known functions and $\theta=(\theta_1,\ldots,\theta_k)'$ is an unknown parameter vector. We assume second order covariance stationarity with covariance function denoted $C(h) = \mathrm{Cov}\,(Z(x+h),Z(x))$, $x, x+h \in D$. We further assume to have prior knowledge in the following form

$$E\,\theta = \mu \text{ and } \mathrm{Cov}\,\theta = T \tag{2}$$

with some $\mu \in R^k$ and some positive definite matrix T. Our goal is to predict $Z(\cdot)$ over some region $D_0 \subset R^d$ such that $Q\{E(\hat{Z}(x)-Z(x))\}^2$ is minimized with respect to the predictor $\hat{Z}$ and the underlying design $d_n=(x_1,\dots,x_n)\in D^n$. Here, attention is restricted to predictors which are linear in the observations $Z(x_1),\dots,Z(x_n)$ and to the maximum operator

$$Q = \sup_{x\in D_0} \{\cdot\} \qquad \text{(G-optimality)} \tag{3}$$

and the integral operator

$$Q = \int_{D_0} \{\cdot\}\, \omega(dx) \qquad \text{(I-optimality)} \tag{4}$$

with respect to some weighting measure ω, respectively. Under the above assumptions, the Bayes linear predictor takes the form

$$\hat{Z}_B(x) = (c_x+FTf(x))'(K+FTF')^{-1}(Z-F\mu) + \mu' f(x) \tag{5}$$

where

$$c_x=(C(x_1-x),\dots,C(x_n-x))',\quad K=(C(x_i-x_j))_{i,j=1,\dots,n}$$

and $\quad F = (f(x_1),\dots,f(x_n))'\ ,\quad Z = (Z(x_1),\dots,Z(x_n))'\ ,$

see e.g. Omre (1987), Omre and Halvorsen (1989). The predictor (5) is called the <u>Bayesian kriging predictor</u> (BKP). In the limiting case $T^{-1} = 0$, which reflects a state of prior ignorance about θ, this predictor coincides with the well-known (universal) kriging predictor introduced by Matheron (1971).

ROBUSTIFICATION OF THE BKP

In practical applications we will rarely have exact knowledge of the prior moments μ and T, also the covariance function is usually unknown and must be estimated from the data. To come up with a robust version of the BKP, we consider the family

$$\mathcal{P}_x = \{P_{\theta,Z_x} : E\theta\in\mathcal{U},\ \mathrm{Cov}\ \theta\in\mathcal{T},\ \mathrm{Cov}\ Z_x\in\mathcal{K}\} \tag{6}$$

of joint probability distributions of θ and $Z_x' = (Z(x),Z')$, where $\mathcal{U}$ is some subset of R^k, assumed to be symmetric around some center point $\mu_0\in R^k$, and $\mathcal{T}$ and $\mathcal{K}$ are given subsets of the sets of positive definite matrices of order k and n+1, respectively. In view of global Bayes robustness, we look for a predictor which minimizes the maximum Bayes risk within the class of linear predictors, where the maximum is taken with respect to the above family $\mathcal{P}_x$. Results are available for two cases:

(i) c_x and $K = \text{Cov}\,Z$ fixed; $E\theta \in \mathcal{U}$, $\text{Cov}\,\theta \in \mathcal{T} = \{T: 0 < T \le \bar{T}\}$ with some positive definite matrix $\bar{T}$, i.e. $\text{Cov}\,\theta \le \bar{T}$

(ii) $c_x \approx 0$, $\text{Cov}\,Z = K \le \bar{K}$; $E\theta$ and $\text{Cov}\,\theta$ as in (i).

In the first case, the robust Bayes linear predictor is given by (5) with μ and T replaced by μ_o and $\bar{T}$, respectively. In the second case it is identical with the hierarchical Bayes linear predictor which arises from (5) replacing μ, K and T by μ_o, $\bar{K}$ and $\bar{T} + T^*$, respectively, where T^* is the solution to a convex optimization problem over the set of second order moment matrices

$$\int_{\mathcal{U}} (\mu - \mu_o)(\mu - \mu_o)' \, \xi(d\mu)$$

generated by the class of probability measures ξ defined on $\mathcal{U}$. For a proof of these results see Pilz (1991 a, b).

BAYES DESIGN OF MONITORING NETWORKS

The Bayes risk associated with the BKP (5) reads

$$B(x,d_n) = C(0) + f(x)'Tf(x) \\ -(c_x + FTf(x))'(K+FTF')^{-1}(c_x+FTf(x)) \qquad (7)$$

With an overcountable domain D_o, the design criteria of G- and I-optimality lead to formidable numerical complexities. For the special case of a constant mean $E\,Z(x) = \theta$, i.e. $f(x) = 1$, tractable design versions can be obtained by suitable asymptotics, see Mitchell, Sacks and Ylvisaker (1991).

Now, let us look at the special case of monitoring design where $D_o = \{x_1^*,\ldots,x_m^*\}$ is usually a finite set of potential sites, which have been selected for geographical, political, logistic and/or other reasons. We are interested in the specific problem of adding a further site x_{n+1} to an existing network $d_n=(x_1,\ldots,x_n)$, i.e. how to choose $x_{n+1} \in D_o$? To this define

$$d_{n+1}^{(j)} = (x_1,\ldots,x_n,x_j^*); \; j=1,\ldots,m$$

and the objective functions

$$G^*(d_{n+1}^{(j)}) = \max_{l=1,..,m;\, l \neq j} B(x_l^*, d_{n+1}^{(j)})$$

and $$I^*(d_{n+1}^{(j)}) = \sum_{\substack{l=1 \\ l \neq j}}^{m} B(x_l^*, d_{n+1}^{(j)})$$

corresponding to the criteria of G- and I-optimality, respectively. Then, one has to add that site $x_{j_o}^*$ which achieves the minimum of $G^*(d_{n+1}^{(j)})$ and $I^*(d_{n+1}^{(j)})$; $j=1,\ldots,m$; respectively. That is, one adds that station which best predicts the remaining sites in D_o. The above design criteria can easily be extended to criteria for detecting hot spots by introducing an additional weight function $g(\cdot)$, e.g. $g(x) = I(E\,Z(x) > m_o)$ where I stands for the indicator function and m_o for some threshold value. In a non-Bayesian setting, this has been done in Cressie et al. (1990).

REFERENCES

Cressie, N., Gotway, C.A. and Grondona, M.O.(1990): Spatial prediction from networks. Chemometrics and Intelligent Laboratory Systems **7**, 251-271

Fedorov, V.V.(1989): Kriging and other estimators of spatial field characteristics (with special reference to environmental studies. Atmospheric Environment **23**, 175-184

Matheron, G. (1971): The Theory of Regionalized Variables and Its Applications. Ecole des Mines, Fontainebleau, France, 211pp.

Mitchell, T., Sacks, J. and Ylvisaker, D. (1991): Asymptotic Bayes criteria for nonparametric response surface design. Technical Report, UCLA, Los Angeles

Omre, H. (1987): Bayesian kriging - merging observations and qualified guesses in kriging. Math. Geology **19**, 25-39

Omre, H. and Halvorsen, K.B. (1989): The Bayesian bridge between simple and universal kriging. Math. Geology **21**, 767-786

Pilz, J. (1991a): Bayesian Estimation and Experimental Design in Linear Regression Models. J. Wiley & Sons, New York, Chichester, Brisbane, Toronto, Singapore

Pilz, J. (1991b): Robust Bayes linear prediction of regionalized variables. Paper presented at the Fourth Int. Valencia Meeting on Bayesian Statistics, submitted to Math. Geology

An Asymptotic Relation Between Elementary Conditional and Purely Finitely Additive Probabilities With Application to Characterizations of Atomless Measures

D. Plachky
Institut für Math. Statistik, University of Münster
Einsteinstr. 62, D-4400 Münster

Abstract

It is shown that for any probability measure P on a σ-algebra $\mathcal{A}$ all subnets of the sequence $P(\ |A_n)$, $n \in \mathbb{N}$, of elementary conditional distributions relative to any decreasing sequence $A_n \in \mathcal{A}$ of positive P-measure, satisfying $P(\bigcap_{n=1}^{\infty} A_n) = 0$, which converge with respect to the weak* topoloty (i.e. setwise convergence) are purely finitely additive probability charges on $\mathcal{A}$. Furthermore, it is proved that the closed convex hull of all purely finitely additive probability charges obtained by the above procedure with respect to the weak* topology consists of all probability charges Q on $\mathcal{A}$ vanishing for all P-zero sets, if and only if P is atomless. Finally, this characterization is generalized to probability charges, which are G-invariant under a finite group G, if one starts from a G-invariant probability measure P.

Motivated by the Kac-Slepian paradox (see [4], p. 442), the starting point is a decreasing sequence $A_n \in \mathcal{A}$ of positive P-measure, $n \in \mathbb{N}$, satisfying $P(\bigcap_{n=1}^{\infty} A_n) = 0$, where P is a probability measure defined on the σ-algebra $\mathcal{A}$ of subsets of a set Ω. Such a sequence exists if and only if P is not purely atomic with a finite number of pairwise disjoint atoms. This follows easily from the uniquely determined decomposition of a finite measure μ on $\mathcal{A}$ according to $\mu = \mu_1 + \mu_2$, where μ_1 is an atomless measure on $\mathcal{A}$ and μ_2 is a purely atomic measure on $\mathcal{A}$ with an at most countable number of pairwise disjoint atoms (see the remark at the end of this note for a probabilistic resp. measure theoretical characterization of atomic probability measures with a finite number of pairwise disjoint atoms). Furthermore, $P(\ |A_n)$ denotes the elementary conditional probability defined by $P(A|A_n) = P(A \cap A_n)/P(A_n)$, $A \in \mathcal{A}$, where $A_n \in \mathcal{A}$ has positive P-measure. Finally, any finitely additive, non-negative set functions Q defined on A satisfying $Q(\Omega) = 1$ is called probability charge on $\mathcal{A}$.

Theorem 1 *Let $(\Omega, \mathcal{A}, P)$ denote a probability space, where P is not purely atomic with a finite number of pairwise disjoint atoms. Then the set $\mathcal{P}$ of setwise limits of a subnet of any sequence $P(\ |A_n)$, $n \in \mathbb{N}$, $A_n \in \mathcal{A}$ decreasing and of positive P-measure satisfying $P(\bigcap_{n=1}^{\infty} A_n) = 0$, consists of purely finitely additive probability charges on $\mathcal{A}$ vanishing for all P-zero sets.*

Proof: According to the theorem of Alaoglu about the weak* compactness of the unit ball of the dual of a Banach space (see [1], V.4.2, p. 424, and VI.5.1, p. 528, for the underlying Banach space), there exists a subnet $P(\ |A_{n_\alpha})$ such that $\lim_\alpha P(A|A_{n_\alpha}) = Q(A)$ exists for all $A \in \mathcal{A}$. In order to show that Q is purely finitely additive, let μ denote a measure on $\mathcal{A}$ satisfying $Q \geq \mu$. Now $Q(A_k^c) = \lim_\alpha P(A_k^c|A_{n_\alpha}) = \lim_\alpha \frac{P(A_{n_\alpha})-P(A_k\cap A_{n_\alpha})}{P(A_{n_\alpha})}$ implies $Q(A_k^c) = 0$ for all $k \in \mathbb{N}$, since the definition of the notion "subnet" (see [2], p. 70) implies for any $k \in \mathbb{N}$ the existence of some $n_\alpha \in \mathbb{N}$, such that $A_{n_\alpha} \subset A_k$ is valid. This yields $\mu(A_k^c) = 0$ for any $k \in \mathbb{N}$, i.e. $\mu(\bigcup_{k=1}^\infty A_k^c) = 0$, from which $\mu(\Omega) = 0$ follows, since $P(\bigcap_{k=1}^\infty A_k) = 0$ yields $Q(\bigcap_{k=1}^\infty A_k) = 0$ and, therefore, $\mu(\bigcap_{k=1}^\infty A_k) = 0$ holds true. □

If in addition the probability measure P is invariant under a group G of transformations $g : \Omega \to \Omega$, which are $(\mathcal{A}, \mathcal{A})$-measurable, P is called G-invariant for short, and $A_n \in \mathcal{A}$, $n \in \mathbb{N}$, are of positive P-measure and belong already to the sub-σ-algebra $\mathcal{I} = \{A \in \mathcal{A} : gA = A, g \in G\}$ of G-invariant measurable sets, then the probability measures $P(\ |A_n)$, $n \in \mathbb{N}$, are invariant under G, too. This yields the following

Corollary 1 *Let $(\Omega, \mathcal{A}, P)$ denote a probability space, where P is G-invariant, and the restriction of P to $\mathcal{I}$ is not purely atomic with a finite number of pairwise disjoint atoms. Then the set $\mathcal{P}$ of setwise limits of a subnet of any sequence $P(\ |A_n)$, $n \in \mathbb{N}$, $A_n \in \mathcal{I}$ decreasing of positive P-measure satisfying $P(\bigcap_{n=1}^\infty A_n) = 0$, consists of G-invariant purely finitely additive probability charges on $\mathcal{A}$ vanishing for all P-zero sets.*

Theorem 1 admits the following characterization of the property of a probability measure to be atomless:

Theorem 2 *P is atomless if and only if the closed convex hull of $\mathcal{P}$ with respect to the weak* topology consists of all probability charges on $\mathcal{A}$, which vanish for all P-zero sets.*

Proof: If there would exist some probability charge $Q_\circ$ on $\mathcal{A}$ vanishing for all P-zero sets, which does not belong to the closed and convex hull of $\mathcal{P}$ with respect to the weak* topology, then according to a separation theorem for convex and compact sets (see [1], V.2.10, p. 427) and since weak* continuous functionals are evaluaton maps (see [1], V.3.9, p. 421), there exists some bounded and $\mathcal{A}$-measurable function f (see [1], IV.8.14, p. 296, for the underlying Banach space), such that the inequality $\int f\,dQ \leq \varepsilon < \int f\,dQ_\circ$ would be valid for all $Q \in \mathcal{P}$ and some real valued number ε. One might work with $\mathcal{A}$ instead of the completion $\mathcal{A}^*$ of $\mathcal{A}$ with respect to P, since any $Q \in \mathcal{P}$ can be extended to $\mathcal{A}^*$ as a probability charge vanishing for all zero sets of the completion of P. Furthermore, one might assume without loss of generality that $0 \leq f \leq 1$ P-a.e. is valid because of $0 \leq Q \leq 1$, $Q \in \mathcal{P}$, and since any $Q \in \mathcal{P}$ vanishes for all P-zero sets. For the same reason one might assume P-ess sup $f = 1$ (and P-ess inf $f = 0$), which implies the existence of a decreasing sequence $A_n \in \mathcal{A}$, $n \in \mathbb{N}$, of positive P-measure, satisfying $P(\bigcap_{n=1}^\infty A_n) = 0$ and $f \geq 1 - \frac{1}{n}$ P-a.e. on A_n. If $P(\{f = P\text{-ess sup } f\}) = 0$ holds true, one might define A_n by $\{f \geq 1 - \frac{1}{n}\}$, $n \in \mathbb{N}$, and in the case $P(\{f = P\text{-ess sup } f\}) > 0$ the existence of a sequence of measurable sets described above follows from the assumption that P is atomless. In particular, one gets $\frac{1}{P(A_n)} \int_{A_n} f\,dP \geq 1 - \frac{1}{n}$, $n \in \mathbb{N}$, which yields $\int f\,dQ_1 = 1$ for any limit $Q_1 \in \mathcal{P}$ of a subnet of the corresponding sequence $P(\ |A_n)$, $n \in \mathbb{N}$, converging relative to the weak* topology (i.e. setwise convergence). Therefore $\varepsilon = 1$ is valid, which is a contradiction to $\varepsilon < \int f\,dQ_\circ \leq 1$, i.e. the condition described by Theorem 1 is necessary for P to be atomless. Conversely, the condition is also sufficient, since $Q(A_o) = 0,\ Q \in \mathcal{P}$, holds true for any P-atom $A_o \in \mathcal{A}$. □

Corollary 2 admits the following characterization of the property of a G-invariant probability measure on $\mathcal{A}$ to be atomless on the sub-σ-algebra $\mathcal{I}$ of $\mathcal{A}$ consisting of all G-invariant subsets of $\mathcal{A}$, if G is in addition finite and where $\mathcal{Q}$ denotes the set of all setwise limits of subnets of any sequence $P(\ |A_n)$, $n \in \mathbb{N}$, $A_n \in \mathcal{I}$ decreasing of positive P-measure and satisfying $P(\bigcap_{n=1}^{\infty} A_n) = 0$.

Corollary 2 *Let P be a G-invariant probability measure on a σ-algebra $\mathcal{A}$ of subsets of a set Ω, where G is a finite group of $(\mathcal{A},\mathcal{A})$-measurable transformations $g : \Omega \to \Omega$. Then the restriction of P to $\mathcal{I}$ is atomless if and only if the closed convex hull of $\mathcal{Q}$ with respect to the weak* topology consists of all G-invariant probability charges on $\mathcal{A}$, which vanish for any P-zero set.*

Proof: The starting point is the inequality $\int f\,dQ \le \varepsilon < \int f\,dQ_o$ of the proof of Theorem 1, where f satisfies in addition $0 \le f \le 1$ P-a.e., from which $\int h\,dQ \le \varepsilon < \int h\,dQ_o$ for h introduced by $h = \frac{1}{|G|}\sum_{g\in G} h \circ g$ ($|G|$ cardinality of G) follows. The remaining part of the proof of Corollary 2 is similar to the proof of Theorem 1, if one takes into consideration that h is G-invariant, i.e. $h \circ g = h$ for all $g \in G$ is valid. □

One might enlarge the set $\mathcal{Q}$ such that the larger set $\hat{\mathcal{Q}}$ is already convex and the closure of $\hat{\mathcal{Q}}$ with respect to the weak* topology coincides with the set of all probability charges, which vanish for all P-zero sets, if P is atomless. This can be realized by replacing the elementary conditional probabilities by elementary conditional expectations $E(I_A|f)$, $A \in \mathcal{A}$, $f \in \mathcal{L}_1(\Omega,\mathcal{A},P)$, defined by $E(I_A|f) = \int_A f\,dP / \int f\,dP$, if $\int f\,dP \neq 0$ is valid. In particular, $\lim_\alpha E(I_A|f_{n_\alpha})$, $A \in \mathcal{A}$, is a purely finitely additive probability charge Q on $\mathcal{A}$, if one starts from a sequence of non-negative functions $f_n \in \mathcal{L}_1(\Omega,\mathcal{A},P)$, $n \in \mathbb{N}$, satisfying $\int f_n\,dP > 0$, $n \in \mathbb{N}$, and $f_n \downarrow 0$, and where f_{n_α} is a subnet such that $\lim_\alpha E(A|f_{n_\alpha})$ exists for any $A \in \mathcal{A}$. The corresponding set $\hat{\mathcal{Q}}$ consisting of all resulting finitely additive probability charges Q vanishing for any P-zero set is convex. This follows from $\lim_\alpha E(I_A|h_{n_\alpha}) = \frac{\lambda}{1+\lambda}\lim_\alpha E(I_A|f_{n_\alpha}) + \frac{1}{1+\lambda}\lim_\alpha E(I_A|g_{n_\alpha})$, $A \in \mathcal{A}$, where $f_n, g_n \in \mathcal{L}_1(\Omega,\mathcal{A},P)$ are non-negative functions satisfying $f_n \downarrow 0$ and $g_n \downarrow 0$, $\int f_n\,dP > 0$ and $\int g_n\,dP > 0$, and where h_n stands for $\lambda(\int g_n\,dP) f_n + (\int f_n\,dP) g_n$, $n \in \mathbb{N}$, with λ being some positive real number. This leads to the following

Corollary 3 *P is atomless if and only if the closure of $\hat{\mathcal{Q}}$ with respect to the weak* topology coincides with the set consisting of all probability charges on $\mathcal{A}$ vanishing for any P-zero set, i.e. for any such probability charge Q on $\mathcal{A}$ there exists non-negative functions $f_{n\beta} \in \mathcal{L}_1(\Omega,\mathcal{A},P)$, $n \in \mathbb{N}$, $\beta \in D$ (D directed set) satisfying $\int f_{n\beta} dP > 0$, $n \in \mathbb{N}$, $\beta \in D$, $f_{n\beta} \downarrow 0$ for $n \to \infty$ ($\beta \in D$ fixed) and $\lim_\beta \lim_\alpha E(A|f_{n_\alpha\beta}) = Q(A)$, for any $A \in \mathcal{A}$ and some subnet $f_{n_\alpha\beta}$ of the sequence $f_{n\beta}$ ($\beta \in D$ fixed).*

Proof: If P is atomless, the proof of Theorem 1 can be carried over to the case $\hat{\mathcal{Q}}$ instead of $\mathcal{Q}$. For the converse direction one should take into consideration that $\lim_\alpha E(I_{A_o}|f_{n_\alpha}) = 0$ is valid for any P-atom $A_o \in \mathcal{A}$ because of $E(I_{A_o}|f_n) = c_n$, where $c_n = I_{A_o} f_n$ P-a.e. on A_o for some real number c_n, $n \in \mathbb{N}$, holds true. □

Remarks.

1. There never exists a subsequence of the sequence $P(\ |A_n)$, $n \in \mathbb{N}$, which converges setwise, since otherwise according to a theorem of Nikodym (cf. [1], III.7.4, p. 106) the corresponding limit $Q \in \mathcal{P}$ would be a probability measure on $\mathcal{A}$, whereas it has been proved that Q is purely finitely additive. The situation of Nikodym's theorem changes drastically, if $\mathcal{A}$ is replaced by a countable algebra of subsets of a set Ω. In this case there exists by a simple diagonal argument a subsequence of the sequence $P(\ |A_n)$, $n \in \mathbb{N}$, which converges setwise on $\mathcal{A}$, such that the limit Q is non-negative, purely finitely additive, and satisfies $Q(\Omega) = 1$.

2. Any atomless probability measure P on a σ-algebra $\mathcal{A}$ of subsets of a set Ω is the setwise limit of a net of purely finitely additive probability charges on $\mathcal{A}$, which vanish for all P-zero sets. If P is G-invariant, where G is a finite group of $(\mathcal{A}, \mathcal{A})$-measurable transformations $g : \Omega \to \Omega$, then P is the setwise limit of a net of G-invariant and purely finitely additive probability charges on $\mathcal{A}$, which vanish for all P-zero sets, provided that the restriction of P to $\mathcal{I}$ is atomless.

3. The class of all probability measures P on a σ-algebra $\mathcal{A}$ of subsets of a set Ω, which are purely atomic with a finite number of pairwise disjoint atoms can be characterized measure-theoretically resp. probabilistically in the following sense (cf. [3]):

   (a) There exists no $\{0,1\}$-valued, purely finitely probability charge on $\mathcal{A}$, which vanishes for all P-zero sets.

   (b) Any sequence X_n, $n \in \mathbb{N}$, of real-valued, $\mathcal{A}$-measurable random variables, which converges P-stochastically to some real-valued, $\mathcal{A}$-measurable random variable X_o, converges P-a.e. uniformly to X_o.

   (c) Any sequence X_n, $n \in \mathbb{N}$, of real-valued and $\mathcal{A}$-measurable random variables, which converges P-stochastically admits some subsequence converging P-a.e. uniformly.

   (d) $L_\infty(\Omega, \mathcal{A}, P)$ is separable.

References

[1] Dunford, N. and J. T. Schwartz: Linear Operators. Interscience Publishers, New York, 1986

[2] Kelley, J. L.: General Topology. Springer, New York, 1955

[3] Plachky, D.: A simple characterization of almost uniform convergence by stochastic convergence. Manuscripta Math. 69 (1990), 27 - 30

[4] Rao, M. M.: Paradoxes in conditional probability. J. Mult. Anal. 27 (1988), 434 - 446

When Should Generalized Shewhart-Charts be Used ?

Michael Sachs
Institut für Angewandte Mathematik und Statistik
Sanderring 2
W-8700 Würzburg, Germany

Consider the case of supervising the mean value μ of a production process with known and constant standard deviation σ^2. To this end in regular distances $n \geq 1$ consecutive produced items are drawn from the production line, for every item i a dimension of interest x_i is measured and the test statistics

$$\bar{x} = \frac{1}{n}\sum_{i=1}^{n} x_i$$

is computed. We assume that the measured values x_i are realisations of independent and identically normal distributed random variables X_i.

Let the process adopt two states: an in-control state (State I), in which the process starts and where the mean value equals the target value μ_0, that is

$$X_i \sim N(\mu_0, \sigma^2).$$

After an unknown amount of time the process changes to the out-of-control state (State II), where

$$X_i \sim N(\mu_0 + \delta\sigma, \sigma^2),$$

with a known shiftparameter $\delta > 0$. Producing in State II the in-control state can only be restored by an inspection and repair of the process.

The present state can only be determined by an inspection of the process. According to the sample result a decision is made whether to inspect the process or not. Let $\bar{x}_i$ be the i-th sample mean. Then the decision rules for the charts with and without warning line are given as follows:

Simple chart without warning line (control scheme (n, k)):
inspection after sample i, iff

$$\frac{\bar{x}_i - \mu_0}{\sigma}\sqrt{n} > k.$$

Generalized chart with warning line (control scheme (N, n, k_1, k_2)):
inspection after sample i, if

$$\frac{\bar{x}_i - \mu_0}{\sigma}\sqrt{n} > k_1$$

or

$$k_2 < \frac{\bar{x}_j - \mu_0}{\sigma}\sqrt{n} \leq k_1$$

for $i \geq N,\ j = i - N + 1,\ \ldots,\ i - 1,\ i.$
(i.e. N consecutive sample results fall into the warning area between warning line k_2 and action line k_1).

For $k_1 = k_2 = k$ we obtain the simple control chart as a special case of a chart with warning line.

As process inspections are costly the control scheme should be designed so that in State I as few alarms as possible occur, while in State II an alarm signal should be given as soon as possible. A widely used criteria to compare the performances of different control charts is the *average run length* (ARL), defined as the expectation of the number of samples until an alarm signal is given by the chart. Let K denote the number of samples to an alarm signal, then we define for the ARL in State I and State II

$$\text{ARL}(0) = E[K \mid \mu = \mu_0] = \sum_{i=1}^{\infty} i \cdot \text{Prob}(K = i \mid \mu = \mu_0),$$

and

$$\text{ARL}(\delta) = E[K \mid \mu = \mu_0 + \delta\sigma] = \sum_{i=1}^{\infty} i \cdot \text{Prob}(K = i \mid \mu = \mu_0 + \delta\sigma)$$

In order to compare control charts with and without warning line we introduce the following notations:

	Chart (n, k)	Chart (N, n, k_1, k_2)
ARL(0)	$A(k)$	$A(k_1, k_2)$
ARL(δ)	$B(k)$	$B(k_1, k_2)$

Page (1955) derives a formula for the ARL of the generalized Shewhart-chart, depending on k_1, k_2 and, for State II, additionally on the amount $\delta\sqrt{n}$. The ARL's of the chart without warning line can easily be derived as

$$A(k) = \frac{1}{\alpha}$$

and

$$B(k) = \frac{1}{1 - \beta},$$

where

$$\begin{aligned} \alpha &= \text{Prob (alarm} \mid \text{State I)} = 1 - \Phi(k) \\ \beta &= \text{Prob (no alarm} \mid \text{State II)} = \Phi(k - \delta\sqrt{n}) \end{aligned}$$

are the probabilities of a Type-1- and a Type-2-error, respectively, and Φ denotes the distribution function of the standard normal distribution.

In order to compare a simple control chart with a chart with warning line we fix the ARL (0) of the in-control period which shall be the same for both charts and try to determine action and warning line so that ARL(δ) becomes smaller than for the original chart. The sample size n shall remain unchanged. This leads to the following conditions:

Given a chart (n, k) and a number $N \geq 2$, determine k_1^* and k_2^* so that for the chart (N, n, k_1^*, k_2^*) holds:

$$\begin{aligned} A(k_1^*, k_2^*) &= A(k) \\ B(k_1^*, k_2^*) &< B(k) \\ B(k_1^*, k_2^*) &= \inf\{B(k_1, k_2) \mid A(k_1, k_2) = A(k),\ k1 > k2 \geq 0\}. \end{aligned}$$

It is shown, that such a chart exists, if

$$\delta\sqrt{n} < 2k,$$

or, equivalently, if

$$\beta = \Phi(k - \delta\sqrt{n}) > \Phi(k - 2k) = \Phi(-k) = \alpha,$$

that is, an improvement of a simple control chart by a chart with warning line in the sense, that ARL(0) remains unchanged, while ARL(δ) gets shorter, is possible, if for the simple chart the probability of a Type-2-error is greater than the probability of a Type-1-error. If in the opposite case $\beta \leq \alpha$ such an improvement is possible, is not known, but numerical examples suggest that it is not so.

The optimal parameters k_1^* and k_2^* depend on $k, \delta\sqrt{n}$ and N. If k_1^* and k_2^* are computed for a fixed pair $(k, \delta\sqrt{n})$ and $N = 2, 3, 4\ldots$, the following observation can be made: $B(k_1^*, k_2^*)$ decreases until a certain N^*, for higher N it increases, that is, a longer consideration of the past only deteriorates ARL(δ).

Furthermore the following empirical conclusions can be drawn from numerical computations:

Even for a high value of the Type-2-error probability $\beta = 0.5$ (a value which is not reached for cost optimal control charts under realistic cost assumptions) the achieved improvement, measurted by the effectivity ratio $B(k_1^*, k_2^*)/B(k)$, is not very high. For $\beta < 0.5$ this ratio is even nearer to 100 %. Therefore we can conclude that a remarkable improvement by the usage of a chart with warning line is only achieved, if the Type-2-error probability β of the original simple chart is high enough.

References

Chiu, W. K. and Cheung, K. C. (1977) An Economic Study of $\overline{X}$-Charts with Warning Limits. *J. Qual. Tech.*, **9**, 166–171.

Collani, E. v. (1986) Shewhart-Karten mit und ohne Warngrenzen. *Statistische Hefte*, **27**, 255–277.

Collani, E.v. (1989) *The Economic Design of Control Charts*. B. G. Teubner, Stuttgart.

Duncan, A. J. (1956) The Economic Design of $\overline{X}$-Charts Used to Maintain Current Control of a Process. *J. Amer. Statist. Ass.*, **51**, 228–242.

Gordon, G. R. and Weindling, J. I. (1975) A Cost Model for Economic Design of Warning Limit Control Chart Schemes. *AIIE Transactions*, **7**, 319–329.

Page, E. S. (1955) Control Charts with Warning Lines. *Biometrika*, **42**, 243–257.

Page, E. S. (1962) A Modified Control Chart with Warning Lines. *Biometrika*, **49**, 171–175

Shewhart, W. A. (1931) *Economic Control of Quality of Manufactured Product*. D. van Nostrand, New York.

Weindling, J. I. (1967) *Statistical Properties of a General Class of Control Charts Treated as a Markov Process*. Ph.D. Dissertation, Columbia University, New York.

Weindling, J. I., Littauer, S. B. and Oliveira, J. T. de (1970) Mean Action Time of the $\overline{X}$ Control Chart with Warning Limits. *J. Qual. Tech.*, **2**, 79–85.

Wetherill, G. B. and Brown, D. W. (1991) *Statistical Process Control*. Chapman and Hall, London.

Classification of type I and II outliers

Wolfgang Schmid
Abteilung Stochastik
Universität Ulm
Helmholtzstr. 18, D - 7900 Ulm

1. Introduction

Frequently time series data contain observations which appear to deviate markedly from the other values. In literature several models have been proposed to describe the occurrence of such observations, e.g. Fox (1972), Martin and Yohai (1985), Schmid (1986).

In the following it is assumed that a realization $x_1, \dots, x_n$ of a process $\{X_t\}$ is given, instead of one of the interesting, however unobservable, process $\{Y_t\}$. $\{Y_t\}$ denotes an AR(p) process, i.e

$$Y_t = \sum_{v=1}^{p} \alpha_v Y_{t-v} + \varepsilon_t \quad , t \in \mathbb{Z},$$

and $\{\varepsilon_t\}$ an i.i.d. random sequence with $E(\varepsilon_t) = 0$ and $Var(\varepsilon_t) = \sigma^2 > 0$.

The processes are connected as follows (δ_{tq} Kronecker delta)

$$X_t = \sum_{v=1}^{p} \alpha_v (X_{t-v} - \sum_{i=1}^{s_1} a_{1i} \delta_{t-v, q_{1i}}) + \sum_{i=1}^{s_1} a_{1i} \delta_{tq_{1i}} + \varepsilon_t + \sum_{j=1}^{s_2} a_{2j} \delta_{tq_{2j}},$$

where $1 \le q_{11} < \dots < q_{1s_1} \le n$ and $1 \le q_{21} < \dots < q_{2s_2} \le n$.

Following Fox (1972), a_{1i} is called a type I outlier at position q_{1i}, if $a_{1i} \neq 0$, and by analogy a_{2j} a type II outlier. $s_1 = s_{1n}$ and $s_2 = s_{2n}$ denote known upper bounds for the number of type I resp. type II outliers.

While a type I outlier only affects a single observation, type II outliers have an influence on all subsequent values. Sometimes type II outliers are also called innovation outliers.

Throughout this paper we interprete q_{1i} and q_{2j} as outlier suspicious positions, which are assumed to be known.

Choosing $s_1 = s_2 = 1$ resp. $s_2 = 0$ we obtain the model of Muirhead (1986) resp. Schmid (1986/88). Consequently a more general outlier model is present.

Here we want to discuss the following problems:

i) Do the data contain an outlier, i.e.

H_1: $a_{1i} = a_{2j} = 0 \ \forall i,j$ against K_1: $a_{1i} \neq 0$ or $a_{2j} \neq 0$ for at least one i, j?

ii) Does a type I outlier, i.e. H_2: $a_{1i} = 0 \ \forall i$ against K_2: $\exists i : a_{1i} \neq 0$, or a type II outlier, i.e. H_3: $a_{2j} = 0 \ \forall j$ against K_3: $\exists j : a_{2j} \neq 0$, occur?

iii) If an outlier occurs at position q, is it a type I or a type II outlier?

The testing problems i) and ii) are special cases of the general linear hypothesis H: $G a = a_0$ against K: $G a \neq a_0$, where G is a $(m, s_1 + s_2)$ matrix with rank $m \leq s_1 + s_2$, $a := (a_{11}, \ldots, a_{1s_1}, a_{21}, \ldots, a_{2s_2})^T$ and G and a_0 are assumed to be known.

In section 2 we extend some results given in Schmid (1986) to the mixed outlier model. An outlier test for the general linear hypothesis is derived.
Several authors have proposed methods for distinguishing between these outlier types, e.g. Fox (1972), Muirhead (1986), Abraham and Yatawara (1988). In section 3 Muirhead's rule is compared with an outlier test of section 2. We determine the probability to conclude on the existence of a type I resp. type II outlier.

2. An outlier test

First we suppose that α and σ are both known and define

$$Z_t := X_t - \sum_{v=1}^{p} \alpha_v X_{t-v} \quad , \; t = p+1, \ldots, n .$$

In order to find estimators for $a_1 := (a_{11}, \ldots, a_{1s_1})^T$ and $a_2 := (a_{21}, \ldots, a_{2s_2})^T$, the method of least squares is applied. Since $Z := (Z_{p+1}, \ldots, Z_n)^T = A a + \varepsilon$ with $a = (a_1^T, a_2^T)^T$, $\varepsilon = (\varepsilon_{p+1}, \ldots, \varepsilon_n)^T$ and $(\alpha_0 := -1)$

$$A = \Big(\big(- \sum_{v=0}^{p} \alpha_v \delta_{t-v, q_{1i}} \big)_{\substack{t = p+1,\ldots,n \\ i = 1,\ldots,s_1}} , \big(\delta_{t q_{2j}} \big)_{\substack{t = p+1,\ldots,n \\ j = 1,\ldots,s_2}} \Big) ,$$

a linear model is present and thus $\hat{a} := (A^T A)^{-1} A^T Z$ is an estimator of a, provided that $rk(A) = s_1 + s_2 \leq n - p$.

The theory of linear models provides the test statistic

$$T := (G\hat{a} - a_0)^T (G (A^T A)^{-1} G^T)^{-1} (G\hat{a} - a_0)/\sigma^2 .$$

If $\varepsilon_t \sim N(0,\sigma^2)$ for all $t \in \mathbb{Z}$, then $T \sim \chi^2_{m,\lambda}$ with

$$\lambda = (G a - a_0)^T (G (A^T A)^{-1} G^T)^{-1} (G a - a_0)/\sigma^2 .$$

Under the null hypothesis λ is equal to 0.

Example

Let $s_1 = s_2 = 1$ and $q_{11} = q_{21} = q \in \{p+1, \ldots, n-p\}$. We obtain as a test statistic for H_2 against K_2 $(G = (1\ 0))$ $T^{(1)} = \hat{a}_1^2 \gamma^2 / \sigma^2$ and for H_3 against K_3 $(G = (0 1))$ $T^{(2)} = \hat{a}_2^2 / ((1 + 1/\gamma^2)/\sigma^2)$, where $\gamma^2 = \sum_{i=1}^{p} \alpha_i^2$, $\hat{a}_1 = - \sum_{i=1}^{p} \alpha_i Z_{q+i} / \gamma^2$ and $\hat{a}_2 = Z_q - \hat{a}_1$. These test statistics are similar to those of Abraham and Yatawara (1988), whose starting-point was an outlier model with $a_{11} = a_{21}$.

Now in general α and σ will be unknown. Let $\hat{\alpha}_n$ resp. $\hat{\sigma}_n$ be arbitrary estimators of α resp. σ, satisfying $\hat{\alpha}_n \xrightarrow[n\to\infty]{P} \alpha$ and $\hat{\sigma}_n \xrightarrow[n\to\infty]{P} \sigma$.

We replace α by $\hat{\alpha}_n$ and σ by $\hat{\sigma}_n$ in T and obtain $\hat{T}_n$. If $rk(A) = s_1 + s_2$ in an open neighbourhood of α and m, s_1, s_2 do not depend on n, then it can be shown that $\hat{T}_n \xrightarrow[n\to\infty]{d} \chi^2_{m,\lambda}$. Thus an outlier test is present for the general linear hypothesis. Suitable estimators of the parameters are e.g. GM - or RA - estimators (see Martin and Yohai (1985)).

If all model parameters are estimated using the least squares method, then an outlier test is obtained with the same arguments as in Schmid (1986/88). The results of these papers can be extended to the above model.

3. Distinguishing between the outlier types

In this section we analyse a slightly modified version of Muirhead's rule for distinguishing between type I and type II outliers. For this, let $s_1 = s_2 = 1$, $p+1 \le q_{11} = q_{21} \le n-p$ and $\hat{a}_1$, $\hat{a}_2$ as in section 2. We restrict us to the case α, σ known, since the case of unknown parameters can be handled as described above.

In order to test, whether an outlier occurs or not, Muirhead uses the test statistic $\tilde{T} = (\hat{a}_1 + \hat{a}_2)^2/\sigma^2$. This test turns out to be bad, if at the position q both outliers occur. For this reason we consider the test statistic of section 2 $(G = I_2)$ $T = (\hat{a}_1 + \hat{a}_2)^2/\sigma^2 + \gamma^2 \hat{a}_1^2/\sigma^2$, which does not have this disadvantage.

If the hypothesis H_1 is rejected, then Muirhead concludes on the existence of a type I resp. type II outlier, provided that $W := \gamma^2 (\hat{a}_1^2 - \hat{a}_2^2/(1+\gamma^2)) > / < 0$. The quantity W is derived from a kind of likelihood - ratio principle.

Now we want to discuss the method in detail. The proofs are omitted.

Proposition 1

Let $\{Y_t\}$ be a stationary, $\sum_{v=0}^{p} \alpha_v z^v \neq 0$ for all $|z| \le 1$ and $\varepsilon_t \sim N(0,\sigma^2)$ $\forall t \in \mathbb{Z}$, then

$$P(W > 0 ; a_1, a_2) = \Phi(m_1/\sigma_1)\, \Phi(m_2/\sigma_2) + \Phi(-m_1/\sigma_1)\, \Phi(-m_2/\sigma_2) \ ,$$

where $\Phi = N(0,1)$, $m_1 = (1+\gamma^2)^{1/2} a_1 - a_2$, $m_2 = (1+\gamma^2)^{1/2} a_1 + a_2$ and

$$\sigma_1^2 = 2\sigma^2 (1+\gamma^2)^{1/2} ((1+\gamma^2)^{1/2} + 1)/\gamma^2 \ , \quad \sigma_2^2 = 2\sigma^2 (1+\gamma^2)^{1/2} ((1+\gamma^2)^{1/2} - 1)/\gamma^2$$

Proposition 2

Suppose that the conditions of Proposition 1 are satisfied, then

$$P(W > 0 \wedge T \le c) = \Phi(-r_2) \, (\Phi(\sqrt{c} + r_1) - \Phi(r_1) - \Phi(\sqrt{c} - r_1) + \Phi(-r_1)) +$$

$$\frac{1}{\sqrt{2\pi}} \int_0^{\sqrt{c}} (\exp(-(x-r_1)^2/2)\, \Phi(\sqrt{c-x^2} - r_2) - \exp(-(x+r_1)^2/2)\, \Phi(-\sqrt{c-x^2} - r_2)) \, dx,$$

where $r_1 = ((1 - 1/(1+\gamma^2)^{1/2})/2)^{1/2} m_1/\sigma$, $r_2 = ((1 + 1/(1+\gamma^2)^{1/2})/2)^{1/2} m_2/\sigma$.

The probability of deciding on the existence on a type I resp. type II outlier is given by $P_1 = P(W > 0 \wedge T > c)$ resp. $P_2 = P(W < 0 \wedge T > c)$, where $\chi_2^2(c) = 1 - \alpha$. With Proposition 1 and 2 we are able to calculate

$$P_1 = P(W > 0) - P(W > 0 \wedge T \leq c) \quad \text{resp.} \quad P_2 = P(T > c) - P_1 .$$

In Table 1/2 the probability P_1 / P_2 is listed as a function of a_1 and a_2.

Table 1: P_1 as a function of a_1 and a_2 ($\alpha = 0.05$, $\sigma^2 = 1$, $\gamma^2 = 1$)

a_2 / a_1	-4	-3	-2	-1	0	1	2	3	4
0	0.984	0.926	0.633	0.173	0.025	0.173	0.633	0.926	0.984
1	0.995	0.891	0.478	0.094	0.040	0.288	0.694	0.890	0.963
2	0.984	0.803	0.346	0.056	0.073	0.331	0.613	0.805	0.919
3	0.960	0.690	0.219	0.028	0.083	0.261	0.473	0.683	0.845
4	0.900	0.487	0.087	0.013	0.057	0.160	0.327	0.537	0.737

Table 2: P_2 as a function of a_1 and a_2 ($\alpha = 0.05$, $\sigma^2 = 1$, $\gamma^2 = 1$)

a_2 / a_1	-4	-3	-2	-1	0	1	2	3	4
0	0.015	0.049	0.085	0.053	0.025	0.053	0.085	0.049	0.015
1	0.002	0.017	0.026	0.039	0.093	0.216	0.214	0.107	0.036
2	0.001	0.013	0.070	0.170	0.343	0.485	0.372	0.194	0.081
3	0.007	0.081	0.285	0.476	0.688	0.706	0.526	0.317	0.155
4	0.057	0.329	0.631	0.803	0.900	0.837	0.673	0.463	0.263

The tables show that the method provides good results in the presence of one outlier. If both outliers occur and have different sign, then P_2 is extremely small. It turns out to be more difficult to detect a type I than a type II outlier.

In comparison with the outlier tests basing on $T^{(1)}$ resp. $T^{(2)}$, Muirhead's rule seems to be better, if a single outlier is present. Since, however, each test does not depend on the other outlier type, they are more powerful in the case of several outliers.

References

Abraham,B. and Yatawara,N. (1988). A score test for detection of time series outliers. J. Time Series Analysis 9(2), 109 - 119.

Fox,A.J. (1972). Outliers in time series. J. Roy. Statist. Soc., Ser.B, 43(3), 350 - 363.

Martin,R.D. and Yohai,V.J. (1985). Robustness in time series and estimating ARMA models. In: Handbook of Statistics Vol.5, Eds. Hannan,E.J., Krishnaiah,P.R. and Rao,M.M., 119 - 155, Elsevier Science Publishers B.V..

Muirhead,C.R. (1986). Distinguishing outlier types in time series. J. Roy. Statist. Soc., Ser.B, 48(1), 39 - 47.

Schmid,W. (1986). The multiple outlier problem in time series analysis. Austral. J. Statist. 28(3), 400 - 413.

Schmid,W. (1988). Asymptotical behaviour of a test of discordancy for an increasing number of outliers. Statistics & Decisions 6, 245 - 260.

ON COLLECTING AND USING INCOMPLETE PRIOR INFORMATION IN ACCEPTANCE SAMPLING

Wilfried Seidel
Universität der Bundeswehr Hamburg
Postfach 70 08 22 D-2000 Hamburg 70

In order to classify incoming lots as acceptable or non acceptable, one often uses a sampling strategy. Frequently records on past inspections contain additional information about the quality of the product, which should be taken into account in order to cut down costs. However, it is not always obvious how to collect and process prior information properly.

Let us assume that a random sample of size n is drawn from a lot, a test statistic T(n) is calculated and the lot is acceptable if T(n) falls in a particular acceptance region A. A statistical model, parametrized over $\vartheta \in \Theta$, describes the quality of the lot and specifies for every $\vartheta \in \Theta$ the distribution $G(t|\vartheta,n)$ of T(n). Given a cost model, the average loss $R(\vartheta;n,A)$ of a sampling strategy (n,A) may be calculated for each $\vartheta \in \Theta$. The function $\vartheta \mapsto R(\vartheta;n,A)$ is called a risk function. Finally, the parameter ϑ is assumed to vary from lot to lot according to a probability distribution π.

Usually π is not known. If we know that π belongs to a particular set Π of probability measures on Θ, we speak about "incomplete prior information". In this case a sampling strategy should be chosen that minimizes

$$\sup_{\pi \in \Pi} \int_{\Theta} R(\vartheta;n,A)\pi(d\vartheta). \qquad [1]$$

Inspecting k lots results in a vector $(T_1(n_1),...,T_k(n_k))$ of observations, here the sample sizes n_i may vary from lot to lot, too. The distribution of $T_i(n_i)$ is the mixture of the family $\{G(t|\vartheta,n_i) : \vartheta \in \Theta\}$ with mixing distribution π. In the case of equal sample sizes $n_i = n$, $i = 1,...,k$, we are given k independent replications of $T = T(n)$.

We do not usually observe ϑ directly, so there is no simple estimator of π. On the other hand, conditions on "generalized moments" of π may be obtained: For each $i = 1,...,r$ let a function $g_i : \Theta \to \mathbb{R}$ and real numbers $a_i \leq b_i$ be given. The set

$$\Pi := \{\pi : a_i \leq \int_{\Theta} g_i \, d\pi \leq b_i, \ 1 \leq i \leq r\} \qquad [2]$$

is called a "moment set", and each of the conditions in [2] a "generalized moment condition". For $g_i(\vartheta) = \vartheta^i$ the integral is simply the i-th-moment of π. Clearly, each moment set is convex. If Π in the optimization problem [1] is a moment set, it can be replaced by the set of its extreme points, see Winkler (4). Winkler also proves that each extreme point is a discrete measure concentrated at not more than r+1 points. Therefore [1] reduces to an optimization problem in not more than 2r+2 real variables.

Generalized moment conditions on π may be obtained by past inspections:

Estimators of moments of π even in the case of different sample sizes can be given if $\{G(t|\vartheta,n):\vartheta\in\Theta\}$ is a natural exponential family with quadratic variance function, a location family or a family of noncentral t distributions, see Morris (1), Hold and Seidel (2) or Seidel (3).

In the case of equal sample sizes, an inequality

$$\mathbb{P}(T\in A) \geq \gamma \qquad [3]$$

can easily be estimated. For instance we can estimate γ by the fraction of lots accepted so far, possibly with a correction that protects against underestimating. In Seidel (3) it is shown that a variety of conditions on T, which includes [3], can be written as moment conditions.

Algorithms for the construction of sampling plans, if an inequality [3] or information about the first two moments of π is given, are constructed in Hold and Seidel (2). They require that Θ is a subset of the real line; the case of a normally distributed quality characteristic with unknown variance and one-sided specification limit is also covered, if ϑ is the noncentrality parameter of the t distribution. The performance of these sampling plans is investigated in a simple model.

References

(1) Morris, C.N., Natural exponential families with quadratic variance functions: Statistical theory, Ann. Statist. 11 (1983), 515-529.

(2) Hold, A., Seidel, W., Algorithms for calculating sampling plans based on generalized moments of the prior distribution, Discussion Papers in Statistics and Quantitative Economics 49 (1991), Universität der Bundeswehr Hamburg.

(3) Seidel, W., Minimax regret sampling plans based on generalized moments of the prior distribution, Frontiers in Statistical Quality Control 4 (Editors: Lenz, Wetherill, Wilrich). Heidelberg, Physica, to appear.

(4) Winkler, G., Integral representation and upper bounds for stop-loss premiums under constraints given by inequalities, Scand. Actuarial J. (1982), 15-21.

A SOLUTION TO THE SCHEDULING PROBLEM TAKING INTO ACCOUNT QUALITY

Christoph Weigand
Institut für Angewandte Mathematik und Statistik
Universität Würzburg
Sanderring 2, D-8700 Würzburg

In statistical process control production processes are investigated which can be affected by assignable causes deterioriating quality by an enhancement of the proportion of defective items. In order to detect assignable causes and renew the process, "inspection schedules" (h,n,c) are used with

h = sampling interval,

n = sample size,

c = test limit.

Every h hour a sample of size n is taken from the current production and a test is performed. The test decides whether or not to give an alarm. If an alarm is released, a process inspection is performed which allows to recognize the actual state of the process with probability 1. If the process is "out of control", a renewal is performed. In the case the process is in control the alarm is called a "false alarm" and wastes time and money.

Traditionally research on statistical process control presents mathematical models which take into account economic input-parameter in order to maximize the profit in the long run. In the first part of this contribution a model which was introduced by v. Collani is extended to the case that the process is operating only during a finite time. Two types of objective functions are defined:

- expected profit per item
- expected number of conforming items per hour.

The following results are obtained:

1. Optimal inspection schedules for the model with infinite time horizon provide excellent approximations for optimal

inspection schedules for the model with finite time horizon.

2. It is posible to give explicit formulas for the expected
   - number of false alarms
   - number of renewals
   - overall time of the process = operating time + down times = processing time.
   - overall profit.
3. The distributions of the (*)
   - number of false alarms and renewals
   - processing time

   can be determined by recursions. Explicit formulas provide good approximations for these probabilities.
4. Collani's economic model can also be used to find approximately optimal schedules which maximize the "expexcted number of conforming items per hour".

In the second part of this contribution we consider a single machine-process which is able to produce different kinds of products. Our aim is to accomplish a given order which is defined by a sequence of individual orders $(D_i,P_i,t_i)_{i=1..N}$ with

D = demand of conforming items

P = type of product

t = due date.

Being impossible to produce more than one product at the same time, set-ups are necessary to change the production from one type of product to the other. The parts of the process between two successive set-ups are described by the model for finite time horizon introduced above and are called "individual processes". Production is governed by "production schedules" $S = (Q_i,\pi_i)_{i=1..M}$ with

Q_i = lot size of the i-th individual process

π_i = product of the i-th individual process.

Because of assignable causes and false alarms, the processing times are random variables. Therefore the starting times as well as the closing times for the individual processes can not be determined in advance. But by means of the results (*) we can calculate the probabilities that production exceeds the due

dates t_i.
Set-ups are time consuming and thus it is obvious that too many set-ups decrease productivity. Minimizing the number of set-ups a solution for the following problem is given:

$$\min_{S} \text{(overall processing time)}$$

subject to
accomplish each individual order with probability of at least α

References:

Collani, E.v. (1989). The Economic Design of Control Charts. Teubner-Verlag, Stuttgart.

Non-zero-sum Dresher inspection games

Rudolf Avenhaus, Bernhard von Stengel
Informatik 5, Armed Forces University Munich
Werner-Heisenberg-Weg 39, D–8014 Neubiberg

Dedicated to the memory of Eckhard Höpfinger (1941–1990)

An inspection game is here a non-cooperative two-person-game between an *inspector* and an *inspectee*. It models a situation where the inspector *controls* the inspectee who has an incentive to *violate* certain legal obligations. A recent survey of inspection games applied to data verification, for example in nuclear material safeguards, is given in [1].

Dresher [2] described a sequential inspection game of n *stages* or time periods. The inspector can allocate m inspections to these periods, $0 \leq m \leq n$. The inspectee knows at each stage the number of past inspections. He can decide to *act legally* or in at most one period to *violate* where he is caught iff the inspector simultaneously inspects. In [2], the game is zero-sum, with payoff zero for legal action and where the gain for the inspectee if he is undetected equals his loss if he is caught. This last assumption has been generalized by Höpfinger [3]. The present paper treats this game $\Gamma(n,m)$ with non-zero-sum payoffs. A closely related game with announced inspection strategies has been solved by Maschler [5].

I \ V	legal action	violation
control	$V(n-1,m-1)$ $I(n-1,m-1)$	$-b$ $-a$
no control	$V(n-1,m)$ $I(n-1,m)$	1 -1

As in [2], the game $\Gamma(n,m)$ can be described *recursively*. For $0 < m < n$, it is shown in the table as a two-by-two game with the choices of the inspector I and the inspectee or "violator" V at the *first period*. As will be shown by induction, the game has a unique equilibrium with payoffs $I(n,m)$ and $V(n,m)$ to I and V. If V violates at the first period, the game continues at the next stage like $\Gamma(n-1,m-1)$ respectively $\Gamma(n-1,m)$ depending on whether I controls at the first stage or not. The equilibrium payoffs of these games are the entries in the first column of the table.

If V violates at the first stage, he will get caught if I controls and receive payoff $-b$ whereas I gets $-a$. The absolute values of these payoffs are $a, b > 0$. The negative sign emphasizes the undesirability of a caught violation for *both* players compared to legal action throughout the game which has reference payoff zero to both. For the inspector, even a caught violation usually represents a failure of the surveillance system that is supposed to induce legal behavior, so I has a *common* interest with V to have legal action instead, which cannot be modeled with a zero-sum game.

A violation at the first period without control does not terminate the game, but determines its payoffs, given by -1 to I and 1 to V (this and payoff zero for legal action normalizes the payoff functions which are unique only up to positive-linear transformations). The additional constraint $a < 1$ indicates that I prefers caught to uncaught violation. For V, the inequalities $1 > 0 > -b$ show the reverse preference and an incentive to violate compared to legal action in order to model adequately the necessity of surveillance.

As pointed out by Kuhn [4, p.174], this recursive description of $\Gamma(n,m)$ tacitly assumes four *subgames* as a result of the actions of the players at stage one. This is actually not true if I did not control since then he *lacks information* about what V did, that is, in which subgame he is in. Nevertheless, I can act as if no violation occurred since otherwise his actions are irrelevant because V will then act legally and cannot be caught anymore. This can be justified formally by describing the game in extensive form with information sets. This description is crucial in a generalization to more than one admitted violation described in [6].

The equilibrium payoffs $I(n,m)$ and $V(n,m)$ of $\Gamma(n,m)$ are defined recursively, with the following base cases. If $m = 0$, then I has no inspections left and

$$I(n,0) = -1, \qquad V(n,0) = 1 \qquad \text{for } n > 0 \tag{1}$$

since then V can safely violate. If $m = n$, then I can (and should) inspect at every remaining period so

$$I(n,n) = 0, \qquad V(n,n) = 0 \qquad \text{for } n \geq 0 \tag{2}$$

since then V prefers legal action; (2) applies also to $n = 0$ where the game is over.

If $0 < m < n$, the game table applies, which has a *mixed equilibrium*. Namely, assume as inductive hypothesis

$$I(n-1,m-1) < I(n-1,m), \tag{3}$$

that is, I prefers not to control if V acts legally (since I can use the inspection later), which is true for $n = 2$, $m = 1$. If V violates, I prefers to control since $-a > -1$. Further inductive hypotheses are

$$V(n-1,m-1) > -b \qquad \text{and} \qquad V(n-1,m) < 1, \tag{4}$$

also true for $n = 2$, $m = 1$, showing that V prefers to act legally if controlled and illegally if not. These preferences are indicated by arrows at the sides of the table. $\Gamma(n,m)$ has then an equilibrium in mixed strategies: I controls at the first period with the unique probability p so that V is indifferent between his actions,

$$p \cdot V(n-1,m-1) + (1-p) \cdot V(n-1,m) = p \cdot (-b) + (1-p) \cdot 1. \tag{5}$$

Both terms of this equation denote the equilibrium payoff $V(n,m)$ to V which after solving (5) for p is

$$V(n,m) = \frac{b \cdot V(n-1,m) + V(n-1,m-1)}{V(n-1,m-1) + b + 1 - V(n-1,m)}. \tag{6}$$

Similarly, the probability q for V of legal action at stage one is determined by

$$q \cdot I(n-1,m-1) + (1-q)\cdot(-a) = q \cdot I(n-1,m) + (1-q)\cdot(-1)$$

yielding the equilibrium payoff $I(n,m)$ to I,

$$I(n,m) = \frac{-a \cdot I(n-1,m) + I(n-1,m-1)}{I(n-1,m) - I(n-1,m-1) + 1 - a}. \tag{7}$$

The functions $V(n,m)$ and $I(n,m)$ are uniquely defined by (1), (2), (6) and (7). Explicit formulas have been found by Dresher [2] for $b = 1$, $a = -1$ and by Höpfinger [3] for the general zero-sum case $b > 0$, $a = -b$ where $a < 0$. This inequality $a < 0$ can be weakened to $a < 1$ as assumed here, with the solution from [3] given by

$$I(n,m) = -\binom{n-1}{m}\Big/ s(n,m) \qquad \text{with} \qquad s(n,m) = \sum_{i=0}^{m} \binom{n}{i} (-a)^{m-i}.$$

This formula clearly fulfills (1) and (2), and (7) can be verified using the identities

$$s(n-1,m) = -a \cdot s(n-1,m-1) + \binom{n-1}{m} \tag{8}$$

and

$$s(n,m) = s(n-1,m) + s(n-1,m-1). \tag{9}$$

The explicit formula for $I(n,m)$ does not depend on the sign of the parameter a. With the formal substitutions $V(n,m) = -I(n,m)$ and $b = -a$, the base cases (1), (2) and the recurrences (6) and (7) are equivalent, so

$$V(n,m) = \binom{n-1}{m}\Big/ t(n,m) \qquad \text{with} \qquad t(n,m) = \sum_{i=0}^{m} \binom{n}{i} b^{m-i}.$$

To complete the induction, the inequalities (4) are seen immediately and (3) is seen as follows: the term $s(n,m)$ is positive since it can also be defined recursively by $s(n,0) = 1$, $s(n,n) = (1-a)^n$ (both positive since $a < 1$) and by (9) for $0 < m < n$. Similarly, one obtains $s(n-1,m) > \frac{n-1-m}{m} \cdot \binom{n-1}{m-1}$ for $0 < m < n$. Since $s(n-1,m-1) \le \binom{n-1}{m-1}$ by (8) with $m-1$ instead of m, this implies $s(n-1,m) > \frac{n-1-m}{m} \cdot s(n-1,m-1)$ or (3).

The probability p of control at the first period in (5) can be simplified to the expression $p = t(n-1,m-1)/t(n,m)$. (A similarly simple expression for q is not known.) This describes the inspector strategy for each stage, which depends on the number of inspections used so far. The resulting ***unconditional*** probabilities of control are ***equal*** for the first $n-m$ periods and monotonically increasing afterwards, where this increase is the higher the greater b is. For $m = 1$, for example, control in one of the first $n-1$ periods is equally probable and in the last period $1+b$ times as probable. This meets the intuition that sequential inspections should in tendency be accumulated towards the end to be optimal.

Finally, the solution of the game $\Gamma(n,m)$ holds also if the constraints $1 > a > 0$ and $b > 0$ are weakened, since the recurrences (6) and (7) are valid as long as the payoff table has the circular structure indicated by the arrows. Keeping the basic equations (1) and (2), the number a can be any real less than 1, where for $a \leq 0$, the inspector receives a nonnegative "reward" $-a$ (then better denoted by an unsigned variable) when he catches the inspectee. This includes the zero-sum game with $-a = b$ that, by induction, results into $V(n,m) = -I(n,m)$. The value $I(n,m)$ of this game has the recurrence (7), which allows to use Höpfinger's [3] solution of this case as mentioned above.

Formally, the solution of $\Gamma(n,m)$ is also valid if the constraint $b > 0$ is weakened to $b > -1$, but for $b < 0$ the inspectee would even with a caught violation gain over legal behavior, which invalidates the assumption $V(n,n) = 0$ in (2). In the case $b = 0$, admitted in [6] for generalizations of $\Gamma(n,m)$, the inspectee neither gains nor loses with a caught violation. It can be seen that then the optimal inspection scheme is very uniform through all stages, which has interesting applications cited in [6, section 5].

REFERENCES

[1] Avenhaus, R. and B. von Stengel, Current research in data verification. Contribution to the IMACS International Workshop on Decision Support Systems and Qualitative Reasoning, Toulouse, France, March 13–15 (1991)

[2] Dresher, M., A sampling inspection problem in arms control agreements: a game-theoretic analysis. Memorandum No. RM–2972–ARPA, The RAND Corporation, Santa Monica, California (1962)

[3] Höpfinger, E., A game-theoretic analysis of an inspection problem. C-Notiz No. 53, University of Karlsruhe, preprint (1971)

[4] Kuhn, H.W., Recursive inspection games. In: Applications of Statistical Methodology to Arms Control and Disarmament, eds. F.J. Anscombe et al., Final report to the U.S. Arms Control and Disarmament Agency under contract No. ACDA/ST-3 by Mathematica, Inc., Princeton, New Jersey (1963), Part III, pp. 169–181

[5] Maschler, M., A price leadership method for solving the inspector's non-constant-sum game. Naval Research Logistics Quarterly 13 (1966), 11–33

[6] von Stengel, B., Recursive inspection games. IASFOR-Bericht S–9106, Fakultät für Informatik, Armed Forces University Munich (1991)

CHARACTERISING THE SOLUTION OF AN AVERAGE COST MINIMISATION PROBLEM WITH RETURNS TO SCALE MEASURES AND A DECOMPOSITION TECHNIQUE

Michael Tow Cheung
Department of Economics
University of Hong Kong
Pokfulam Rd., Hong Kong

and

David W.K. Yeung
Department of Economics
University of Hong Kong
Pokfulam Rd., Hong Kong

In standard microeconomic theory, the competitive firm operates to minimise average cost in long period equilibrium. Assuming the sufficient conditions for minimisation are satisfied, it is possible to show that the firm's input demand functions exist, and to describe its responses to parametric changes in the prices of inputs (comparative statics). It has, however, not been possible to obtain definite results for own derivatives: e.g., the change in labour services, when its wage changes.

This paper develops properties of two measures of returns to scale, and constructs with their aid a decomposition technique, to express comparative statics derivatives in terms of the slopes elements of a "technically optimal surface". Under certain conditions, the own derivatives may be signed. Suppose the firm has a production function $x = f(\mathbf{v})$, where $\nabla \mathbf{f} > \mathbf{0}$, and contour lines of f are strict convex. Choosing an arbitrary base vector $\mathbf{v}^\circ$, we may express inputs as $\mathbf{v} = \lambda \mathbf{v}^\circ$, and measure the firm's scale of production by the variable ratio $\lambda \geq 0$ along a ray. Writing $x = f(\lambda \mathbf{v}^\circ) = g(\lambda)$, the proportional measure of returns to scale is the elasticity of output with respect to λ along a ray: $\epsilon \equiv (dx/d\lambda)(\lambda/x)$. If ϵ (>/=/<) 1, there is (increasing/constant/decreasing) returns to scale. The marginal measure of returns to scale derives from the acceleration of $x = g(\lambda)$ along a ray: $\theta \equiv d^2x/d\lambda^2$. If θ (>/=/<) 0, there is (increasing/constant/decreasing) returns to scale. The two measures give the same information, when the production function is homogeneous. For an inhomogeneous or general production function, the value of ϵ reveals the extent that output is exhausted when inputs are paid their marginal products, while θ measures its curvature.

The results of this paper are contained in Propositions 1-6, the proofs of which may be found in the full text.

PROPOSITION 1. If $x = f(\mathbf{v})$ is a general production function, and ϵ (>/=/<) 1 at a point $\mathbf{v}$, then $f(\mathbf{v}) - \nabla \mathbf{f} \mathbf{v}$ (</=/>) 0.

PROPOSITION 2. If $x = f(\mathbf{v})$ is a general production function, and θ (>/=/<) 0 at some point $\mathbf{v}$, the Hessian matrix H_f is (positive definite/singular/negative definite).

Consider a competitive market with a large number of firms. As Silberberg (1974, 1990) has shown, in long period equilibrium the representative firm operates to:

$$\text{minimise average cost} = \mathbf{wv}/f(\mathbf{v}), \tag{1}$$

where $\mathbf{w}$ are parametric prices of inputs. Sufficient conditions to problem (1) are:

$$\frac{f(v)w_i - (\sum_{j=1}^{n} w_j v_j) f_i}{[f(v)]^2} = 0, \qquad i = 1,2,\ldots,n. \tag{2}$$

$$J = -\frac{\sum_{j=1}^{n} w_j v_j}{[f(v)]^2} H_f . \tag{3}$$

If (2) has a locally unique and economically unique solution, the firm's long period equilibrium inputs $\mathbf{v}^*$ and output $x^* = f(\mathbf{v}^*)$ are determined. From (2), if the Jacobian determinant:

$$\det(J) = \left[-\frac{\sum_{j=1}^{n} w_j v_j}{[f(v)]^2} \right]^n \det(H_f). \tag{4}$$

$\neq 0$ at $\{\mathbf{v}^*, \mathbf{w}\}$, by the implicit function theorem the C^1 class long period equilibrium input demand functions $v_i = h_i(\mathbf{w})$, $i = 1,2,\ldots,n$ exist in some neighbourhood of the solution. If the second order sufficient condition in (2) holds, this condition would be satisfied ipso facto.

An expansion path is the locus of inputs where total cost $\mathbf{wv}$ is minimised subject to $f(\mathbf{v}) = x$. If ϵ decreases monotonically through 1 along any expansion path, we may visualise a solution

$\{x^*, v^*, w\}$ in which the firm operates in long period equilibrium at the (unique) minimum of a U-shaped average cost curve (Frisch 1965). The following may be established.

PROPOSITION 3. At the solution $\{v^*, x^*, w\}$, $\epsilon = 1$ and $\theta < 0$.

PROPOSITION 4. If $\theta < 0$ at some output x, then $x < x^*$.

Since $\epsilon = 1$ there is product exhaustion, so that profit = 0 in long period equilibrium. With $\theta < 0$, H_f is negative definite. This guarentees that the second order sufficient condition for problem (2) is satisfied (see above). The firm is operating at a "technically optimal scale" by the ϵ measure, but at a "technically post optimal scale" by the θ measure (Frisch op. cit.): i.e., it is not optimising at both margins.

Let us imagine parametric changes in w_j, and plot the locus of the corresponding long period equilibrium inputs $v_i = h_i(w)$, i = 1,2,...,n. By Proposition 3, these points are characterised by the technical optimality condition $\epsilon = 1$, and they lie on the surface $\phi(v) = 0$.

PROPOSITION 5. The slope elements of the $\epsilon = 1$ locus at any point v is:

$$\left.\frac{dv_i}{dv_j}\right|_{\epsilon=1} = \frac{-\sum_{k=1}^{n} v_k f_{kj}}{\sum_{k=1}^{n} v_k f_{ki}} . \tag{5}$$

It is possible to express the slopes of the firm's long period input demand functions in terms of (5). Decompose (2) into:

$$\frac{f_i}{w_i} - \frac{f_j}{w_j} = 0, \; j = 1,2,\ldots,n, \; j \neq i, \tag{6.1}$$

$$f(v) - \sum_{j=1}^{n} f_j v_j = 0. \tag{6.2}$$

The first n-1 equations involve w, while the nth equation does not. We may select an input i, and provisionally treat v_i as a parameter in addition to w. In subsystem (6.1), there are then n-1 equations in n-1 unknowns $\{v_1, v_2, \ldots v_{i-1}, v_{i+1}, \ldots, v_n\}$, and n+1 parameters $\{v_i, w\}$. If a locally unique solution exists and if the n-1 order matrix with jkth element:

$$a_{jk} \equiv (f_{ik}/w_i) - (f_{jk}/w_j), \; j,k = 1,2,\ldots,n, \; j \neq i, \; k \neq i$$

is non-singular at this point, we may obtain the C^1 class functions $v_j = \gamma_j(v_i, w)$, $j = 1,2,\ldots,n$, $j \neq i$. Substituting into (6.2):

$$f(\gamma_1,\gamma_2,\dots,\gamma_{i-1},v_i,\gamma_{i+1},\dots,\gamma_n)$$

$$- f_i(\gamma_1,\gamma_2,\dots,\gamma_{i-1},v_i,\gamma_{i+1},\dots,\gamma_n)v_i$$

$$- \sum_{\substack{j=1\\ j\neq i}}^{n} f_j(\gamma_1,\gamma_2,\dots,\gamma_{i-1},v_i,\gamma_{i+1},\dots,\gamma_n)\gamma_j \equiv \Gamma^i(v_i,w) = 0. \tag{7}$$

(7) defines an implicit function with dependent variable v_i and independent variables **w**. If $\{v_i^{**}, \mathbf{w}\}$ is a locally unique solution to (7) and if: $\partial\Gamma^i/\partial v_i$ =

$$- v_i f_{ii} - \sum_{\substack{k=1\\ k\neq i}}^{n} v_i f_{ik}\frac{\partial\gamma_k}{\partial v_i} - \sum_{\substack{j=1\\ j\neq i}}^{n} \gamma_j f_{ji} - \sum_{\substack{j=1\\ j\neq i}}^{n}\sum_{\substack{k=1\\ k\neq i}}^{n} \gamma_j f_{jk}\frac{\partial\gamma_k}{\partial v_i} \neq 0 \tag{8}$$

at this point, then again by the implicit function theorem the C^1 class function $v_i = \psi_i(\mathbf{w})$ would exist in its neighbourhood. This gives the firm's long period equilibrium demand function for input i. The long period equilibrium demand functions for inputs j, $j \neq i$, are then: $v_j = \gamma_j(v_i,w) = \gamma_j(\psi_i(w),w) \equiv \psi_j(w)$,

PROPOSITION 6. The own derivative $\partial v_i/\partial w_i$ may be expressed as:

$$\frac{\partial v_i}{\partial w_i} = \frac{- \sum_{\substack{k=1\\ k\neq i}}^{n} v_i f_{ik}\frac{\partial\gamma_k}{\partial w_i} - \sum_{\substack{k=1\\ k\neq i}}^{n}\sum_{\substack{j=1\\ j\neq i}}^{n} \gamma_j f_{jk}\frac{\partial\gamma_k}{\partial w_i}}{\sum_{\substack{k=1\\ k\neq i}}^{n} v_i f_{ik}\frac{\partial\gamma_k}{\partial v_i} + v_i f_{ii} + \sum_{\substack{j=1\\ j\neq i}}^{n} \gamma_j f_{ji} + \sum_{\substack{k=1\\ k\neq i}}^{n}\sum_{\substack{j=1\\ j\neq i}}^{n} \gamma_j f_{jk}\frac{\partial\gamma_k}{\partial v_i}}$$

$$= - \sum_{\substack{k=1\\ k\neq i}}^{n} \frac{\phi_k}{\phi_i}\frac{\partial\gamma_k}{\partial w_i} \Big/ \{1 + \sum_{\substack{k=1\\ k\neq i}}^{n} \frac{\phi_k}{\phi_i}\frac{\partial\gamma_k}{\partial v_i}\} \tag{9}$$

We may, with additional assumptions, sign (7). If expansion paths are rising and the $\epsilon = 1$ surface slopes downwards, and if the cross substitution effect of a change in w_i are positive, < 0. The result also obtains if f is homothetic, and n = 2.

References

Frisch, R. Theory of Production. Chicago: Rand McNally, 1965.

Silberberg, E. The Theory of the Firm in Long Run Equilibrium. American Economic Review, LXIV:4, 1974, 734-741.

Silberberg, E. The Structure of Economics. New York: McGraw Hill, 1990.

THE DISTRIBUTION OF CONSUMERS' TASTES AND THE EXISTENCE OF BERTRAND EQUILIBRIA

Egbert Dierker and Konrad Podczeck
Department of Economics
University of Vienna
Dr. Karl Lueger-Ring 1, A-1010 Vienna

We consider a market for an indivisible good of which a typical consumer buys at most one unit. It is assumed that the good is offered by several firms each of which produces and sells one brand. In addition to these brands there is a composite commodity which represents everything else including similar products of higher or lower quality. This commodity is divisible and serves as numéraire.

It suffices to assume that there are three producers and hence three brands indexed by $j \in \{1,2,3\}$. Each firm j reacts to the prices charged by its competitors by adjusting its own price in such a way that its profit is maximized given the prices of its rivals. A *Bertrand equilibrium* is a price vector (p_1^*, p_2^*, p_3^*) such that every p_i^* is an optimal response to p_{-i}^*, i.e. a Nash equilibrium in pure strategies on a market with price competition. Since mixed strategies are ruled out, one would like to know under which conditions the optimal response of a firm is always unique. If it is, then it is given by a continuous function and the existence of a Bertrand equilibrium can be derived from a fixed point argument.

Consider the optimization problem of, say, firm 1. Given the prices $\bar{p}_2$ and $\bar{p}_3$ of its competitors, the demand for brand 1 is a function of p_1 which we denote by F. If unit costs are equal to c, the profit of firm 1 is $(p_1 - c) \cdot F(p_1)$. The first order condition can, for instance, be written as

$$\frac{1}{p_1 - c} = -\frac{F'(p_1)}{F(p_1)} = -(log F(p_1))'.$$

The left hand side is monotonically decreasing w.r.t. p_1. Hence the optimal price is unique if *log* F is a concave function of p_1. Observe that we could also have said that the optimal response of firm 1 is unique if $log\ F$ is a concave function of $\pi_1 = log\ (p_1)$. (To see this, multiply the first order condition as written above by p_1). Prékopa's theorem on logconcave functions and measures will be of central importance.

To obtain the logconcavity of aggregate demand F, we shall make assumptions on the distribution of consumers' tastes. Let w_j^a be consumer a's willingness to pay for brand j. If a's net benefit derived from the consumption of brand j is maximal for $j = 1$ and if, furthermore, a's willingness to pay for brand 1 exceeds the price p_1, then a will choose brand 1. Thus we have to model the joint distribution of (w_1^a, w_2^a, w_3^a). Consider the hypothetical case of pure Bertrand competition, in which the product is homogeneous. Then $w_1^a = w_2^a = w_3^a = b^a$. To model product differentiation we introduce random perturbations d_j which are supposed to summarize statistically all effects of all particular attributes of the individual brands on the consumers. These perturbations could, for instance, act additively, i.e. $w_j = b + d_j$, or they could act multiplicatively as in the Weber-Fechner-law, i.e. $log\ (w_j) = log\ (b) + log\ (d_j)$.

We are not aware of any empirical or theoretical studies that explain the actual shape of the distribution of the willingnesses to pay. However, considering studies of the income distribution one observes that it is the logarithm of the income rather than income itself that is distributed with a logconcave density.

We examine a class of quasiadditions that contains the additive and the multiplicative examples as polar cases. If $f :]0, \infty[\rightarrow I\!R$ is strictly monotone and continuous, then a quasiaddition is defined by $f^{-1}(f(x) + f(y))$ for $x, y > 0$. Results on functional equations suggest that the functions $f_r(x) = \frac{1}{r}(x^r - 1), 0 < r \leq 1$, and their limit $f_o(x) = log\ (x)$ yield a reasonable class of quasiadditions. We use these functions to relate b and d_j to w_j and we are particularly interested in the multiplicative case $r = 0$, i.e. $log\ (w_j) = log\ (b) + log\ (d_j)$.

Assume that prices range within $[c, c + \Delta]$. The upper bound $c + \Delta$ can be viewed as the price of a similar product of a higher quality that everybody prefers to the brands

$j \in \{1,2,3\}$. Let $\bar{p}_2, \bar{p}_3 \in [c, c+\Delta]$ be given. We want to use Prékopa's theorem, which states that logconcave densities give rise to logconcave measures, in order to show that the optimal response of firm 1 to $\bar{p}_2$, $\bar{p}_3$ is unique.

Consumers' tastes are described by $\beta = log\ (b)$ and $\delta_j = log\ (d_j)$, $j = 1,2,3$, if $r = 0$, and by $\beta = \frac{1}{r}(b^r - 1)$ and $\delta_j = \frac{1}{r}(d_j^r - 1), j = 1,2,3$, if $0 < r \leq 1$. However, the clientele of firm 1 at a price p_1 in terms of the characteristics $(\beta, \delta_1, \delta_2, \delta_3)$ will not in general be convex (unless $r = 1$). Hence Prékopa's theorem is not directly applicable. Therefore, we define a coordinate transformation $\delta_1 \mapsto \hat{\delta}_1$, such that the sets of customers of firm 1 in terms of $(\beta, \hat{\delta}_1, \delta_2, \delta_3)$ satisfy the convexity properties that make Prékopa's theorem useful for our purpose. If we assume that the original characteristics, e.g. $(\beta, \delta_1, \delta_2, \delta_3)$, have a logconcave joint density and if, furthermore, the necessary coordinate transformation $\delta_1 \mapsto \hat{\delta}_1$ does not destroy the logconcavity of the density, then the optimal price p_1 is uniquely determined.

To study the effect of the coordinate transformation $\delta_1 \mapsto \hat{\delta}_1$ on the logconcavity of the density, we consider the case in which the untransformed coordinates are stochastically independent. Observe that this does not imply the stochastic independence of the willingnesses w_j to pay, since each w_j is the quasisum of b and d_j. We state conditions that are sufficient for the logconcavity of the transformed density and, therefore, for the uniquess of the optimal response of firm 1.

The assumption that the perturbations $(\delta_1, \delta_2, \delta_3)$ have a logconcave density can best be motivated if these perturbations are i.i.d.. In the case of pure Bertrand competition without product differentiation, $\delta_1 = \delta_2 = \delta_3 = 0$ by definition. If product differentiation is introduced, one still wants to express the idea that the perturbations cluster around 0 and that extreme perturbations are rare. Therefore, assume that the joint density is unimodal. Then it is Schur concave. Schur's inequality implies that the density is log concave if $\delta_1, \delta_2, \delta_3$ are i.i.d.. The concept of Schur concavity can also be used to derive the logconcavity of the density if the δ_j's are stochastically independent without being i.i.d., the underlying principle again being that "more equal perturbations are more likely".

REFERENCES

Caplin, A. and B. Nalebuff (1991): "Aggregation and imperfect competition: On the existence of equilibrium", *Econometrica* 59, 25-95.

Dierker, E. (1991): "Competition for Costumers", to appear in *Equilibrium Theory and Applications,* Cambridge University Press.

Dierker, E. and K. Podczeck (1991): "The distribution of consumers' tastes and the existence of Bertrand equilibria", discussion paper, University of Vienna, in preparation.

Eichhorn, W. (1978): *Functional Equations in Economics,* Addison-Wesley.

Heckman, J. and B. Honoré (1990): "The empirical content of the Roy model", *Econometrica* 58, 1121-1149.

McDonald, J. (1984): "Some generalized functions for size distribution of income", *Econometrica* 52, 647-663.

Prékopa, A. (1973): "On the logarithmic concave measures and functions", *Acta Sci, Math.* 34, 335-343.

HOW TO PLAY A GAME WHEN UTILITIES CHANGE WHILE PLAYING

Jose Luis Ferreira, Itzhak Gilboa
Department of Managerial Economics and Decision Sciences
J.L. Kellogg Graduate School of Management
Northwestern University
Evanston, Illinois 60208
and
Michael Maschler
Department of Mathematics
The Hebrew University Jerusalem

The first game of this kind that appeared in the literature is, perhaps, the story of Odysseus and the sirens. Odysseus wanted to hear their music but knew that if he did, his personality would change and he would be unable to suppress a desire to follow the sirens to his death. The way he (or rather, Homer) solved that dilemma was to take precautions, so that it would be impossible for him to follow the sirens.
In this paper we shall outline a way to generalize the concept of Nash equilibrium to games in which utilities change during the play.

The Model

The model we consider is an n–person game form in extensive form, with perfect recall. An information set of a player will be said to belong to an *agent* of this player. To this game form we add payments at each endpoint — one for each information set encountered on the path from the root to the endpoint. These payments represent the utilities of the various agents along the path. For agents not on the path we may, if we wish, also add utility payments. However, if this does not make sense, because such agents "did not come to existence", we simply leave their payments blank. At any rate, our solution concept will not depend on the payments to agents not along the paths. Thus, when an agent comes to play he has a complete von–Neumann Morgenstern utility function for all endpoints he may encounter, but different agents of a player may have different utilities.

Credible Equilibria

Since our game Γ has perfect recall, we can employ only behavioral strategies. Let $s = (s^1, s^2, ..., s^n)$ be an n-tuple of behavioral strategies in our game. Here. $s^i = (s_{i.1}, s_{i.2}, ..., s_{i.k_i})$ is the strategy of player i, where $s_{i.j}$ is the strategy of agent $i.j$.

Definition 1. A *credible deviation* from s by an agent $i.j_0$, using a set of agents C. is $\acute{s}_C$. where $i.j_0 \in C$, all other members of C are agents of i playing after $i.j_0$. and $\acute{s} := (\acute{s}_C . s_{-C})$ satisfies:

i. Agent $i.j_0$ prefers $\acute{s}$ to s.

ii. Each agent $i.j$ of C, other than $i.j_0$, prefers $\acute{s}$ to $(\acute{s}_{-i.j}, s_{i.j})$.

iii. No agent $i.j$, that comes to play after $i.j_0$ with positive probability under $\acute{s}$. has a credible deviation in the game $\Gamma^{\acute{s}}_{i.j_0}$ resulting from Γ by converting all agents except those that play after $i.j_0$ to chance moves playing $\acute{s}$.

This is a legitimate recursive definition. It yields

Definition 2. Let s an n-tuple of behavioral strategies in an n-person game Γ. Strategy n-tuple s will be called *credible* if no agent has a credible deviation.

Results

That the concept of credible deviation is a generalization of Nash equilibrium follows from the following.

Theorem 1. *If, for each player, all its agents have the same utility function, then s is credible iff it is a Nash equilibrium.*

The following theorem characterizes some of the credible equilibria, and proves that they always exist.

Theorem 2. *Every agent form (trembling hand) perfect equilibrium is credible.*

To generalize the definition of a credible equilibrium to games without perfect recall is an open problem. If this could be done, then the concept would be applicable to other situations in which the requirement of perfect recall does not make sense. One such application is games in which a player (= a decision–making unit) does not have a utility function of its own, but represents several groups, each having its own utility function. For example, the player may be a state, representing farmers, manufacturers, etc.

ON THE EVALUATION OF BUDGET SITUATIONS

Susanne Fuchs-Seliger
Institut für Wirtschaftstheorie und OR
Universität Karlsruhe
Am Schloß Bau IV, D-7500 Karlsruhe

1. ON RANKING SITUATIONS

If we have to decide whether we go to Norway or to Marocco for holidays, then we have to balance the advantages and disadvantages of these countries against each other. Therefore, we have to look for criteria to make a decision.

According to Gärdenfors [2] we can consider a situation A to be better than a situation B, if for all alternatives x of A and for all alternatives y of B we have, x is better than y. This is a very simple form of ranking situations. Formally, we can proceed as follows:

Consider a set X of alternatives. In every choice situation the individual has to decide which of two choice situations $A,B \subseteq 2^X \setminus \{\phi\}$ is the better one or if they are equivalent. The ranking of these situations will usually depend on the individual's preferences on X. Therefore, we assume that the individual has a preference relation R on X. We can rank two situations A,B of X, which are also called budget sets, by the following way:

$$A \succsim_G B :\Longleftrightarrow \forall x \in A, \forall y \in B: xRy.$$

Another version of ranking situations is the following one:

$$A \succsim_M B :\Longleftrightarrow \max(A)\ R\ \max(B),$$

supposed that the maximum of A and B with respect to R exists. An alternative $\bar{x}$ is a maximum (with respect to R) in a set C if there does not exist an $y \in C$ such that $yP\bar{x}$, where P is the asymmetric part of R. When the individual also takes the worst alternative into account, it can for instance rank two budget sets A and B according to the following criterion:

$$A \succsim_e B :\Longleftrightarrow \max(A)\ R\ \max(B) \text{ and } \min(A)\ R\ \min(B).$$

The relations $\succsim_G$, $\succsim_M$, and $\succsim_e$ are simple examples of the individual's way of ranking situations.

2. EXISTENCE CONDITIONS

We will now investigate the question under which conditions a maximum (minimum) of a set A with respect to a given relation R exists, so that the relations $\succeq_M$ and $\succeq_e$ are well defined. An important tool for proving the following theorem is the finite intersection property, which says: If $\{C^i/i\varepsilon I\}$ is a family of compact subsets of the IR^n, and if every finite subcollection of the sets C^i has a nonempty intersection, then the entire collection has a nonempty intersection.

Theorem 1

If R is a complete, transitive and continuous relation on $X \subseteq IR^n$, then $\succeq_e$ is well defined on every family $\mathcal{T}$ of compact subsets of X.

In the following theorem we will give up the assumptions of completeness and transitivity of R, and replace it by a property which is defined by the following way:

For any relation R on X, a finite set $\{x^1,\ldots,x^m\} \subseteq B$ is said to be dominated in B if there exists an element $y\varepsilon B$ such that yRy and yRx^j for all $j=1,\ldots,m$. Let us denote the family of all compact and convex subsets of $X \subseteq IR^n$ by $\mathcal{D}$. We can then establish the following theorem.

Theorem 2

Let R be an upper semicontinuous and convex[1)] relation on $X \subseteq IR^n$. Then the relation $\succeq_M$ is well defined on $\mathcal{D}$ if for all $B\varepsilon\mathcal{D}$, every subset $K \subseteq B$ with $|K| = n+1$ is dominated in B.

We will now turn to properties of relations on 2^X induced by the properties of R.

3. PROPERTIES OF BUDGET PREFERENCES

We can show

Theorem 3

Let R be an upper semicontinuous and antisymmetric relation on $X \subseteq IR^n$, and for every $B\varepsilon\mathcal{T}$ assume that every finite subset A of B is dominated in B. Then

---

1) A relation R on X is convex if for all $x\varepsilon X$, $R(x) = \{y/yRx\}$ is convex.

$\succsim_M$ is complete.

Theorem 4

Assume the conditions of Theorem 3 except of the antisymmetry of R, and let R be transitive. Then $\succsim_M$ is an order, i.e. $\succsim_M$ is complete and transitive.

Theorem 5

Under the conditions of Theorem 4 there exists a linear order $\succsim_L$ on $\mathcal{T}$ such that

$$B^1 \succ_M B^2 \Rightarrow B^1 \succsim_L B^2.$$

The proof of Theorem 5 uses the well-ordering theorem.

The next theorem presents properties of R under which $\succsim_e$ is reflexive and transitive.

Theorem 6

Assume the conditions of Theorem 4. Additionally require that R is lower semicontinuous on X, and that for every $B \in \mathcal{T}$ and for every finite set $\{x^1, \ldots, x^k\} \subseteq B$ there exists $y \in B$ such that yRy and $x^i Ry$ for all $i=1,\ldots,k$. Then the relation $\succsim_e$ is reflexive and transitive.

According to Kannai and Peleg [3] we will call a relation $\succsim$ on $\mathcal{B} \subseteq 2^X \setminus \{\phi\}$ an extension of R if: For all alternatives $a, b \in X$,

$$aRb \Leftrightarrow \{a\} \succsim \{b\} .$$

By application of the well-ordering theorem one can show

Theorem 7

Consider $X \neq \phi$ and a linear order R on X. Then there exists a linear order on $\mathcal{B} \subseteq 2^X \setminus \{\phi\}$ which is an extension of R.

4. A RELATIONSHIP TO RATIONAL CHOICE

In the theory of rational choice we can also introduce preferences on a family of budget sets by means of the choice correspondence. By this notion we mean the following:

Consider a subset $\mathcal{B} \subseteq 2^X$. A map $h: \mathcal{B} \to 2^X$ is called a "choice correspondence" $:\Leftrightarrow \forall B \in \mathcal{B}: h(B) \neq \phi \wedge h(B) \subseteq B$.

Given a relation R on X, we will call a choice correspondence "rational" with respect to R $:\Leftrightarrow \forall B \in \mathcal{B}: h(B) = \{x \mid x \in B \wedge \forall y \in B : xRy\}$.

Based on the individual's choice behaviour we can define a relation on $\mathcal{B}$ by:

$B' \succeq' B :\Leftrightarrow \exists x \in X : x \in h(B) \wedge x \in B'$.

Kannai and Peleg required two postulates for extending a linear order R on X. These postulates are:

(GP) If $A \in 2^X$ is finite and $x \in X \setminus A$, then $A \cup \{x\} \succ A$ if $xR \max (A)$, and $A \succ A \cup \{x\}$ if $\min (A) Rx$.

(M) If $a \in X$, $B, C \in 2^X$, $a \notin B \cup C$ and $B \succ C$, then $\{a\} \cup B \succeq \{a\} \cup C$.

The following theorem shows that the relation $\succeq'$ satisfies condition (M) but not (GP).

<u>Theorem 6</u>

Given a linear order R on X, and let $h: \mathcal{B} \rightarrow 2^X$ be a choice correspondence rational with respect to R. Then $\succeq'$ satisfies (M) but not necessarily (GP).

REFERENCES:

1. Fuchs-Seliger, S.: "An Application of Helly's Theorem to Preference-Generated Choice Correspondences", Int. Econ. Review, 25 (1984), 71-77.

2. Gärdenfors, P.: "On Definition of Manipulation of Social Choice Functions", in "Aggregation and Revelation of Preferences" (J.-J. Laffont, Ed) pp. 29-36, North Holland, Amsterdam, 1979.

3. Kannai, Y. and B. Peleg: "A Note on the Extension of an Order on a Set to the Power Set", J. of Econ. Theory, 32 (1984), 172-175.

THE SHAPLEY-ENTRANCE GAME

HERBERT HAMERS
Tilburg University
P.O. Box 90153, 5000 LE Tilburg
The Netherlands

extended abstract

One story that is told in textbooks to introduce the Shapley value is as follows. The players of the grand coalition enter one by one. When a player enters he will get his marginal contribution to the coalition that is already present. If each order of entrance has the same probability then the Shapley value is the expected payoff to the players.

We study whether the assumption that each order of entrance is equally likely is justified if players choose their entry time strategically. To that end we study the (non-cooperative) Shapley entrance-game (SEG). In this game each player independently selects an entrance time. The payoff of a player is his marginal contribution with regard to the cooperative game (N, v), discounted over time. It is assumed that the discount parameter is the same for each player. The two person SEG, that is discussed here, defines a "silent" game of timing [see Karlin (1959)].

Formally, let (N, v) be a two person cooperative game such that $v\ (1)= \alpha$, $v\ (2)= \beta$ and $v\ (N)=1$ and $\alpha > 0, \beta > 0$ and $\alpha+\beta \leq 1$. Taking (N, v) fixed, the SEG is defined as follows. The set of pure strategies of player i is $S_i = [0, \infty)$ where $t_i \in S_i$ represents the time player i will enter. If (t_1, t_2) is a strategy pair, then the corresponding payoff vector is

$$\pi(t_1, t_2) = \begin{cases} (\alpha\delta^{t_1}, (1-\alpha)\delta^{t_2}) & t_1 < t_2 \\ (\{p\alpha + (1-p)(1-\beta)\}\delta^{t_1}, & \\ \quad \{p(1-\alpha) + (1-p)\beta\}\delta^{t_2}) & t_1 = t_2 \\ ((1-\beta)\delta^{t_1}, \beta\delta^{t_2}) & t_1 > t_2 \end{cases}$$

Hence each player receives his discounted marginal contribution, where $p \in [0, 1]$ is the probability that player 1 has to enter first when the arrival times of both players are identical.

Further we suppose that the discounting parameter satisfies $0 < \delta < 1$. A mixed strategy of a player i is a probability distribution function P_i on $[0, \infty]$.

This model is similar with the models analysed by Hendricks et al. and Baye et al. Hendricks et al. analyzed the continuous War of Attrition, a special class of "noisy" games. In a "noisy" game the entrance time of the follower is equal to the entrance time of the leader, since the follower is informed when the leader enters, contrary to the "silent" game. They showed that there exists a Nash equilibrium (NE) where at least one of the players uses a pure strategy. They also provided conditions that guarenteed the existence of a mixed NE.

Baye et al. analyzed the set of NE of the n-player ($n \geq 3$) first price sealed bid, all pay auction. They gave a full discription of the set of NE in these games.

The main result we derive on the two person SEG is shown in the next theorem.

Theorem 1 *If $\alpha + \beta < 1$ and $\alpha \leq \beta$ then the Shapley-entrance game has a unique Nash Equilibrium given by the strategy- pair :*

$$P_1^*(t) = \begin{cases} \frac{\beta - \beta\delta^t}{(1-\alpha-\beta)\delta^t} & 0 \leq t \leq c \\ 1 & t > c \end{cases}$$

and

$$P_2^*(t) = \begin{cases} \frac{\beta(1-\beta)-\alpha(1-\alpha)\delta^t}{(1-\alpha)(1-\alpha-\beta)\delta^t} & 0 \leq t \leq c \\ 1 & t > c \end{cases}$$

with c such that $\delta^c(1-\alpha) = \beta$. *Moreover, the payoff is given by* $\pi(P_1^*, P_2^*) = \frac{\beta}{1-\alpha}(1-\beta, 1-\alpha)$.

In case $\beta < \alpha$ similar results can be obtained. Interesting is that the payoff of the NE is independently of the discount-parameter. This means that the discount-parameter can only affect the duration of the game but not the equilibrium-payoff of the players. Moreover, the equilibrium-payoff is not equal to the Shapley value of (N, v). This implies that when players can choose their entrance time strategically, they cannot choose an equilibrium strategy that supports the Shapley value.

Clearly, if $\alpha + \beta = 1$ than the Shapley value is the payoff of the unique NE (0,0) of the SEG.

Finally, it is easy to see that the SEG with no discounting does not contain an equilibrium, since both players become "infinite patient".

References:

BAYE M., KOVENOCK D. and VRIES DE C. (1990) The All-pay auction with complete information, *Working Paper: june 1990*

HENDRICKS K. , WEISS A. and WILSON C. (1988) The War of Attrition in continuous time with complete information, *International Economic Review*, **29** 663–680.

KARLIN S. (1959), Mathematical Methods and Theory in Games, Programming and Economics, Volume 2.

SHAPLEY L. (1953), A value for *n* -person games, *Annals of Math Studies* , **28**, 307–317.

HOUSEHOLD PRODUCTION ECONOMIES:
A DUAL APPROACH

Theo Junius
Faculty of Economics, University of Groningen
P.O. Box 800, 9700 AV Groningen
The Netherlands

The purpose of this paper is to reconsider *the theory of household production economies* (*THPE*) by the application of the results of *duality theory*. We derive:

(1) the decomposition into cost minimization and utility maximization;

(2) the conditions for deriving the cost price of household activities;

(3) variants of the so-called Hicks–Slutsky equation.

As an example we illustrate that – by extending *THPE* – the issue of *emancipation* can be studied.

1. On the mathematical background

(α) The Lagrange function Φ of the optimization problem

$$(\mathbf{x}^*,\mathbf{y}^*) := (x_1^*,\ldots,x_k^*,y_1^*,\ldots,y_l^*) =$$

$$\text{argmax}_{(\mathbf{x},\mathbf{y})}\{f(\mathbf{y}) \text{ s.t. } g(\mathbf{x}) = 0,$$

$$h_1(\mathbf{x},\mathbf{y}) = 0,\ldots, h_l(\mathbf{x},\mathbf{y}) = 0\} \tag{1}$$

$$u^* = f(\mathbf{y}^*) \tag{2}$$

$$f\colon \mathsf{R}^l \to \mathsf{R},\ g\colon \mathsf{R}^k \to \mathsf{R},\ h_i\colon \mathsf{R}^{k+l} \to \mathsf{R},\ i = 1,\ldots,k \tag{3}$$

reads

$$\Phi(\mathbf{x},\mathbf{y},\lambda,\gamma_1,\ldots,\gamma_m) = f(\mathbf{y})) - \lambda[g(\mathbf{x}) - \Sigma_i\gamma_i h_i(\mathbf{x},\mathbf{y}] \tag{4}$$

As an example: the l–vector $\mathbf{y}$ may be considered as outputs, the k–vector $\mathbf{x}$ as inputs, the function f as a utility function, the function g as net expenditure on inputs and the functions $h_1,\ldots,h_l$ as transformation functions of inputs into outputs.

The shape of eq. (4) implies that problem (1) can be decomposed into two stages. I.e.

$$\mathbf{x}(\mathbf{y}) = \text{argmin}_{\mathbf{x}}\{g(\mathbf{x}) \text{ s.t. } h_1(\mathbf{x},\mathbf{y}) = 0,\ldots,h_l(\mathbf{x},\mathbf{y}) = 0\} \tag{5}$$

and

$$\mathbf{y}^* = \text{argmax}_{\mathbf{y}}\{f(\mathbf{x}(\mathbf{y}),\mathbf{y}) \text{ s.t. } g(\mathbf{x}(\mathbf{y})) = 0\},$$

$$\mathbf{x}^* = \mathbf{x}(\mathbf{y}^*),\ u^* = f(\mathbf{y}^*) \tag{6}$$

(β) Let $\boldsymbol{\alpha}$ be a vector of given parameters entering the function g, e.g. input prices and income. Then

$$\mathbf{y}^* = \mathbf{y}^*(\boldsymbol{\alpha}),\ \mathbf{x}^* = \mathbf{x}^*(\boldsymbol{\alpha},\mathbf{y}^*(\boldsymbol{\alpha})),\ u^* = f(\mathbf{y}^*(\boldsymbol{\alpha})) \tag{7}$$

Furthermore define $G(\mathbf{y},\boldsymbol{\alpha}) = g(\mathbf{x}(\mathbf{y}),\boldsymbol{\alpha})$ and

$$\bar{\mathbf{y}}(\boldsymbol{\alpha},u) = \text{argmin}_{\mathbf{y}}\{G(\mathbf{y},\boldsymbol{\alpha}) \text{ s.t. } f(\mathbf{y}) = u\} \tag{8}$$

Then the following identities must hold in equilibrium

$$\bar{\mathbf{y}}(\boldsymbol{\alpha},u) = \mathbf{y}^*(\boldsymbol{\alpha}) \tag{9}$$

$$\bar{\mathbf{x}}(\boldsymbol{\alpha},u) = \mathbf{x}(\mathbf{y}^*(\boldsymbol{\alpha},u),u) \tag{10}$$

which can be used for deriving results concerning the effects of perturbations in $\boldsymbol{\alpha}$ (*comparative statics*).

2. On *THPE*

The Lagrange function Φ of the *THPE* model reads

$$\Phi(z_1,\ldots,z_n,x_1,\ldots,x_n,t_1,\ldots,t_n,\lambda,\gamma_1,\ldots,\gamma_n)$$

$$= f(z_1,\ldots,z_n)+\lambda[w(T-\Sigma_i t_i)-\Sigma_i p_i x_i]$$

$$+ \Sigma_i[\gamma_i\{z_i-\phi_i(x_i,t_i)\}] \tag{11}$$

with f given utility function, z_i household good i, x_i market good i, t_i transformation time market good i, T given labor time available for household and non-household activities, ϕ_i given production function, w given wage rate and p_i given price market good i, $i = 1,...,n$. So each market good x_i has to be transformed into a *household good* z_i by the use of *household* time t_i. It is obvious that problem (11) is a particular case of eq. (4). Hence household utility maximization can be viewed as *the decomposition* into n independent conditional cost minimization problems over transformation inputs

$$C_i(p_i,t_i,z_i) = \min_{x_i,t_i}\{p_ix_i+wt_i \text{ s.t. } z_i=\phi_i(x_i,t_i)\} \tag{12}$$

and utility maximization over households goods only

$$V(p_1,...p_n,w) = \max_{z_i}\{f(z_1,...,z_n)$$

$$\text{s.t. } \textstyle\sum_i C_i(p_i,t_i,z_i)=M^*\} \tag{13}$$

With C_i conditional minimum cost of producing z_i, V indirect utility and $M^* = wT$ maximum income available when no household activities will take place.

If in particular each household production function ϕ_i is *homothetic* with respect to inputs, i.e. $\phi_i = \psi_i(\hat{\phi}_i)$, $\hat{\phi}_i$ linear-homogeneous, the budget restriction in (13) reads

$$\textstyle\sum_i c_i(p_i,w)\psi^{-1}(z_i) = M^* \tag{14}$$

with c_i the *unit cost* of producing househuld good i. Problem (11) can then be viewed as 'standard' utility maximization.

For investigating *comparative statics* we define the expenditure function

$$e(p_1,...,p_n,w,U)$$

$$= \min_{z_1,...,z_n}\{\textstyle\sum_i C_i(p_i,w,z_i) \text{ s.t. } f(z_1,...,z_n)=U\} \tag{15}$$

Let ζ_i be the compensated demand for household good i. In equilibrium the following system of identities must hold

$$\zeta_i(p_1,...,p_n,w,V) = z_i(p_1,...,p_n,w,e(p_1,...,p_n,w,V)) \tag{16}$$

This equation is the basis for deriving Hicks–Slutsky equations for the ordinary demand for household goods z_i, market goods x_i and transformation time t_i. For example, we obtain for the total effect of a change in wage rate w on the ordinary demand of transformation time t_i the decomposition

$$dt_i/dw = \partial t_i/\partial w + (\partial C_i^2/\partial z \partial w_i)[\partial \zeta_i/\partial w + (T - \Sigma_j t_j)(\partial z_i/\partial M^*)] \quad (17)$$

i.e. a substitution effect over inputs, a substitution effect over household goods and an income effect with respect to household goods.

3. On emancipation

One way of studying the issue of emancipation is the following restatement of the budget restriction in eq. (11)

$$\Sigma_i p_i x_i = w_f[T_f - (1-\varepsilon)\Sigma_i t_i] + w_m[T_m - \varepsilon \Sigma_i t_i] \quad (18)$$

with w_f given female wage rate (w_m given male wage rate), T_f given female labor time available (T_m given male labor time available) and ε given male participation rate of household activities. If e.g. $\varepsilon = 0$, household activities are only fullfilled by women. From eqs. (12) and (17) it follows that, within the structure of problem (16), the issue of emancipation must be considered as a 'conditional cost problem'.

Hence the comparative statics of changes in male participation with respect to household activities can be analyzed in a standard way by defining the appropriate expenditure function.

Distributive Effects Implied by the Path Dependence of the Nash Bargaining Solution

Marlies Klemisch–Ahlert
Department of Economics
University of Osnabrück
Postfach 4469
W–4500 Osnabrück, Germany

If we think of the division of a certain amount $0 < M$ of a divisible good between two persons, we can compare different types of procedures. The persons may bargain about the division of the whole amount in one step, or they can split the amount into pieces and divide one piece after the other. The last type of procedure may be used if the whole amount is not available at once. Intuitively it seems clear that the result of the bargaining procedure after dividing the whole amount M depends on how the amount is split. This means that the bargaining outcome is path dependent.

The question arises under which conditions statements on the comparison of the final results of those bargaining procedures can be proven. In the following models we apply the Nash bargaining solution to this problem and afterwards we give an outlook on corresponding results for the Kalai–Smorodinsky solution.

Model 1

Person 1 and person 2 have to divide an amount $0 < M$ of a divisible good by bargaining. Person 1 has a linear utility function on the commodity space. After a suitable positive affine transformation the utility function of person 1 is $u_1(y) = y \;\; \forall y \in \mathbb{R}_0^+$. The utility function u_2 of person 2 is strictly increasing and concave. Therefore, u_2 can be represented as a strictly increasing concave transformation of u_1. $u_2(y) = k(u_1(y)) = k(y)$ with $k : \mathbb{R}_0^+ \to \mathbb{R}_0^+$ is twice differentiable with $k(0) = 0$, $k'(z) > 0 \;\; \forall z \in \mathbb{R}_0^+$, and $k''(z) < 0 \;\; \forall z \in \mathbb{R}_0^+$.

Both persons have the initial endowment of 0.

In the first procedure the persons divide M in one step. We receive the bargaining situation (S_M, d^0) with

$$S_M = \{(s_1, s_2) \mid \exists\, (x_1, x_2) \in P_M \text{ with } (0,0) \leq (s_1, s_2) \leq (x_1, x_2)\}$$

and $d^0 = (0, k(0)) = (0,0)$, where

$$P_M = \{(s_1, s_2) \mid \exists\, 0 \leq m \leq M \text{ with } s_1 = m \text{ and } s_2 = k(M - m)\}$$

is the set of Pareto efficient points of the bargaining situation.

Let $F(S_M, d^0) = (m^*, k(M - m^*))$ be the Nash solution of (S_M, d^0). In this solution person 1 receives m^* units of the amount M.

In the first step of the other procedure the two persons divide $0 < L < M$ units of the good. This leads to the bargaining situation (S_L, d^0) with the Nash solution $F(S_L, d^0) = (l^*, k(L - l^*))$ where l^* is the number of units of the good person 1 receives in the first bargaining step. Afterwards the two persons divide the remaining $M - L$ units of the good by bargaining. The status quo of this second bargaining step is the agreement of the first step, $d_L = (u_1(l^*), u_2(L - l^*)) = (l^*, k(L - l^*))$. The set of feasible utility pairs of the second step is

$$T_{M-L} = \{(s_1, s_2) \mid \exists 0 \leq m \leq M \text{ with } l^* \leq s_1 \leq m \text{ and } k(L - l^*) \leq s_2 \leq k(M - m)\}.$$

$F(T_{M-L}, d^L) = (m^{**}, k(M - m^{**}))$ is the Nash solution of the situation (T_{M-L}, d^L) and m^{**} is the total amount of the good person 1 receives after both steps.

We prove the following results:

Lemma 1

$$m^* > l^* \text{ and } M - m^* > L - l^* .$$

Lemma 2

$$\frac{k(L - l^*)}{l^*} > \frac{k(M - m^*)}{m^*} .$$

Theorem 1

$$m^{**} < m^* .$$

The result of Theorem 1 means that in the two–step–procedure person 1 receives a smaller amount than in the one-step-procedure. Person 2, the more risk averse person, prefers the two-step-procedure.

Model 2

We consider the same problem as in Model 1 but we assume that person 1 has an arbitrary utility function u_1 with $u_1'(y) > 0$ and $u_1''(y) < 0 \; \forall y \in \mathbb{R}^+$ and person 2 has a utility function u_2 with $u_2(y) = k(u_1(y))$, where $k : \mathbb{R}_0^+ \to \mathbb{R}_0^+$ is a twice differentiable transformation with $k'(z) > 0$ und $k''(z) < 0 \quad \forall z \in \mathbb{R}^+$. This means that person 2 is more risk averse than person 1.

The Nash solutions $F(S_M, d^0)$, $F(S_L, d^0)$ and $F(T_{M-L}, d^L)$ are defined analogously to Model 1.

We prove the following results under some weak technical requirements on the utility functions.

Lemma 3

$$\frac{u_2'(L-l^*)}{u_1'(l^*)} > \frac{u_2'(M-m^*)}{u_1'(m^*)} \iff m^{**} < m^* .$$

Lemma 3 gives a necessary and sufficient condition for the fact that the more risk averse person 2 prefers the two-step-procedure.

In Lemma 4 we show that if the derivative of k is large enough for small utility values, then for small values of L we have $m^{**} < m^*$.

In this case too, the more risk averse person prefers to bargain in two steps, with a small amount to be divided in the first step.

For the Kalai-Smorodinsky solution we derive conditions on the utility functions of the two persons under which the more risk averse person prefers a split of the bargaining procedure into two steps.

References

Kalai, E. (1985): *Solutions to the Bargaining Problem,* in: Hurwicz, L., Schmeidler, D. and Sonnenschein, H. (eds.): Social Goods and Social Organization, Essays in Memory of Elisha Pazner, C.U.P., Cambridge.

Kalai, E. and Megiddo, N. (1980): *Path Independent Choices,* Econometrica 48, 781–784.

Kalai, E. and Smorodinsky, M. (1975): *Other Solutions to Nash's Bargaining Problem,* Econometrica 43, 513–518.

Kihlstrom, R.E., Roth, A.E. and Schmeidler, D. (1981): *Risk Aversion and Solutions to Nash's Bargaining Problem,* in: Moeschlin, O. and Pallaschke, D. (eds.): Game Theory and Mathematical Economics, North-Holland Publishing Company, Amsterdam.

Nash, J.F. (1950): *The Bargaining Problem,* Econometrica 18, 155–162.

Plott, C.R. (1973): *Path Independence, Rationality and Social Choice,* Econometrica 41, 1075–1091.

Roth, A.E. (1979): *Axiomatic Models of Bargaining,* Springer Verlag, Berlin, Heidelberg.

NEW VERSIONS OF THE MINIMAX THEOREM

Heinz König
Fachbereich Mathematik
Universität des Saarlandes
D-6600 Saarbrücken

In recent years the minimax theorem of John von Neumann has found numerous new extensions, due to Irle [1985], Kindler [1990], Simons [1990][1991] and others, with the aim to remove from the assumptions the last remnants of linear and convex structures, and to install assumptions of more comprehensive kinds instead. The talk wants to present an extension and unification, due to the author in cooperation with Frank Zartmann, of the recent main contributions. The principal results are a *quantitative* theorem in the spirit of the *concave-convexlike* minimax theorem of Ky Fan [1953], and a *topological* theorem in the spirit of the *quasiconcave-convex* minimax theorem of Sion [1958]. A further main contribution is to decompose the minimax relation into independent halfs, such that the minimax theorems quoted above - and hence the bulk of the minimax theorems known so far - appear as unions of one-sided theorems, which then can be combined at will to minimax theorems of mixed types in the spirit of Terkelsen [1972].

Let X and Y be nonvoid sets and $F: X\times Y \to \mathbb{R}$ (one can also consider functions $\to \overline{\mathbb{R}}$ with additional care). We form as usual

$$F_*(X,Y) := \operatorname*{Sup}_{x\in X} \operatorname*{Inf}_{y\in Y} F(x,y) \quad \text{and} \quad F^*(X,Y) := \operatorname*{Inf}_{y\in Y} \operatorname*{Sup}_{x\in X} F(x,y).$$

Then $F_*(X,Y) \leqq F^*(X,Y)$. The function F is defined to fulfill the *minimax* relation (=:MM) iff $F_*(X,Y)=F^*(X,Y)$. The recent minimax theorems can be subdivided into the *quantitative* versions, where the assumptions are quantitative relations between certain formations in terms of F, the *topological* versions, where the assumptions are of pure topological nature, and the versions of *mixed* types.

QUANTITATIVE MINIMAX THEOREMS

The ancestor of the more comprehensive quantitative versions is the result of Ky Fan [1953].

Ky Fan Theorem: Assume that F is concave-convexlike in the sense that

(I) for each $0<\alpha<1$ one has: for any $u,v\in X$ there exists $w\in X$ such that $F(w,y) \geqq (1-\alpha)F(u,y)+\alpha F(v,y)$ $\forall y\in Y$;

(II) for each $0<\beta<1$ one has: for any $u,v\in Y$ there exists $w\in Y$ such that $F(x,w) \leqq (1-\beta)F(x,u)+\beta F(x,v)$ $\forall x\in X$.

Assume in addition that Y carries a compact topology such that $F(x,.)\in LSC(Y)$ (=:lower semicontinuous on Y) $\forall x\in X$. Then F fulfills MM.

In König [1968] the assumptions (I)(II) had been reduced to hold but for *some* $0<\alpha<1$ and $0<\beta<1$, which opened the road for the further development. Irle [1985] and Kindler [1990] did the basic step to pass from convex combinations to wide classes of mean functions. A parallel achievement in different terms was in Simons [1990][1991]. Then König-Zartmann [Preprint] unified all these results in the theorem below, which is in terms of comparison functions of one variable.

For real $\sigma<\tau$ define $M(\sigma\uparrow\tau)$ to consist of the monotone increasing functions $\varphi:\mathbb{R}\to\mathbb{R}$ with $\varphi(t)\geqq t$ $\forall t\in\mathbb{R}$ such that

$$\lim_{n\to\infty} \varphi^{\langle n\rangle}(t) \geqq \tau \text{ for all } t\geqq\sigma,$$

where $\varphi^{\langle n\rangle}$ denotes the nth iterate of the function φ. Likewise for $\tau<\sigma$ define $M(\sigma\downarrow\tau)$. Then the theorem reads as follows.

<u>Quantitative MM Theorem</u>: Assume that F fulfills

(IQ) for any real $\sigma<\tau<\lambda$ there exists $\varphi\in M(\sigma\uparrow\tau)$ such that: for any $u,v\in X$ there exists $w\in X$ with

$$F(w,y) \geqq \left\{\begin{array}{ll} F(u,y)\wedge F(v,y) & \forall y\in Y \\ \varphi\big(F(u,y)\wedge F(v,y)\big) & \forall y\in Y \text{ with } F(u,y)\vee F(v,y)\geqq\lambda \end{array}\right\};$$

(IIQ) for any real $\lambda<\tau<\sigma$ and nonvoid finite $S\subset X$ there exists $\varphi\in M(\sigma\downarrow\tau)$ such that: for any $u,v\in Y$ there exists $w\in Y$ with

$$F(x,w) \leqq \varphi\big(F(x,u)\vee F(x,v)\big) \quad \forall x\in S \text{ with } F(x,u)\wedge F(x,v)\leqq\lambda.$$

Assume in addition that Y carries a compact topology such that $F(x,.)\in LSC(Y)$ $\forall x\in X$. Then F fulfills MM.

TOPOLOGICAL MINIMAX THEOREMS

The ancestor of the topological minimax theorems is the result of Sion [1958].

<u>Sion Theorem</u>: Let X and Y be convex subsets of topological vector spaces such that

(I) $F(.,y)\in USC(X)$ $\forall y\in Y$, and $[F(.,y)\geq\lambda]\subset X$ is convex $\forall y\in Y$ and $\lambda\in\mathbb{R}$;

(II) $F(x,.)\in LSC(Y)$ $\forall x\in X$, and $[F(x,.)\leq\lambda]\subset Y$ is convex $\forall x\in X$ and $\lambda\in\mathbb{R}$.

Assume in addition that Y is compact. Then F fulfills MM.

This is of course not a theorem of topological nature. In search of natural topological assumptions which qualify to replace the convexity assumptions in (I)(II) above, one is led to the conditions that certain kinds of intersections of the level sets in question be connected. This idea occurs as early as in Wu [1959]; more comprehensive versions are due to Hoang Tuy [1974] and others. However, all these results are not in exclusive terms of the above natural connectedness conditions, but have to impose other less natural topological assumptions. Other results circumvent this in terms of additional structure, like the interval spaces in Stachó [1980] and Kindler-Trost [1989]. The first topological minimax theorem with no other assumptions is in König [1991].

<u>Topological MM Theorem</u>: Let X and Y be topological spaces such that

(IT) $F(.,y)\in USC(X)$ $\forall y\in Y$, and for each real $\lambda>F_*(X,Y)$ the intersections of all families of subsets $[F(.,y)\geq\lambda]$ $\forall y\in Y$ are connected;

(IIT) $F(x,.)\in LSC(Y)$ $\forall x\in X$, and for each real $\lambda>F_*(X,Y)$ the intersections of all *nonvoid finite* families of subsets $[F(x,.)\leq\lambda]$ $\forall x\in X$ are connected.

Assume in addition that Y is compact. Then F fulfills MM.

The theorem remains true for all combinations of levels $\geq$ and $>$ with $\leq$ and $<$. Furthermore the two semicontinuity requirements can be replaced by the assumption that $F\in LSC(X\times Y)$.

MINIMAX THEOREMS OF MIXED TYPES

The quantitative and the topological minimax theorems are, at least in their more comprehensive forms, quite far from each other, so that there is not much hope for substantial and transparent theorems which encompass both of them. But there is a remarkable way to combine the two kinds of theorems: Terkelsen [1972] discovered that an assumption (I) of quantitative kind and an assumption (II) of topological kind can combine to produce the MM conclusion. After certain intermediate steps Simons [Preprint] and König-Zartmann [Preprint] independently obtained decompositions of the MM relation which open a systematic way to produce minimax theorems of mixed types. We formulate the latter result, but without the explicit description of (MMI) and (MMII) which is somewhat technical.

Theorem: There are properties (MMI) and (MMII) such that

0) MM implies (MMI)&(MMII), and (MMI)&(MMII) implies MM whenever Y carries a compact topology such that $F(x,.)\in LSC(Y)\ \forall x\in X$;

I) each of the assumptions (IQ) and (IT) implies (MMI);

II) each of the assumptions (IIQ) and (IIT) implies (MMII).

The combination of (IQ) and (IIT) furnishes an extension of Terkelsen [1972], whereas the combination of (IT) and (IIQ) produces a minimax theorem of a new mixed type. Little variations in (MMI) and (MMII) allow to incorporate the variants of the topological assumptions (IT) and (IIT) mentioned above.

REFERENCES

Ky Fan [1953] Minimax Theorems. Proc.Nat.Acad.Sci.USA 39,42-47.

A.Irle [1985] A General Minimax Theorem. Z.Oper.Res.29,229-247.

Jürgen Kindler [1990] On a Minimax Theorem of Terkelsen's. Arch.Math.55,573-583.

J.Kindler and R.Trost [1989] Minimax Theorems for Interval Spaces. Acta Math. Hung.54,39-49.

Heinz König [1968] Über das von Neumannsche Minimax-Theorem. Arch.Math.19,482-487.

Heinz König [1991] A General Minimax Theorem based on Connectedness. Arch.Math.

Heinz König and Frank Zartmann [Preprint] New Versions of the Minimax Theorem.

S.Simons [1990] An Upward-Downward Minimax Theorem. Arch.Math.55,275-279.

Stephen Simons [1991] Minimax Theorems with Staircases. Arch.Math.

S.Simons [Preprint] A Flexible Minimax Theorem.

Maurice Sion [1958] On General Minimax Theorems. Pacific J.Math.8,171-176.

L.L.Stachó [1980] Minimax Theorems beyond Topological Vector Spaces. Acta Sci. Math.42,157-164.

Frode Terkelsen [1972] Some Minimax Theorems. Math.Scand.31,405-413.

Hoang Tuy [1974] On a General Minimax Theorem. Soviet Math.Dokl.15,1689-1693.

Wu Wen-Tsün [1959] A Remark on the Fundamental Theorem in the Theory of Games. Sci.Rec.(N.S.)3,229-233.

SHORT-TERM AND LONG-TERM INTEREST RATES IN A MONETARY MODEL OF A CLOSED ECONOMY

Manfred Krtscha
Institut für Mathematische Stochastik, Universität Karlsruhe
Englerstr.2, D-7500 Karlsruhe 1

In 1976 Dornbusch published a paper on exchange rates which is often quoted. It explains the so-called overshooting of the exchange rate after a shock or an expansion of the nominal money supply. Introducing a long-term interest rate and simplification of Dornbusch's model lead to the following system of equations.

$$\ln D_t = \beta_1 - \beta_2 r_t , \tag{1}$$

$$\ln \frac{M}{p_t} = \alpha_1 - \alpha_2 i_t, \tag{2}$$

$$\frac{\dot{p}_t}{p_t} = \gamma \cdot (\ln D_t - \ln \overline{D}) , \tag{3}$$

where

D_t = real aggregate demand,

$\overline{D}$ = stationary aggregate supply, taken to be fixed,

r_t = long-term interest rate,

i_t = short-term interest rate,

M = nominal money supply,

p_t = price level,

α_1, α_2, β_1, β_2, γ are positive constants. The four variables D_t, r_t, i_t, M of this system depend on time t, and their time paths are allowed to jump, whereas the fifth variable p_t doesn't jump in normal economies. Hence the function $p_t : \mathbb{R} \to \mathbb{R}$ is assumed to be continuous and, for unchanged M ,even differentiable.

Assuming M = constant and $i_t = r_t$, the equations (1), (2), (3) imply the differential equation

$$(\ln^{\cdot\cdot} p_t) = -\gamma \frac{\beta_2}{\alpha_2} (\ln^{\cdot} p_t).$$

Solving this simple differential equation, we obtain the inflation rate

$$\frac{\dot{p}_t}{p_t} = c \cdot e^{-\gamma \frac{\beta_2}{\alpha_2} t} \quad \text{and the price level} \quad p_t = d \cdot \exp\left(-\frac{c\,\alpha_2}{\gamma\,\beta_2} e^{-\gamma \frac{\beta_2}{\alpha_2} t}\right).$$

Being interested in the influence of the expansion of M at time t=0 on the price level, we assume the following situation: $M = M_0$ for $t < 0$ and $M = M_1$ for $t \geq 0$, $p_t = p_0$ for $-1 \leq t < 0$. Then our model implies

$$d = \frac{M_1}{M_0} p_0, \qquad c = \gamma \frac{\beta_2}{\alpha_2} \ln \frac{M_1}{M_0}.$$

This result however didn't satisfy von Kalckreuth, an economist of the university of Mannheim, for he considered an overshooting time path of the price level more natural than a monotonic time path. Therefore, in accordance with Turnovsky, he distinguished between r_t and i_t and assumed perfect foresight, which implies the arbitrage equation

$$r_t = \int_t^{t+\omega} i_\tau \, d\tau \quad \text{or} \quad \dot{r}_t = \frac{1}{\omega}(i_{t+\omega} - i_t), \tag{4}$$

where ω is the average term of long-term credit contracts.

Adding equation (4) to the equations (1), (2), (3) , he could derive the functional differential equation

$$(\dot{\ln} \, p_t) = -\frac{\gamma \beta_2}{\omega \alpha_2}(\ln p_{t+\omega} - \ln p_t). \tag{5}$$

In order to get all solutions of (5), we prove the following theorem.

THEOREM 1:

All solutions of the functional differential equation with advancing argument

$$f'(x) = B \cdot (f(x+\omega) - f(x)) \qquad (x \geq 0) \tag{6}$$

form a vector space with an uncountable basis.

That unexpected result seems to make the second model worthless, but fortunately there exists only one economically interesting solution which can be obtained by the next theorem.

THEOREM 2:

For $\omega > 0$, $a > 1$, $e^{a|B|\omega^2} < a^2|B|\omega^2 + 1$ exists only one solution of the equation (6), where $f(0) = \alpha$, $f'(0) = \beta$, $|f(x)| \leq M \cdot e^{a|B|\omega x}$. This "not exploding" solution has the form

$$f(x) = \frac{\beta}{\lambda} e^{\lambda x} + \alpha - \frac{\beta}{\lambda}, \tag{7}$$

where λ is the suitable real solution of the equation $\lambda^2 + B = B \cdot e^{\lambda \omega}$.

Moreover for negative B one can show that the last equation has only one negative solution λ_1 and, inserting λ_1 in (7), we obtain the only not exploding solution of (6).

What is now the economic meaning of theorem 2 ? First we can say that the addition of the arbitrage equation (4) to the simple model (1), (2), (3) doesn't admit an overshooting, bounded time path of p_t , for the character of the uniquely determined not exploding solution of the functional differential equation (5) is the same as the character of the solution of the simple model. Moreover we can perceive the influence of ω on the adjustment path of the price level by the following theorem.

THEOREM 3:

There exists only one solution of the model (1), (2), (3),(4) with $0 \leq i_t \leq 1$, $M = M_0$ for $t < 0$, $M = M_1$ for $t \geq 0$, $p_t = p_0$ for $-1 \leq t < 0$ .This solution is given by

$$p_t = \frac{M_0}{M_1} p_0 \cdot \exp\left(e^{\lambda t} \cdot \frac{\gamma \beta_2}{\lambda \alpha_2} \cdot \ln \frac{M_0}{M_1}\right),$$

where λ is the only negative solution of the equation

$$\lambda^2 - \frac{\gamma \beta_2}{\omega \alpha_2} = -\frac{\gamma \beta_2}{\omega \alpha_2} \cdot e^{\lambda \omega}.$$

Increasing ω causes decreasing speed of adjustment of the time path of p_t to the new stationary price level, i. e. $|\lambda|$ decreases if ω increases.

Roughly spoken, the effect of long-term credit contracts on the time path of p_t is a delay of the adjustment to the new stationary price level.
This result confirms that the economic model (1), (2), (3), (4) is not unreasonable.

REFERENCES

Dornbusch, R."Expectations and Exchange Rate Dynamics", Journal of Pol. Economics, Volume 84 (1976): 1161 - 1176.

Turnovsky, S. J."Short-term and Long-term Interest Rates in a Monetary Model of a Small Open Economy", Journal of International Economics, Vol. 20 (1986):291 - 311.

ECONOMIES WITH LAND: A GAME THEORETIC APPROACH

J. LEGUT, Wroclaw
J.A.M. POTTERS, Nijmegen
S.H. TIJS, Tilburg/Nijmegen

EXTENDED ABSTRACT

An economy with land consists of a finite set of agents N and a finite measure space $(L, \mathcal{B}, \nu)$. The collection $\mathcal{B}$ is a σ-algebra on L and $\nu: \mathcal{B} \to R_+$ is a finite measure on $\mathcal{B}$. Each agent $i \in N$ has an initial endowment $A_i \subset L$ and a non-negative bounded ν-measurable (utility) function f_i on L. If $C \in \mathcal{B}$ and $i \in N$ then $\int_C f_i d\nu$ denotes agent i's appreciation for the parcel C (cf. Berliant 1982, Dunz 1984, Legut 1990).

If we take a TU-point of view (i.e. if we assume that there is an exogeneous commodity 'money' suited to transfer utilities and $\int_C f_i d\nu$ is the 'monetary' appreciation of agent i for C) it is senseful to define the TU-game $(N, v_{\mathcal{E}})$ by

$$(0.1) \qquad v_{\mathcal{E}}(S) := \sup\{\textstyle\sum_{i\in S} \int_{Y_i} f_i d\nu \mid \{Y_i\}_{i\in S} \text{ is a } \mathcal{B}\text{-partition of } A(S) = \bigcup_{i\in S} A_i\}$$

for all $S \subset N$. To reach the value $v_{\mathcal{E}}(S)$ we must allocate every piece of $\bigcup_{i\in S} A_i$ at the agent of S with the highest appreciation for that parcel. This means that $v_{\mathcal{E}}(S)$ is the maximally attainable social welfare for coalition S.

We call the game $(N, v_{\mathcal{E}})$ the *fair division game* belonging to the economy $\mathcal{E}$ (cf. Legut 1990).

If we take an NTU-point of view (i.e $\int_C f_i d\nu$ is the utility which agent i assigns to parcel C in his personal utility scale, not comparable with the utility scale of other agents) we define an NTU-game $(N, V_{\mathcal{E}})$ by

$$(0.2) \qquad V_{\mathcal{E}}(S) := \text{Compr. Hull}\{(\textstyle\int_{Y_i} f_i d\nu\}_{i\in S} \in R^S \mid (Y_i)_{i\in S} \text{ is a } \mathcal{B}\text{-partition of } A(S)\}$$

for each coalition $S \neq \emptyset$.

In order to place the main result of this paper in the right context we will briefly recall the idea of λ-transfer of an NTU-game. Let (N, V) be an NTU-game and let b be a vector in $R^N_+ \backslash \{0\}$. Then we can associate with the game (N, V) and the vector b a TU-game $(N, t_b(V))$ with values

$$(0.3) \qquad t_b(V)(S) := \max\{(b^S, x) \mid x \in V(S)\}$$

where $b^S \in R^S$ is the projection of b onto R^S and $(.,.)$ denotes the inner product. By the introduction (and acceptation by the agents) of the transfer vector b a trade-off between the utilities of the agents becomes possible and the inner product (b^S, x) is

a measure for the social welfare in the point x with respect to the transfer vector b. In his 1969-paper Shapley uses this idea to *define* the NTU-value of an game as follows: a utility vector $x \in V(N)$ is an element of the NTU-value $\Phi(V)$ if there is a transfer vector b such that $t_b(V)$ is well defined (i.e. the maximum of (b^S, x) exists for all coalitions S) and the Shapley value $\varphi(t_b(V))$ equals the vector $b \star x := (b_i x_i)_{i \in N}$.
In this paper we introduce the concept of competitive equilibrium in a TU-context as well as in a NTU-context. We shall *prove* that a vector of utility levels $x \in V_{\mathcal{E}}(N)$ is attained in an NTU- competitive equilibrium if and only if there is a transfer vector $b > 0$ such that $b \star x$ is an TU-equilibrium payoff in the economy $b \star \mathcal{E}$ (which generates the fair division game $t_b(V_{\mathcal{E}})$). The economy $b \star \mathcal{E}$ has the same initial endowments as the economy $\mathcal{E}$ but utility densities $\{b_i f_i\}_{i \in N}$ instead of $\{f_i\}_{i \in N}$.
Before we can prove this main result we need a careful description of the equilibrium payoffs in the TU-setting. This will be done in section 1. Section 2 gives an idea of the proof of the main result.

1. Fair division games

Let $(L, \mathcal{B})$ be a measurable space and ν a finite measure on $\mathcal{B}$. An *economy with land* $\mathcal{E}$ consists of a finite set of agents N each having an initial endowment $A_i \in \mathcal{B}$ and a utility density f_i, a non-negative ν-measurable bounded function on L. The *fair division game* belonging to $\mathcal{E} = \{N, \{A_i, f_i\}_{i \in N}\}$ is the TU-game $v_{\mathcal{E}}$ defined by (0.1).
Let us introduce the following notation:

$$\bar{f}^S := \bigvee_{i \in S} f_i \qquad \underline{f}^S := \bigwedge_{i \in S} f_i.$$

for all $S \subset N$. The symbols $\bigvee$ and $\bigwedge$ denote the maximum and the minimum of a finite set of functions. Further we define $\bar{f} := \bar{f}^N$ and $\underline{f} := \bigwedge_{i \in N} \bar{f}^{N \setminus i}$. The function $\underline{f}$ has in every point of L the second highest value. With this notation it is immediately clear that for every coalition $S \subset N$:

$$(1.1) \qquad v_{\mathcal{E}}(S) = \int_{A(S)} \bar{f}^S \, d\nu.$$

Further the game $v_{\mathcal{E}}$ has a canonical decomposition $v_{\mathcal{E}} = \sum_{i \in N} v_{\mathcal{E},i}$ where $(N, v_{\mathcal{E},i})$ is defined by

$$(1.2) \qquad v_{\mathcal{E},i}(S) := \begin{cases} \int_{A_i} \bar{f}^S \, d\nu & \text{if } i \in S \\ 0 & \text{if } i \notin S \end{cases}$$

Theorem 1 describes the set of fair division games as a cone generated by the following simple games

$$(1.3) \qquad u_i(S) := \begin{cases} 1 & \text{if } i \in S \\ 0 & \text{if } i \notin S \end{cases} \qquad \text{and} \qquad u^{\star}_{T,i}(S) := \begin{cases} 1 & \text{if } i \in S \text{ and } S \cap T \neq \emptyset \\ 0 & \text{else} \end{cases}.$$

Theorem 1. *A cooperative game (N, v) is a fair division game if and only if the game can be decomposed into a non-negative linear combination of the games of type (1.3).*

Proof: If (N, v) is the fair division game of the economy $\mathcal{E} = \{N, \{A_i, f_i\}_{i \in N}\}$ then it is not difficult to prove that $v = \sum_{i \in N} (\lambda_i u_i + \sum_{T \neq \emptyset, T \subset N \setminus i} \lambda_{T,i} u^{\star}_{T,i})$ with

(1.4) $\lambda_{T,i} := \int_{A_i} (\underline{f}^T - \bar{f}^{N \setminus T})^+ d\nu$ and $\lambda_i := \int_{A_i} f_i d\nu.$

We use the notation $a^+ := \max(a, 0)$. This gives the only-if-part of the proof.
To prove the 'if-part' we show that games of type (1.3) are fair division games and that the set of fair division games is a cone.
Let g be a non-negative C^∞-function on $L := [0, 1]$ with $\int_0^1 g(t) dt = 1$. We assume that all derivatives of g in the points $t = 0$ and $t = 1$ vanish (g is a 'bell-shaped' function). The game $u^{\star}_{T,i}$ is generated by an economy with $A_i = [0, 1], A_j = \emptyset$ for $j \neq i$ and utility densities $f_k = g$ if $k \in T$ and $f_k = 0$ if $k \notin T$. The game u_i is generated by an economy with the same initial endowments and utility densities $f_i = g$ and $f_j = g$ for $j \neq i$.
If (N, v) is the fair division game generated by an economy $\mathcal{E}$ and λ is a non-negative real number then λv is generated by the economy $\lambda \mathcal{E}$ with the same set of agents N and the same initial endowments but with utility densities $\{\lambda f_i\}_{i \in N}$ instead of $\{f_i\}_{i \in N}$.
The sum of two fair division games (N, v) and (N, v') generated by economies $\mathcal{E}$ and $\mathcal{E}'$ is generated by an economy with the following data:

(1.5) $\bar{L} := L \cup L', \bar{\nu}(\bullet) := \nu(\bullet \cap L) + \nu'(\bullet \cap L'), \bar{A}_i := A_i \cup A'_i$ and $\bar{f}_i := \begin{cases} f_i & \text{on } L \\ f'_i & \text{on } L'. \end{cases}$

Hence the set of fair division games contains the cone generated by games of type (1.3). QED

From the special choice of the function g we can infer that every fair division game can be represented by an economy wherein L is an segment of the reals with the Lebesgue measure and the utility densities are C^∞-functions.

In the TU-context we call a pair $(X^\star, g)$ a *price equilibrium* if $X^\star = \{X^\star_i\}_{i \in N}$ is a measurable partition of L, g is a bounded ν-measurable function on L and

(1.6) (Maximality condition) $\int_{X^\star_i} (f_i - g) d\nu = \max \{\int_C (f_i - g) d\nu \mid C \in \mathcal{B}\}.$

If $(X^\star, g)$ is a price equilibrium we call $X^\star$ a *competitive equilibrium* and the vector x with coordinates $x_i = \int_{X^\star_i} (f_i - g) d\nu + \int_{A_i} g \, d\nu$ a *(TU)-equilibrium payoff.*
As we are in a TU-context every agent can balance the difference between selling and purchasing by a transfer of the exogeneously given commodity 'money' and therefore he will, given the price density g, purchase every parcel of land for which his private 'monetary' appreciation is higher than the price, and no other parcels. To describe the set of equilibrium payoffs of an economy $\mathcal{E}$ we introduce an other economy $\hat{\mathcal{E}}$ with the same set of agents and the same initial endowments but with utility densities $\{f_i \vee \underline{f}\}_{i \in N}$ instead of $\{f_i\}_{i \in N}$. Note that every agent in the economy $\hat{\mathcal{E}}$ has in every point of L at least the second highest utility level. It is not difficult to see that $v_{\hat{\mathcal{E}}} \geq v_{\mathcal{E}}$ and that both games give the same values to coalitions with $n := |N|$ or $n - 1$ agents. In particular, the core of $v_{\hat{\mathcal{E}}}$ is a subset of the core of $v_{\mathcal{E}}$.

Theorem 2. *The set of equilibrium payoffs of an economy $\mathcal{E}$ coincides with the core of the game* $(N, v_{\mathcal{E}})$.

The proof of this theorem relies mainly on the fact that the core of $v_{\mathcal{E},i}$ and $v_{\mathcal{E},i}$ are the same, the fact that the core of $v_{\mathcal{E}}$ is the sum of the cores of the games $v_{\mathcal{E},i}$ because of the convexity of these games (Dragan et al. 1989) and the fact that the equilibrium payoffs of $\mathcal{E}$ are the points of the (algebraic) sum of the cores of $v_{\mathcal{E},i}$.

2. NTU-games associated with economies with land.

In this section we lay some restrictions on the economies we consider.

(a) The measure ν is a finite *non-atomic* measure.

(b) At least two players have an initial endowment with positive ν-measure. Otherwise the economy is trivial.

(c) For every pair of agents $i \neq j$ and every real number $\mu \geq 0$ the ν-measure of the set $\{x \in L \mid f_i(x) = \mu f_j(x)\}$ vanishes. This is a kind of transversality condition.

In an economy $\mathcal{E}$ a (NTU-)price equilibrium (X^*, g) must satisfy two conditions

(2.1) Budget constraint: $\int_{X_i^*} g\, d\nu \leq \int_{A_i} g\, d\nu$.

(2.2) Maximality: If $\int_C f_i\, d\nu > \int_{X_i^*} f_i\, d\nu$ then $\int_C g\, d\nu > \int_{A_i} g\, d\nu$.

If (X^*, g) is a price equilibrium we call the vector x with coordinates $x_i := \int_{X_i^*} f_i\, d\nu$ the *equilibrium payoff* belonging to the (price) equilibrium (X^*, g). Note that equilibrium payoffs are points of the set $V_{\mathcal{E}}(N)$ where $V_{\mathcal{E}}$ is the NTU-game defined in (0.2). In fact by a standard argument one can prove that for no coalition S the vector x^S (the projection of x onto R^S is in the interior of $V_{\mathcal{E}}(S)$ i.e. equilibrium payoffs lie in the core of the game $V_{\mathcal{E}}$. The main theorem gives a connection between equilibrium payoffs in the NTU-case and the TU-equilibrium payoffs of section 1.

Theorem 3. *A utility vector $x \in V_{\mathcal{E}}(N)$ is an equilibrium payoff of an economy $\mathcal{E}$ satisfying the conditions (a), (b) and (c), if and only if there is a (transfer) vector $b > 0$ such that $b \star x$ is a TU-equilibrium payoff for the economy $b \star \mathcal{E}$.*

References.

Berliant, M. (1982). "A general equilibrium model of an economy with land", PhD. Thesis University of California, Berkeley.

Dragan, I., Potters, J. A. M. and S. H. Tijs (1989). "Superadditivity for solutions of coalitional games", *Libertas Mathematica* **9,** 101–110.

Dunz, K. (1984). "Some results of economies with land", PhD. Thesis University of California, Berkeley.

Legut, J. (1990). "On totally balanced games arising from cooperation in fair division," *Games and Economic Behavior* **2,** 47–60.

Shapley, L. S. (1969). "Utility comparison and the theory of games", *La décision* **2,** 251–263.

Regression Analysis of Cooperative Payoff Divisions - A Contribution to Experimental Economics

Ulrike Leopold-Wildburger
University of Graz, A-8010 Graz, Austria

1. Introduction

The experiment presented in this paper examines the influence of varying grand coalition in 3-person games in characteristic function form, which differ only in one respect, namely concerning the rewards for the subjects who run the experiment. The game was run 108 times. 12 independent groups of 9 subjects played each of nine games once. Within the first half of the experiment the subjects received substantial monetary rewards (case I).

Within the second half the subjects did not receive any reward (case II). Another paper [Leopold-Wildburger (1991)] refers in more details to the first part of the experiment.

2. Games played

Briefly described, an n-person game in characteristic function form is defined by a pair (N,v), where $N = \{1,2,...,n\}$ is the set of players and v is a real valued function on the set of coalitions $P(N) = \{S: S \subseteq N\}$. The possible subsets of players are called coalitions. The payoff amount which is assigned to a coalition can be distributed among the players of the coalition in various ways, which way eventually will be chosen is a matter of bargaining.

In this study we shall be concerned only with 3-person games with players 1, 2 and 3.

In the game played in the experiment we always have:

(1) $$v(\{1\}) = v(\{2\}) = v(\{3\}) = 0,$$

(2) $$v(\{1,2\}) = a = 80 ,$$

(3) $$v(\{1,3\}) = b = 60 ,$$

(4) $$v(\{2,3\}) = c = 40 .$$

The value $v(\{1,2,3\})$ of the grand coalition is also denoted by g. This value varies in steps of 5 from 80 to 120:

(5) $$g = 80, 85, ... , 120$$

The games have been selected with the intention to study the influence of varying g with everything else kept constant and the influence of monetary rewards (case I vs. case II).

3. Procedure

The procedure permitted free and unrestricted face to face communication. When a group of players had formed a coalition and when they had agreed upon the payoff distribution they had to announce this to their referee.

Agreements were takes as final if they had been stable for 10 minutes. Within this time an agreement could be nullified by a unilateral decision of one of the members of the coalition. Bargaining times were unrestricted.

The following interesting observation can be drawn from the proceedings: For games with $g > 90$ all players tend clearly toward the grand coalition, yet they try to find out how well they can do on the basis of their position in the small coalition. Figure 1 shows the final payoff divisions.

4. Theoretical solutions

The nucleolus [Schmeidler (1969)] for our 3-person game with non-negative quotas can be described as that payoff division which adds to the quota the evenly divided surplus of the grand coalition over the sum of the quotas among the players.

Let (y_1, y_2, y_3) be the nucleolus for one of the nine games. Then we have

(6) $$y_i = q_i + (g - q_1 - q_2 - q_3)/3 ,$$

(7) $$y_i = q_i + (g - 90)/3.$$

This yields in our case

(8) $$(y_1, y_2, y_3) = (g/3 + 20, g/3, g/3 - 20) .$$

For the games examined here the nucleolus is equivalent to the kernel.

For games with $2g < a+b+c$ the nucleolus/kernel is identical to the bargaining set for the grand coalition [Aumann and Maschler (1964)]. For three-person games the bargaining set for the grand coalition coincides with the core, if the core exists.

	g	pl 1 (case I)	pl 2 (case I)	pl 3 (case I)	pl 1 (case II)	pl 2 (case II)	pl 3 (case II)
1	120	57	41	22	57	41	22
2	120	40	40	40	40	40	40
3	120	40	40	40	40	40	40
4	120	40	40	40	40	40	40
5	120	41	40	39	41	40	39
6	120	41	39	0	41	39	0
7	115	60	36	19	60	36	19
8	115	38	39	38	38	39	38
9	115	0	20	20	0	20	20
10	115	38	38	39	38	38	39
11	115	52	27	36	52	27	36
12	115	45	40	30	45	40	30
13	110	50	36	24	50	36	24
14	110	38	36	36	38	36	36
15	110	40	38	32	40	38	32
16	110	55	35	20	55	35	20
17	110	40	40	30	40	40	30
18	110	37	37	36	37	37	36
19	105	49	34	22	49	34	22
20	105	41	39	25	41	39	25
21	105	40	35	30	40	35	30
22	105	40	35	30	40	35	30
23	105	35	35	35	35	35	35
24	105	35	35	35	35	35	35
25	100	45	40	15	45	40	15
26	100	33	33	34	33	33	34
27	100	30	0	30	30	0	30
28	100	40	30	30	40	30	30
29	100	38	38	24	38	38	24
30	100	34	33	33	34	33	33
31	95	43	33	19	43	33	19
32	95	32	32	31	32	32	31
33	95	40	40	15	40	40	15
34	95	35	30	30	35	30	30
35	95	32	32	31	32	32	31
36	95	0	22	18	50	22	18
37	90	55	20	15	55	20	15
38	90	50	30	0	50	30	0
39	90	35	35	20	35	35	20
40	90	30	30	30	30	30	30
41	90	31	30	29	31	30	29
42	90	47	24	19	47	24	19
43	85	50	30	5	50	30	5
44	85	29	28	28	29	28	28
45	85	40	40	5	40	40	5
46	85	43	32	10	43	32	10
47	85	35	35	15	35	35	15
48	85	32	27	26	32	27	26
49	80	35	25	20	35	25	20
50	80	30	26	24	30	26	24
51	80	45	35	0	45	35	0
52	80	33	30	17	33	30	17
53	80	40	40	0	40	40	0
54	80	40	30	10	40	30	10

Fig. 1: Representation of the final payoffs for the 108 games for the case with monetary rewards (case I) and without monetary rewards (case II)

Let (s_1, s_2, s_3) be the Shapley value of one of the nine games [Shapley (1953)]. The Shapley value s_i of player i can be described as i's expected mean contribution $v(C) - v(C\setminus\{i\})$ in a process where one player after the other enters C in arbitrary sequence until finally the grand coalition is formed. In our case for three-person games there are just 6 sequences to consider and the computation yields

(9) $$(s_1, s_2, s_3) = (g/3 + 10, g/3, g/3 - 10).$$

The payoff division vector

(10) $$(e_1, e_2, e_3) = (g/3, g/3, g/3)$$

is called the even split.

These concepts have been selected since they provide unique point predictions when the grand coalition forms.

5. Final payoff divisions and regression analysis

In this section a regression analysis of the bargaining results will be presented as a descriptive model.

A traditional linear regression (OLS) of the payoffs

(11) $$x_i = b_o^i + b_1^i g \quad \text{for } i = 1,2,3 ,$$

obtained for players i = 1,2 and 3, respectively, on g under the constraint

(12) $$x_1 + x_2 + x_3 = g ,$$

is done for both cases of the experiment.

The regression analysis yields for case I for N = 52 (i.e. excluding the two cases where player 3 got (nearly) nothing the following result:

(13) $$x_1 = 12.245 + 0.365g$$

(14) $$x_2 = 2.698 + 0.306g$$

(15) $$x_3 = -14.954 + 0.329g .$$

For case II: (N = 48, all cases where the grand coalition was formed)

(16) $$x_1 = 17.354 + 0.229g$$

(17) $$x_2 = 6.8 + 0.271g$$

(18) $$x_3 = 24.154 + 0.5g .$$

In both cases, however, the means respectively the medians of the six games perform even better than the original data.

6. Statistical tests

The values of the test statistic T of the slope b_1^i in the linear regression model also indicates a good fit. A rather small test level a = 0.0001 can be choosen for both cases.

For case I it is reasonable to represent the central tendency of the payoff division in the grand coalition by a convex linear combination of the nucleolus kernel and the even split:

(19) $x_1 = (1-\gamma)g/3 + (\gamma)(g/3+20) = g/3 + 20\gamma$

(20) $x_2 = (1-\gamma)g/3 + (\gamma)g/3 = g/3$

(21) $x_3 = (1-\gamma)g/3 + (\gamma)(g/3-20) = g/3 - 20\gamma.$

The best fit is obtained by approximately $\gamma = 0.748$.

Such a convex linear combination can be supported as a good predictor of the final outcomes.

For case II we have the following remarkable facts:
Player 2 behaves in a way very similar to case I, he receives the same average payoffs, the most remarkable difference between the two cases refers to the payoffs of player 1 resp. player 3 whereas player 1 gives part of his payoff to player 3 (see fig. 2).
The protocols convey the impression that the subjects tried to look for a compromise between obvious ordinal power comparisons and equitable shares. Of course this result may be due to the special structure of the games underlying the face to face experiment. Nevertheless, it is interesting that the kernel/nucleolus overestimates the inequality of the three players payoff, whereas the Shapley value underestimates it in the case with monetary rewards, whereas in the case without monetary rewards accumulation points near the kernel/nucleolus are good explanations for small g, and equal payoff for larger g.

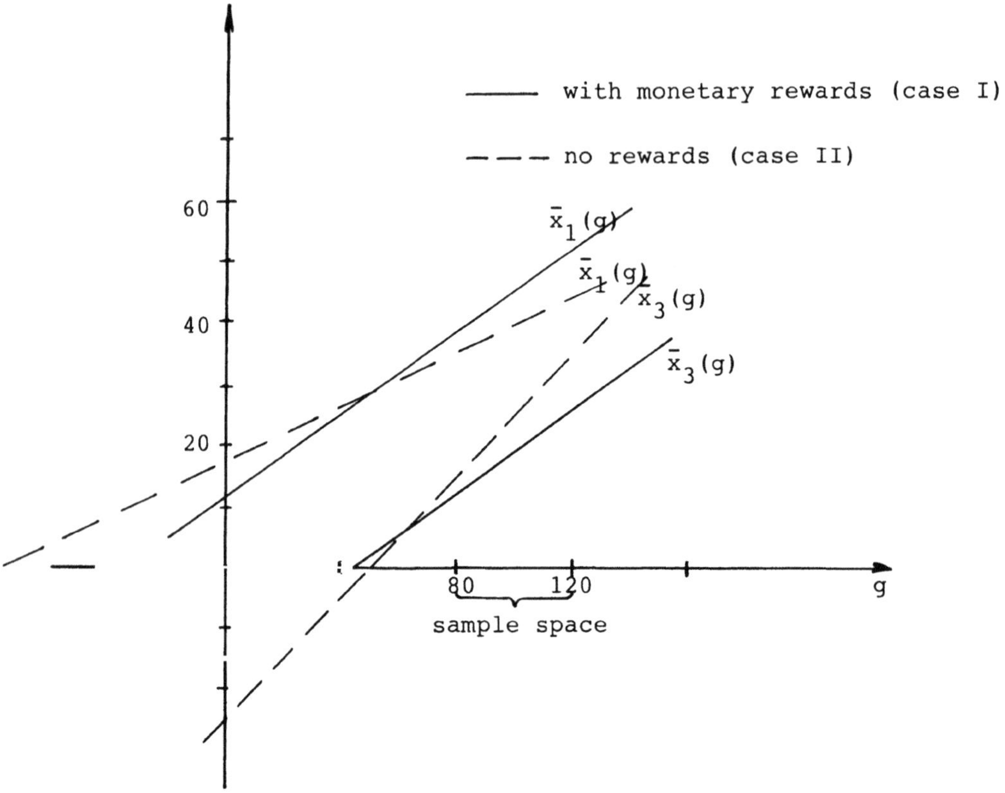

Fig. 2: Payoffs for player 1 and player 3 for both cases.

References:

Aumann, R.J. and M.Maschler, 1964, The bargaining set for cooperative games, in: M.Dresher, L.S.Shapley and A.W.Tucker, eds., Advances in game theory (Princeton, NJ).

Leopold-Wildburger, U., Payoff divisions on coalition formation in a three-person characteristic function experiment, JEBO 1991 (to appear).

Schmeidler, D., 1969, The nucleolus of a characteristic function game. Siam Journal of Applied Mathematics 17, 1163-1170.

Selten, R., 1978, The equity principle in economic behavior, in: W.Gottinger and W.Leinfellner, eds., Decision theory and social ethics, issues in social choice (Dordrecht), 289-301.

Selten, R., 1985, Equity and coalition bargaining in experimental 3-person-games, Working Paper No. 154 (University of Bonn).

Shapley, L.S., 1953, A value for n-person-games. Annals of Mathematics Studies 52, 307-317.

AN ESTIMATE AND DISCUSSION ABOUT THE IMPROVEMENT OF LABOUR FORCE QUALITY FOR INDUSTRY OUTPUT CONTRIBUTION IN QINGDAO

Haohao Li, Shuxia Li. Keren Sun
Department of Management Science
Ocean University of Qingdao
Qingdao (266003), P.R. of China

Consider the Cobb–Douglas production function on the assumption of constant returns to scale

$$Y = A\,e^{bt}\,L^{1-\beta}\,K^{\beta} \tag{1}$$

we can calculate the proportion of outputs increase depending on composite technical progress:

$$k_1 = \frac{b}{\dfrac{\Delta Y}{Y}} \tag{2}$$

the proportion of outputs increase depending on labour force:

$$k_2 = \frac{(1-\beta)\dfrac{\Delta L}{L}}{\dfrac{\Delta Y}{Y}} \tag{3}$$

the proportion of outputs increase depending on fixed assets:

$$k_3 = \frac{\beta\dfrac{\Delta K}{K}}{\dfrac{\Delta Y}{Y}}. \tag{4}$$

It is impossible to extract directly the factor of the improvement of the labour force quality which effects the proportion of output growth. Therefore, we adopt an indirect method. Suppose, we take a worker of scale 1 as a standard labour force, then letting the total amount of wages in a sector divide by the wage of scale 1 worker, the result is the quantity of the standard labour forces in that sector. Generally speaking, under such a definition the quantity of standard labour forces in a sector should be larger than that of actual labour forces.

Let's the formula (1) into

$$Y = A'\,e^{b't}\,L'^{\,1-\beta'}\,K^{\beta'} \tag{5}$$

where L' is the standard labour forces at time t, and b' is the rate of technical progress. β' and $1-\beta'$ are output–elasticity coefficients of the fixed assets and the standard labour force. In general, under such circumstances $b' < b$, $\beta' > \beta$ and $0 < \beta, \beta' < 1$.

We can also calculate under such being the case the proportion of outputs increase depending on composite technical progress:

$$k_1' = \frac{b'}{\frac{\Delta Y}{Y}} \tag{6}$$

the proportion of outputs increase depending on standard labour force:

$$k_2' = \frac{(1-\beta')\frac{\Delta L}{L}}{\frac{\Delta Y}{Y}} \tag{7}$$

the proportion of outputs increase depending on fixed assets:

$$k_3' = \frac{\beta' \frac{\Delta K}{K}}{\frac{\Delta Y}{Y}}. \tag{8}$$

In the latter consideration, however, the factor of the improvement of the labour force quality (the part of composite technical progress) has already been transfered into the investment of the standard labour force. Therefore, $k_1 > k_1'$. While $\bar{k}$, the proportion of outputs increase depending on the improvement of labour force can be estimated by the following formula:

$$\bar{k} = \frac{(b-b') + (\beta' - \beta)\frac{\Delta K}{K}}{\frac{\Delta Y}{Y}}. \tag{9}$$

When estimating the k, we do not take the variations between k_2 and k_2' into consideration. This is because at present the wage differences in China among different technical ranks of workers are not so noticeable. Besides, they have an equalitarian tendency. If in the formula (9) the factor of variation between k_2 and k_2' is to be introduced, there might occur great interference, as well have as other effects. Based on the above mentioned situations, we deem that our estimate on $\bar{k}$ will be a bit conservative as compared to the real facts.

According to the above thought, we make an estimate through calculations on the improvement of labour force quality in the stateowned enterprises of Qingdao (one of the 14 China's coastal open cities), which makes effects on the proportion of outputs increase.

Using regression analysis, we have obtained from 1951 to 1988 the Cobb–Douglas production function which corresponds to (1)

$$Y = 0.702\, e^{0.0372t}\, L^{0.499}\, K^{0.501} \tag{10}$$

and the Cobb–Douglas production function agreeable with (5)

$$Y = 1.145\, e^{0.0205t}\, L'^{\,0.252}\, K^{0.748}. \tag{11}$$

Therefore, we have $b = 0.0372$, $b' = 0.0205$, $\beta = 0.501$, $\beta' = 0.748$. Using statistical data, we have made estimate as well as calculations that the improvement of labour force quality had effected k, the proportion of industrial output of Qingdao, during the 1983–1988 fiscal years. The results are given in table 1.

Table 1

Year	k
1983	0.394
1984	0.315
1985	0.262
1986	0.359
1987	0.216
1988	0.182

In relation to the above mentioned results, estimates and calculations we have some discussions. First of all, it can be concluded that from 1983 to 1988, with the exception in 1986 (because the wage adjustment in enterprises and the area adjustment of wage scales from Rank 5 to Rank 6 were carried out, which as a result, brought a rise of total wages), the improvement of labour force quality had gradually decreased in proportion of industrial output in Qingdao. During this time industrial increase went up at a high speed in Qingdao. The annual increase rate at 1980 constant prices for example reached 19.6 %. But such an increase became more and more dependent on extensively expanded reproduction. It can be seen from the increase of original value of fixed assets (annual increase rates: 1977–82: 9.5 %; 1983–88: 14.9 %). Since the mid–eighties the staff and workers' training has gradually slowed down, resulting in a sluggish increase of staff and workers' quality in municipality. These factors have led to gradual decrease proportion of labour force quality enhancement in giving effective municipal industrial output.

References

Abramovitz, M. (1989): Thinking About Growth, Cambridge Univ. Press.
Black, J. (1962): The Technical Progress Function and the Production Function, Economica, 29.
Denison, E.F. (1962): The Sources of Economic Growth in the United States and Alternatives Before Us, New York.
Denison, E.F. and Chung, W.K. (1976): How Japan's Economy Grew So Fast, Brookings Institution, Washington D.C.
Eltis, W.A. (1973): Growth and Distribution, Macmillan, London.
Han, Z.L. (1990): A Study on the Economic Benifit of Educational Investment in China, Educational Research, No. 1.
Hemmer, H.R. u.a. (1984): Die Bedeutung menschlicher Ressourcen fr den Entwicklungsprozess, Weltforum Verlag, Köln.
Li, H.H. (1989): Perspektiven der Hochschulplanung in der Volksrepublik China, Schultz–Kirchner Verlag, Idstein.
Lindbeck, A. (1983): The Recent Slow–down of Productivity Growth, Economic Journal, 93.
Pascharopoulos, G. (1987): Economics of Education, Research and studies, Pergamon Press, Oxford.
Scott, M.Fg. (1989): A new View of Economic Growth, Oxford Univ. Press.
Schultz, T.W. (1963): The Economic Value of Education, Columbia Univ. Press, New York.
Solow, R.M. (1970): Growth Theory, Clarendon Press, Oxford.
Statistical Bureau of Qingdao: Statistical Yearbook of Qingdao 1984, 1985, 1986, 1987, 1988, 1989.
Strumiling, S.G. (1924): Die Bedeutung der Volksbildung fr die Volkswirtschaft, in: Strumiling, konomische Schriften 1919–1973, Band 1: Sozialismus und Planung, Berlin 1977.
Swan, T.W. (1956): Economic Growth and Capital Accumulation, Economic Record, 32.
Wang, S.M. (1989): An Introduction to Economics of Education, Beijing Normal Univ. Press 9.

ON THE ROLE OF FINANCIAL FACTORS IN THE BUSINESS CYCLE - A COMPARATIVE DYNAMIC ANALYSIS -

Thomas Lux
Department of Economics, University of Würzburg
Sanderring 2, D-87 Würzburg, Germany

In the light of recent attempts to include financial variables into Keynesian models of the business cycle we are interested here in carrying out a comparative dynamic analysis of business cycle models with respect to these factors. The main question to be examined will be: In what way will the amplitude of a cycle change if one takes into consideration additional features of the financial side of the economy, or: how does a change concerning financial variables effect the amplitude of the cycle?
In order to isolate the effects in question we pick out two recent studies (Semmler 1987, Jarsulic 1989) that incorporate an explanation of business cycles from the real side and add several financial ingredients.

Methods

The mathematical method applied for these comparative dynamics is the so-called method of averaging for oscillator differential equations in R^2 which dates back to the Russian mathematicians Krylov and Bogoliubov (1947) but has been applied to economic problems only very recently by Chiarella (1990). For *small non-linearities* this method allows to study the behavior of two-dimensional systems by the investigation of a proxy for their amplitude (ϕ), where ϕ is the "average" of the Euclidian distances on the interval $[0,2\pi]$. We may assume that such small non-linearities prevail in economic applications, i.e. there are no sudden, strong changes in the behavior of economic agents.

Results

Semmler's profit-accumulation (p,k) dynamics is formally very similar to that of the Kaldor-Chang/Smyth model (profits replacing income) and limit cycles can be analyzed in a similar way. This theory of an interaction of accumulation and profit rates generating endogenous cycles is modified by several arguments stemming from the financial side of the economy in Semmler (1987). Most interestingly, the role of debt payment commitments is measured by a function h which is either $h_1 = -\max[0, vPK^2]$ or $h_2 = \min[0, vPK^2]$, or even both h_1 and h_2 are effective. $h_1(\cdot)$ is thought of as measuring the negative impact of debt payment commitments in expansionary and $h_2(\cdot)$ in contractionary periods. Semmler's simulation studies show that $h_1(\cdot)$ has stabilizing and $h_2(.)$ destabilizing effects (P,K: deviations from equilibrium values). The formal investigation confirms that these results remain valid for arbitrary parameter values. Therefore the increase of debt payment in the expansion dampens the cycle whereas the same effect aggravates fluctuations if it appears in recessions.

As an additional result we show that the limit cycle may be unstable if only h_2 is valid. In this case it separates the basin of attraction of the equilibrium (p^*, k^*) from the unstable outer region. This last scenario may be identified with the view of the debt-deflation-mechanism described by Fisher (1933). A further interesting result is that the effects of both $h_1(\cdot)$ and $h_2(\cdot)$ cancel out with respect to ϕ, i. e. the mean distance of all points on the cycle from equilibrium is the same as before.

Jarsulic's concern is mainly to introduce endogeneity of credit supply into a business cycle model of the accelerator type. He seems to suggest that this endogeneity is the cause of fluctuations in his model where the real side of the economy is described by an adjustment process of the actual growth rate of the economy towards the desired rate of accumulation and a interest rate dynamics is derived from the equilibrium condition on the credit market. The formal analysis, however, shows that endogenous credit is not responsible for the emergence of a cycle. There would also be oscillations in the case of a steady growth of loanable funds. They are mainly caused by a strong accelerator coefficient and the existence of a floor for capacity growth. On the other hand the comparative dynamics show that increased flexibility of endogenous credit as well as expansive monetary policies lead to an aggravation of the business cycle. The explanation is that increased flexibility of supply leads to a comparatively less significiant rise of the interest rate in the upswing of the cycle thus leading to a later upper turning point of the growth rate.

References:

Chiarella, C., 1990, The Elements of a Nonlinear Theory of Economic Dynamics (Lecture Notes in Economics and Mathematical Systems, Vol. 343, Springer, Berlin)

Fisher, I., 1933, The Debt-Deflation Theory of Great Depressions, Econometrica 1, pp. 337 - 357

Jarsulic, M., 1989, Endogenous Credit and Endogenous Business Cycles, Journal of Post-Keynesian Economics 12, pp. 27 - 48

Krylov, N. M. and Bogoliubov, N. N., 1947, Introduction to Nonlinear Mechanics (University Press, Princeton)

Semmler, W., 1987, A Macroeconomic Limit Cycle with Financial Perturbations, Journal of Economic Behavior and Organization 8, pp. 469 - 495

Impatience, Risk Aversion and the Optimal Relationship Between Consumption and Wealth

H. Molana
Department of Economics and Management
University of Dundee
Dundee DD1 4HN
Scotland, U.K.

The problem of determining the optimal consumption/saving strategy has been studied by a number of authors. These studies usually conclude that: (i) the level of consumption is determined by current nonhuman wealth and the present value of human wealth, and (ii) the rate of change of consumption depends on the real interest rate and the subjective rate of time preference. The differences between these studies are due to their assumptions concerning the degree of uncertainty, attitude towards risk and the formation of expectations; these factors affect the shape of the functional forms in (i) and (ii) above. This paper concentrates on the relationship between consumption and nonhuman wealth and demonstrates how the shape of such a relationship is affected by an agent's degree of impatience and its attitude towards risk. To keep the analysis simple, it shall be assumed that the real labour income and interest rate remain constant and that, at any time t, the typical agent wishes to maximise a separable utility function,

$$\Sigma_{i=o}^{\infty}\delta^{-i}\ U(C_{t+i}) \tag{1}$$

subject to the intertemporal budget constraint

$$W_{t+i+1} = r(W_{t+i} + Y - C_{t+i}),\quad i\geq 0 \tag{2}$$

where U(.) is the instantaneous utility function, Y is the real labour income, W is the beginning of period real nonhuman wealth invested as a riskless asset with the real rate of return (r-1), C is real consumption and (δ-1) is the subjective rate of time preference. It is assumed that $U'>0$ and $U''<0$. The first order conditions imply the following relationship between current and future marginal utilities

$$U'(C_{t+i})] = (\delta/r)^{i}\ U'(C_t),\quad i>0 \tag{3}$$

Thus, in general, consumption will increase (decrease) if $r>\delta$ ($r<\delta$), and remain constant when $r=\delta$. The relationship between C_t and W_t can be derived as follows. First, from (2) we can derive the life time budget constraint,

$$\Sigma_{i=o}^{\infty}r^{-i}\ C_{t+i} = W_t + [r/(r-1)]Y \tag{4}$$

Next, from (3) and the specific U(.) that is assumed we can determine C_{t+i} in terms of C_t, which can be substituted in (4) and solved to obtain the required relationship. The interesting observation is that for all popular functional forms that are usually used to characterise U(.), namely

$$U(X) = \begin{cases} k - \tfrac{1}{2}\beta(X - \alpha)^2, & k>0,\ \beta>0,\ \alpha>0 \quad (5.1) \\ k + [\beta/(1-\sigma)]X^{1-\sigma}, & k>0,\ \beta>0,\ \sigma>0,\ \sigma\neq 1 \quad (5.2) \\ k + \beta\log(X), & k>0,\ \beta>0 \quad (5.3) \\ k - (\beta/\sigma)\exp(-\sigma X), & k>0,\ \beta>0,\ \sigma>0 \quad (5.4) \end{cases}$$

C happens to be positively and linearly related to W. This outcome, however, is not entirely satisfactory and excludes a concave or a convex relationship between C and W, which are more interesting possibilities. The main point made in this paper is that by modifying the utility function in (5.4) above one may obtain a relationship between C and W which displays variable curvature. The utility function is

$$U(C_{t+i}) = k \pm \alpha^i C_{t+i} - (\beta/\sigma)\exp(-\sigma C_{t+i}) \qquad (6)$$

where k, α, β and σ are positive coefficients chosen to ensure a large $U'(0)$ and negative U''. It can be easily seen that the role of α is crucial in determining the risk attitude. In fact, the parameters may be chosen so as to satisfy Arrow's risk criteria. The result of using (6) is that, unless $\delta=r$, one may obtain a convex or a concave relationship between C and W (when $\delta=r$ the relationship is independent of the other parameters and C remains constant. This can then be used to check the plausibility of the theoretical relationship in the light of the degree of impatience (size of δ relative to r) and the risk attitude (sizes of α, β and σ).

In conclusion, the shape of the relationship between consumption and nonhuman wealth may be linear, concave or convex. It is nevertheless interesting to note that the attitude towards risk is not the only determinant of the shape of the relationship between consumption and wealth; the magnitude of the subjective rate of time preference, relative to the real interest rate, is equally important and can reverse the outcome. In fact if these rates happen to be equal then the shape of the relationship turns out to be a linear one, independent of the risk attitude.

IMPLEMENTATION OF EFFECTIVITY FUNCTIONS BY GAME CORRESPONDENCES

Gert-Jan Otten, Peter Borm, Ton Storcken, Stef Tijs
Department of Economics
Tilburg University
P.O. Box 90153, NL-5000 LE Tilburg

Effectivity functions, introduced by Moulin and Peleg (1982), describe the power distribution among a group of people. In this paper we discuss an implementation of upper cycle free effectivity functions by special game correspondences, called claim game correspondences. The idea of claim game correspondences is derived from Borm and Tijs (1989) who introduced strategic claim games corresponding to NTU-games. We show that these claim game correspondences are tight and furthermore, we give necessary and sufficient conditions for the effectivity function such that it coincides with the α- and β-effectivity function of the associated claim game correspondence. Finally we establish relationships between solution concepts for effectivity functions and solution concepts of the associated claim game correspondences.

Let A be a set of alternatives and N a finite set with n members. N is called a society, members of N are called players and non-empty subsets of N are called coalitions. We shall use the following notations. Let D be a set. By $\mathcal{P}(D)$ we denote the power set of D and $\mathcal{P}(D)\backslash\{\phi\}$ we denote by 2^D. Furthermore, if R^i is a preference relation on A for each player $i \in N$, then $R^S := (R^i)_{i\in S}$ is an S-profile on A. An N-profile is called a profile. By P^i we denote the asymmetric part of R^i. Let R be a preference relation on A. The extension $\tilde{R}$ of R to 2^A is defined by: for all $B, B' \in 2^A$: $B'\tilde{R}B$ if and only if (i) for all $b' \in B'\backslash B$ and all $b \in B$ we have $b'Rb$ and (ii) for all $b' \in B'$ and all $b \in B\backslash B'$ we have $b'Rb$. The asymetric part of $\tilde{R}$ is denoted by $\tilde{P}$.

An *effectivity function* is a map $E : 2^N \to \mathcal{P}(2^A)$ such that (i) $E(N) = 2^A$ and (ii) $A \in E(S)$ for all $S \in 2^N$.
Let $E : 2^N \to \mathcal{P}(2^A)$ be an effectivity function. We say that E is *weakly A-monotonic* if for all $B, B' \in 2^A$, with $B \subset B'$, and all $S \in 2^N$: if $B \in E(S)$, then there is a partition $S_1, \ldots, S_K$ of S and there are $B_i' \in E(S_i)$ for all $i \in \{1, \ldots, k\}$ such that $B' = \bigcap\{B_i' | i \in \{1, \ldots, k\}\}$. E is *superadditive* if for all $S_1, S_2 \in 2^N$ with $S_1 \cap S_2 = \phi$ and all $B_1 \in E(S_1)$ and all $B_2 \in E(S_2)$ we have $B_1 \cap B_2 \in E(S_1 \cup S_2)$. Furthermore, we say that E is *upper cycle free* if there is no collection $S_1, \ldots, S_k \in 2^N$ which is pairwise disjoint and $B_i \in E(S_i)$ for all $i \in \{1, \ldots, k\}$ such that $\bigcap\{B_i | i \in \{1, \ldots, k\}\} = \phi$.
Let $E : 2^N \to \mathcal{P}(2^A)$ be an effectivity function and R^N a profile on A. An element

$B \in 2^A$ is called an *imputation* of E at R^N if (i) there does not exist an $i \in N$ and a $B' \in E(\{i\})$ such that $B'\tilde{P}^iB$ and (ii) there does not exist a $B' \in E(N)$ and an $i \in N$ such that $B'\tilde{R}^NB$ and $B'\tilde{P}^iB$. B is called a *strong core element* of E at R^N if there exists no $S \in 2^N$, an $i \in S$ and a $B' \in E(S)$ such that $B'\tilde{R}^SB$ and $B'\tilde{P}^iB$.

Let N be a society and A a set of alternatives. A *game correspondence* (Peleg (1984b)) is an $(n+2)$-tuple $G = (X_1, \ldots, X_n, A, \pi)$ where X_i is a non-empty finite set for all $i \in N$ and π is a function from $\Pi_{i \in N} X_i$ to 2^A which is non-imposed, i.e. for all $a \in A$ there exists a $\sigma_N := (\sigma_1, \ldots, \sigma_n) \in X_N := \Pi_{i\in N} X_i$ such that $\pi(\sigma_N) = \{a\}$. A pair (G, R^N) where G is a game correspondence and R^N a profile on A is called a *game*.
The *α- and β-effectivity function* associated with a game correspondence $G = (X_1, \ldots, X_n)$ are defined as follows. For each $S \in 2^N$

$$E_\alpha^G(S) := \{B \in 2^A | \exists \sigma_S \in X_S \forall \tau_{N\setminus S} \in X_{N\setminus S}[\pi(\sigma_S, \tau_{N\setminus S}) \subset B]\},$$
$$E_\beta^G(S) := \{B \in 2^A | \forall \tau_{N\setminus S} \in X_{N\setminus S} \exists \sigma_S \in X_S[\pi(\sigma_S, \tau_{N\setminus S}) \subset B]\}.$$

It is easy to verify that E_α^G and E_β^G are indeed effectivity functions and that $E_\alpha^G(S) \subset E_\beta^G(S)$ for all $S \in 2^N$. A game form G is *tight* if $E_\alpha^G(S) = E_\beta^G(S)$ for all $S \in 2^N$ or shortly, $E_\alpha^G = E_\beta^G$.
Let (G, R^N) be a game. $\sigma_N \in X_N$ is called a *Nash equilibrium* of (G, R^N) if there does not exist an $i \in N$ and a $\tau_i \in X_i$ such that $\pi(\tau_i, \sigma_{N\setminus i})\tilde{P}^i\pi(\sigma_N)$. σ_N is called a *strong Nash equilibrium* of (G, R^N) if there is not a $S \in 2^N$, an $i \in S$ and a $\tau_S \in X_S$ such that $\pi(\tau_S, \sigma_{N\setminus S})\tilde{R}^S\pi(\sigma_N)$ and $\pi(\tau_S, \sigma_{N\setminus S})\tilde{P}^i\pi(\sigma_N)$. Furthermore, σ_N is called *Pareto undominated* if there does not exist a $B \in 2^N$ and an $i \in N$ such that $B\tilde{R}^N\pi(\sigma_N)$ and $B\tilde{P}^i\pi(\sigma_N)$.

Given an upper cycle free effectivity function $E : 2^N \to \mathcal{P}(2^A)$ we will now construct a tight game correspondence $G(E)$ and we give necessary and sufficient conditions such that $E = E_\alpha^{G(E)} = E_\beta^{G(E)}$. Therefore, we define $G(E) = (X_1, \ldots, X_n, A, \pi)$ by

$$X_i := \{(S, B) \in 2^N \times 2^A | i \in S, B \in E(S)\} \text{ for all } i \in N$$

and for $\sigma_N = (S_i, B_i)_{i\in N}$ $\pi(\sigma_N) \in 2^A$ is defined by

$$\pi(\sigma_N) := \bigcap\{B \in 2^A | B \in F(\sigma_N)\} \text{ if } F(\sigma_N) \neq \phi \text{ and } \pi(\sigma_N) := A \text{ if } F(\sigma_N) = \phi,$$
where $F : X_N \to 2^A$ is defined by
$$F(\sigma_N) := \{B \in 2^A | \exists S \in 2^N[B \in E(S), \forall i \in S[\sigma_i = (S, B)]]\} \text{ for all } \sigma_N \in X_N.$$

This game correspondence is called the *claim game correspondence associated with E*. Note that $\pi(\sigma_N) \neq \phi$ for all $\sigma_N \in X_N$ because E is upper cycle free.
In the claim game correspondence $G(E)$ the strategy (S_i, B_i) of player $i \in N$ can be interpreted as follows. Player i wants to form coalition $S_i \ni i$ and claims a subset $B_i \in 2^A$ of alternatives for which S_i is effective. His claim is only accepted if everybody in S_i proposes the same coalition, S_i, and claims the same subset B_i.

Now we are ready to formulate our results.

Theorem 1: Let $E : 2^N \to \mathcal{P}(2^A)$ be an upper cycle free effectivity function. Then

(i) $E \subset E_\alpha^{G(E)} = E_\beta^{G(E)}$,

(ii) $E = E_\alpha^{G(E)}$ if and only if E is superadditive and weakly A-monotonic.

Theorem 2: Let $E : 2^N \to \mathcal{P}(2^A)$ be an upper cycle free effectivity function and R^N a profile on A. Let (G, R^N) be the associated claim game. Then we have

(i) B is an imputation of E at R^N if an only if there exists a Pareto undominated Nash equilibrium σ_N of $(G(E), R^N)$ such that $\pi(\sigma_N) = B$.

(ii) if σ_N is a strong Nash equilibrium of $(G(E), R^N)$ then $\pi(\sigma_N)$ is a strong core element of E at R^N.

(iii) in case E is superadditive then for each strong core element B of E at R^N there exists a strong Nash equilibrium σ_N of $(G(E), R^N)$ such that $\pi(\sigma_N) = B$.

REFERENCES

Borm, P.E.M. and Tijs, S.H. (1989), Strategic claim games corresponding to an NTU-game, to appear in International Journal of Game Theory.

Moulin, H. (1983), The strategy of social choice, Amsterdam: North-Holland.

Moulin, H. and Peleg, B. (1982), Cores of effectivity functions and implementation theory, Journal of Mathematical Economics, 10, 115-145.

Peleg, B. (1984a), Game theoretical analysis of voting in committees, Cambridge University Press, Cambridge.

Peleg, B. (1984b), Core stability and duality of effectivity functions, in G. Hammer and D. Pallaschke, eds., Selected Topics in Operations Research and Mathematical Economics (Springer-Verlag, New York) 272-287.

STRATEGY-PROOFNESS FOR GENERAL DOMAINS OF ALTERNATIVES AND RESTRICTED DOMAINS OF PREFERENCES

Hans Peters, Hans van der Stel
Department of Mathematics
University of Limburg
P.O. Box 616, NL-6200 MD Maastricht

Ton Storcken
Department of Philosophy,
University of Brabant,
P.O. Box 90153, NL-5000 LE Tilburg

1. Introduction This abstract is a summary of the main recent results obtained by the three authors concerning strategy-proofness in social choice problems with general (and typically, continuous) domains of alternatives and restricted domains of preferences. Contrary to the classical papers by Arrow (1963), Gibbard (1973), and Satterthwaite (1975), in many cases possibility results are found, typically involving median-like solutions and extensions thereof.

2. The Model Let $m \in \mathbb{N}$ and let A, a nonempty subset of $\mathbb{R}^m$, denote the *set of alternatives*. Let $n \in \mathbb{N}$ and $N := \{1, 2, \ldots, n\}$ denote the *set of individuals*. A point $p = (p(1), \ldots, p(n)) \in A^N$ is called a *profile*, and a map $\varphi : A^N \to A$ a *solution*. The idea is that each individual $i \in N$ reports a point $p(i) \in A$, and φ assigns the 'compromise' point $\varphi(p) \in A$ to the profile p of reported points $p(i)$.

In what the individuals report, they are guided by their preferences. A *preference* R is a binary relation $R \subset A \times A$. Important is the set $\text{best}(R) := \{x \in A | \forall y \in A [< x, y > \in R]\}$ of *best elements* of R. Attention throughout will be restricted to preferences R satisfying:

(i) $\text{best}(R) \neq \emptyset$

(ii) $< v, y > \in R$ whenever $x \in \text{best}(R)$, $v, y \in A$ and v_j is in-between x_j and y_j for every $j = 1, 2, \ldots, m$.

Preferences satisfying (i) and (ii) are called *admissable*. Let $\mathcal{P}$ be some set of admissable preferences. The solution φ is called *strategy-proof w.r.t.* $\mathcal{P}$ if for every $R \in \mathcal{P}$, $i \in N$, $p, q \in A^N$ with $p(i) \in \text{best}(R)$ and $p(j) = q(j)$ for every $j \neq i$, it holds that $< \varphi(p), \varphi(q) > \in R$. If φ is strategy-proof, then for each individual it is optimal to report a best element of his (true) preference.

3. Euclidean Preferences A preference R is called *Euclidean* if there is an $x \in A$ with $< y, z > \in R \Leftrightarrow d(y, x) \leq d(z, x)$, where d denotes Euclidean distance. Let $A = \mathbb{R}^m$ and let $\mathcal{E}$ denote the set of Euclidean preferences on A. The solution $\varphi : A^N \to A$ is *anonymous* if $\varphi(p \circ \sigma) = \varphi(p)$ for every $p \in A^N$ and every permutation σ of N. φ is called *Pareto optimal w.r.t.* $\mathcal{E}$ if $d(p(i)), x) = d(p(i)), \varphi(p))$ for all $i \in N$, $p \in A^N$, and x with $d(p(i), x) \leq d(p(i), \varphi(p))$ for all $i \in N$. It is standard to prove that φ is Pareto optimal w.r.t. $\mathcal{E}$ if and only if $\varphi(p)$ is in the convex hull of the points $p(i)$ for every $p \in A^N$. Moulin (1980) proves:

Theorem 1. *Let $m = 1$. Then $\varphi : (\mathbb{R}^m)^N \to \mathbb{R}^m$ is Pareto optimal and strategy-proof w.r.t. $\mathcal{E}$, and anonymous, if and only if there exist points $a_1, a_2, \ldots, a_{n-1} \in \mathbb{R} \cup \{-\infty, \infty\}$*

such that $\varphi(p)$ is the median of the points $p(1), \ldots, p(n), a_1, \ldots, a_{n-1}$, for every $p \in \mathbb{R}^N$.

Furthermore, Moulin (1980) shows that the result is true without Pareto optimality if we take $n+1$ 'fixed ballots' instead of $n-1$.

Let $x \in \mathbb{R}^m$ and let b denote another orthonormal basis of $\mathbb{R}^m$. By x^b we denote the representation of x with respect to the basis b. Let n be odd. The *coordinatewise median solution* φ^b is defined by requiring $\varphi^b(p)_j$ to be the median of the numbers $p(1)^b_j, \ldots, p(n)^b_j$. PSS[1] (1990) prove the following theorem:

Theorem 2. *(a) Let $m = 2$ and n odd. The solution $\varphi : (\mathbb{R}^m)^N \to \mathbb{R}^m$ is anonymous, strategy-proof and Pareto optimal w.r.t. $\mathcal{E}$, if and only if there exists an orthonormal basis b such that $\varphi^b = \varphi$.*

(b) If $m > 2$ or n is even, then there exists no solution with the three properties mentioned under (a).

A possibility result in theorem 2(b) could be obtained by relaxing Pareto optimality to coordinatewise Pareto optimality (i.e., $\varphi(p)_j$ must be in the convex hull of the points $p(1)_j, \ldots, p(n)_j$, for every $p \in A^N$ and $j = 1, 2, \ldots, m$). A complete characterization, however, is not yet available. PSS (1991b) extend theorem 2 to the case of preferences derived from any strictly convex norm instead of the Euclidean norm.

4. A Central Theorem A solution $\varphi : A^N \to A$ is *uncompromising* if $\varphi(p) = \varphi(q)$ for any profiles $p, q \in A^N$ satisfying, for all $t = 1, 2, \ldots, m$ and all $i \in N$: $p(i)_t < \varphi(p)_t \Leftrightarrow q(i)_t < \varphi(p)_t$ and $p(i)_t > \varphi(p)_t \Leftrightarrow q(i)_t > \varphi(p)_t$. This property was introduced by Border and Jordan (1983). φ is *confirmatory* if $\varphi(p) = \varphi(q)$ whenever $q(i)_t \in \{p(i)_t, \varphi(p)_t\}$ for every $i \in N$ and $t = 1, 2, \ldots, m$. In general, there is no logical relation between the two properties. However, for example, if A is open, then confirmatoriness is implied by uncompromisingness. A map $\delta : 2^N \to (\mathbb{R} \cup \{-\infty, \infty\})^m$ is an *assignment of disagreements*, if, for all $t = 1, 2 \ldots, m$ and $S \subset T \subset N$, $\delta(\emptyset)_t > -\infty$, $\delta(N)_t < \infty$, $\delta(S)_t \geq \delta(T)_t$. Given an assignment of disagreement δ and a profile $p \in A^N$, we define, for every $t = 1, 2, \ldots, m$: $\varphi_\delta(p)_t := \min_{S \subset N}\{\max_{i \in S}\{p(i)_t \vee \delta(S)_t\}\}$. If $\varphi_\delta(p) \in A$ for every $p \in A^N$, φ_δ is called a *coordinatewise vetosolution*. In PSS (1991c) the following theorem is derived:

Theorem 3 *Let $\emptyset \neq A \subset \mathbb{R}^m$ and let $\varphi : A^N \to A$ be a solution. Then φ is uncompromising and confirmatory if and only if it is a coordinatewise vetosolution.*

This theorem extends Border and Jordan (1983). It is a central theorem in the sense that many results involving strategy-proofness can be derived from it. Note that the class of coordinatewise vetosolutions is a very large class (although more information about A is needed to determine it exactly): it contains constant and dictatorial solutions, but may also contain the coordinatewise median solutions. Some results which can be derived from theorem 3 are given by theorems 4–6.

Theorem 4 *The solution $\varphi : A^N \to A$ is strategy-proof with respect to the class of admissable preferences, if and only if it is a coordinatewise vetosolution.*

The set $A \subset \mathbb{R}^m$ is called a *grid* if for every $t = 1, 2, \ldots, m$ there is a natural number m^t and a set $L^t = \{l^t_1, \ldots, l^t_{m^t}\} \subset \mathbb{R}$ with $l^t_1 < \ldots < l^t_{m^t}$ such that $A = \{x \in \mathbb{R}^m | \exists t[l^t_1 \leq x_t \leq l^t_{m^t}$

[1] Peters, Van der Stel, and Storcken

& $x_s \in L^s$ for all $s \neq t]\}$. A solution φ is *strictly strategy-proof w.r.t. the* l_1-norm if for all $i \in N$ and $p, q \in A^N$ with $p(j) = q(j)$ for all $j \neq i$, we have either $\sum_{t=1}^{m} |p(i)_t - \varphi(q)_t| > \sum_{i=1}^{m} |p(i)_t - \varphi(q)_t|$ or $\varphi(p) = \varphi(q)$. Note that these are natural preferences to consider on a grid.

Theorem 5 *Let $\emptyset \neq A \subset \mathbb{R}^m$ be a grid and let $\varphi : A^N \to A$ be a solution. Then φ is strictly strategy-proof w.r.t. the l_1-norm if and only if φ is a coordinatewise vetosolution.*

Call A *coordinatewise mid-point closed* if for all $x, y \in A$ and $t = 1, 2, \ldots, m$ there is a $z \in A$ with $z_t = \frac{1}{2}(x_t + y_t)$. For $k = 1, 2, \ldots$ let $Q^k := \{R \subset A \times A | \exists x \in A, \alpha_1, \ldots, \alpha_m > 0 \forall y, z \in A$ $[< y, z > \in R \Leftrightarrow \sum_{t=1}^{m} \alpha_t |x_t - y_t|^k \leq \sum_{t=1}^{m} \alpha_t |x_t - z_t|^k]\}$. Call φ *unanimous* if $\varphi(p) = p$ whenever $p(1) = \ldots = p(n)$.

Theorem 6 *Let $\emptyset \neq A \subset \mathbb{R}^m$ be coordinatewise midpoint-closed, and let $\varphi : A^N \to A$ be a unanimous solution. Let $k \in \mathbb{N}$. Then φ is strategy-proof w.r.t. Q^k if and only if φ is a coordinatewise vetosolution.*

For $k = 2$ and $A = \mathbb{R}^m$, theorem 6 reduces to the main result of Border and Jordan (1983).

5. Independence of Irrelevant Alternatives (IIA) In PSS (1991a), it is shown that in the framework with a continuum of alternatives, IIA is in general stronger than strategy-proofness, and is bound to lead to impossibility results. Let $\mathcal{P}$, $\mathcal{P}'$ be classes of admissable preferences. A map $F : \mathcal{P}^N \to \mathcal{P}'$ is called a *preference solution*. F is said to satisfy IIA if $r =_{\{x,y\}} r'$ implies $F(r) =_{\{x,y\}} F(r')$ for all $r, r' \in \mathcal{P}^N$ and $x, y \in A$. Here, $R =_{\{x,y\}} R'$ for $R, R' \in \mathcal{P}$ or $\mathcal{P}'$ means $< x, y > \in R \Leftrightarrow < x, y > \in R'$, $r =_{\{x,y\}} r'$ means that $r(i) =_{\{x,y\}} r'(i)$ for every $i \in N$. So, if at the profiles r and r' all individuals order x and y in the same way, then the group preference should do the same. One of the results in PSS (1991a) is the following theorem:

Theorem 7 *Let $A \subset \mathbb{R}^m$ be open ($m \geq 2$) and let $F : \mathcal{E}^N \to \mathcal{E}$ satisfy IIA. Then F is constant or dictatorial.*

In particular, theorem 7 implies that the preference solutions derived from coordinatewise median solutions (cf. theorem 2) do not satisfy IIA.

6. Related literature We list the references cited above as well as some other related literature.

Arrow, K.J. (1963): *Social Choice and Individual Values.* Wiley, New York.

Border, K.C., and J.S. Jordan (1983): "Straightforward Elections, Unanimity and Phantom Voters", *Review of Economic Studies*, 50, 153–170.

Bordes, G., G. Laffond and M. le Breton (1990): "Strategy-Proofness Issues in Some Economic and Political Domains", Working Paper, GREQE, Marseille.

Gibbard, A. (1973): "Manipulation of Voting Schemes: A General Result", *Econometrica*, 41, 587–601.

Kim, K.H., and F.W. Roush (1984): "Nonmanipulability in Two Dimensions", *Mathemati-*

cal Social Sciences, 8, 29–43.

Moulin, H. (1980): "On Strategy-Proofness and Single Peakedness", *Public Choice*, 35, 437–455.

Peters H., H. van der Stel and T. Storcken (1990): "Pareto Optimality, Anonymity, and Strategy-Proofness in Location Problems", Report M 90-06, Maastricht, The Netherlands.

Peters H., H. van der Stel and T. Storcken (1991a): "Independence of Irrelevant Alternatives and Strategy-Proofness on Economic Domains", Report M91-05, Maastricht, The Netherlands.

Peters H., H. van der Stel and T. Storcken (1991b): "Generalized Median Solutions, Strategy-Proofness and Strictly Convex Norms", Report M91-11, Maastricht, The Netherlands.

Peters H., H. van der Stel and T. Storcken (1991c): "On Uncompromisingness and Strategy-Proofness", Report, Maastricht, The Netherlands (forthcoming).

Satterthwaite, M. (1975): "Strategy-Proofness and Arrow's Conditions: Existence and Correspondence Theorem for Voting Procedures and Social Choice Functions", *Journal of Economic Theory*, 10, 187–217.

FAIR DIVISION GAMES

Hans Reijnierse, Nijmegen
Jos Potters, Nijmegen
Stef Tijs, Tilburg

EXTENDED ABSTRACT

In Legut et al. [1991] economies are considered in which a measurable good (like land) is the unique commodity. Such a game 'generates' a TU-game which the authors call a *fair division game* (FDG for short). An economy with land has competitive equilibria and equilibrium payoffs associated with such equilibria. Economies which generate the same FDG may have different sets of equilbrium payoffs. We can however define the set of all imputations of a FDG which are equilibrium payoff in *some* economy generating the FDG. In Sprumont [1990] the concept of a *population monotonic allocation scheme* (*Pmas* for short) has been defined as a kind of extension of a core allocation. It has been proved that an equilibrium payoff is *Pmas*-extendable.

In this paper we describe the set of all fair division games. Secondly we provide an algorithm which separates FDG's from non-FDG's.

Furthermore, we shall give an example of a 4-person FDG with an element of the core which is not *Pmas*-extendable and a core element which is *Pmas*-extendable but not an equilibrium payoff. Finally we will give a way to find all *Pmas*-extendable core elements of a 4-person FDG.

We use the following notations: Let $N := \{1, 2, \ldots, n\}$. Let us introduce some classes of games:

For $T \subset N$ with $|T| \geq 2$ let w_T be the game defined by: $w_T(S) := \max\,(0, |S \cap T| - 1)$ for all $S \subset N$.

Further we introduce the following simple games u_T, $u_{T,i}$ and $\mathbb{1}_T$ ($T \subset N, i \in N$): $u_T(S) := 1$ iff $T \subset S$, $u_{T,i}(S) := 1$ iff $T \subset S$ or $i \in S$, $\mathbb{1}_T(S) := 1$ iff $S = T$.

The dual of v, is the game v^* defined by $v^*(S) := v(N) - v(N \backslash S)$. E.g. $u^*_{T,i}(S) = 1$ iff $S \cap T \neq \emptyset$ and $i \in S$. Note that $w_{\{i,j\}} = u_{\{i,j\}} = u^*_{\{i\},j}$ (henceforth we will write w_{ij} and $u^*_{i,j}$). A game is called an *i-veto* game if every coalition without player i gets 0. A game is *0-normalized* if every single-person coalition gets 0. The 0-normalization of v, denoted by $(v)_0$, is $v - a$ where $a(S) = \sum_{i \in S} v(i)$. We call a game v *convex* if $v(S) + v(T) \leq v(S \cup T) + v(S \cap T)$ $(S, T \subset N)$. It is called *concave* if $v(S) + v(T) \geq v(S \cup T) + v(S \cap T)$ $(S, T \subset N)$. When v is both convex and concave, it is called ***additive***. The *top down convexification* of v, denoted by v_c, is the game recursively defined by: $v_c(S) := v(S)$ if $|S| \geq n - 1$ and $v_c(S) := \max\,\{v(S), v_c(S \cup i) + v_c(S \cup j) - v_c(S \cup \{i, j\}) \mid i, j \notin S\}$.

An imputation is a vector $x \in \mathbb{R}^N_+$ with $x(N) := \sum x(i) = v(N)$. The *Core* of v is the set of imputations with $x(S) \geq v(S)$ for all $S \subset N$.

In the following lemma we summarize some elementary properties of the set of games w_T:

Lemma:

(1) $w^*_T = \sum_{i \in T} u_i - u_T$

(2) w_T is an extreme direction in the cone of convex games.

(3) $\{w_T \mid T \subset N, |T| \geq 2\}$ is a base of the 0-normalized n-player games.
(4) For $T = \{i_1, \dots, i_m\}$, $m \geq 2$, we have $w_T = u^*_{\{i_1,\dots,i_{m-1}\},i_m} + \dots + u^*_{\{i_1\},i_2}$.

From this lemma we obtain the following algorithm to write a 0-normalized game v as linear combination of w_T's:
Step 1: Take the dual game of v.
Step 2: 0-normalize and multiply by -1.
Step 3: Write the resulting game as (unique) linear combination of u_A's, say $\sum_i v^*(i)u_i - v^* = \sum_{|A|\geq 2} \lambda_A u_A$.
Then $v = \sum \lambda_A w_A$. The proof follows immediately from (1).

1. An algorithm to determine whether a game is a FDG.

In Legut et. al. [1991] it is proved that a game v is a FDG iff there are reals $\lambda_{T,i}$'s ≥ 0 such that $v = \sum_{T,i} \lambda_{T,i} u^*_{T,i}$. In this paper we take this as a definition for a FDG. Or equivalently, a 0-normalized game v is a FDG iff there are non-negative coefficients λ_T and $\mu_{S,T}$ such that

$$v = \sum \lambda_T w_T + \sum_{T \subset S} \mu_{S,T}(w_S - w_T) \qquad (*)$$

Note that for $|T| \geq 2 : u^*_{T,i} = w_{T \cup i} - w_T$.
If N is small, say $N \leq 5$, it is easy to see whether such λ's and μ's exist, once we have decomposed the game into a linear combination of w_T's. For instance: let v have the values

$$\begin{matrix} & & v(1234) & & & \\ & v(123) & v(124) & v(134) & v(234) & \\ v(12) & v(13) & v(14) & v(23) & v(24) & v(34) \end{matrix} \quad = \quad \begin{matrix} & & 8 & & & \\ & 5 & 6 & 5 & 5 & \\ 2 & 0 & 4 & 3 & 2 & 3 \end{matrix}$$

Then $v = w_{12} - w_{13} + w_{14} + w_{23} - 2w_{24} - w_{34} - w_{123} + w_{124} + w_{134} + 2w_{234} + w_{1234}$. It can be written as $(w_{134} - w_{13}) + (w_{124} - w_{24}) + (w_{234} - w_{24}) + (w_{234} - w_{34}) + (w_{1234} - w_{123}) + w_{12} + w_{14} + w_{23}$. This gives the composition $u^*_{13,4} + u^*_{12,4} + u^*_{24,3} + u^*_{34,2} + u^*_{123,4} + u^*_{1,2} + u^*_{1,4} + u^*_{2,3}$.
For larger N it is not that simple to find a decomposition $(*)$, if it exists. The following algorithm, which is in fact a flow algorithm, does the job.
Step 1: Write v as a linear combination of w_T's (see before):
$v = \sum_T \lambda_T w_T - \sum_T \mu_T w_T$ with $\lambda_T \geq 0, \mu_T \geq 0, \lambda_T \mu_T = 0$ for all T.
Step 2: Write the w_T's with $\lambda_T > 0$ on one line, and write the w_T's with $\mu_T > 0$ on a line below. If $T \supset S$ with $\lambda_T, \mu_S > 0$ connect them with a 'pipeline' of capacity min (λ_T, μ_S). Put above the top line a node D (distributor) and below the bottom line a node C (collector). D is connected with all elements of the top line with capacity λ_T. C is connected with all elements of the bottom line with capacity μ_T.

For instance, if v is

$$\begin{matrix} 6 \\ 5\ 5\ 4\ 3 \\ 4\ 2\ 2\ 2\ 0\ 2 \end{matrix}$$

the flow problem will be:

$$\begin{matrix} & & D & & \\ w_{12} & 2w_{123} & & w_{1234} & w_{134} \\ & w_{23} & 2w_{13} & w_{24} & \\ & & C & & \end{matrix}$$

Now, v is a FDG if and only if the maximum flow from D to C equals $\sum_T \mu_T$. We find the maximum flow with the maximum flow algorithm of Ford & Fulkerson [1956].

2. Allocation schemes and equilibrium payoffs.

In this section v is a 0-normalized FDG. In Sprumont [1990] the concept of a *population monotonic allocation scheme* has been defined as a kind of extension of core allocations. A *Pmas* gives a core allocation x^S for every subgame $v_{|S}$ of a game v such that every player i gets a weakly higher payoff in larger coalitions:
$\sum_{i \in S} x_i^S = v(S)$ for every non-empty coalition $S \subset N$ and $x_i^S \leq x_i^T$ whenever $i \in S \subset T$.
The set of *Pmas*-extendable core-elements is denoted by $PMAS$.
In Legut [1991] equilibrium payoffs are defined for economies. In this paper an equilibrium payoff of any economy which generates a FDG v will be called an equilibrium payoff of v. In Legut [1991] it is proved that this is equivalent with:

Definition: Let v a FDG. A *Core*-element x is an *equilibrium payoff* iff there exist *i-veto* FDG's v_i, such that $v = \sum_i v_i$ and $x \in \sum Core(v_i)$. The set of equilibrium payoffs is called EP. It can be seen easily that EP is a convex set. In Legut [1991] is proved that $EP \subset PMAS$, and of course $PMAS \subset Core$.

Lemma: If v is a 3-person FDG, then $EP = Core$.

Here is an example of a 4-person game with $Core \supsetneq PMAS \supsetneq EP$:

Example: Let v be:

7
5 4 3 4
2 1 2 2 2 2

Take $x :=$ (3,2,2,0). Then x is an element of the core. Suppose it lies in $PMAS$ too. Since $v(14) = 2$ and $x(4) = 0$, we have $x_1^S = 2$ for $S = \{1,4\}$. Further, $v(34) = 2$ and $x(4) = 0$ gives $x_3^S = 2$ for $S = \{3,4\}$. Therefore $x_1^S + x_3^S \geq 4$ for $S = \{1,3,4\}$, which is more than $v(134)$. Let $y :=$ (2,2,2,1). The following table shows that y is *Pmas*-extendable.

N	(123)	(124)	(134)	(234)	(12)	(13)	(14)	(23)	(24)	(34)	(1)	(2)	(3)	(4)
2	2	1	1	-	1	1	1	-	-	-	0	-	-	-
2	2	2	-	1	1	-	-	1	1	-	-	0	-	-
2	1	-	1	2	-	0	-	1	-	1	-	-	0	-
1	-	1	1	1	-	-	1	-	1	1	-	-	-	0

We prove that y does not lie in EP. The decomposition of v has the form: $v = 2w_{12} + w_{13} + 2w_{23} - 2w_{123} + 2w_{1234}$. We see that the flow problem has only one solution. If $v = \sum_i v_i$ with v_i *i-veto* games, it is necessary that $v_4 = 2u^*_{123,4}$. Therefore every equilibrium payoff gives player 4 two units. □

In the following lemma we prove that for 4-person FDG's the set of *Pmas*-extendable allocations is just the $Core$ of v_c.

Lemma: If v is a 4-person FDG, then $PMAS(v) = Core(v_c)$.

Proof: Without loss of generality we may assume that v is already 0-normalized. Let $x \in Core(v_c)$. Since v_c is convex, $x \in PMAS(v_c)$. (cf. Sprumont [1990]). The games v

and v_c may have only different values from each other in the 1- and 2-person coalitions. Given the $PMAS$ of x with respect to v_c, we can easily change it into a $PMAS$ of x with respect to v by reducing the values of x_i^S ($i \in S \subset N, |S| \leq 2$). So $Core(v_c) \subset PMAS(v)$. To prove the converse, first note that for an element x of the core and $A \subset S \subset N$ we have: $x(S) \geq v(S)$, $x(N\backslash S) + x(A) \geq v((N\backslash S) \cup A)$ and $-x(N) = -v(N)$. This gives:

$$x(A) \geq v(S) + v((N\backslash S) \cup A) - v(N) \qquad \text{for } A \subset S \subset N \qquad (**)$$

Let $x \in PMAS(v)$ and $\{i,j,k,l\} = N$. Because $x \in Core(v)$ we have that:

(1) $x(i) \geq v(ij) + v(ikl) - v(N)$ (see (**) with $S = \{i,j\}, A = \{i\}$).

(2) $x(i) \geq v(N) - M(j) - M(k) - M(l)$ (because $x_p \leq M(p)$ for $p \in \{j,k,l\}$).

Because x is $Pmas$-extendable x^T lies in the core of $v_{|T}$ for all $T \subset N$. So:

(3) $x(i) \geq v(ij) + v(ik) - v(ijk)$ (see (**) with $T = \{i,j,k\}, A = \{i\}$, S={i,j}).

Let $S \subset N$. We are finished if $x(S) \geq v_c(S)$. For $|S| \geq 3$, there is nothing to prove. For $|S| = 2$, say $S = \{i,j\}$ we have $x(S) \geq \max\ \{v(S), v(ijk) + v(ijl) - v(N)\} = v_c(S)$. Now let $|S| = 1$, say $S = \{i\}$. By definition $v_c(i) = \max\ \{v(i), v_c(ip) + v_c(iq) - v_c(ipq) \mid p,q \in N\backslash i\}$. This gives the following cases:

- If $v_c(i) = v(i)$, then $x(i) \geq v(i)$.
- If $v_c(i) = v(ij) + v(ik) - v(ijk)$, then the lemma follows from (3).
- If $v_c(i) = v(ij) + (v(ikl) + v(ikj) - v(N)) - v(ijk) = v(ij) + v(ikl) - v(N)$, and (1) gives the result.
- If $v_c(i) = (v(ijk) + v(ijl) - v(N)) + (v(ikj) + v(ikl) - v(N)) - v(ijk) = v(N) - M(j) - M(k) - M(l)$, then it follows from (2). So in any case $x(S) \geq v_c(S)$ and the lemma is proved. □

References

Ford, L.R., Fulkerson, D.R. (1956). "Maximal flow through a network", *Canadian Journal of Mathematics* 8, 399-404.

Legut, J., Potters, J.A.M., Tijs, S.H. (1991)."Economies with land - A game theoretic approach", Report 9111, Department of Mathematics, University of Nijmegen, The Netherlands.

Sprumont, Y. (1990). "Population monotonic allocation schemes for cooperative games with transferable utility", *Games and Economic Behavior* 2.

MACROECONOMICS AS VIEWED THROUGH THE LOOKING GLASS OF THE NEW INSTITUTIONAL ECONOMICS

Rudolf Richter
D–6600 Saarbrücken

Brief Survey of the New Institutional Economics

The New Institutional Economics (NIE) deals primarily with contracts. Yet opposite to neoclassical economics, in which the concept of "perfect" contracts prevails (everything is fixed ex ante for all contingencies and the entire duration of the contract), the NIE focusses on relational or "incomplete" contracts (which are open—ended because it is impossible to agree ex ante on all future eventualities, see Williamson [1985]). The outcome of such contracts may be improved by specific investments. Yet, if the investment cost are "sunk", there is a lock–in effect which may invite opportunistic ("bad") behavior of parties. Court orderings are not sufficient to prevent opportunism. They need to be supplemented by "private orderings" (Williamson [1985], 48), e.g., building up a reputation. Reputation works only if the action of, e.g., the authority is observable by third parties and conforms to some pattern. Kreps [1990] identifies this pattern in his theory of the firm with the concept of corporate culture, or more generally: organizational culture.

Some Institutional Economic Microfoundations of Macroeconomics

Contract theory plays an increasing role in the microfoundation of macroeconomics. Monopolistic practices (New Keynesians) or efficiency purposes (e.g., NIE, Williamson [1985], 23) are offered as explanations. Insider–outsider theory of unemployment belongs to the monopolistic branch, efficiency wage theory to the efficiency branch of contract theory. The latter, though, is short–term and therefore further away from NIE than, e.g., Lazaer's [1981] bonding mechanism. The NIE literature itself has a quite simple argument for fixed nominal wages and "layoffs": it is a device to prevent employers from unjustifiable reducing wages. Similarly in the case of good markets: rational contracts (e.g., customer relationships) develop with specific investments (search costs etc.). The NIE argument is: quantity adjustments have much better incentive compatibility properties than price adjustments (Williamson [1985], 76). — In monetary macroeconomics a relational contract exists between money supplier and money users. Credible commitments of the money supplier are important. One argument is that delegation to an independent central bank, which is instructed to keep inflation low, could credibly commit the government to a policy of sound money. We argued that this may not suffice. The organizational culture of money users must not be neglected. — International economic relations raise the credible commitment issue as well, e.g., in typical relational contracts like the Louvre Accord of 1987. Transaction costs are considered: the costs to open up markets may explain the apparent failure of PPP. — Finally the coordination of investment and saving is discussed under institutional economic aspects. Failing future markets, the central issue of Keynes's General Theory, may be substituted by all sorts of collective action, e.g., firms or other networks of relational contracts. Misinvestments and organizational change play an important role in a world driven by economic change. They may explain, inter alia, the hysteresis phenomenon in unemployment.

Towards a New Consensus View of Macroeconomics ?

With some fantasy one can picture a new consensus view on the basis of the NIE. Its center piece would be the concept of relational contracts. Macroeconomics could be imagined as the theory of a network of relational contracts which explain how individuals grope their way into an unknown future. Informal norms are more stable and therefore better predictable than formal rules or, worse, numbers. Therefore, an environment which is conducive to the development and cultivation of informal rules may stabilize an economy more successfully than legal or administrative activism. Yet discretion of the government, the central bank etc. cannot be completely supplemented by rules. Part of the relational contract between public authorities and constituents is that the authorities have to decide what should be done in an unforeseen contingency. But the reputation argument says they have to observe some principle: organizational culture plays a role. Its cultivation is an important part of a policy of economic stability and adequate economic growth. All things considered, the magic formula to achieve a prosperous economy is neither classical "free markets and sound money" nor Keynesian "appropriate monetary and fiscal policies". It is a policy conducive to the formation and growth of an adequate network of relational contracts as just described. Clearly, the NIE approach would demand radical changes in the way we think about macroeconomics.

Literature

Kreps, D.M. [1990], Corporate Culture and Economic Theory, in: Alt, J.E. and Shepsle, K.A. (eds.), Perspectives on Positive Political Economy, Cambridge, Mass.
Lazaer, E.P. [1981], Agency, Earnings Profiles, Productivity and Hours Restrictions, American Economic Review, 71, 606–20.
Williamson, O.E. [1985], The Economic Institutions of Capitalism, New York and London.

AUCTION BIDDING AND EVOLUTIONARY STABLE STRATEGIES

Minoru Sakaguchi
Department of Management Information
Nagoya University of Commerce and Business Administration
Sagamine, .Nisshin-cho, Aichi, 470-01, JAPAN

1. INTRODUCTION

One of the most unusual applications of game theory in recent years has been to model how animal behavior evolves from generation to generation. Maynard-Smith [1974] modelled conflicts among animals in their mating behavior, for example, in terms of game theory by introducing the concepts of "strategy" and "fitness" (i.e., payoffs in other terminology) that are considered to be "thought and used" by animals. He defined evolutionary stable strategies(ESS) and showed that animals use ESS in order to secure revolution of their species (this explains why snakes wrestle rather than bite). Now we understand that some examples are observed in the animal world that can be thought of as n-player game rather than two-player game. (Thomas [1984; pp. 186-187]). The aim of the present paper is to extend the two-player ESS originally defined by Maynard-Smith to the n-player ESS, and to apply this concept to some types of n-bidder auction. In Section 2 n-player ESS are defined by extending the concept of two-player ESS to the n-player case. Three types of n-bidder auctions, i.e., second-bid, first-bid, and sad-loser auctions (in Section 3) and a guessing game, as a variant of auction, (in Section 4), are discussed and a unique mixed-strategy ESS (if it exists) is derived for each of these four examples in auction.

2. EVOLUTIONARY STABLE STRATEGIES

Consider an n-player non-zero-sum, competitive, and "symmetric" game where the payoff to player i, when he uses a strategy x_i and his opponents use a (n-1)-tuple of strategies $X^{-i} = (x_1, \ldots x_{i-1}, x_{i+1}, \ldots x_n)$, is represented by

$$M_i(x_1, \ldots, x_n) = e(x_i, X^{-i}) \qquad i=1, .., n.$$

Here the function $e(x_1, \ldots, x_n)$ is called an <u>n-player fitness function</u> and has the property that $e(x_i, X^{-i})$, for each i, is unchanged under any permutation over the components of X^{-i}.

We state the following definition. Let x^{*n-1} be an (n-1) repetition of the same x^*. A strategy x^* is an n-player evolutionary stable strategy (ESS) if it satisfies

$$e(x^*, x^{*n-1}) \geq e(y, x^{*n-1}), \text{ for any strategy } y \neq x^*, \tag{2.1}$$

and if $e(x^*, x^{*n-1}) = e(y, x^{*n-1})$, then

$$e(x^*, y^{n-1}) > e(y, y^{n-1}). \tag{2.2}$$

This is a natural extension of the two-player ESS, originally given by Maynard-Smith [1974], to the n-player case. For each player, an ESS x^* is the best response to x^{*n-1} employed by his competitors, and if there exists an equivalent strategy $y \neq x^*$, then, to y^{n-1}, x^* is a better response than y^*. Note that, if x^* is an n-player ESS, x^{*n} will be an equilibrium n-tuple for the corresponding non-zero-sum game, but not all such equilibrium n-tuples are n-player ESS because of (2.2).

3. ESS IN AUCTION BIDDING

In sealed auctions n players bid for an item which has an identical worth $V > o$ for all players. The bidder who bids highest obtains the item, and when more than one bidder bid highest the item is given to a single bidder chosen by an equal-chance lottery. According to how the price is paid to the seller by the winner we have several types of auction. (See Thomas [1984; Chapter 9] and Vickrey [1962]). We discuss 1. Second-Bid auction, 2. First-Bid auction and 3. Sad-Loser auction. In the last type of auction the loser forfeits the amount of his bid, and the winner obtains the item without paying the price. The fitness function is

$$e(x_1, x_2, \ldots, x_n) = \begin{cases} -x_1, & \text{if } x_1 < y_{-1} \\ (V - x_1)/m_1(x), & \text{if } x_1 = y_{-1} \\ V & \text{if } x_1 > y_{-1} \end{cases}$$

where $y_{-i} = \max_{j \neq i} x_j$ and $m_i(x) = |\{j \mid x_j = x_i\}|$, $i = 1, \ldots, n$. We prove

Proposition 3. In the sad-loser auction with the above fitness function the mixed strategy

$$F^*(x) = \left(\frac{x}{V+x}\right)^{1/(n-1)}, \quad 0 \leq x < \infty$$

is an n-player ESS. The equilibrium value is zero.

4. A GUESSING GAME

As a final example we will give an auction-like n-player symmetric game. This is a Guessing Game as follows: Player O picks up a random number t uniformly distributed on $0 \le t \le 1$. Each of n players guesses t independently of other players' guess. They know only that the distribution of t is uniform. A player, whose guess is nearest to t among the guesses not greater than t, wins, and is rewarded by a unit amount. The loser gets nothing. Each player seeks to find the strategy that maximizes his expected reward. The fitness function in this game is given by

$$e(x_1,x_2,\dots,x_n)=(z_1(x)-x_1)/m_1(x), \quad x=(x_1,\dots,x_n)\in[0,1]^n$$

where $z_i(x)=\begin{cases} \min\{x_j \mid x_j>x_i\}, & \text{if } x_j>x_i \text{ for some } j \\ 1, & \text{if otherwise} \end{cases}$

A unique mixed-strategy ESS when it exists is derived.

References

Maynard-Smith, J.: The theory of games and the evolution of animal conflicts, J. Theor. Biol 47 (1974), 209-221.

Thomas, L.C.: Games, Theory and Applications, Ellis Horwood, Chichester, 1984.

Vickrey, W.: Auction and bidding games, in Recent Advances in Game Theory, Princeton University Press, 1962 pp.15-27.

THE COPELAND DECISION MECHANISM

Ton Storcken
Department of Philosophy
Tilburg University
P.O. Box 90153, NL - 5000 LE Tilburg

The so called Copeland preference rule is characterized. A preference rule is a function which assigns to every profile or combination of individual preferences over a fixed finite population N a collective preference. Here preferences are considered to be weak orderings on a fixed finite set of alternatives A. $\mathbf{W} := \{R \subseteq A\text{x}A \mid R \text{ is transitive and complete}\}$ is <u>the set of weak orderings</u>. So a <u>preference rule</u> is a function F from $\mathbf{W}^N$ to $\mathbf{W}$. Let $M(r) := \{\langle x,y\rangle \in A^2 \mid \#\{i \in N \mid \langle x,y\rangle \in r(i)\} \geq \#\{i \in N \mid \langle y,x\rangle \in r(i)\}\}$ denote the simple pairwise majority rule at profile $r \in \mathbf{W}^N$. Let $R(x) := \{y \in A \mid \langle x,y\rangle \in R\}$ for all relations R on A. The <u>Copeland preference rule</u> F_{Cop} is defined at profile $r \in \mathbf{W}^N$ as follows

$$F_{Cop}(r) := \{\langle x,y\rangle \in A^2 \mid \#(M(r))(x) \geq \#(M(r))(y)\}.$$

So $\langle x,y\rangle$ is in $F_{Cop}(r)$ if x weakly dominates as least as much alternatives as y in the simple pairwise majority rule M at r. See also Moulin [1983].

To the author's knowledge this rule has never been characterized. Appart from characterizations of dictatorship see Arrow [1978] or Kelly [1978] he has only found characterizations of so called score rules see Young [1974] and [1975] and of the simple majority rule in a two alternatives case see May [1952].

There are five characterizing conditions. The first three mentioned below are adjustments of May's conditions to the two or more alternatives situations. The fourth condition is a weak Pareto-optimality condition. The last condition is a relaxation of the independence of irrelevant alternatives condition.

Let F be a preference rule. F is <u>neutral</u>, if for all profiles $r \in \mathbf{W}^N$ and every permutation σ of A, $F(\sigma r) = \sigma F(r)$. Here $\sigma R := \{\langle\sigma(x),\sigma(y)\rangle \mid \langle x,y\rangle \in R\}$ for all $R \subseteq A\text{x}A$ and $(\sigma r)(i) := \sigma(r(i))$ is for all $i \in N$ and all $r \in \mathbf{W}^N$. F is anonymous, if for all profiles $r \in W^N$ and every permutation τ of A, $F(r \circ \tau) = F(r)$. F is monotonic, if for all profiles $r, r' \in W^N$ and $x, y \in A$ such that $r \neq r'$, $\langle x,y\rangle \in F(r')$, $Ax(A-\{x,y\}) \subseteq r(i) \cap r'(i)$, $\langle x,y\rangle \in r'(i)$ implies $\langle x,y\rangle \in r(i)$ and $\langle y,x\rangle \notin r(i)$ implies $\langle x,y\rangle \notin r'(i)$ for all $i \in N$, it holds that $\langle y,x\rangle \notin F(r)$.

For a profile $r \in W^N$, $x, y \in A$ and $i \in N$ let $r_{xy}(i) := r(i)|_{\{x,y\}^2} \gg (A - \{x,y\})^2$. For $B, C \subseteq A$ with $B \cap C = \emptyset$ and $R \subseteq B^2$, $R' \subseteq C^2$ $R \gg R' := R \cup R' \cup (BxC)$. r_{xy} is the profile which orders x,y above the rest which is total indifferent for each individual and which orders x and y as in r. Intuitively $F(r_{xy})|_{\{x,y\}^2}$ expresses the collective preference between x and y at F(r) disregarding the other alternatives. These preferences form the base relation rule, $B(F,r) := \{\langle x,y\rangle \mid \langle x,y\rangle \in F(r_{x,y})|_{\{x,y\}^2}\}$. Now using May's proof we have

THEOREM 1 Let $F : W^N \to W$ be neutral, anonymous, and monotonic. Then for all $r \in W^N$, $B(F,r) = M(r)$.

■

F is globally Pareto-optimal if for all $r \in W^N$ and all $x \subseteq A$ such that $r(i) = r(i)|_{X^2} \gg r(i)|_{(A-X)^2}$, $F(r) = F(r)|_{X^2} \gg F(r)|_{(A-X)^2}$. Global Pareto-optimality can only be applied whenever the whole profile is known this explains the word global. F depends on pairwise comparison, if for all profiles $r, r' \in W^N$ and $x, y \in A$ such that $B(F,r)(x) = B(F,r')(x)$ and $B(F,r)(y) = B(F,r')(y)$, $F(r)|_{\{x,y\}^2} = F(r')|_{\{x,y\}^2}$. Now we can formulate the main result.

THEOREM 2 Let $F : W^N \to W$. Then (i) and (ii) are equivalent, where

(i) $F = F_{Cop}$

(ii) F is neutral, anonymous, monotonic, globally Pareto-optimal and depends on pairwise comparisons.

The proof of (i) ⇒ (ii) is straightforward. We give an outline of the proof of (ii) ⇒ (i). First by theorem 1 and the dependence on pairwise comparisons there is a function $f : M(W^N) \to W$ such that $F = f \circ M$. Let $f_{out}(R) := \{\langle x,y\rangle \mid \#R(x) \geq \#R(y)\}$. Then it is sufficient to prove that $f = f_{out}$. Now f <u>commutates with every permutation</u> σ on A [i.e. $f(\sigma R) = \sigma f(R)$ for all $R \in M(W^N)$] since F is neutral. Furthermore, f commutates with concatenations [i.e. $f(R|_{X^2} \gg R|_{(A-X)^2}) = f(R)|_{X^2} \gg f(R)|_{(A-X)^2}$ for all $R|_{X^2} \gg R|_{(A-X)^2}$ in $M(W^N)$] since F is globally Pareto-optimal. f <u>depends on pairwise donimances</u> [i.e. for all $R, R' \in M(W^N)$ and $x, y \in A$, $R(x) = R'(x)$ and $R(y) = R'(y)$ implies $f(R)|_{\{x,y\}^2} = f(R')|_{\{x,y\}^2}$] since F depends on pairwise comparisons. Now similarly as in Delver, Monsuur & Storcken [1991] these three conditions characterize f_{out}. This completes the outline of the proof.

REFERENCES

Arrow K.J., 1978, Social choice and individual values, Yale University Press (9th ed.).

Delver R., Monsuur H., Storcken T., 1991, Ordering pairwise comparison structures, Theory and Decision (to appear).

Kelly J.S., 1978, Arrow impossibility theorems, Academic Press, New York.

May K.O., 1952, A set of independent neccessary and sufficient conditions for simple majority decision, Econometrica, 20, p.680 - 684.

Moulin H., 1983, The strategy of social choice, North-Holland, Amsterdam.

Young H.P., 1974, An axiomatization of Borda's rule, Journal of Economic Theory, 9, p.43 - 52.

Young H.P., 1975, Social choice scoring functions, SIAM Journal of Applied Mathematics, 28, p. 824 - 838.

ACKNOWLEDGEMENT

We gratefully acknowledge the support by the Co-operation Centre of Tilburg and Eindhoven University.

Some Bilateral Approach to the Generalized Secretary Problem

K. Szajowski
Institute of Mathematics
Technical University of Wrocław
Wybrzeże Wyspiańskiego 27
PL-50-370 Wrocław, Poland

Two employers, Player 1 and Player 2, are to view sequentially a group of N applicant for vacancies in their enterprise. The aim of the players is to accept the best or the second best (**BOS**) applicant but better than another player. Their decisions are based on relative ranks of applicants and previous decisions of the opponent. If the applicant is viewed the employer must either accept or reject her. The applicant once accepted cannot be rejected, once rejected cannot be reconsidered. Each employer can accept at most one applicant. When both players want to accept the same applicant the priority is given to Player 1. The considered problem is a game variant of the double choice problem (see [5] for a review) and a generalization of the priority game approach to the generalized secretary problem [4], [6], [7]. This model and other game approaches to the problem differs in, among others, the structure of payoff functions. It is the first example in which the gain of both players depends on the candidates accepted by the opponent. The formal model of the problem is given and the numerical solution of the problem posed is presented. The most relevant game model has been investigated by Ano [1]. The aim of the players in his model is to choose **BOS** but when one player stops another one cannot choose any other object.

Two decision makers stopping problem

Let $(X_n, \mathcal{F}_n, \mathbf{P}_x)_{n=0}^N$ be a homogeneous Markov process defined on a probability space $(\Omega, \mathcal{F}, \mathbf{P})$ with a state space $(\mathbb{E}, \mathcal{B})$ and let $f : \mathbb{E} \times \mathbb{E} \to \Re$ be a $\mathcal{B} \otimes \mathcal{B}$ real valued measurable function. The horizon N is finite. The players observe the Markov chain and they try to accept the "best realization" according to function f and possible selections of another player. Each realization x_n of X_n can be accepted by only one player and each player can accept at most one realization. Player 1 has priority i.e. when both want to accept the same realization it is assigned to Player 1. If Player 1 and 2 have accepted states x and y, respectively, then Player 2 pays to Player 1 $f(x,y)$. When only Player 1 (Player 2) accepts a state x (y) then Player 1 obtains $f_1(x) = \sup_{y \in \mathbb{E}} f(x,y)$ ($f_2(y) = \inf_{x \in \mathbb{E}} f(x,y)$). If both players finish the decision process without any accepted state then they have gain 0.

Let $\mathcal{S}^N$ be the aggregation of Markov times with respect to $(\mathcal{F}_n)_{n=0}^N$. We admit that $\mathbf{P}_x(\tau \leq N) < 1$ for some $\tau \in \mathcal{S}^N$. The elements of $\mathcal{S}^N$ are possible strategies for the players with the restriction that Player 2 cannot stop at the same moment as Player 1. The aim of Player 1 is to maximize the expected gain and Player 2 tries to minimize his expected loss. When one of the players accepts realization x_n at moment n, the second one will try to maximize his gain without any disturbance from another player. It means that if there is not acceptance of states till moment n, the players have to take into account the potential danger from a future decision of the opponent before accepting or rejecting the realization x_n of X_n. Let us formalize this consideration. Let $\mathcal{S}_k^N = \{\tau \in \mathcal{S}^N : \tau \geq k\}$. Denote M_k^N and Λ_k^N copies of $\mathcal{S}_k^N$. Define $\tilde{\Lambda}^N = \{(\lambda, \{\sigma_n^1\}) : \lambda \in \Lambda^N, \sigma_n^1 \in \Lambda_{n+1}^N$ for every $n\}$ and $\tilde{M}^N = \{(\mu, \{\sigma_n^2\}) : \mu \in M^N, \sigma_n^2 \in M_{n+1}^N$ for every $n\}$. Let Player 1 and 2 choose $s = (\lambda, \{\sigma_n^1\}) \in \tilde{\Lambda}^N$ and $t = (\mu, \{\sigma_n^2\}) \in \tilde{M}^N$, respectively. Define $\tilde{R}(x,s,t) = E_x f(X_s, X_t) = E_x f(X_{\tau_1}, X_{\tau_2})$ where $\tau_1 = \lambda \mathbb{I}_{\{\lambda \le \mu\}} + \sigma^1_\mu \mathbb{I}_{\{\lambda > \mu\}}$ and $\tau_2 = \mu \mathbb{I}_{\{\lambda > \mu\}} + \sigma^2_\lambda \mathbb{I}_{\{\lambda \le \mu\}}$. In this way the normal form of the game $(\tilde{\Lambda}^N, \tilde{M}^N, \tilde{R}(x,s,t))$ is defined.

Definition 1. *A pair* $(s^*, t^*) \in \tilde{\Lambda}^N \times \tilde{M}^N$ *is an equilibrium if for every* $x \in \mathbb{E}$, $s \in \tilde{\Lambda}^N$ *and* $t \in \tilde{M}^N$ *we have*

$$\tilde{R}(x,s,t^*) \le \tilde{R}(x,s^*,t^*) \le \tilde{R}(x,s^*,t).$$

To solve this game we consider the following auxiliary game. Let $\mathcal{S}^n_{f+} = \{\tau \in \mathcal{S}^n : E_y f^+(x, X_\tau) < \infty,\ x,y \in \mathbb{E}\}$ and $\mathcal{S}^n_{f-} = \{\tau \in \mathcal{S}^n : E_y f^-(X_\tau, y) < \infty,\ x,y \in \mathbb{E}\}$. Define $s_0(x,y) = S_0(x,y) = f(x,y)$ and $s_n(x,y) = \inf_{\tau \in \mathcal{S}^n_{f+}} E_y f(x, X_\tau)$, $S_n(x,y) = \sup_{\tau \in \mathcal{S}^n_{f-}} E_x f(X_\tau, y)$ for all $x,y \in \mathbb{E}$, $n = 1,2,\ldots,N$. If Player 1 is the first to accept x at moment n then his expected gain is $h(n,x) = E_x s_{N-n-1}(x, X_1)$, for $n = 0,1,\ldots,N-1$ and $h(N,x) = f_1(x)$. When Player 2 is the first then the expected gain of Player 1 is $H(n,x) = E_x S_{N-n-1}(X_1, x)$, for $n = 0,1,\ldots,N-1$ and $H(N,x) = f_2(x)$. The functions $h(n,x)$ and $H(n,x)$ are well defined. They are $\mathcal{B}$-measurable of the second variable. Admit as the set of strategies for Player 1 and Player 2 in auxiliary game the copies of $\mathcal{S}^N$ and denote them M^N and Λ^N, respectively. For $\lambda \in \Lambda^N$ and $\mu \in M^N$ define payoff function

$$r(\lambda,\mu) = \begin{cases} h(\lambda, X_\lambda)\mathbb{I}_{\{\lambda \le \mu\}} + H(\mu, X_\mu)\mathbb{I}_{\{\lambda > \mu\}} & \text{if } \lambda \le N \text{ or } \mu \le N, \\ 0 & \text{otherwise,} \end{cases} \tag{1}$$

where $\mathbb{I}_A$ is a characteristic function of the set A. This game is a special case of Neveu's stopping problem considered by Yasuda [8]. As a solution of the game we search for an equilibrium pair (λ^*, μ^*) such that

$$R(x,\lambda,\mu^*) \le R(x,\lambda^*,\mu^*) \le R(x,\lambda^*,\mu) \qquad \text{for all} \quad x \in \mathbb{E}, \tag{2}$$

where $R(x,\lambda,\mu) = E_x r(\lambda,\mu)$. Let us construct the equilibrium pair for the auxiliary game. Define the sequence $v_n(x)$, $n = 0,1,\ldots,N+1$ on $\mathbb{E}$ by setting $v_{N+1}(x) = 0$ and

$$v_n(x) = \operatorname{val}\begin{bmatrix} h(n,x) & h(n,x) \\ H(n,x) & \tilde{v}_{n+1}(x) \end{bmatrix} \tag{3}$$

for $n = 0,1,\ldots,N$, where $\tilde{v}_k(x) = Tv_k(x) = E_x v_k(X_1)$ and denote $A^{ss}_n = \{x \in \mathbb{E} : h(n,x) \ge H(n,x), H(n,x) \le \tilde{v}_{n+1}(x)\}$, $A^{sf}_n = \{x \in \mathbb{E} : h(n,x) \ge H(n,x), H(n,x) > \tilde{v}_{n+1}(x)\}$, $A^{fs}_n = \{x \in \mathbb{E} : h(n,x) < H(n,x), H(n,x) \le Tv_{n+1}(x)\}$ and $A^{ff}_n = \mathbb{E} \setminus (A^{ss}_n \cup A^{sf}_n \cup A^{fs}_n)$. Define $\lambda^* = \inf_n\{X_n \in A^{ss}_n \cup A^{sf}_n\}$ and $\mu^* = \inf_n\{X_n \in A^{ss}_n \cup A^{fs}_n\}$. Since the matrix in (3) has always an equilibrium in pure strategies and by results of [8] there exists a solution of the auxiliary game.

Theorem 1. *The auxiliary game with payoff function (1) has the solution and* (λ^*, μ^*) *is an equilibrium pair. The value of the game is equal to* $v_0(x)$.

Define (see [3])

$$\begin{aligned} \sigma^{1^*}_n &= \inf\{m > n : S_{N-m}(X_m, X_n) = f(X_m, X_n)\}, \\ \sigma^{2^*}_n &= \inf\{m > n : s_{N-m}(X_n, X_m) = f(X_n, X_m)\}. \end{aligned}$$

Theorem 2. *The pair of strategies* (s^*, t^*), *where* $s^* = (\lambda^*, \{\sigma^{1^*}_n\})$ *and* $t^* = (\mu^*, \{\sigma^{2^*}_n\})$, *is the solution of the game* $(\tilde{\Lambda}^N, \tilde{M}^N, \tilde{R}(x,s,t))$. *The value of the game is equal to* $v_0(x)$.

Bilateral problem of choosing the best or the second best

Let $I\!K$ be the set of characteristics (real numbers), assuming that the values are different. The players observe a permutation $\xi_1, \xi_2, \ldots, \xi_N$ of the elements of $I\!K$ sequentially. We assume that all permutations are equally likely. Let Z_k and Y_k denote the absolute rank and the relative rank of the object with the characteristics ξ_k, respectively. The aim of the players is to accept (basing on the relative ranks) **BOS** but better than the opponent. Each employer can accept at most one applicant and both players together can accept at most 2 objects. It is assumed Player 1 has priority. If the applicant is viewed the employer must either accept or reject her. Once the applicant is accepted, she cannot be rejected, once rejected cannot be reconsidered. The player obtains +1 from another one if he has chosen the required applicant, −1 when the opponent has done it and 0 otherwise. Denote S^N the set of all Markov times τ with respect to the σ-fields $\{\mathcal{F}_k\}_{k=1}^N = \sigma(Y_1, Y_2, \ldots, Y_k)$, $k = 1, 2 \ldots, N$. The problem considered can be formulated as follows. For $s \in \tilde{\Lambda}^N$ and $t \in \tilde{M}^N$ denote $A_{ij} = \{\omega : X_{\tau_i} = 1\} \cup \{\omega : X_{\tau_i} = 2, x_{\tau_j} \neq 1\}$. Define the payoff function $g(s,t) = I\!I_{A_{12}} - I\!I_{A_{21}}$ and the expected payoff $G(s,t) = Eg(s,t)$. We are looking for (s^*, t^*) such that for every $s \in \tilde{\Lambda}^N$ and $t \in \tilde{M}^N$

$$G(s, t^*) \leq G(s^*, t^*) \leq G(s^*, t).$$

The problem can be reformulated to the two decision makers double stopping problem of a homogeneous Markov chain (**AMC**) $(W_t, \mathcal{G}_t, \mathbf{P}_{(1,1)})_{t=1}^N$, where $W_t = (\rho_t, Y_{\rho_t})$ and $\rho_1 = 1$, $\rho_t = \inf\{r > \rho_{t-1} : Y_r \in \{1,2\}\}$ for $t > 1$ (see [2]). Denote $\varsigma^*(r, l_r)$ the strategy such that

$$h(r, l_r) = E_{(r,l_r)} g(r, \varsigma^*(r, l_r)) = \inf_{\sigma \in S_{r+1}^N} E_{(r,l_r)} g(r, \sigma) \tag{4}$$

where the expectation is taken with respect to $\mathbf{P}_{(r,l_r)}$ of **AMC**. We have $h(r, l_r) = -H(r, l_r) = h_1(r, l_r) - h_2(r, l_r)$, where, since $\sigma_n^{i\,*} = \varsigma^*(n, Y_n)$,

$$\begin{aligned} h_1(r, l_r) &= \mathbf{P}\{A_{12} \mid \tau_1 = r, Y_r = l_r\} \\ &= \begin{cases} \frac{r}{N} + \begin{cases} 0 & \text{if } r \geq r_b \\ \sum_{s=r+1}^{r_b - 1} \frac{r}{s(s-1)} \frac{s(s-1)}{N(N-1)} & \text{if } r < r_b \end{cases} & \text{for } l_r = 1, \\ \frac{r(r-1)}{N(N-1)} & \text{for } l_r = 2 \end{cases} \end{aligned}$$

and

$$\begin{aligned} h_2(r, l_r) &= \mathbf{P}\{A_{21} \mid \tau_1 = r, Y_r = l_r\} \\ &= \begin{cases} \sum_{s=r+1}^{N} \frac{r}{s(s-1)} \max\left\{\frac{s(2N-s-1)}{N(N-1)}, \tilde{c}_{\mathbf{BOS}}(s)\right\} & \text{if } l_r = 1, \\ \tilde{c}_{\mathbf{BOS}}(r) & \text{if } l_r = 2. \end{cases} \end{aligned}$$

$\tilde{c}_{\mathbf{BOS}}(r) = E_{(r,l_r)} c_{\mathbf{BOS}}(W_1)$ and $c_{\mathbf{BOS}}(r, l_r) = \sup_{\tau \in S_r^N} \mathbf{P}\{Z_\tau \in \{1,2\} \mid Y_\tau \in \{1,2\}\}$. We have

$$\varsigma^*(r, l_r) = \begin{cases} \begin{cases} \vartheta_r & \text{if } \vartheta_r \geq r_b, \\ \sigma^*_{\vartheta_r} & \text{if } \vartheta_r < r_b \end{cases} & \text{for } l_r = 1, \\ \sigma^*_r & \text{for } l_r = 2, \end{cases} \tag{5}$$

where $\vartheta_r = \inf\{s > r : Y_s = 1\}$ and $\sigma_r^* = \inf\{s > r : (s, Y_s) \in \Gamma(r_b, r_a)\}$, $\Gamma(r_b, r_a)$ is the optimal stopping set for one player problem of choosing **BOS**. By analytical consideration the problem solution is as follows. Denote

$$\begin{aligned} w(r,s,t,u) &= \sum_{j=r+1}^{s-1} p(r,j)[H(j,1) + w(j,s,t,u)] + \sum_{j=s}^{t-1} [h(j,1) + w(j,j+1,t,u)] \\ &\quad + \sum_{j=t}^{u-1} p(r,j)[h(j,1) + H(j,2)] + \sum_{j=u}^{N} p(r,j)[h(j,1) + h(j,2)] \end{aligned}$$

and $B_{st}(k) = \{(r, l_r) : s \le r \le t,\ l_r = k\}$. Solving recursively (3) we obtain that there exist $r_\alpha = \min\{r < r_a : H(r,2) > \tilde{v}(r)\}$, $r_\gamma = \min\{r < r_\alpha : h(r,1) \ge 0\}$, $r_\beta = \min\{r < r_\gamma : H(r,1) > \tilde{v}(r)\}$ such that

$$v_r(r,l_r) = v(r,l_r) = \begin{cases} h(r,l_r) & (r,l_r) \in B_{r_\gamma N}(1) \cup B_{r_a N}(2), \\ H(r,l_r) & (r,l_r) \in B_{r_\beta r_\gamma - 1}(1) \cup B_{r_\alpha r_a - 1}(2), \\ \tilde{v}(r) & (r,l_r) \in B_{1 r_\beta - 1}(1) \cup B_{1 r_\alpha - 1}(2) \end{cases} \tag{6}$$

where

$$\tilde{v}(r) = Tv(r,l_r) = \begin{cases} w(r,r+1,r+1,r+1) & \text{if } r_a \le r \le N, \\ w(r,r+1,r+1,r_a) & \text{if } r_\alpha \le r < r_a, \\ w(r,r+1,r_\alpha,r_a) & \text{if } r_\gamma \le r < r_\alpha, \\ w(r,r_\gamma,r_\alpha,r_a) & \text{if } r_\beta \le r < r_\gamma, \\ w(r_\beta,r_\gamma,r_\alpha,r_a) & \text{if } 1 \le r < r_\beta. \end{cases} \tag{7}$$

The optimal first stop strategy is given by the sets $A_t^{ss} = B_{r_\gamma N}(1) \cup B_{r_a N}(2)$, $A_t^{fs} = B_{r_\beta r_\gamma}(1) \cup B_{r_\alpha r_a}(2)$, $A_t^{ff} = I\!E \setminus (A_t^{ss} \cup A_t^{fs})$, $t = 1,2,\ldots,N$. When $N \to \infty$ so that $\lim_{N\to\infty} \frac{r}{N} = x$ we have $a = \lim_{N\to\infty} \frac{r_a}{N} = \frac{2}{3}$, $b = \lim_{N\to\infty} \frac{r_b}{N} \cong 0.3470$, $\alpha = \lim_{N\to\infty} \frac{r_\alpha}{N} \cong 0.5365$, $\gamma = \lim_{N\to\infty} \frac{r_\gamma}{N} \cong 0.4639$, $\beta = \lim_{N\to\infty} \frac{r_\beta}{N} \cong 0.3263$ and the limit of value function is

$$\hat{v}(x) = \lim_{N\to\infty} \tilde{v}(r) = \begin{cases} \hat{w}(x,x,x,x,x) & \text{if } a \le x \le 1, \\ \hat{w}(x,x,x,x,a) & \text{if } \alpha \le x < a, \\ \hat{w}(x,x,x,\alpha,a) & \text{if } \gamma \le x < \alpha, \\ \hat{w}(x,x,\gamma,\alpha,a) & \text{if } b \le x < \gamma, \\ \hat{w}(x,b,\gamma,\alpha,a) & \text{if } \beta \le x < b, \\ \hat{w}(\beta,b,\gamma,\alpha,a) & \text{if } 0 \le x < \beta. \end{cases} \tag{8}$$

where $\hat{w}(x_1,x_2,y_1,y_2,z) = \lim_{N\to\infty} w(r,s,t,u)$. We have $\hat{v}(0) \cong 0.1789$. For a comparison, the value of the game considered in [1] is 0.2704.

Theorem 3. *In the competitive two person problem of choosing* BOS *but a better one than the opponent the optimal strategy of the first stop is described by sets* A_t^{ss}, A_t^{fs} *and* A_t^{ff}. *The second stop is according to (5). The value function of the problem is given by (6), the expected value with respect to* $\mathbf{P}_{(r,l_r)}$ *of* AMC *by (7) and its limit by (8).*

REFERENCES

[1] K. Ano, *Bilateral secretary problem recognizing the maximum or the second maximum of a sequence*, J. Information & Optimization Sciences, 11 (1990), pp. 177 – 188.

[2] E. Dynkin and A. Yushkevich, *Theorems and Problems on Markov Processes*, Plenum, New York, 1969.

[3] R. Eidukjavicjus, *Optimalna ostanovka markovskoj cepi dvumia momentami ostanovki*, Lit. Mat. Sbornik, 19 (1979), pp. 181–183. Inf. XIX conf. math.

[4] E. Enns and E. Ferenstein, *On a multi-person time-sequential game with priorities*, Sequential Analysis, 6 (1987), pp. 239–256.

[5] J. Preater, *A survey of secretary problems with multiple appointments*, Research Report 88-12, Dept. of Math., Univ. of Keele, Keele, ST5 5BG, UK, 1988.

[6] T. Radzik and K. Szajowski, *Sequential games with random priority*, Sequential Analysis, 9 (1990), pp. 361–377.

[7] M. Sakaguchi, *Some two-person bilateral games in the generalized secretary problem*, Math. Japonica, 34 (1988), pp. 637–654.

[8] M. Yasuda, *On a randomized strategy in Neveu's stopping problem*, Stochastic Proc. and their Appl., 21 (1985), pp. 159–166.

On the Existence of Structural Saddle-Points in Variational Closed Models of Capital Formation

Reiner Wolff
Department of Economics, University of Siegen
P.O. Box 101240, D-5900 Siegen

I. Introduction

The so-called turnpike theorem can be regarded one of the most striking results of modern growth theory. It confirms the catenary behavior of efficient capital accumulation paths around a ray of fastest proportional capital stock expansion in finite-horizon models of efficient economic growth. Standard proofs of the theorem assume that the underlying production technology set is a convex cone (see L.W. McKenzie [4]). More recent research by this author (see R. Wolff [7]) indicates that the theorem also applies in the case of a non-convex production technology set if this set can be assumed a biconvex set in the sense of L.J. Lau [3] with its input and output partitions independent of each other. The present paper tries to shed light on the subsequent, yet open question if there exist production technologies different from the ones just mentioned and still compatible with the catenary property of efficient capital formation paths.

This question will be posed within the common framework of a continuous-time neoclassical optimum growth model to be introduced in Section II. The model assumes as given an instantaneous production technology set which may be time-dependent and represented by a smooth transformation frontier function with some further restrictions imposed upon the change of technology over time. We will then establish and prove in Section III the theorem that for there to exist a turnpike expansion ray the transformation frontier must have *along this ray* a representation of the form *globally* assumed in R. Wolff [7].

Our use of notation will be as follows. Throughout the paper elements of R^n, $n > 1$, will be referred to as column-vectors or simply called 'vectors'. They will be denoted by lowercase letters and set in a bold typeface for ease of reading. Component i of vector $\mathbf{x}$ will be written as x_i. Furthermore, let $S \subset R^n$ and $T \subset R$ be two sets and consider a differentiable function $f: S \rightarrow T$. Then for each element $\mathbf{x} \in S$ and image $f(\mathbf{x})$ we use f_{x_i} as short-hand notation for $\partial f(\mathbf{x})/\partial x_i$. Much in the same way, $f_{\mathbf{x}}$ stands for the gradient $\nabla f(\mathbf{x})$. Differentiation with respect to 'time' will be indicated by a dot '·' and a prime ' ' ' signifies transposition.

II. Statement of the Problem

We will be concerned with the standard optimum investment problem of maximizing under technological constraints a positive linear combination of a vector of capital stocks

$\mathbf{k}$ in some future period t_1:

(1) $$\max_{\mathbf{k}(t)} \mathbf{a}'\,\mathbf{k}(t_1)$$

$$\text{subject to} \quad T(\mathbf{k},\dot{\mathbf{k}},t) = 0\,, \ t \in [t_0, t_1]\,, \quad \text{and} \quad \mathbf{k}(t_0) = \mathbf{k}_0\,.$$

$T(\cdot)$ is assumed a transformation frontier function with domain $R^n_+ \times R^n \times R_+$, where $n > 1$. It thus completely describes all efficient one-period input-output combinations of a firm or of an economy. It shall be increasing in $\mathbf{k}$, decreasing in $\dot{\mathbf{k}}$ and twice-continuously differentiable as well as strictly quasi-concave in both $\mathbf{k}$ and $\dot{\mathbf{k}}$. Differentiability is also assumed with regard to t. Finally, Inada regularity conditions shall hold for $\mathbf{k}$.

Note that (1) is a classical problem of Mayer in the calculus of variations. We call it closed in the sense that all input variables other than capital stocks $\mathbf{k}$ and all output variables other than investments $\dot{\mathbf{k}}$ are assumed to be given from some external decision process and supposed to enter $T(\cdot)$ via t. Most of all, however, will t reflect autonomous technical progress.

Standard practice suggests to define a Lagrangian functional associated with (1) and solve the corresponding system of Euler differential equations for optimum time paths $\mathbf{k}(t)$. These equations are long known to be equivalent to the familiar own-rates of interest relationships of optimum growth theory:

Lemma 1: *If $\mathbf{k}(t)$ is a solution to (1) then*

(2) $$\frac{T_{k_i}}{T_{\dot{k}_i}} = \frac{T_{k_n}}{T_{\dot{k}_n}} + \frac{d}{dt} ln\left[\frac{T_{\dot{k}_i}}{T_{\dot{k}_n}}\right], \quad \textit{for all} \ \ i \neq n\,.$$

Proof: see H.Y. Wan, Jr. ([6], pp. 277-278).

The above $n-1$ equations along with $2n$ boundary conditions and the technology constraint $T(\cdot) = 0$ completely determine the dynamics of $\mathbf{k}(t)$. In particular, the following theorem holds:

Theorem 1: *If the transformation frontier of (1) assumes the form*

(3) $$T(\mathbf{k},\dot{\mathbf{k}},t) = J\big(G(\mathbf{k}),t\big) - H(\dot{\mathbf{k}})$$

with first-order homogeneous functions $G(\cdot)$ and $H(\cdot)$ then there exists a real-valued scalar function $\theta(t)$ and a vector of $n-1$ positive constants $\bar{\mathbf{s}}^*$ such that $\mathbf{k}(t) = \theta(t)(\bar{\mathbf{s}}^{*\prime}, 1)'$ is a solution to (2) *and $\bar{\mathbf{s}}^*$ constitutes a turnpike expansion ray of (1).*

Proof: see R. Wolff [7].

Theorem 1 refers to the case of a production technology set which is globally biconvex and has independent input and output partitions. Biconvexity of the production technology set then involves (additive) separability of the transformation frontier function (see L.J. Lau [3]). Note that our theorem does not imply constant returns to scale. Finally, as $\bar{\mathbf{s}}^*$ is indicative of the composition of the capital stocks $\mathbf{k}(t)$, we label it a 'structural saddle-point' of (1).

III. A Representation Theorem

We may now introduce our basic

Theorem 2: *Suppose a turnpike expansion ray $\bar{\mathbf{s}}^*$ of (1) exists. Also suppose that along this ray all marginal substitution and transformation rates between inputs $\mathbf{k}$ and outputs $\dot{\mathbf{k}}$, respectively, are independent of t. Then the production technology set will possess a local frontier function representation of the form in (3).*

Proof: Our proof consists of two parts. To begin with the first part, define as w the rate of growth uniformly assigned to all stock variables along an arbitrary expansion ray at a given point in time. Hence, $\dot{\mathbf{k}} = w\mathbf{k}$ such that $T(\mathbf{k}, w\mathbf{k}, t) = 0$ must hold. As $T(\cdot)$ is decreasing in $\dot{\mathbf{k}}$ we may solve for w as a function of $\mathbf{k}$ and t: $w = f(\mathbf{k}, t)$. Furthermore, assume that $k_n > 0$ and let $\mathbf{s} := (k_1/k_n, ..., k_{n-1}/k_n)'$ in which case $w = f(\mathbf{s}k_n, k_n, t)$. Now observe as an intrinsic necessary condition for a given expansion ray to be efficient that it must never pay, in terms of levels of w, to move off the ray as $\mathbf{k}$ increases over time. In other words, every efficient ray $\bar{\mathbf{s}}^*$ must always point in the direction of the maximum increase or minimum decrease, respectively, of w. Therefore, we conclude from the envelope theorem that along $\bar{\mathbf{s}}^*$:

$$(4) \qquad -\frac{T_{k_n}}{T_{\dot{k}_n}} = \frac{\partial \dot{k}_n}{\partial k_n} = \frac{\partial (w k_n)}{\partial k_n} = \sum_{i=1}^{n-1} f_{k_i} \bar{s}_i^* k_n + f_{k_n} k_n + w = \sum_{i=1}^{n} f_{k_i} k_i + w\,.$$

Since k_n is really any capital stock the above sequence applies accordingly to all components of $\mathbf{k}$. We thus obtain from (4) a system of $n-1$ necessary conditions for there to exist a ray of efficient proportional capital stock formation. They require that the own-rates of interest be the same for all capital stocks:

$$(5) \qquad \frac{T_{k_i}}{T_{\dot{k}_i}} = \frac{T_{k_n}}{T_{\dot{k}_n}} \quad \text{for all } t \text{ and all } \; i \neq n\,.$$

Equivalently, we may also say that all corresponding marginal substitution and transformation rates must coincide:

$$(6) \qquad \frac{T_{k_i}}{T_{k_n}} = \frac{T_{\dot{k}_i}}{T_{\dot{k}_n}} \quad \text{for all } t \text{ and all } \; i \neq n\,.$$

Plugging (5) into (2) reveals that intertemporal efficiency is achieved only if the second term on the right-hand side of (2) drops to zero for all t and i. Therefore, and because of (6), we find that

$$(7) \qquad \frac{d}{dt}\left(\frac{T_{k_i}}{T_{k_n}}\right) = \frac{d}{dt}\left(\frac{T_{\dot{k}_i}}{T_{\dot{k}_n}}\right) = 0 \quad \text{for all } t \text{ and all } \; i \neq n\,.$$

These equations establish an invariant relationship between $\bar{\mathbf{s}}^*$ and the ratios in (6) and end the first part of our proof.

We will now discuss in the final part of the proof what is implied by (5)-(7) for the functional form of the transformation frontier. First of all, let $\tilde{T}(k_n, \dot{\mathbf{k}}, t) := T(\bar{\mathbf{s}}^* k_n, \dot{k}_n, \mathbf{k}, t) = 0$. Since $\tilde{T}(\cdot)$ is increasing in k_n we can solve for k_n in terms of $\mathbf{k}$ and t: $k_n = \tilde{F}(\mathbf{k}, t)$. Now recall that all output transformation rates are by assumption independent of t. Therefore, and considering (7), it follows from the quasi-concavity of $T(\cdot)$ with respect to $\dot{\mathbf{k}}$ that $\tilde{F}(\cdot)$ must be a homothetic and quasi-convex function of $\dot{\mathbf{k}}$, at least if evaluated along $\bar{\mathbf{s}}^*$ (see R. Färe [1] and [2], pp. 49-61; also see Shephard [5]). Hence, $k_n = F\big(H(\dot{\mathbf{k}}), t\big) = F\big(wH(\mathbf{k}), t\big)$. Consequently, multiplying both sides of $w = f(\mathbf{k}, t)$ by $H(\mathbf{k})$ yields

$$wH(\mathbf{k}) = H(\dot{\mathbf{k}}) = f(\mathbf{k}, t) H(\mathbf{k}) =: \tilde{J}(\mathbf{k}, t) \tag{8}$$

and thereby separates $T(\cdot)$ into a homothetic and quasi-convex output branch $H(\cdot)$ and a remaining input branch $\tilde{J}(\cdot)$. At this point note that the gradients $H_{\mathbf{k}}$ and $\tilde{J}_{\mathbf{k}}$ always indicate the same direction because of (6). Also note that we have assumed all input substitution rates not to be affected by t. Finally, remind that $T(\cdot)$ is a quasi-concave function of $\mathbf{k}$. As a result, $\tilde{J}(\cdot)$ must be both homothetic and quasi-concave in $\mathbf{k}$ along $\bar{\mathbf{s}}^*$: $\tilde{J}(\mathbf{k}, t) = J\big(G(\mathbf{k}), t\big)$. We thus obtain from (8) a frontier function representation of the form

$$T(\mathbf{k}, \dot{\mathbf{k}}, t) := J\big(G(\mathbf{k}), t\big) - H(\dot{\mathbf{k}}) \tag{9}$$

which is quasi-concave in both $\mathbf{k}$ and $\dot{\mathbf{k}}$ and with $H(\cdot)$ and $G(\cdot)$ homogeneous of degree one. This completes our proof of Theorem 2. Q.E.D.

References

1. R. Färe, "On Linear Expansion Paths and Homothetic Production Functions", in: W. Eichhorn et al. (eds.), *Production Theory*, Springer Verlag, Berlin 1974, pp. 53-64.
2. R. Färe, *Fundamentals of Production Theory*, Springer Verlag, Berlin 1988.
3. L.J. Lau, "A Characterization of the Normalized Restricted Profit Function", *Journal of Economic Theory* **12** (1976), pp. 131- 164. Reprinted in D. Cass and K. Shell (eds.), *The Hamiltonian Approach to Dynamic Economics*, Academic Press, New York 1976.
4. L.W. McKenzie, "Optimal Economic Growth, Turnpike Theorems and Comparative Dynamics", in: K.J. Arrow, M.D. Intriligator (eds.), *Handbook of Mathematical Economics, Vol. III*, North-Holland, Amsterdam 1986, Chapter 26, pp. 1281-1355.
5. R.W. Shephard, *Theory of Cost and Production Functions*, Princeton 1970.
6. H.Y. Wan, Jr., *Economic Growth*, Harcourt Brace Jovanovich, New York 1971.
7. R. Wolff, "Efficient Stationary Capital Accumulation Structures of a Biconvex Production Technology", Discussion Paper No. 13-90, Department of Economics, University of Siegen, Siegen 1990, 9 pages.

PREDICTION MODELS AND TREND ANALYSIS FOR TIME-NONHOMOGENEOUS STOCHASTIC PROCESSES

Menachem P. Berg
Department of Statistics
University of Haifa
Haifa, Israel

Predictions on future evolution of stochastic processes is our main concern in this study. Based on past data of the process as well as on any relevant information or "beliefs" we have, we may wish to make predictions on future evolution of process characteristics of interest. The particular focus of this work is on time-nonhomogeneous (TN) stochastic point processes and the more general case of marked point processes (i.e. processes with jumps).

TN processes arise either as direct modelling tools or as a result of qualitative-type assumptions on processes' properties. Illustrations in that regard are provided for the application areas of Reliability (including Software Reliability) and Maintenance as well as Insurance and Epidemiology which, indeed, motivated this work.

A detailed analysis is carried out for families of TN stochastic processes with appropriatly chosen Bayesian revision models which are of special relevance to the application areas mentioned above. Some of the results obtained provide interesting insights into the processes considered.

One particular instance in which TN stochastic processes are of clear relevance is when a trend may exist and need to be allowed for in the model construction. As a matter of fact such a trend may exist in the point process and in the jump process and both cases are considered. When a trend does exist we may also want to be able to detect it on the basis of our information about the process and the predictions obtained for it.

Such trend detecting procedures, although essentially qualitative in nature, still require appropriate mathematical trend-formulation which are based on process' characteristics as well as on probabilistic ordering notions (because the formers are random quantities). Some possible trend-formulations of this type, technically referred to as process monotonicity properties, are presented and applied for trend detection in the special cases mentioned above.

PREFERENCE REVERSAL AND THE SYMMETRIC CHOQUET INTEGRAL

Extended Abstract

Dieter Denneberg
FB Mathematik/Informatik
Universität Bremen
Postfach 33 04 40, W-2800 Bremen 33, Germany

We regard decisions over uncertain or risky prospects X (or, in another terminology, acts). It is a well established empirical fact (cf. Kahneman and Tversky) that a majority of decision takers behaves risk or uncertainty averse if the prospects offer gains but the same persons are attracted by risk or uncertainty if they have to decide over losses. A real functional Γ represents these preferences if it has the following properties:

(1) $\quad \Gamma(X+Y) \geq \Gamma X + \Gamma Y \qquad$ for $X, Y \geq 0$,

(2) $\quad \Gamma(-X) = -\Gamma X \qquad$ for $X \geq 0$.

Superadditivity (1) reflects risk aversion for gains and it is equivalent to convexity of Γ for gains if, in addition, one has

(3) $\quad \Gamma(cX) = c\,\Gamma X \qquad$ for $c \geq 0$.

Using the reflection property (2) Γ is subadditive or concave for losses, hence Γ represents risk seeking behavior in the domain of losses. We show that a very natural modification of the Choquet-integral results in functionals of this type. This symmetric Choquet-integral, as we shall call it, is fully characterized through conditions (2) and (5), (9) below. Furthermore continuity properties are presented.

We start with the usual (asymmetric) Choquet integral. Let Ω be the set of elementary events (or states of nature) and $\mathfrak{A} \subset 2^{\Omega}$ a σ-algebra. We regard monotone, finite set functions $\mu: \mathfrak{A} \to \mathbb{R}$ with $\mu(\emptyset) = 0$. For an $\mathfrak{A}$-measurable function $X : \Omega \to \mathbb{R}$ we denote with $\check{G}_{\mu,X}$ the pseudo-inverse function of the descending distribution function $G_{\mu,X}(x) := \mu(X>x)$, $x \in \mathbb{R}$. The **Choqet-integral** is defined as $\int X d\mu := \int_0^{\mu(\Omega)} \check{G}_{\mu,X}(t)dt$. A crucial property of the integral is comonotonic additivity

(4) $\int X + Y\, d\mu = \int X d\mu + \int Y d\mu$ for comonotonic X,Y.

X,Y are **comonotonic** iff there is no pair $\omega_1, \omega_2 \in \Omega$ with $X(\omega_1) > X(\omega_2)$, $Y(\omega_1) < Y(\omega_2)$. It is well known that $\int \cdot d\mu$ is superadditive iff μ is supermodular, i.e. $\mu(A \cup B) + \mu(A \cap B) \geq \mu(A) + \mu(B)$. Similarly the integral behaves subadditive iff μ is submodular.

We describe the topological properties of the integral connected with the "norm" $\|X\|_1 = \|X\|_{\mu,1} := \int |X| d\mu$. For general μ the set $\mathfrak{L}_1(\mu) := \{X \mid X\ \mathfrak{A}\text{-measurable}, \|X\|_1 < \infty\}$ is no vector space but we have (cf. Denneberg).

Theorem 1. If μ is submodular then $\mathfrak{L}_1(\mu)$ and $\mathfrak{N} := \{X \in \mathfrak{L}_1(\mu) \mid \|X\|_1 = 0\}$ are vector spaces and $L_1(\mu) := \mathfrak{L}_1(\mu)/\mathfrak{N}$ is a normed linear space. The integral is a contracting functional $L_1(\mu) \to \mathbb{R}$,

$$\left| \int X d\mu - \int Y d\mu \right| \leq \|X-Y\|_1, \quad X,Y \in \mathfrak{L}_1(\mu).$$

If μ is continuous from below, $L_1(\mu)$ is a Banach space.

$\mathfrak{L}_\infty(\mathfrak{A}) := \{X \mid X\ \mathfrak{A}\text{-measurable, bounded}\}$ together with the supremum norm $\|\cdot\|_\infty$ is a normed linear space. For submodular μ the embedding $\mathfrak{L}_\infty(\mathfrak{A}) \subset \mathfrak{L}_1(\mu)$ is continuous. Applying theorem 1 we can add a continuity assertion to **Schmeidler's representation theorem:**

Theorem 2. Given a functional $\Gamma : \mathfrak{L}_\infty(\mathfrak{A}) \to \mathbb{R}$ with

(5) $X \leq Y$ implies $\Gamma X \leq \Gamma Y$,

(6) $\Gamma(X+Y) = \Gamma X + \Gamma Y$ for comonotonic X,Y.

Define the set function γ through $\gamma(A) := \Gamma 1_A$, $A \in \mathfrak{A}$. Then

$$\Gamma X = \int X d\gamma \quad \text{and} \quad \Gamma \text{ is } \|\cdot\|_\infty\text{-continuous.}$$

If, in addition Γ is subadditive then γ is submodular and Γ is $\|\cdot\|_{\gamma,1}$-continuous. The conjugate functional $\overline{\Gamma}(X) := -\Gamma(-X)$ is superadditive and $\|\cdot\|_{\gamma,1}$-continuous.

An important special case is worth mentioning. We say that a **functional** Γ on $\mathfrak{L}_\infty(\mathfrak{A})$ or $\mathfrak{L}_1(P)$ **valuates risk** given through a probability measure P on $\mathfrak{A}$ if Γ is compatible with stochastic dominance (of first order), i.e.

(7) $\qquad G_{P,X} \le G_{P,Y}$ implies $\Gamma X \le \Gamma Y$.

Then Γ can be perceived as monotone functional on the P-distribution functions. In the general situation, where no P is supposed to be given, we say that Γ **valuates uncertainty** if (5) holds. If, in theorem 2, (5) is replaced by the stronger condition (7) one easily concludes that γ is a **distortion** of P, i.e. $\gamma = g \circ P$ with distortion function $g : [0,1] \to [0, \Gamma 1]$, increasing and $g(0) = 0$, $g(1) = \Gamma 1 = \gamma(\Omega)$. Then the functionals $\int \cdot\, d(g \circ P)$ are dual (cf. Yaari) to the very popular expected utilities $\int u(\cdot) dP$ with increasing utility functions u.

Each finite set function μ has a natural partner, it's **conjugate** $\bar{\mu}(A) := \mu(\Omega) - \mu(A^c)$. Both are coupled through the **asymmetry** formula **of the integral**

(8) $\qquad \int -X\, d\mu = -\int X\, d\bar{\mu}$.

Furthermore μ is submodular iff $\bar{\mu}$ is supermodular and in that case $\bar{\mu} \le \mu$ so that $\mathfrak{L}_1(\mu) \subset \mathfrak{L}_1(\bar{\mu})$. But $\mathfrak{L}_1(\bar{\mu})$ is, in general, no vector space and $\|\cdot\|_{\bar{\mu},1}$ no norm. Nevertheless the $\bar{\mu}$-integral is continuous on $L_1(\mu)$

$$\left|\int X d\bar{\mu} - \int Y d\bar{\mu}\right| \le \|X-Y\|_{\mu,1}, \quad X,Y \in \mathfrak{L}_1(\mu), \ \mu \text{ submodular}.$$

Back to general μ we can decompose by (4), (8) the asymmetric integral as $\int X d\mu = \int X^+ d\mu + \int -X^- d\mu = \int X^+ d\mu - \int X^- d\bar{\mu}$. Omitting the bar we define the **symmetric integral**

$$⨏ X d\mu := \int X^+ d\mu - \int X^- d\mu .$$

We have symmetry

$$⨏ -X d\mu = -⨏ X d\mu$$

and, for submodular μ, continuity

$$|⨏ X d\mu - ⨏ Y d\mu| \le 2\|X-Y\|_{\mu,1}, \quad X,Y \in \mathfrak{L}_1(\mu), \ \mu \text{ submodular}.$$

This inequality remains true if we write $\bar{\mu}$ in place of μ on the left hand side only. Altogether we have seen that the four integrals $\int \cdot d\mu$, $\int \cdot d\bar{\mu}$, $\oint \cdot d\mu$, $\oint \cdot d\bar{\mu}$ live all on the normed vector space $L_1(\mu)$ if μ is submodular. The latter integral, $\oint \cdot d\bar{\mu}$, is a functional valuating uncertainty and for submodular μ it has the desired properties (1), (2), (3). Hence it is a candidate for modelling the preference reversal phenomenon. Finally we ask what additional properties have to be imposed on a functional Γ in order that it becomes a symmetric integral. With the same methods as theorem 2 one proves:

Theorem 3. Given a functional $\Gamma : \mathfrak{L}_\infty(\mathfrak{A}) \to \mathbb{R}$ with (2), (5) and restricted comonotonic additivity

(9) (i) $\Gamma(X+Y) = \Gamma X + \Gamma Y$ for comonotonic $X, Y \geq 0$,

(ii) $\Gamma X = \Gamma X^+ + \Gamma(-X^-)$.

Define γ as in theorem 2 through $\gamma(A) = \Gamma 1_A$. Then

$$\Gamma X = \oint X d\gamma .$$

If, in addition, (1) holds then $\bar{\gamma}$ is submodular and Γ is $\|\cdot\|_{\bar{\gamma},1}$-continuous. If Γ valuates risk, γ and $\bar{\gamma}$ are distorted probabilities.

Denneberg, D. (1991): "Subadditive Measure and Integral". Preprint, University of Bremen (Part of this paper appeared 1990 under the same title in the series: Mathematik-Arbeitspapiere Preprint Nr. 39, Universität Bremen).

Kahneman, D. and A. Tversky (1979): "Prospect Theory: An Analysis of Decision under Risk". Econometrica 47, 263-291.

Schmeidler, D. (1986): " Integral Representation without Additivity ". Proceedings of the American Mathematical Society 97, 255-261.

Yaari, M. E. (1987): " The Dual Theory of Choice under Risk". Econometrica 55, 95-115.

STOCHASTIC PROCESS MODELS FOR INSURANCE

Hans M. Dietz
Fachbereich Mathematik
Humboldt-Universität zu Berlin
PF 1297, D-O-1086 Berlin

Consider the accumulated amount S_t of a capital (at time t) that is established by a process R of cumulative payments and disbursements and that yields interest according to a certain interest process D, and admit both R and D to be random (say: semimartingales). Then S is the solution of the linear stochastic differential equation

$$S_t = R_t + S_{-} \bullet D_t \ , \quad t = 0,$$

that can be given explicitly by means of the Doléans exponential $\mathcal{E} = \mathcal{E}(D)$ of the interest process D. If R is of finite variation (and $[\Delta D = -1]$ is negligible) then another quantity of interest is

$$B_t = \mathcal{E}_t^{-1} \int_{]t,\infty[} \mathcal{E}_s^{-1} dR_s \ ,$$

i.e. the present value of all future payments. Thus

$$Z_t = S_t + B_t$$

can be considered as the temporary value of all payments . Then it holds

$$Z_t = \mathcal{E}_s^{-1} \mathcal{E}_t \, Z_s \quad , \quad s,t \geq 0.$$

In life insurance, typically R can be taken as the cumulative sum of the insurant's benefits from the contract and his negative premiums, whereat D is assumed to be non-random. The history of a contract can be described with the help of a suitable filtration $(\mathcal{F}_t)$. As at time t the future is not known yet the best predictor of the temporary value of the insurer's total loss at time t is

$$\hat{Z}_t = E(Z_t | \mathcal{F}_t) = S_t + E(B_t | \mathcal{F}_t),$$

where (up to the additive constant ΔR_t) $E(B_t|\mathcal{F}_t)$ is the net policy reserve. It turns out that

$$E(Z_t|\mathcal{F}_s) \rightarrow Z_t \quad \text{a.s. as } s \rightarrow \infty ,$$

hence the predictor $\hat{Z}_t$ is "consistent" in this sense.

DECOMPOSITION OF MULTIVARIATE UTILITY FUNCTIONS IN NON-ADDITIVE EXPECTED UTILITY THEORY

Rainer Dyckerhoff
Institut für Statistik und quantitative Ökonomik
Universität der Bundeswehr Hamburg
Postfach 70 08 22, D-2000 Hamburg 70

EXTENDED ABSTRACT

In many decision problems the consequences of different alternatives cannot be described by a single attribute but only by a set of several attributes. Thus, the space of consequences is a Cartesian product of several single attribute spaces. In general for a given decision maker it is a difficult and tedious job to assess the utilities of all possible consequences.

The assessment of the utility function can be considerably simplified if the utility function is decomposable in a certain functional form. The following decompositions are standard in expected utility (EU).

A utility function is said to be *multilinear decomposable* if it can be written in the form

$$u(x_1, \ldots, x_n) = \sum_{\emptyset \neq I \subset N} \gamma_I \prod_{i \in I} u_i(x_i) , \tag{1}$$

where $u_1, \ldots, u_n$ are utility functions on the attribute spaces, and the γ_I, $\emptyset \neq I \subset N$, are scaling constants, $N = \{1, 2, \ldots, n\}$.

If u can be written in the form

$$u(x_1, \ldots, x_n) = \sum_{\emptyset \neq I \subset N} \beta^{|I|-1} \prod_{i \in I} \alpha_i u_i(x_i) , \tag{2}$$

where $\alpha_1, \ldots, \alpha_n$ and β are scaling constants, u is said to be *multiplicative decomposable*.

Finally, if

$$u(x_1, \ldots, x_n) = \sum_{i=1}^{n} \alpha_i u_i(x_i) , \tag{3}$$

where $\alpha_1, \ldots, \alpha_n$ are again scaling constants, then u has an *additive decomposition*.

In these cases only univariate utility functions on the attribute spaces and a set of scaling constants have to be assessed. In expected utility (EU) many results are known that give necessary and/or sufficient conditions for a multivariate utility function to be decomposable, cf. Keeney/Raiffa [4], Fishburn [2]. These are conditions on the decision maker's preferences which postulate independence properties between the attributes. They can be checked in practical situations.

A set of attributes I is said to be *utility independent* of its complement if preferences over two lotteries which have a common fixed outcome for sure in the attributes not belonging to I do not depend on that fixed outcome.

The *marginality condition* is satisfied if preferences over lotteries depend on their marginal probability distributions only.

The following results are standard in EU.

- A utility function is multiplicative decomposable iff every set of attributes is utility independent of its complement.
- A utility function is multilinear decomposable iff every single attribute is utility independent of its complement.
- A utility function is additive decomposable iff the marginality condition is satisfied.

In recent years empirical observations have shown that in real life decision problems people tend to violate the axioms of EU, in particular the independence axiom. Many models have been developed to cope with such systematical violations of EU. One class of them makes use of non-additive probability measures. In these models the preferences between acts or lotteries are represented by the Choquet integral of a utility function with respect to a non-additive probability measure. In decision making under risk these models are known as anticipated utility (AU), rank dependent expected utility (RDEU), or expected utility with rank dependent probabilities (EURDP) and have been investigated by Quiggin [6], Segal [8], and Chew, Karni, and Safra [1]. Here the non-additive probability measure is derived as a distortion of a given additive probability measure. In decision making under uncertainty Gilboa [3], Schmeidler [7], Wakker [9] and Nakamura [5] gave axiomatizations of models with non-additive probability measures which we will refer to as Choquet expected utility (CEU). Since in these models not only the utility function has to be assessed but also a distortion function (in AU) or a non-additive probability measure (in CEU) the more important is the need for conditions that simplify these assessment procedures. We show that many of the results about decomposition of multivariate utility functions in EU carry over to AU and CEU. In particular we prove the following theorems.

Theorem 1 *In AU and CEU the following two conditions are equivalent:*

1. *The utility function u has a multiplicative decomposition.*
2. *Every nonempty subset of attributes is utility independent of its complement.*

Theorem 2 *In AU and CEU the following two conditions are equivalent:*

1. *The utility function u has a multilinear decomposition.*
2. *Every single attribute is utility independent of its complement.*

We further characterize bivariate risk aversion and risk proneness in AU. In EU a decision maker having a multiplicative utility function is bivariate risk averse (risk prone) iff the parameter β in the multiplicative decomposition is less (greater) than zero, respectively. In AU the bivariate risk posture depends also on the value of the distortion function q at 0.5. A decision maker in AU having a multiplicative utility function can be bivariate risk averse for every value of the parameter β. If we abbreviate the ratio $(1 - q(0.5))/q(0.5)$ by c the theorem can be stated in the following form.

Theorem 3 *In an AU-model with bivariate consequence space $C = C_1 \times C_2$, $C_i \subset \mathbb{R}, i = 1, 2$, let the utility function be continuous and multiplicative decomposable according to (2). Then the following statements hold:*

1. *The DM is bivariate risk averse if and only if one of the following conditions holds:*
   (a) $\beta \leq 0,\ c \geq 1$
   (b) $\beta > 0,\ c \geq \max\{1 + \beta\alpha_1, 1 + \beta\alpha_2\}$
2. *The DM is bivariate risk seeking if and only if one of the following conditions holds:*
   (a) $\beta \geq 0,\ c \leq 1$
   (b) $\beta < 0,\ c \leq \min\{1 + \beta\alpha_1, 1 + \beta\alpha_2\}$
3. *The DM is bivariate risk neutral if and only if $\beta = 0$ and $c = 1$.*

We further state two theorems concerning additive decompositions. It is shown that the marginality condition as well as bivariate risk neutrality are sufficient for an additive decomposition. However, none of them is necessary since they both pose additional restrictions on the form of the distortion function.

Theorem 4 *In AU the marginality condition is satisfied iff the following two conditions hold:*

1. *The utility function is additively decomposable.*
2. *The distortion function is the identity.*

The above theorem says that there is no non-trivial AU-model that satisfies the marginality condition. This is the case since an AU-model in which q is the identity reduces to an EU-model.

Theorem 5 *In AU the decision maker is bivariate risk neutral iff the following two conditions hold:*

1. *The utility function is additively decomposable.*

2. *The distortion function q satisfies $q(0.5) = 0.5$.*

References

[1] S.H. Chew, E. Karni, and Z. Safra. Risk aversion in the theory of expected utility with rank-dependent probabilities. *Journal of Economic Theory*, 42:370–381, 1987.

[2] P.C. Fishburn. *The Foundations of Expected Utility.* D. Reidel, Dordrecht, 1982.

[3] I. Gilboa. Expected utility with purely subjective nonadditive probabilities. *Journal of Mathematical Economics*, 16:65–88, 1987.

[4] R.L. Keeney and H. Raiffa. *Decisions with Multiple Objectives: Preferences and Value Tradeoffs.* J. Wiley, New York, 1976.

[5] Y. Nakamura. Subjective expected utility with non-additive probabilities on finite spaces. *Journal of Economic Theory*, 51:346–366, 1990.

[6] J. Quiggin. A theory of anticipated utility. *Journal of Economic Behavior and Organization*, 3:323–343, 1982.

[7] D. Schmeidler. Subjective probability and expected utility without additivity. *Econometrica*, 57:571–587, 1989.

[8] U. Segal. Nonlinear decision weights with the independence axiom. Working Paper 353, Department of Economics, University of California, Los Angeles, 1984.

[9] P.P. Wakker. Continuous subjective expected utility with nonadditive probabilities. *Journal of Mathematical Economics*, 18:1–27, 1989.

MODELLING QUESTIONS IN SECURITY VALUATION

Ernst Eberlein
Institut für Mathematische Stochastik
Universität Freiburg
D - 7800 Freiburg

The standard model for the valuation of options and other derivative securities, which has been accepted by the financial markets, is the *continuous-time Black-Scholes* model. Stock prices are assumed to be given by a geometric Brownian motion

$$S_t = S_0 \exp(\sigma B_t + (\mu - \frac{\sigma^2}{2})t) \qquad (0 \leq t \leq T),$$

where $(B_t)_{0 \leq t \leq T}$ denotes a standard Brownian motion and the constants $\sigma > 0$ and μ represent the volatility and the drift of the price process. It is assumed that securities can be and actually are traded continuously over time. In the real world, however, new stock prices appear at certain discrete time points only and prices remain constant in between. This raises the question of the relation between realistic discrete-time and idealized continuous-time models. More precisely we ask how close one class does approximate the other and in which sense. Various results have appeared recently (see e.g. [1], [3]) where approximation is discussed in terms of weak convergence of distributions. Willinger and Taqqu [4] study *pathwise approximation*. This is our goal here, too, since traders are used to look at the paths of stock prices as they appear on charts or on electronic boards and not at distributions.

Let ν be any mean-zero probability measure on the line. We require that a finite moment of order $2 + \delta$ exists for some $\delta > 0$. ν serves as the so-called *return distribution* which describes the possible price changes in each discrete step. Let σ and μ be the parameters from above and $(k_n)_{n \geq 1}$ an increasing sequence of integers. Consider the discrete price process

$$S_t^n = S_0 \exp\left(\sum_{i=1}^{[tk_n T^{-1}]} (\sigma x_{n,i} + T(\mu - \frac{\sigma^2}{2})k_n^{-1})\right) \qquad (0 \leq t \leq T),$$

where $(x_{n,i})_{1 \leq i \leq k_n, n \geq 1}$ is a triangular array of row-wise independent random variables such that $\mathcal{L}((k_n/T)^{1/2} x_{n,i}) = \nu$. If $\|\cdot\|_T$ denotes the supremum norm on functions on $[0,T]$, we show that given a Brownian motion $(B_t)_{0 \leq t \leq T}$ an array $(x_{n,i})$, for (k_n) sufficiently large, can be constructed on the same probability space such that

$$\|S_t^n - S_t\|_T \ll n^{-\lambda}$$

holds almost surely for some $\lambda > 0$. This result means that the continuous-time model is ***robust*** in the sense that more realistic discrete-time models are pathwise as close as one wishes.

As a consequence results on ***trading strategies*** and on the ***financial gains*** process can be obtained. Let (T_k^n) be stopping times defining a grid on $[0,T]$ whose mesh size converges to 0 almost surely as n goes to infinity. As an example consider the deterministic net $T_k^n = kTk_n^{-1}$ $(0 \leq k \leq k_n)$. Let $f: \mathbb{R} \times [0,T] \to \mathbb{R}$ be a continuous function and define the trading strategy θ_t^n corresponding to f and the price process S_t^n by

$$\theta_t^n = f\,(S^n(T_k^n)\,,\,T_k^n\,) \qquad \text{if } t \in]T_k^n, T_{k+1}^n]\,.$$

Then if $\theta_t = f(S_t,t)$, $\|\theta_t^n - \theta_t\|_T$ converges to 0 almost surely as well. The most interesting example for f here is the Black-Scholes trading strategy $C_x(x,t) = \frac{\partial}{\partial x} C(x,t)$, where $C(S_t,t)$ denotes the Black-Scholes value of a call option. The financial gains resulting from the trading strategies (θ_t^n) are given be the stochastic integrals $\int_0^t \theta_s^n dS_s^n$. It can be shown that the sequence of stochastic integrals $(\int_0^t \theta_s^n dS_s^n)_{n\geq 1}$ converges in probability with respect to the supremum norm to $\int_0^t \theta_s dS_s$, the financial gain resulting from (θ_t) under (S_t). For an appropriate subsequence convergence holds even almost surely.

References:

[1] Duffie, D. and P. Protter (1988): From Discrete to Continuous Time Finance: Weak Convergence of the Financial Gain Process. (forthcoming)

[2] Eberlein, E. (1991): On Modelling Questions in Security Valuation. (submitted to Mathematical Finance)

[3] He, H. (1990): Convergence from Discrete to Continuous Time Financial Models. (forthcoming)

[4] Willinger, W. and M. Taqqu (1991): Toward a Convergence Theory for Continuous Stochastic Securities Market Models. Mathematical Finance 1, 55-99.

A Bootstrap Procedure for Estimating the Lundberg Coefficient

Paul Embrechts
ETH Zürich
Dept. of Mathematics
CH-8092 Zürich

Thomas Mikosch
TU Dresden
Inst. f. Math. Stochastik
Mommsenstr. 13, D-8027 Dresden

1. Efron's bootstrap method

Efron (1979) introduced a new resampling method, the bootstrap: Let $\mathbf{X}_n = (X_1,\ldots,X_n)$ be a given sample of i.i.d. random variables (r.v.'s) with distribution function (d.f.) F. From $\mathbf{X}_n$ construct the empirical d.f. F_n and draw a bootstrap sample $\mathbf{X}^*_{nm} = (X^*_{n1},\ldots,X^*_{nm})$ of (conditionally) i.i.d. r.v.'s with d.f. F_n, given $\mathbf{X}_n$. Consider a statistic $T_n = T(\mathbf{X}_n|F)$ and its bootstrap version $T^*_{nm} = T(\mathbf{X}^*_{nm}|F_n)$. Then, drawing a large number of i.i.d. bootstrap samples $\mathbf{X}^*_{nm}(1),\ldots,\mathbf{X}^*_{nm}(B)$ and applying the SLLN, one can approximate the d.f. $P^*(T^*_{nm}\le x)=P(T^*_{nm}\le x|\mathbf{X}_n)$ or parameters of the d.f. as exactly as one wishes. But one also has to guarantee that T_n and T^*_{nm} are "close" in some sense. The usual way is to show bootstrap consistency in the sense that $\sup_x | P(T_n\le x) - P^*(T^*_{nm}\le x) | \longrightarrow 0$ a.s. or in probability.

We will say that a bootstrap estimator is *strongly consistent* if $T_n-T^*_{n,m(n)} \longrightarrow 0$ a.s. along a given subsequence $m(n) \longrightarrow \infty$, $n \longrightarrow \infty$.

2. The classical risk model

We consider the cumulative claim process

$$S(t) = x + c\,t - \sum_{i=1}^{N(t)} C_i$$

with initial reserve $x>0$, premium rate $c>0$, the claims C_i

occur at times T_1, $T_1+T_2,\ldots$, and $N(t)=\text{card}\{k\geq 0: T_1+\ldots+T_k\leq t\}$. We put $X_i = C_i-cT_i$ and suppose that (X_i) is a sequence of i.i.d. r.v.'s. The probability of ruin with initial reserve x is then given by

$$\psi(x) = P(\inf_{t>0} S(t) < 0) = P(\sup_{n>0} \textstyle\sum_{i=1}^{n} X_i).$$

It is well known (e.g. Gerber (1979)) that $\psi(x)$ behaves like e^{-Rx} as $x \longrightarrow \infty$ provided that there exists a positive solution of the equation $Ee^{RX_1} = 1$. The number R is called the Lundberg or adjustment coefficient.

Csörgö, Steinebach (1990) proposed a new estimator of the Lundberg coefficient R: Put $M_0=0$, $M_k=[M_{k-1}+X_k]^+$, $\nu_0=0$, $\nu_k=\min\{i: i\geq\nu_{k-1}+1,\ M_i=0\}$, $Z_k= \max_{\nu_{k-1}\leq l\leq\nu_k} M_l$. The Z_i form a sequence of i.i.d. r.v.'s. Let $Z_{n1}\leq\ldots\leq Z_{nn}$ denote the order statistics corresponding to $Z_1,\ldots,Z_n$. Then the following assertion holds:

Proposition. Suppose that the following conditions are satisfied:

(1) The moment generating function of X_1 exists in $(-r_0,r_0)$.

(2) There exists a solution $R\in(0,r_0)$ of the equation $Ee^{RX_1} = 1$.

If the integer sequence k_n satisfies the condition $k_n/n \longrightarrow 0$ then $\lim_{n\to\infty} Z_{n,n-k_n+1} / \ln(n/k_n) = 1/R$ a.s.

3. A bootstrap procedure for estimating R

Given a sample $\mathbf{X}_n=(X_1,\ldots,X_n)$ with common d.f. F, construct the empirical d.f. F_n and draw a sufficiently large bootstrap sample $(X^*_{n1},\ldots,X^*_{nl})$ as described in Section 1. In a similar way as in Csörgö, Steinebach (1990) (see Proposition 1 above) we define for fixed n: $M^*_{n0}=0$, $M^*_{nk}=[M_{n,k-1}+X^*_{nk}]^+$, $k\geq 1$, $\nu^*_{n0}=0$, $\nu^*_{nk} = \min\{i: i\geq\nu_{n,k-1}+1,\ M^*_{ni}=0\}$, $Z^*_{nk}= \max\{M^*_{nl}: \nu^*_{n,k-1} \leq l \leq \nu^*_{nk}\}$. Then the Z^*_{ni} form a sequence of (conditionally) i.i.d. r.v.'s. Let $Z^*_{n,1,l_n}\leq\ldots\leq Z^*_{n,l_n,l_n}$ denote the order statistics corresponding to $Z^*_{n1},\dots,Z^*_{nl_n}$.

We first consider an empirical estimator R_n for R defined as follows: $R_n=R_n(X_1,\dots,X_n)$ is the solution of the equation

$$E^*\exp\{R_nX^*_{n1}\} = n^{-1}\sum_{i=1}^{n} \exp\{R_nX_i\} = 1,$$

where E^* denotes expectation with respect to P^*.

This estimator for R was first proposed in Csörgö, Teugels (1990). Because $E^*\exp\{rX^*_{n1}\}$ is finite for all real r, it follows from Mammitzsch (1986) that there exists a unique solution $R_n>0$ if and only if $E^*X_{n1} = n^{-1}\sum_{i=1}^{n} X_i < 0$ and $P^*(X^*_{n1}>0) = n^{-1}\sum_{i=1}^{n} I(X_i>0) > 0$.

So we can rewrite the above conditions as

(3) at least one of the observations X_i is positive,

(4) $\sum_{i=1}^{n} X_i < 0$.

If the Lundberg coefficient R exists, then $EX_1<0$ and $P(X_1>0)>0$, so that, by the SLLN, the conditions (3) and (4) are satisfied for sufficiently large n, with probability 1. It now follows from Proposition 1 that

$$\Delta^*_{n,k_n,l_n} = Z^*_{n,l-k_l+1,l} \,/\, \log(1/k_l) \longrightarrow 1/R_n \text{ a.s., } l \longrightarrow \infty$$

for almost all samples $\mathbf{X}_n$, provided that $k_l/l \longrightarrow 0$. Moreover, it is not difficult to see that, whenever R exists, $R_n \longrightarrow R$ a.s. Simple diagonalization suggests that there should exist nonrandom integer sequences (k_n) and (l_n) such that $1\le k_n\le l_n$, $k_n/l_n \longrightarrow 0$ and $\Delta^*_{n,k_n,l_n} \longrightarrow 1/R$ P-a.s. In the spirit of Section 1 this would amount to a strong consistency result of the bootstrap estimator of R. That this procedure really works is the content of our result:

Theorem. Let (k_n), (l_n) be integer sequences such that $1\le k_n\le l_n$, $k_n/l_n \longrightarrow 0$, as $n\longrightarrow\infty$, and one of the following conditions is satisfied:

i) $\underline{\lim}\ k_n / \log n > 2$;

ii) $\log k_n / \log l_n = o(1)$ and $\forall\ \eta>0$: $\sum_n l_n^{-\eta} < \infty$.

If (1) and (2) hold then $\Delta^*_{n,k_n,l_n} \longrightarrow 1/R$ a.s., $n \longrightarrow \infty$.

The proof uses ideas of Bartfai (1970) and Csörgö, Steinebach (1990). Our main tool is a Chernoff type bound for $P^*(Z^*_{n1} \geq x)$: Under the conditions of Theorem 2,

$$\exp\{-R_n x_n\}\, C_1\, x_n^{-3/2} \leq P^*(Z^*_{n1} \geq x_n) \leq \exp\{-R_n x_n\}\, C_2\, (x_n+1),$$

for a sequence $x_n \longrightarrow \infty$, sufficiently large n, with probability 1.

Computer simulations show that this procedure works quickly even for "small" sample sizes (n=100,...,500).

References

Bartfai P. (1970) Limes-Superior-Sätze für die Wartemodelle. Studia Sci. Math. Hung. **5**, 317-325.

Csörgö M., Steinebach J. (1990) On the estimation of the adjustment coefficient in risk theory via intermediate order statistics. Technical report.

Csörgö S., Teugels J.L. (1990) Empirical Laplace transform and approximation of compound distributions. J. Appl. Probab. **27**, 88-101.

Efron B. (1979) Another look at the jackknife. Ann. Statist. **7**, 1-26.

Embrechts P., Mikosch T. (1991) A bootstrap procedure for estimating the adjustment coefficient. Technical report.

Gerber H.U. (1979) An Introduction to Mathematical Risk Theory. Huebner Foundation Monograph, no 8, Irwin Homewood

Mammitzsch V. (1986) A note on the adjustment coefficient in ruin theory. Insurance: Math.and Econ. **5**, 147-149.

SWAP POLICY AND UTILITY THEORY

G.GUGLIELMONE
Industrial Engineering Dept.
University of Genoa
N.DAZZI
Systems Engineering Dept.
Italimpianti s.p.a. Genoa (Italy)

The possibility of applying Utility Theory to the problem of evaluating the best covering policy (swap), when future revenues in a foreign currency are foreseen, is examined in the present paper.

1) Problem's Description

"Swap" is a financial technique widely used by companies operating in international environment in order to reduce exposure to risk due to uncertainty in exchange rate values. Financial managers have to decide about which part of the future revenues is to be covered by swap.

A representation of this problem is given in fig. 1: rows represent possible actions, which in this case are related to different percentages (0%,33%,66%,100%) of the whole amount to be swapped; columns represent possible states of exchange rate values (in decision theory language "states of the world").

In this paper only three states are taken in to account: an optimistic one (θ_3), a "status quo" one (θ_2), and a pessimistic one (θ_1).

Each entry in the matrix represents the monetary outcome of the selected action and the corresponding state of the world.

2) Hints of Utility Theory

Utility Theory assumes that Decision Maker selects the action which presents the maximum result in terms of expected utility [1].

In mathematical terms Decision Maker selects the action a_k such that:

$$\Sigma_j\, p(\theta_j)^* u(x_{kj}) = \max_i\, [\Sigma_j\, p(\theta_j)^* u(x_{ij})]\text{ , where:}$$

x_{ij} is monetary outcome in local currency corresponding to action a_i and state θ_j;

$u(x_{ij})$ is decision maker utility of outcome x_{ij};

$p(\theta_j)$ is probability of state θ_j.

In fig. 2 is shown an example of utility function.

3) Geometrical interpretation

In order to achieve a better understanding of implications of Utility Theory, the three states geometrical representation, suggested by Machina [3], was used.

In fig. 3, the points within the triangle (simplex space) represent all possible values that probability over the three states can assume.

Lines are the "isopreference" curves between couple of actions; there is a link between the shape of Utility function and the type of curve in the simplex space.

In particular we are interested on the isopreference curves between the two following couple of actions:

a_4 (100% coverage) and a_3 (66% coverage)

a_2 (33% coverage) and a_1 (0% coverage).

Analytical expressions of isopreferences are the following:

$$p(\theta_1)*[u(X_{41})-u(X_{31})] + p(\theta_3)*[u(X_{43})-u(X_{33})] = 0$$

$$p(\theta_1)*[u(X_{21})-u(X_{11})] + p(\theta_3)*[u(X_{23})-u(X_{13})] = 0 .$$

Isopreference curves are straight lines passing through the axes origin and with angular coefficients respectively equal to:

$$m_{43} = [u(X_{41})-u(X_{31})]/[u(X_{33})-u(X_{43})]$$

$$m_{21} = [u(X_{21})-u(X_{11})]/[u(X_{13})-u(X_{23})] .$$

It will be $m_{21} > m_{43} > 1$ if utility function is concave.

For probabilities at the right of isopreference line $a_3 \sim a_4$, "total swap" is the preferred action, while above line $a_1 \sim a_2$ "no swap" is the best action. For probability states between the two lines, partial swap is the best action.

It is clear that from Utility Theory point of view only the two extreme actions (a_4 , a_1) appear to be robust.

Moreover it has to be observed that decision about the best action is taken depending only on the ratio $p(\theta_1)/p(\theta_3)$, being the value of $p(\theta_2)$ uninfluential.

A new approach to our problem by means of Decision Theory Under Risk, which is a development of classical Utility Theory [3,4], is being investigated.

In this approach the utility isopreference curves pass through the axes origin but are not straight lines.

4) Test results

An investigation about risk attitude was carried out by interview.

Many company's managers and employees were asked about two types of questions; by first they had to evaluate probability states ($p(\theta_1)$, $p(\theta_3)$) for which they are indifferent between the following couple of actions: a_4-a_3 , a_3-a_2 , a_2-a_1.

Subsequently their utility function was estimated using the standard method [1].

Examination of first type of answers reveals that:

- only 20% are in accordance with risk-adverse Utility Theory;
- 35% stated that $m_{21} > m_{32} > m_{43}$ but with $m_{43} < 1$.

Examination of second type of answers reveals that:

- 35% are in accordance with Prospect Theory [5], which implies risk proness for losses and risk adversion for gains;
- 50% are risk-prones.

5) References

1] Keeney R.L., Raiffa H.; Decisions with Multiple Objectives; J.Wiley & Sons (1976);

2] Machina M.J.; Choice under uncertainty : Problems solved and unsolved; Economic Perspectives; Vol. 1, n° 1 (1987);

3] Machina M.J.; Expected Utility analysis without independence axiom; Econometrica; n° 50 (1982); Vol. 1, n° 1 (1987);

4] Quigging J.; A theory of anticipated utility; Journal of Economic Behavior and Organization; n° 3 (1983);

5] Tversky A.,Kahneman D.; Prospect Theory: An Analysis of Theory under risk; Econometrica; n° 47 (1979).

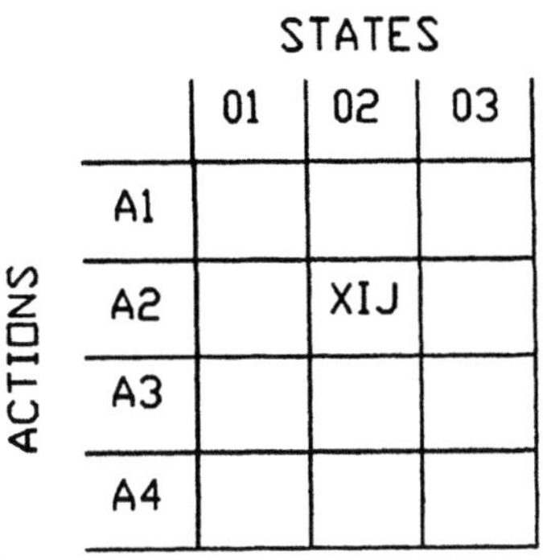

FIG.1 PROBLEM REPRESENTATION

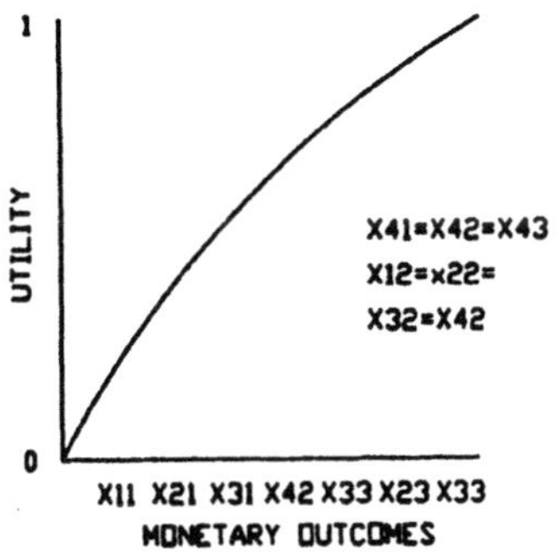

FIG.2 UTILITY FUNCTION

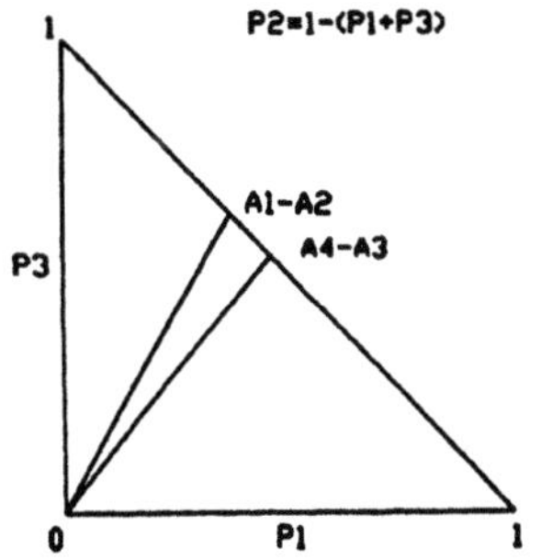

FIG.3 THREE STATES MODEL

INTERTEMPORAL PORTFOLIO SELECTION AND RISK BUSINESS

Christian Hipp
Institute for Mathematical Stochastics
University of Hamburg
Bundesstrasse 55, D-2000 Hamburg 13

1. Introduction

Modern finance is a challenging field for the application of modern probability and statistics. The emphasis in this talk is on discretization of continuous time stochastic processes and its application to problems in finance. Pioneering work on discretization is done by Kloeden and Platen (1991). Their work has implications on the understanding of stochastic differential equations (SDE), on Monte Carlo simulation and on estimation theory for SDE. With discretization methods we can simulate complex models for asset prices and investigate the effect of intertemporal portfolio selection in these models. And one can estimate the parameters in these models.

2. Portfolio selection

The intertemporal portfolio selection considered here is Merton's (1973) modification of the classical Markowitz diversification. It is based on mean variance analysis, which clearly shows that there is a tradeoff between high expected return (mean) and low risk (variance). For intertemporal portfolio selection it is assumed that for each time point the means and covariances of all returns on risky assets are given. For prescribed (maximal) variance of the portfolio a portfolio is chosen which maximizes expected return in the class of portfolios with prescribed variance. Our model for asset prices is a linear system of SDE

$$dX_t = A_1 X_t\, dt + A_2 Y_t\, dt + BX_t\, dW_t$$

with X_t the vector of asset prices, W_t multivariate Wiener process, and Y_t another observable process of economic quantities (such as interest rates). This model covers the Black Scholes model as a special case. It allows, however, for periodic drifts, interaction between asset prices and interaction between interest rates and asset prices. In this model, at time t the conditional means and covariances of returns for a time interval of length dt in the future are

$$1 + \{A_1X_t + A_2Y_t\}^{(i)}/X_t^{(i)}\quad dt$$

and

$$\sum_{l,m,k} B_{lim}\, B_{ljk}\, X_t^{(m)}\, X_t^{(k)}/X_t^{(i)}\, X_t^{(j)}\quad dt$$

respectively. Here, B_{lim} are the entries of the matrix B. Write B_i for the matrix with entries B_{lim}. The system of SDE can be solved explicitely only if all matrices A_1, B_i commute. If not, then Monte Carlo simulations for the X_t process can be obtained with Kloeden and Platen's methods.

3. Combination with risk business

The comments on combination of portfolio selection and risk business are restricted to the case of life insurance business. For the general case one should consult Cummins (1990). Life insurance business has the following special properties: i) it is a long-term business with little risk, ii) at maturity, policy holders expect to get their sum with certainty, together with a high bonus. Since long-term returns on stock is higher than return on riskless assets, investment in stock will yield a higher bonus. The investment risk can be controlled by a prescribed variance which may depend on maturities, on the present value of the portfolio, and on the value of reserves.

4. Discretization

Stochastic calculus (based on Wiener process) with its concept of Ito-integral and with Ito's and Girsanov's formula can easily be understood using discretization. For the SDE

$$dX_t = a(X_t,t)\,dt + b(X_t,t)\,dW_t$$

and discretization $t_n = \frac{n}{N}$, $n=0,\dots,N$, of $[0,1]$ the so-called Euler scheme is the following: define the approximating process $Y_N(t)$ at t_n by

$$y_0 = x_0$$

$$y_{n+1} = y_n + a(y_n,t_n)\,\frac{1}{N} + b(y_n,t_n)\,\Delta W_n$$

and $Y_N(t_n) = y_n$. Here x_0 is the deterministic value of X_0, and ΔW_n are iid $N(0,\frac{1}{N})$. In the case of a linear SDE

$$dX_t = aX_t\,dt + bX_t\,dW_t$$

the values y_n can be calculated explicitely, and it is easily seen that $Y_N(t)$ converges to X_t at the rate $N^{-1/2}$. In this simple example it can be seen how to adjust the recursion for y_n to obtain an approximating process $\tilde{Y}_N(t)$ converging to X_t at the rate N^{-1}, $N^{-3/2}$, etc. Kloeden and Platen define higher order discretizations for the general nonlinear and multivariate case. Their recursions are written using multiple Wiener integrals. The univariate order N^{-1} scheme due to Milstein (1978) might serve as an appetizer:

$$y_{n+1} = y_n + a\,\frac{1}{N} + b\Delta W_n + \frac{1}{2}\,bb'\left[(\Delta W_n)^2 - \frac{1}{N}\right].$$

Here, the functions a and b are evaluated at y_n, t_n, and $b' = \partial b/\partial x$. Finally, discretization can help to find estimators for the parameters of SDE. This statistical problem is most important for successful intertemporal portfolio selection, and it is unsolved. To define estimators derived from higher order discretization we consider the linear SDE

$$dX_t = aX_t dt + bX_t dW_t$$

with a unknown and b known. Use first the Euler scheme, solve for ΔW_n, and form the joint density of the y_n's, n=1,...,N. Then compute the maximum likelihood estimator (MLE) for a and replace all y_n's by the observations $X(t_n)$. The resulting estimator converges to the continuous time MLE when N tends to infinity. The speed of this convergence is of order $N^{-1/2}$. Next consider the Milstein scheme, solve for ΔW_n, and expand:

$$\Delta W_n \sim \frac{y_{n+1}}{y_n} - 1 - a/N$$

$$\Delta W_n \sim \frac{y_{n+1}}{y_n} - 1 - a/N - \frac{1}{2} b^2\left[\left(\frac{y_{n+1}}{y_n} - 1 - a/N\right)^2 - \frac{1}{N}\right].$$

The corresponding MLE for a equals

$$\arg\min \sum_{n=0}^{N-1} \left[\frac{y_{n+1}}{y_n} - 1 - \frac{a}{N} - \frac{1}{2} b^2\left[\left(\frac{y_{n+1}}{y_n} - 1 - \frac{a}{N}\right)^2 - \frac{1}{N}\right]\right]^2$$

which is - up to terms which can be neglected, equal to

$$\frac{1}{N} \sum_{n=0}^{N-1} \left[\frac{y_{n+1}}{y_n} - 1 - \frac{1}{2} b^2\left[\left(\frac{y_{n+1}}{y_n} -1\right)^2 - \frac{1}{N}\right]\right].$$

We obtain a second order estimator for a when we replace y_n by $X(t_n)$, n=0,...,N.

5. Open problems

i) The multivariate Milstein scheme contains the following double Wiener integral

$$\int_0^t \int_0^s dW_r^{(1)}\, dW_s^{(2)}$$

where $W_s^{(1)}$, $W_s^{(2)}$ are independent standard Wiener processes. For this integral, a simple (in the sense of Monte Carlo simulations) approximation for $t \to 0$ is needed.

ii) In our portfolio selection, transaction costs were neglected. Incorporation of transaction costs in intertemporal Markowitz diversification is an unsolved problem. For option pricing, the incorporation of transaction costs was recently solved by Boyle and Vorst (1990).

iii) The short term prediction of asset prices in our model is not satisfactory. This observation was made in an empirical study with time series of nine stock prices, two investment fonds and three option prices. It is unknown whether this phenomenon is caused by a nonlinear drift in the real world stock prices.

REFERENCES

Ph. Boyle and T. Vorst (1990). Option replication in discrete time with transaction costs. Preprint, University of Waterloo.

J.D. Cummins (1990). Asset pricing models and insurance ratemaking. ASTIN Bulletin 20, 125-166.

P. Kloeden and E. Platen (1991). The numerical solution of stochastic differential equations. Springer. To appear.

R.C. Merton (1973). An intertemporal capital asset pricing model. Econometrica 41, 867-880.

G.N. Milstein (1978). A method of second-order accuracy integration of stochastic differential equations. Theor. Probab. Appl. 23, 396-401.

ON THE UNIQUENESS OF SUBJECTIVE PROBABILITIES

Ed Karni

The John Hopkins University

and

David Schmeidler

Tel Aviv University and The Ohio State University

Summary

The Purpose of this paper is twofold: First, within the framework of Savage (1954), we suggest axiomatic foundations for the representation of event-dependent preference relations over acts. This representation has the form of expectation of event-dependent utility with respect to non-unique subjective probabilities on the set of states. Second, we give an economic-theoretic motivation for selecting a unique probability distribution as an appropriate concept of "subjective probabilities". However, unlike in Savage's theory, this notion of subjective probabilities does not necessarily represent the decision-maker's belief regarding the likelihood of events.

Our approach involves a departure from Savage's postulate P4, which guarantees the completeness of Savage's likelihood relation on the set of all events. Instead, we assume the existence of a finite partition of the set of states, $\{S_1, ..., S_n\}$, such that, for events within each element of this partition P4 is satisfied. This weakening of Savage's axioms suffices for the existence of an expected event-dependent utility representation, but not for the uniqueness of the subjective probabilities. In many economic problems involving decision-making under uncertainty the existence of a unique probability is presumed and, in fact, is essential for the statement of the result. For example consider Arrow's (1965) finding that all risk averse decision-makers will invest in a risky asset provided its expected rate of return exceeds that of an alternative risk-free asset. We show that a unique probability distribution can be chosen so as to render such results meaningful, i.e., any risk averse decision-maker will hold a positive position in the risky asset if and only if its expected rate of return with respect to the chosen probability exceeds that of the riskless asset.

THE EFFECTS OF SKEWNESS FOR INSURANCE RATEMAKING

Winfried Schott
Universität Hamburg
Seminar für Bank- und Versicherungsbetriebslehre
Von-Melle-Park 5, D- W 2000 Hamburg 13

Introduction

In Risk Theory only the actuarial risk is considered; the description of the actuarial risk is the probability distribution of the claims. On this basis an insurer's necessary premium for covering the risk is derived. Financial models intend to develop "fair" market rates of return and thus a normative price for a risky investment, or any asset in general. A fair insurance premium is derived following the idea that the fair rate of return when covering a risk by means of an insurance contract should be the same as the fair rate of return from any other risky investment. The most applied financial models are the Capital Asset Pricing Model (CAPM), the Arbitrage Pricing Model (APM) and the Option Pricing Model (OPM); for all these models a competitive market or, at least, market equilibrium is assumed, and there is no financial model which can be applied for any arbitrary probability distribution without suppressing substantial information being included in a probability distribution. The Capital Asset Pricing Model (CAPM), for instance, is based on a (μ,σ)-model, which means: Every asset or investment is regarded only in respect to μ, the expected rate of return, and σ, its standard deviation. Every other information about a probability distribution is neglected; in Option Pricing Theory solutions are only considered on the basis of very special assumptions about the probability distributions.

The loss of general applicability would not be of any relevance to insurance ratemaking if the real claim distributions were taken into consideration sufficiently; and the loss of information would not be of any relevance if this information were not important. But it is shown that in fact more information about a probability distribution than only μ and σ is required, and it is, of course, necessary for decision making to specify which probability distributions should be taken into account and which information about the probability distributions is required.

Relevant probability distributions and decision theoretic consequences

In financial theory investment returns very often are assumed to be normally distributed. As a normal distribution is characterized by the parameters μ and σ, the use of a (μ,σ)-model might be reasonable if the assumption of the normal distribution is realistic. But obviously losses greater than the invested amount cannot occur to the investor if he does not cover any other risk. On the other hand, there is no natural upper bound for positive profit margins. Very high profit margins will of course only occur with very small probabilities. So it seems to be more realistic to assume a distribution for investment profit margins which is bounded from below, unbounded from above and positively skewed, with $\gamma_X = \frac{E(X-EX)^3}{\sigma^3}$ being the skewness of a random variable X, as it is performed in Option Pricing Theory for deriving the Black-Scholes formula where the investment returns are assumed to be log-normally distributed.

Considering insurance business we have to distinguish between the underwriting business and the investment business. For the latter the assumption of positively skewed rates of return will hold, but it will not hold for the underwriting business. A typical claim distribution X is positively skewed so that the random variable of the return $\boldsymbol{R} = -X+\pi_X$, with π_X the premium received for covering the risk X, is negatively skewed. As the total risk of an insured portfolio is also negatively skewed there is a difference between underwriting and investment business. So the decision theoretic relevance of skewness is considered. On the basis of the Bernoulli Principle it can be developed that decisions based on a (μ,σ)-model might be unreasonable, and it is shown that a monotonically nonincreasing risk aversion function (Arrow-Pratt measure) will imply a preference for skewness. Therefore a (μ,σ,γ)-model is considered, and the effects of skewness for insurance ratemaking are analysed.

Consequences of the integration of skewness for the market rates of return of actuarial and financial risks

Preference functions $\Psi(\mu,\sigma,\gamma):=a\cdot\gamma\cdot\sigma^3+3\cdot a\cdot\sigma^2\cdot\mu+a\cdot\mu^3+b\cdot\sigma^2+b\cdot\mu^2+c\cdot\mu+d$, $a>0$, $b,c,d\in\mathbb{R}$, $3ac\geq b^2$, are the only (μ,σ,γ)-rules which are generally rational (i.e.: in conformity with the Bernoulli Principle). They correspond to cubic utility functions $u(x)=ax^3+bx^2+cx+d$, which do not seem to be very reasonable. Though cubic utility functions are monotonically increasing for $a>0$ and $3ac\geq b^2$ there must be a segment $[c,\infty)$ of the function where risk sympathetic decisions are made so that the assumption of risk aversion cannot hold in general. In the risk averse segment, like the quadratic utility function, the risk aversion function is, at least in most of its parts, increasing, and as a cubic function is unbounded paradoxa like the well known paradox of the St.Petersburg Game can be caused. So it does not seem to be very reasonable to make decisions on the basis of the expected value μ, the standard deviation σ and the skewness γ. But nevertheless, there is a progress compared to decisions based on (μ,σ)-rules.

If there are homogeneous assumptions about the probability distributions there will be a market price for the skewness of risks, for skewness preference can be assumed. Therefore the expected return of an investment in a negatively skewed actuarial risk must be higher than the expected return of an investment in a normal financial risk. And though the skewness is no description for a ruin probability it can be interpreted that the danger of being ruined in underwriting business is taken into account by the market price for skewness. These are very reasonable consequences of the integration of skewness effects into financial models. Having covered negatively skewed actuarial risk a decision maker can combine his risk with positively skewed financial risks. So there is a reasonable explanation why insurance companies are existing which do business by combining underwriting and investment risks. Quantitative remarks can only be made depending on special stochastic assumptions. But it can be noticed that for a large portfolio of actuarial risks less positively skewed investments are needed in order to avoid an excessively negative value of skewness than this is the case for a small portfolio. These are effects which are rather similar to the effects of collective risk reduction for the standard deviation.

Finally it is examined whether the integration of the skewness into the most applied financial model, the CAPM, produces more reasonable results than in the two-moment case. Under the assumptions of the two-moment CAPM one gets the result that any risk R_j has to be assessed by calculating the risk free rate of return r_f and a charge which depends linearly on the correlation of the risk to the market portfolio M, being reflected by the CAPM-formula of the capital market line: $ER_j=r_f+\beta_j\cdot(ER_M-r_f)$. This formula can of course be applied to underwriting business. We can assume the actuarial risk to be nearly uncorrelated to the risk of the market portfolio which depends on business cycles etc., but not on stochastical claims. We therefore set $\beta_U=0$, where β_U is the beta-factor of the underwriting business. Hence, as there is no difference between an insurer and an insured in that model, we get the result that an insurer has to pay the market price of r_f for "buying" the insurance contract. So he gets an expected technical loss of r_f without receiving any risk premium. This result is in contradiction to the risk theoretic result that the expected value of the claims risk is the absolutely lowest premium which is necessary for covering the risk. We therefore examine whether this paradox can be avoided if a three-moment CAPM including a market price for skewness is considered. It is supposed that the expected utility is maximized and that only the first three moments of a probability distribution are relevant for decision making.

Integrating a co-skewness factor $\gamma_{iP}=\frac{E(R_i-ER_i)(W-EW)^2}{E(W-EW)^3}$, if $E(W-EW)^3\neq 0$, W the random variable of the investor's wealth, as a measure for systematic skewness a function $\Phi(EW,\sigma_W,m_W)$, with $m_W^3=E(W-EW)^3$, is maximized subject to the initial wealth by Lagrange's method of multiplyers, analogously to the two-moment portfolio selection. If $E(W-EW)^3=0$, separate considerations are unavoidable, but they will not lead to other results than the following. We get the result that for an optimal individual portfolio the expected return will grow for bearing systematic risk and fall for receiving systematic skewness. Unfortunately very strong assumptions are needed if these reasonable results are to be generalized from one decision maker's portfolio to the market portfolio. In a two-moment CAPM only risk aversion has to be assumed to get the result that each investor will invest in a combination of the market portfolio and the risk-free asset, the proportion depending on the level of risk aversion. The "fair" market rate of return can easily be developed knowing the beta-factor. In a three-moment CAPM there is a conflict between minimizing the standard deviation and maximizing the skewness. So assumptions are required on how a compromise can be found in order to fulfil these two aims; this means that a market with homogeneous proportions of the relevance of these two aims is needed, a requirement which seems unrealistic. But even if this is guaranteed we get the result of the "fair" rate of return of the underwriting business again being $-r_f$, for in a three-moment CAPM the expected return depends linearly on r_f, the beta-factor β_U and the gamma-factor γ_U of the underwriting business; and having assumed that actuarial risk is independent from the market risk we get $\gamma_U=\beta_U=0$.

So we can summarize: Taking skewness into consideration for individual risk assessment leads to more reasonable results than decisions based on a (μ,σ)-model. But rational decisions based on the first three moments of a probability distribution correspond to unrealistic utility functions. So it seems to be advisable to use more of the information about a risk than the first three moments. The capital market assumptions, however, are so restrictive that the results developed in a (μ,σ,γ)-model are as unreasonable as they are in a (μ,σ)-model. Modifying the capital market assumptions and considering the consequences for insurance ratemaking seems to be a sensible idea for undertaking further research.

References

D'Arcy,S.P./Doherty,N.: The Financial Theory of Pricing Property-Liability Insurance Contracts; Homewood 1988.
Bühlmann,H.: Mathematical methods in risk theory; Berlin/Heidelberg/New York 1970.
Cummins,J.D.: Asset Pricing Models and Insurance Ratemaking; in: The Astin Bulletin 20/2 (1990), p.125-166.
Von Eije,J.H.: Reinsurance Mangement; Rotterdam 1989.
Heilmann,W.-R.: Fundamentals of Risk Theory; Karlsruhe 1988.
Ingersoll, J.E.: Theory of Financial Decision Making; Totowa (New Jersey) 1987.
Kraus,A./Litzenberger,R.H.: Skewness Preference and the Valuation of Risk Assets; in: The Journal of Finance 31/4 (1976), p.1085-1100.
Müller,W.: Finanztheoretische Analyse der Versicherungsunternehmen und der Versicherungsmärkte; in: Zeitschrift für die gesamte Versicherungswissenschaft 72 (1983), p.535-574.
Schneeweiß,H.: Entscheidungskriterien bei Risiko; Berlin/Heidelberg/New York 1966.
Sterk,H.-P.: Selbstbeteiligung unter risikotheoretischen Aspekten; Karlsruhe 1979.

On a Family of Counting Distributions and Recursions for Related Compound Distributions

Klaus J. Schröter
University of Karlsruhe
Lehrstuhl für Versicherungswissenschaft
Kronenstr. 34
7500 Karlsruhe 1

1. Introduction

Willmot & Sundt (1989) have considered compound Delaporte distributions and have developed a recursive algorithm to evaluate their counting densities in the case with integer-valued severities. An important point in the derivation is the fact that the Delaporte distributions represent compound Poisson distributions. This leads to a kind of twofold Panjer-type algorithm, cf. Panjer (1981).
After presenting notation and preliminary results in Section 2, a class of counting distributions containing the Delaporte and other non-trivial distributions is considered in Section 3. The members of this class are characterized by the property that their counting densities fulfill a certain second order difference equation. This property is used to generate a recursive Panjer-type algorithm in order to evaluate related compound distributions. In comparison to the algorithm presented by Willmot & Sundt (1989) the computational effort can be reduced.
Section 4 investigates the question whether a counting distribution is fully determined by the above-mentioned difference equations, examines which parameters of the recursions are feasible, and works out some special cases, especially compound Poisson distributions.

2. Notation and Preliminaries

The random variables considered are assumed to be defined on a fixed probability space $(\Omega, \mathfrak{A}, \mathbb{P})$. A non-negative random variable representing a number of claims or a (total) claim amount is called a **risk**. The distribution of a risk Y is denoted by $\mathbb{P}^Y$. If $\mathbb{P}^Y = Q$, then we use the notation $Y \sim Q$.
Throughout we adopt the assumptions of the collective model of risk theory. Let us

consider a fixed collective of risks in one period, and let N be a non-negative integer-valued random variable representing the number of claims, with counting density

$$p_n = \mathbb{P}(N=n) \quad , \quad n = 0, 1, 2, \ldots$$

Let $X_1, X_2, \ldots$ be a sequence of stochastically independent and identically distributed random variables representing the single claim sizes. They are assumed to take their values in the set of non-negative integers, with probability density function

$$f_k = \mathbb{P}(X=k) \quad , \quad k = 0, 1, 2, \ldots$$

The n-fold convolution of $\{f_k\}_{k=0,1,\ldots}$ is denoted by $\{f_k^{*n}\}_{k=0,1,\ldots}$, $n = 0,1,\ldots$
We also assume that N and $(X_1, X_2, \ldots)$ are stochastically independent.
The random sum $S = X_1 + \ldots + X_N$ represents the total claim. The probability density function of S is denoted by

$$g_i = \mathbb{P}(S=i) = \sum_{n=0}^{\infty} p_n f_i^{*n} \quad , \quad i = 0, 1, \ldots$$

Finally, for a non-negative integer-valued random variable Y with $Y \sim Q$ let ρ_Y or ρ_Q be its probability generating function.
We write $N \sim \Pi(\lambda)$, $N \sim B(m,p)$, $N \sim NB(r,p)$ or $N \sim L(p)$ if N has a Poisson, binomial, negative binomial or logarithmic distribution, respectively. If N is concentrated on the integer $m \in \{0,1,\ldots\}$, then we write $N \sim \delta_m$.
By $Del(\alpha,\beta,\gamma)$ we denote the Delaporte distribution with parameters $\alpha > 0$, $\beta > 0$ and $\gamma > 0$ which is defined as the convolution of $NB(\beta, \frac{\alpha}{1+\alpha})$ and $\Pi(\gamma)$.
For an arbitrary probability distribution Q and a weight $p \in [0,1]$ we denote by $M(p;Q)$ the finite mixture distribution of δ_1 with weight p and Q with weight $1-p$.
Let $N \sim L(p)$ with $p \in (0,1)$. Then the (conditional) distribution of N, given $N \geq 2$, is denoted by $L^*(p)$.
If the random number N in the random sum $S = X_1 + \ldots + X_N$ has a Poisson distribution with parameter λ and $X \sim Q$ for an arbitrary probability distribution Q, then we write $S \sim CP(\lambda;Q)$ or $S \sim CP(\lambda;X)$.

Definition. *If the counting density $\{p_n\}$ of N satisfies the second order recursion*

$$p_n = (a+\tfrac{b}{n})\, p_{n-1} + \tfrac{c}{n}\, p_{n-2} \quad , \quad n = 1, 2, \ldots, \tag{2.1}$$

$(p_{-1}=0)$ for some constants $a < 1$, b and c, then we write
$N \sim R2(a,b,c)$.

Obviously, (2.1) comes to the well-known Panjer-recursion for the case $c = 0$, cf.

Panjer (1981). In Sundt & Jewell (1981) it is shown that the resulting recursion

$$p_n = (a+\tfrac{b}{n})\, p_{n-1} \quad , \quad n = 1, 2, \ldots , \tag{2.2}$$

is satisfied if and only if N has a Poisson, a binomial or a negative binomial distribution or $N \sim \delta_0$, respectively.

3. Recursions for compound *R2*-distributions

Using the recursion

$$f_i^{*n} = \frac{n}{ki} \sum_{j=1}^{i} j\, f_j^{*k} f_{i-j}^{*(n-k)} \quad , \quad i = 1, 2, \ldots \tag{3.1}$$

for $k = 1$ and $k = 2$ one obtains for $N \sim R2(a,b,c)$

$$g_i = \frac{1}{1-af_0} \sum_{j=1}^{i} [(a+\tfrac{bj}{i})f_j + \tfrac{c}{2i}\, j\, f_j^{*2}]\, g_{i-j} \quad . \tag{3.2}$$

In comparison to the recursive algorithm introduced by Willmot & Sundt (1989) especially in case of Delaporte distributed claim numbers ($Del(\alpha,\beta,\gamma)$ is contained in the *R2*-family), the computational effort of the recursion (3.2) reduces to about the half.

4. Characterization of the *R2*-distribution

4A. Considering the probability generating function ρ_N of $N \sim R2(a,b,c)$ the recursion (2.1) yields the so-called separated differential equation

$$\rho_N'(s) = \frac{a+b+cs}{1-as}\, \rho_N(s) \quad , \quad s \in [0,1] \quad . \tag{4.1}$$

Together with the condition $\rho_N(1) = 1$ the unique solution of (4.1) in case of $a \neq 0$ is

$$\rho_N(s) = e^{-\frac{c}{a}(s-1)} \left(\frac{1-a}{1-as}\right)^{\kappa} \tag{4.2}$$

with

$$\kappa = \frac{a(a+b)+c}{a^2}$$

and, in the case $a > 0$

$$\rho_N(s) = e^{\frac{c}{2}(s^2-1)+b(s-1)} \tag{4.3}$$

It is easy to see that for $a \to 0$ the expression in (4.2) converges to (4.3).
Thus, by the recursion (2.1) alone, the probability generating function of $N \sim R2(a,b,c)$ and therefore the distribution itself is determined.

4B. We will not specify the parameter space of *R2*-distributions completely, but the following proposition gives some answers with respect to the feasibility of the parameters a, *b* and *c*.

Proposition. *If* $N \sim R2(a,b,c)$, *then* $a+b \geq 0$, $a+b+c \geq 0$, $b > -1$ and $a > 0$ *if* $c < 0$.

4C. In this subsection we will specify most of the members of *R2*-distributions. A very helpful basis is provided by the theory of **infinitely divisible distributions**, which are closely related to compound Poisson distributions, cf. Feller (1968).
To specify the members of the *R2*-family it is useful to separate our considerations into the three cases $0 < a < 1$, $a = 0$ and $a < 0$, respectively. For $a \in (0,1)$ and $a = 0$ *R2*-distributions appear as compound Poisson distributions whose severity distributions are certain variations of the logarithmic distribution and the binomial distribution, respectively. For $a < 0$ there exist non-trivial members of the *R2*-family which are not *CP*-distributions, e.g. the convolution of Poisson and binomial distributions. The following table summarizes most of the results of this section.

Table. *R2*(a,*b*,*c*)-distributions

	$a < 0$		$a = 0$		$0 < a < 1$	
$c < 0$	not possible		not possible		$\Pi(-\frac{c}{a})$ $Del(\frac{1-a}{a},\kappa,-\frac{c}{a})$	if $\kappa = 0$ if $\kappa > 0$
$c = 0$	δ_0 $B(-\kappa,\frac{\lvert a\rvert}{1+\lvert a\rvert})$	if $b = -a$ if $-\kappa \in \{1,2,\ldots\}$	δ_0 $\Pi(b)$	if $b = 0$ if $b > 0$	δ_0 $NB(\kappa,1-a)$	if $b = -a$ if $b > -a$
$c > 0$	$\Pi(-\frac{c}{a})$ $\Pi(-\frac{c}{a})*B(-\kappa,\frac{\lvert a\rvert}{1+\lvert a\rvert})$	if $b = -a$ if $-\kappa \in \{1,2,\ldots\}$	$CP(\frac{c}{2};\delta_2)$ $CP\left(b+\frac{c}{2};M(\frac{2b}{c+2b};\delta_2)\right)$	if $b = 0$ if $b > 0$	$CP(\mu\ ;\ M(\frac{a+b}{\mu};L^*(a)))$ if $b \geq -a$ $(\mu = -\frac{c}{a} - \kappa\ \ln(1-a))$	

References

Feller, W. (1968). *An introduction to probability theory and its applications*. Vol. I (3rd ed.). Wiley and Sons, New York.

Panjer, H.H. (1981). Recursive evaluation of a family of compound distributions. *ASTIN Bulletin* 12, 22 – 26.

Sundt, B. & Jewell, W.S. (1981). Further results on recursive evaluation of compound distributions. *ASTIN Bulletin* 12, 27 – 39.

Willmot, G.E. & Sundt, B. (1989). On evaluation of the Delaporte distribution and related distributions. *Scandinavian Actuarial Journal*, 101 – 113.

ON THE DISTRIBUTION OF DISCOUNTED SUMS

Werner Wolf
Institut für Mathematische Stochastik
Technische Universität Dresden
D-8027 Dresden

Imagine a fair coin with faces labeled -1 and 1. Suppose that by each toss of the coin we have profit or loss of 1 Dollar. The infinite sequence of tosses of the coin can be described by a sequence of independent identically distributed random variables $X_1, X_2, \ldots$ with $P(X_k = -1) = P(X_k = 1) = 1/2$, $k = 1, 2, \ldots$ and the sum of all future profits or losses by

$$\lim_{n\to\infty} \sum_{k=1}^{n} X_k$$

But the limit doesn't exist (a.s.).
By a rate of interest p, we have from 1 Dollar in n days $(1+p)^n$ Dollars, and 1 Dollar received or lossed in n days has now the value $(1+p)^{-n}$. Therefore, introduce the discount factor

$$\delta = \frac{1}{1+p}, \; 0 < \delta < 1.$$

As the sum of all profits or losses we consider

$$S(\delta) = \sum_{k=0}^{\infty} \delta^k X_k$$

These sums are random variables and we may ask how are they distributed for each fixed $\delta \in (0,1)$.
The following results will be discussed and proved:

- If $0 < \delta < 1/2$ then the distribution of $S(\delta)$ is singular.
- The random variable $S(2^{-1/n})$ has a density for any positive integer n.
- If $x_0 \in (1,2)$ is a Pisot number then the distribution of $S(1/x_0)$ is singular.
- The characteristic function of $S(\delta)$ tends to zero at infinity if and only if δ^{-1} is not a Pisot number

- The distribution of $S((\sqrt{5}-1)/2)$ - of the Golden section - is singular.

A general criteria for the existence of a density of $S(\delta)$, $\delta \in [1/2, 1)$ can be found in Sasvári, Wolf.

In the next part general discounted sums $\sum_{k=0}^{\infty} a_k(\delta)X_k$, where $X_0, X_1, \ldots$ independent random variables and $a_k(\delta)$, $k = 0, 1, \ldots$ are nonnegative functions defined on the interval (0,1) will be investigated. For $\delta \to 1-0$ and special weights different central local limit theorems will be obtained under additional assumptions on X_k.

REFERENCE:

Sasvári, Z. and Wolf, W. (1987) On the existence of the density of weighted sums. In: Limit theorems in probability theory and related fields. TU Dresden, Wissenschaft, Theory and Praxis, pp. 89 - 102.

Stock Market Prediction with Neural Networks

Jürgen Graf
SGZ Bank
Südwestdeutsche Genossenschafts-
Zentralbank AG
Postfach 6960
D-7500 Karlsruhe 1

1. Abstract

Providing non-linear learning and smooth interpolation capabilities neural networks are presenting an interesting alternative to traditional concepts for solving problems with regard to prediction of financial markets.
This paper discusses a buying and selling timing prediction system for the DAX (German Stock Exchange Price Index).
In this system, a neural network learned the relationship between various technical and economic indexes and the timing for when to buy and sell stocks on the German Stock Exchange.
The results obtained lead to the conclusion that neural networks can be considered as useful instruments to improve the analysis of non-linear relationships in financial markets.

2. Introduction

In the past, many different methods for the prediction of stock prices were applied. The most important ones are the technical stock analysis, the fundamental analysis and various linear statistical methods of time series analysis.
As we have learned from former research, it seems, however, that economic data are not simple autoregressive-integrated-moving-average (ARIMA) processes; they are not describable by simple linear structural models; they are not simply white noise; they are not random walks ([6] p.82).
In this paper, we demonstrate the application of neural networks to develop a system for predicting the best time to buy and sell stocks for one month in the future. In section three, some remarks about the stock market prediction will be presented. Section four discusses the architecture of the backpropagation network which we have used. The results obtained by simulation with the trading system will be shown in section five.

3. Stock Market Prediction

The first models for predicting stock prices with neural networks are purely autoregressive ([2], [7]). But facing the results which were obtained by neural networks, one can recognize that the predicted values tend to run after the true values ([2] p.176).
This feature is typical of many statistical methods of time series analysis relating to exponential smoothing.
The problem is, that neural networks can only process information, make data transformations and detect pattern. Assuming that stock prices are nearly random on a day-to-day basis, then neural networks cannot be expected to predict the next day's stock price autoregressively.
So for more successful results, however, a more sophisticated set of inputs, with a variety of sources for pertinent financial data would be needed ([1] p.221).
This can be done by elaborating the networks to allow additional inputs (e.g., volume, other stock prices and volume, leading indicators, macroeconomic data, etc.) ([7] p.456).

4. Neural Network Architecture

Neural networks are computational systems, either hardware or software, which mimic the computational abilities of biological systems by using large numbers of simple, interconnected artificial neurons.
The neural network architecture used for this prediction system consists of four layers: the input layer, two hidden layers, and the output layer. The four layers are completely connected to form a hierarchical network.
Empirically, one has found that the optimum ratio of first to second hidden layer nodes remains 3:1, even for higher dimensional inputs ([4] p.242).
Using one hidden node per pattern type leads to the loss of ability of generalization.
The learning rates for those layers close to the output were set lower than those layers near the input. Lowering the learning rates over time improves learning.
As we know from experience, the values for the learning rates should start between 0.3 and 0.5.
Instead of a standard sigmoid function, we use the hyperbolic tangent transfer function ([5] p.UN-57)

5. Results

The prediction system uses a moving average of weekly average data of each index for minimizing influence due to random walk ([3] p.I-3). The learning period begins 01/01/88 and stops 08/10/90. The next 40 weeks are representing the recall time.

Table 1 lists the most technical and economic indexes which were used as input data. The timing for when to buy and sell (output layer) is a weighted sum of the weekly returns transformed in the [0,100] section.

Table 1: Input data

1. Technical Indicators	4. Interest rates
2. Foreign stock exchange indexes	5. Turnover
3. Foreign exchange rate	

To verify the effectiveness of the prediction system, a simulation of buying and selling the DAX was done. In the prediction system, an output of 80 or more indicates buy, and an output less than 20 indicates sell.

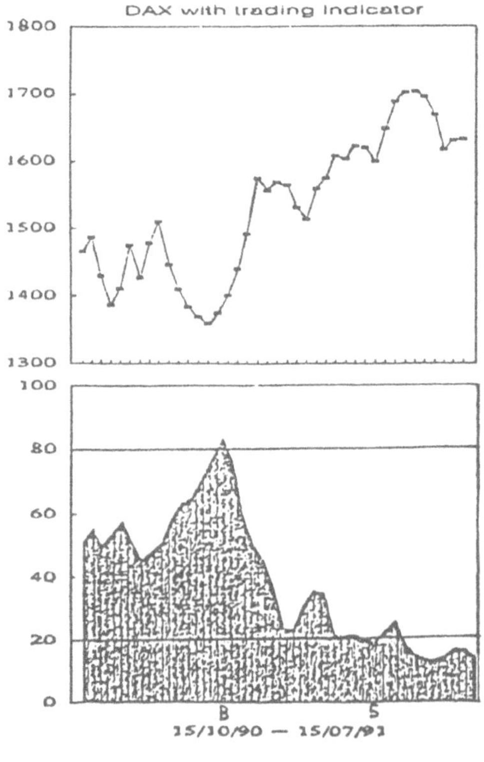

Figure 1:
Trading signals with the prediction system:
B = buy ; S = sell

Comparing the results, we recognize that the prediction system was more profitable than the buy- and hold-strategy:

	buy	sell	hold	profit
buy & hold:	15/10/90 1466.51		15/07/91 1631.65	165.14 **11.26%**
trading system:	21/01/91 1376.26	06/05/91 1619.84		243.58 **17.70%**

6. Summary

This paper discussed a possibility of developing a system that advises the right timing for buying and selling stocks. The model made a better profit than the buying and holding in a simulation. Further research should be carried out in two subjects:

- The teaching data should be generated by a combination of statistical methods and future returns.
- We have to develop theoretical methods to verify neural network systems.

References:

[1] *Dayhoff, J.E.* (1990)
Neural Network Architectures. An Introduction. New York

[2] *Graf, J.* (1990)
Klassische statistische Methoden zur kurzfristigen Prognose des Aktienmarkts und deren Vergleich mit den Methoden der künstlichen Intelligenz. University of Karlsruhe

[3] *Kimoto, T./ Asakawa, K./ Yoda, M./ Takeoka, M.*
Stock Market Prediction System with Modular Neural Networks.

[4] *Maren, A.J./ Harston, C.T./ Pap, R.M.* (1990)
Handbook of Neural Computing Applications. San Diego

[5] *NeuralWare, Inc.*
Using Nworks. An Extended Tutorial for NeuralWorks Professional II/PLUS and NeuralWorks Explorer. Pittsburgh

[6] *Ramsey, J.B.* (1990)
Economic and Financial Data as Nonlinear Processes. In Dwyer, G.P./ Hafer, R.W.: The Stock Market: Bubbles, Volatility, and Chaos: Proceedings of the Thirteenth Annual Economic Policy of the Federal Reserve Bank of St. Louis, p.81-134. London

[7] *White, H.* (1988)
Economic Prediction Using Neural Networks: The Case of IBM Daily Stock Returns. In IEEE International Conference on Neural Networks, Volume II, p.451-458. San Diego

RISK MANAGEMENT IN BANKS

Ulla-Christiane Kopp
Institut für Unternehmensforschung (Operations Research)
an der Hochschule St. Gallen
Bodanstr. 6, CH-9000 St. Gallen

1 Introduction

The following paper is divided into three parts. In the first part, a risk measure is developed to handle the three most important risks (interest rate risk, currency risk and default risk) in a consistent manner. Then follows a short description of the decision model that uses the risk measure introduced before which optimizes balance and off-balance sheet instruments simultaneously. The aim of the model is to limit the risks to a given amount while the bank's result is maximized. Finally, we briefly summarize some practical experiences with the model.

2 The risk measure

Risk is defined as losses or reduced returns because of unexpected and/or unforeseen changes of market parameters (interest rates and exchange rates) or occurences of defaults. (In the following, market parameters and default probabilities are both refered to as market data.)
As risk manifests itself in reduced returns it has to be treated analogously to them. The only difference between risk and return is that the risk has to be measured ex ante and the result is calculated ex post by comparing real market data with the deals' conditions. As the future market data is uncertain one has to consider either forecasts or scenarios of market data when trying to measure the risk. For several reasons that are not to be discussed here it is more convenient to use scenarios than forecasts. Here we use pairs of worst case assumptions that represent a corridor around the actual or expected data. (For more details see [6].)
Risk is in this study measured by the difference between the market value of the deal or the position and the value calculated with the worst case scenario. How risk is splitted into its three main components - interest rate risk, currency risk and default risk - is demonstrated with an example of a foreign currency loan.
The loan has maturity T and cash flows cf_t. In t=0 we have a given exchange rate structure k_{0t} and an interest rate structure i_{0t}. Furthermore, we suppose that the loan does not default in the time period considered. The market value V of the loan is then:

$$V = \sum_{t=1}^{T} cf_t \, k_{0t} \left(\frac{1}{1+i_{0t}}\right)^t \tag{1}$$

With our worst case assumptions for exchange rates k_t and interest rates i_t we can calculate the present value of the future result R which is the same as the total risk:

$$R = \sum_{t=1}^{T} cf_t \, k_t \left(\frac{1}{1+i_t}\right)^t - V \tag{2}$$

The total risk is now splitted into its components. The currency risk component C is given by the following equation:

$$C = \sum_{t=1}^{T} cf_t \, (k_t - k_{0t}) \left(\frac{1}{1+i_t}\right)^t \tag{3}$$

The currency risk depends not only on future exchange rates but on future interest rates as well. This is usually known as swap rate risk.

Neglecting the default risk for the time being, the interest rate risk I has the following value:

$$I = \sum_{t=1}^{T} cf_t \, k_{0t} \left(\frac{1}{1+i_t}\right)^t - V \tag{4}$$

Equation (3) and (4) sum up to equation (2).

Now the default risk is also considered. Because banks have variable conditions for borrowers with different credit ratings we assume that the cash flows cf_t can be splitted into an interest rate part cf_{ti} and a default risk part cf_{td} that depends on the creditworthiness of the borrower. Thus, the pure interest rate risk I' can be written as:

$$I' = \sum_{t=1}^{T} cf_{ti} \, k_{0t} \left(\frac{1}{1+i_t}\right)^t - V \tag{4'}$$

The present value of the default risk premium D is:

$$D = \sum_{t=1}^{T} cf_{td} \, k_{0t} \left(\frac{1}{1+i_t}\right)^t \tag{5}$$

The default risk premium is always greater or equal to zero. In a complete market the risk premium reflects the default expectations. To check if the default risk premium charged is actually adequate one has to compare the sum of all expected default risk premiums with the value of all expected defaults. Therefore one needs default probabilities that depend on the customers' ratings and the time of default. Ideally, the default risk premiums cover the default losses.

If the loan is refinanced with matching conditions ($cf_t = cf_t^{ref}$) then apart from the default risk there are no risks. If it is a home currency loan, then k_{0t} and k_t both equal one (no currency risk). If the borrower is the government then the charged default risk premium cf_{td} equals zero (no default risk).
The risk shares C, I' and D given by equations (3), (4') and (5) sum up to the risk total V given by equation (2). Thus, we can measure the three essential risks consistently and separately.

3 The decision model

In the literature various optimization models for bank asset & liability management and risk management can be found. They can be distinguished according to various characteristics like consideration of off-balance sheet deals, number of decision functions, etc. Most of them deal with interest rate risk only, e.g. the models described in [1], [2], [3] and [5]. Some of them are single period decision models, others are multiperiod decision models. Examples for multiperiod models are given in [2], [3], [4] and [5].
The model introduced here is a single period linear programming model that considers three kinds of risks and off-balance sheet deals.
The given parameters are:
- cash flows of all existing assets, liabilities and off-balance sheet deals in their currencies at time t,
- market data (interest rates, risk premiums dependent of customers' ratings and deal categories, exchange rates for all currencies and default probabilities),
- capital to cover all risks,
- etc.

Estimated parameters are:
- worst-case assumptions for market data.

Decision variables are:
- amount of new balance sheet deals with maturity t in currency c and fixed or variable conditions,
- amount of new off-balance sheet deals (futures and swaps),
- limits for all risks.

The following restrictions are considered in the model:
Market restrictions:

For all decision variables there are upper and lower bounds given by market demands. Off-balance sheet deals are not restricted. Every risk limit has also an upper bound to make sure that there is a diversification of risks. The lower bounds of risk limits are zero.

Balance sheet restriction:

The market value of assets as well as the market value of liabilities are equal to the balance. The balance is restricted to a range of values.

Interest rate risk restrictions:

For the two worst case scenarios (rising and falling interest rates) the difference between present values of all (old and new) assets and liabilities and the value of off-balance sheet deals plus the interest rate risk limit has to be greater or equal to zero.

Currency risk restrictions:

For all currencies the present value of exchange rate differentials of balance and off-balance sheet deals has to be less or equal to the exchange rate risk limit.

Default risk restriction:

The present value of expected defaults has to be greater or equal to the default risk limit. Off-balance sheet deals are assumed to have no default risk at all.

The other restrictions like e.g. the liquidity restriction are not discussed here.

The objective funktion is:

Maximize the expected result of balance sheet deals minus the transaction cost of off-balance sheet deals minus the cost of capital to cover the risks. To avoid speculations, off-balance sheet deals are not considered to contribute something to the result.

All risks are calculated as shown in part one of this paper.

The variable cash flows are calculated with the given worst case data, assuming that the future interest rates can be calculated with spot rates.

4 Summary

By testing the model with real data it became clear how important it is to manage balance and off-balance sheet deals simultaneously. By comparing decisions with and without off-balance sheet deals we got quite different decision structures. With off-balance sheet deals we obtained a higher objective function value and also a better risk/return ratio. Of course the choice of worst case parameters is essential. Therefore, we advise practicians to test the stability of the results with different scenarios.

5 References

[1] W. Bessler/ G. G. Booth, Controlling interest rate risk in commercial banks, conference paper, Fifth Symposium on Money, Banking and Insurance, 1990

[2] G. G. Booth/ W. Bessler/ W. G. Foote, Managing interest-rate risk in banking institutions, European Journal of Operational Research, 1989

[3] A. J. Brodt, Optimal bank asset and liability management with financial futures, The Journal of Futures Markets, 1988

[4] A. Korhonen, A dynamic bank portfolio planning model with multiple scenarios, multiple goals and changing priorities, European Journal of Operational Research, 1987

[5] H. Meyer zu Selhausen, Erfassung und Steuerung des Zinsänderungsrisikos einer Bank mit Hilfe eines Modells der Aktiv-Passiv-Koordination, Kredit und Kapital, 1988

[6] J. K. Speakes, Fixed-income risk measurement and risk management, The Journal of Portfolio Management, 1989

ON THE UNIQUENESS OF DISCOUNT FACTORS

Prof. Dr. Andreas Pfingsten
VWL I, FB 5, Universität GH Siegen
Hölderlinstr. 3, D - 5900 Siegen

The evaluation of bank products is based on an opportunity cost approach for which the terms "Marktzinsmethode" or "Marktzinsmodell" (e.g., Schierenbeck [1987] and Marusev [1990]) have been established. It is the objective of this approach to provide a preference-free valuation of each single activity. The method used is the duplication (or rather the compensation) of the activity to be evaluated.

The calculations, which will be described in more detail below, yield as results the profit contribution of the activity (in present value) and, among others, certain discount factors. These discount factors are present values of future payments. Together with some additional pieces of information, they show how money can be shifted between periods without arbitrage and without effects on scarce resources (see Pfingsten/Marusev [1991] for a discussion of this latter aspect).

The central question examined here is the uniqueness of the derived discount factors, i.e., are the discount factors independent of the activity evaluated? (They will, of course, in general depend on parameters which describe relevant bank and market conditions.)

This issue is not only of theoretical interest but also of practical importance. In cases where the discount factors are unique (given the "state of the world"), the valuation of activities is simply obtained by a few multiplications, whereas in other cases it is necessary to solve a linear programming problem.

In the basic model, the contribution to profits of a single activity was derived by duplicating (with negative sign) its cash flow only. Instruments for this compensation were, besides the extraction of present value profits, assets and liabilities on money and capital markets. The virtual compensation could be derived most easily by simply solving a system of linear equations (e.g., Kotissek [1987]). The corresponding matrix equation

matrix of cash flows of instruments * vector of instruments
= - cash flow of activity

had a unique solution, because the used matrix had a full rank equal to the number of payments. The reason lies in the assumption that for each future date of payment, i.e. for each period, there is one and only one relevant instrument available for the bank on its money and capital market.

The natural way to find the solution is to invert the matrix and multiply it by the right-hand-side (RHS). In addition, the inverse contains the discount factors looked for. Since the matrix (and hence its inverse) is the same for any RHS, these discount factors are unique (as long as the money and capital market instruments, i.e. the matrix, do not change).

(Strictly speaking, the matrices are not the same for activities that differ in their time horizon. The matrices are, however, all triangular. Their size increases with the time until the last payment. And since the matrices for shorter activities are simply upper triangular parts of the matrix used for the longest one of all offered contracts, the same holds for the inverse.)

In the extended model, other scarce resources (e.g., equity requirements) can also be included. Likewise, the number of instruments available to the bank is increased (by additionally taking into account, e.g., loans to prime rate customers and swaps). In probably most practical cases the number of instruments will exceed the number of constraints which is equal to the number of payments and other resource requirements. It is now not obvious anymore which of the instruments should be used for duplication.

Marusev/Siewert [1991] have shown how the profit contribution can be derived by linear programming: it is maximized subject to the condition that all resource uses are compensated for.

When solving this problem, discount factors are automatically derived. They appear as dual variables and provide the present values for changing the constraints by one unit. Again with some additional pieces of information, they show how arbitrary resources can be transformed into (present value) money.

(The discount factors also appear in an inverse as they did in the basic model: When the linear programming problem is solved, it is known which instruments together are basic variables. Collecting the columns of the constraints that belong to a basis into a square matrix, we are back in the situation of the original model.)

The possible non-uniqueness of the discount factors stems from the fact that the basic variables may be different when the RHS is different. In the remainder we will suggest a method to verify uniqueness and we will indicate the proof why it works.

Firstly, solve the LP problem with the following RHS: one entry is 1 and all other entries are 0. Do so for all such unit vectors. (Basically, the LP problem is solved successively for the columns of an identity matrix.) Note that every activity is a unique linear combination of these unit vectors. Also, taking the same linear combination of the corresponding solutions yields a feasible solution for the LP problem with the activity on the RHS.

Secondly, compare the basic variables of the different problems. If they are always identical (or in the case of non-unique sets of basic variables: if there exists one basis which supports all optimal solutions) then we can be sure that the linear combination is also optimal, and the discount factors are unique.

The proof of optimality makes use of one of the landmarks of duality theory, namely the complementary slackness condition (e.g., Intriligator [1971, p.83] or Neumann [1975, p.67]). It can be shown that the feasible solution derived above satisfies complementary slackness, i.e. a necessary and sufficient optimality condition.

Summing up, the discount factors were unique in the basic version of the Marktzinsmodell, but will not necessarily be unique in the extended version. However, if the instruments available to the bank are such that the same set of instruments can serve as a basis for the optimal solutions of all unit vectors, then uniqueness of discount factors is guaranteed.

References

Intriligator, M.D. [1971]: "Mathematical Optimization and Economic Theory", Prentice Hall.

Kotissek, N. [1987]: "Zur Berechnung des Konditionsbeitrages bei konstanter effektiver Marge", Bank und Markt, No. 1, 34-37.

Marusev, A.W. [1990]: "Das Marktzinsmodell in der bankbetrieblichen Einzelgeschäftskalkulation", Fritz Knapp Verlag.

Marusev, A.W. and K.-J. Siewert [1991]: "Engpaßbezogene Einzelgeschäftskalkulation als LP-Ansatz", Die Bank, No. 1, 168-171.

Neumann, K. [1975]: "Operations Research Verfahren I", Carl Hanser Verlag.

Pfingsten, A. and A.W. Marusev [1991]: "Kalkulation von Anschlußgeschäften mit der Marktzinsmethode im Multi-Engpaßfall", forthcoming in: W.R. Heilmann (ed.), "Geld, Banken und Versicherungen".

Schierenbeck, H. [1987]: "Ertragsorientiertes Bankmanagement", 2nd ed., Gabler.

I am indebted to Hans Ulrich Buhl for significant help.

THE INFORMATION CONTENT IN OFFICIAL GERMAN TERM STRUCTURE DATA - SOME NEW EVIDENCE ON THE EXPECTATIONS THEORY OF THE TERM STRUCTURE OF INTEREST RATES -

Klaus Schmidt
Institut für öffentliche Wirtschaft, Geld und Währung
Johann-Wolfgang-Goethe-Universität Frankfurt
Zeppelinallee 29, D-6000 Frankfurt/Main

The term structure of interest rates (TS) is an important analytical device in monetary economics. The central bank controls short-term rates, but decisions to invest rather depend on the long-term rate. Thus the TS appears central to the transmission process of monetary policy. The expectations theory of the TS states that the slope of the yield curve, the empirical approximation of the TS, "has something to do with expectations about future interest rates" (Shiller 1990, p. 644). If this were true, the TS could be a reliable indicator for the credibility and the effect of monetary policy decisions (cf. Gebauer 1991). Unfortunately the evidence for the expectations theory is, at best, mixed. In the following sections I will analyse the information contained in the 'official' German TS, published monthly by the Deutsche Bundesbank (Statistische Beihefte, Reihe 2, Wertpapierstatistik, table 8d), with respect to the expectations theory.

THE DATA

Let r(m) denote the m-period interest rate, i.e. by approximation the yield to maturity of a bond with m years to maturity. The yield curve relates the r(m)-values to their term m. To construct the yield curve, the yields on bonds of the federal government, post and railway offices with terms m=1...10 years are used. Because the original values reflect market imperfections, the yield curve is found by 'drawing' a smooth regression line through the original values. The regression explicitely accounts for the 'coupon effect', i.e. it eliminates the effect which the coupon (and not the term) has on the yield, mainly due to German tax laws and/or different duration. In the following, these estimated values are examined.

The basic sample period is 1970(1) to 1990(12) with monthly data. The sample shows well-known properties: the short rates are usually below the long rates and are more volatile: (maximum=13.1%, minimum=3.2%, mean=6.8%, standard deviation=2.2%) for r(1) and (10.3%, 5.7%, 7.9%, 1.2%) for r(10). Let SP(m) denote the long-short-spread r(m)-r(1) for m=2...10. Normally the yield curve is gently upward slooping, the mean is 1.1% for SP(10); an inverse TS on the other hand is not unusual, because negative values for SP(10) are already contained in the 1-σ-intervall (standard deviation=1.2%). Flat or inverse yield curves are correlated with high and rising average interest rates: the correlation coefficient for SP(10) and the average interest rate, $r(\phi) \equiv 1/10\,[r(1)+r(2)+...+r(10)]$, is -0.69 for levels and -0.36 for first differences.

THEORETICAL CONSIDERATIONS

Consider the following equation:

$$(1) \qquad r_{t+n}(m) - r_t(m) = f_t(n,m) - r_t(m) - \phi_t^f(n,m) \quad .$$

The left hand side indicates the expected change of the m-period rate in n periods. (Expectations are proxied by realisations, assuming rational expectations.) This depends on the forward-spot-spread, $FSSP_t(n,m) \equiv f_t(n,m)-r_t(m)$ - i.e. the slope of the yield curve, whereby $f_t(n,m)$ denotes the forward rate - and the expected forward term premium, denoted as $\Phi_t^f(n,m)$. Using this framework, the expectations theory states that the term premium is constant through time, i.e. it does not depend on t, but only on n, the forcast horizont, and m, the term of the forward rate. Hence, a changing slope of the yield curve is <u>solely</u> caused by changed expectations of future short rates (and not by changed term premia). Calling the left hand side 'expected-spot-spread', $ESSP_t(n,m)$, leads us to equation (1a), which is a popular basis for empirical tests:

$$(1a) \qquad ESSP_t(n,m) = FSSP_t(n,m) - \phi^f(n,m) \quad .$$

Other testable implications can be deferred. The variance of the ex post rational or perfect foresight long-term interest rate, $r^*(m)$, defined as

$$(2) \qquad r_t^*(m) = \sqrt[m]{[1+r_t(1)]\prod_{n=1}^{m-1}[1+r_{t+n}(1)]} - 1 \quad ,$$

puts an upper bound on the variance of r(m), because the expectations theory implies, that the ex post rational long-term rate $r_t^*(m)$ equals the actual long-term rate $r_t(m)$ minus a constant - $\Phi^r(m)$ - plus a random forcast error, $u_t(m)$:

$$(3) \qquad r_t^*(m) = r_t(m) - \phi^r(m) + u_t(m)$$

The constant is the roll-over term premium, defined as $\Phi_t^r(m) \equiv r_t(m) - r_t^*(m)$, which the expectations theory assumes to be independent of t. Since expectations are rational, $u_t(m)$ can not be correlated with anything known at t. Hence, $r_t(m)$ and $u_t(m)$ are independent, i.e. the variance of $r^*(m)$ puts an upper bound to the variance of r(m). By subtracting $r_t(1)$ from both sides of equation (5), we will get the same expression in spreads ($SP_t^*(m)$ denotes the ex post rational long-short spread, $r_t^*(m)-r_t(1)$):

$$(4) \qquad SP_t^*(m) = SP_t(m) - \phi^r(m) + u_t(m) \quad .$$

EMPIRICAL RESULTS

Equations (3) and (4) imply, that Var r(m) ≤ Var $r^*(m)$, resp. Var SP(m) ≤ Var $SP^*(m)$. I conducted these excess variability tests for the period 1970(1) until 1991(12)-m, for m=2,...,10. The variance inequalities do not hold for m greater than 2 in the case of the r(m)-values, but they do hold for all SP(m)-values. Therefore I will concentrate on spreads in the following.

Testing the expectations theory on the basis of equation (1a) amounts to running the regression:

$$(5) \qquad ESSP_t(n,m) = \beta_1 FSSP_t(n,m) + \beta_0 + u_t \quad .$$

If the expectations theory were true, then $(\beta_0,\beta_1)=(-\Phi^r(n,m),1)$. The literature on testing equation (3a) or near approximations is enormous and normally rejects the expectations theory (cf. Shiller 1990, p. 656). I conducted (augmented) Dickey-Fuller tests to examine the degree of integration of ESSP(n,m) and FSSP(n,m) for (n,m)=(1,1), (1,4), (1,9), (2,1), (2,4), (2,8), (4,1), (4,4), (4,6) (6,1), (6,4), (9,1), showing that they are all I(1), but not cointegrated with a cointegrating parameter K=1, which one would expect from the theory. The sample period was 1971(2) until 1990(12)-n. Running regressions on levels is thus inadmissible. Such regressions yield inconsistent parameter estimates and may explain the bad results of other researches.

A plot of $SP^*(m)$ and $SP(m)$ across time reveals very similar curves (cf. Shiller 1990, p. 660f). The German data confirm this finding for $SP^*(10)$ and $SP(10)$. Indeed, running the regression:

$$(6) \qquad SP_t^*(m) = \beta_1 \, SP(m) + \beta_0 + u_t \quad ,$$

is another way of testing the expectations theory, based on equation (4). One would expect $(\beta_0,\beta_1)=(-\Phi'(m),1)$. But again, for m=2,5,10, the variables are I(1) and fail to be cointegrated. The sample period was 1970(2) until 1991(12)-m. Clearly, the regressions (5) and (6) yield unsatisfactory results, because the (forward and roll-over) term premia vary in time and are I(1). Variables explaining the term premia are thus needed to get cointegrated variables. Flow-of-funds or risk proxies have been suggested with disappointing results (cf. Mankiw 1986, Shiller 1990).

I estimated the models (5) and (6) in first differences. Clearly, one would expect $(\beta_0,\beta_1)=(0,1)$ for both models - i.e. a changing slope of the yield curve is solely caused by changing expectations. I ran static OLS-regressions for all specifications mentioned above, and in no case the estimated betas differed significantly from (0,1).

Thus, expectations play a significant, but not the only role in explaining the slope of the yield curve. Although one can not infer the future level of interest rates from the slope ot the yield curve within any range of certainty, because term premia are time varying, one knows, that a changing slope points in the right direction. Hence, in Germany the TS has something to do with expectations. But the expectations theory is only half of the truth and the explanation of the term premia should still "remain high on the research agenda" (Mankiw 1986, p.92).

REFERENCES

Deutsche Bundesbank (ed.): Statistische Beihefte zu den Monatsberichten der Deutschen Bundesbank, Reihe 2, Wertpapierstatistik; published monthly.

Gebauer, W. (1991): Geld versus Zins - Überlegungen zu einer Europäischen Zentralbankpolitik, Geld und Währung Working Paper No. 18.

Mankiw, N. G. (1986): The term structure of interest rates revisited, in: Brookings Papers on Economic Activity; No. 1; pp. 61 - 91.

Shiller, R. J. (1990): The term structure of interest rates; in: Handbook for Monetary Economics, Vol. 1; ed. by B.M. Friedman, F.H. Hahn; Amsterdam et. al.; pp. 627 - 722.

FLEXIBLE OPTIMIZATION: OPERATION RESEARCH MODELS AND APPLICATIONS

by Dr. Virgil Chichernea
Informatics Division
Ministry of Education and Science
Str. General Bertholet nr.12
70738 Bucharest ROMANIA

The complex requirement of modern management prompt the utilization an large scale of mathematical models and informatic instruments that are groupe toghether under the title of "management informatics".

The paper goes beyond the rigid framework of conventional optimization and presents the alternative concept of flexible optimization. The concept enables this avoidance of major obstacles encountered in solving decision-making problems through the identification of several work directions such as:

- *development of multicriterial optimization techniques;*
- *consideration of qualitative jumps;*
- *relaxing of restrictions and for acceptance of solutions that transgress certain restrictions;*
- *extending simulation as a method to seek satisfactory solutions.*

The flexible optimization is an extension of conventional optimization in order to include criterion functions with inexact data. As objective functions, we consider the real functions f defined on the subsets $M_i * X$ *in* $R^n * R^n$:

$$f_i(C_i, x) = f_i(C_{i1}, \ldots, C_{is}, x_1, \ldots x_n)$$

where:

$x = (x_1, \ldots, x_n) \in X \subseteq R^n$, *is the vector of decision variables;* c_{ik} $(i \in I = \{1,2,\ldots,p\}$, $k \in J = \{1,2,\ldots,s\}$ *represent the objective coefficients and* $C_i \in M_i \subseteq R^s$: *Let C be the matrix having the rows* C_i $(i \in I)$.

We suppose that the columns coefficient vectors C_j $(j \in J)$ *belong to some given domains of variation* $K_j \subseteq R^p$.

We assume that:

I. K_j $(j \in J)$ *are convex, compact and nonempty sets in* R^p *and the sets* M_i $(i \in I)$ *are given by:*

$$M_i = \{C_i = (c_{i1}, \ldots, c_{is}) \ : c_j \in K_j, \ j \in J\}$$

II. The objectives f_i $(i \in I)$ *are continous functions on* $M_i * X$.

The assumption I. implies that M_i $(i \in I)$ *are convex and compact sets. Then, by the continuity of the function* f_i , *for any given point* x' *in X, the set:*

$$f_i(M_i, x') = \{f_i(C_i, x') \ : C_i \in M_i\}$$

is a bounded closed interval. Therefore, when the coefficients of the function f_i *in a point* $x' \in X$, *lie in an interval.*

Hence, it is natural that certain notions of performance solution for the multiobjective programing with inexact objectives $f_i (i \in I)$, *are related to a semiorder relation defined on the set*

$$I(R) = \{[a,b] \ : a,b \in R, \ a \leq b\}$$

of the bounded closed intervals in R.

Find the lexicographic optimization with inexact data:

$$\text{Lex}\begin{bmatrix}\min\\ \max\end{bmatrix}\left\{g^j\ (x,y,z)\quad : j\in L\right\}$$

subject to:

- $f_i(C_i,x) + y_i - z_i = h_i$, *for all* $i \in I = \{1,2,\ldots,p\}$,
- $x \in X \subseteq R^n$, $y \geq 0$, $z \geq 0$.

where:

- $f_i (i \in I)$ *are the criterion function* $(C_i \in R^n)$;
- *the numbers* $h_i \in R$ $(i \in I)$ *are the desired goal levels of achivement for the criterion functions* $f_i (i \in I)$;
- y_i *and* z_i *are respectively underachivement and overachivement deviational variables;*
- $L = \{1,2,\ldots,q\}$ *denotes the set of the priority levels ;*
- g^j $(j \in J)$ *represents the deviational objective function of the j-th priority level;*
- *X is the feasible region of the problem.*

We assume thoughout that X is a polyhedral nonempty and bounded subset of R^n, *defined by*

$$X = \{x \in R^n \ :\ Ax = b,\ x \geq 0\},$$

*where A is a given m*n real matrix and* $b \in R^m$.

To ilustrate all these the paper presents the solution to some operations research models by the use of flexible optimization in the case of two applications:

A. OPTIMIZATION OF CAPITAL REPAIRS SCHEDULING IN ENTREPRISES HAVING CONTINOUS FLOW MANUFACTURING PROCEEESSES:

Problem set:

The equipment of a company with a continous flow manufacturing process is structured in the form of graph where the nodes represent the Unit of Repair (UR) and arcs the connections among UR's according to technological processes. The characteristics of the UR's (plants, storehaus/tanks, utilities) are known.
The problem consists in scheduling repair work for all the UR's so that there should be a minimum less of output in all the company caused by stopping the equipment during capital repairs.

The qualitative and quantitatve questions:

1. *identify all the UR's involved in manufacturing a finished product or, in other words, identify the components of the technological flow of each finished product;*
2. *identify all the flow in which a unit of repair is involved;*
3. *classify UR's according to their value impact, i.e. calculate the total value of products in whose manufacture the respective UR is involved;*
4. *calculate repair start time and ending time for each UR, using constant and variable elements of state of the analysed system;*
5. *schedule capital repairs of technological flow so as to make resonable use of manpower, material and financial resources throughout the process.*

The graph associated to the production process is the

material support we can use in a systematic and through study of the derived problems mentioned before.

TEROFLUX programme package, realised in our computer centre, is enable generation by the computer of the graph associated to the UR's in the company, and performance by the computer of calculations for solving the qualitative and quantitative aspects of the problem set. The input data and the output of package are presented.

B.OPTIMIZATION OF ACCESS OF PUBLIC MEANS OF TRANSPORT (ELECTRICAL) THROUGH A RE-ALLOCATION OF LINES INTO SHEDS.

Problem set:

There are known:

- the transport network with the precise layout of sheds and with the precise route of every public transport line;

- the maximum capacity of operation/maintenance of every shed;

- the number of vehicles required by every line during the six specific intervals of each day;

- the transport services is calculated to include the number of complete rides ;

- one transport line is served only by vehicles belonging to one and the some shed;

The required: Optimization of Access of Public means of Transport through a re-allocation of lines into Sheds/Garrage.

The mathematical model differs from classical allocation model, since:

- some input data are uncertain (number of vehicles/lines /characteristics intervals in a day);

- X_{ij} *variables of the accepted solution must lead to a situation in which every line is served by vehicles starting from the same shed;*

- there is an artificial separation between the notion of full ride and that of access ride (arrivels/departures) to/from the route.

We look for a starting point in flexible optimization and it is using a simulation method for the various alternatives and evaluation of the objective function (total minimization of access distance) in each case.

In real application it was four allocation models have been solved for four types of vehicles (trams,trolleybusses, long busses and short busses). The solutions of allocations lines in sheds generate a shotering of distance for arrival/departures to and from shelds/garrage to and from terminals.

The input and the output data of programme package are presented.

PERFORMANCE MODELLING of a BUSINESS SOFTWARE SYSTEM

Werner E. HELM
Inge STEINMETZ
FB MN , STAT & OR , FH Darmstadt
Schoefferstr. 3 , D-6100 DARMSTADT

INTRODUCTION . Today the success and even survival of many business companies critically depends on certain operational on-line transaction processing systems . To ensure permanent availability and adequate performance many companies take considerable investment in hardware, in software and in consulting experts . Cost-effectively planning the necessary hardware and accordingly configuring the software for the first time at a new site or when increasing the transaction rates due to the installation of new components is an extremely difficult management task. Especially since due to their critical nature no experimentation with the production systems will be allowed.
Performance evaluation and prediction of such software systems can lead to greatly improved management decisions .
The system we studied is the SAP-System R/2 RB (SAP AG, Walldorf). SAP offers a unique line of integrated business application software systems and is market leader in Germany and all of Europe .
As a modelling technique we chose SIMULATION . We used NETWORK II.5 (CACI International, La Jolla) as a simulation tool .
Pre- and post-simulation statistical analysis was done with SAS (SAS Institute, Cary) .
All computational work was performed on PC's (386/486).
In this paper we give a brief overview of the project and discuss some major steps when creating and validating the present simulation model. We then present some first results of our approach and also comment on the suitability of the techniques and tools employed in this performance evaluation study .

TARGET SYSTEM . TOOLS . The whole SAP-system is organized in modules or components, the most of which are concerned with one specific business domain such as sales, cost accounting , materials managemet, etc . At present the best-selling component is RF which is devoted to Financial Accounting . So a starting installation could just comprise the basic component RB and RF . The RB Basis System is the heart of any SAP-installation . RB is designed to provide

- standardized interfaces across all applications
- complete control and supervision mechanisms (w.r.t. system, dialogue, DB/DC ,etc)
- a complete development environment (including the language ABAP/4, data dictionary,etc)
- the separation of the application modules from the operating (system) environment .

The real SAP-system which we use as a reference and which is also the (first) target of our modelling effort runs in a medium-sized engineering company in a MVS/CICS/VS-environment on an IBM 3090-30 J and processes about 330 000 transactions per day . The database behind CICS is built up from VSAM-files .
In order to keep the development-time within reasonable bounds we decided to build up the simulation model with NETWORK II.5 . NETWORK II.5 is an application module based on SIMSCRIPT II.5 and is aimed at the design and analysis of computer and communication networks . The first phases of our project were set up to answer the fundamental questions :

- Can the task-handling of SAP R/2 RB be simulated at all (to a reasonable accuracy) ?

- Can it be done with NETWORK II.5 (which had been used before mainly for hardware modelling) ?

SIMULATION MODEL . NETWORK II.5 contains the following basic building blocks :

- Processing Elements (PE)
- (Software) Modules
- Messages, Instruction Mixes
- Statist. Distribution Functions (SDF)
- NETIN, NETGIN
- Storage Devices (SD)
- Transfer Devices (TD)
- Semaphores, Flags, Macros
- Reports, Plots, Gplots
- NETANIMATION

Apart from SD´s and TD´s we employed most of these basic elements within our simulation model. To give a brief outline, we used PE´s to model the entities TERMINAL, CPU and I/O PROCy (y=1,...,5) , we implemented about 44 software MODULES, 13 different statistical distribution functions (SDF) and 23 SEMAPHORES .
At present we incorporated the following features :

- SAP - working areas
- SAP - tasks
  Update, Dialogue, Long-running and Spool
- task priorities (Update highest, Long-running lowest priority)
- time-sliced operation of CPU

We followed the internal SAP-syntax rules . So the model contains software modules named SAPZTTADx, SAPZTTALx, ZTTADxIO, ZTTALxIO (x=2, .. , 7) which represent the CPU- or I/O- activity of Dialogue- or Long-running- tasks being processed in working area no. x . Space does not permit to go into further details here .
The resulting model in it´s present form reflects the SAP - task handling in a CICS-environment. The primary goal was to achieve such a degree of refinement in the model that allows to produce reasonable values of dialogue- response times and CPU-utilization by simulation.
With respect to general methodology in simulation modeling and statistical evaluation we closely followed the lines of Jain [3] and Law and Kelton [4] .

VERIFICATION and VALIDATION . To check the internal consistency and correctness of the model and it´s implementation we made use of the trace- and debug- options of NETWORK II.5 . Thus the resulting verification of our simulation model largely depends on the correctness and verification of NETWORK , which is at present in release no. 6.0 and is being constantly improved through worldwide feedback between users and developers .
We took several series of measurements from the real SAP-system (test- and production version) via the SAP -trace - facility , where we concentrated on the fairly stable transaction load in the business hours between 10.00 and 12.00 a.m. (see figure 1) .
When we tried to fit theoretical distributions to our data no single classical distribution gave an acceptable fit . This forced us to resort to mixtures and smoothed empirical distribution functions . For example, we had to approximate the distribution of CPU-service times of certain dialogue tasks by 93 : 7 - mixtures of shifted Gamma(26.9 , 2.2) - and Exponential(232) - distributions . Note the large scale differences as expressed in the means of 26.9 and 232 , respectively . Where no twofold mixtures did work we used 4-6 - point piecewise linear approximations to the empirical distribution function (SDF RANDOM.LINEAR in NETWORK) . This method provided also a good matching of the first (two) moments .
Extensive statistical data analysis was done with SAS . We took considerable advantage of the module SAS/QC esp. of PROC CAPABILITY which we used intensively for maximum-likelihood-fitting of various types of distribution functions to the measurement data . The graphical assessment of goodness-of-fit was supported by PP- , QQ- and CDF- Plots .

FIRST RESULTS . When we chose all the input parameters in accordance with the measurements and the experience we gained through the validation we could reproduce all essential characteristics of the (real) target system very closely by simulation .
So we calculated a 90 % confidence interval for the mean response time of SAP-dialogue tasks as [345.9 , 384.4] (n=8 independent replications , ≥ 50 000 tasks) . This interval covers the mean of measurements which was 355 . Moreover, the complete distributions of measured and simulated response times were in good agreement . However the simulation model has the advantage that it is much more amenable to quickly set and vary a large number of parameters and to study the resulting behaviour than it is possible with the test-version of SAP.
Any experimentation with the production-version is strictly forbidden .

With the exception of a few peaks the CPU-utilization in our default state was about 35 % .
It could be demonstrated what will happen if additional SAP-modules are installed and lead to a certain increase of the transaction rates (= system load) . The corresponding increase of the (mean) response times is shown in figure 2 .
The real bottleneck preventing further increase of the transaction rates are the I/O-processors.
We could empirically determine the range of system load where the I/O´s become critical.

In a typical simulation run we chose a simulation time of 11 minutes, resetting our statistics after the first or second minute . This left us about 6350 tasks that were generated, processed and evaluated in such a run . Running the simulation with the very first stage of the model and on a PC-286 took about 20 hours . After several refinement steps and after moving on to a PC-486 we finally needed about 7 minutes of computing time .

CONCLUSIONS . We could establish that the transaction behaviour of SAP R/2 ´s basic component RB can be successfully modeled by simulation and that this can be carried out efficiently with NETWORK II.5 from CACI . The simulation model could produce answers and insight about the stochastic nature of the production-version of SAP that could not be obtained through the test-version . In general the model proved to be an excellent means to rapidly formulate and answer WHAT-IF-questions with respect to the behaviour of a SAP-system .
The results of our performance study were a valuable support for the company´s internal decision processes w.r.t. efficient hardware planning for optimal SAP-performance .

SELECTED REFERENCES .

[1] Banks, J. ; Carson, J. Discrete-Event System Simulation ; Prentice-Hall, London, 1984
[2] Fishman, G.S. Concepts and Methods in Discrete Event Digital Simulation ; J.Wiley, New York, 1973
[3] Jain, R. The Art of Computer Systems Performance Analysis ; J.Wiley, New York, 1991
[4] Law, A.M. ; Kelton, W.D. Simulation Modeling and Analysis, 2nd ed. , Mc Graw-Hill, New York, 1991
[5] CICS/MVS Version 2.1 Application Programmer´s Reference, IBM Corporation, 1987
[6] System RB Funktionsbeschreibung Basis-Technologie, Entwicklungsumgebung , Allgemeine Dienste; SAP AG , Walldorf, 1.10.1990
[7] Network II.5 User´s Manual Release 6.0 ; CACI-Products Company, La Jolla, August 1990
[8] SAS/QC Guide for Personal Computers, Version 6 Edition, SAS Institute, Cary, NC, 1989

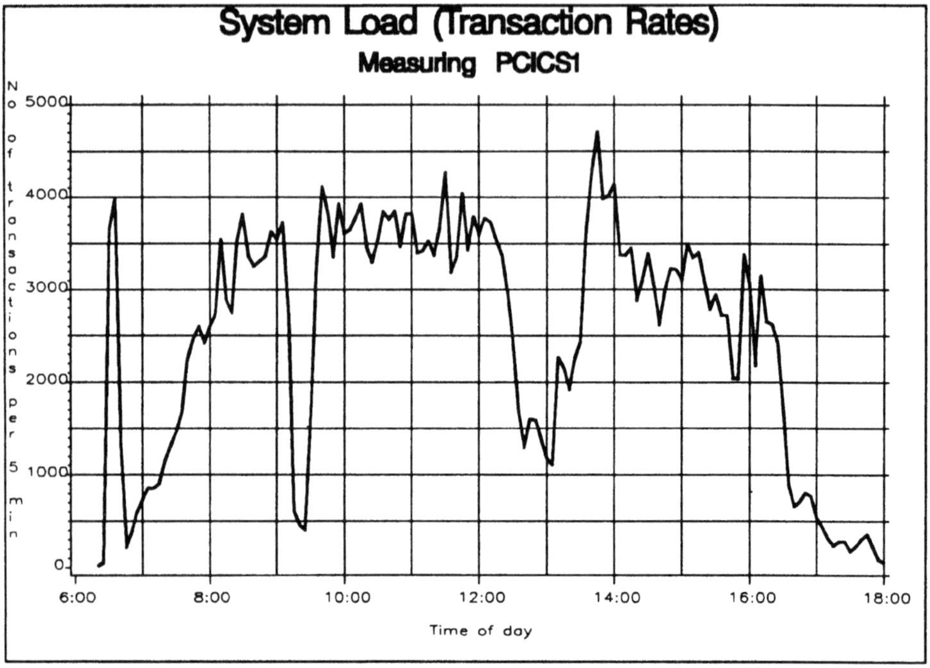

Figure 1 : Transaction rates of the production-version of SAP during a typical work day

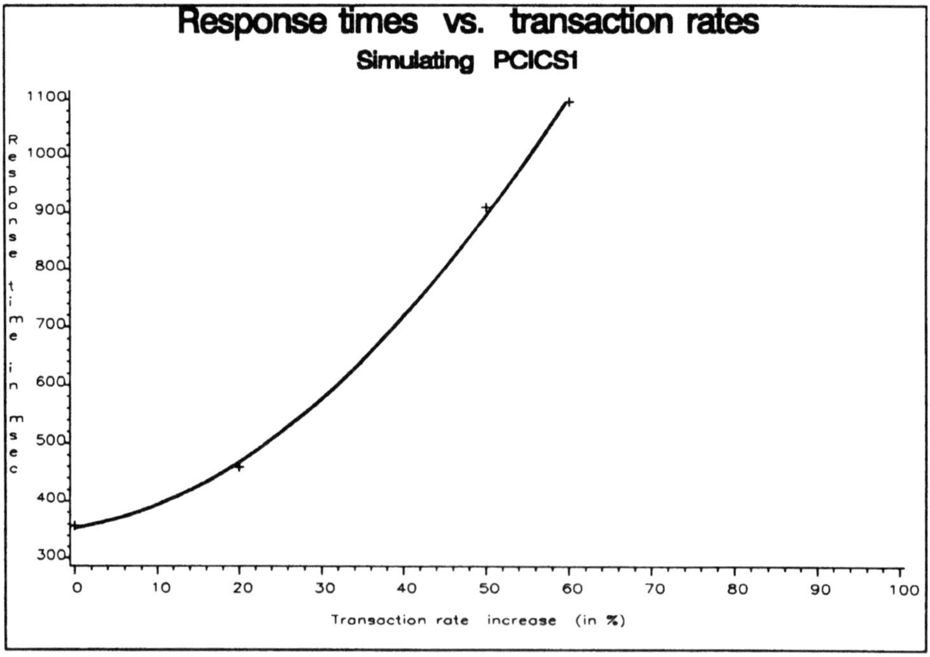

Figure 2 : Predicted increase of response times vs. increase of transaction rates

THEORETICAL AND EMPIRICAL EVALUATION OF SOME INDUCTIVE BASED METHODS IN ARTIFICIAL INTELLIGENCE AND STATISTICS

Fariba Jafar-Shaghaghi
Institute of Statistics and Mathematical Economics
University of Karlsruhe,
Rechenzentrum Zirkel 2, 7500 Karlruhe

1. Introduction

Besides The statistical methods there are also some totally different methods in Machine Learning, which are appropriate for classification.
This paper discusses the comparison of one classification method in statistics (discriminance analysis) with one machine learning algorithm (ID3), theoretically and empirically through using two data sets. In section 2 the definition of induction and some philosophical aspects will be disscussed. Section 3 is devoted to thoeretical aspects of inductive methods in statistics and machine learning. Theoretical and empirical comparison of algorithm (ID3) and discriminance analysis will be presented in the last section.

2. Induction:

One of the most controvercial issue in philosophy has been the concept of induction, its definition and justification. Induction is regarded as an inference in terms of universal statements derived from singular statements. The justification of this definition has been the battlefield of many philosophers such as Hume, Kant, Wittgenstein and Popper. The most relevant point of view to both underlying areas of statistics and machine learning is the view of Karl Popper.
Popper maitains that "inductive inference although not 'strictly valid', *can attain some degree of reliability* or of *probability*" (Popper:1960:29). According to his doctrine "inductive inferences are probable inferences" (ibid:29). The justification of induction is the matter most concerned in the area of philosophy. But the inductive methods are the matter of concern in statistics and machine learning and therefore the subject of this paper.

3. Inductive methods

3.1 in statistics

Finding meaning hidden in masses of data is an old problem which was the main motivating force behinde developing statistical methods for classification. In this regards some statistical techniques such as regression analysis and discriminance analysis, cluster analysis and factor analysis have been evolved.
There are different types of discriminance analysis in regards of the normality or non-normality of population and homogenity or heterogenity of covariance matrix assumption

1) Classical (Fisher's) two-class linear discriminance analysis.
Assumption: normal population and equal covariance matrixes.
2) Several-classes linear discriminance analysis
Assumption: normal population and equal covariance matrixes.
3) The quadratic discriminance function or best linear discriminance function.
Assumption: normal population heterogenous or unequal covariance matrixes.
4) Classification by logistic regression.
Assumption: non-normal population .
5) Kernel and nearest neighbour method.
Assumption: non parametric.

The advantages and disadvantages of the above mentioned methods and the problem of misclassification and the test of hypothesis by normal population and equal covariance matrix and also the problem of proper variable selection are the topics of this section.

3.2 in machine learning

In order to overcome the "knowlege acquisition bottleneck" and to eliminate the need for knowlege engineers who capture expertise for creating expert system, a new area in artificial intelligence called machine learning was developed.
One of the main purpose in machine learning is analyzing data. Historically statistics has been used to analyze the data numerically. Machine learning solves the same problem by using logic.
One of the central topics in machine learning is inductive learning. This means inductive inference from facts given by teachers (learning from examples) or by environment (learning from observations). Here we are concerned mainly with the inductive methods

of learning from examples, by using one of the well known allgorithm called Quinlan's ID3 (Quinlan 1979).
ID3 can be categorized as one of the TDITD family (Top-Down Induction of Decision Trees) of algorithms. The main idea behinde the ID3 is : First of all, to take instances (objects) whose classes are predefined through a fixed amount of properties (attributes). Then to draw a decision tree over these properties (attributes), such that, all instances can be correctly classified.

4. Comparison of the above two inductive methods

4.1 Common issues :

1. Selection of variables.
2. Misclassification cost.
3. Estimation of prior probabilities.
4. Estimation of error rates.

4.2 Advantages and disadvantages :

The result of statistical methods are mathematical equations, but machine learning produces rules which are much easier to understand, to follow and to use.
The linear dependency between groups of attributes and the independency between the attributes in one group are important assumptions in multivariate statistical analysis, which do not reflect the reality although simplify the calculation procedure. Decision trees are more robust to the complexity in the data set but they are very sensitive to outliers. Machine learning algorithms are flexible non-parametric methods for classification and appropriate for logical tasks.

4.3 Summary of the result of data analysis :

data set area	# of data	analysis method	software paket	accuracy rate
marketing	295	disc.	SPSS	% 71.56
marketing	295	ID3	Assistant Profetioal	% 71.86
bank note	200	disc.	SAS	% 99
bank note	200	ID3	Assistant Professionl	% 96
bank note	200	ID3	KET	% 89

The marketing data set is taken from "Multivariate Analysemethode" .
The bank note data set is taken from "Angewandte multivariate Statistik".

Refrences :

Backhaus, K. et al (1989), *Multivariate Analysemethoden*. Springer Verlag, Heidelberg.

Breiman, L. et al (1984), *Classification and Regression Trees*. Wadsworth, Belmont, Calif.

Flury, B. & Riedwyl, H. (1983), *Angewandte multivariate Statistik*. Gustave Fischer Verlag, Stuttgart.

Lachenbruch, P.A. (1975), *Disriminant Analysis*. Hafner, New York.

Michalski, R.S. et al (ed.) (1983), *Machine Learning I*. Tioga Press, Palo Alto.

Popper, K. (1960), *The Logic of Scientific Discovery*. Basic Books, N. Y..

Quinlan, J.R. (1979), *Induction over Large Databases*: Report HPP 79-14, Stanford Universty.

Quinlan, J. R. (1982), *Semi-autonomous Aquisition of Pattern-based Knowledge*: in Michi, D. (ed.) Intrductory Readings in Expert Systems. Gordon & Breach.

Simulating Chaotic Dynamics in a Macroeconomic Trade–Off–Model

Carsten Lange and Markus Pasche
Institut für Volkswirtschaftslehre, Universität Hannover
Wunstorfer Str. 14, D-3000 Hannover 91, Germany

1 Introduction

An expansive monetary impulse is analyzed in the framework of a nonlinear macroeconomic employment model. The analysis concentrates on the timepath and not on the trade off between inflation and unemployment rates. Solving nonlinear dynamical systems is often difficult or impossible, therefore computer simulation techniques are used.

2 Model

The model consists of four equations. There are only minor differences from common trade–off–models.

Wage Equation $$\widehat{w}_t = \widehat{q}_t + \gamma \widehat{P}^e_t + \beta(u^* - u_{t-1})^3 \quad \text{with} \quad \beta > 0, 0 < \gamma < 1 \tag{1}$$

The wage growth rate is determined by the sum of productivity growth, the expected inflation rate, which trade unions can push through only with a quote[1] γ, and the influence of the employment market in $t-1$ (natural unemployment rate (u^*) minus effective unemployment rate (u_{t-1})) multiplied with the proportional factor β. It is assumed that this influence is nonlinear[2].

Price Equation $$\widehat{P}_t = \widehat{w}_t - \widehat{q}_t \tag{2}$$

The inflation rate is determined by the amount the wage growth rate exceeds the productivity growth rate.

Demand Equation $$\Delta u_t = -\zeta(\widehat{M}^{ex}_t - \widehat{P}_t) \qquad \text{with} \quad \zeta > 0 \tag{3}$$

Like in many trade-off-models it is assumed that unemployment decreases, if real balance increases (real–balance–effect).

Inflation Expectations $$\widehat{P}^e_t = \widehat{P}_t \qquad \text{for all t} \tag{4}$$

Under common assumptions it can be shown that the inflation rate is expected correctly, if economic agents use the relevant economic model. Usually, a stochastic term is introduced, but here it is not taken into consideration in order to prevent the deterministic dynamics from beeing covered by stochastic motions.

Menu of Choice $$\widehat{P}_t = \frac{\beta}{1-\gamma}(u^* - u_t)^3 \tag{5}$$

The reduced form of the model is the Menu of Choice . Policy makers can choose a prefered $(u_t, \widehat{P}_t)$-combination by using monetary policy ($\widehat{M}^{ex}_t$). Whether the chosen combination will be reached depends on the stability of the model. In the following this will be analyzed by computer simulations.

---

[1]See *Fischer, S.* 1977.
[2]See *Lange/Pasche* 1991, p. 2.

3 Simulation of expansive monetary policy

The simulation equations of the endogenous variables can be derived by some arithmetic transformations. For simplificity, $\widehat{q}_t$ is set to zero. This is unproblematic because $\widehat{q}_t$ has no influence on the timepath.[3]

Simulation Equation for u_t: $u_t = \frac{\beta\zeta}{1-\gamma}(u^* - u_{t-1})^3 - \zeta\widehat{M}_t^{ex} + u_{t-1}$ (6)

Simulation Equation for $\widehat{w}_t$: $\widehat{w}_t = \frac{\beta}{1-\gamma}(u^* - u_{t-1})^3$ (7)

Simulation Equation for $\widehat{P}_t$: $\widehat{P}_t = \widehat{w}_t$ (2)

Simulation Equation for $\widehat{P}_t^e$ $\widehat{P}_t^e = \widehat{P}_t$ (4)

A period transformation in (6) leads to the difference equation of the system.

$$\Phi(u_t) = u_{t+1} = \frac{\beta\zeta}{1-\gamma}(u^* - u_t)^3 - \zeta\widehat{M}_{t+1}^{ex} + u_t \quad (8)$$

A steady-state–equilibrium $u_0 = u^* = 4\%$ and $\widehat{P}_0^e = \widehat{P}_0 = \widehat{w}_0 = \widehat{M}_0^{ex} = 0\%$ is choosen as initial condition for the following simulations. This equilibrium will be disturbed by an expansive monetary impulse $\widehat{M}_{1,2,3,\ldots}^{ex} = 2.5\% > \widehat{M}_0^{ex}$.

For visualization of the results a *phase diagram* will be used, in this case a cartesic $(u_t, \widehat{P}_t)$–diagram. The state of the system in t is plotted as a *phase point* in the diagram. Starting with an initial point $(u_0, \widehat{P}_0)$, while time is running, all phase points create a timepath (*trajectory*), each point representing a special solution of the system in t.

3.1 Fixpoint attractor

Using the parametrization: $\beta = 0.3, \zeta = 0.4, \gamma = 0.5$, the simulation exhibits a trajectory, which converges to a local stable point (*fixpoint attractor*), representing a new steady–state–equilibrium ($u_\infty \approx 2.39\%$, $\widehat{P}_\infty = 2.50\%$) given by the menu of choice. The economic policy was successful.

In general, an attractor is a compact set of points attracting all trajectories in the neighbourhood. Here the attractor is only the local stable point $\bar{u}$. Local stability means, if the initial point is far enough from $\bar{u}$, the trajectory will not converge any more.

3.2 Periodic attractor

Choosing the same initial condition but a different parametrization: $\beta = 0.3, \zeta = 0.5$, $\gamma = 0.6$, the simulation yields a timepath, which is not reaching the new steady–state–equilibrium (see ⊗ in figure 1), determined by the menu of choice ($\widehat{P}_\infty = 2.5\%, u_\infty \approx 2.51\%$). The policy failed.

After adaption, a cycle with period 4 is realized, called *periodic attractor*. After n iterations a point of a n–periodic attractor will be reached again. For $t \to \infty$ in these points $u_t = u_{t+n}$ with $u_t \neq u_{t+k}$ $(1 \leq k < n)$. In this case n is 4. Hence $u_t - u_{t+4} = 0$ for $t \to \infty$. If $\Phi^{(4)}(u_t)$ is defined as the fourth application of the recursive function $\Phi(u_t)$, then the function $u_t - \Phi^{(4)}(u_t)$ must intersect the abscisse at u_t, if u_t is a point of the periodic attractor.[4] This is shown in figure 1, where u_t is plotted against $u_t - \Phi^{(4)}(u_t)$.

[3]For a more detailed argumentation see *Lange/Pasche* 1991, p. 3.

[4]See *Baumol/Benhabib* 1989, pp. 87.

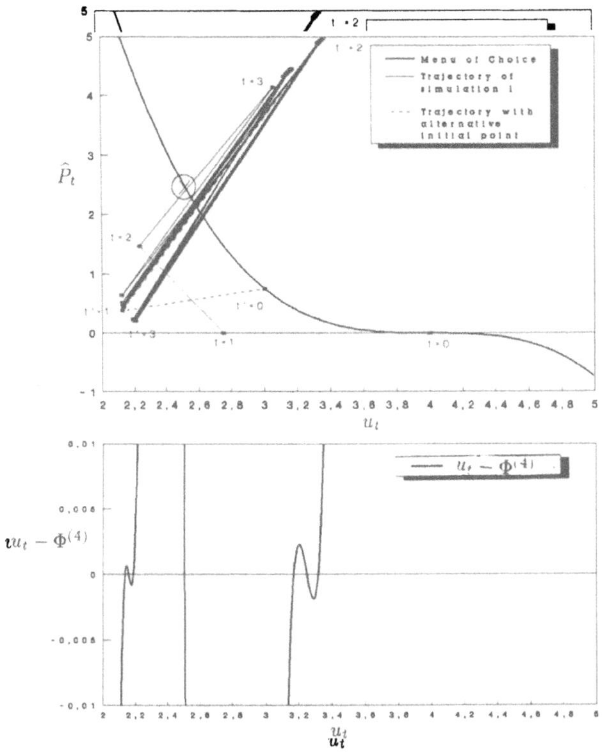

Figure 1: Simulation 2

3.3 Strange attractor

In this simulation the parametrization is: $\beta = 0.3, \zeta = 0.5, \gamma = 0.7$. The timepath, shown in figure 2, converges neither to a fixpoint nor to a periodic attractor. It is attracted to a special area of the phase space, called *strange attractor*. On this attractor the trajectory moves aperiodic so that the dynamics seems to be random although the model is strictly deterministic. This dynamical behaviour is called *deterministic chaos*. There might not be a big difference between this strange attractor and a periodic attractor with a very high period, if the timepath could be forecasted.
But figure 3 illustrates that two timepaths, namely the timepath of simulation 3 and one starting very close to it, diverge after some iterations. Even minimal variations of initial conditions lead in the long run to totally different timepaths. This characteristic is called *sensitive dependence on initial conditions*[5].

If a system is in a chaotic regime, the impact of political interventions are not forecastable, because in empirical research the initial conditions and parameters are not given exactly.

4 Impact of monetary policy on the dynamics

The dynamical behaviour of the model can be investigated with Ljapunov exponents. The Ljapunov exponent ist the geometric average of all relative changes, occuring when the initial

[5]See *Baumol/Benhabib* 1989, p. 92, *Stahlecker/Schmidt* 1991, p. 191.

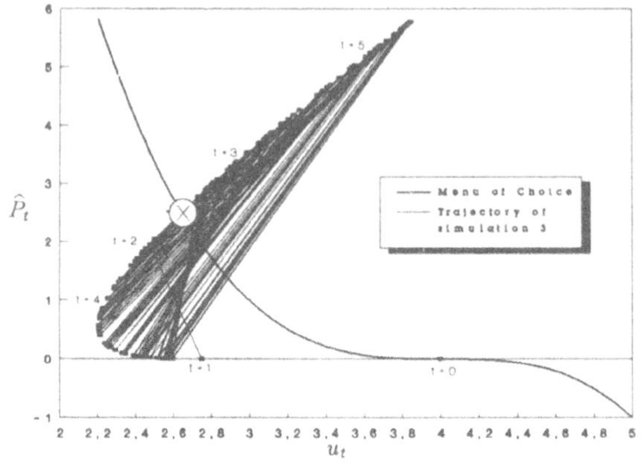

Figure 2: Simulation 3

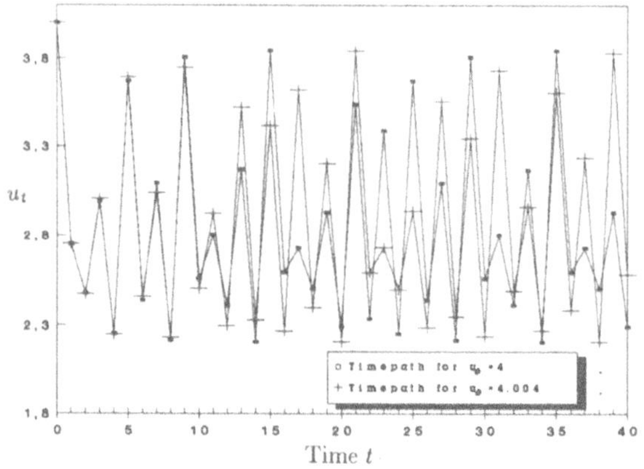

Figure 3: Diverging timepaths

condition is infinitesimally disturbed[6]. Here $f'(x)$ is the first derivation of (8).

$$L = \lim_{N\to\infty} \frac{1}{N} \sum_{n=0}^{N} \ln |f'(x_n)| < 0$$

If $L < 0$, deviations in the initial conditions die out during the iteration process. So $L > 0$ (trajectories diverge) indicates a chaotic dynamic. In the following, it will be shown how the dynamic changes when monetary policy changes. Therefore, (8) is transformed in a compact form by introducing two variables a and b:

$$u_{t+1} = a(u^* - u_t)^3 - b + u_t \qquad \text{with} \quad a = \frac{\beta\zeta}{1-\gamma}, \quad b = \zeta \widehat{M}^{ex}_{t+1}$$

In a series of simulations the stability of the model with different (a, b)–combinations was tested. In figure 4 the dynamic behaviour depending on a and b is characterized by using the concept of the Ljapunov exponent.

[6]For the mathematical background of the Ljapunov exponent see *Lorenz* 1989.

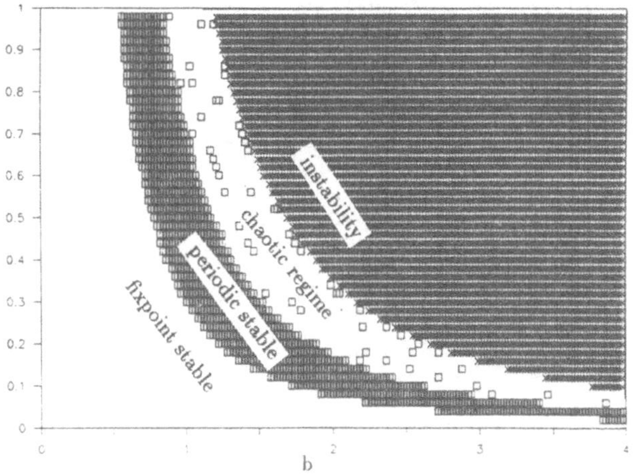

Figure 4: Stability regions of the model

C.p. a variation of monetary policy changes the parameter b (horizontal moving in figure 4). Hence figure 4 shows that in a wide range of parameters ($a \gtrsim 0.1$) a variation of $\widehat{M}_t^{ex}$ can yield either a fixpoint, a periodic, or a chaotic attractor or unstable dynamics (explosion). So even in a stable situation a modification of monetary policy can lead to a chaotic regime.

5 Conclusions

Nonlinear models exhibit the limits of applicability of economic models. The sensitivity of the timepath in a chaotic regime makes a long run forcast of economic phenomena questionable, because initial conditions have to be estimated. This is a limit of empirical research in general, because no bias is negligible.

References

Baumol, W.J./Benhabib, J. (1989), Chaos: Significance, Mechanism, and Economic Applications; in: Journal of Economic Perspectives 3, S. 77–105.

Fischer, S. (1977), Long–Term Contracts, Rational Expectations, and the Optimal Money Supply Rule; in: Journal of Political Economy 85, S. 191–205.

Lange, C./Pasche, M. (1991), Chaotische Dynamik am Beispiel eines Beschäftigungsmodells mit rationalen Erwartungen, Diskussionspapier Nr. 157, Universität Hannover

Lange, C./Pasche, M. (forthcoming), Chaos und Stabilität in einem Beschäftigungsmodell mit rationalen Erwartungen, in: Zeitschrift für Wirtschafts- und Sozialwissenschaften.

Lorenz, H.-W. (1989), Nonlinear Dynamical Economics and Chaotic Motion, Berlin.

Stahlecker, P./Schmidt, K.(1991), Chaos und sensitive Abhängigkeit in ökonomischen Prozessen; in: Zeitschrift für Wirtschafts- und Sozialwissenschaften 111, S. 187–206.

EXECUTIVE INFORMATION SYSTEMS RESEARCH: STATUS AND FUTURE DIRECTIONS

Charles A. Snyder
&
R. Kelly Rainer, Jr.
Department of Management
Auburn University
Auburn, AL 36830 U.S.A.

I. Introduction

This study reports on a comprehensive review of the Executive Information System (EIS) literature. In compiling the sources for EIS it was useful to categorize them in three groups: academic, practitioner, and mixed in the cases where appropriate. The purpose of this research was to assess the state of research in an important, emerging category of information systems applications. Because the topic of EIS is relatively new, there is not a great deal of reported research. The characteristics of EIS make the topic of great interest and importance for researchers, but a topic that currently lacks a research framework. Consequently, an important purpose of the present research was to help provide suggested research designs and methodologies within a research framework.

We report on the results of our literature review and the methodology of categorizing the EIS sources by content dimensions. The few academic sources are discussed in more detail and research designs and methodologies are outlined. The review and categorizations are designed to aid in determining directions for future and more rigorous EIS research. We offer suggestions for a framework to guide this future research.

II. Methodology

An extensive review of the literature pertaining to EIS was

undertaken. In the literature review, it was quickly evident that most of the sources were not academic. Because most of the EIS sources were oriented towards practitioners, they were separated into a **practitioner** category. If the sources appeared to fit into both an **academic** and **practitioner** category, they were placed into a **mixed** category. Thus, each source was placed into only one of three categories as a first step in the evaluation process. Sources were placed in the academic category based on (1) the journal, e.g., Management Information Systems Quarterly is academic while The Wall Street Journal is practitioner; and (2) methodological rigor, e.g., a case study versus a report.

Each of the sources was next examined along several major content dimensions. For example, the EIS definition, EIS characteristics, EIS development or implementation, evaluation, functions or capabilities, executive use and training, benefits, requirements, data management, and architecture were some of these content dimensions. A total of fourteen dimensions was used in the research.

The investigation and summarization of the categories and content of the existing EIS literature helped to determine the present status of EIS research. The content analysis provided a means for mapping areas to a research framework.

In addition, the categorization of the content and thrust of the articles allowed better analysis of the design, methodology, and research direction employed by EIS researchers and practitioners. Four major IS frameworks were examined: Gorry & Scott Morton (1971); Mason & Mitroff (1978); Ives, Hamilton, & Davis (1980); and Nolan & Wetherbe (1980).

III. EIS Research

The review of the EIS literature found a total of 231 articles.

Of these articles, only 61 were classified as **academic**. Of the remainder, 22 were classified as **mixed**. Thus, 148 of the sources were found to be **practitioner** oriented. Based on the categories and the content of the articles, one might conclude that the EIS topic has not attracted much attention from academic researchers. Because the EIS field is relatively new, little published academic research might be expected. In this case, the number of academic EIS sources was very small relative to the total degree of interest and impact of the systems reflected by the total practitioner sources.

IV. Academic EIS Literature

Of the 61 sources that were classified as academic, most were case studies. There were also several sources that remain working papers rather than being widely reported journal publications.

V. Proposed Research Framework

In order to address the research requirements in EIS, it is useful to have a framework. Although several frameworks for information systems research have been proposed, none has been extended for EIS. The Nolan & Wetherbe (1980) framework was chosen as the framework on which to map our content dimensions. We mapped the content dimensions to positions in the framework that appeared most appropriate. The frequency of appearance of the content dimensions indicates where most emphasis has been placed by EIS researchers and points out directions for future research.

VI. Methodologies and Designs for Future EIS Research

The adoption of a framework such as that proposed above should help guide future EIS research. Because EIS is as yet an immature information systems application, there remains a great deal of useful research at the exploratory level. Some of the most useful EIS studies to date have employed the case study methodology; e.g., Houdeshel & Watson (1987); Applegate & Osborn (1988). A few sources reported on results of survey research; e.g., Watson, Rainer, & Koh (1991).

As EISs become more widespread, the opportunity to perform more rigorous research will need a framework and research designs should evolve to provide more empirical evidence of their effectiveness. More survey research to test hypotheses and longitudinal research designs will be possible. Only after the EIS matures somewhat and researchers, provided with the proper framework and employing good research designs, can we expect to have sufficient evidence to properly assess and assure the success of this important executive support system.

VII. References

References available upon request.

FROM BUSINESS MODELS TO AUTOMATIC SOFTWARE PRODUCTION

Arne Sølvberg
Information Systems Group
Dept. EECS, The Norwegian Inst. Technology
University of Trondheim
Norway

Information Systems Engineering is the discipline of developing and maintaining computerized Information Systems. In the past these systems have mostly been developed in a "tailor-made" fashion. Companies have developed their own in-house systems from scratch. This practice has led to increasing maintenance burdens on their DP-departments, and to embarrassingly high information systems expenses.

Information system design comprises organisational design, application software design, and computer system configuration, plus appropriate interface design between the layers. Some of the most important developments that will influence Information Systems development techniques in the years to come are found in the realms of:

- application platforms
- system development environments
- integrated specification models

An application platform contains basic software functions for a particular application domain, plus possibilities for the platform user to add on company-specific software. An application platform is a vendor supplied "common system". It is intended to comprise 40-80% of the software that is required in an information system within some particular application area.

The rationale for developing an application platform is economy of scale. Information systems are becoming more and more complex and expensive to develop and maintain. It makes sense to share costs through standardisation of business functions and software. We may therefore expect to see more platforms in new domains in the years to come.

Even if application platforms are domain oriented, they will have to contain a number of general data processing functions, e.g. word processors. This may lead to problems with the integration of a platform with other software packages that are already used by the platform buyer. The platform buyers - the companies - will face additional problems. Integration of information systems applications is also today a formidable challenge. The databases of the many information systems that are in operation in a large company reflect various views of the company and its environment. Systems integration requires that the databases are integrated. This requires that a common world view is developed within the company.

Information systems used to be built from scratch, because there were few, if any, components available to base the new systems upon. This is not the case any more. Information systems are increasingly being built through the re-use, modification, integration and interfacing of commercially available software components. Programming, in the original meaning of writing commands for a computer to follow, is not as dominant an activity as it used to be only a few years ago.

More of the total effort of a development project has been shifted from the actual writing of the software, to finding out which software to write. This change has come about because too many projects failed, in order to secure that the software is useful for some worthwhile purpose when it is finally written.

A system development environment is a particular type of platform, which provides an infrastructure for the integration of available system development tools, beyond the conventional level of compilers and database systems. A most important component of system development platforms is the system encyclopedia (data dictionary, repository, specification database), which makes it possible to integrate the various application systems of a company, so that it may become possible to obtain control over the evolution of a company's software.

In spite of the recognition of the need for standardization, there is a plethora of available development methods, specification techniques, and programming languages. There is, so far, no indication of that the industry, as a whole, will settle for a broad agreement on standards for information systems development in the forseeable future. Therefore, support systems must be able to incorporate various techniques and tools as they become available and are offered in the marketplace.

The most critical problem in developing information systems is the communication problem. It is crucial to the success of the system that the users can participate in the development of the information system requirements because the users are the specialists of the application domain where the information system is built.

An integrated specification model makes it possible to formally express a system's properties on every level of abstraction, from the business policy level to the operational data processing level, such that the specifications may be formally massaged and analysed. "Automatic programming" based on functional application systems specifications may be within reach.

Most modelling approaches are either process-oriented, data-oriented or logic-oriented.

Process-oriented approaches take as a starting point the description of the processes of the system which are supported by separate data models.

Data-oriented approaches take as their starting point the description of data structures and data semantics which are made common to all of the applications. The approach stems from the database area, where the specification of the data items, records, and their relationships were focused.

In a logic-oriented approach, knowledge about the application is represented by a set of formal assertions, such as logical formulae. These assertions constitute a theory of the application.

A logic-oriented approach aims at specifying WHAT the informationsystem is going to do rather than HOW to do it. In dataoriented approach and the processoriented approach, the emphasis is on HOW the information system is to process the information rather than WHAT it is supposed to do. Therefore, the logic-oriented approach has a higher degree of data processing independence than the two other approaches. However, logic-oriented approaches are more difficult to implement and the performance is usually low.

Specification languages with automatic abstraction facilities would improve the current situation. A "super language" would contain sufficient modelling constructs for the specification of every conceivable system detail. In addition, abstraction facilities would be available, so that e.g. a data flow diagram could be derived from the detailed algorithmic specification, plus a specification of the systems structure. This situation is clearly beyond the current state of the art.

A "super-language" may be developed over the next decade. Such a language will combine logic-orientation with process-oriented and data-oriented approaches. The key concept of a "super language" is "constructivity", that is, it must be possible to formally derive the external properties of a system structure when the properties of its components are known, so that the system structure can be replaced by a "black box" with the properties of that system.

Completing A KBS-Shell With A Module For Uncertain Reasoning

Christof Weinhardt, BWL-Wirtschaftsinformatik, University of Giessen

I Introduction

In most economic applications of Knowledge Based Systems (KBS) - as well as in many other fields of applications (e.g., medicine, meteorology) - the available data are uncertain; i.e., the input facts to the reasoning process are affected with some degree of *uncertainty*. Furthermore, the rules of the *inference process* are uncertain, too. These two sources of uncertainty influence the results of reasoning and can be represented in different ways; one of them is the *method of certainty factors*, on which this note will focus. In many KBS tools or KBS Shells, especially in PC tools (e.g., in KBMS, Nexpert Object, TIRS), there exist no modules capable to cope with uncertain knowledge. In this paper we deal with the question, how such a tool without the capability of handling uncertain knowledge may be completed with a module for uncertain reasoning. For applications requiring uncertain reasoning two main problems need to be solved:

1. An appropriate concept for evaluation and aggregation of uncertainty factors as mentioned above needs to be determined.
2. An external module has to be "added " to the KBS Shell representing the uncertainty concept choosen.

Especially the second problem must be solved in an easily handable manner from the knowledge engineer's point of view.

II The Extended Aggregation Approach for Certainty Factors

In Buhl/Pfingsten/Weinhardt[1991] the EMYCIN approach to uncertain reasoning (see Buchanan/Shortliffe[1984]) - a mixture of fuzzy and probabilistic aggregation of output and/or input certainty factors, respectively - three main disadvantages are discussed in detail: discontinuity, dependence on rule formulation and dependence on the firing sequence. It is shown that these disadvantages are an implication of the implicit EMYCIN-assumption that input (conditional) facts are independent but output (i.e. fired) facts are completely dependent (see also figure 1); e.g., for the rules

$$R1: \quad A \,\&\, B \Rightarrow e \qquad\qquad R2: \quad C \vee D \Rightarrow e,$$

the input facts (A,B) and (C,D) are assumed to be independent - their certainty factors are aggregated probabilistically - whereas the rules firing the output fact e are assumed to be (completely) dependent and are therefore aggregated according to the fuzzy approach (see Zadeh[1965], Zimmermann[1985]).

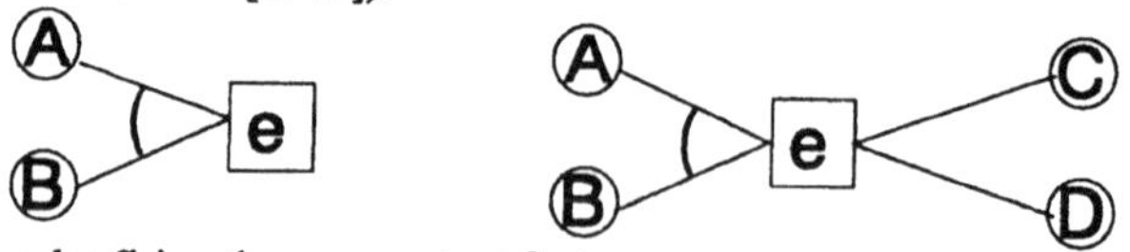

Figure 1: Two rules firing the same output fact

For some output e, the certainty from rule R_r with conclusion certainty s_r is given by

$C^r(e) = s_r\, aggi(n, \mu, o, C(A1), C(A2), ..., C(An))$.

As rules are considered as OR-connected, the incremental and extended aggregation of certainties for any output fact implied by more than one rule works exactly in the same way as for input facts, that means for two rules R_r and R_s firing fact e we have:

$$C^{r,s}{}_{\mu'}(C^r(e), C^s(e), v, \mu') = \mu' \max\{C^r(e), C^s(e)\} + (1-\mu')\, C_p(C^r(e), C^s(e), v).$$

Thus, the procedure "*aggo*" performs the second aggregation step for the certainty factors in the reasoning process:

$$aggo(\mu', s^r, C^t(e), aggi(n, \mu, o, C(A1), ..., C(An)),$$

where $C^t(e)$ can be either a default value or the current aggregated certainty of the output fact. For $\mu = \mu'$ this procedure ensures continuity, independence of rule formulation and - at least - local independence of the reasoning sequence.

III The implementation of the Extended Aggregation Procedure

As mentioned above, in most PC-KBS-Shells are incapable of coping with uncertain reasoning. Since many applications handle uncertain data, a procedure is necessary to complete such Shells with a suitable module. Adding certainty components to slots and/or parameters is the first step to realize such a certainty aggregation. Hence, these components can be processed in a module, e.g., implemented in a procedural language like C being appended to the KBS-Shell. This procedure, named *AGG*, should be called from the rule action in rule R_r with the following list of parameters:

$$AGG(\mu', s^r\, C^t(e),\ n, \mu, o, C(A1), ... , C(An)),$$

where the notation corresponds to section II.

The transformation of the extended aggregation approach of section II into a C-procedure only allows the certainty aggregation of one kind of logical connection of the input facts of the rule considered, namley AND or OR. That means, no mixed "chains" of input facts nor brackets in these chains are tractable with the corresponding procedure - a rather unsatisfying result for our problem.

As the procedure developed should be easily handable for potential knowledge engineers, it is not very helpful adding a long list of special (C-) procedures - one for every imaginable case each (with different lists of parameters etc.) to the KBS-Shell. A better approach is the following: Using fixed values for some of the parameters of AGG, we can find something like the neutral element for the output aggregation in the following sence:

Starting with some reasonable aggregation axioms the following aggregation procedure for input and output facts is introduced: With C(A) denoting the certainty factor of fact A and s_r denoting that of conclusion r (i.e. rule R_r), μ and μ' representing the degree of dependence of inputs (i.e. rule's conditions) and outputs (i.e. facts in the rule's action, fired by two or more rules), respectively, the certainty factor of the output considered is computed in - at least - two steps: First, the inputs of the conditional part of the rule are aggregated incrementally (by "*aggi*"). Second this aggregation result is aggregated again with the current certainty of the output fact (by "*aggo*"). Initially the current certainty of the output fact may be default (e.g., zero). After output aggregations it represents aggregated certainties. Due to this incremental approach for input certainties as well as for output certainties successive application of the (two argument) formula $C_{p/f}$ with $o \in \{\&,v\}$:

$$C_{p/f}: [-1,+1]^2 \times \{\&,v\} \text{-->} [-1,+1]; \qquad (C(A1), C(A2), o) \text{-->} C_{p/f}(C(A1), C(A2), o).$$

C_p represents the probabilistic aggregation,

$$C_p(C(A1), C(A2), o) = \begin{cases} C(A1)\,C(A2) & \text{for } o = \text{"\&"}, C(A1), C(A2) >= 0 \\ -C(A1)\,C(A2) & \text{for } o = \text{"\&"}, C(A1), C(A2) < 0 \\ 0 & \text{for } o = \text{"\&"}, \text{for all others} \\ C(A1) + C(A2) - C_p(C(A1),C(A2), \&) & \text{for } o = \text{"v"}, \end{cases}$$

and C_f the fuzzy aggregation approach,

$$C_f(C(A1), C(A2), o) = \begin{cases} \max\{C(A1), C(A2)\} & \text{for } o = \& \\ \min\{C(A1), C(A2)\} & \text{for } o = v. \end{cases}$$

The extended aggregation C_μ of input certainty factors is defined in the following way:

$$C_\mu: [-1,+1]^2 \times \{\&,v\} \times [0,1] \text{ -->} [-1,+1] \quad (C(A), C(A2), o, \mu) \text{-->} C_\mu(C(A1), C(A2), o, \mu),$$

$$C_\mu(C(A1), C(A2), o, \mu) = \mu\, C_f(C(A1), C(A2), o) + (1-\mu)\, C_p(C(A1), C(A2), o).$$

The procedure "*aggi*" finally aggregates a number of input facts and requires the following parameters:

aggi(n, μ, o, C(A1), C(A2), ..., C(An)),

where n denotes the number of input facts in the rule, μ the degree of (in)dependence of these input facts, o the logical connection of the inputs and C(.) the certainties of input facts considered, respectively.

Let μ' be +1, $s_T = +1$ and $C^t(e) = -1$, we obtain the pure input aggregation of all inputs of the rule under consideration; formally

$$AGG(+1, +1, -1, n, \mu, o, C(A1), C(A2), ..., C(An)) = aggi(n, \mu, o, C(A1), ..., C(An)),$$

which is the aggregated certainty of all input facts of the "o"-chain A1o A2 o ... o An. Thus, with these fixed parameters we are able to aggregate certainties of all mixed chains of input facts: Taking out the corresponding parts of this chain we can simulate its pure input aggregation and put its result into the final *AGG* procedure as one of all input facts; thereby we obtain a recursive call of *AGG*. A short example will make this clear:

Example: For rule R_1: (A v B) & C & (A v F) => x the following procedure call computes the correct certainty factor for x

$$\begin{array}{ccccc} & (A \vee B) & \& \;\; C \;\; \& & (A \vee F) \\ AGG(\mu', s_1, C^t(x), 3, \mu, \&, & AGG(1,1,-1,2,\mu,v,C(A),C(B)), & C(C), & AGG(1,1,-1,2,\mu,v,C(A),C(F))) \end{array}$$

Hence, all logical combinations of input facts can be mapped with these recursive procedure calls; thus, only one single procedure head and its structure must be learned by the knowledge engineer.

IV Outlook

The procedure introduced above performs the aggregation of certainty factors in the reasoning process of a knowledge based system in an external C-module appended to any KBS-Shell. In this paper only the logical connection of pure input fact certainties was treated. In practical applications other problems arise as, e.g., how to handle relations/comparisons between two or more input facts, or how to treat the logical NOT operator, what to do if the inference machine cuts OR-conditions into a list of OR-less rules, etc.

In a cooperation project with IBM Germany the introduced kind of uncertain reasoning is currently implemented and tested. We hope that the empirical results will support the theory founded extension approach to uncertain reasoning.

References

Buchanan, B.G. and E. Shortliffe [1984]: *Rule based Expert Systems*, Addison Wessley, Reading, Massachusetts.

Buhl, H.U., A. Pfingsten and Ch.Weinhardt [1991]: *Gibt es in wissensbasierten Systemen Alternativen zur EMYCIN-Gewißheitsverarbeitung?*, erscheint in Wirtschaftsinformatik, 4/91, Vieweg, Wiesbaden.

ON THE BAYESIAN APPROACH TO LEARNING

S. ACID, L.M. DE CAMPOS, A. GONZALEZ,

R. MOLINA, N. PEREZ DE LA BLANCA

Departamento de Ciencias de la Computación e I.A.

Universidad de Granada. 18071 Granada, España.

1 INTRODUCTION

The aim of this work is to introduce CASTLE (Causal Structures from Inductive Learning), a tool based on the bayesian approach to learning. CASTLE can be used so far to learn causal structures from raw data, propagate knowledge throughout polytrees, simulate and also edit polytree dependent distributions. CASTLE ([1] and [2]), is currently being developed by the authors in the DECSAI at the University of Granada. Basically, CASTLE estimates, from a file of examples, the (in)dependencies among the variables involved in the examples in order to build a polytree displaying such (in)dependencies. The steps to construct such polytree are: setting constrains among the variables, selecting a criterion to calculate the skeleton of the polytree and, finally, selecting the criterion to direct the obtained skeleton. Once the polytree is built, CASTLE allows the user to propagate knowledge throughout the obtained singly-connected graph using what has been called the bayesian approach to the knowledge propagation task. CASTLE can be also used as a platform where to test learning methods since it allows the users to create polytrees and simulate data from them and use the generated sample as learning samples.

2 CASTLE IN LEARNING MODE

CASTLE is a C program which can be run either in batch or in interactive modes. In this section, we show how CASTLE can be used to learn a causal network from raw data and how we can use this network to propagate our knowledge about some facts to get new knowledge about other related facts, through the causal network.

For learning, CASTLE needs a sample data file with a particular format where the name of the variables, the cases and the values appear ([2] for details). So, let us assume we have a sample data file and we want to learn about the causal network representing the probability distribution where the data come from. The first step to learn about the polytree associated to the read data sample is to estimate the skeleton of such polytree.

CASTLE have the option **Learning** with the following structure: **Set Constrains, Skeleton, Polytree Recovery** and **Complete.**

Before learning the skeleton the user could be interested in introducing constrains on its topology. The first option of **Learning** gives the user the opportunity to include constrains on the skeleton topology, linking in advance those couples of nodes on which you have strong evidence on their dependency. According to the kind of evidence the user has on the nodes he/she will be interested in introducing arrows, edges or both. Edges means causal dependence relationship between variables without specifying precedence between them. Arrows means causal dependence relationship, the sense of the arrow indicating the cause and effect node respectively. Once the user have finished introducing constrains, CASTLE will have stored the constrains together with the network structure, giving us the opportunity to estimate the skeleton with or without constrains.

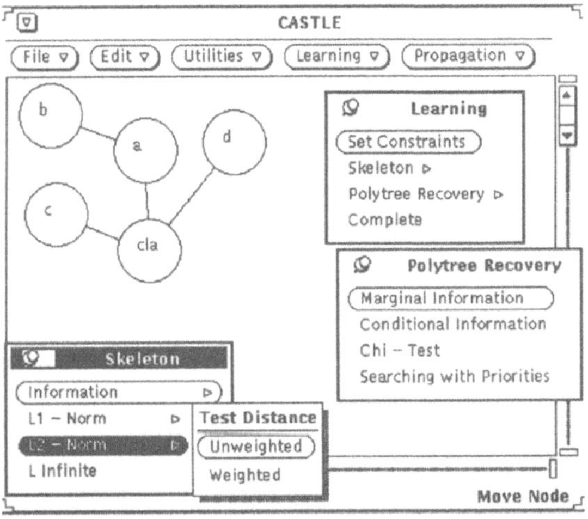

Figure 1: Learning options in CASTLE

The second option of **Learning** allow us to estimate the skeleton associated to a data set using different algorithms all of them roughly based on the Chow-Liu algorithm ([3]). To estimate the skeleton CASTLE uses a maximum weight spanning tree (MWST) algorithm with different kinds of dependence measures: **Information** (Kullback-Leibler, Rajski), **L1-norm** (Weighted, Unweighted), **L2-norm** (Weighted, Unweighted), L_∞.

The next step in the learning procedure is to direct the edges of the skeleton. CASTLE uses several criteria for directing edges: **Marginal Information, Conditional Information, Chi-Square Test, Searching with Priorities**. Each one uses a different independence test. CASTLE is an experimental software that allow us several freedom degrees for testing bayesian learning algorithms, and the user can combine the above criteria with those in Skeleton to get different methods for polytree estimation. Some on the above criteria (**Marginal Information, Searching with Priorities**) used to direct edges need a threshold to detect independence. CASTLE has an option to modify the thresholds and by selecting the **Set Thresholds** option the user can see and modify the default values. The **Chi-Square Test** option is built fixing the confidence level at 95%. (see [2] for theoretical detail).

Complete is the last step in the CASTLE learning procedure. This option allow us to direct the edges which could not be directed using the algorithms implemented in the Polytree Recovery option, and to attach to each node the corresponding probabilities.

Once we have in memory a network with probabilities defined on each node we could be interested in propagating the marginal probabilities through out the network or in fixing observed cases on some nodes and propagate these pieces of information through out the network. In both cases the idea is to know how these pieces of information affect the probabilities on the cases of the variables in the remainder nodes. The option **Propagation** in CASTLE allow us **Show Bel, Set Observation** and **Propagation.** Selecting **Show Bel** and a node CASTLE shows the probabilities associated to the cases of that node. The option **Set Observation** allows the user to fix what cases of a node are considered observed before propagate this information. To fix in a node more than one case means that we have observed one of these cases but we don't know which of them exactly. The facts of fixing observed cases doesn't mean that CASTLE propagates this information. In order to do this CASTLE has the option **Propagation**.

3 CASTLE IN TESTING MODE

CASTLE was thought as an experimental software for testing the behaviour of the bayesian learning algorithms, that is the reason CASTLE has the testing mode. The user can use the graphical utilities of CASTLE to edit a polytree, i.e., to draw nodes, link them by arrows, give name to the nodes and cases, and define the conditional or marginal probabilities in each node.

CASTLE can also simulate samples from edited or learned polytree-dependent distributions. The aim of this utility is to offer a way of testing the performance of the algorithms implemented in CASTLE, since you can edit a polytree, simulate a sample from it, and compare your original network with that obtained from the learning algorithms.

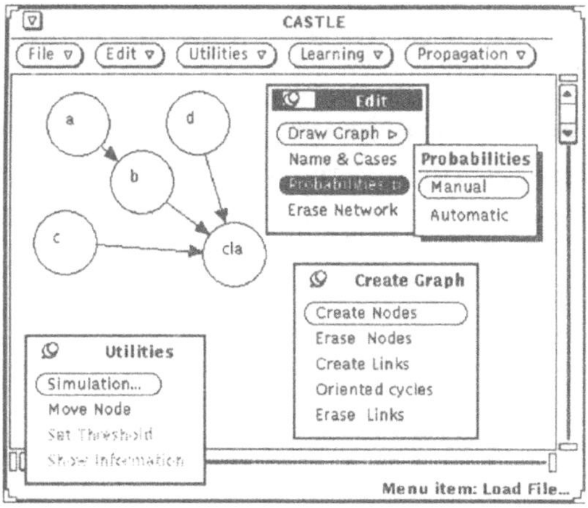

Figure 2: Testing options in CASTLE

4 CASTLE UTILITIES

In order to facilitate the use of the learning algorithms CASTLE has some other graphical utilities as **Move node, Show Information**, etc. and moreover CASTLE can also be run in batch mode. Really, the batch mode is a new version of CASTLE. This one creates a file containing the estimated network. Furthermore, the user can provide to the program with a new type of file containing a set of samples of observed values of any variable but the last one (the one thought as classifier), in this case CASTLE propagates the observed knowledge through out the net and outputs a file containing the posterior probability of the cases of the classifier given the observed value of the rest of the variables.

Acknowledgements

This work has been supported by the Commission of the European Communities under ESPRIT project no 5170: Comparative Testing of Statistical and Logical Learning, Statlog.

References

[1] Acid, S., Campos,L.M.de, González, A., Molina, R. and Pérez de la Blanca, N. (1991): Bayesian Learning Algorithms in CASTLE. *Technical Report no 91-4-2.* Dept of Computer Science and A.I. (DECSAI). University of Granada.

[2] Acid, S., Campos,L.M.de, González, A., Molina, R. and Pérez de la Blanca, N. (1991) CASTLE: Causal Structures from Inductive Learning. Release 2.0. *Technical Report no 91-4-3.* Dept of Computer Science and A.I. (DECSAI). University of Granada.

[3] Pearl, J. (1988) *Probabilistic Reasoning in Intelligent Systems: Networks of Plausible Inference.* Morgan and Kaufmann.

SOME RESULTS ON THE AUTOMATIC CONSTRUCTION OF BAYESIAN NETWORKS

S. Acid, L.M. de Campos, A. González, R. Molina, N. Pérez de la Blanca
Departamento de Ciencias de la Computación e I.A.
Universidad de Granada. 18071 Granada, Spain

1. Introduction

When dealing with systems that contain a great quantity of knowledge, that one of the main problems we need to solve is to determine how much and what sort of knowledge is necessary to perform a given task (e.g. an inference or a diagnosis). In other words, it is essential to know what information is relevant to the question we are interested in.

Bayesian networks are powerful knowledge representation tools able to efficiently represent and manipulate relationships of relevance. As defined by Pearl [3], Bayesian networks are directed acyclic graphs (DAGs) in which the nodes represent propositions or variables, the arcs signify the existence of direct causal dependencies between the linked propositions, and the strengths of these dependencies are quantified by conditional probabilities (in this context (ir)relevance is identified with (in)dependence). Once the network has been built, it constitutes an efficient device to perform probabilistic inferences. However, the problem of building such a network remains. The usual way to obtain the structure and conditional probabilities necessary for characterising the network is from the experts, however it would be very interesting to know if they could be partially replaced or complemented by learning the net directly from empirical observations.

Our work here will be focused on learning structure (the topology of the network) rather than parameters (conditional probabilities). We restrict our attention to a particular kind of bayesian networks: polytrees or singly connected networks, where no more than one path exists between any two nodes. These networks do not require too much storage and lengthy procedures to produce predictions or explanations and they allow a local extremely efficient

---

This work has been supported by the Commission of the European Communities under ESPRIT Project no 5170: Comparative Testing of Statistical and Logical Learning, Statlog

propagation procedure (see [3]).

The two more important steps when building up the structure of Bayesian polytrees from raw data are, first, the estimation of the polytree's skeleton (the graph stripped of the arrows) and then the orientation of such skeleton. This work can be divided in two parts. In the first part we propose several dependency measures that can be used, instead of the Kullback-Leibler information measure, in order to build up the skeleton of a polytree. In the second part we examine several methods to deal with the inconsistencies, in terms of the (in)dependencies, that could appear when directing the skeleton of the polytree. Using CASTLE, a software developed for the Esprit Project Statlog [6], we compare the methods to give direction to a polytree (see [1] for details about CASTLE).

2. Learning the Skeleton of a Polytree

In order to learn the skeleton of the polytree associated to a nondegenerate distribution P, Rebane and Pearl [5] proved that a Maximum Weight Spanning Tree (MWST) algorithm will recover the skeleton, where the weight of the branch connecting any two nodes is defined as the Kullback-Leibler information measure, $KL(X,Y)=\sum_{x,y} P(x,y)\log[P(x,y)/P(x)P(y)]$. The crucial part of the proof is that the function KL verifies the following property:

$$\min(KL(X,Y),KL(Y,Z)) \geq KL(X,Z) \qquad (1)$$

One problem that arises in real cases is that we do not have the exact distribution P but an estimation $\hat{P}$ obtained from the data. So, we do not have neither KL but $\hat{KL}$. Depending on the sample size this estimation could be more or less accurate. It is then interesting to consider other ways to weight the branches of the MWST. These functions Dep (the substitutes of KL) should measure the dependence degree between any two nodes in an increasing way (with Dep(X,Y)=0 for independent variables and Dep(X,Y) maximum for functionally dependent ones). So far we have implemented in CASTLE the following Dep functions:

- -Kullback-Leibler: $KL(X,Y)$
- -L1 unweighted: $L1U(X,Y) = \sum_{x,y} |P(x,y)-P(x)P(y)|$
- -L1 weighted: $L1W(X,Y) = \sum_{x,y} P(x,y)|P(x,y)-P(x)P(y)|$
- -L2 unweighted: $L2U(X,Y) = \sum_{x,y} [P(x,y)-P(x)P(y)]^2$
- -L2 weighted: $L2W(X,Y) = \sum_{x,y} P(x,y)[P(x,y)-P(x)P(y)]^2$
- -L∞: $LINF(X,Y) = \max_{x,y} |P(x,y)-P(x)P(y)|$
- -Rajski [4]: $R(X,Y) = -\dfrac{\sum_{x,y} P(x,y)\log[P(x,y)/P(x)P(y)]}{\sum_{x,y} P(x,y)\log[P(x,y)]}$

In practical terms, the small-sample behaviour of the estimator and the degree of difficulty of the associated computations are probably the most important considerations in the choice of the Dep function. All the functions but Rajski are faster to compute than the measure of Kullback-Leibler. With respect to how robust our Dep functions are, we are simulating experiments with different sample sizes for simple cases. From a theoretical point of view, we have found that only L1 unweighted and Rajski together with KL verify the property (1) in all the cases. We are also looking for more functions with this property. For example, the Onicescu Informational Energy [2] is a promising candidate.

3. Directing the Skeleton of a Polytree

To recover the directions of the polytree's branches we will take into account the following facts: given the branches X—Y—Z:

(1) For the pattern $X \longrightarrow Y \longleftarrow Z$ we have:

-Dep(X,Z)=0 (X and Z are marginally independent)

-Dep(X,Z|Y)>0 (X and Z are conditionally dependent given Y).

(2) For the patterns $X \longrightarrow Y \longrightarrow Z$, $X \longleftarrow Y \longleftarrow Z$ or $X \longleftarrow Y \longrightarrow Z$, we have:

-Dep(X,Z)>0 (X and Z are marginally dependent)

-Dep(X,Z|Y)=0 (X and Z are conditionally independent given Y).

Remark: The conditional Dep function Dep(X,Z|Y) is defined as the mean with respect to P(y) of the functions Dep(X,Z|Y=y), which are analogous to Dep(X,Z), but each marginal distribution being replaced by the corresponding conditional distribution given Y equal to y.

Using these facts we can recover the head-to-head patterns, $X \longrightarrow Y \longleftarrow Z$. The rest of the branches can be assigned any direction as long as we do not produce more head-to-head patterns. The problem is again that we do not have an exact distribution but a sample from it. So, conditions like $\widehat{Dep}(X,Z)=0$ or $\widehat{Dep}(X,Z|Y)=0$ are hardly satisfied when X and Z are independent or when X and Z are independent given Y, respectively. It is even possible to have inconsistencies: some of the dependencies and/or independencies estimated from the data could be in contradiction with each other and then some of them should not be taken into account in order to obtain a polytree structure.

To detect the head-to-head patterns, we have implemented in CASTLE three different tests: $\widehat{Dep}(X,Z)<c$, $\widehat{Dep}(X,Z)<\widehat{Dep}(X,Z|Y)$ and a standard χ^2 test of independence, where c is a threshold used to detect independencies. Using the Rebane and Pearl algorithm [5] with any of the previous tests, CASTLE will recover the directions of the branches. However, the problem with such algorithm when applied to data is that there is no criterion to decide the (in)dependencies that should be preserved in the case of a conflict. In other words, the selection is blind, it depends on the order in which the nodes are examined.

CASTLE has a second method to orientate the skeleton based on the same previous criteria to distinguish head-to-head patterns, but providing some guidance to decide which (in)dependencies to preserve. The method is a search with priorities. The key idea is to take into account some measure of the strength of the (in)dependencies, in order to include the most important first.

The idea is simple, when we are using to detect the head-to-head patterns: (a) the marginal information criterion ($\hat{D}ep(X,Z) < c$) or (b) the conditional information criterion ($\hat{D}ep(X,Z) < \hat{D}ep(X,Z \mid Y)$), then:

-If (a) $\hat{D}ep(X,Z) < \hat{D}ep(U,W) < c$ or (b) $0 < \hat{D}ep(U,W \mid V) - \hat{D}ep(U,W) < \hat{D}ep(X,Z \mid Y) - \hat{D}ep(X,Z)$, in both cases X and Z, U and W are independent, then the independence between X and Z has more priority and should be preserved first.

-If (a) $c < \hat{D}ep(X,Z) < \hat{D}ep(U,W)$ or (b) $0 < \hat{D}ep(X,Z) - \hat{D}ep(X,Z \mid Y) < \hat{D}ep(U,W) - \hat{D}ep(U,W \mid V)$, in both cases X and Z, U and W are dependent, then the dependence between U and W has more priority and should be preserved first.

Using CASTLE, the user can decide whether he/she prefers to preserve dependencies or independencies first, using always the above rules between dependencies or independencies. In the case of a conflict, obviously we will loose the weaker (in)dependencies compatible with the selected criterion.

The simulation experiments we have carried out show an improvement (with a very small increase in the complexity) in the fitness of the recovered polytree when using the searching with priorities strategy instead of the blind method. Perhaps using other, more global control structures would still help to improve the results.

References

[1] Acid, S., Campos, L.M. de, González, A., Molina, R. and Pérez de la Blanca, N. (1991) CASTLE: Causal Structures from Inductive Learning. Release 2.0. *Technical Report no* 91-4-3. DECSAI. Universidad de Granada.

[2] Onicescu, O. (1966) Energie Informationnelle. *C.R.S.A. Paris, ser. A.*, 263, 841-842.

[3] Pearl, J. (1988) *Probabilistic Reasoning in Intelligent Systems: Networks of Plausible Inference*. Morgan and Kaufmann.

[4] Rajski, C. (1964) On the Normed Information Rate of Discrete Random Variables. Trasl. of the *Third Praga Congress*, 583-585.

[5] Rebane, G. and Pearl, J. (1987) The recovery of causal polytrees from statistical data. *Proc. 3rd Workshop on Uncertainty in AI*, Seattle, 222-228.

[6] Statlog (1990). Technical Annex of ESPRIT Project: *Comparative Testing of Statistical and Logical Learning, Statlog*.

Estimation of Error-rates in Classification Rules

R.J. Henery, R. King, A. Sutherland, J.M.O. Mitchell (University of Strathclyde) and P. Brazdil (University of Porto).

1. Introduction

In conjunction with several other partners, both industrial and academic, the authors are engaged in an Esprit Project (StatLog) that has as one of its principal aims the comparison of Statistical and Machine Learning Algorithms on large-scale and complex classification problems. One of the main difficulties in classification problems is to estimate the true mis-classification error rate, and there are several methods available, although it is widely known that error rates tend to be biased if they are estimated from the same set of data used to construct the rules. Stone (1974) describes cross-validation methods for giving unbiased estimates of the error rate. Watkins (1987) gives a description of cross-validation in the context of testing decision-tree classification algorithms, and Weiss and Kapouleas (1989) discuss the methodology for evaluating different classification methods.

The main objection to cross-validation is that the error estimates it produces are too random, so that the confidence intervals for the true error-rate are too wide. The bootstrap procedure (Efron 1983) produces much narrower confidence limits, but the penalty paid is that the estimated error-rates are biased (usually downwards), i.e. the estimated error-rates are again optimistic. The trade-off between bias and random error means that, as a general rule, the bootstrap method is preferred when the sample size is small, and cross-validation when the sample size is large. In conducting comparative trials, the amount of bias is not so important so long as the bias is the same for all methods. *Since the bootstrap represents the best way to reduce variability, the most effective way to conduct comparisons in small datasets is to use the bootstrap.* However, there are several variants of the bootstrap.

This paper describes a small-scale experiment to compare the performance of bootstrap and cross-validation. Some empirical results are presented to show that the simplest form of the botstrap is most suited for comparative studies between methods as it gives the smallest random error.

2. Cross-Validation

Stone (1974) describes cross-validation methods for giving unbiased estimates of the error rate. Watkins (1986) gives a description of cross-validation in the context of testing decision-tree classification algorithms, and uses cross-validation as a means of selecting better decision trees.

In its most elementary form, cross-validation consists of dividing the data into two subsamples: one subsample is used to construct the classification rule which is then applied to the second subsample. More generally, n-fold cross-validation is used: the original data are partitioned into n subsamples. Each sub-sample is predicted via the classification rule constructed from the remaining (n-1) subsamples, and the estimated error rate is the average error rate from these n subsamples. Cross-validation estimates are approximately unbiased.

3. Bootstrap

The basic idea of the bootstrap is to re-use the original data (of size n) to give new datasets also of size n by re-sampling with replacement. See Efron (1983) for the definitive introduction to the subject and Crawford (1989) for an application to CART.

In the context of classification, the bootstrap is used to estimate the error rate in small samples (of size n say) by creating a large number (B) of bootstrap replicates. That is, a random sample of size n is taken from the original sample by sampling *with replacement.* Sampling with replacement means, for example, that some data points will be omitted (on average about $1/e = 37\%$ of data will not appear in the bootstrap sample). Also, some data points will appear more than once in the bootstrap sample.

3.1. Simple bootstrap

Each bootstrap sample is used to construct a classification rule which is then used to predict the classes of the original data. This gives one estimate of the error rate for each bootstrap sample: the average error rate over all bootstrap samples is then the estimated error rate for the classification rule.

3.2. e0 estimate

The same classification rule derived for each bootstrap is used to make predictions, but this time predicitons are made only for the examples which were not selected in the bootstrap, so that the test set is distinct from the training set. The number of predictions will vary slightly here but will usually consist of around 37% of the original data.

4. Method.

The example follows the recognition of digits example of Breiman et al. (p47), except that our simulation concerns only the two digits '0' and '1'. Thus the dataset comprises two classes and there are seven binary attributes with random noise added. The probability P that any attribute value is in error is controlled by the experimenter. All attribute values independently have the same error probability P in one run of the experiment. By construction, the exact probability of misclassification may be calculated via the binomial probability law.

Sets of 20 noisy examples of each class are analysed. The classification procedure to be tested is the linear discriminant algorithm [Mardia et al., pp318ff] as implemented in the Minitab statistical package. Firstly, the 'apparent' error rate is noted. The 'leave-one-out' cross validation procedure is also carried out.

Then two forms of bootstrapping are carried out. A random sample of size 40 is selected with replacement from the examples. The 'simple bootstrap' is obtained by finding the discriminant rule for each bootstrap sample and using this rule to predict the class of the original 40 observations. The e0 bootstrap uses the same classification rule on the omitted observations only. The whole bootstrapping cycle is repeated 20 times, and the mean error rates for both types of bootstrap estimate are stored.

The whole exercise is repeated usually 25 times in all. The parameters used for the generation of noise gave the following error probabilities for each attribute value: 0.40, 0.35, 0.28, 0.23, 0.20.

5. Results.

Table

P is the probability of error in each attribute value (noise level).
The figure which follows P is the mean of the calculated exact error rates.

	Mean	S.D.	Bias	Rms error
P=0.40	.245			
e0	.436	.078	.191	.208
bootstrap	.308	.059	.063	.095
apparent	.267	.050	.021	.088
cross validation	.428	.096	.182	.206
P=0.35	.200			
e0	.368	.075	.168	.191
bootstrap	.248	.058	.047	.090
apparent	.212	.074	.012	.093
cross validation	.331	.089	.131	.167
P=0.28	.180			
e0	.259	.079	.079	.113

bootstrap	.164	.053	-.015	.059
apparent	.127	.049	-.053	.073
cross validation	.212	.072	.033	.080
P=0.23	.174			
e0	.194	.072	.020	.083
bootstrap	.118	.048	-.056	.079
apparent	.085	.049	-.088	.102
cross validation	.169	.070	-.005	.075
P=0.20	.181			
e0	.153	.058	-.028	.080
bootstrap	.085	.037	-.096	.109
apparent	.052	.048	-.129	.143
cross validation	.131	.049	-.050	.081

In all cases the correlation between the e0 error rates, the bootstrap error rates and the crossvalidation error rates are over 0.84, the highest usually being for the correlation between the two bootstrap error rates. The correlations of the other error rates with the apparent error rate are in the range 0.64-0.93.

For the higher noise levels (P > 0.25), the bootstrap and apparent mean error rates are close to the exact ones, while the e0 and crossvalidation mean error rates are higher. The bias, the standard deviation and the root mean square discrepancy from the exact error rate are all smaller for the bootstrap and the apparent error rates than for e0 and crossvalidation.

For less noisy data these effects change. The mean apparent and bootstrap error rates are lower than the exact figure, while the e0 and crossvalidation mean error rates are closer to it. The standard deviations for the apparent and bootstrap error rates are lower. The bias is least for e0 and crossvalidation, and the root mean square discrepancy from the exact error rate becomes less for these also.

6. Conclusions.

These corroborate results reported by Weiss (1991), viz. that no one method is best in all situations. In the situation studied here, for high noise levels e0 and crossvalidation have a larger bias and variance than the bootstrap and apparent errors. For lower noise levels e0 and crossvalidation have less bias and, despite their slightly larger variance, also a lower root mean square error. No simple rule is available for choosing the best error estimate.

For the purposes of comparative studies however, it is clear that the simple bootstrap method usually has the smallest standard deviation and that this is the estimate to use for preference.

7. References

Breiman, L., Friedman, J.H., Olshen, R. & Stone, C. (1984) *Classification and Regression Trees* Wadsworth and Brooks, Monterey, Ca.

Crawford, S.L. (1989). Extensions to the CART algorithm. *Int. J. Man-Machine Studies* **31**, 197-217.

Efron, B. (1983). Estimating the error rate of a prediction rule: improvements on cross-validation. *J. Amer. Stat. Ass.* **78**, 316-331.

Mardia, K.V., Kent, J.Y. and Bibby, J.M. (1979). *Multivariate Analysis*, Academic Press.

Stone, M. (1974). Cross-validatory Choice and Assessment of Statistical Predictions. *J. Roy. Statist. Soc. B* **36**, 111-133: discussion 133-147.

Watkins, C.J.C.H. (1987). Combining Cross-Validation and Search. *Progress in Machine Learning* (eds. I.Bratko and N.Lavrac) Sigma Books, Wimslow, 79-87.

Weiss, S.M. (1991). Small sample error rate extimation for k-NN classifiers. *IEEE Trans. Patt. Anal.and Mach. Intell.*, **13**, pp 285-289.

Weiss S.M. and Kapouleas I. (1989) An empirical comparison of pattern recognition, neural nets, and machine learning classification methods. In: *International Joint Conference on Artificial Intelligence*, Detroit, Morgan Kaufmann, 781-787.

August, 1991

A LOGICAL FORMALISM FOR KNOWLEDGE-BASED CONTROL

Antoni Ligęza
Institute of Automatics, Academy of Mining and Metallurgy
al. Mickiewicza 30, 30-059 Kraków, Poland

Knowledge Engineering methods can be applied for analysis and control of various natural and technological systems having no precise mathematical models in the classical meaning, but still manageable by human experts having domain experience. In this paper we deal with finite, discrete, dynamic, logical systems. A logic-based formalism for modelling such systems is presented in brief. The approach is aimed at describing the behaviour of dynamic systems with use of state formulae and state transformation rules. A set of such rules, together with inference control mechanism, can model a finite, discrete system of arbitrary complexity. Some basic characteristics of such systems are defined, and a formal approach to verifying them is outlined. A more detailed presentation of the proposed formalism and most important proofs of the presented theorems can be found in [3].

Knowledge Representation

The proposed language for knowledge representation is based on *first-order predicate calculus* (see [1,2]). Definitions of new concepts are presented in brief.

Definition 1 *Let $q_1, q_2, \ldots, q_k$ be literals (atomic formulae or their negations). A formula $\phi = q_1 \wedge q_2 \wedge \ldots \wedge q_k$ is called a* simple formula *(a simple formula is a finite conjunction of literals).*

Definition 2 *Let $\phi_1, \phi_2, \ldots, \phi_m$ be some simple formulae. A* normal formula *is any formula of the form*

$$\Phi = \phi_1 \vee \phi_2 \vee \phi_3 \vee \ldots \vee \phi_m. \tag{1}$$

Any formula containing no quantifiers can be transformed into equivalent normal formula (disjunctive normal form).

Substitutions [1,2] are denoted with lower case Greek letters. If Υ is a formula and σ is a substitution, then $\Upsilon\sigma$ is the formula resulting from replacing the variables of Υ with the appropriate terms of σ; $\Upsilon\sigma$ is called a *factor* of Υ.

Generalization

Let Υ and Γ be some two logical formulae. Any of them can be regarded as a description of a possible dynamic world in some physical state (states). To any formula one can assign the set of states for which the formula is true. We say that a *more general formula* describes more states than a *less general one*. Thus Γ is more general than Υ if and only if any state described by Υ belongs to the set of states described by Γ.

Definition 3 . *Let Γ and Υ be two formulae. Formula Γ is said to be* more general *than formula Υ (Γ generalizes Υ, Γ is less restrictive than Υ, or Γ matches Υ) if and only if, for any interpretation I, if Υ is satisfiable under I, then also Γ is satisfiable under I; we shall write shortly $\Gamma \geq \Upsilon$.*

In order to introduce a method of checking whether generalization holds a way of reasoning within the proposed formalism is introduced. By "combining" some two simple formulae of a normal formula another simple formula can be generated. Let Ψ be a normal formula,

$$\Psi = \psi_1 \vee \psi_2 \vee \psi_3 \vee \ldots \vee \psi_n, \tag{2}$$

such that $\psi_1 = \psi_1' \wedge q_1$ and $\psi_2 = \psi_2' \wedge \neg q_2$. If atoms q_1 and q_2 are unifiable, then it is possible to build a new simple formula ψ' by "combining" together ψ_1 and ψ_2 in an analogous (dual) way to the resolution method (for resolution see [1,2]). Since, roughly speaking, the new formula is obtained in a backward manner for a formula dual to the one in resolution method, the result will be called a ***backward dual resolvent*** or ***bd-resolvent***, for short. The formal definition is given below.

Definition 4 *Let Ψ be a normal formula of the form (2), where $n \geq 2$, $\psi_1 = \psi_1' \wedge q_1$ and $\psi_2 = \psi_2' \wedge \neg q_2$ and let there exists a unifying substitution σ for atoms q_1 and q_2. Then, a formula ψ'*

$$\psi' = \psi_1'\sigma \wedge \psi_2'\sigma \tag{3}$$

will be called a backward dual resolvent *(bd-resolvent) of ψ_1 and ψ_2 (within Ψ).*

The defined as above bd-resolvent can be viewed as a formula corresponding to binary resolvent in resolution theorem proving. A bd-resolvent is a formula less or equally general to the initial alternative formula consisting of the two initial simple formulae; thus, assuming that all the variables appearing in the normal formula are existentially quantified (dually to resolution method) the initial formula is a logical consequence of its bd-resolvent. This observation gives rise to a simple method of theorem proving. Let there be given a formula Ψ to be proved. If, starting from Ψ, we are able to generate a sequence of simple formulae, such that any formula in the sequence is a bd-resolvent of the former generated formulae (or the ones belonging to Ψ), then, if the sequence eventually ends up with an empty formula (always true), the initial formula Ψ is proved. The proof is found in a backward manner, *i.e.* with regard to the sequence a former generated formula is the logical consequence of a later generated one. The above considerations are justified by the following theorem.

Theorem 1 Soundness of bd-resolution *Let Ψ be a formula of the form (2) and let ψ' be the bd-resolvent defined as above (3). Then $\psi_1 \vee \psi_2 \geq \psi'$ and $\Psi \geq \psi'$.*

Further, an idea of *derivation* with use of bd-resolution is defined.

Definition 5 *A* bd-derivation *(or derivation, for short) of a simple formula ψ' from a normal formula Ψ is a sequence of simple formulae $\psi^1, \psi^2, \ldots, \psi^k$, such that for any $i \in \{1, 2, \ldots, k\}$ ψ^i is a bd-resolvent or a factor of simple formulae either belonging to Ψ or generated earlier, and, $\psi' = \psi_k$. Formula ψ' is said to be* derived *from Ψ.*

A simple formula derived from any normal formula is less or equally general to the initial formula. Thus, if all the variables in both of the formulae are existentially quantified, the initial formula (Ψ) is a logical consequence of the derived formula (ψ').

Theorem 2 *Let Ψ and Φ be some two normal formulae defined by (2) and (1). Then $\Psi \geq \Phi$ if and only if, for any simple formula $\phi \in \Phi$ there exists a derivation of a simple formula ψ' from Ψ such that $\psi' \geq \phi$.*

For simple formulae there exists a direct way of checking whether a formula generalizes another formula.

Theorem 3 *Let ψ and ϕ be two simple formulae, $\psi = p_1 \wedge p_2 \wedge \ldots \wedge p_n$ and $\phi = q_1 \wedge q_2 \wedge \ldots \wedge q_m$, where p_i and q_j are literals, $i = 1, 2, \ldots, n$, $j = 1, 2, \ldots, m$. Then ψ is more general than ϕ if and only if there exists a substitution σ, such that $\psi\sigma \subseteq \phi$, or if ϕ contains a complementary pair of literals (q and $\neg q$).*

We shall also state the following auxiliary theorem.

Theorem 4 Separability of generalization *Let Ψ and Φ be two normal formulae defined by (2) and (1). Then $\Psi \geq \Phi$ if and only if $\Psi \geq \phi_i$ for any $i \in \{1, 2, \ldots, m\}$.*

Logical Representation of Physical States

Consider a finite, discrete system, which can be described with logical (relational) expressions. Let **P** be a finite set predicates (relations) which can be used to characterize elements of the system behaviour and let I be some assumed interpretation. Let **S** denote a finite state-space of the system.

Definition 6 *A state formula ϕ_s of a state s is the only simple formula containing no variables and satisfiable under the assumed interpretation I, such that for any predicate symbol $p \in$ **P** of arity n and any ground terms $t_1, t_2, \ldots, t_n$, $p(t_1, t_2, \ldots, t_n) \in \phi_s$ if $\models_I p(t_1, t_2, \ldots, t_n)$ and $\neg p(t_1, t_2, \ldots, t_n) \in \phi_s$ if $\not\models_I p(t_1, t_2, \ldots, t_n)$.*

Clearly, any state $s \in$ **S** has one and only one corresponding state formula. For intuition, a state formula corresponding to some state s is a conjunction of all the facts which are true in this state and are possible to be expressed in the assumed language.

Definition 7 *Let* $S = \{s_1, s_2, \ldots, s_n\}$ *be a subset of the state space* **S**. *Further, let any state* s_i *be described with its state formula* ϕ_i, $i = 1, 2, \ldots, n$. *A* situation formula *of situation* S *is any normal formula* Ψ_S*, such that* $\Psi_S \geq \phi_i$ *for* $i = 1, 2, \ldots, n$*, and* Ψ_S *does not generalize any state formula* ϕ *of any state* s *for any* $s \notin S$.

A simple but important theorem concerns inclusion of situations (situations are subsets of state space).

Theorem 5 *Let* Ψ_1 *and* Ψ_2 *be situation formulae for situations* S_1 *and* S_2 *respectively. Then* $S_1 \subseteq S_2$ *if and only if* $\Psi_2 \geq \Psi_1$.

Theorem 6 *Let* Ψ_1 *and* Ψ_2 *be situation formulae for situations* S_1 *and* S_2 *respectively. Then* $\Psi_1 \wedge \Psi_2$ *is the situation formula for* $S_1 \cap S_2$ *and* $\Psi_1 \vee \Psi_2$ *is the situation formula for* $S_1 \cup S_2$.

Knowledge Representation and Inference for Control Systems

A special transformation rule scheme for dealing with dynamic knowledge is proposed. The idea of the scheme is based on the STRIPS representation of operators (see [4,2]). The basic format for any reasoning rule used in the system is as follows:

```
if              precondition(s)
then
        do        action(s)
        retract   delete_result(s)
        assert    add_result(s)
next            rule(s)
```

Let Φ denote the formula of the current knowledge base (i.e. the state or situation formula). Let also Ψ stay for *precondition(s)*, r - for *add_result(s)*, d - for *delete_result(s)*, a - for *action(s)* and finally n - for next *rule(s)* to be executed. The basic transformation process with the use of reasoning rules proceeds as follows:

1. Check if $\Psi \geq \Phi$. If so, go to 2; otherwise, the rule cannot be applied.
2. Let σ be the substitution defining parameters. Execute the actions specified by $a\sigma$.
3. Retract (delete) the facts specified by $d\sigma$.
4. Assert (add) the facts specified by $r\sigma$.
5. As a next rule(s) try to apply the one(s) specified by n.

The above algorithm defines the basic one-step state transformation process. Some further details concerning the nature of facts used to provide some control of this process are discussed in [4].

Theoretical Properties of Knowledge-Based Systems

In this section we shall briefly define the basic theoretical properties of knowledge-based control systems.

Definition 8 (Determinism) *A knowledge-based system system is (weakly) deterministic if and only if for any state* s *described with formula* S *there exists at most one state transformation rule applicable to* s.

Definition 9 (Completeness) *A knowledge-based system is complete if and only if for any state* s *described with formula* S *there exists at least one transformation rule applicable to* S.

Definition 10 (Correctness (potential)) *A knowledge-based system is potentially correct if and only if it is complete and deterministic.*

The defined above correctness is, of course, potential – the system is able to react in any physical situation and there is exactly one rule applicable in any situation. However, this does not guarantee that the only rule is really correct, i.e. that the action performed will achieve the required results.

Assume that there are given k transformation rules, each of them having its precondition formula Ψ_i, $i = 1, 2, \ldots, k$ (normal formulae). The outlines of the proposed algorithms for verifying determinism and completeness are as follows.

Algorithm for checking determinism

1. For any two formulae Ψ_i and Ψ_j, $i \neq j$, $i, j \in \{1, 2, \ldots, k\}$ build a formula $\Psi_{i,j} = \Psi_i \wedge \Psi_j$ describing the intersection of the appropriate situations.

2. Transform any formula $\Psi_{i,j}$ in an equivalent normal formula.

3. From any formula $\Psi_{i,j}$ delete any unsatisfiable simple formula (a simple formula is unsatisfiable if and only if it contains a pair of complementary literals); delete any formula $\Psi_{i,j}$ containing no simple formula.

4. If the set of remaining formulae is empty, then the initial set of transformation rules (the control systems) is deterministic; in other case the obtained formulae $\Psi_{i,j}$ indicate situations in which the i-th and the j-th transformation rules can be applied.

If, after application of the above algorithm there remains some formulae $\Psi_{i,j}$, then further analysis of them may be necessary. In particular systems one can find a number of rules defining impossible situations (consisting of potentially definable but physically unfeasible states). Thus further elimination of remaining formulae $\Psi_{i,j}$ is possible.

Algorithm for checking completeness

1. Build a formula describing the sum of all the appropriate situations (the normal formula of the form $\Psi_1 \vee \Psi_2 \vee \ldots \vee \Psi_k$).

2. Perform any possible derivation of bd-resolvent, *e.g.* by applying the level-saturation method [1], or any other strategy.

3. If empty formula is eventually generated, then the system is complete. The constructed formula describes any possible state.

4. In other case (due to the completeness of the bd-resolution) the system is incomplete. The derived formulae describe the situations which are "served".

Conclusions

The presented formalism provides theoretical bases for improving the design and implementation of knowledge based control systems by providing the possibility of checking the system for determinism and completeness. For practical applications the proposed algorithms must be equipped with domain-specific knowledge, hierarchization mechanisms and possibly – heuristics.

References

1. Chang,C.L. and R.C.T.Lee: *Symbolic Logic and Mechanical Theorem Proving.* Academic Press, New York and London, 1973.

2. Genesereth,M.R. and N.J.Nilsson: *Logical Foundations of Artificial Intelligence.* M.Kaufmann Publ. Inc., Los Altos, California, 1987.

3. Ligęza, A.: A Logical Formalism for Knowledge-Based Control Systems. Technical Report of the Institute of Automatics AGH, No. 8, Cracow, 1991.

4. Tzafestas,S. and A.Ligęza: A framework for knowledge based control. *Journal of Intelligent and Robotic Systems*, Vol.1, No.4, 407-425, 1989.

APPLICATION OF ARTIFICIAL INTELLIGENCE METHODS TO PREDICTION OF FINANCIAL TIME SERIES

A. Merkel
Universitaet Heidelberg
Institut fuer Statistik
Grabengasse 14
6900 Heidelberg

G. Nakhaeizadeh
Daimler-Benz AG
Forschung und Technik
Eberhard-Finckh-Str.11
7900 Ulm

1. Introduction

Beside the methods based on classical statistic and econometrics, some artificial intelligence (AI) based approaches can be applied to predict the future development of financial time series data. In this paper some AI based algorithms which come from the area of Machine Learning (ML) and Neural Nets (NN) will be introduced and their practicability to predict the development of financial time series will be demonstrated. To make prediction with ML algorithms the regression tree algorithm is used. This algorithm can be seen as a modified form of Quinlan's ID3 algorithms (see [2]). It is described in detail by Breiman et al in their book about the CART (classification and regression trees) algorithm (see [1]). Using NN for prediction, a backpropagation algorithm is used (see [4]).

In this paper the algorithms shall not be described. One shall only get an idea of how prediction with these algorithms works. The ability of these algorithms to solving the prediction problems will be shown by prediction the interest rate in Germany.

2. The algorithms

The regression tree and backpropagation algorithms which can be used to predict the development of financial time series belong to a class of procedures called "Learning from examples" which is a subarea of ML. In this section we describe the main idea of these algorithms.

First a classification problem will be described to demonstrate how the ML algorithm works. While using a ML-algorithm, the program seeks to find rules which classify the examples of a given dataset used to induce the rules correctly. Quinlan describes in [2] a decision problem. It shall be decided whether one shall do something special today or not. To make up once mind, one has some information about the day, e.g. information about the humidy, the temperatur, the wind and the weather. The input to the algorithm is a set of examples. Each example is representing a special day which is described by the information about this day and the chosen decision on this day. The algorithm induces from these examples a rule set, which is able to determine the correct decision by giving only the information about this day as input.

This rule set can be used now to classify new examples. One rule for the weather problem would be R1:

R1: if weather = sunny & humidy = high then class = negativ

Now a short discription of the induction of such a rule set shall be given. Beginning with the complete dataset the algorithm starts splitting up this set in subsets by formulating conditions for the examples. Formulating of conditions is done using the attribute values, that means in a new subset all example do have the same value (e.g. weather = suny) for a selected attribute. This procedure stops if all examples in the subsets have the same class. If there are examples in a subset with different classes, a new condition is added for this subset. A condition is selected by an entropy measure, which is described by Quinlan in [2].

Neural Nets simulate the functionality of the human brain to solve different problems. A NN consists of some connected input, hidden and output processing units. The Backpropagation algorithm which is used in this study to predict the interest rate belongs to the well-known NN-algorithms. In this procedure, the internal weights between the different layers of the net are as long modified until the system output reaches the same value as the desired output. The modification is based on a pre-determined learning rule.

3. Prediction of the interest rate using AI algorithms

In this section we demonstrate the ability of AI algorithms to predict the financial time series. Using the regression tree and backpropagation algorithms described in the last section, the yearly interest rate for Germany for the period from 01/86 to 12/90 is predicted with the help of information about the interest rate in the past and some economic attributes like exchange rate of US Dollar/D-Mark, US bonds and the german price index.

One of the rule induced by the regression tree algorithm is R2.

R2: if price ≤ 0.75 & interest_21 ≤ 0.65 & interest_22 ≤ - 0.93 then interest_1 = 0.5

It can be seen that in contrast to the statistical algorithms, the output of the learning system is not a mathematical function but some if-then-rules. It is the same for NN. The obtained prediction system in NN is a trained net which is charactrized by some internal weights.

To get an idea of the goodness of the prediction the dataset is splited up in 7 different training and test samples. The training samples are used to induce the rule set and the corresponding test sample which has different examples then the training sample is used to test the goodness of the predictor. This is done for every test sample 3 steps in the future. In the test sample, the RMSE (Root Mean Square Error) is calculated for every step and it is examined if the prediction has the same direction like the real value (does the prediction increase if the real value increases? etc.).

step	ML	NN	Regression
1	0.2737	0.2515	0.1996
2	0.2856	0.1888	0.3137
3	0.4042	0.4052	0.3500

Table 1: Mean Root Square Errors for the interest rate predictor

Table 1 shows the average RMSE of the predicted interest rates using the ML and NN algorithms and the linear regression over the different samples.

It can be seen that all predictors have good accuracy. The best 1 and 3 step predictor is given by the linear regression and the best 2 step predictor is given by NN.

step	ML	NN	Regression
1	5	4	4
2	5	6	4
3	4	4	3

Table 2: Number of correct direction predictions

Now the ability of the predictors to get the right direction of the change of the interest rate shall be examined. Table 2 shows the results of this experiment. It can be seen, that ML and NN deliver better results for the prediction of the direction than the linear regression.

This study shows that the AI algorithms deliver competitiv results to the statistical methods. As additional advantage, the ML algorithm delivers a rule set which can be read and discussed with experts. One can use this rule set for the implementation of an expert system that can be extended step by step. Experiments done by Merkel with car registration number (see [3]) and Graf with stock prices (see [4]) have also shown that the AI based methods can be regarded as a compotent alternative to the statistical procedures.

References

[1] L.Breiman, J.H. Friedman, R.A.Olshen, and C.J. Stone (1984). *Classification and Regression Trees.* The Wadsworth & Brooks/Cole Statistics/Probability Series.

[2] J.R Quinlan (1986). Induction of decision trees. *Machine Learning*, pages 81–106.

[3] A. Merkel(1991). Einsatz des Maschinellen Lernens zur Prognose von Zeitreihendaten *Diplomarbeit*, Universitaet Karlsruhe.

[4] J. Graf (1990). Klassische statistische Methoden zur kurzfristigen Prognose des Aktienmarkts und deren Vergleich mit den Methoden der kuenstlichen Intelligenz *Diplomarbeit*, Universitaet Karlsruhe.

Application of Machine Learning to Solving Industrial Problems

G. Nakhaeizadeh
Daimler-Benz AG, Forschung und Technik
Eberhard-Finckhstr. 11
7900 Ulm, Germany
E-Mail: unido!fuzi!reza and reza@fuzi.uucp

1. Introduction

Although the research in the field of Machine Learning (ML) is nearly 50 years old, one can find its successful commercial and industrial applications, firstly, since early eighties. Such applications are based, mostly, on a subarea of ML called learning from examples. The basic research in this subarea is due to Hunt et al (1966), Michalski (1972) and Quinlan (1979). Further developments of these works can be found in Michalski et al (1978), Quinlan (1986) and Niblett and Clark (1987). A number of commercial and industrial applications of ML are discussed in Mowforth(1986) and Clark et al (1991). Regarding the volume of research done in the last years in ML, one can easily conclude that the number of successful applications of ML in commerce and industry is too limited. Some reasons for this limitation are discussed in the joint paper of Clark et al (1991) which can be summarized as follows:

- The ML-algorithms mainly handle synthetic data while the solution of real world problems usually requires handling of analytic large-scale datasets.
- The incorporation of domain-specific properties in the acquired knowledge has not been sufficiently considered yet in the ML research.
- To handle the applications of real-world, several methods should be combined together.
- Scientific and engineering domains tend to require more structured representation. Due to this reason, research in constructive induction and learning relation is necessary.
- Success of ML-applications depends on the skill of the "ML-expert" as on the ML-technique used.

The above points cover some of the shortcomings of ML-methods in handling the real world applications. The problem can be regarded, however, from another point of view. Generally, most of the real-world applications of ML deal with one of the following tasks:
- Classification
- Prediction
- Control

To perform these tasks, one can use a series of sophisticated statistical procedures. Besides the statistical methods, however, a lot of ML-algorithms can handle also, at least, the classification and prediction tasks appropriately. It means, in many circumstances the ML-algorithms are potentially interesting for the users of the statistical methods. But, why do these users pay no attention to ML-methods but to statistical procedures? One can mention here three general reasons:

- Most of the users of the statistical procedures are not familier at all with ML-Methods. ML-methodology is not very known as Statistics in the scientific community. In almost every scientific area at the universities, there are elementary and advance courses in Statistics but not in Machine Learning.
- There is no comprehensive study dealing with the performance of machine learning algorithms when they are compared with statistical procedures.
- Contrary to the statistical procedures, thers is no developed package, as a toolbox, involving a variety of ML-algorithms needed for different applications.

To overcome the last two difficulties, two ESPRIT-Projects are runing at present. The first project (StatLog) evaluates different stattistical and logical learning algorithms using the real-world applications. This project and some of its initial results will be discussed in the next sections. The second project (MLT) develops a Machine Learning Toolbox which provides the users a number of different ML-algorithms and helps selecting of appropriate learning methods. For more information about this project, see Morik (1991).

2. Esprit-Project StatLog

Since October 1990, different European research institutions from industry and universities work on the Esprit-Project StatLog funded by the European Community. StatLog will complete an evaluation of the performance of machine learning algorithms on large-scale commercial and industrial problems.

The learning algorithms to be evaluated in StatLog cover a variety of statistical, logical, neuronal and genetic algorithms. To statistical algorithms belong the algorithms of traditional Statistics like linear discriminance analysis and algorithms of modern Statistics like HELEN which uses the Bayes-Theorem without assuming independence of attributes. Among the traditional ML-algorithms, one can find C4.5 and CN2. Relational ML-algorithms are represented, for example, by ALPHAGOLEM and FOIL (see Henery et al (1991) for a complete description of algorithms).

The learning methods consists of supervised, unsupervised and reinforcement learning. The industrial and commercial applications deal mainly with classification tasks. There are, however, some applications in the field of prediction and also one application in the area of adaptive control. The objectives of StatLog are to:

1. provide critical performance measurments and criteria for the measurment of available learning algorithms which improve confidence in their full exploitation.
2. indicate the nature and scope of the next developments which particular algorithms will require in order to meet commercial performance expectations.

3. indicate the most promising avenues of development for the more commercially immature approaches.

Selected learning algorithms will be evaluated using a number of criteria which can be devided into two main groups: objective and subjective criteria (see Henery et al (1991) for more detail). To the objective criteria belong measurments of :
- Success rate
- Training time
- Size of learned structure
- Test time
- Memory requirements in training

The subjective criteria involve the parameters like comprehensibility and ease of use.

In StatLog, there are about twenty datasets which should be analysed using different learning algorithms. Almost, every considered dataset demonstrates a complex application of commercial or industrial importance. Most of the datasets are larege-scale.

3. Selected applications

In the followings, some of the industrial applications introduced to StatLog by Daimler-Benz should be presented in summary. For more information about the other industrial and commercial applications which are of interest of the other StatLog's partners see Nakhaeizadeh and Mellis (1991) or Henery et al (1991).

In many departments of Daimler-Benz like economic survey departement, department for strategic planing, marketing department etc., different management decision models are used. A very important component of such decision models is the long and short term forecasting of different time series.

Especially, the prediction of the development of the registered cars and trucks are of interest. The aim of the prediction is to develop a system that predicts automatically the number of registered cars and trucks. To the attributes used belong different economic indicators like gross social product, private and public consume, services, investment assets, prices etc.

At present, the department of marketing research applies the classical statistical methods based on the concept of Moving-Average and Box-Jenkins approach to predict the development of registered cars and trucks in different countries. The regression analysis approach has been used as well. The deparment of marketing research is interested, however, in application of symbolic ML and Neural Networks.

The first experiments within this application are performed using the learning algorithm NEWID which can handle continuous-valued classes. The initial results are promising. Especially in dealing with the number of registered trucks, NEWID delivered results which are almost as accurate as the results of regression analysis (see Merkel(1991) for more details). Other learning algorithms should be evaluated using this dataset.

The second application which is introduced to StatLog by Daimler-Benz is the recognition of hand written digits. This is a large-scale dataset contains about 20000 examples and 256 attributes. There are already some initial experiments with this datasets in Daimler-Benz using statistical and neural classifiers (see Kreßel (1991)). The performance of symbolic learning algorithms like ID3, NEWID etc is also of interest. Some tests have shown that NEWID can not handle this dataset at all. Experiments using other symbolic learning algorithms are running. In cooperation with its associated partner MBB, Daimler-Benz is also interested in application of neural nets and symbolic learning algorithms to adaptive control of dynamic systems.

References

Clark, P. Cestik, B. Sammut, C. and Stender J. (1991). Applications of Machine Learning: Notes from the Panel Members. In Kodratoff, Y. (Ed.), Machine Learning-EWSL-91, 457-462, Springer-Verlag.

Henery, R. J., King, R., Sutherland, A., Mitchell, J. and Brazdil, P. (1991). StatLog: Comparative Testing of Statistical and Machine Learning Algorithms. Mimeo, Uiversity of Strathclyde.

Hunt, E. B. ,Marin, J. and Stone, P. T. (1966). Experiments in Induction, Academic Press, New York.

Kreßel, U. (1991). The impact of the Learning-Set Size in Handwritten-Digit Recognition. Mimeo, Daimler-Benz, Forschung und Technik, Germany.

Merkel, A. (1991). Einsatz des maschinellen Lernens zur Prognose von Zeitreihen. Diplomarbeit, Universität Karlsruhe.

Michalski, R. S. (1972). A variable-valued logic system as applied to picture description and recognition. In: Nake, F. et al (Eds.), Graphic Languages, North Holland.

Michalski, R. S. and Larson, J. B. (1978): Selection of most representative training example and incremental generation of VL1 hypotheses: The underlying methodology and description of programs ESEL and AQ11, Report 867, University of Illinois.

Morik, K. (1991). Machine Learning Toolbox (MLT). KI:34-35.

Mowforth, P. (1986). Some Applications with Inductive Expert System Shells. Turing Institute, Glasgow.

Nakhaeizadeh, G. and Mellis, W. (1991). Esprit-Projekt StatLog. Evaluierung statistischer und logischer maschineller Lernalgorithmen anhand realer Anwendungen. KI:36-39.

Niblett, T. and Clark, P. (1987). Induction in noisy domains. In: Lavrac, N. and Bratko, I. (Eds.), Progress in Machine Learning. Sigma Press, Wilmslow.

Quinlan, J. R. (1979). Discovery rules from large collections of examples; a case Study. In: Michie, D. (Ed.). Expert Systems in the Micro Electronic Age. Edinburgh, University Press.

Quinlan, J. R. (1986). Induction of decision trees. Machine Learning, Vo 1, 81-106.

Bounded Perception and Learning How to Decide

Karl Schlag
MEDS Department
Northwestern University
2001 Sheridan Rd, Evanston IL 60208, USA

The profitability of a decision (or action) is often dependent on the occurrence of a phenomenon, say drill for oil only when it is indeed there or invest only when the market is favorable. So the decision maker aims to coordinate his decisions with the occurrence of this phenomenon. However whether or not the phenomenon occurs is usually not revealed until after the decision is made. Hence the outcome of the decision is very much dependent on how well the decision maker can forecast the occurrence of the phenomenon. For this he evaluates the present circumstances and compares this with what he knows about what determines the occurrence of the phenomenon. The process of learning the circumstances surrounding a phenomenon in preparation of such a (critical) decision is the subject of this paper.

A standard framework for learning when a phenomenon occurs is learning from examples. Its analysis is a frequent topic in the field of knowledge acquisition, found mostly in the machine learning and artificial intelligence literature. The emphasis is on programming computers to "learn". One widely adopted model is "non Bayesian" and was developed by Valiant [1984]. Other approaches using the standard Bayesian analysis are also quite frequent (see Buntine [1989] et al.).

The approaches in the knowledge acquisition literature analyze what can be inferred from the presented examples. The learning "individual" has no influence on which examples are presented to him and there are no bounds on how much information the "individual" can process at once. Slight modifications are made in Valiant's model who allows the learner to specify for each example whether he wants to observe a positive or a negative one.

The capability of human perception and processing is known to be limited (see Miller [1956]). These limits force the individual (for each example) to select what he wants to observe. This selection is strongly influenced by the individual's bias about what causes the phenomenon. And this in turn often causes aspects of a decision to be predetermined during the gathering process.

Therefore, to properly capture human decision making in this context, it is necessary to impose bounded perception restrictions and incorporate the gathering of information into the optimization. Bounded perception means that only a fixed number of attributes may be observed in each example.

For clarity and simplicity, it is assumed that for each example the individual may only observe one of its attributes. This makes some additional assumptions necessary: the individual will only be given examples in which the phenomenon occurs (called positive examples) to learn from. Additionally it will be assumed that positive examples can be characterized as a boolean conjunction (i.e. logically connected by "AND") of the circumstances surrounding the phenomenon. (E.g. the market is favorable if and only if the dollar is strong and the economy is growing.)

Now to a brief description of the progress of the decision making and how it will be modelled:

An individual wants to coordinate his decision with the occurrence of a phenomenon. He uses a fixed number of binary valued characteristics (attributes) of the state of the world to analyze the circumstances surrounding the occurrence of the phenomenon. These attributes are assumed to be sufficient for determining whether or not the phenomenon occurs.

The individual is given a fixed number of rounds to learn about these circumstances. In each round, nature presents the individual with a state of the world (independent of the previous rounds) in which the phenomenon occurs (i.e. a positive example). For each presented state the individual specifies the attribute he wants to observe and then he observes its value in that state.

After the learning phase is over, the opportunity for the individual to make his decision arrives. Nature presents him with a sequence of random states of the world. For each presented state, the individual observes the values of all of the attributes but not whether the phenomenon occurs. The individual may make his decision in at most one of these states.

It is assumed that the individual only makes his decision in a state in which the phenomenon occurs and prefers to do this as early as possible.

The model will be set in a Bayesian framework: the individual assesses priors to the occurrence of states of the world and to the possibility that a characteristic is necessary for the phenomenon to occur.

The main result of this paper is the following: assume that the occurrence of each attribute and its effect on the occurrence of the phenomenon are independent and independent of the other attributes. Then it is shown that an optimal algorithm (specification of attributes to be observed in the learning phase and when to decide in the decision phase) is essentially a local "hill-climbing" algorithm, i.e. it is constructed as if each round of the learning phase were the last round before the decision has to be made.

The decision is made in the first presented state in which the values of the attributes were all observed in the learning phase. If there is no such state, the decision will not be made.

These locally optimal algorithms are easy to implement and are independent of the length of the learning phase. Additionally after the learning phase has lasted a while, the specification essentially follows a simple pattern: specify each attribute a fixed number of times (dependent on the attribute) and then proceed to the next one. If both values 0 and 1 are observed then stop specifying this attribute.

A model of learning is presented that uses priors to aid in the gathering of information, but avoids "guessing" in the critical decisions. The results underline the importance of diversifying attention when acquiring knowledge.

Finally, there is a lot of room for future research: a counter-example can be found which demonstrates that without the independence assumption, these locally optimal algorithms are not necessarily (globally) optimal.

References:

Buntine Wray, "Learning Classification Rules Using Bayes", 6th Int. Work. Mach. Learn., 94-98 (1989).
Buntine Wray, "A Critique of the Valiant Model", IJCAI-89, 837-842 (1989).
Miller George, "The Magical Number Seven, Plus or Minus Two: Some Limits on our Capacity for Processing Information", Psychological Review 63, 81-97 (1956).
Valiant Leslie G., "A Theory of the Learnable", Proc. 16th Annu. ACM Symp. Theory of Comp., 436-445 (1984).

Combining Adaptive Learning Techniques in Solving Economic Prediction Problems

Joachim Stender, Brainware GmbH 1991
Gustav-Meyer-Allee 25, W-1000 Berlin 65

Abstract

In solving complex adaptive control problems, it is necessary to consider different tasks: partitioning the state space (preferably into "optimal" or "near-optimal" groups or categories) and setting up a learning system which allows the handling of sequences of actions which might be determined by a "path dependency". The talk suggests that, for solving complex adaptive control problems as well as for some complex economic prediction problems, it is useful to combine different learning paradigms, each of which provides an adequate solution for one of the above-mentioned tasks. An application in the area of economic modelling and prediction will be presented.

1. The Task: Getting Rich by Correctly Predicting the Exchange Rate Dollar - DM.

In an attempt to forecast the correct actions (buy/sell/do nothing) in exchanging \$/DM (resulting in profit maximization), a data series spanning from 02.01.78 to 08.12.89 was utilized. The tests involve 3000 time steps and data acquired daily (assuming open stock market). The combined algorithm receives 100 KDM, and aims to maximize the profit by buying and selling at the appropriate moments.

2. Partitioning the State Space: Keep It Simple

An important problem with many learning algorithms is that they require the space of input vectors to be **partitioned into classes** by some form of preprocessor before they can do any useful learning. This partitioning is itself a learning process and is often carried out by unsupervised learning algorithms (such as Competitive Learning or Kohonen Nets).

In experiments, three different approaches have been investigated: *Kohonen´s* Structured Vector Quantization (SVQ), *Lynne´s* Competitive Reinforcement Learning and, last but not least, a straight-forward partitioner.

Kohonen´s Structured Vector Quantization enables units in a neural net to become sensitive to specific occurrences (or "features") in an input data set. A collection of such units forms a **feature map** in which "similar" features are detected by units which are spatially close together, and "dissimilar" features by those which are spatially far apart. The model is inspired by biological brain maps such as the auditory cortex (see [1]).

The structure is normally a 2-dimensional layer of neurons. The simplest learning algorithm is as follows:

(1) Apply an input vector;

(2) Determine the unit with the maximum response (Umax). This is also the one whose weight vector is "nearest" (in Euclidean distance) to the input vector;

(3) For all units within a specified neighbourhood of Umax: change the weight vectors slightly so that they are closer to the input vector than before.

After several thousand such iterations, the responses of the units should have "self-organized" to reflect the structure of the input data. Details of this process, along with a mathematical proof, are given in [2].

Lynne´s Competitive Reinforcement Learning [3] combines the function of unsupervised competitive learning with the form of a reinforcement learning scheme, which takes into account feedback from outside the system. It should thus be able to assess the suitability of the categorizations being learned and to deal with categorizations which depend on more than vectors superficial similarity.

This approach is inherently more stable than traditional paradigms and can be easily adapted to function in reinforcement learning networks.

The most simple of the paradigms to be considered , the straight-forward partitioner, basically divides up values into several equidistant groups. Once this has been achieved, the results are combined using a specific encoding technique.

Disappointingly, the results of Kohonen´s approach were of no great use. A possible reason for this is that the actual problem is not a question of Structured Vector Quantization. In comparison, Lynne´s Competitive Reinforcement Learning performed quite well. However, the algorithm requires a considerable overhead, and the various learning tasks may tend to interfere with each other. This current implementation was unable to match the results which could be achieved with the straight-forward partitioner, the simplest model of all.

On this basis, it seems that the most suitable partitioning method for Second-Order-Learning is the least sophisticated **partitioner**, which reinforces the claim that the partitioner should be kept simple.

3. Second-Order-Learning: Handling Sequences of Actions

The Second-Order-Learning algorithm was designed to learn from a particular type of system environment which is more complex than the "datasets" normally handled by Machine-Learning algorithms. Instead of static, repetitive information of the type normally found in databases, the system environment is in the form of dynamic events and changes continually over time in a "non-linear" fashion. This learning algorithm belongs to the class of "Non-Linear Adaptive Systems" and is, therefore, particularly suited to real-time control problems.

The algorithm can normally solve the "credit assignment" problem; i.e. if feedback from the environment occurs as the result of a decision or action taken considerably earlier in the sequence of actions, it is usually possible to identify this earlier action as the cause of the environmental occurrence.

This identification is done by the **parasystem** which marks all successive states leading to a failure as "bad". The objective of the parasystem is to develop a collection of rules which can classify states as "dangerous", "bad", "uncritical" or "good".

The objective of the **performance system** is to develop a collection of rules which can enable a correct control decision to be made when presented with an input vector. The interaction between these two systems is described in detail in [4].

When the SOL system core is incorporated into a concrete application, it must be extended and modified as follows:

(1) The "environmental" Input-Output interface for the **performance system** must be adjusted according to the application's environment,

(2) The interfaces to the **parasystem** must be adjusted according to the particular "credit assignment" problem.

4. Empirical Results

Several tests have been carried out on this time series, comprising some 3000 steps. In the first test, a set figure of 100 KDM was used. In the ensuing investigations, the algorithm could make use of the total amount accumulated by earlier actions.

The best result was obtained when it was assumed that the process is noisy, and represent an increase by a factor of 21, i.e. 2145.77 KDM.

References:

[1] Ritter, H., Martinetz, T., Schulten, K., **Neuronale Netze**, Addison-Wesley, Bonn (1990).

[2] Kohonen, T., **Self-Organization and Associative Memory**, Springer-Verlag, 3rd edition (1989).

[3] Lynne, K. J., "Competitive Reinforcement Learning" in **Proceedings of the Fifth International Conference on MACHINE LEARNING**, The University of Michigan, Ann Arbor, June 12-14, 1988.

[4] Stender, J. (1989), "Second-Order-Learning-System auf Transputerbasis" in **Vorträge und Begleittexte zum 7. Entwicklerforum:"Transputer"** Munich, 24 & 25 October 1989. Markt & Technik Verlag, Germany.

MACHINE LEARNING AND ITS APPLICATION TO PROCESS CONTROL

Fritz Wysotzki
Institute of Automation Berlin
Rudower Chausse 5, O-1199 Berlin

Methods of Machine Learning - a main topic of AI-research-are to day in a state to get major industrial applications.They can be especially applied to the analysis, diagnosis and control of complicated processes for example in production automation, ecology or economy which cannot (or only partly) be modelled by conventional mathematical methods. By an automatic analysis of a set of examples (training set) of measured input-output behaviour of the process learning algorithms can find out important causal relationships between process variables and construct classification procedures for the detection of dangerous or unwanted process states /1/, /3/, /5/. Additionally, by classification learning partitions of the process states are induced which may be used for the construction of optimal control trajectories in process planning or even in real time process control.

Two main possibilities of application of classification learning to process diagnosis will be considered: decision trees, and artificial neuronal nets of the MADALINE-type. Details of the learning algorithms using examples of measured and preclassified process states can be found for example in /5/. Now modifications and extensions are elaborated within the ESPRIT-project StatLog.

DECISION TREES

Fig. 1 shows (in part) a decision tree for the diagnosis of non-optimal states in gas production /4/.

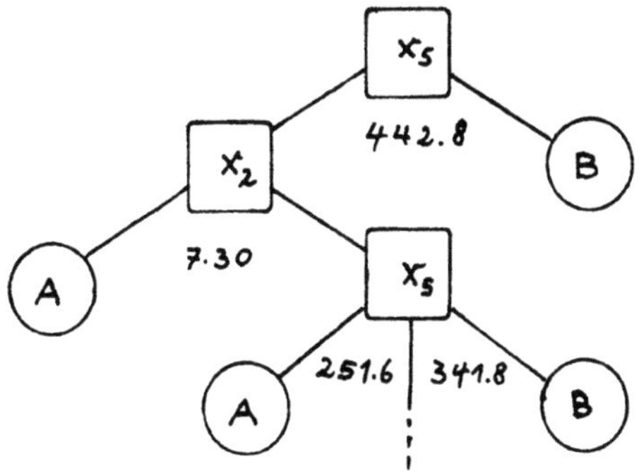

Fig.1 Decision tree (in part) for the classification of process states in gas production

Non-optimal states are those ones with high emission of coal dust (B). The process must be controlled in such a way that states with low dust emission (A) are reached. The nodes of the tree denote tests (measurements) to be performed on process variables (x_2, x_5), the arcs intervals for the corresponding measured values (outcome of the test). Numbers between arcs indicate the boundary between adjacent intervals. The tree is passed by a measured process state recursively until a terminal node is reached giving the classification.

In the example of fig.1 the process variable x_2 (vapour/oxygen ratio in the gas generator) can be controlled only (x_5 is the temperature at a certain height of the gas generator and cannot be controlled). It must be shifted to a value < 7.30 to get into a low-dust-emission region.
The tree was learned with the help of a training set of about 150 measured process states consisting of measurements of 13 process variables and the corresponding dust emission. The intervals are constructed by the learning algorithm automatically and are the results of an optimal analog-to-digital conversion of the continuous parameters. Only 4 variables are found to be relevant for the classification, i.e. must be measured for diagnosis. Each path in the tree represents a "macrostate", i.e. a set of process states equivalent for classification forming an n-dimensional interval.

EXTENDED MADALINE

By decision trees the boundaries of class regions in the parameter space are approximated by hyperplanes which are parallel to the axes. In general one gets a better approximation by using discriminating hyperplanes in arbitrary position.

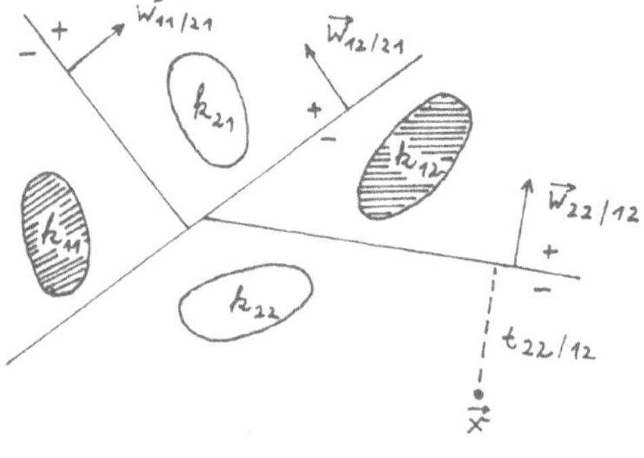

Fig.2 System of discriminating hyperplanes

In fig.2 an example is shown for two classes, consisting of two subclasses each.
By the hyperplanes new features (parameters)

$$t_r = \vec{w}_r \cdot \vec{x} + w_{o,r}$$

in the direction of their normals are defined, consisting of the scalar products of the original (measured) parameter vector $\vec{x}$ with a weight vector w_r plus a threshold $w_{o,r}$ (MADALINE /6/). The weights can be adapted by a learning procedure to get an optimal discrimination of the classes.
This is done by minimising an error functional using a gradient method or stochastic approximation. The necessary number and start position of the hyperplanes is found by an initial cluster analysis /5/.
The system of hyperplanes divides the parameter space into a set of class or subclass regions (sections). Each section can be uniquely described by a conjunction of Boolean variables

$$y_r = \text{sign } t_r$$

denoting the directions of the normals of its defining hyperplanes. In the original MADALINE the sign of $\sum y_r$ ("majority function") is used for decision of the class membership of a vector $\vec{x}$, but the efficiency and generality of the solution of the classification problem can be greatly increased by allowing general Boolean decision functions /5/, i.e. a combined symbolic/subsymbolic approach.

Local optimal control has to be performed perpendicular to the boundary (hyperplane) of a desired goal region in the parameter space.

The amount of control is given by the weigths of the parameters x_i. Additionally, the partitioning of the process space into discrete "macrostates" (sections) provided by both algorithms (learning decision trees and general hyperplanes respectively) can be used to apply problem solving methods to construct global optimal control trajectories which avoid undesired (dangerous or instability) regions.

References:

/1/ Kiendl, H. et al.: Regelbasierte Analyse und Synthese von Regelsystemen, in: Automatisierungstechnik '90, VDI-Berichte 855, VDI-Verlag 1990, 153-162

/2/ Nilsson, N.: Learning Machines, McGraw Hill 1965.

/3/ Wehenkel, L. et al.: Artificial Intelligence Applied to Online Transient Stability Assessment of Electric Power Systems, Proc. 10th World Congress on Automatic Control, Vol. 6, Munich 1987, 308-313.

/4/ Unger, S.; Sobik, F.; Türschmann, M.; Wysotzki, F.: Anwendung von Klassifizierungsverfahren auf Meßdaten der Kohlevergasung am Generator 24 des Gaskombinates Schwarze Pumpe, Research Report (unpublished), ZKI der AdW, June 1980.

/5/ Unger, S.; Wysotzki, F.: Lernfähige Klassifizierungssysteme, Akademieverlag, Berlin 1981.

/6/ Widrow, B.: "Bootsharp Learning" in Threshold Logics, Proc. 3rd IFAC-Congress, London 1966.

MULTI-LEVEL INVENTORY SYSTEMS WITH STOCHASTIC DEMAND

Sven Axsäter
Luleå University of Technology
S-951 87 Luleå, Sweden

When products are distributed over a large region it is common to have several local stocking locations close to the final customers. These local inventories are, in turn, customers of a higher level stocking site, for example a central warehouse. The resulting inventory system (see Figure 1) is denoted a *distribution* system or an *arborescent* system:

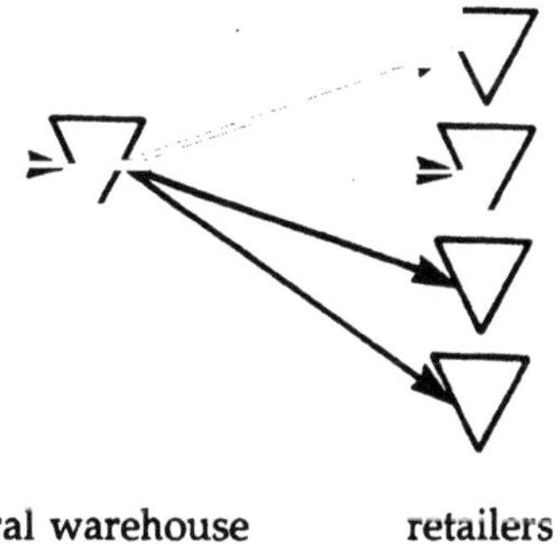

Figure 1 Two-level distribution system

In the special case when there is just a single retailer we have a *serial* system.

The fundamental problem in connection with such a two-level inventory system is to find the best balance between central stock (at the warehouse) and local stock (at the retailers). The optimal solution will depend on system structure, demand distributions, leadtimes, costs etc. It has been shown (Muckstadt and Thomas, 1980) that special multi-level methods may reduce the costs substantially compared to an application of single-level techniques.

It is important to note that quite different physical systems may lead to identical inventory systems. For example, several of the most important models have been developed in connection with military applications where the inventory items are repairable instead of consumable. Repairable items can be handled in essentially the same way as consumable items. The system in Figure 1 could also represent a production system where a number of different end products are all produced from a common basic module.

Among different multi-level inventory models there are two basic frameworks that have been very important for the development in the field: the Clark-Scarf framework and the METRIC framework.

Clark-Scarf Framework

The original finite horizon model was presented by Clark and Scarf (1960). For more recent infinite horizon models see Federgruen and Zipkin (1984), Rosling (1989) and Van Houtum and Zijm (1990).

The model assumes periodic review and order-up-to-S policies. The period demands are independent stochastic variables. The solution method, that is exact for serial systems, can be described as a decomposition technique. First we solve the retailer's problem. Furthermore we determine the additional cost due to insufficient supply at the warehouse. This cost is the shortage cost when optimizing the inventory policy at the warehouse. This means that the solution can be obtained from a sequence of single location models. When dealing with more than one retailer, the standard approximation is to assume that the retailers after ordering always have inventory positions with an optimal distribution among the retailers.

METRIC Framework

This framework assumes continuous review, one-for-one inventory policies and Poisson or compound Poisson demand.

Sherbrooke (1968) suggested a simple approximate method for policy evaluation, that can also be described as a decomposition technique. First we analyze the warehouse and determine the average holding costs and the average time delay. When evaluating the costs at a retailer the average time delay at the warehouse is added to the transportation time from the warehouse to the retailer. This means that a stochastic leadtime is replaced by its mean and leads to a lower bound for the costs.

Sherbrooke's technique can be seen as an one-parameter approximation. Graves (1985) has suggested a more accurate two-parameter approximation. Recently a simple exact recursive procedure was given by Axsäter (1990a).

Graves (1985) and Axsäter (1991b) have shown that a slightly modified Clark-Scarf model can be solved in essentially the same way as a METRIC-model. The two considered frameworks are therefore in a sense very related.

Batch-Ordering Policies

It is much more difficult to analyze general batch ordering policies. Exceptions are serial systems and two-level systems with batches only at the warehouse.

One approach is to consider a batch as a number of individual units following different one-for-one policies. The costs are consequently obtained as an average over costs for different one-for-one policies. See Axsäter (1990b, 1991a). A different approach is to use a decomposition technique similar in spirit to the METRIC approach. Examples of such methods are Deuermeyer and Schwarz (1981), Lee and Moinzadeh (1987a, b), Moinzadeh and Lee (1986) and Svoronos and Zipkin (1988).

REFERENCES

AXSÄTER, S. 1990a. Simple Solution Procedures for a Class of Two-Echelon Inventory Problems. Opns. Res. 38, 64-69.

AXSÄTER, S. 1990b. Evaluation of (R, Q)-Policies for Two-Level Inventory Systems with Poisson Demand, Luleå University of Technology.
AXSÄTER, S. 1990c. Modelling Emergency Lateral Transshipments in Inventory Systems. Mgmt. Sci. 36, 1329-1338.
AXSÄTER, S. 1991a. Exact and Approximate Evaluation of Batch-Ordering Policies for Two-Level Inventory Systems. Luleå University of Technology, Sweden.
AXSÄTER, S. 1991b. Optimization of Order-up-to-S Policies in Two-Echelon Inventory Systems with Periodic Review, Luleå University of Technology, Sweden.
CLARK, A. J. and H. SCARF 1960. Optimal Policies for a Multi-Echelon Inventory Problem, Mgmt. Sci. 6, 475-490.
FEDERGRUEN A. and P. ZIPKIN 1984. Computational Issues in an Infinite-Horizon Multi-Echelon Inventory Model, Opns. Res. 32, 818-836.
DEUERMEYER, B. and L. B. SCHWARZ 1981. A Model for the Analysis of System Service Level in Warehouse/Retailer Distribution Systems: the Identical Retailer Case. In Studies in the Management Sciences, Vol. 16. Multi-Level Production/Inventory Control Systems, 163-193. L. B. Schwarz (ed), North Holland.
GRAVES, S. C. 1985. A Multi-Echelon Inventory Model for a Repairable Item with One-for-One Replenishment, Mgmt. Sci. 31, 1247-1256.
GRAVES, S. C. 1989. A Multi-Echelon Inventory Model with Fixed Reorder Intervals, WP#3045-89-MS, Sloan School of Management, MIT.
LEE, H. L. 1987. A Multi-Echelon Inventory Model for Repairable Items with Emergency Lateral Transshipments. Mgmt. Sci. 33, 1302-1316.
LEE, H. L. and K. MOINZADEH 1987a. Two-Parameter Approximations for Multi-Echelon Repairable Inventory Models with Batch Ordering Policy. IIE Transactions 19, 140-149.
LEE, H. L. and K. MOINZADEH 1987b. Operating Characteristics of a Two-Echelon Inventory System for Repairable and Consumable Items under Batch-Ordering and Shipment Policy, Naval Res. Logist. Quart. 34, 365-380.
MOINZADEH, K. and H. L. LEE 1986. Batch Size and Stocking Levels in Multi-Echelon Repairable Systems. Mgmt. Sci. 32, 1567-1581.
MUCKSTADT, J. A. 1973. A Model for a Multi-Item, Multi-Echelon, Multi-Indenture Inventory System. Mgmt. Sci. 20, 472-481.
MUCKSTADT, J. A. and L. J. THOMAS 1980. Are Multi-Echelon Inventory Methods Worth Implementing in Systems with Low-Demand Rates? Mgmt. Sci. 26, 483-494.
ROSLING, K. 1989. Optimal Inventory Policies for Assembly Systems under Random Demands, Opns. Res. 37, 565-579.
SHERBROOKE, C. C. 1968. METRIC: A Multi-Echelon Technique for Recoverable Item Control. Opns. Res. 16, 122-141.
SVORONOS, A. and P. ZIPKIN 1988. Estimating the Performance of Multi-Level Inventory Systems. Opns. Res. 36, 57-72.
VAN HOUTUM, G. J. and W. H. M. Zijm 1990. Computational Procedures for Stochastic Multi-Echelon Production Systems, Eindhoven University of Technology.

DE NOVO PROGRAMING IN MCDM

ZORAN BABIĆ, IVAN PAVIĆ
FACULTY OF ECONOMICS
RADOVANOVA 13, 58000 SPLIT
YUGOSLAVIA

De Novo presents a special approach of optimization. Instead of "optimizing a given system" M.Zeleny (1982, 1986) suggests a way of "designing an optimal system". The basis of the standard approach is a production model with resources defined in advance, so that the constraints, and the feasible set are fixed. In the case of multiple criteria the result is a compromise solution that gives to some targets a value lower than the optimal or ideal one. However, De Novo approach does not limit the resources as most of the necessary resource quantities can be obtained at certain prices. Resources are actually limited because its maximum quantity are governed by the budget which is an important element of De Novo. There are also demand and capacity constraints which can be incorporated in the modelUsing De Novo approach most various cases can be handled more effectively than by the standard programming models. Changes in prices, tehnological coefficients, increasing costs of raw materials, quantity discounts and other similar and real production situations can be easily incorporated in De Novo model and can give very satisfactory solutions.
In the case of multiple criteria De Novo formulation of the model make it possible to readjust the resource constraints in such way that the originally infeasible ideal solution becomes feasible with the same or often with lower costs than previous ones. If the budget restriction does not allow readjustment to cause full achievement of the ideal solution, De Novo shows the way how to find near satisfaction of the ideal solution. However, if we are able to take more money for the budget using De Novo we can find the optimal way how to design our sistem for such amount of money.
This paper shows the application of De Novo in the real production system which produces various products mainly from milk such as yogurt, cheese, pudding and so on.

This factory produces ten different products A_j in quantities x_j using 19 different raw materials y_j which are available only in limited quantities. The production plan for next period (1 month) must assure the maximum profit.
However, because of the foreign currency restriction it is important to spend the less possible on import of raw materials. We can summarize the problem as follows:

$$\text{Max} \quad z_1 = \sum_j c_j x_j \qquad (1)$$

$$\text{Min} \quad z_2 = \sum_j t_j x_j \qquad (2)$$

$$\text{s.t.} \quad \sum_j a_{ij} x_j \le b_i , \; i = 1,\dots,19 \qquad (3)$$

$$x_j \ge 0, \; j = 1,\dots,10 \qquad (4)$$

where c_j represents the production profit per unit, t_j is the cost of imported raw materials per unit of the j-th product, and a_{ij} are technological coefficients.
In production process last month, net income achieved the sum of $4.412 \; 10^7$ din, while the relevant raw materials costs were about $3.527 \; 10^7$ din.
If we consider the necessary quantities of raw materials (b_i) as variables, and the resource constraints (3) as equations, it is possible to express the required amount of money by the budget constraint:

$$\sum_j v_j x_j \le B \qquad (5)$$

where v_j are total raw material costs required for one unit of the j-th product.
Solving this problem with respect to z_1, with no additional constraints, the optimal solution consists of the only one and most profitable product x_r, which satisfy $c_r/v_r = \max (c_j/v_j)$.
However, our problem has a number of capacity constraints, related especially to the filling and packaging machines, as well as those demand constraints which should be introduced into the model. In order to reduce the model dimensions the demand constraints

$L_j \leq x_j \leq G_j$ are introduced into the model by transformation of variables x_j into x_j', where $x_j' = x_j - L_j$, and the model is solved with respect to both objective functions.
Since there are specific budget constraints two possibilities are taken into consideration: in first, the budget amounts to $B = 3.5\ 10^7$ din and in second $B = 3.4\ 10^7$ din. In the first case, with the given constraints, we obtain greater profit of $z_1 = 4.658\ 10^7$ din due to more efficient purchase of raw materials. In the second case (lack of money) we obtain the profit almost equal to those achieved in real process production but with considerably less money spent.
Solving the problem with respect to both objective functions the ideal solution can be obtained only by corection of budget, e.i. by additional purchase of raw materials. Optimal solution in this case, is determined in such way that minimaization of budget is required on condition that both objective functions should achieve their optimal values as follows:

$$\text{Min } B = \sum_j v_j x_j \tag{6}$$

$$\text{s.t. } z_1 = z_1^* = 4.658\ 10^7 \tag{7}$$

$$z_2 = z_2^* = 1.032\ 10^7 \tag{8}$$

Consequently, all demand and capacity constraints must be sastisfied as well.
In order to obtain ideal solution, it is necessary to increase the budget to $4.044\ 10^7$ din, if not, the approved budget (B') should be allocated on raw materials according to the solution of the problem (6)-(8), so that the optimal solution can be easily obtained by solving the equation system

$$\sum a_{ij} x_j = b_i'$$

or simply, by a corection of optimal solution for problem (6)-(8) accordingly to the ratio B'/B.

REFERENCES:

1. Zeleny,M.,1982. Multiple Criteria Decision Making, McGraw-Hill, New York.
2. Zeleny,M.,1986. Optimal System Design with Multiple Criteria: De Novo Programming Approach, Engineering Costs and Production Economics, 10, 89-94.
3. Tabucanon,T.M.,1988. Multiple Criteria Decision Making in Industry, Elsevier, Amsterdam.

OPERATIONS RESEARCH AND SERVICE QUALITY

Klaus Fischer
Friedrich List University of
Transport and Communications Dresden
Division Transportationsystemtheory and quality assurance
Friedrich-List-Platz 1 / PF 82
D-O-8010 Dresden

1. INTRODUCTION

Service quality gains more and more importance and can be considered as the new battleground for competition. That's why the service sector including the number of employees grows in size permanently (unstoppable) on the one hand and the produced products must be sold on the other.
Quality is simply the permanently fulfilling of the customer's expectations /1/.
The decision concerning the quality (good or poor) is finally met by the customer only and it includes the decision to buy or not to buy. Hence it follows the companies need a customer-oriented quality strategy focussed on the customer's satisfaction. This is the only way for a service company if it will be successfull today and above all in the future.
Don't forget service quality differs from product quality strongly. Customer's satisfaction is closely connected with individuality and individuality cannot be evaluated by mean values. On the other hand the customer is mostly involved in the service process and so he experiences the service quality directly. That means even if a product of poor quality can be touched up a service of poor quality never can be "improved" because in this moment the customer has already "consumed" the service of poor quality (e.g. delayed train or plane).
Last but not least the human factors (expressed by the employees of service companies) take a great influence on customers satisfaction.

2. CUSTOMERS AND SERVICE QUALITY

Every day a lot of customers are coming to a service company very hopefully, surely also with different expectations (see fig.1) and each customer wants to be the most important one.

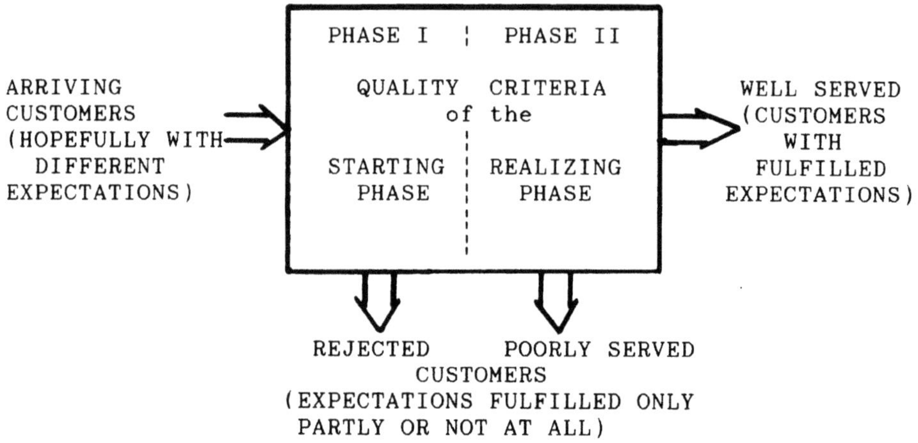

Fig.1 : Arriving customers - a service system - possible results

Now, let us have a look at the reality /2/ .

Already in the very beginning of the service process a few of customers get difficulties (e.g. no free capacity available, long waiting times, bad waiting conditions, behaviour of the employees not encouraging) and consequently they are rejected directly or indirectly because they are already disappointed in this phase of the service process. Undoubtedly, there was no conformance to their expectations and so they don't belong to the satisfied customers. Consequently we have to ask : has the company a real chance that these customers will be comming to it with their next wishes? Scarcely.

The remaining customers are served. A part of them very well, their expectations were fulfilled they are satisfied, and consequently, they will surely come with their next needs again to the same company. An other (small) part of the served customers has not experienced a high service quality, their expectations were fulfilled only partly or even not at all. Some of them will look for an other service company, some of them may be will make a second try with the same company.

The required calculation of satisfied/ dissatisfied customers is a great challenge to Operation Research.

3. METHODS

Service quality must be developed, designed and (its benefit for the customer) presented. That means that the service quality must aim of the needs of the customers from the very first beginning. This requirement can only be fulfilled if the process of developing and designing is supported by scientific foundations on the one hand and by knowledge of the behaviour and attidude of the customers/ employees on the other.
What has to be taken into account?
Firstly, service quality is essentially influenced by the following elements of services

a) the creation of high quality service products
b) a customer-oriented utilization/application of the service products
c) a well designed service system to offer and to sell services on a high quality level
d) a well and customer-oriented trained staff
e) a service process which is carried out in a pleasant atmospere and environment

Secondly, these are some important aspects which have to be recognized and integrated into provided mathematical models step by step or must be taken into account if new models have to be developed.
1) The quality criteria have to be defined and quantified. Hence it follows that the quality criteria must be measurable or observable. It is worth mentioning that the achieved level of the single quality criteria should be compared with a non-plus-ultra-quality /3/ . In some cases it is easy e.g. zero failure, no delay, in other cases a broad field for discussions is open e.g. frequency of transport means, comfort, behaviour, attitude, experiences of the employees of the service company, aspects of the environment and last but not

least waiting time.

2) We should always keep in mind two essential aspects :
The quality criteria are valued by the customers and their own evaluation and not the company's one is decisive for the customer's decision to buy or not to buy.
The customer usually evaluates the quality of service in a more or less complex way. That's why the customer mostly does not use only one but a sequence of services being closely connected and so it is important for him that the whole sequence of services was fulfilled in an excellent way.

3) The sequence of services is mostly done by some different companies or agencies. Therefore in many cases the service companies should replace displacing by cooperation. For example a bad accomodation in a hotel can be decisive for the evaluation of the whole holiday trip as of poor quality.

4) We must take into account the customer influence function (influence of quality on customer's behaviour and how the influenced customer acts). Here are comprehensive investigations necessary /4/ .

5) A very close connection between the customers and the service companies is necessary in order to experience the actual expectations and evaluations of the customers. Notice, that a happening but one question of the customers is not sufficient because their evaluations are not static but dynamic ones - that means the changes must be known at any time.

6) Coming back to OR. It is not sufficient to calculate the number of served customers. On the contrary we have to try to compute both the well and poorly served customers, only in this way the company can evaluate the own results. However, in a lot of cases customers are rejected directly or indirectly before the service process starts really and these customers are surely also dissatisfied ones like poorly served customers.

7) The calculation of results by means of OR should be directed more and more to the instantaneous values instaed of mean values. The latter one is doubtless useful for long-term planning, however, the customers never experience the mean

values but the instanteous values - he likes individuality.
8) The experiences of product quality can only partly used for service quality. Why? The customer is mostly involved into the service process and therefore e.g. a quality control is worthless concerning the served customer because at this time he has already "consumed" the poor quality (e.g. a delayed arrival).
9) The mathematical models of OR should be extended to such aspects as reliability, maintainability, waiting time, behaviour of the employees etc. /5/ .
10) It must be taken into account that we have to find a suitable relationship between grade of customer's satisfaction, the expense to realize this grade and the changeable share of the market. That means one has to proof if the marketing strategies must be changed by taking into account aspects of quality. Does the aim satisfied customers require changes in the economical consideration of strategies? A consideration of the development in the field of transportation seems to show the importance of such a question in a very characteristic way!
11) The influence of the employees on service quality must be investigated thoroughly.

4. MATHEMATICAL MODELS

The well-known models of queueing and reliability theory, resp. should be combined. This can be realized by extending of reliability models to performance aspects and vice versa of queueing models by extending to reliability aspects /5/. Based on these models we are able to compute RELIABILITY RELATED SYSTEM PERFORMANCE MEASURES including the distribution function of the system parameters. Beyond it the quality criteria which the employees responsible for must also be taken into account. Otherwise the results don't correspond with the reality.
If we succeed in solving the last mentioned task we will be

able to compute a QUALITY-RELATED SYSTEM PERFORMANCE MEASURE also. That means we have only one statment concerning the "system quality". That must not mean that the result is only one number.
The colour of individuality has to be introduced into the consideration and the mathematical models slowly but consequently. Only in this way we get knowledge about the numbers of customers who had to wait for a longer time ..., experienced a longer delay time ... etc. However, only in this way we can develop improvement of service quality with the aim : the satisfied customer.

5. CONCLUSION

The "production" of highly satisfied customers is an important contribution for a high quality of life if we don't forget the environment as an important quality criterion.
The quality management is responsible for the development of such a strategy. For that it urgently needs scientific support by OR and last but not least a new thinking if it wants to start this process already in the developing phase.
Mathematical models and quality-related system performance measures could be important tools to offer a high service quality. The integration of service quality aspects into OR could be challenge and further chance for OR.

REFERENCES

/1/ Rosander,A.G. : The quest for quality in services
Quality Press.,American Society for Quality Control, 1989
/2/ Fischer,K. : Reliability-Related Performance Measures -
Aims and tools,Proc. EURO XI, Aachen, 1991, pp 84
/3/ Kürzl,A. : Qualität und Qualitätsmanagement
W. de Gruyter, Berlin/ New York, 1989
/4/ Ullah,P. : The Psychology of Total Quality Management
ICQCC'91, Bali, Special sheets
/5/ Bär,M., Fischer,K., Hertel,G. : Leistungsfähigkeit -
Qualität - Zuverlässigkeit, transpress Verlag, Berlin, 1988

Capacity Oriented Scheduling
- A method to control FMS -

Prof. Dr. K. - W. Hansmann
Dipl.-Kfm. K. Kleeberg
University of the Bundeswehr
Holstenhofweg 85, D - 2000 Hamburg 70, Germany

I. Capacity Oriented Scheduling (COS)

Capacity Oriented Scheduling (COS) is based on the "Load Oriented Order Release", first published by Bechte [1] and Wiendahl [2].

In contrast to MRP II a customer order is not yet released to the shop floor when the required materials are available but only when it is certain that all required work stations have enough available capacity.

The five steps of our Capacity Oriented Scheduling (COS) procedure can be described as follows:

1) Determine the bottleneck work stations

   Our experience shows that load limits are only to be calculated for those work stations which are known as bottlenecks because they determine the mean flow-time of the jobs, and so the in-process inventory in front of the bottlenecks needs to be controlled properly.
   Although it's very difficult to realize the bottlenecks in advance as they are dependent on the production program, the MRP II production and capacity planning or the experience of people on the shop floor could give some hints for determining actual bottlenecks.

2) Assign load limits to the bottlenecks

   By using a load limit for each work station the COS-strategy tries to get a relatively constant level of in-process inventory in front of each work station in each period. A properly chosen load level shall contribute to the solution of three problems: First to keep the work station from being idle, second to reduce the mean flow-time of the orders and third to reduce the standard deviation of the mean-flow-time of each part type.

3) Calculate the expected capacity requirements of the orders

Capacity has to be reserved only for those orders which reach a work station within the planning horizon. This depends on

- the work content of the work station and
- the number of work stations to be passed before the work station in question.

We calculate a probability for this expected capacity requirement as follows:

$$P_{ij} = \frac{T - \sum_{k=i}^{j-1} RW_k}{T} \cdot \frac{n - (j - i)}{n}, \quad \text{if} \sum_{k=i}^{j-1} RW_k \leq T$$

$$P_{ij} = 0, \quad \text{if} \sum_{k=i}^{j-1} RW_k > T$$

$$P_{ii} = 1$$

$$\forall \quad \begin{array}{l} i = 1, \ldots\ldots, n-1 \\ j = i+1, \ldots\ldots, n \end{array}$$

with :

i: work station where the order is at the moment

j: work station to be reached

n: maximum number of work stations

T: Length of the planning period

RW_k: Remaining work on work station k

4) Release those orders for which the expected capacity requirement on each work station is available

Those orders which do not exceed the load limit of any work station within the planning period have to be released in the sequence that the order which has the earliest start-date is released first.

5) Schedule the released orders at each work station according to suitable priority rules.
In this way we can combine the controlling parameters of order release (load limit) with scheduling on the shop floor.

To compare the priority rules we employ a simulation model comprising 24 priority rules and combinations of rules. It shows for a pure job shop system that the combination of order release and scheduling leads to a considerable reduction of the mean flow-time by using capacity oriented scheduling but an increase of the tardy jobs [3].
The satisfying results of this job shop scheduling problem encouraged us to extend our method to flexible manufacturing systems.

II. Flexible Manufacturing Systems

We define a flexible manufacturing system (FMS) similarly to Stecke [4] as an

integrated production system consisting of
- a set of NC machine tools, linked by
- automated material handling devices,
- all controlled by an integrated computer system.

Our data for the simulation model stem from a company where one small FMS representing one production stage is embedded in a job shop system.

III. Capacity Oriented Scheduling for FMS

The company tries to achieve the two objectives
- minimization of the mean flow-time and
- minimization of the mean tardiness

equally weighed. That means a combinatorial objective function (COF) represented by a linear combination of the goals with weight of 0.5.

After some experimental simulation runs with various load limits and priority rules on the shop floor we introduce a load limit only in the refixturing/remounting station and in the machining centers of the FMS. To show the effect purely no load limit is applied on the shop floor. By varying the FMS load limit, we are able to prove that an optimal load limit in the FMS exists. The mean flow-time grows almost linearly with an increasing load limit while the mean tardiness shows at first a decreasing tendency and increases subsequently. These contrary tendencies of mean flow-time and mean tardiness lead to a konvex objective function which actually has a minimum.

The simulation model shows that the optimal load limit of the bottleneck (FMS) determines the load limit of the shop floor. The scheduling results have been improved further as the load limits in the shop floor and the FMS are optimized integratively and simultaneously. If the load limit is close to the optimum the scheduling results of the various priority rules do not differ essentially from each other.
The results support our hypothesis that an integration of load oriented order release and scheduling improves shop floor control and scheduling performance considerably.

References

1. Bechte, W.,
   Steuerung der Durchlaufzeit durch belastungsorientierte Auftragsfreigabe bei Werkstattfertigung,
   Universität Hannover 1980.
2. Wiendahl, H.-P.,
   Belastungsorintierte Fertigungssteuerung,
   München - Wien 1987.
3. Hansmann, K.W., Kleeberg, K.,
   Comparison of New Approaches to Job Shop Scheduling with an Interactive Simulation Progamm on PC,
   Paper at ORSA/TIMS meeting in Vancouver 1989.
4. Stecke, K.E.,
   Formulation and Solution of Nonlinear Integer Production Planning Problems for Flexible Manufacturing Systems,
   in: Management Science, Vol.29, No.3, March 1983, S.273-288.

A Simulation-Based Investigation of Some Recent Developments in Priority Rule Research

Reinhard Haupt, Volker Schilling
Allgemeine Betriebswirtschaftslehre
Universität Bayreuth
Postfach 10 12 51, D-8580 Bayreuth

Production scheduling is part of the operative shop management decision system. In particular, manufacturing resource planning systems involve a Shop Floor Control (SFC) System which implies day-to-day scheduling and dispatching of jobs through the shop. The simulated shop is characterized by arbitrary routings of different, inhomogenous job types (job shop) in contrast to the identical routing in a flow shop.

The scheduling problem is defined as the determination of the order in which a set of jobs $\{i/i=1,\ldots,n\}$ is to be processed through a set of machines $\{j/j=1,\ldots,m\}$. The complexity of the scheduling problem is due to the fact that jobs arrive intermittently during the planning period, i.e. they are not available in whole at the start time of the planning cycle. This requires a new scheduling procedure each time a job arrives.

The lack of practicable, analytical procedures has led to the development of heuristic methods. The most important method is the priority rule. Priority rules can be defined as sequencing decision criteria according to which a job, among those waiting to be processed by a machine, is selected at the time a machine becomes free.

The simulated priority rules were tested under different conditions. A simulation run is determinded by the configuration of the mean interarrival time (workload level) and the due date setting. The latter follows the TWK method, where the due date is defined as the sum of a multiple of the job's total processing time and the arrival time of the job. The investigated priority rules as well as the main results are shown in Table 1. The rules can be divided into different classes of priority functions the rules of which are expected to yield a similar performance behavior. The observed criteria mean flow time ($\bar{F}$), mean tardiness ($\bar{T}$), and fraction of tardy jobs (n_T%) reflect about the performance of the rules. In addition, the root mean square (T_{RMS}) gives information about the distribution of (especially heavy) tardy jobs.

The best figures of $\bar{T}$ are shown by the SL-rule, which belongs to the due date class. Concerning $\bar{F}$ and T_{RMS}, SL behaves on the average in a mediocre way. The spread is low in comparison to the other rules.

The versions of the CoverT- and ATC-rules by *Vepsalainen et al.* (1987) produce low fractions of tardy jobs. Specifically, ATC performs acceptable $\bar{F}$- and $\bar{T}$-results in contrast to the bad behavior of CoverT (with respect to $\bar{T}$). Both rules are characterized by high figures of T_{RMS}, produced by a small fraction of jobs being heavily late.

The exact definition of the look-ahead- (LA) and the alternate operation- (AltOp) heuristics by *Gere* (1966) are given by *Haupt* (1989). The simple AltOp-rule shows medium results in the main figures in connection with relative high values of n_T%. The implementation of the LA-heuristic reduces $\bar{F}$, and (under a high workload level) n_T% too. On the other hand, $\bar{T}$ and T_{RMS} are increased by LA.

The rules of the SPT-class are not sensitive to the due date setting multiplier with respect to $\bar{F}$. The $\bar{F}$-values of SPT are low; they are reducable by two variants of truncation, which is based on an idea of *Conway et al.* (1967). It is characteristic of the SPT-class too that the n_T%-figures are relatively low. Again, the mean tardiness appears high, if the fraction of tardy jobs is low. In contrast to SPT and $TSPT_C$, the performance of $TSPT_F$ shows extremely high figures in $\bar{T}$ and T_{RMS}.

Generally, the priority rules of a specific class tend to produce similar results. Furthermore, the n_T%- and $\bar{T}$-values exhibit a significant trade-off-behavior. Finally, the performance measures are more sensitive to the workload level than to the tightness of the due dates.

Table 1

S1	High workload level (91,88 %), tight due date
S2	High workload level (91,88 %), extensive due date
S3	Low workload level (82,5 %), tight due date
S4	Low workload level (82,5 %), extensive due date

Priority Rule	Configuration	$\overline{F}$	$\overline{T}$	n_T%	T_{RMS}	Definition $(Z_i(t))$
SL	S1	1203	669	84,01	759	$d_i - t - \sum_{q=j}^{m_i} p_{iq}$
	S2	978	412	45,21	368	
	S3	442	107	8,31	41	
	S4	439	24	0,25	1	
SPT	S1	905	1128	37,68	950	p_{ij}
	S2	905	1181	28,59	836	
	S3	364	287	7,79	124	
	S4	364	405	2,53	87	
$TSPT_C$	S1	848	882	40,53	720	$\begin{cases} Z_i(i \in R)_{SPT} & \text{for } \sum_{q=1}^{j} W_{iq} \leq f \\ -\sum_{q=1}^{j} W_{iq} & \text{for } \sum_{q=1}^{j} W_{iq} > f \end{cases}$ $f \in \{1740; 459\}$
	S2	848	865	30,53	394	
	S3	385	152	13,17	63	
	S4	385	57	2,40	12	
CoverT	S1	1193	2828	25,22	3283	$\frac{1}{p_{ij}} \cdot \left[1 - \frac{\left[d_i - t - \sum_{q=1}^{m_i} p_{iq}\right]^+}{k \cdot \sum_{q=j}^{m_i} W_{iq}}\right]^+$ $k = 2$
	S2	1270	3732	17,30	4289	
	S3	480	825	3,69	282	
	S4	485	294	0,09	52	
ATC	S1	932	804	41,38	1411	$\frac{1}{p_{ij}} \cdot \exp\left(-\left[\frac{d_i - t - \sum_{q=j+1}^{m_i}(W_{iq} + p_{iq}) - p_{ij}}{k \cdot \hat{p}}\right]^+\right)$ $k = 3$
	S2	848	514	19,36	437	
	S3	436	192	3,75	58	
	S4	454	34	0,09	0	
AltOp	S1	1011	579	68,51	874	$-\sum_{h \in R, h \neq i}\left[d_h - (t + p_{ij}) - \sum_{q=j}^{m_h} p_{hq}\right]^- - \left[d_i - (t + p_{ij}) - \sum_{q=j+1}^{m_i} p_{iq}\right]^-$
	S2	943	462	48,39	1222	
	S3	477	323	12,48	268	
	S4	467	47	11,01	29	
LA(AltOp)	S1	996	2610	25,60	3173	$\sum_{h \in (P \cup R), h \neq i}\left(\left[d_h - t - \sum_{q=j}^{m_h} p_{hq} - \left[p_{ij} + [d_{i,j-1} - t]^+ - [d_{h,j-1} - t]^+\right]^+\right]^-\right) + \left[d_i - t - \sum_{q=j}^{m_i} p_{iq}\right]^-$
	S2	868	2985	18,52	2208	
	S3	378	902	15,57	534	
	S4	363	857	11,42	388	
$TSPT_F$	S1	795	1115	30,04	1907	$\begin{cases} Z_i(i \in R)_{SPT} & \text{for } \sum_{q=1}^{j} W_{iq} \leq g \cdot \left(\overline{W} + \frac{\overline{W}^2}{\sigma_W + 1}\right) \\ \sum_{q=1}^{j} W_{iq} & \text{for } \sum_{q=1}^{j} W_{iq} > g \cdot \left(\overline{W} + \frac{\overline{W}^2}{\sigma_W + 1}\right) \end{cases}$ $g \in \{1,9166; 1,8250\}$
	S2	795	1516	17,98	1864	
	S3	426	944	8,16	644	
	S4	426	2466	2,62	614	

Literature:

Conway, R.W./Maxwell, W.L./Miller, L.W., Theory of scheduling, Reading (Mass.), 1967.

Gere, William S., Heuristics in job shop scheduling, in: Management Science 13(1966), P. 167-190.

Haupt, R., A survey of priority rule-based scheduling, in: OR Spektrum 11(1989), P. 3-16.

Vepsalainen, A.P./Morton Th.E., Priority rules for job shops with weighted tardiness costs, in: Management Science 33(1987), P. 1035-1047.

Notation:

$Z_i(t)$	Priority value of job i at time t
d_i	Due date of job i
t	Actual time
q	Index of remaining operations $(q=j,\ldots,m_i)$
p_{ij}	Processing time of job i on machine j
W_{ij}	Waiting time of job i before it is processed by machine j
k	"Look-ahead-" parameter
$\hat{p}$	mean processing time of the jobs in the queue
R	Set of jobs in queue of operation j
P	Set of jobs which are currently processed on machines preceding operation j

$$T_{RMS} = \sqrt{\frac{\sum_{i=1}^{n_T} T_i^2}{n_T}}$$

$$[x]^- = \min\{0; x\}$$

$$[x]^+ = \max\{0; x\}$$

AN INTEGRATED SYSTEM FOR QUALITY FUNCTION DEPLOYMENT

Werner Jammernegg, Günther Schönleitner
Department of Information Processing
Vienna University of Economics and Business Administration
Reithlegasse 16, A-1190 Wien, Austria

There are four important developments in production management that are cornerstones for the implementation of greater integration in manufacturing: Just-in-Time manufacturing (JIT), Design for Manufacturability (DFM), Quality Function Deployment (QFD) and Computer Integrated Manufacturing (CIM). Of these approaches, only CIM deals with factory automation and is therefore directly related with information and manufacturing technology. JIT, DFM and QFD are organizational approaches that should be implemented before or at least in parallel with CIM in order to avoid the automation of inefficient practices.

QFD is a concept which channels the knowledge from marketing, product and process design and production with the single goal to satisfy customer needs. An essential characteristic is that during all stages of QFD teams are formed from these functional areas. Four stages of QFD can be identified: product selection, part design, process design and production and process planning. Starting from the customer needs the design requirements of the product are specified by a brainstorming team using the concept of the house of quality (cp. Hauser and Clausing (1988)). At the part design stage the design requirements are translated into part characteristics. Here DFM and experimental design can be employed. During process design the optimal levels of the process parameters are dertermined that minimize the so-called quality loss. Finally, at the last stage the process parameters constitute the necessary input for production planning (e.g. bill of material) as well as process planning (e.g. tool requirements).

Like other organizational approaches QFD is also a descriptive concept. In order to make this concept more operative we developed for the first two stages, product selection and part design, DESIGNEXPERT, an integrated expert system and decision support system. For a related system we refer to Knight and Kim (1991).

The goal of DESIGNEXPERT is to supply the non-expert with knowledge in experimental design containing information about different methods, references and analyses of the results of the experiments. To apply the system successfully knowledge about products and processes is necessary. Furthermore, it can be seen as a kind of prototype as only up to 15 part characteristics each with 2 or 3 levels are covered. But from our practical experiences this seems to be enough for many real-world applications.

The development tool of DESIGNEXPERT was VP-Expert, a rule-based expert system shell. VP-Expert allows the access to external programs like data base systems and spread sheets what was very convenient for our application. In this respect DESIGNEXPERT is an integrated expert system and decision support system.

DESIGNEXPERT consists of 7 modules with about 300 rules. The knowledge is composed of interviews with experts and of extensive search in the literature. Module 1 gives advice in selecting the members of the brainstorming team in dependence on the problem to solve. Also information is given how to perform brainstorming using Ishikawa diagrams.

In Module 2 the part characteristics found in the brainstorming meeting are evaluated with respect to several criteria, like significance, availability, cost, time and accuracy of measurement. A weighting scheme is used to compute a score for each part characteristic. In this way the relevance of the part characteristics is determined.

Module 3 selects an appropriate method for experimental design. First the user is asked about the knowledge on the interactions between different part characteristics. Then the method for experimental design is suggested in dependence on the number of relevant part characteristics, the number of levels of each characteristic and the cost of an experiment. DESIGNEXPERT offers the following methods: full factorial design, fractional factorial design and Taguchi design (cp. e.g. Phadke (1989)).

Modules 4, 5 and 6 contain guidelines for the 3 types of design methods. Additionally, in these modules statistical analyses, like the analysis of variance, can be performed with the results of the experiments. In this way the optimal levels of the significant part characteristics are obtained.

Finally, Module 7 contains a guideline for Taguchi's tolerance design. Building on his concept of the quality loss function, tolerancing aims at reducing the distance between the lower bound and the upper bound of a control chart in order to achieve an improvement of product and/or process quality.

For a complete description of DESIGNEXPERT we refer to Schönleitner (1990).

The usefulness of DESIGNEXPERT was first tested in a paper-mill. The goal was to improve the fiber of Xerox-paper. The project-team which has been selected by means of DESIGNEXPERT worked very efficiently in the brainstorming meeting. The members found about 70 characteristics. For performing the experiments this number was reduced to 11 characteristics (Module 2). As method for experimental design the Taguchi design was chosen. The statistical analyses of the experiments resulted in an improvement of the fiber of the Xerox-paper. As an important by-product an increased insight in the production process has been encountered. This might be valuable for future experiments.

References

Hauser, John R. and Don Clausing (1988): The House of Quality. Harvard Business Review, May-June, 63-73.

Knight, Thomas P. and Steven H. Kim (1991): A Knowledge System for Integrated Product Design. Journal of Intelligent Manufacturing 2, 17-25.

Phadke, Madhav S. (1989): Quality Engineering Using Robust Design. Prentice Hall, Englewood Cliffs.

Schönleitner, Günther J. (1990): Die Bedeutung der Taguchi- Methode des Experimental Design unter dem Aspekt des Einsatzes von Expertensystemen. Dissertation, Vienna University of Economics.

DUE DATE ASSIGNMENT AND SCHEDULING TO MINIMIZE TARDINESS CRITERIA

H.G. Kahlbacher,
Department of Mathematics,
University of Kaiserslautern,
D-6750 Kaiserslautern, Germany.

We discuss the computational complexity of a combined due date assignment and scheduling problem. In the literature, usually job due dates are treated as externally given data and only the scheduling or sequencing of the jobs is part of the decision.

We use a completely different approach. Now both decisions, assigning due dates to the jobs and schedule them on a single machine or parallel, identical machines, respectively, are included in the optimization problem. Our aim is to avoid tardiness costs and to assign acceptable due dates to each of the customers (jobs). Both goals are conflicting and we try to find a compromise solution by combining both components, tardiness costs and due date assignment costs, to derive a performance measure.

The tardiness cost for a single job j measures the linear deviation of the job completion time and its assigned due date, hence it is rather an earliness/tardiness cost than a pure tardiness cost. It turns out that including earliness costs, too, will ensure that no job is finished early. Formally, we may express the earliness/tardiness cost (ETC) of a single job j by

$$ETC_j = v_j \cdot |C_j - d_j|,$$

where v_j denotes the tardiness cost per unit, C_j the completion time and d_j the assigned due date of job j, respectively.

We discuss four different due date assignment cost models to provide an insight to the resulting scheduling problems. The most simple due date assignment cost model is called *simple model* and takes a multiple of the due date as due date assignment costs (DAC) for each job j,

$$DAC_j^{simple} = u_j \cdot d_j,$$

where u_j denotes the cost per unit for assigning a due dates to job j. The main disadvantage of this simple model is that we may assign a job due date to zero for some of the jobs. Since processing of job j takes a given amount of time, the processing time p_j of job j, assigning a zero due date to the job is unrealistic and it is a priori impossible to meet this due date.

This observation leads to an alternative due date assignment cost model which is called *extended simple model*. In this model we avoid the assignment of too small due dates by introducing additional constraints for the n job due dates, namely

$$DAC_j^{extended\ simple} = u_j \cdot d_j,$$

with the additional contraints

$$d_j \geq p_j,$$

for all jobs j.

But there is another possibility to avoid the assignment of too small due dates which will result in the assignment of more realistic due dates. We call this model *more realistic model*, it introduces due date assignment costs only for due dates exceeding the processing time of the job,

$$DAC_j^{more\ realistic} = u_j \cdot (d_j - p_j)^+,$$

where x^+ denotes the positive part of a number x,

$$x^+ := max\{0, x\}.$$

Then we discuss the most realistic model, where the customer may tell a *lead time* for the due date to be assigned to the job. This lead time, denoted by A_j, of customer (job) j can be seen as largest due date which is accepted by the customer without causing due date assignment costs. A simpler version of this lead time model is discussed in Seidmann, Panwalkar and Smith (1981) [6], where a *constant* lead time is assigned to all jobs. The resulting due date assignment cost model is called *lead time model* and can be expressed by

$$DAC_j^{lead\ time} = u_j \cdot (d_j - A_j)^+.$$

As mentioned before, for a single job j we combine these two components, ETC_j and DAC_j, either by the mean or the maximum to get the combined cost for job j, called $COST_j$,

$$COST_j^{mean} = ETC_j + DAC_j$$

and

$$COST_j^{max} = max\{ETC_j, DAC_j\}.$$

To derive a performance measure for a schedule and the due date assignment decision, we combine all these cost parts for the single jobs either by the mean or the maximum operator. This results in four different objective function models:

$$(\sum - \sum) \qquad \sum_{j=1}^{n} COST_j^{mean},$$

$$(\sum - max) \qquad \sum_{j=1}^{n} COST_j^{max},$$

$$(max - \sum) \qquad \max_{j=1}^{n} COST_j^{mean},$$

and

$$(max - max) \qquad \max_{j=1}^{n} COST_j^{max}.$$

For the basic single machine model from Baker (1974) [1], we derive the following complexity results for the sixteen different due date assignment and sequencing problems.

Performance measure ↓ / *DAC − model* →	*simple*	*more realistic*	*extended simple*	*lead time*
$\sum - \sum$	$O(n \cdot logn)$	$O(n \cdot logn)$	$O(n \cdot logn)$	$NP - hard$
$\sum - max$	$O(n \cdot logn)$	$O(n \cdot logn)$	$NP - hard$	$NP - hard$
$max - \sum$	$O(n \cdot logn)$	$O(n^2)$	$O(n^2)$	$O(n^2)$
$max - max$	$O(n \cdot logn)$	$O(n^2)$	$O(n^2)$	$O(n^2)$

The polynomial algorithms are strongly related to either Smith's ratio rule for $n|1|\ |\sum w_j \cdot C_j$, Smith (1956) [7] for the sum performance measures or Lawler's algorithm for $n|1|\ |f_{max}(C_j)$, Lawler (1973) [3] for the max performance measures. In the latter case it is possible for the simple due date assignment model to explore the special structure of the resulting sequencing problem to derive an O($n \cdot logn$) algorithm, whereas Lawler's algorithm works in O(n^2). For the three NP-hardness results, we use the *weighted tardiness sequencing problem*, $n|1|\ |\sum w_j \cdot (C_j - d_j)^+$, for a reduction. This sequencing problem is proved to be NP-hard by Lenstra, Rinnooy Kan and Brucker (1977) [4].

Extending this approach to systems of parallel, identical machines leads to scheduling problems which are NP-hard for all sixteen different models. For the reduction we use either the $n|2|P|\sum w_j \cdot C_j$

problem which is NP-hard, see e.g. Rinnooy Kan (1976) [5] or the *makespan problem for parallel, identical machines*, $n|m|P|C_{max}$, which is proved to be NP-hard by Garey and Johnson (1979) [2].

But it is possible to solve the max- problems on a single machine polynomially, if we include *job precedence constraints*. This is due to the fact that Lawler's algorithm, Lawler (1973) [3], may be used, even if precedence relations are considered for the jobs.

With this classification of the combined due date assignment and scheduling problem we provide several polynomial algorithms and the basis for heuristic approaches in case of the NP-hard problems. This may help both, researchers and practitioners, to make use of this combined decision approach.

References

[1] Baker K.R. 1974, 'Introduction to Sequencing and Scheduling', Wiley.

[2] Garey M.R. and Johnson D.S. 1979, 'Computers and Intractability - A Guide to the Theory of NP-Completeness', Freeman.

[3] Lawler E.L. 1973, 'Optimal Sequencing of a Single Machine Subject to Precedence Constraints', Management Science 19, 5, 544-546.

[4] Lenstra J.K., Rinnooy Kan A.H.G. and Brucker B. 1977, 'Complexity of Machine Scheduling Problems', Annals of Discrete Mathematics 1, 343-362.

[5] Rinnooy Kan A.H.G. 1976, 'Machine Scheduling Problems', Nijhoff.

[6] Seidmann A., Panwalkar S.S. and Smith M.L. 1981, 'Optimal Assignment of Due Dates for a Single Processor Scheduling Problem', Int. J. Prod. Res. 19, 4, 393-399.

[7] Smith W.E. 1956, 'Various Optimizers for Single-Stage Production', Naval Research Logistics Quarterly 3, 1, 59-66.

Towards a Generalization of Production Theory "Soft" Production Functions Using Fuzzy Set Theory

Jürgen Klein

(Universität Köln), Severinswall 52, D-W-5000 Köln 41 (priv.)

Production functions are formal models of the relations between the output and input quantities of a production system. Classical production theory has constrained its focus on industrial production of material goods where problems of uncertainty or vagueness are often secondary. Only some few extensions were made by using probability theory (e.g. [3]).

The paper presents a new model of a "soft" production function by using *fuzzy set theory*. This "vague" representation is closer to reality than classical functions. This holds especially for the case of *information production* where vagueness and uncertainty are more important issues than in material production.

Generalization of traditional production theory is obtained in two dimensions:

- fuzzy production functions contain classical "crisp" functions as special case;
- fuzzy production functions are beneficially applicable to information production which extends the scope of production theory on immaterial goods.

Static Crisp Production Function

Figure 1 shows an input-output-model of a production system. Nodes denote production units i, $i = 1, \ldots, n$ which produce an output and consume inputs. Flows of input and output are represented by arcs. For more details see [4].

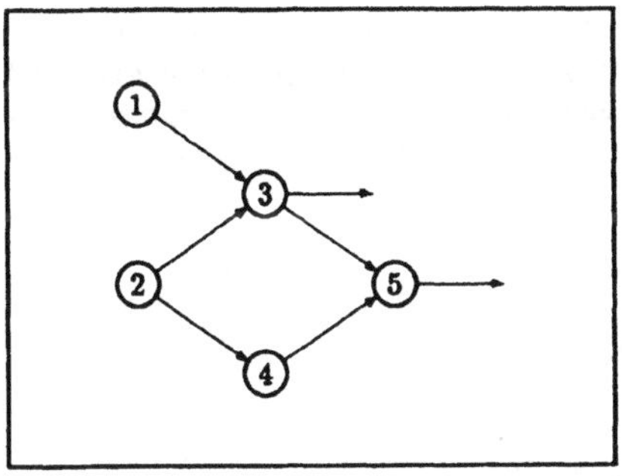

Figure 1: Input-output-model

The total output quantity of production unit i, r_i, equals the deliveries r_{ij} from i to all other units j of the system, augmented by its output x_i leaving the system (marketed output):

$$r_i = \sum_j r_{ij} + x_i \tag{1}$$

The relationship between output and input quantities is assumed to be linear–limitational (LEONTIEF–Model) with constant production coefficients a_{ij}:

$$r_{ij} = a_{ij} \cdot r_j \qquad a_{ij} = \text{const.} \tag{2}$$

An aggregation of (1) and (2) over all i, j leads to matrix equation (3) as a static crisp multi-stage/multi-product production function:

$$\begin{pmatrix} r_1 \\ \vdots \\ r_n \end{pmatrix} = \begin{pmatrix} a_{11} & \cdots & a_{1n} \\ \vdots & \ddots & \vdots \\ a_{n1} & \cdots & a_{nn} \end{pmatrix} \cdot \begin{pmatrix} r_1 \\ \vdots \\ r_n \end{pmatrix} + \begin{pmatrix} x_1 \\ \vdots \\ x_n \end{pmatrix} \tag{3}$$

Static Fuzzy Production Function

Equation (3) will be fuzzified in two dimensions:

- fuzzy production coefficients (e.g. to model vague knowledge about input quantities for a given output),
- fuzzy input-output structure (e.g. to model vague knowledge about the constituents of the output and the required types of input).

Fuzzy Production Coefficients

In reality, relationships between input and output quantities often cannot precisely be determined. E.g., when an author starts the preparation of a paper for a symposium (which is a case of information production, the paper being the information product) he has no accurate knowledge on how much labor will be required to complete the paper.

This can be represented by *fuzzy numbers* ([2], [5]) or *fuzzy intervals* ([2]) as production coefficients. Fuzzy numbers are convex normalized fuzzy sets on the set of real numbers $\Re$ with exactly one element x_0 (*fuzzy numbers*) with a membership value of $\mu(x_0) = 1$. Fuzzy numbers of the *L-R* type are represented by the mean value m, left and right spreads α and β and the functions L and R which describe the shape of the membership function left and right of the mean value. Thus, a fuzzy production coefficient $\tilde{a}_{ij}$ is denoted as

$$\tilde{a}_{ij} = (m; \alpha; \beta)_{LR} \tag{4}$$

This is analogously applicable to fuzzy intervals.

Fuzzy Input-Output Structure

In information production, the constituents of the output and the required inputs are often only vaguely known. E.g., an author starting the preparation of a paper for a symposium often does not precisely know which chapters will be the elements of the paper (constituents of information output) and which informations have to be gathered in order to complete the paper (required types of input).

In the fuzzy model, each production unit (node) has a fuzzy set of inputs (arcs). Each output (output arcs) is a member of a fuzzy output set. Thus, each arc ij in the graph can be denoted with a membership value z_{ij} representing the fuzzy membership of the output of unit i to the set of inputs of unit j. E.g., $z_{ij} = .4$ means that the output of unit i PERHAPS is an input of j. Analogously, $z_{X_i} = .9$ says that the output of unit i MOST LIKELY is a required output of the system.

For the manager of production unit i, besides the membership values z_{ij} on a micro level, it is interesting to know how the membership values of the whole system aggregate to a resulting membership on the macro level z_i. This number in general is different from z_{ij} because i delivers its output to several other units with different values z_{ij}, and because z_{ij} says nothing about the membership values of the unit outputs located later in the chain of production.

Two operators have to be used expressing how parallel membership values (operator $\oplus$) and membership values along a chain (operator $\odot$) are aggregated. For the ease of understanding the max-operator ($\oplus$) resp. min-operator ($\odot$) can be used. Experimental and empirical research have to show if other operators (e.g. parametric adaptable operators, [5]) better justify human behavior.

Applying the above mentioned a twofold *fuzzy static production function* is obtained:

$$\begin{pmatrix} \tilde{r}_1 \\ \vdots \\ \tilde{r}_n \end{pmatrix} = \begin{pmatrix} \tilde{a}_{11} & \cdots & \tilde{a}_{1n} \\ \vdots & \ddots & \vdots \\ \tilde{a}_{n1} & \cdots & \tilde{a}_{nn} \end{pmatrix} \cdot \begin{pmatrix} \tilde{r}_1 \\ \vdots \\ \tilde{r}_n \end{pmatrix} + \begin{pmatrix} \tilde{x}_1 \\ \vdots \\ \tilde{x}_n \end{pmatrix} \tag{5}$$

$$\begin{pmatrix} z_1 \\ \vdots \\ z_n \end{pmatrix} = \begin{pmatrix} z_{11} & \cdots & z_{1n} \\ \vdots & \ddots & \vdots \\ z_{n1} & \cdots & z_{nn} \end{pmatrix} \odot \begin{pmatrix} z_1 \\ \vdots \\ z_n \end{pmatrix} \oplus \begin{pmatrix} z_{X_1} \\ \vdots \\ z_{X_n} \end{pmatrix} \tag{6}$$

(5) models the flow of fuzzy input and output quantities, whereas (6) represents the fuzziness of the system. Matrice algebra allows the elegant similarity of the two equations.

Fuzzy Dynamic Production Function

For paractical applications (e.g. PPC systems) it is most useful to incorporate the concept of *time* into the model. Here, besides the flow of goods and the inventory changes over time it interesting to know *how fuzziness changes over time*. In the beginning of an information production process we are facing a highly vague situation. After completion of the process there is complete information of what has happened, i.e. vagueness has disappeared during the process.

It is successively incoming *information* which gives more and more certainty about the production situation. Information with impact on the membership values of the model — which express fuzziness — is called *strucutural information*. Its linkage to the fuzzy variables of the system has to be mapped in a dynamic production function.

The deterministic flow of goods over time has been modeled in [1]. A fuzzy dynamic production function additionally has to incorporate the fuzzy flow of goods (e.g. by using *fuzzy numbers* as in equation (5)) and the dependencies between the fuzziness of the production structure (expressed in equation (6)) and the availability of the incoming structural information.

Outlook

Through application of fuzzy production functions production planning models can be used to find "optimal uncertainty" of vague production situations. Production planning and control (PPC) of information production (e.g. consulting, engineering), still rather intuitive, could become rationalized.

References

[1] Küpper, Hans-Ulrich, Interdependenzen zwischen Produktionstheorie und der Organisation des Produktionsprozesses, Berlin 1980

[2] Rommelfanger, Heinrich, Entscheiden bei Unschärfe, Berlin Heidelberg New York 1988

[3] Schwarze, Jochen, Diskussion eines einfachen stochastischen Produktionsmodells, in: ZfbF 24 (1972), S.666–681

[4] Schweitzer, Marcell / Küpper, Hans-Ulrich, Produktions- und Kostentheorie der Unternehmung, Reinbek bei Hamburg 1974

[5] Zimmermann, Hans J., Fuzzy Set Theory — And Its Applications, Boston Dordrecht Lancaster 1986

A SOFTWARE FOR MULTICRITERIA SELECTION PROBLEMS IN PRODUCTION SCHEDULING

Marc J.A. Lescrenier
ARBED Information Systems s.a.
19, Avenue de la Liberté
L-2930 Luxembourg

Description of the industrial problem

The new rolling mill of ARBED Dudelange is one of the major assets of the Luxembourg steel industry. It is based on Continuous Variable Crown technology which allows for optimal rolling of very thin sheet.

Given the coils sequence the rolling mill is directly controlled by the process computer in view of the thickness to reach.

The choice of the coils sequence remained to be automated. This lead the production engineers of ARBED Dudelange to propose the search and development of a software that would address this question.

The coils are selected amongst the coils available in the stock. Each coil is associated with a set of characteristics such as

- its weight, width, post-rolling thickness, ...
- its post-rolling treatment
- its ultimate delay at the CVC rolling mill

and other informations that are production decisions dependent such as

- coil to produce during the next eight hours,
- coil not to be selected in the next selection process.

Production requires the establishment of the sequence of coils that are to be produced during the next eight hours. A list of criteria that are to be applied for determining the coils sequence is used for this purpose. Criteria of the following type are commonly used:

(a) the selected coils amount to a total of 2000 tons,

(b) 30 percent of the selected coils are to be galvanized,

(c) if a coil is selected in a given class of width, then at least 4 coils are selected in this class,

(d) the most urgent coils are selected in order to respect the delivery delay,

but this list is periodically revised to reflect new production decisions.

Given this information, the required automated tool should select a list of coils which is then scheduled using simple rules based on the width and thickness of the material to produce. A multicriteria scheduling tool [1] can also be used for this purpose in cases of more sophisticated ordering criteria.

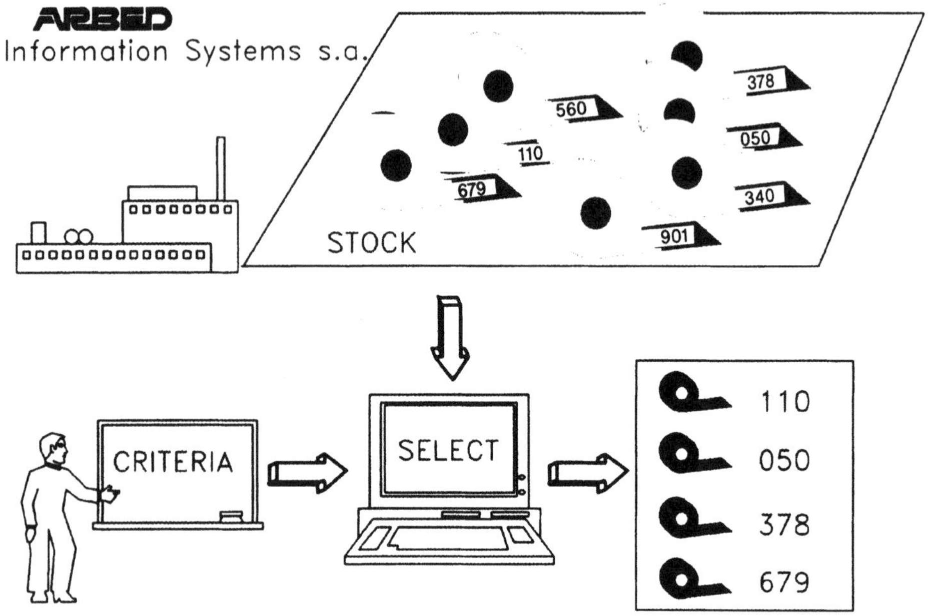

Figure 1: the automated multicriteria selection process

Multiple competing selection criteria should be taken into account using user defined priorities for each criterion.

Identical coils (in the sense of the above characteristics) that are to be produced for a given customer are gathered together and define a so-called order unit. The selection tool should provide the number (possibly zero) of coils selected in each order unit.

Features of the implemented tool

The selection problem we consider here is not confined to the scheduling of the Dudelange CVC rolling mill. Problems of this type are often encountered in the context of production scheduling as it is indeed observed in practice at other production plants of ARBED s.a. But selection can also play an important role in other activities such as sampling techniques in statistics.

This is why the implemented tool developed by ARBED Information Systems s.a. addresses a generalized selection problem. This tool is currently being integrated in the general on-line planning and tracking tool used at ARBED plants so that it can be used, if required, at every production step.

The generalized problem is that of selecting a set of objects among a population of objects classified in families. Each object of a family shares the parameters associated with the family. Real or alphanumeric parameters are permitted. The set of selection criteria is specified by instanciating predefined selection criteria such as, for instance,

(a) the sum of the values of the i-th real parameter for the selected objects is greater than NMIN and smaller than NMAX,

(b) the percentage of selected objects (in terms of the i-th real parameter) whose j-th parameter is equal to VALUE is greater than NMIN and smaller than NMAX,

(c) if an object is selected in a class defined by a given value of the i-th alphanumeric parameter, then at least N objects are selected in this class,

(d) minimise the sum of the i-th real parameter.

Multiple competing selection criteria are taken into account using user defined priorities for each criterion.

The implemented tool takes the form of a FORTRAN 77 routine. Its input parameters are the population of objects and the selection criteria together with their priorities. As output the routine provides the number (possibly zero) of objects selected in each family.

A more detailed specification of the selection routine can be found in [2].

Description of the method

The generalized selection problem belongs to the class of multicriteria optimization problems. A goal programming model has been chosen for dealing with conflicting criteria. In these now well established techniques in multicriteria optimization (see [3] and [5] for instance) the criteria are not considered as absolute constraints but are instead associated with target levels for achievement and relative priorities on achieving these levels. A solution that comes as close as possible to the targets is then searched for.

All criteria of the model lead to linear equations. The variables representing the number of objects selected in each family must receive integer values only. Criterion (c) above gives rise to two equations involving an associated binary variable for each class.

The goal programming model consequently belongs to the class of mixed integer linear programming problems and is solved using a branch and bound algorithm (see [3]).

Results of industrial experimentation

The model has been experimented on a set of problems proposed by the production engineers of Dudelange. These problems consist in selections of about 100 coils among 500 coils (from 150 order units) in the stock.

The model then involves a set of real variables, 150 integer variables for the selection decision, and 16 binary variables introduced by the use of a criterion of type (c).

Experimentation has shown that about 30 minutes of CPU time are required to obtain the first integer solution of this problem on a VAX 8530 under VMS. This has been considered unacceptable in the context of the on-line production tracking tool even if this first integer solution was generally very near the optimal one.

The integrity constraint on the 150 selection variables has then been ignored but the one on the binary variables is necessarily kept active. The same mixed integer linear programming solver is used for solving the new model. A rounding procedure is applied to the selection variables if required.

This approach already quite acceptable in the context of goal programming has proved to be extremely adequate in the case we consider. Indeed, experimentation shows that very few of the selection variables are not at integer values at the optimum of the new model. Moreover, the rounding procedure results in insignificant changes in the criteria achievement.

A satisfactory selection proposal is now delivered by the new model in no more than 30 seconds CPU.

The setting of the relative priorities for the criteria that are used appears to be fairly straightforward according to the production engineers. In worst cases, the model is used two or three times successively in order to find the adequate compromise. This process is facilitated by the use of an interactive menu of the on-line production tracking tool for defining the selection parameters. Complementary mathematical interactive procedures [4] designed for approaching the best compromise in view of the decision taker could also be implemented at low additional costs if required.

Acknowledgments

The author would like to thank R. Bausch, A. Goy and M. Pauly for their constructive remarks when defining the functionalities of the selection tool together with T. Lamouline for his careful implementation of the software.

References

[1] Bausch Raymond, "A multicriteria scheduling tool using a Branch and Bound algorithm", presented at Decision Support Systems, IFORS, Bruges, March 1991, ARBED s.a., L-2930 Luxembourg, 1991.

[2] Lescrenier Marc J.A., "Sélection multi-critères: manuel d'utilisation et d'exploitation", référence SC.DE.LM.MANU.02, ARBED s.a., L-2930 Luxembourg, 1991.

[3] Ravindran A., Phillips Don T. and Solberg James J., "Operations Research: principles and practice", John Wiley & Sons, New York, 1987.

[4] Vanderpooten Daniel and Vincke Philippe, "Description and analysis of some representative interactive multicriteria procedures", Math. Comput. Modelling, Vol. 12, No. 10/11, pp. 1221-1238, 1989.

[5] Zanakis Stelios H. and Gupta Sushil K., "A categorized bibliographic survey of goal programming", OMEGA Int J. of Mgmt Sci., Vol 13, No. 3, pp. 211-222, 1985.

FRACTIONAL PIECEWISE LINEAR OPTIMIZATION

Ivan Meško
University of Maribor, Department of Economics
YU-62000 Maribor, Razlagova 14, Slovenija

In business optimization, the piecewise linear programming problem arises [1]. When taking into account the investments, the cost is a discontinuous piecewise linear function of decision variables. In this paper, a transformation of a fractional piecewise linear programming problem into a linear mixed integer programming problem is described. This transformation can be used while maximizing the quotient of the revenue and the cost. A similar transformation can be applied when a constraint contains this quotient.

The piecewise linear function can be expressed in the form,

$$f(z) = \sum_{k=1}^{n} c_k x_k + \sum_{k=1}^{n} d_k u_k \tag{1}$$

subject to zero-one variables u_k and,

$$0 \leq x_k \leq a_k u_k, \qquad a_k > 0, \qquad k = 1, \dots, n \tag{2}$$

$$x_k - a_k u_{k+1} \geq 0, \qquad k = 1, \dots, n-1 \tag{3}$$

$$z = a_0 + x_1 + \cdots + x_n$$

where a_k, c_k and d_k are given parameters.

Let us consider the programming problem,

$$maximize \frac{\sum_j f_j(z_j)}{q_0 + \sum_j g_j(z_j)} \tag{4}$$

with the following constraints,

$$\sum_j h_{ij}(z_j) \geq b_i, \qquad i \in I \tag{5}$$

where $f_j : \Re \to \Re$, $g_j : \Re \to \Re$ and $h_{ij} : \Re \to \Re$ are piecewise linear functions. Each piecewise linear function in (4) and (5) can be substituted by function (1) subject to (2) and (3). Consequently, the following programming problem is obtained,

$$maximize \frac{\sum_j c_j x_j + \sum_k d_k u_k}{q_0 + \sum_j q_j x_j + \sum_k r_k u_k}$$

subject to nonnegative variables x_j, zero-one variables u_k and,

$$\sum_j a_{ij} x_j + \sum_k p_{ik} u_k \geq b_i, \qquad i \in I \cup J.$$

Here, J is the set of indices of the transformed constraints (2) and (3).

If,

$$q_0 + \sum_j q_j x_j + \sum_k r_k u_k \geq s > 0$$

the Charnes-Cooper transformation,

$$(q_0 + \sum_j q_j x_j + \sum_k r_k u_k)t = 1$$

$$t x_j = y_j, \qquad \forall j$$

where $t > 0$, can be used. This results in,

$$maximize \sum_j c_j y_j + \sum_k d_k t u_k$$

subject to nonnegative variables y_j and t, zero-one variables u_k and,

$$t q_0 + \sum_j q_j y_j + \sum_k r_k t u_k = 1$$

$$\sum_j a_{ij} y_j + \sum_k p_{ik} u_k t \geq b_i t, \qquad i \in I \cup J.$$

The nonnegative product tu_k can be replaced by v_k subject to,

$$t = v_k + w_k \qquad 0 \leq s v_k \leq u_k \qquad 0 \leq s w_k \leq 1 - u_k. \tag{6}$$

Using this result, the programming problem (4) and (5) is transformed into the linear mixed integer programming problem,

$$maximize \sum_j c_j y_j + \sum_k d_k v_k$$

subject to (6) for each zero-one variable and,

$$q_0 t + \sum_j q_j y_j + \sum_k r_k v_k = 1$$

$$\sum_j a_{ij} y_j + \sum_k p_{ik} v_k - b_i t \geq 0, \qquad i \in I \cup J.$$

Several computer programs are available for solving such a programming problem [2].

References

[1] Meško, I. : Nonsmooth and Nonconvex Models of the Business Process. Ekonomska analiza XXII (1988), 63-80.

[2] Suhl, U.H. : Solving Large-Scale Mixed Integer Programms with Fixed Charge Variables. Mathematical Programming, (1985), 165-182.

A Decomposition Method for the Approximate Evaluation of an Unreliable Kanban Production System

Harald Schmidbauer / Angi Rösch
Seminar für Angewandte Stochastik
Universität München
Akademiestr. 1/IV
D - 8000 München 40

1 Introduction

In the present paper, we consider a stochastic model of an unreliable one-card Kanban production system. The basic idea of this system is that several processing units (machines) are arranged in series, workpieces move sequentially from one unit to the next upon request. The request is signalled by a Kanban card. There is a finite capacity buffer behind each machine. The processing times at all units are assumed to be constant and equal. Randomness enters as the machines may break down. Time until repair is geometrically distributed. We present a method of analysing a serial Kanban system of k units via decomposition to k single-unit Kanban systems.

2 A Stochastic Model of a Kanban System

The system with which we will deal consists of k stages in series (fig. 1). Stage i consists of machine M_i and buffer B_i, which has a finite capacity $N_i \geq 1$. Workpieces from outside the production system enter M_1 for being processed and will be stored in B_1 until requested by M_2 for processing. This mechanism continues downstream until the workpiece reaches B_k. A demand will be satisfied if B_k is not empty; in this case, a workpiece is taken from B_k, and a new production in M_k is triggered. The supply from outside to M_1 is inexhaustible. The following assumptions are the pull system version of standard assumptions (see [4]).

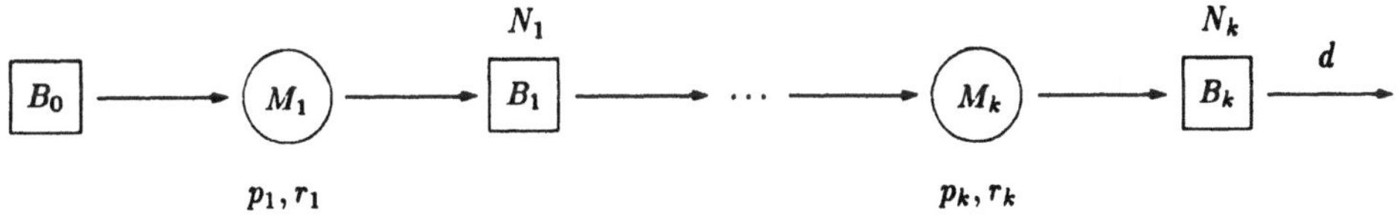

Figure 1: The k-stage Kanban line L

We will assume that all the machines have constant service times which are equal to one time unit. Denote by $n_i(t)$ the number of workpieces in buffer B_i at epoch t ($t = 0, 1, \ldots$). Machine M_i is called blocked during $(t, t+1]$ if $n_i(t) = N_i$ and starved if $n_{i-1}(t) = 0$. The operating condition of M_i during $(t, t+1]$ is denoted by $\alpha_i(t+1)$. If M_i is neither starved nor blocked it may break down at the beginning of $(t, t+1]$ with probability p_i; in this case, $\alpha_i(t+1) = 0$. If M_i is broken at the beginning of $(t-1, t]$, it will be repaired within one time unit with probability r_i, which means a transition from $\alpha_i(t) = 0$ to $\alpha_i(t+1) = 1$. At the beginning of $(t, t+1]$, there is a demand (i.e., $de(t+1) = 1$) with probability d which will take one workpiece from B_k if $n_k(t) > 0$, or it will be lost (if $n_k(t) = 0$). With probability $1 - d$, $de(t+1) = 0$.
This system is called a pull system because a production in M_i takes place only upon request from B_i. The state of the production line at epoch t can hence be described by a random vector

$$\vec{s}(t) = (n_1(t), \ldots, n_k(t), \alpha_1(t), \ldots, \alpha_k(t), de(t)),$$

and $(\vec{s}(t))_{t=0,1,\ldots}$ is a Markov chain with state space

$$S = \{(n_1,\ldots,n_k,\alpha_1,\ldots,\alpha_k,de):\ 0 \le n_i \le N_i,\ \alpha_i, de \in \{0,1\}\}.$$

If the buffers are neither empty nor full, it holds that

$$n_i(t+1) = n_i(t) + \alpha_i(t+1) - \alpha_{i+1}(t+1) \quad (i = 1,\ldots,k),$$

where $\alpha_{k+1}(t+1) = de(t+1)$. Obviously, the number of elements in S is equal to $2^{k+1} \cdot \prod_{i=1}^{k}(N_i+1)$, and it is practically impossible to calculate steady state probabilities if $k \ge 3$. It is, however, easy to compute them with a matrix partitioning technique (as in [5]) in the case $k = 1$.
We are interested in

i) the long-run average number of workpieces in buffer B_i,

ii) the long-run percentage of satisfied demand.

3 Relation to a $k+1$-stage Push System

There is flow from the final buffer B_k if there is a demand (i.e., $de = 1$) that will be satisfied. Therefore, it is possible to interpret the demand in the pull system as an additional machine in a push system which breaks down with probability $1-d$ and is repaired with probability d (cf. [2]). This idea, however, does not not lead to a starting point for a steady-state analysis because the sets of transient states in both systems are different: The last machine in the push system cannot break down if starved, whereas there may be a demand in the pull system even if the final buffer is empty. Hence, we will not try to apply a decomposition algorithm for push systems (see, e.g., [1], [3]), but develop an analogous algorithm for the pull system.

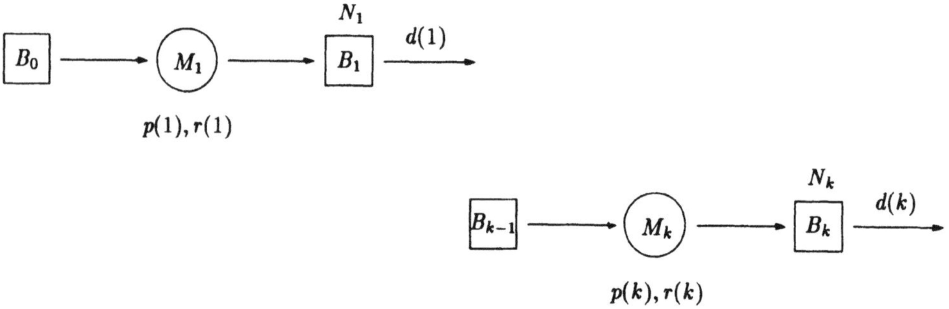

Figure 2: Decomposition of line L to k single-stage Kanban lines $L(1), \ldots, L(k)$

4 Decomposition

We will now decompose the k-stage pull system L to k single-stage pull systems $L(1),\ldots,L(k)$ in such a way that some quantities of interest will remain unchanged. Each single-stage system $L(i)$ with parameters $p(i), r(i), d(i)$ corresponds to a pair M_i, B_i in L, as shown in fig. 2. An important quantity is the actual throughput of machine M_i which is defined as

$$E_i := P\{\alpha_i(t+1) = 1, n_{i-1}(t) > 0, n_i(t) < N_i\}.$$

First, we observe that E_i must be the same for all machines. The long-run fraction of satisfied demand is then E_k/d. The problem is that E_k is unknown. To carry out the decomposition, we must find the parameters $p(i), r(i), d(i)$ subject to the following conditions:

- The actual throughput in each $L(i)$ should equal the actual throughput in the system L.
- The probability that buffer B_i is either empty or full should be the same in $L(i)$ and L.

We assume further that the probability that M_i is blocked and starved at the same time is close to zero. It can then be shown that

$$\frac{p(i)}{r(i)} + \frac{1}{d(i-1)} = \frac{p_i}{r_i} + \frac{1}{E(i-1)}, \tag{1}$$

where $E(i-1)$ is a preliminary quantity and denotes the actual throughput of $L(i-1)$. This equation is similar to what is called flow rate / idle time relationship in [3]. Equation (1) permits the calculation of $p(i)/r(i)$, given the parameters of $L(i-1)$. By modifying the notion of breakdown of a machine in $L(i)$, it can be shown that

$$r(i) = r_i\left(1 - \frac{r(i)}{p(i)}\frac{p_s(i-1)}{E(i-1)}\right) + r(i-1)\frac{r(i)}{p(i)}\frac{p_s(i-1)}{E(i-1)}, \tag{2}$$

where $p_s(i-1)$ denotes the probability that B_{i-1} is empty in $L(i-1)$. Equation (2) permits the calculation of $r(i)$ and therefore $p(i)$.

5 The Algorithm

Equation (1) serves two purposes: First, calculation of $p(i)/r(i)$, given the parameters of $L(i-1)$ (as described), second, calculation of $d(i-1)$, given the parameters of $L(i)$ (subject to the assumption $E(i-1) = E(i)$). This is expressed in the following algorithm:

Initialisation: $r(1) := r_1, p(1) := p_1, d(i) := \dfrac{r_{i+1}}{r_{i+1} + p_{i+1}}$ $(i = 1, \ldots, k-1)$, $d(k) := d$.
Step 1 ("forward"): For $i = 2, \ldots, k$, calculate $r(i), p(i)$ by means of (1), (2).
Step 2 ("backward"): For $i = k-1, \ldots, 1$, calculate $d(i)$ by means of (1).
Step 3 (test of accuracy): Stop if $\max_{i,j} |E(i) - E(j)| < \varepsilon$.

References

[1] Dallery, Y., David, R., Xie, X.-L.: Approximate Analysis of Transfer Lines with Unreliable Machines and Finite Buffers. *IEEE Transactions on Automatic Control* **34** (1989), 943–953.

[2] Deleersnyder, J.-L., Hodgson, T. J., Muller (-Malek), H., O'Grady, P. J.: Kanban Controlled Pull Systems: An Analytic Approach. *Management Science* **15** (1989), 1079–1091.

[3] Gershwin, S. B.: An Efficient Decomposition Method for the Approximate Evaluation of Tandem Queues with Finite Storage Space and Blocking. *Operations Research* **35** (1987), 291–305.

[4] Gershwin, S. B., Schick, I. C.: Modelling and Analysis of Three-Stage Transfer Lines with Unreliable Machines and Finite Buffers. *Operations Research* **31** (1983), 354–380.

[5] Lal, R., Bhat, U. N.: Reduced Systems in Markov Chains and Their Applications in Queueing Theory. *Queueing Systems* **2** (1987), 147–172.

MONITORING FACE MILLING USING FUZZY LOGIC

Gabriella, Szöllôsi
Department of Production Engineering
Budapest Technical University
BME, H-1521 Budapest

INTRODUCTION

Cutting process monitoring is mainly aimed at preventing undesirable damage to the machining system components caused by the failure of cutting tools. Additionally in order to optimize adaptive control, tool wear and the changes in the process should continuously be sensed. The purpose of our monitorimg system is to provide continuous report of the tool system and the cutting process.

Certain industrial processes can be monitored and controlled with better results by an experienced operator than by conventional diagnostic and control systems. The difficulty is that the strategies employed by an operator use qualitative rather than quantitative termes since this is the way human beings make decisions. We tried to simulate this decision making using fuzzy logic.

THE ALGORITHM

The aim of this section is to outline our application of fuzzy logic to process monitoring. We drew up 35 rules of following structure:

> if MEANFORCE is VERYSMALL and VARIANCE is VERYBIG and MAXIMUM is SMALL then our diagnosis: ENTERING with 0.8% chance or CUTOFF with 0.2% chance.

All the terms MEANFORCE (mean of the Fx force component in the feed direction over 1.5 revolutions), VARIANCE (or to be more precise the ratio of the variance and the mean over the same time) and the MAXIMUM (maximum of the Fx component over the given time) had the subjective fuzzy values: VERYSMALL, SMALL, MEDIUM, BIG, VERYBIG. The definitions are:

	1 .	2.	3.	4.	5.	classes
VB	1.0	0.6	0.0	0.0	0.0	
B	0.3	1.0	0.3	0.0	0.0	
M	0.0	0.3	1.0	0.3	0.0	
S	0.0	0.0	0.3	1.0	0.3	
VS	0.0	0.0	0.0	0.6	1.0	

The diagnosis is "only" probabilistic; nevertheless it is handled in a fuzzy way. Let us assume for a moment that the diagnosis is deterministic and the extended fuzzy definitions are:

classes	1.	2.	3.	4.	5.	6.	7.	8.	9.	10.
1. diag.	1	0	0	0	0	0	0	0	0	0
...										
10. diag.	0	0	0	0	0	0	0	0	0	1

These outputs were NORMAL, UNSTABLE, ENTERING, BOREHOLE, WARN, etc. Now one can build the fuzzy inference matrix (a similar application [1]). Since we had probabilistic rules as well, two rules had to be taken into consideration (instead of one), which had previously been scaled by the probability percents before. Thus we used a 4 dimension matrix when monitoring.

EXPERIMENTAL RESULTS

The experimewntal setting contains a UF22 horizontal milling machine, a KISTLER 9281B piezoelectric three component force sensor, a KISTLER 9863A charge amplifier, a GOULD 1600 digital storage oscilloscope and an IBM PC. The results showed 70% success, and furthermore they were very informative and graded. In some cases they revealed incorrect or missing rules.

[1] Zhu, Shumshreduddin, Bollinger, Control of Machine Tools, Annals of the CIRP, 31/1/1982, pp. 347-352.

THE INFLUENCE OF SERVICE QUALITY ON THE CUSTOMERS' BEHAVIOUR

Sabine Thümmel
Hochschule für Verkehrswesen Dresden
Bereich Verkehrssystemtheorie und Qualitätssicherung
Friedrich-List-Platz 1 / PF 82
D-O-8010 Dresden

The importance of quality increases in all fields of life. Many products and services are offered with an information about their quality. The customers are paying attention to the quality of a product or service more and more.
People often use the expression "quality", but do we really know the customers' expectations regarding quality? Do we know the influences or the effects of quality on the customers' behaviour or can we only speak about quality?
I think it is necessary to make investigations regarding the influence of quality on the customers' behaviour - especially the service quality - we should also use mathematical methods. I want to demonstrate some results of my research work regarding the effects of transportation quality on the behaviour of the customers.
The increasing production and the growing mobility of the people are generating more and more transport. Some results of the increasing transport are traffic jams, parking problems and a growing environmental pollution. What can be done?
Isolated solutions - the improvment of an unique means of transport - are able to decrease some effects of the present situation of transport only. But they cannot change the causes of the present situation.
A solution of these problems is only possible by a complex thinking - a new thinking - about the whole system of transport.
It is necessary for the transport companies to work together, to cooperate. If they work against, they all together will lose more and more customers. Transport is an essential part of our life. Trips to work, business or holiday trips are taking up much of our time.

So one can say that quality of transport produces quality of life.
The aim of the transport companies (or in generally the service companies) should be the satisfaction of the customers. This is only possible by cooperation.
If a traveller wants to make a trip from place A to place B in generally he has more then one opportunity.
He can go the whole way by his own car. In this case he is relatively independent, but he must expect traffic jams. This is not the best solution with regard to the environmental pollution.
An other opportunity is to go by the own car, a rented car or a public means of transport to the railway then by train to a railway near the destination and then by a rented car or a public means of transport to the destination. It seems to be a good variant, but often in practice there are many problems. The traveller has to wait for the next means of transport, he often gets not enough information. The delays grow more and more if the first means of transport is not in time.
The whole trip is *one single service product* in the oppinion of the traveller - or a potential customer of a transport company. He will be dissatisfied with the whole trip if one part of the trip has a poor quality.
With regard to the aim to solve the present transport problems it is necessary to develop such a transport system that a traveller *wants* to use the public means of transport. In this way it is also possible to improve the environmental problems which are connected with the transport. However, that is only possible by a new quality in dealing with the customers.
Therefore it has to be developed a complex system of transport including quality aspects and the cooperation of the service companies.
It is necessary to make theoretical investigations about the construction and organisation of such a system.
It begins with the structure of the transportation network. There are some mathematical models describing the transport flows or the distribution of various means of transportation.

These models are a help in the planning of a transport network and it's use. There are some attempts including quality aspects into the modelling, e.g. the attractivity of a route or a means of transport. But in most cases has included only one parameter of quality.
As quality is playing an increasing role in our life, the models have to include quality aspects also. But the quality cannot be limited to one parameter. Many investigations are necessary to find out the relations between the different quality parameters.
The models have to include quality parameters regarding the transportation network and the construction of the points of intersection.
Because the customer is interested in the whole product - the whole trip - the models must include the combination of more than one service company.
The main reason for decision on a means of transport is quality. It should be possible to exercise an influence on the further behaviour of the customers by using the findings of these investigations.

References

/1/ Bär, M. and Fischer, K. and Hertel, G. :
Leistungsfähigkeit - Qualität - Zuverlässigkeit
Transpress Verlag, Berlin, 1988

/2/ Fischer, K. and Hertel, G. :
Dienstleistungsqualität versus Produktqualität ?
(to be published)

/3/ integrated traffic safety manegement in urban areas
report prepared by an OECD scientific expert group
OECD, Paris, 1990

/4/ Mäcke, P.A. and Switaiski, B. :
Untersuchungen der Verkehrsteilung im Güterverkehr zur Verbesserung durch Quantifizierung vorliegender Modellansätze;
Forschung Straßenbau und Straßenverkehrstechnik, Heft 437, Bonn, 1985

MULTIATTRIBUTE DECISION ANALYSIS: THE ANALYTIC HIERARCHY PROCESS

Karl Weber
Department of Business Administration
University of Giessen
Licher Strasse 74, D-6300 Giessen

Multiattribute decision methodologies are gaining recognition. Among the various approaches the Analytic Hierarchy Process (AHP) represents a powerful means for systematic and easily understood project assessment. In the area of business administration AHP is especially suited for the analysis and/or justification of CIM (Computer Integrated Manufacturing) systems.

The AHP method is characterized by a multi-stage approach, whereby the first and most important step aims at a precise definition of the system being studied as well as a hierarchically structured list of relevant evaluation criteria (attributes). The top level (focus) consists of only one element which reflects the overall objective of the system. The following layers systematically lead to groups of logically related attributes and subattributes (tree structure). The next steps relate to the allocation of priority weights to the attributes within each level of the hierarchy. The weights have to be determined successively by pairwise comparison of the relevant criteria, whereby the use of matrices is highly recommended. Furthermore, a standardized evaluation scheme (1 = equally important/preferred; 3 = weakly more important; 5 = strongly more important; 7 = very strongly more important; 9 = absolutely more important) should be used. The next step involves the stepwise computation of the eigenvector of each basic evaluation matrix, and then normalizing it to sum to 1. Similar calculations have to be made for the matrices relating to higher levels in the system hierarchy. Finally the composite weights have to be determined by aggregating the weights through the hierarchy. This evaluation process has to be made for each path leading from the top level through specific bifurcations to the lowest level of the tree and by multiplying the weights along each segment of the path. The final result is a normalized vector of the overall priority weights (score) of the system being studied. Similar studies can be made on the basis of modified weights (sensibility analysis) or for alternative (e.g. existing) systems.

The calculations to be made for AHP studies will usually prove to be fairly complex and they will call for the use of special software packages. Such programs will usually give way to additional tests (such as the calculation of special indicators of consistency in making pairwise comparisons). One of the most valuable software programs is AutoMan (Decision Support Software for Automated Manufacturing Investments). The following example illustrated the AHP methodology with respect to a CIM justification case.

Table 1. CIM Project Evaluation Criteria

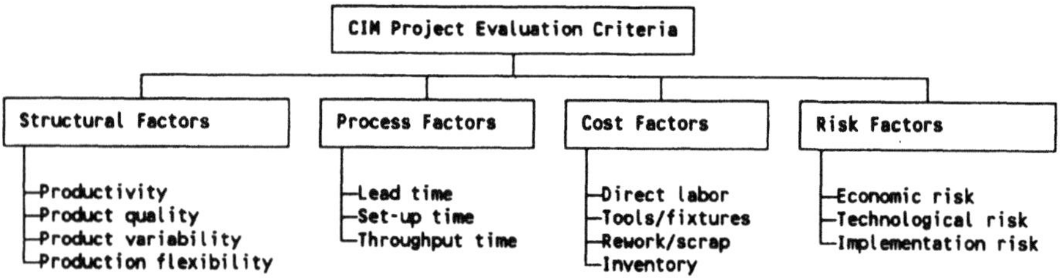

Table 2. AHP Method. Basic Structure

K	K1 K2 ... Kn	K1 K2 ... Kn	Group Results	
K1 K2 Kn	1 original matrix (M1) 1 Pair-wise Comparison 1	Matrix of the normalized values (M2 = M1/V1)	Row sums (V3)	Average values (V4 = V3/n)
Sum (V1)		1 1 ... 1	-	1

Table 3. AHP Method. Example

K	K1	K2	K3	K4	K1	K2	K3	K4	Group Results	
K1	1	2	3.5	2	.437	.400	.583	.333	1.755	.439
K2	(.5)	1	1	1	.219	.200	.167	.167	.753	.188
K3	(.286)	(1)	1	2	.125	.200	.167	.333	.825	.206
K4	(.5)	(1)	(.5)	1	.219	.200	.083	.167	.669	.167
	2.286	5.0	6.0	6.0	1.0	1.0	1.0	1.0	-	1.0

Table 4. AHP Method. AutoMan Example

Model: 16th Symposium on Operations Research

Pairwise Comparison Data for Weighting Categories and Criteria and for Rating Alternatives

Comparisons between Categories

See Table 2, M1

	Structur	Process	Cost	Risk
Structur		2.000	3.500	2.000
Process			1.000	1.000
Cost				2.000
Risk				

Comparisons between Criteria within Category: Structur

	Producti	Quality	Variabil	Flexibil
Producti		0.500	3.000	5.000
Quality			5.000	7.000
Variabil				2.000
Flexibil				

Comparisons between Criteria within Category: Process

	LeadTime	Set-up T	Throuthp
LeadTime		2.000	0.200
Set-up T			0.150
Throughp			

Comparisons between Criteria within Category: Cost

	DirLabor	Tools	RewScrap	Inventor
DirLabor		2.000	2.000	0.200
Tools			0.500	0.100
RewScrap				0.150
Inventor				

Comparisons between Criteria within Category: Risk

	EconRisk	TechRisk	ImplRisk
EconRisk		2.000	3.000
TechRisk			2.000
ImplRisk			

Model Structure, Weights, Shares, and Inconsistency Ratios

CATEGORY — See Table 2, V4

CATEGORY	CRITERION	WEIGHT	SHARE	RATING INCONSISTENCY
STRUCTUR	Producti	0.301	0.135	0.000
	Quality	0.527	0.236	0.000
Weight = 0.447	Variabil	0.110	0.049	0.000
Inconsistency = 0.007	Flexibil	0.063	0.028	0.000
PROCESS	LeadTime	0.168	0.031	0.000
	Set-up T	0.096	0.018	0.000
Weight = 0.187	Throughp	0.735	0.137	0.000
Inconsistency = 0.016				
COST	DirLabor	0.153	0.031	0.000
	Tools	0.064	0.013	0.000
Weight = 0.203	RewScrap	0.101	0.021	0.000
Inconsistency = 0.017	Inventor	0.682	0.138	0.000
RISK	EconRisk	0.540	0.088	0.000
	TechRisk	0.297	0.048	0.000
Weight = 0.163	ImplRisk	0.163	0.027	0.000
Inconsistency = 0.008				

[Inconsistency of pairwise comparisons between categories = 0.056]

*Pairwise comparisons with inconsistency values > 0.1 should be redone.

Ratings by Criterion and Overall Ratings of Alternatives

CATEGORY: CRITERION	RATINGS Old-Syst	New-Syst
1: Producti	0.333	0.667
1: Quality	0.333	0.667
1: Variabil	0.200	0.800
1: Flexibil	0.250	0.750
2: LeadTime	0.333	0.667
2: Set-up T	0.286	0.714
2: Throuthp	0.333	0.667
3: DirLabor	0.333	0.667
3: Tools	0.222	0.778
3: RewScrap	0.250	0.750
3: Inventor	0.091	0.909
4: EconRisk	0.333	0.667
4: TechRisk	0.667	0.333
4: ImplRisk	0.800	0.200
OVERALL RATING	0.315	0.685

Ranking of Alternatives by Overall Rating

RANK	ALTERNATIVE	RATING
=>1	New-Syst	0.685
2	Old-Syst	0.315

Literature

Canada, John R. and Sullivan, William G.: Economics and Multiattribute Evaluation of Advanced Manufacturing Systems. Englewood Cliffs: Prentice-Hell, 1989.

Saaty, Thomas L.: Multicriteria Decision Making. The Analytic Hierarchy Process. Pittburgh: RWS Publications, 1990.

Weber, Stephan F.: AutoMan. Decision Support Software for Automated Manufacturing Investment. User Manual. New York: U.S.Department of Commerce, National Institute of Standards and Technology, 1989 = NISTIR 89-4116.

Zahedi, Fatemeh: The Analytic Hierarchy Process. A Survey of the Method and its Applications. Interfaces 16(1986)4, July-August, p. 96-108.

How to deal with Uncertainty in Inventory Control?

J. Wijngaard, University of Groningen

In many situations inventory is necessary to buffer against short term disturbances in demand and/or supply. The amount of inventory that is necessary is generally assumed to be determinable by some proper stochastic model. The most straight forward stochastic model is the one-product inventory model with periodic review and stationary stochastic demand (normally distributed for instance) and fixed leadtime.

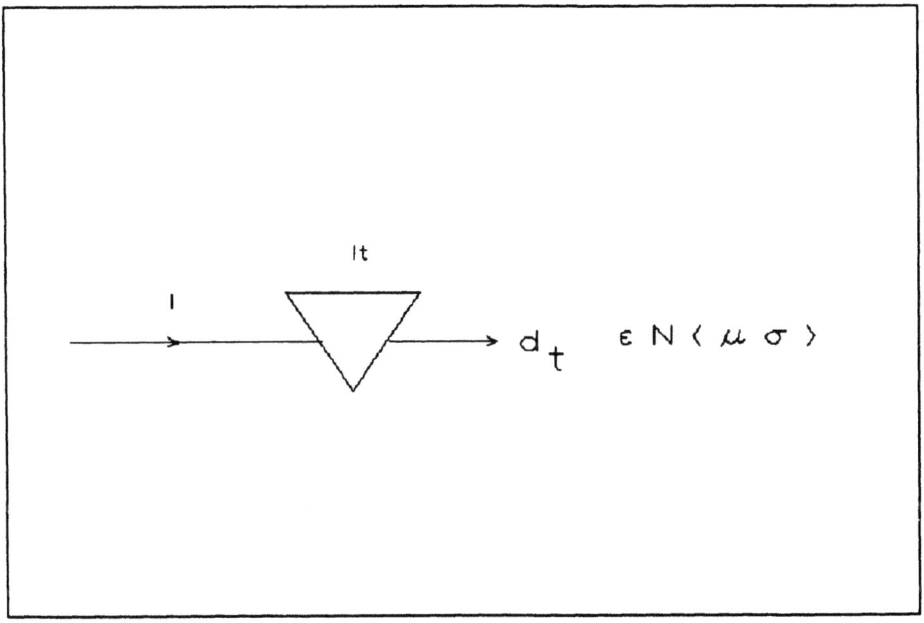

Figuur 1: Stationary stochastic demand, fixed leadtime.

The safety stock that is necessary according to such a model is due to the uncertainty during the leadtime. Independently normally distributed demand with standard deviation σ leads to a safety stock of

$$k \, \sigma \, \sqrt{l + 1}$$

With k some factor that depends on the delivery performance that

is required, taking into account the order sizes that are applied.
If the leadtime is also assumed to be stochastic the required safety stock is instead

$$k\sqrt{(l+1)\sigma^2 + \mu^2\sigma_l^2}$$

with l+1 the average leadtime and σ_l the standard deviation of the leadtime. In applying such models μ, σ, l and σ_l are generally estimated by averaging past realizations.

If demand is partly known beforehand, it is in principle possible to use the same type of models although the situation is more complex already. Now the expression

$$(l+1)\sigma^2 + \mu^2\sigma_l^2$$

has to be replaced by the variance of the forecast error of the demand during leadtime. Complicating here is that forecasts are adapted. In case of fixed leadtime, the conceptually easiest way to handle this is to compare the forecast of the demand during the interval [t,t+l+1], made at the beginning of period t and the realization of that demand. In case of stochastic leadtime one could use here the most recent realization of l.
It is clear that there are problems left in case of combinations of uncertainty and predictability. But as long as demand and leadtime are autonomous stationary processes albeit partly predictable ones, one may expect to be able to solve the problems. The situation gets more severe if variations are of an incidental character and even worse if variations are partly controllable. Unfortunately that is what happens generally in practice. Uncertainty, predictability and controllability are elements that are difficult to seperate and keeping inventory is mainly directed to the occurence of incidental variations.
This will be made more specific for the case of component inventory.

component requirement follows from the explosion of a schedule at final product level. One of the reasons to keep inventory is to be able to react on changing customer requirements by changing the final product schedule. When these changes occur however the changes are checked for component availability to keep the plan feasible. This leads to disturbances of the "real" demand. In fact "real" demand is an abstraction that is difficult to find back in practice. What can be observed is what is used eventually. But it is not easy to translate that to "real" demand.

Another reason to keep component inventory is to be able to react properly on internal disturbances in the execution of the final product schedule. Capacity problems or component availability problems may lead to a situation where it is not possible to execute the schedule.

If there is some extra inventory of (most of) the components it may be possible by rescheduling to keep the volume of final product production at norm. Here the shortage of certain components leads to earlier requirement of other components. This again makes the difference between "demand" and use of components larger.

A third reason for keeping inventory is to be able to keep the schedule also in case of possible supply disturbances, leadtime variations for instance. With respect to leadtime the assumption of an autonomous process generating the leadtime variations is even further away from practice than the assumption of autonomous demand. The component planners spend a major part of their time in influencing leadtime in a very specific way (expediting). Variations in the leadtimes are partly the effect of control and it is impossible to separate leadtimes that are not influenced from leadtime that are influenced.

So far with respect to the question of controllability, now the question of stationarity. Important factors leading to the need to keep component inventory are:

- certain components are difficult to produce and the supplier may get manufacturing problems

- the BOM contains errors leading to systematic misestimates of component requirement
- customer requirement mix changes significantly
- the spare parts requirement is higher than average because of a change in the spare parts distribution structure
- the production location is changed leading to other offsets.

All these factors are of a rather incidental character. It is not something to model stationary. Of course there are also more structural causes of variations, but, again, it is not easy to distinguish variations caused by structural factors and variations caused by incidental factors. It is difficult therefore to estimate future variations from historical data. Direct knowledge about the actual state of the processes determining requirement and leadtimes and the expert interpretation of requirement and leadtime data are more valuable than a mechanistic calculation of mean and standard deviation of demand and leadtime. But such knowledge and expertise leads to control behaviour that does not fit well in a stationary stochastic model. In a stationary stochastic inventory model parameter setting (reorder level) is neatly distinguished from ordering. In practice, with many incidental variety generating factors, such a distinction is less easy.

The stationary stochastic inventory models are fundamentally inadequate to support inventory control at the individual item level. On the other hand some support is necessary, certainly in case of hundreds or thousands of products per (component) planner. Controlling many products just having available plain data on actual and historical orders (procurement, assembly, customer) and inventories is beyond the information processing capability of most planners. Procurement order suggestions and signals demanding for extra attention are necessary. The question is how to generate such order suggestions and signals if stationary stochastic inventory models are inadequate.

It will be sketched how this problem can be tackled by more

explicitly formulating inventory control as an aggregate control problem. The heavy attention payed in Silver / Petersen [1] on aggregate performance can be interpreted as a first (implicit) step in this direction.

[1] Silver, E.A., Peterson, R. "Decision Systems for Inventory Management and Production Planning". Wiley, 1985.

Author Index

GPSR Compliance

The European Union's (EU) General Product Safety Regulation (GPSR) is a set of rules that requires consumer products to be safe and our obligations to ensure this.

If you have any concerns about our products, you can contact us on ProductSafety@springernature.com

In case Publisher is established outside the EU, the EU authorized representative is:

Springer Nature Customer Service Center GmbH
Europaplatz 3
69115 Heidelberg, Germany

Batch number: 10725962

Printed by Printforce, the Netherlands